BOOK OF PEOPLES
OF THE WORLD

BOOK OF PEOPLES OF THE WORLD

A GUIDE TO CULTURES

EDITED BY
WADE DAVIS AND K. DAVID HARRISON
WITH
CATHERINE HERBERT HOWELL

NATIONAL GEOGRAPHIC
WASHINGTON, D.C.

Candles glimmer as Thai monks
process ceremonially near
Bangkok's Marble Temple,
the Wat Benchamabophit.
Preceding pages: A fisherman
heads out for the day's catch from
a port in Senegal, West Africa.

CONTENTS

Introduction by Wade Davis | 6
The Genographic Project by Jason Blue-Smith | 12
Editor's Note | 14
Map of Regions of the World | 16

SUB-SAHARAN AFRICA | 18

WHEN LANGUAGES DIE
by K. David Harrison • 58

NORTH AFRICA & THE MIDDLE EAST | 62

A LIFE ON THE MOVE
by K. David Harrison • 86

ASIA | 90

TO SAIL BY THE WISDOM OF THE STARS
by Elizabeth Kapu'uwailani Lindsey • 142

OCEANIA | 146

NOTES ON THE WORLD'S SCALES
by Miranda Weinberg • 188

EUROPE | 192

WRITTEN WORD, ORAL WORLD
by Robert E. Hart • 252

NORTH AMERICA | 256

MAKING A SPACE TO LIVE IN
by K. David Harrison • 300

CENTRAL & SOUTH AMERICA | 304

Ethnic Groups of the World | 358
Contributors | 376   Illustrations Credits | 377
Readings and Resources | 378   Index | 379

Introduction

BY WADE DAVIS

Culture is born of the imagination—and the human imagination as we know it arose in the distant past as our species, *Homo sapiens,* evolved from its direct ancestor, *Homo erectus,* and, infused with consciousness, embarked on a journey that would carry it to every habitable domain on the planet. It is an extraordinary story.

The first evidence of our existence is found in Africa, dating back to some 150,000 years ago. For most of our history we shared the world with another branch on the hominid tree, our remote cousins the Neandertals, who were descendants of the same progenitor. Neandertals clearly had some spark of awareness. They used tools, and there is evidence of deliberate burial as early as 70,000 years ago. But whether it was an increase in the size of the brain, the development of language, or some other evolutionary catalyst, competitive advantages developed in our species that were to launch its destiny in an astonishing manner.

The turning point

Beginning about 60,000 years ago, two waves of human migration moved out of Africa. One followed the southern shores of Asia, reaching Australia 45,000 years ago. The second went north through the Middle East into Central Asia, with one pulse heading west into Europe, another going east, ultimately reaching the Americas. Sparking this journey was an explosion of intellect that left Neandertal man gasping for survival.

By the time the last vestiges of Neandertal life slipped away in Europe, some 27,000 years ago, stunning Upper Paleolithic cave art created by our direct ancestors was already several thousand years old. Reaching deep into the Earth, through narrow passages that opened into chambers illuminated only by the flicker of tallow lamps, men and women drew with stark realism the animals they revered, singly or in herds, using the contour of the stone to animate the forms so dramatically that entire caverns come alive even today with creatures long since lost to extinction.

The sophistication of the figurative art found in caves near Chauvet, France, and at later sites such as Lascaux and Altamire, is astonishing not only for its transcendent beauty but also for what it tells us about the florescence of the human potential once brought into being by culture. The technical skills—the exploitation of ochre and manganese, iron oxide, and charcoal to yield a full palette of colors; the use of scaffolding; the diverse techniques to apply the pigments—are themselves remarkable. All suggest relatively high levels of social organization and specialization, which are echoed in the genius of the Upper Paleolithic tool kit, the elegant scrapers and blades pounded from flint. The use of negative space and shadow, the sense of composition and perspective, the superimposition of animal forms through time—all indicate a highly evolved aesthetic that itself implies the expression of some deeper yearning.

The cave art does much more than invoke the magic of the hunt. It pays homage to that moment when human beings through consciousness separated themselves from the animal realm, emerging as the unique entity that, whether we like it or not, we know ourselves to be. Viewed in this light, the art may be seen almost as postcards of nostalgia, laments for a lost time when animals and people were as one. Proto-shamanism, the first great spiritual impulse, grew as an attempt to reconcile and even reestablish through ritual a separation that was irrevocable. What is perhaps most remarkable is the fact that the fundamentals of Paleolithic art remained essentially unchanged for

The genius of early human artistic expression emanates from the Upper Paleolithic cave art in Altamira, Spain. These lifelike, fully realized figures were created some 14,000 years ago.

25,000 years, six times the chronological span that separates us today from the builders of the Great Pyramid at Giza. Ours was a long farewell.

The prehistoric existential

This art also marked the beginning of our discontent, the restless yearning for meaning that has ever since propelled the human dream. Our entire experience as a species over the past 50,000 years may be distilled into two words: how and why. These are the departure points of all inquiry, the slivers of insight around which cultures crystallize.

All peoples face the same adaptive imperatives. We all must give birth; raise, educate, and protect our children; console our elders as they move into their final years. Virtually all cultures would endorse most tenets of the Ten Commandments, not because the Judaic world was uniquely inspired, but because they are the rules that allow a social species to thrive. Few societies fail to outlaw murder or thievery. All create traditions that bring consistency to coupling and procreation. Every culture honors its dead, even as it struggles with the meaning of the inexorable separation that death implies.

Given these common challenges, the range and diversity of cultural adaptations is astonishing. Hunting and gathering societies have flourished, from the rain forests of Southeast Asia and the Amazon to the dry, flat deserts of Australia; from the Kalahari of Africa to the remote, icy reaches of the high Arctic; from the broad American plains to the pampas of Patagonia. Wayfarers and fishermen have settled virtually every island chain in all of the world's oceans. Complex societies have been built on the bounty of the sea alone, the salmon and herring that brought life to the First Nations of the Pacific Northwest.

With the Neolithic revolution some 10,000 years ago, human beings came to domesticate plants and animals. Pastoral nomads settled the most marginal reaches of the planet: the sands of the Sahara, the Tibetan plateau, the windswept expanses of the Asian steppe. Agriculturists took a handful of domesticated grasses—wheat, barley, rice, oats, millet, and maize—and from their bounty generated surpluses, food that could be stored, thus allowing for hierarchy, specialization, and sedentary life: all the hallmarks of civilization as traditionally defined. Great cities arose, and, in time, kingdoms, empires, and nation-states.

No one book can do justice to the full wonder of the human cultural experience. The very word "culture" defies precise definition, even as the concept embraces multitudes. A small, isolated society of but a few hundred men and women in the mountains of New Guinea has its own culture, but so, too, do countries such as Ireland and France. Distinct cultures may share similar spiritual beliefs—indeed this is the norm in lands that have been inspired by Christianity, Islam, and Buddhism. While language in general tends to delineate unique worldviews, there are peoples in Alaska, for example, that have lost the ability to speak their native tongues, yet they still maintain a thriving and vibrant sense of culture.

Perhaps the closest we can come to a meaningful definition of a culture is the acknowledgment that each is a unique and ever-changing constellation, which we recognize as a whole through the observation and study of its language, religion, social and economic organization, decorative arts, stories, myths, ritual practices and beliefs, and a host of other adaptive traits and characteristics. The full measure of a culture embraces both the actions of a people and the quality of their aspirations, the nature of the metaphors that motivate them. And no description of a people can be complete without reference to the character of their homeland, the ecological and geographical matrix in which they have determined to live

out their destiny. As landscape defines character, a culture springs from a spirit of place.

The future of the ethnosphere

What we have tried to do in this book is to provide a representative sampling of the cultures of the world, drawn from every continent and way of life, not only with the goal of celebrating the brilliance and wonder of the human experiment, but also with the hope of drawing attention to a greater theme. All of these cultures, as well as the thousands of others that might readily have found a place in this book, make up an intellectual, social, and spiritual web of life that envelops the Earth and is every bit as important to the well-being of the planet as is the biological web of life that we know as the biosphere. You might think of this cultural web of life as being an ethnosphere, a term perhaps best defined as the sum total of all thoughts and intuitions, myths and beliefs, ideas and inspirations brought into being by the human imagination since the dawn of consciousness. The ethnosphere is humanity's great legacy. It is the product of our dreams, the embodiment of our hopes, the symbol of all that we are and all that we have created as a wildly inquisitive and astonishingly adaptive species.

And just as the biosphere, the biological matrix of life, is being severely compromised with the destruction of habitat and the resulting loss of plant and

A Chipaya sheep herder in Bolivia confronts a universal parenting challenge: helping his daughter with her math homework.

animal species, so, too, is the ethnosphere, only at a far greater rate. No biologist, for example, would suggest that 50 percent of all species are moribund or on the brink of extinction. Yet this, the most apocalyptic scenario in the realm of biological diversity, scarcely approaches what we know to be the most optimistic scenario in the realm of cultural diversity.

The key indicator is language loss. A language, of course, is not merely a set of grammatical rules or a body of vocabulary. It is a flash of the human spirit, the vehicle by which the soul of each particular culture comes into the material realm. Every language is an old-growth forest of the mind, a watershed of thought, an ecosystem of spiritual possibilities. Of the nearly 7,000 languages spoken today, fully half are not being taught to children. Effectively, they are already dead. Every two weeks, on average, somewhere on Earth an elder dies and carries with him or her into the grave the last syllables of an ancient tongue. What this really means is that within a generation or two, we may witness the disappearance of fully half of humanity's social, cultural, and intellectual legacy. This is the hidden backdrop of our age.

Redefining progress

But what exactly is at stake? What is being lost? Biologists and geneticists have at last proven something that philosophers have always dreamed to be true. We are all brothers and sisters. The unveiling of the human genome reveals that all of humanity may trace its ancestry to as few as a thousand individuals. We are all cut from the same genetic cloth.

It follows, by definition, that all cultures share the same mental acuity, the same raw genius. Whether this intellectual capacity and potential is exercised in stunning works of technological wizardry, as has been the great achievement of the West, or through the untangling of the complex threads of memory inherent in a myth, a primary concern, for example, of the Aborigines of Australia, is simply a matter of choice and orientation, adaptive insights, and cultural priorities.

While we have been sending men and women into space, it is not as if the other peoples of the world have been intellectually idle. For 2,500 years the Buddhists of Tibet have turned inward and, with intense empirical rigor, have sought an understanding of the nature of mind. In the Amazon, shamans have learned to manipulate and combine plants with specific pharmacological results that astonish modern science. The same latent genius that allowed Americans to place men on the moon enabled Polynesian navigators, equipped only with the power of observation, to establish the largest culture sphere in the history of humanity, tens of thousands of islands flung like jewels upon the southern seas.

By definition there is no hierarchy of progress in the history of culture, no social Darwinian ladder to success. The Victorian notion of civilization—with European industrial society sitting proudly at the apex of a pyramid of advancement that widens at its base to include the so-called primitives of the world—has been utterly discredited, indeed scientifically ridiculed for the racial and colonial conceit that it was. Throughout history, cultures have come and gone, absorbed by other more powerful societies or eliminated altogether by violence and conquest, famines, or natural disasters. But the current wave of assimilation and acculturation, in which peoples all over the Earth are being drawn away from their past, has no precedent.

To grasp fully the significance of what is at risk and what is being lost, and perhaps to find ways of ameliorating the situation, it is essential to distinguish cultural change from, in effect, cultural annihilation. One can lament the transformation of small-town U.S.A., for example, and identify any number of causes: technological innovations, such as television and air conditioning, which lured families away from the front porch and the social realm of the street; or the automobile and the network of roads and interstate highways, which changed the architecture of place. While it is true that all of these developments provoked profound changes in the cultural landscape, none challenged the fundamental existence of the United States as an idea, a nation, a sphere of life and inspiration.

Similarly, the arrival of digital technology in India, or even the flood of genetically modified seed crops into Indian agriculture, will not fundamentally threaten a nation and a culture that for 4,000 years has absorbed every conceivable intrusion, from the Moguls to the British. In Canada, recent immigrations have affected the country, mostly for the better, in little more than a decade. In Vancouver, once an Anglo bastion, 50 percent of schoolchildren today consider English their second language. Toronto hospitals provide medical advice to patients speaking 80 different languages, and the city plays host to peoples from some 150 nations.

Such changes are not, in and of themselves, threats to culture. The Kiowa Indians did not cease being Kiowa when they gave up the bow and arrow, any more than Americans stopped being Americans when they gave up the horse and buggy and embraced the car. The notion that small, indigenous societies are frozen in time and thus fated to slip away, reduced by circumstance to the sidelines of history as the modern world moves inexorably forward, is simply wrong. No culture, however isolated, is static. Traditional cultures have survived precisely because of their ability to cope with change, the one constant in history. People disappear only when they are overwhelmed by external forces, when drastic conditions imposed on them from the outside render them incapable of adapting to new possibilities. Sadly, these are the circumstances confronting most of the world's indigenous peoples today.

In the upper reaches of the Orinoco, a gold rush brings disease to the Yanomami, killing a quarter of the population in a decade and leaving the survivors destitute. In Colombia, Barasana men and women are reduced to being coca-growing serfs by drug lords and their allies, the revolutionary guerrillas of the left. In Nigeria, pollutants from the oil industry so saturate the floodplain of the Niger River, homeland of the Ogoni people, that their once fertile soil can no longer be farmed. A vortex of violence and war-induced famine claims the lives of tens of thousands of Nuer people in the Sudan. The Efe, forest dwellers of the Congo, dwindle toward extinction as sexually transmitted diseases ravage the population. In Borneo, the nomadic Penan drift toward settlements as their forest homeland is ruined by the unsustainable extraction of timber.

These are not cultures destined to fade away. On the contrary, in virtually every instance, these peoples are being torn from their past and propelled into an uncertain future because of specific political and economic decisions made by powerful outside entities.

The ultimate tragedy, as anthropologist David Maybury-Lewis has written, is not that archaic societies are disappearing, but rather that vibrant, dynamic living cultures and languages are being forced out of existence. It is not change that threatens the integrity of cultures; it is power, the crude face of domination.

Genocide, the physical elimination of a people, is universally condemned by all nations. Ethnocide, the destruction of a people's way of life, is too often embraced as appropriate development policy.

If governments and institutions are the agents of cultural destruction, they can also be the agents of cultural survival. Their organizers, and we as individuals, need to remember that our modern way of life, however wondrous it seems with its technological wizardry and cities dense in intrigue, is but one cultural possibility, one model of reality. It is the consequence of only one set of choices that our particular intellectual ancestors made, albeit successfully, generations ago.

Changing course

The great revelation of anthropology is the realization that there are other ways of being, morally inspired and inherently right. Whether it be the nomadic Penan in the rain forests of Borneo, the Voudou acolytes in Haiti, the Rendille pastoralists in the searing deserts of northern Kenya, or any one of the many cultures celebrated in this book—all of these peoples teach us that there are other options, other possibilities, other ways of thinking and interacting with the Earth itself.

The myriad cultures of the world are not failed attempts at being modern, failed attempts at being us. They are unique answers to a fundamental question: What does it mean to be human and alive? When asked that question, humanity responds with 7,000 distinct voices, which collectively become our repertoire for dealing with the challenges we will face as a species in the coming millennia.

The idea is not to freeze peoples in time or space. You cannot make a rain forest park of the mind. One cannot reduce a people to some kind of zoological specimen. The very thought is immoral. The goal is to find a way in which all peoples of the world may benefit from the genius of modernity, without that engagement implying the loss of their ethnicity.

This is neither a sentimental issue nor a gesture of nostalgia. It is a matter of geopolitical survival. Culture is not decorative. It is the raiment of ethical and moral values that wraps the body of every individual and keeps at bay the barbaric heart that history suggests lies beneath the surface of every one of us. Culture allows us to make sense out of sensation, to find order and meaning in a universe that may have none. It is

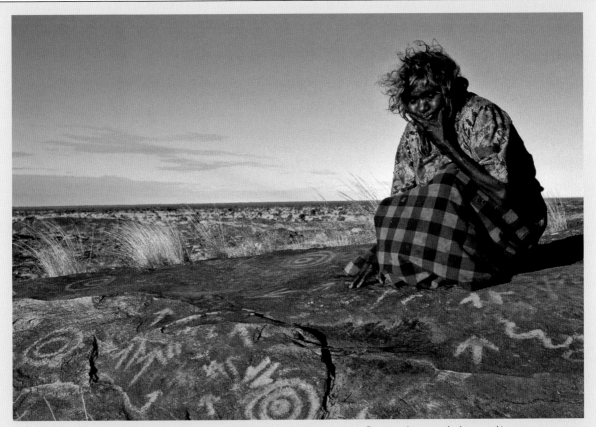

At Corroboree Rock, in Australia's eastern Macdonnell Ranges, an Arrernte woman reflects on the petroglyphs carved into stones centuries before. These symbols speak to her as they did to her ancestors.

culture that allows us to reach, as Abraham Lincoln implored us to do, for the better angels of our nature.

What matters

As cultures are lost, individuals remain, often shadows of their former selves. They find themselves caught in time, unable to return to the past yet denied any real possibility of securing a place in the world whose values they seek to emulate and whose wealth they may long to acquire. Anthropology suggests that when peoples are squeezed, extreme ideologies frequently emerge, inspired by strange and unexpected beliefs. The Shining Path in Peru, Pol Pot and the homicidal mania of the Khmer Rouge in Cambodia, Osama bin Laden and al Qaeda are all examples of malevolent, atavistic movements that have sprung from conditions of chaos and disintegration, disenfranchisement and disaffection.

Culture, in other words, matters. It provides the vital constraints of tradition and comfort that allow true civilization to exist.

Before she died, anthropologist Margaret Mead expressed her concern that, as we drift toward a more homogeneous world, all of human potential might be reduced to a single modality, a blandly amorphous generic culture, a monochromatic world of monotony. Her greatest fear was the possibility that we might awake one day, as if awaking from a dream, and discover that we have forgotten that there had ever been any other options.

Does it matter, I am often asked, to a community in Kansas if a tribe in Kenya disappears? Perhaps not, or at least no more than it matters to that people in Kenya if Kansas disappears. But would not the entire world be a more impoverished place if either tragedy were to unfold?

There is a fire burning over the Earth, taking with it plants and animals, human languages, ancient skills, and visionary wisdom. Quelling this flame, and kindling in its wake a new respect for the value and importance of both biological and cultural diversity, is one of the great challenges of our age.

The Genographic Project

BY JASON BLUE-SMITH

Over the past 50 years, genetics research has changed our understanding of human origins. Early work on protein and blood group markers paved the way for discoveries such as "mitochondrial Eve," a name given to the most recent common ancestor of all living humans, and "Y-chromosome Adam," the most recent common ancestor of all men, firmly establishing the origin for all humans in Africa. As genetics defined its role in a field traditionally dominated by paleoanthropology and archaeology, skepticism within the anthropological community gave way to acceptance of its validity. Today it would be difficult to discuss the origin and spread of our species without drawing on the genetic data.

By calculating patterns of genetic diversity, geneticists are coming to understand both the age and the ancestry of groups living in different geographic regions. The data clearly show that African populations have a much greater diversity than non-African populations and that their mutations are ancestral to the genetic signals found in non-African groups. It is now widely accepted that humans originated in Africa, left that continent around 60,000 years ago, and proceeded to populate the planet. But many gaps remain in our knowledge, and we lack sufficient data to answer some questions fundamental to human evolutionary history, particularly events that have occurred over the past 15,000 years, during the period separating the end of the last ice age from recorded history.

Current efforts by geneticists to shed light on this period of human prehistory are facing increasing challenges. While the Internet and globalization have brought the world closer together, that closeness and the pressures of rapid industrial development also threaten indigenous populations. Their numbers are dwindling, languages are dying out at alarming rates, and oral traditions and customs are dispersing as generations pass on. When indigenous peoples move to cities and lose touch with their traditional ways of life, the geographic and cultural context in which their genetic diversity arose is lost.

Today this process is happening with shocking speed. We may have only a single generation left to capture a genetic snapshot of the history of our species before it is lost forever. It may be that our best chance to work with indigenous communities is now.

A new archaeology

In 2005 the National Geographic Society and IBM launched a research partnership called the Genographic Project. Led by Dr. Spencer Wells, the project's mission is to retrace the earliest human migrations through the use of DNA donated from people around the world. Rather than gazing earthward in search of the stones and bones familiar to archaeologists and paleoanthropologists, the Genographic Project research team uses the DNA of people living today as a historical document to delve into our ancient past.

To trace recent migrations with scientific rigor, geneticists must pool data on the same set of markers from tens of thousands of individuals, representing a cross-section of global genetic diversity. With funding from the Waitt Family Foundation, a consortium of ten scientific centers around the world is now collaborating with indigenous populations in their respective regions. The work conducted by these centers is guided by a core ethical framework that ensures the highest respect for the traditions of each participating indigenous community. Many in those communities consider the genetic information resulting from their participation in the Genographic Project as new pieces of the

EARLY HUMAN MIGRATIONS

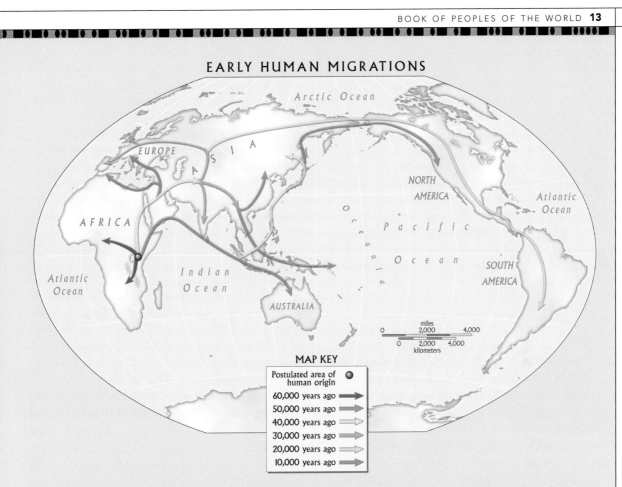

Genetic research findings provide new evidence for understanding the paths and pace at which human beings migrated out of Africa and, through tens of thousands of years, established communities and cultures in all the habitable continents of the world.

puzzle, potentially helpful in understanding their own histories. Participants around the world have overwhelmingly engaged in the project with great interest.

A broader spectrum

Work with indigenous communities constitutes one aspect of the Genographic Project. Members of the general public can participate as well, by purchasing a participation kit from the project's website (www.national geographic.com/genographic). Participants donate a cheek swab sample, learn about their own ancestors' migratory journey, and track the overall progress of the research through the project's website. Proceeds from the sale of these kits are helping to fund both the field research and the Genographic Legacy Fund, which provides grants to indigenous communities for cultural conservation and revitalization efforts. The end goal is to leave a lasting legacy by empowering indigenous and traditional peoples on a local level while helping to raise

global awareness of the challenges and pressures facing these communities.

In this book on the ethnic identities of peoples around the world, the National Geographic Society's Genographic Project serves as a backdrop and an illuminating thread to help us understand the remarkable diversity described in its pages. Appearing throughout are essays, "Genographic Insights," that offer further evidence for the history of the human occupation of a wide range of geographic regions. In many places these essays draw directly from the research and writings of Dr. Wells. They provide a perspective on the major migration movements by which humans departed from an African homeland and populated all the corners of our planet.

These essays, and the work they reflect, show how other scientific disciplines combine with the genetic data, helping us construct a richer and more accurate understanding of our shared human past.

Editor's Note

A first edition of this book, titled *Peoples of the World*, appeared in the fall of 2001. It was an inauspicious time to publish any book, given current events, and yet a moment in world history when the urgent need for such a book—with its messages of respect and understanding, unity in diversity—was heightened.

In an effort to bring *Peoples of the World* up to date and to improve the ways in which it fulfilled its vital mission, certain fundamental changes were made. First of all, we noted the harmonies between the content of this book and the groundbreaking research underway with the National Geographic Society's Genographic Project, initiated in 2005. The grand sweeps of human migration and the interactions of ethnic groups over millennia already formed the core content of this book. We decided to make room for some of the genographic findings and, further, to reorganize the chapters of the book so that their order mirrors the movement of humans through time and into world regions, as evidenced by those findings.

The groups featured here

The list of groups featured in the book has undergone thorough reconsideration. The final list here, which features 50 groups not found in the first edition, was compiled by consensus among the anthropologists, linguists, and consultants working on this book. Decisions were made in part with an eye to the diversity and fascination of little-known groups, particularly those that teeter on the verge of extinction and therefore deserve our recognition. Also added, however, were a number of groups that might as fairly be called nationalities—Egyptians, English, Japanese, New Zealanders—with an understanding that in many lives, national identity is cultural identity.

This book features 222 different ethnic groups, and yet it still represents a mere sampling of the world's ethnosphere. In recognition of all world cultures, we devote 18 pages in the appendix to a list of more than 5,000 known ethnic groups of the world—and even it, as editor and ethnolinguist K. David Harrison notes in his introduction to it, cannot be said to be complete.

The fact boxes

Equally elusive, and yet important for understanding world cultures, are the statistics of population and language use that we have compiled for each of the book's 222 ethnic groups. For each group, we list the most reliable population statistic, representing the numbers of that ethnic group living in their homeland. We also list alternate names, native lands, and language families for each group.

In many cases, the population figures can only begin to express the widespread appearance of that group's people in places around the world. In the case of the Jewish people, for example, whom we feature in the chapter that includes the Middle East, our population figure counts only those Jews living in Israel and does not take into account the hundreds of thousands of Jewish people living elsewhere in the world. In the case of the French, likewise, we count only those living in France and not those living in places such as the French-speaking Canadian province of Québec. For groups that have no country of their own, such as the Kurds or the Roma, we have done our best to compile transnational statistics.

Similarly, when we state the location of each ethnic group, we are highlighting the central and identifying habitation of that group. Secondary habitations are often mentioned in the text beyond those listed in the fact box as a group's primary locations.

For each group featured in this book, we provide a statistical snapshot, featuring alternate names for that people, current population statistics, the group's primary home location, and the language family to which the group's language belongs.

For population, our research began with census tables provided by the United Nations or by national census bureaus, adjusted as necessary, resulting in figures reflecting the population of each ethnic group within its primary location.

To help you hear the sounds of the peoples of the world, we note those regions that are represented by music samples on the National Geographic Society's World Music website.

And, to help you hear the voices of the peoples of the world, we include translations of proverbs, hoping that through them readers can glimpse the characters of peoples far and wide and recognize that wisdom in one culture often serves as wisdom for all.

Ordinary life, extraordinary wisdom

Our intention for illustrating this new edition, *Book of Peoples of the World,* was to find a new selection of photographs that bring to light the small details, passing moments, and authentic lives of people: working and playing, laughing and crying, and, in many cases, facing the challenge and enjoying the benefits when traditions intersect with modernity. While occasional photographs picture costumes and demeanors assumed for the sake of a festival or a once-a-year ceremony, more often we show the ordinary moments of existence that all people share no matter where they live or who they are.

The grand panorama of peoples of the world is an ever-shifting tableau, and this book by definition can only represent a snapshot in time, intricate and rich yet precarious in its detail, given our changing times. At the same time that the population of our world is increasing at an unprecedented pace, the number of discrete ethnicities and languages alive in the world, paradoxically, is dwindling. This trend makes all the more urgent the need to record and remember today.

May this journey around the globe, through the pages of this book, be one valuable step in your continuing exploration of the human experience.

Following divisions both geographic and ethnic, this book divides the world into seven major regions, reflected in its chapters. Each of those chapters is divided into subregions, as shown on this map.

A M E R I C A N   A R C T I C

ARCTIC CIRCLE

60°

NORTH

NORTHWEST COAST

PLAINS

NORTHEAST

PLATEAU AND GREAT BASIN

SOUTHWEST & FAR WEST

SOUTHEAST

30°

TROPIC OF CANCER

CARIBBEAN

MESOAMERICA

N

W

P O L Y N E S I A

0°

EQUATOR

AMAZON AND ORINOCO BASINS

A N D E S

Pacific Ocean

Atlantic Ocean

TROPIC OF CAPRICORN

CENTRAL SOUTH AMERICA

30°

miles
0   1,000   2,000

0   1,000   2,000
kilometers

PATAGONIA

60°

ANTARCTIC CIRCLE

150°   120°   90°   60°   30°

30° 60° 90° 120° 150°

rctic Ocean

ARCTIC CIRCLE

ASIAN NORTH

60°

ROPE

EASTERN EUROPE

CENTRAL ASIA

CENTRAL
EUROPE

CAUCASUS

EAST ASIA

SOUTHERN
EUROPE

30°

MIDDLE EAST

AFRICA

SOUTH ASIA

TROPIC OF CANCER

Pacific Ocean

SOUTHEAST ASIA

MICRONESIA

ICA

CENTRAL AFRICA

EAST AFRICA

Indian

Ocean

EQUATOR 0°

MELANESIA

SOUTHERN
AFRICA

TROPIC OF CAPRICORN

AUSTRALIA

30°

Map Key

— International boundary

Sub-Saharan Africa

North Africa and the Middle East

Asia

Oceania

Europe

North America

Central and South America

PATAGONIA Regional subdivision

*Note: Regional divisions in this book do not correspond
to traditional geophysical continental boundaries.*

ANTARCTIC
CIRCLE

60°

TARCTICA

30° 60° 90° 120° 150°

SUB-SAHARAN AFRICA

SOUTHERN AFRICA
Afrikaners • San • Shona
Tswana • Zulu

WEST AFRICA
Asante • Bambara • Dogon • Fang • Fulani
Hausa • Igbo • Wolof • Yoruba

CENTRAL AFRICA
Efe • Kongo • Mangbetu
Tutsi & Hutu

EAST AFRICA
Amhara • Baganda • Beta Israel • Dinka • Kikuyu
Malagasy • Masai • Somali • Swahili

Masked and costumed men prepare to dance
at a festival in Bamako, Mali.

Africa is the birthplace of humankind, an ancient land where our hominid, or humanlike, ancestors lived more than four million years ago. Extraordinarily diverse in its geography and cultures, this immense continent measures about 5,000 miles north to south and 4,600 miles east to west—from the Horn of Africa to the tip of Senegal—and over the millennia it has given rise to a rich mix of peoples now inhabiting deserts and rain forests, mountains and valleys.

Even within similar geographic areas, one finds a wide range of social and political organizations. The Nuer of Sudan, for example, have no indigenous leadership roles, while the Zulu of southern Africa are known for their once heavily militarized kingdom. Societies such as the Asante and Yoruba in the west and the Baganda, Bunyoro, and Tutsi in the east maintained large states, while numerous others, like southern Africa's Shona and Tswana, composed smaller states or kingdoms. The Mbuti and Efe of central Africa and the San of the Kalahari Desert continue to live by hunting and gathering and have a fluid political organization without any recognized political authority.

Language The languages spoken by Africa's many peoples can be grouped into a few general families, such as Bantu or Sudanic, but one group may include several different tongues. European languages are also spoken throughout Africa because of the long colonial period, which lasted until the 1960s. French is spoken in the former French and Belgian colonies of western and central Africa; English is heard in the west, east, and south; and Portuguese is spoken in the former Portuguese-occupied areas of Angola, Mozambique, and Guinea-Bissau.

Although African societies vary considerably in the ways they organize their families and social lives, some general patterns can be found. Marriage, for example, is usually considered a union of groups rather than individuals, and that union is symbolized and made legal by the transfer of bridewealth from the groom's family to the bride's. In many societies, a man must first pay a certain amount of money to the bride's father to set the marriage in process; later, he must make childwealth payments for rights to his offspring. Most Africans permit polygamy, the marriage of a man to more than one woman, although one area in Nigeria once permitted polyandry, the marriage of a woman to more than one man. Among the Lese of the Democratic Republic of the Congo, and in some other

A Madagascar market offers bread, bananas, and baskets of rice, providing opportunities, especially for women, to earn cash from prepared and surplus foods and crafts.

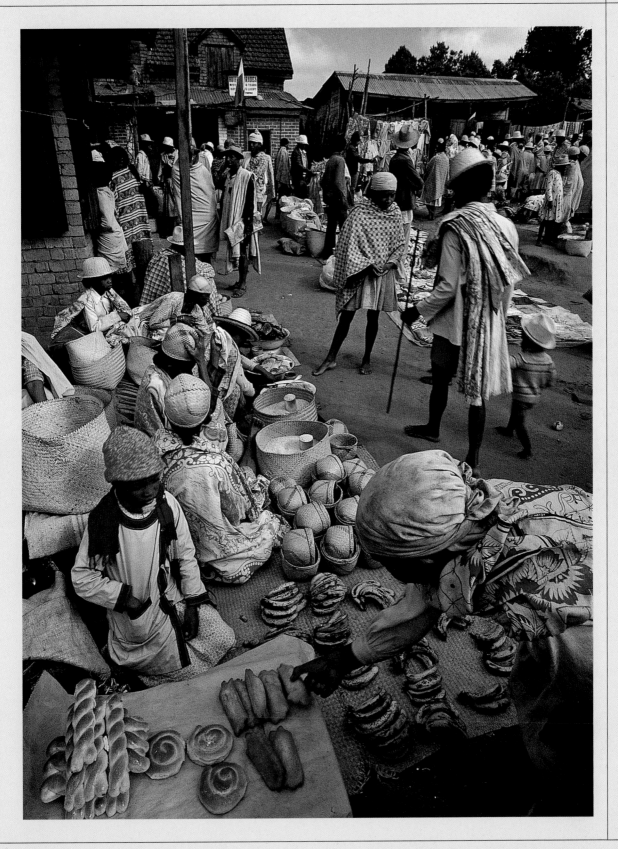

societies of western and central Africa, an infertile wife may marry another woman. In a woman-to-woman marriage, the other wife reproduces with the husband, helping to make sure that he does not abandon the infertile wife for lack of children.

The vast majority of African societies reckon descent unilineally, either through the mother in matrilineal societies or through the father in patrilineal societies. In both cases, however, the men have most of the authority. In matrilineal societies, one traces descent through the mother's brother and is subject to his authority, not the mother's. A small number of African societies reckon descent in the same way that most Americans do: bilaterally, but with a bias toward the male side of the family.

Some African societies are well known for art that is both useful and aesthetic. Styles vary greatly, but the most common products are figurines used in sacrifice and worship, generally with heads oversized in relation to the body, and masks worn in ritual performances. Among the Dan of Liberia, masks hide the faces of secret-society members and protect the identity of judges involved in settling disputes. The Akan of Ghana rely on wooden figures to facilitate childbirth. Africans also produce an enormous amount of "tourist art," much of which is distributed in Europe and North America; despite the name, this art is often of the same style and quality as art not created for export.

African people practice many religions, including Islam, Christianity, Judaism, and Hinduism. In western Africa, Islam now has numerous adherents. This is especially true among the Hausa of Nigeria and other societies that have engaged in trade with northern Africa, where Muslim Hamitic-speaking peoples have long been distinguished both culturally and religiously from the sub-Saharan societies.

East African girls share a confidence on a special occasion for their tribe.

The economies of Africa are also diverse, as disparate as hunting and gathering in the central African rain forest; diamond and gold mining in southern Africa; and large-scale farming in western Africa. Often, the differences between the urban and rural areas are quite dramatic. Some families occupy cable-ready high-rise apartments and perhaps hold positions as engineers, teachers, doctors, lawyers, or software developers. But many of their countrymen dwell in thatched-roof huts, with no plumbing, no electricity, or, in some cases, with no access to cities. They may spend their lives as pastoralists, hunters, or farmers who grow crops of rice, yams, bananas, cassava, or coffee. In remote areas of economically challenged countries like Ethiopia and the Democratic Republic of the Congo, people trying to eke out a living sometimes dwell in unsanitary conditions, even more marginalized from economic and political power than they were during European colonialism. Some Africans still follow nomadic lifestyles, taking only what they can carry with them and using shelters that they can quickly build and take apart.

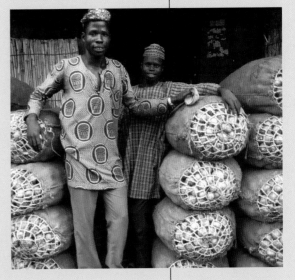

In Ibadan, Nigeria, a market wholesaler shows off his supply of bagged onions. Producers also sell their crops directly at many African markets.

Culturally interwoven Despite a tendency by many people to study Africa as a collection of distinct cultures, the reality is that various groups have had long, extensive contacts with one another, with much cultural exchange. Neighboring societies may have borrowed elements of each other's rituals over the years, sometimes in a manner so subtle and inconspicuous that trying to determine the precise origins of a particular ritual becomes an impossible task. The continent's so-called distinct cultures are, in fact, composed of many threads.

This rich cultural pluralism in Africa allows alternative beliefs and practices to coexist. Here, major religions of the world are practiced alongside indigenous religions, and a range of medical treatments are made available to everyone; different illnesses may be treated with therapies that are religious in nature, indigenous or traditional, or even based on Western medicine. A spectacular example of how cultures can coexist, work together, and even borrow elements from one another can be seen in the hometown of Felix Houphouet-Boigny, a former president of Cote d'Ivoire and a devout Roman Catholic: It is an extra-large replica of St. Peter's Basilica in Vatican City. Engineered by Lebanese architects and built by French and Israeli contractors, the European-style structure incorporates Greek columns, Italian marble, and French stained glass. In 1990, the basilica was consecrated by Pope John Paul II amid traditional dancing performed by the Baule society of Cote d'Ivoire. ■

Southern Africa

Two rivers delineate this region in the southern quarter of the African continent. The Okavanga originates in Angola and flows southeast, emptying not into a sea or ocean but into a broad delta in the center of the Kalahari Desert. The Zambezi, with headwaters in the Katanga Plateau, flows east to the Indian Ocean, swelling to a mile wide and plummeting more than 340 feet at Victoria Falls.

Namibia, Botswana, Zimbabwe, and Mozambique form the northerly stretch of this region; South Africa encompasses the tip of the continent at the Cape of Good Hope, and is home to the region's larger cities.

To listen to music from Mozambique, South Africa, and Zimbabwe, visit http://worldmusic.national geographic.com.

AFRIKANERS

Population: 2.5 million
Location: South Africa
Language family: Germanic

In 1652, Dutch farmers arrived at the Cape of Good Hope near the southern tip of Africa. They initially called themselves Boers—literally, "peasants" or "farmers" in Dutch—but in time they developed a distinctive South African identity and a Dutch dialect with many loanwords from English and local African languages. They began to see themselves as Africans, or Afrikaners, the term used today by their Afrikaans-speaking descendants. Today, approximately two and a half million Afrikaners live in South Africa, which has a total population of almost 43 million.

The history of the Afrikaners is both heroic and tragic. On the one hand, their struggle for religious and economic freedom in a sometimes inhospitable land illustrates their endurance. On the other hand, their struggle entailed countless violent clashes with native Africans who had been dispossessed of their lands after the Boer arrival. The expansion of the Boers in South Africa was motivated in part by a deep-seated religious conviction that Africans, or Kaffirs—Afrikaans for "heathen"—were descended from Ham and created by God to serve whites.

Working for the Dutch East India Company, the settlers of 1652 set up a trading post on the southwest coast of South Africa. But soon the company released many of the increasing number of workers to settle the land, grow food for its fleets, and expand eastward. In 1795, the Dutch East India Company ended its rule of the Cape colony, and the Boers found themselves in direct opposition to the British.

The British colonized all the Cape settlements, outlawed slavery, and gave native black Africans many civil rights previously denied them by the Boers. In 1835, feeling threatened by both Africans and the British, the Boers began their Great Trek into the Transvaal, where gold and diamonds would eventually be found. Neither the Boers (they called themselves Voortrekkers) nor any of the local African societies they encountered along the way would ever be the same. From that point on, the history of native South Africans would be inextricably tied to the history of white expansion.

In 1899, President Paul Kruger of the South African Republic declared war on the British, who wanted to

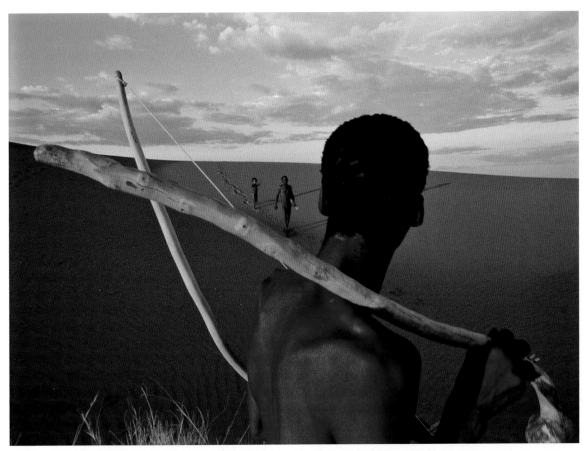

A San hunter may track game for days across the red sands of the Kalahari in Botswana before achieving success.

stop the rise of Afrikaner power and get control of the gold. Thus began the Boer War, a bloody conflict won by the British in 1902. The victors controled South African politics until 1948, when Afrikaners won the legislature on a nationalist platform that advocated increased segregation between blacks and whites. During the Boer War, many Afrikaners had lost their land and become impoverished; they had also been forced to travel from their farms to the cities, where they competed with black South Africans for employment.

Once in control, the Afrikaner government designed a system of apartheid, or separateness, which divided the people racially, geographically, socially, economically, and politically. The people were grouped into four categories: White, Bantu (all-black Africans), Colored (people of mixed race), and Asian (Indians and Pakistanis); all were separate and unequal.

Beginning in the early 1990s, South Africans began to dismantle the apartheid system, but the legacy of differential access to economic and political resources remains. Many white South Africans, especially those who have descended from the Boers, have continued to farm.

Today, the ethnic identity of Afrikaners is characterized by the Afrikaans language; by their membership in the Dutch Reformed Church; by their continued celebration of holidays remembering early historical struggles; and by the realities of contemporary class and political relations within South Africa, particularly their relations with non-Afrikaner whites. Afrikaner identity continues to be defined by a long-standing, ambivalent relationship with South Africans of British descent.

SAN

Alternate name: Bushmen   Population: 80,000
Location: Namibia, Angola, Botswana, South Africa
Language family: Khoisan

After the Pygmies of central Africa, the San peoples of southern Africa are the best known hunter-gatherers in the world. Often referred to

An Afrikaner couple celebrates their enduring marriage with a kiss. While proud of their European heritage, Afrikaners see themselves as Africans.

collectively and pejoratively as "Bushmen," they call themselves the *Zhun/twasi:* "the real people." They live in small camps composed of loosely organized kinship groups with no formal system of leadership.

The name "San" applies to a large group of people who have been living in remote desert regions of Botswana, Namibia, and Angola for perhaps thousands of years, but they are nonetheless ethnically and, to some extent, linguistically diverse. The San in the western Kalahari, for example, have a very different history from people in the desert's eastern part. Some San have lived closely with Bantu pastoralists for several hundred years and were much affected by the wars and population movements that followed the rise of the Zulu empire in the early 1800s; other San have remained relatively isolated from other ethnic groups.

In the European and American media, the San have been depicted as living in total isolation or, as they might have lived long before the advent of agriculture 10,000 years ago. Commercially successful films such as *The Gods Must be Crazy* have perpetuated the false image of these people as living fossils. In fact, the San have interacted with neighboring societies for hundreds of years, and archaeological evidence strongly suggests that they were engaging in regional trade as far back as A.D. 500. Today, the San maintain relationships with cattle herders such as the Herero and the Tswana. They pay taxes, and they have even served in the South African and Namibian armies, despite the fact that the South African government has resettled San-speaking peoples on a number of occasions.

Compared with their neighbors, the San maintain a peaceful and egalitarian society in which sharing is highly valued but private property and individualism are disdained. They are known for their skills as hunters of small mammals, and they occasionally can bring down an elephant or a giraffe by using poisoned arrows.

Once the arrow finds its mark, the hunter follows the wounded animal, sometimes for several days, until it collapses. This is one reason why the San have been enlisted by military forces as trackers. In a remarkably inhospitable environment, the San people can collect enough food and water to survive. But they must travel often to find resources, and sometimes the only available water that they can find is what they can squeeze out of deep roots.

The San also have a rich medical knowledge that they have incorporated into a series of rituals. During the medicine trance rituals, for example, audiences dance and clap, and ill people who have come to be cured watch as healers go into a trance state. The healers may administer medicines, derived from local plants or roots, and they may touch the patients to draw the sickness out of them and into their own bodies.

SHONA

Population: 10 million
Location: Zimbabwe, Mozambique
Language family: Bantu

About nine million Shona live in Zimbabwe and southern Mozambique, the majority of them residing in Zimbabwe. Like many African ethnic groups, the Shona are actually a collection of peoples speaking mutually intelligible languages, such as Korekore, Ndau, and Karanga. The Shona language is among the most widely spoken in southern Africa.

Many contemporary archaeologists believe that Great Zimbabwe, the ruins of which make up one of Africa's most formidable archaeological sites, was built by ancestors of today's Shona. The rich artistic tradition of these people has continued into the 21st century, with intricate wooden headrests perhaps their best known creations.

The Shona people are primarily an agricultural group. Maize is their main crop, but the people grow millet, sorghum, rice, peanuts, and a variety of tubers, too. They also raise cattle, sheep, and chickens; the cattle work, though, is taboo for women and is therefore done exclusively by men. Women may supplement their income by selling utilitarian pottery and baskets.

In their traditional political organization, Shona people still live mostly in villages that typically accommodate one or more interrelated families and consist of clustered mud-and-wattle huts, granaries, and common cattle kraals. Although villages have often been quite distant from each other, they were once part of central states with hereditary kings who made large-scale decisions for the territory, such as waging war. These policies were financed by substantial tributes from the surrounding settlements. Local decision-making was left to elders residing within each village, a policy that has changed somewhat because of the practice of centralized decision-making in the nation-states where today's Shona live.

In Shona traditional religion, the *vadzimu*, or ancestor spirits, play major roles. They represent the essence of the Shona way of life and embody the ideals and values of greatest importance, such as preserving and maintaining harmonious social networks. Vadzimu may be recently departed ancestors

A San man peers from his canoe into the flooded Okavango River in Botswana. The San, also known as Bushmen, supplement hunting, gathering, and fishing with cultivation.

or heroes from the past. They will offer protection if it is merited, but they will disappear if Shona values are not upheld.

TSWANA

Population: 4.4 million
Location: South Africa, Botswana, Namibia, Zimbabwe
Language family: Bantu

The Tswana people constitute most of the population in Botswana—"land of the Tswana." Twice as many, however, live in northeastern South Africa, where they inhabit what was known as Bophuthatswana—"the place of gathering of the Tswana"—during the time of apartheid. Tswana also live in neighboring Namibia and Zimbabwe.

A southern Bantu people, the Tswana are closely related to the Sotho of Lesotho and South Africa. Both groups speak mutually intelligible languages, have agricultural economies, share certain customs, and trace their descent from a common ancestor known as Mogale. The meaning of "Tswana," essentially an

---

The human heart is not a bag into which one can plunge one's hand.
KONGO PROVERB

---

invention of European colonists who encountered the group, is not known, but the name is believed to derive from a Bantu word. The people themselves have no common name; instead, they use the various names of their eight constituent subgroups.

During the second half of the 19th century, the Ngwato subgroup's Chief Khama III converted to Christianity while still a boy. He attended a missionary school and recognized the growing European interest in the area. By the 1880s, most Tswana were at least nominal Christians.

Traditionally, the Tswana have included ancestors along with the living as members of their society; they call the ancestor spirits dwelling among them and possessing metaphysical powers the *Badimo*. But European settlers did not understand the powerful role of social networks among the Tswana, including

their ongoing relationships with ancestors.

With their Victorian notions of privacy and individualism, the Europeans did not comprehend the subtlety of Tswana life, where prestige and power are gained by obtaining followers and allies. In this way of life, a person is nothing if he is not part of a larger group. Through a highly developed system of clientage, men gained rights over others in Tswana society, a connection that was once known as "eating" one another.

Since gaining independence from Britain in 1966, the Tswana of Botswana have maintained a stable, democratic government, proving themselves one of the few African peoples to do so.

ZULU

Population: 10 million
Location: South Africa
Language family: Bantu

Perhaps best known for having one of the most powerful state and military organizations in 19th-century Africa, the Zulu remain a vital political and cultural force in present-day South Africa.

Under Shaka (circa 1787-1828), its founder, the Zulu empire dominated sub-Saharan Africa. Shaka's military actions led to political consolidation elsewhere, with new kingdoms rising and stimulating large population movements into frontier territories. But behind the florescence of the Zulu and other African kingdoms, such as the Swazi and Sotho, were oppression and the ejection of many people from their homelands. And the political intrigue sometimes rivaled the best fiction: Shaka was assassinated by his half-brother Dingane, who was deposed by Mpande, another brother.

Though dominant over other African societies, the Zulu eventually found themselves in conflict with the Boers, Dutch colonists who escaped British oppression by trekking east to occupy Zululand. Dingane agreed to let the Boers into Zululand in early 1838 but then changed his mind and sent his men to murder dozens of men, women, and children. On December 16, 1838, the Boers retaliated against Dingane in a fight that became known as the Battle of Blood River. Thousands of Zulu were killed; not a single Boer soldier died.

The Zulu nation has long been defined as several hundred clans held together by their loyalty to the king, who owned all land. Men demonstrated their allegiance by fighting for the king's regiments and chiefs; in the

Our Human Birthplace

We are intrigued with our own humanity. That this book is open before you is itself testament to the fact that humans are fascinated with the sea of faces around us. Celebrating our differences is a wonderful part of being human—learning new languages and traveling to exotic places are practically universal curiosities, uniting people in a way that underscores the fact that our own DNA is 99.9 percent identical to that of everybody else on this planet. But somehow simply recognizing diversity falls short of answering the fundamental questions motivating this global phenomenon. In short, what of that other 0.1 percent? After all, who hasn't asked at some point, "Where do we all come from, really? And if we're all so closely related, why do we look so different?"

Looking for home

Getting to the root of these differences really boils down to questions of origin, which have fueled centuries of scientific research in search of the putative homeland of our species. Archaeology and paleoanthropology have focused on the evolutionary emergence of modern humans from a number of ancestral species spread geographically and temporally throughout the fossil record. With each new finding, theories became more refined, and over time a clearer picture emerged, placing the origin of our species squarely in sub-Saharan Africa, a region now widely referred to as the "cradle of humanity."

In fact, southern Africa itself is home to a number of sites containing some of the earliest evidence of modern humans found anywhere in Africa. Border Cave,

a rock shelter in the Lembombo Mountains between South Africa and Swaziland, has produced both anatomically modern human skeletal remains and advanced tool artifacts dated to 75,000 years ago. East of the Klasies River, a series of caves at the southernmost tip of South Africa show human

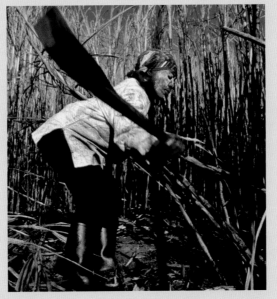

In South Africa, a Zulu woman harvests sugarcane with a machete.

habitation over the past 125,000 years and provide important clues into what life might have been like during the Middle Stone Age. Plant and animal remains show that these people knew how to seasonally hunt and gather, cook and fish. Each new finding seems to produce a new theory of human evolution, and only recently have these remains been put to the test.

What genes begin to tell us

Geneticists help by studying DNA for signals of the past. Most of our genome is passed down in equal parts from our

parents, with each half representing a shuffled combination of genetic material from their ancestors. The shuffling process, called recombination, is vital to maintaining the genetic diversity that enables species to adapt to changing environments and survive new diseases. But it makes life difficult for anthropological geneticists, because it creates a genetic mix of everyone who has come before.

Fortunately, some segments of our genome—such as the maternally inherited mitochondrial DNA (mtDNA) and the paternally inherited Y chromosome—get passed down unshuffled from parent to child and vary only through occasional mutations. When inherited by the next generation, these mutations become markers of descent that geneticists can use to decipher human prehistory.

Studies of mtDNA have shown that the Khoi and the San, groups indigenous to southern Africa, are among the oldest on the continent. Matching the genetic patterns with the archaeological findings suggests that in times of drastic climate fluctuation, the ancestors of these groups did the smartest thing possible and headed to the coast. Offering abundant shellfish, the sea acted as a buffer against changing conditions; picking up camp and moving with the shoreline kept life relatively stable. Meanwhile, distant inland populations around the same time were probably struggling in East and Central Africa to survive on the changing savannahs. Even in the evidence of the earliest humans, we see signs of the same ingenuity and adaptability that set in motion the technological innovations of today.

time of Shaka, a man was called *isihlangu senkosi,* meaning "the war-shield of the king." Today the Zulu remain a stratified society that values political power. The Zulu chief plays an important role in South African national politics and civil rights. Now numbering more than three million, the Zulu generally live in the Natal region of eastern South Africa and speak a language that contains the clicking sounds common to the Bantu languages. Many contemporary Zulu live in cities or near the gold mines where they work, but a large number live in the countryside, herding cattle and growing vegetables. They are known for their beadwork, basketry, and circular houses.

Zulu men and women are easily recognized by their distinctive traditional dress. Men tie a beaded belt over a goatskin apron and wear certain clothing for rituals and other special occasions. The Zulu identify themselves as a warrior people, and various shields and spear designs distinguish different regiments. Zulu women make elaborate and multicolored beaded necklaces in symbolic colors. Blue, for example, means fidelity, and white means purity.

Zulu society is patrilineal. Descent is thus reckoned through the male line, and after marriage women almost always move to the homes of their husbands. Marriages continue to be conducted with the exchange of *lobola,* or bridewealth—goods given by the groom's kin to the bride's kin. Although cattle are preferred, money and other goods are being given more and more. On the surface, the practice appears to be a sort of bride "purchase," but like other societies that have bridewealth customs, the Zulu consider it more of an entitlement to domestic and sexual rights. Bridewealth also makes the marriage legal, and so women are able to hold their husbands responsible for their actions.

Believing in a single creator called Nkulunkulu, the Zulu look to a spiritual world inhabited by ancestors who intervene in everyday life. These ancestors are known as shades and appear as dreams and omens. They are not considered distant from the living, and they may even be called the living dead.

Many Zulu are Christian, but many follow the faith first revealed by Isaiah Shembe, a Zulu prophet who brought Christian and Zulu beliefs and practices together in a religion he called Zionism.

Zulu men don traditional 19th-century warrior garb for rituals, a stark contrast with the Western clothing they may wear daily.

West Africa

The Gold Coast, the Ivory Coast, the Grain Coast, the Slave Coast—the many names of commodity and abundance that have been attached to this region indicate its history of importance in world trade and economics. These lands once saw great empires built over centuries: the Mali Empire from the 13th century, the Songhay from the 15th. Great rivers, including the Gambia and the Niger, flow from mountains to shore, through forests, savannahs, and arid plains to an often swampy coastline. Numerous small countries cluster in West Africa today, including Senegal, Gambia, Guinea-Bissau, Guinea, Sierra Leone, Liberia, Côte d'Ivoire, Ghana, Togo, Benin—as well as the larger surrounding countries of Mauriania, Mali, Niger, and Nigeria. The complex patchwork of national boundaries signals the region's long and complicated tribal, colonial, and political history.

To listen to music from Cameroon, Cape Verde, Côte d'Ivoire, Gambia, Guinea, Nigeria, and Senegal, visit http://worldmusic.nationalgeographic.com.

ASANTE

Alternate name: Ashanti
Population: 2.8 million   **Location:** Ghana
Language family: Kwa

Nearly 1.5 million Asante dwell in southern Ghana. They speak the Asante language, which is part of the Akan cluster of Twi languages, and they are perhaps best known for their colorful, geometrically designed Kente cloth.

The mighty Asante kingdom emerged in the forests of central Ghana in the late 17th century, after the union of several smaller states. At that time, the Golden Stool—symbol of Asante statehood—appeared. This sacred relic is said to have descended from the heavens in answer to the prayers of Okomfe Anokye, a legendary priest and adviser. The stool came to rest on the knees of Osei Tutu, who ascended to power as the first Ashantehene or Asante ruler. Treated with the reverence given to a king, the Golden Stool travels with a retinue and occupies its own palace. It has never been sat upon.

In the early Asante economy, the people depended on the gold-and-slave trade that developed between them and the Manding and Hausa, other peoples of West Africa, as well between them and the Europeans who came to their shores. By acting as middlemen in the slave trade, the Asante received firearms, which increased their already dominant power in the region. Other luxury goods became symbols of status and political office. The Asante turned to the surrounding forest for another economically important item: kola nuts, sought after as gifts and used as a mild stimulant among the Muslim peoples to the north.

Today the Asante are primarily farmers, growing cocoa for export and planting yams, plantains, and other produce for local consumption. They also include master stool makers and accomplished carvers, jewelers, metalsmiths, and weavers. Originally worn by rulers, the famous kente cloth is now donned by commoners and has become an important cultural symbol for many African Americans.

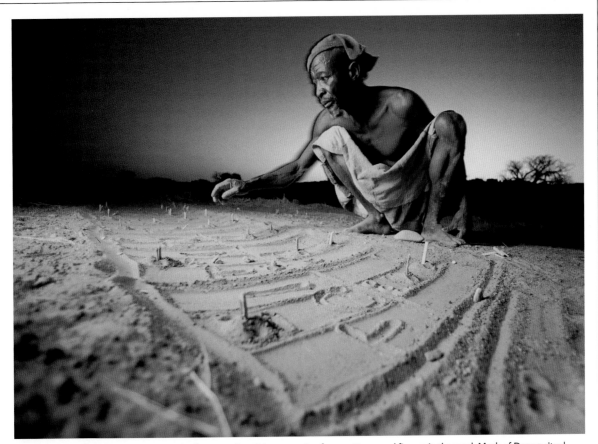

Steeped in a complex cosmology, a Dogon fortune-teller divines meaning from patterns and figures in the sand. Much of Dogon ritual aims at success in agriculture.

Most of the Asante reside in south-central Ghana's Asante region, which is centered around Kumasi, the country's second largest city, after Accra. Villages include the extended families of clans that descend from common female ancestors along the maternal lines. The Asante maintain customs and beliefs in the spirit world that all share, while some practice Christianity, Islam, and animism as well.

BAMBARA

Population: 3 million
Location: Mali
Language family: Mande

Mali's largest ethnic group, the Bambara live primarily in the western part of the country and along the Niger River. They speak Bamana, a language widely used throughout Mali, particularly in the areas of business and trade.

During the 1700s, there were two Bambara kingdoms: Segu and Karta. Muslim groups overthrew these kingdoms in the 1800s, and many Bambara remained wary of Islam until the arrival of the French as a colonial power. As resistance to French colonialism grew, so did Islam, and today nearly 80 percent of Bambara peoples are Muslim.

The Bambara are farmers who produce large quantities of sorghum and groundnuts; their main crop is millet. They also grow maize, cassava, tobacco, and numerous other plants in private gardens. Environmental hardships such as drought often make farming difficult, so people may keep livestock to supplement their diet. Often they trust their neighbors, the Fulani herdsmen, to look after their domestic animals. This arrangement lets the Bambara focus on farming during the short rainy season from June to September. Both men and women share the farming duties, although the division of labor allows women to leave the fields earlier to prepare meals for their families.

Bambara villages are collections of different family units, usually all from one extended family or lineage, and each *gwa*, or household, provides for all of its members and helps them with their farming duties. The members of each gwa work together every day except Monday, usually considered market day. Generally larger than the homes of other West African groups, Bambara dwellings may house 60 or more people.

For the Bambara, marriage carries heavy expenses, but most men are prepared to sacrifice a great deal because they view it as an investment. The return on that investment is the arrival of children, who then help with farming and contribute to the growth of a family's fortunes. Many Bambara women give birth to eight or more children. All adults marry, and it is not unusual for widows in their 70s or 80s to have suitors, for marriage enhances a person's reputation.

Although most Bambara are Muslims, old beliefs and rituals persist. In many areas, traditional male religious societies perform ceremonies to honor ancestors and promote the fertility of both the land and the people. Each society has its own distinctive masks, carved in wood and often depicting animals.

DOGON

Population: 600,000
Location: Mali
Language family: Dogon

Now inhabiting the Bandiagara cliffs region of south-central Mali, as well as parts of Burkina Faso, the Dogon are thought to be descended from the first inhabitants of the Niger River Valley. From there, the Dogon probably migrated to Burkina Faso between the 13th and 15th centuries. Then, around 1490, they fled an onslaught of their territory by Mossi people and found a haven among the cliffs of southern Mali.

Contemporary populations speak a language also known as Dogon. They live in a stratified society, with each individual's status determined by his position within important subgroups, such as his clan, village, male lineage, and age set. Each subgroup has a hierarchy based on age and rules of descent, meaning that individuals who enjoy high status in their families are the people most likely to occupy important positions in society.

A jeans-clad Dogon youth perches on a rock above his village in Mali. In this remote area, Dogon build their settlements on both towering cliffs and in the valleys.

The Dogon build their dwellings into and atop the dramatic cliffs of their homeland, as well as on the land below. Family homes are made of stone or adobe and are arranged around a courtyard open to domestic animals. Often set above the corners of this courtyard are thick-walled, fortress-like towers where millet and wheat are stored; such towers have also been used in defensive efforts against attackers.

Because the Dogon are an agricultural people, the land is of great importance in their lives and in their religious views and practices. For example, the Lebe cult is dedicated to agricultural renewal; its altars contain clumps of earth to encourage fertility. Perhaps the most significant agricultural rite is called the *bulu,* performed before the rains come and the planting begins.

Dogon religion involves the worship of ancestors, as well as spirits the people encountered as they moved across the landscape of West Africa. An important institution is the Awa society, whose rituals enable the deceased to leave the world of the living for the world of the dead. Many ceremonies are public, and these include funerary rites known as *bago bundo,* with masks and dancing, and the *dama* ceremony to mark the end of mourning. The society's most important responsibility is the planning of the *sigui* ceremonies, held every 60 years, when the star Sirius appears between two mountain peaks.

Rites and ceremonies involve masks and are performed by males who personify supernatural beings and speak their special language, *sigi so.* The Dogon's carved masks and wooden figurative art—usually in red, black, and white, with spirals and checkerboard patterns—draw admiration around the world.

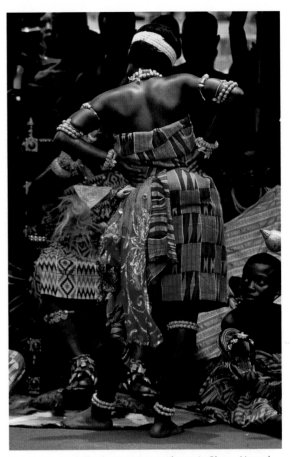

Colorful kente cloth adorns an Asante dancer in Ghana. Named for past rulers, textile designs reflect Ghana's rich history.

FANG

Population: 3.3 million
Location: Gabon, Equatorial Guinea, Cameroon
Language family: Bantu

The Fang people have not occupied their rain forest territories for very long, having migrated from the northeast a couple of centuries ago. Although they were feared at first by Europeans on the coast, they later traded ivory and forest products with them; they did not, however, take part in the widespread slave trade.

The Fang grow crops such as manioc and plantains using swidden cultivation, an agricultural technique that creates temporary growing plots. They rotate crops to help preserve fertility and prevent erosion. Many Fang cultivate cash crops of cocoa and coffee, while others make a living by working in cities.

Outside of Africa, the Fang are perhaps best known for their wooden reliquary figures, stylized carvings meant to embody aesthetic and social values of opposition and vitality. Features in Fang art reflect the idea that through opposition will come strength, growth, and energy. From antagonism or difference comes new life; the simplest example of this concept is the joining of men and women to produce children.

The principle of dichotomies also extends to architecture: Entering a Fang village, one sees straight rows of houses flanking a central courtyard or plaza, creating a square of houses. Those who build opposite one another often say that "it is better to shout insults to your brother across the court than to whisper them to his ear as your neighbor." They believe conflict is best resolved in the open, since it festers in secret.

FULANI

Alternate names: Fula, Fulbe Population: 13 million
Location: Nigeria, Guinea, Senegal
Language family: Atlantic

One of the most wide-ranging African tribes, the Fulani are found from Senegal and Gambia on the western coast of Africa as far east as western Sudan. They speak many dialects of the Fulfulde language. Though some animist practices continue, the majority of Fulani are Muslim, and many Fulani men have become respected religious leaders and teachers.

Traditionally, the Fulani are pastoralists who practice transhumance: They move their herds seasonally from one area to another in search of pasturage and available water, away from diseases that affect cattle, and to the markets where they can transact business and learn important news. The pastoral Fulani exist for their cattle, doing everything they can to manage their herds successfully. In return, the cattle give them the dairy products on which they base their nutrition. Fulani migrate as households of one man with from one to four wives and numerous children. They travel light, with minimal household possessions—with one exception: the decorated calabashes that Fulani women tend to accumulate in numbers far greater than any domestic need.

Today's Fulani pursue economic strategies on the spectrum between nomadism and a totally sedentary lifestyle. Those who remain pastoralists are known as Cattle Fulani, while those who are assimilated into urban life and follow a profession such as religious leader, teacher, trader, or government worker are known as Town Fulani. Variations combine a connection to cattle—sometimes only owning a herd managed by others—with settled life, either as a farmer or in a town. Some Town Fulani have allied themselves with the Hausa of Nigeria and now are totally sedentary (and nearly indistinguishable from the Hausa).

Fulani people have a reputation of being aloof and inscrutable, traits that have been linked to their values of reserve, patience, and gentleness. They view themselves as proper Muslims and look askance at those who are lax. This attitude drew the Fulani into jihads, or holy wars, in the 18th and 19th centuries and allowed them to achieve ethnic dominance in parts of West Africa.

Fulani carry personal decoration to the height of elaboration for both men and women. As women do in many nomadic societies, Fulani women make and wear large amounts of jewelry as a way to transport and safeguard wealth. Their treasures may include beads of glass and bronze, silver, gold, and coins. In times of need, they can sell a piece of jewelry to raise cash.

Fulani clothing differs from group to group but includes embroidered and brightly colored and patterned tunics, skirts, pants, turbans, and head wraps.

> In the woman's womb,
> a child takes shape through
> the ancient stories of the world.
> **DOGON PROVERB**

Many Fulani people practice body decoration in the form of multiple tattoos, colorful face powders and paints, and intricately braided hairstyles.

Fulani have strongly developed notions of both male and female physical beauty, or *boodal,* that perhaps is carried out to the extreme among the Wodaabe, a nomadic Fulani group found mainly in Niger and northern Nigeria. At the annual *geerewole* ceremony, the men dress and make themselves up painstakingly to appear as a group in front of eligible young women. They jump, dance, and make facial contortions that they hope will catch the eye of a potential second wife, or perhaps just start a dalliance, as first wives usually are chosen in a more circumspect way among first cousins by the young man's family.

HAUSA

Population: 25 million
Location: Nigeria, Niger
Language family: Chadic

The history of the Hausa, who inhabit northern Nigeria and southern Niger, is marked by the rise of powerful kingdoms built on lucrative trade markets. Living along caravan routes that reached to the Middle East, the Hausa became expert traders, even though the majority of the people were, and remain, settled farmers.

Hausa origin myths hold that the hero Bayajidda rescued the queen of Daura and her people from

Hausa tribesmen pick up their nets from Lake Chad, on the border of Nigeria and Niger. Many Hausa also farm and others excel in trade.

a powerful serpent. As a reward, the queen married Bayajidda and gave birth to seven sons, each of whom founded a Hausa kingdom. Allied politically, all of the kingdoms specialized in economic and military activities that were based on their locations and natural resources. These substates were known for indigo, slaves, markets, government, war, and so forth. Constant military vigilance was required to fend off such aggressive neighbors as the Akan and Songhay.

From at least the 11th century, the history of the region has been intimately tied to Islam and the Fulani ethnic group, which seized power from the Hausa in the early 1800s through a series of jihads. In many areas, intermarriage has since blurred the distinctions between Hausa and Fulani, and they are considered one group in contemporary Nigeria. Together they form the largest ethnic group in the country and the most numerous Muslim group in sub-Saharan Africa.

Political leadership in the early Hausa states was based on ancestry, with individuals who could trace their relations back to Bayajidda considered royal.

When Islam arrived, many Hausa rulers embraced the religion and combined it with traditional ways. Rulers also welcomed praise singers, known as *maroka,* who were historians of lineage and were granted access to important personages.

In the early 20th century, as the British colonized the region, the Hausa became part of Nigeria. Today they are still traders and farmers, well known for their production of indigo-dyed cloth. Hausa, a language related to Arabic, Berber, and Hebrew, is spoken throughout Africa as a language of trade.

IGBO

Alternate name: Ibo Population: 20 million
Location: Nigeria
Language family: Benue-Congo [Igboid]

In the corner of southeastern Nigeria divided by the Niger River and encompassing its delta, the Igbo (EE-boh) people have been a dominant presence for at least a thousand years, the age of their earliest surviving art. They may have come from an area a hundred miles to the north of the confluence of the Niger and Benue Rivers, from which they fanned out to the south. Today, some 18 million Igbo inhabit a region referred to as Igboland. The Igbo language is spoken by most contemporary Igbo people, and they also often speak English, Nigeria's official language, which has gained them access to educational opportunities ever since the British colonial period.

Unlike neighbors to the north such as the Yoruba and the Hausa, the Igbo did not establish kingdoms or hereditary chiefdoms. They traditionally live in villages composed of households formed mostly on the basis of patrilineal descent. Village size ranges anywhere from a few dozen members to several thousand. Igbo men often have several wives who share the same homestead but keep their own rooms, kitchens, and storage areas for their provisions.

Villages are governed by a council of elders, who include the village's oldest members and titled men. Igbo women form their own political organizations under the leadership of respected matriarchs, which sometimes rally together, as they did against the colonial British in the 1929 Women's War.

An Igbo man accrues status by obtaining a number of titles that indicate particular achievements. For example, the "killer of cows" has acquired enough cows to slaughter and then hold a large feast. Igbo men work hard to prove they are worthy of the titles, and some may spend quite a bit of money in this quest. Women can acquire titles independently and can also receive them by association from their titled husbands. Other villagers morally judge titled and important Igbo by whether they use their high positions to help their less successful kin.

Traditionally, the Igbo are farmers. They follow a division of labor by gender, with the men growing yams—culturally, their most important crop—and the women growing cassava, cocoyams, pumpkins, peppers, and their own varieties of yams. Igbo also cultivate and process the fruit of the palm to obtain products to use and also sell, such as palm oil, which is even exported to Europe.

All Igbo, particularly the women, participate very actively in a local market economy. Women sell surplus crops along with mats that they weave and pottery that they make, almost exclusively, sometimes with considerable economic success. Women also decorate their homes with painted geometric patterns and participate in the construction and decoration of *mbari*, elaborately decorated houses built in honor of gods that often incorporate life-size pottery figures. Igbo men are renowned blacksmiths and woodcarvers, specializing in stylized painted masks, their designs inspired by the deities whose images artisans create to be worn in ritual dances.

During the British colonial period, most Igbo converted to Christianity. Today they combine the Christian religion with their traditional beliefs, which revolve around a creator god, Chukwu, and a pantheon of lesser gods, goddesses, and spirits. Divination priests and priestesses discern the deities' wishes, so that appropriate actions can be taken to thwart misfortune and promote good consequences.

The period leading up to and following Nigerian independence was tumultuous for the Igbo. In 1967 the largely Igbo region of Nigeria's southeastern coast seceded from the rest of the country and became known

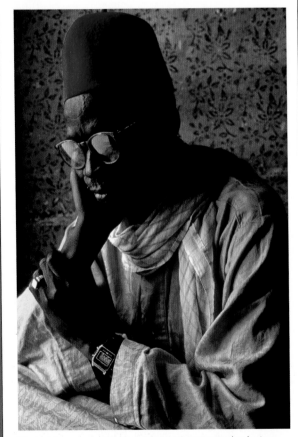

The red fez worn by this Senegalese man suggests that he is Muslim, the religious affiliation of many West Africans.

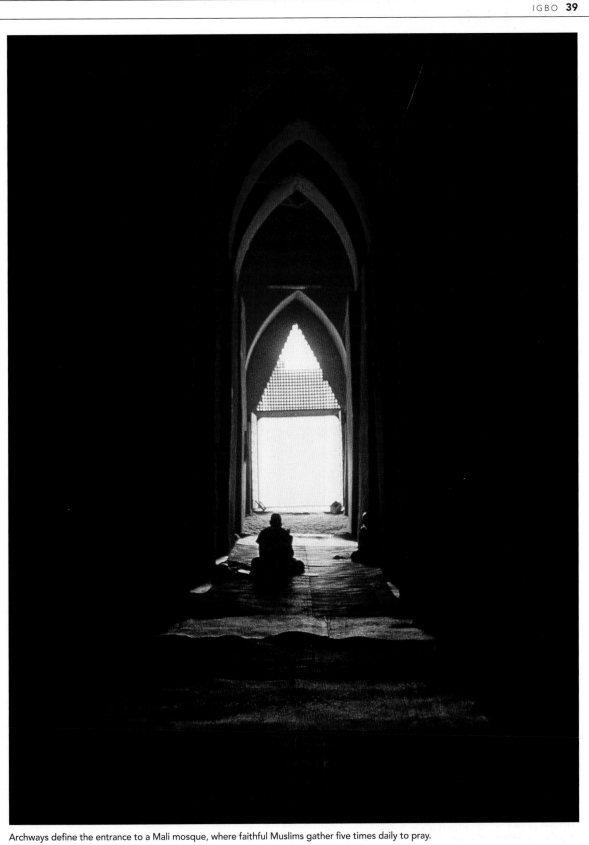

Archways define the entrance to a Mali mosque, where faithful Muslims gather five times daily to pray.

as Biafra. During the ensuing civil war, many Igbo were killed, and mass starvation mobilized international relief efforts. Biafra became reincorporated into Nigeria in 1970, but regional instability led to a diaspora that took many Igbo to overseas destinations including the United Kingdom and the United States.

WOLOF

Population: 5.7 million
Location: Senegal
Language family: Atlantic

Neighbors to the Mandika and the Fulani, the Wolof are the dominant ethnic group of coastal Senegal. Their history dates from about the 12th or 13th century and is preserved in the art of the griots, or oral praise singers.

After the fall of the Ghana Empire in the 11th century, the ancestors of today's Wolof no longer felt protected in their old territory and migrated westward from Mali to the Atlantic coast. By the 15th century, they had established a powerful presence in what is now the Wolof homeland. The Portuguese established a presence on the African continent around that time as well, building a fort on Gorée Island, off the coast of Dakar; that fort would be used in the Atlantic slave trade. Islam arrived in the 15th century, brought to Senegal by Mauretanian imams. Today, the majority of Wolof people are Muslims, and many of the men belong to Muslim brotherhoods, each with its own unique features.

The traditional Wolof political system involved the rule of powerful headmen from elite lineages. These headmen acted as a sort of parliament, electing a supreme ruler from a pool of candidates. Slavery was a part of Wolof society, and the people were themselves involved in the slave trade. In West Africa, there were two types of enslaved people: those born into a household as slaves and those who were either captured in war or purchased.

In today's world, the Wolof people are well known for their rich musical tradition. They have developed an enormously sophisticated body of percussion instruments and harps, the most famous of which may be the *tama,* or talking drum, so called because its resonance

Women's voluntary associations, such as this group in Côte d'Ivoire, play major roles in promoting progressive political causes and gender solidarity throughout the sub-Saharan region.

can be altered by pressing strings that attach the drumhead to the drum, resulting in changing pitches that sound like human speech. Also important is the *xalam,* a five-stringed guitarlike instrument. Some contemporary Wolof musicians—Youssou N'Dour and Baaba Maal, to name two of them—have established international reputations and made the sounds of Wolof music better known around the world.

The Wolof are known for their spicy stews, too. Sorghum and millet are the staple crops, but tomatoes, peanuts, beans, and peppers are important fare as well. Fish and rice are also staples, and all of these ingredients find their way into the stews and other dishes that are characteristic of Wolof cooking.

YORUBA

Population: 28 million
Location: Nigeria
Language family: Benue-Congo [Yoruboid]

One of the largest groups in Africa, the Yoruba people live primarily in southwestern Nigeria and the neighboring countries of Benin and Togo. While some of the Yoruba make their homes in grasslands and forests, members of this group have also been city dwellers for centuries. They are therefore among the most urbanized people of all those living on the African continent.

> The cock with the very fine comb
> is the one we kill for a sacrifice.
> WEST AFRICAN PROVERB

In the past, Yoruba city-states were governed by an *oba,* or king, and a supreme council. Ancient city-states frequently went to war, and in the mid-18th century the Oyo kingdom became dominant, providing a cohesive identity among the Yoruba that continues to this day.

Religion has always been very important in Yoruba society, with traditional beliefs still exercising a major influence on daily life, even though both Christianity and Islam are now widespread. Olorun is the high god, but he has no specific shrines. People consider him relatively inactive in human affairs and instead seek

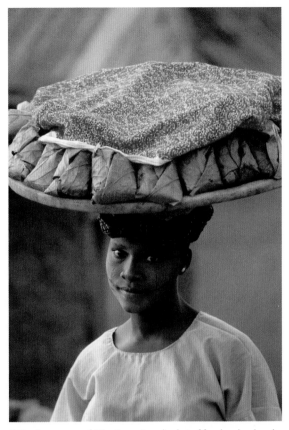

A Yoruba woman of Nigeria carries a basket of food on her head.

help from traditional deities known as *orisha,* which are said to number 401. The Yoruba believe that when they die, they enter the ancestors' realm, from which they continue to influence earthly affairs. In rare instances, they may even become orisha like Shango, the thunder god who was once a celebrated king. Yoruba spiritual beliefs have had an enormous influence on New World religions such as Cuba's Santería, Trinidad's Orisha, and Brazil's Candomblé.

Along with their skills in woodcarving, weaving, potterymaking, and metalwork, the Yoruba are famous for something else: their high incidence of twinning. With 45 births in 1,000 producing twins, the rate is four times that of the United States or Great Britain. This biological phenomenon has yielded a special status for twins in the Yoruba cosmology; they are known as thunder children, because the first twins were believed to be the children of Shango. Twins are considered both a burden and a blessing: Twice as much trouble to raise, they also bring twice as much good fortune to parents who give them proper care.

Central Africa

South of the Sahara, west of the Great Rift Valley, and intersected by the Equator, the region of Central Africa (also called Middle Africa) contains some of the densest tropical rain forest of the world. Through it flow the Congo River and its tributaries, a complex river system that drains a total of about 1,425,000 square miles into the Atlantic. The nations of Central Africa include Chad, Sudan, Gabon, Cameroon, Angola, the Central African Republic, the Democratic Republic of the Congo, and the People's Republic of the Congo, often called simply the Congo.

♫ To listen to music from Congo, the Democratic Republic of the Congo, Gabon, and Tanzania, visit http://world music.nationalgeographic.com.

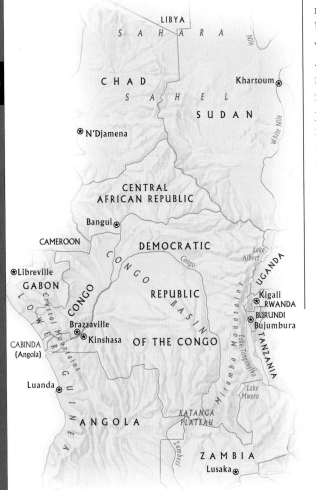

EFE

Population: 20,000
Location: Democratic Republic of the Congo
Language family: Central Sudanic

The central African rain forest is home to the Efe, one of several hunter-gatherer groups known as Pygmies, a term increasingly viewed in the region as a pejorative. With a total population of nearly 200,000, these groups also include the Mbuti, the Sua, and the Aka.

Today the Efe—like their immediate neighbors, the Mbuti—are almost exclusively hunter-gatherers. Some Efe men may reach a height of five feet, but the vast majority of both men and women never exceed four feet, ten inches. Researchers believe that their shortness is an adaptation: Smaller individuals have more surface area in proportion to volume and can therefore dissipate body heat better in the hot rain forest.

The Efe live in camps of between four and twenty people, occupying quickly built huts for only a few months before moving on to new hunting territory. Unlike the Mbuti, who use nets, the Efe hunt exclusively with bows and arrows, usually for monkeys and small African antelopes known as duikers. But the Efe cannot survive by eating only what they find in the rain forest. For carbohydrates they depend on cassava, rice, peanuts, potatoes, and yams collected from their farmer neighbors, with whom they engage in long-term, hereditary exchange partnerships, conversing in mutually understandable dialects of the same language.

Ideally, a Lese farmer inherits as his partner the son of his father's Efe trading partner. The Efe give their partners meat, honey, and other forest foods in return for cultivated foods and metal. Farmers sometimes marry Efe women, but it is taboo for Efe men to marry farmer women. Hence the farmer group has lost height over time while the Efe have remained the same.

With a somewhat nomadic lifestyle, the Efe do not possess property or wealth that they cannot move. Artistically, they are perhaps best known for their bark cloth paintings with simple black geometric designs that are common to nearly all Pygmy groups.

Central African Pygmy peoples live in small camps, their homes hemispherical huts made from leaves and sticks. Huts rise quickly in the forest when the group moves to a new area.

KONGO

Population: 2.2 million
Location: Democratic Republic of the Congo, Congo
Language family: Bantu

More than two million Kongo live in the southwest part of the Democratic Republic of the Congo, in northwestern Angola, and in southern Congo. These people reckon descent through the maternal line, believing they descend from 12 female ancestors who assisted the founders of the ancient kingdom of Kongo.

In 1482 Portuguese explorers first encountered this kingdom. They saw a vibrant and complex political and economic organization of chiefs, governors, and judicial officers, with a strong military and a system for collecting taxes. Though the Portuguese had limited success in converting the people to Christianity, they still retained respect for them and later agreed to help when the Kongo were plundered by the Jaga in the 16th century. Even so, the Kongo never fully recovered, and in 1885 they became colonial subjects of Belgium. Over the years, the Kongo have occasionally gained power in national politics, especially in 1960 when Joseph Kasavubu, a Kongo, became the first head of state of the newly independent Republic of Congo.

The economy of the ancient kingdom depended on taxes, tribute, and proceeds from the slave trade, but now the Kongo subsist, primarily through agriculture and fishing. The people maintain a conventional division of labor: Women harvest fields of cassava, beans, and squash, while men tend orchards of palm oil trees.

Kongo live in cities and in the countryside, but in the Democratic Republic of the Congo many live in independent religious communities, some arising from the religion of the prophet Simon Kimbangu (1889-1951), a Zulu Zionist who developed a syncretic religion based on Christianity and native beliefs. Kimbangu became so powerful that the Belgian colonial government emprisoned him for life, and he died a martyr. Kimbangu's church was the first in Africa to be admitted to the World Council of Churches.

MANGBETU

Population: 50,000
Location: Democratic Republic of the Congo
Language family: Central Sudanic

The Mangbetu live in the northern part of the Democratic Republic of the Congo. Like their neighbors, the Efe and the Azande, they speak a Sudanic, tonal language. The Mangbetu and other Sudanic-speaking populations in central Africa most likely originated in the Sudan, from which they either migrated or were displaced into the Congo basin.

Until the late 19th century, the Mangbetu people formed a vibrant group of kingdoms. Leadership positions were hereditary, and social organization was founded on the smallest societal unit: the house. More than just a rectangular, physical structure made of mud and sticks, a "house" might refer to a whole village or a group of villages. Houses of varying size could incorporate nonlineage members such as wives, sisters' children, slaves, and even non-Mangbetu people.

The Mangbetu are one of the most physically distinctive groups in central Africa, since they value women with a conical head shape. During much of the 20th century, high-status families would bind the heads of infant girls so that as their craniums hardened, they became elongated. This procedure is seldom practiced today, but for the Mangbetu a conical head is still a sign of great beauty and status, reflecting the right to authority and political power. A unique, elaborate hairstyle emphasizes the distinctive shape of the head.

Mangbetu artistic traditions have spread throughout the northern Democratic Republic of the Congo, making them one of the most artistically influential societies in central Africa. The Mangbetu are known for their decorated harps, trumpets, knives, pots, and boxes—many of which bear elongated-head sculptures.

TUTSI & HUTU

Alternate name: Watutsi (for Tutsi) **Population:** 18 million
Location: Rwanda, Burundi **Language family:** Bantu

The Hutu and the Tutsi, along with the Twa, a Pygmy people, occupy the nations of Rwanda and Burundi. While the Hutu and Tutsi have lived side by side for several centuries, their relationship has been marked by hostility and occasional violence.

For a long time the Tutsi, the minority group, ruled the Hutu. According to tradition, the cattle-herding Tutsi came into the area in the 14th or 15th century and began to incorporate the Twa hunter-gatherers and the Hutu farmers into their society as subordinates. They established a hierarchical political system headed by a king, or *mwami,* considered divine. The German and Belgian colonists who took control of the area in the 19th and early 20th centuries reinforced the distinctions, calling the Tutsi "lords" and the Hutu "vassals."

The integration of these two peoples socially and economically was achieved primarily through a patron-client relationship. Since cattle were the key to social power, the dominant Tutsi needed to retain control over livestock, and they achieved this through a process called *ubuhake.* A Tutsi cattle owner or patron permitted his less well-off client—a Hutu or perhaps another Tutsi—to use his cattle in return for labor and goods. Thus most Hutu and Tutsi families have long been linked in some way, including by intermarriage. The Hutu and Tutsi cultures also became integrated through language, with Tutsis adopting mutually intelligible Bantu languages, and religion: Tutsi and Hutu animism has largely given way to Christianity.

The colonial powers continued to perpetuate these socioeconomic distinctions, and the powerful Tutsi received greater access to European resources and education, fueling resentment among the Hutu. Following independence in 1962, two countries emerged from what had been Ruanda-Urundi, or Belgian East Africa. The Hutu seized power, and some of the worst violence of the 20th century ensued. Military campaigns on both sides resulted in the deaths of thousands.

In 1994, civil war erupted after Rwanda's and Burundi's Hutu presidents were killed when their helicopter was shot down. The retaliation left half a million Tutsis dead and created one of the largest groups of refugees in African history. The Tutsis took back power in Rwanda, and the country became enmeshed in complex regional politics. Many Hutu and Tutsi have stood trial before the United Nations for crimes of genocide, and many others have been judged in communal grassroots courts called *gacaca.*

In 2004 the Rwandan government dedicated a memorial in Kigali, the capital, to the estimated 250,000 genocide victims from that area alone. New legislation was passed forbidding political parties to make any reference to ethnic, religious, regional, or clan differences in their names or operations.

A Tutsi man performs a ritual dance in Rwanda, scene of civil warfare in recent decades.

East Africa

East Africa includes the lands sometimes called the Horn of Africa, bordering the Gulf of Aden; the great island of Madagascar and companion islands in the Indian Ocean; and the lands defined by the Great Rift Valley, a 3,000-mile-long north-south fault line caused by massive tectonic plate shifts some hundreds of thousands, perhaps a million, years ago. Some of the most complete remains of hominid ancestors have been found in this terrain. The geographical highlights of East Africa include Mounts Kilimanjaro and Kenya, Africa's highest peaks, and Lake Victoria, Africa's largest lake (and the world's second largest freshwater lake) and the source for the White Nile, the largest branch of the Nile River, which flows northward through this region and eventually empties into the Mediterranean Sea.

To listen to music from Ethiopia, Kenya, and Tanzania, visit http://worldmusic.nationalgeographic.com.

AMHARA
Population: 16 million
Location: Ethiopia
Language family: Semitic

The Amhara people live in the highlands of Ethiopia. For most of their history, they have been farmers and part-time pastoralists, but they have also been the most powerful ethnic group in the region. Amhara kings fought for power in Ethiopia throughout the 18th and 19th centuries, and in 1889 Menelik II, an Amhara, declared himself emperor of an area nearly equal in size to today's country. Except for its occupation by Italy from 1935 to 1941, when Emperor Haile Selassie went into exile, Ethiopia escaped European domination in the 20th century—the only African nation to do so.

Like many other residents of the highlands, the Amhara maintain religious traditions that derive from extensive and early contacts between Ethiopia and the Near East. Some groups practice Islam, others a form of Coptic Christianity, which was widely practiced in Egypt until the Arab conquest in the seventh century. The Ethiopian Orthodox Church eventually emerged from early Greek and Coptic influences.

According to linguists, the Amharic language is from the Afro-Asiatic group of languages spoken mostly in parts of Mediterranean Africa; these tongues are also spoken by certain peoples of west and central Africa, as well as small numbers in the Horn of Africa. Some linguists suggest that Amharic is most closely related to Hebrew.

The Amhara economy is based primarily on cultivation of maize, wheat, sorghum, and a cereal grass called teff. In the past, land ownership was bestowed by the emperor in thanks for loyalty and military service, and new landowners would then become patrons to client farmers.

Throughout history, the social organization of the Amhara kingdom has been patriarchal, with women having little authority or potential to own property. To some extent, the status of a woman is tied to the kind of marriage she has. The most common form, called *serat*, is a civil union not bound by religious restrictions. In such a union, a woman is more likely to be able to seek divorce or to air a dispute with the help of a mediator; she may also claim part of her husband's wealth

Masai women head to a ritual gathering in Tanzania. Masai are one of the few East African tribes to practice pastoralism almost exclusively, foregoing involvement in agriculture.

if they divorce. A smaller number of people marry in the Ethiopian Church, a process called *qurban,* and this kind of marriage cannot be dissolved even if a partner is an Ethiopian priest. The form of marriage giving a woman the lowest status, *damoz,* occurs often, despite its being illegal in Ethiopia. In this arrangement, women are paid to become short-term wives or sexual partners, sometimes for just a few weeks.

In the 20th century, the Amhara expanded militarily and became the political elite of Ethiopia. People who did not speak Amharic, the language of the elite, were soon at a disadvantage in everyday life and before the law. By the middle of the century, after Amharic had become the national language, neighboring groups declared they would no longer be dominated by the Amhara. One of the central forces behind the rebellion was the growth of Oromo nationalism; although the Oromo have far greater numbers, they were long subordinate to the Amhara. Ethiopia continues to struggle for the national integration of its different ethnic groups, and in this respect Ethiopia shares much with the rest of sub-Saharan Africa.

BAGANDA

Population: 5.1 million   Location: Uganda
Language family: Bantu

Uganda's largest ethnic group, the Baganda live on the northern and western shores of Lake Victoria. They speak Luganda, or Ganda, which also is an alternate name for the people.

British explorers coming to the area in the mid-1800s encountered a kingdom, called Buganda, ruled by a powerful *kabaka,* or hereditary king. The king presided over a network of patrilineal clans headed by chiefs who administered his policies, distributed land, and collected tribute in the form of food, livestock, and services. The kabaka took wives from many different clans, inspiring loyalty by keeping open the possibility that a future king could come from any clan. Behavior in the presence of the kabaka was highly ritualized and

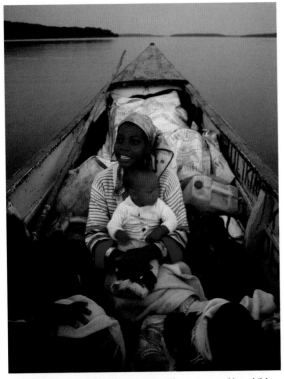

After a visit to her tribal home, a Baganda woman and her child head out across Lake Victoria in Uganda.

cotton, coffee, and tea—and they also hunt and fish. Even Baganda who reside in towns often cultivate a kitchen garden.

From early childhood, Bagandan children are encouraged to be loquacious and to manipulate the Luganda language for fun. With peers, they engage in games of *ludikya,* or talking backward, often to

> From cleverness of hand,
> you get serfdom.
> From cleverness of mouth,
> you become boss.
>
> AMHARA PROVERB

befuddle adults. All ages participate in riddle contests, a favorite pastime in the evening. These games, along with a rich folklore tradition, have helped make modern Bagandans some of Africa's most prolific novelists, playwrights, poets, and songwriters.

Since the mid-1980s, many Baganda people have succumbed to the effects of HIV/AIDS, and the population includes large numbers of orphaned children as a result. The Ugandan government now maintains one of Africa's most far-reaching and effective programs for dealing with the disease and within a relatively short time has managed to reduce rates of infection significantly.

BETA ISRAEL

Alternate name: Falasha   Population: 2,500
Location: Ethiopia, Israel
Language family: Semitic

required that all commoners lie prone on the ground before him. The Baganda trace their kinship to the first kabaka, Kintu, who ruled about seven centuries ago. Myths attribute a heavenly origin to Kintu, regarded by some as the progenitor of all Baganda.

The Bagandan kingship remained intact during the British colonial period, and when Uganda gained its independence, in 1962, the king of Buganda became the nation's first president. Within a few years, however, all kingships in Uganda were abolished, not to be reinstated until 1993.

The majority of Bagandans are Christian, about equally divided between Catholic and Protestant, and about 15 percent are Muslim. Some Baganda believe in sorcery and witchcraft as the cause of misfortune and death; some also practice ancestor worship.

Bagandan villages occupy flat-topped hills on an elevated plateau and contain a number of households, each representing a patrilineage. Family compounds are surrounded by their own banana groves, which provide the Baganda's staple food, along with yams. Bagandans grow a number of other food crops—sweet potatoes, taro, millet, and peanuts, along with cash crops such as

Outsiders have often referred to the African Jews of Ethiopia as Falasha, meaning "moved" or "gone into exile" in the ancient Ge'ez language. Today, the community considers the word derogatory and prefers Beta Israel, a Hebrew term for "House of Israel." For millennia, this ethnic group from northwestern Ethiopia has practiced a form of Judaism. Now only a few thousand of its people remain in Africa, where they are concentrated in Addis Ababa, Ethiopia's capital city. Since the 1980s, most Beta Israel have migrated to Israel—many in a series of airlifts dubbed Operation Moses—and tens of thousands of Beta Israel currently reside there.

Although the origins of Judaism in Ethiopia remain a mystery, it is likely that the community's roots go back 2,500 years. Until relatively recent times, the Beta Israel were cut off from the rest of the Jewish world. This isolation left them unaware of the presence of other Jews and without access to important Jewish scripture, such as the Talmud. Furthermore, most Ethiopian Jews had no idea that many other Jews were white. Despite this situation, the Beta Israel have always considered themselves to be exiles from the land of Israel, followers of Moses, and one of the lost tribes. Some trace the group's history to the biblical parting of the Red Sea, claiming that the Jews of Ethiopia were those who did not cross before the waters returned and so had to escape from Egypt by heading south.

Some scholars have suggested that the Beta Israel descend from a people who spoke Agaw, a Cushitic language, and were converted roughly 2,000 years ago by Jews from southern Arabia (today's Yemen). In the 2nd century A.D., the Ethiopian kingdom of Aksum arose. It adopted Christianity as its religion in the 4th century, and the Beta Israel relocated to the mountains around Lake Tana. During the 13th century, the people numbered in the hundreds of thousands and ruled a powerful state in what is now Ethiopia. But beginning around 1400, the Solomonic Dynasty of Ethiopia gradually subdued the Beta Israel. In the 17th century, the Ethiopian emperor finally defeated the Jewish state and seized their lands. Most Beta Israel eventually gave up their Agaw language and adopted the Tigrinya or Amharic language of their neighbors.

The religious life of the Beta Israel is based on the Torah, on oral interpretations passed down through generations, and on the community's holy writings. Beta Israel strictly adhere to the kosher diet, observe the Sabbath, and celebrate all the festivals mentioned in the Torah, as well as those of their own tradition. The timing of holidays is determined by their own religious lunar calendar.

For century upon century, the Ethiopian Jews have

A Dinka herder drives his cattle into a forest to escape attack during Sudan's civil war. Years of warfare destroyed traditional economies throughout southern Sudan.

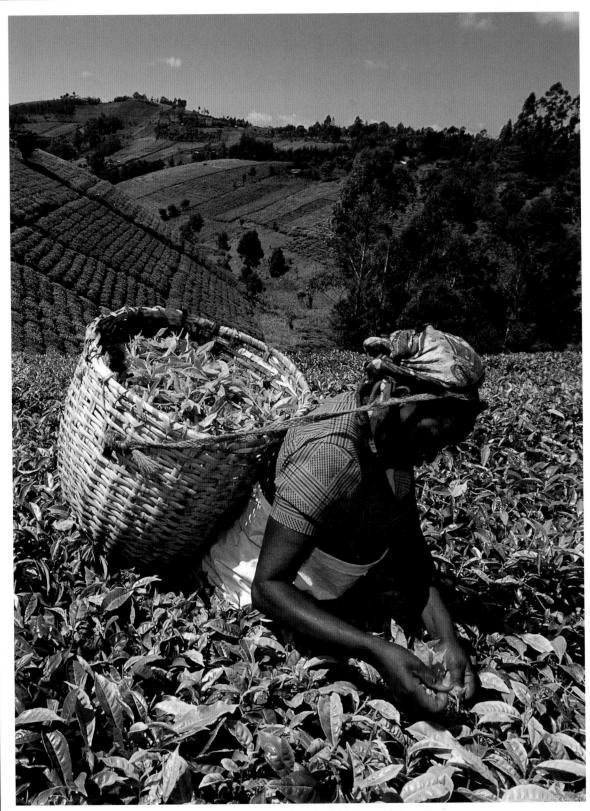

Many Kikuyu women work on large farms, such as this tea plantation on the fertile slopes of Mount Kenya.

grouped their Sabbaths into seven-week cycles. The seventh Sabbath, called Legata Sanbat, is considered particularly holy and includes special prayers, festivities, and a sanctification service; at this time, priests may have their sins absolved completely. A traditional priesthood, the Kohanim, leads the community's religious life, and its importance as the repository of the group's traditions has increased during the upheavals of the past century.

DINKA

Population: 2 million
Location: Sudan
Language family: Nilotic

Decades of civil strife in southern Sudan have dramatically altered the way of life of the tall, stalwart Dinka, who revere and rely on the herds of long-horned cattle that have formed the basis of their economy for centuries.

Traditionally, the tribe moves between dry-season camps near the Nile's banks, where Dinka men pasture and manage their herds, and rainy-season settlements away from Nile flooding that turns those grasslands into swamps. Spears at their shoulders, they guard the cattle vigilantly from animal predators and possible marauders from rival Nuer and other groups. They also hunt and fish to supplement their diet, sometimes taking down hippopotamuses. At their settlements, women work in gardens, cultivating crops such as millet, pumpkins, okra, and cassava.

Dinka live in patrilineal groups that are linked by descent from a common ancestor, but they observe no overall tribal leadership. Traditionally, men often supported more than one wife, and some wealthy men could have upwards of 50. Each wife contributed to the compound's chores but raised her own children. While newborn daughters are welcome for the cattle they bring at marriage, a newborn son will carry on a man's name and lineage.

As children, Dinka boys milk the cows, tie them up, and collect their dung. As youth, they are initiated with others of their age into warriorhood, never again to milk the cows but to assume adult responsibility for their protection. During initiation, the boys' foreheads are incised with tribal marks, and the ritual leaves distinctive permanent scars.

Every part and product of the cow has a use, and often several. While alive, the cow provides milk and butter and also blood, which is sometimes mixed with milk and drunk. Cow urine is used for washing hair, as an astringent for insect stings, and for tanning hides. Cow dung provides fuel for fires, and the ash becomes a tooth powder and an insect repellent for cows and people. Cattle are not slaughtered, except as a sacrifice on ceremonial occasions, such as a birth, a wedding, or a death. When a cow dies, either naturally or ritually, it provides meat and hides that are tanned. Cow horns and bones are used as musical instruments.

As the traditional form of wealth among the Dinka, cattle are offered as bride-price to secure spouses for young Dinka men. It can take as many as 40, 50, or 100 cows to seal a deal, depending on the bride's status. The recent widespread disruption of Dinka life has affected many aspects of their culture. Many have lost their cattle, and so they can only offer the promise of cows in the future to a prospective bride's family.

In the 1980s, civil war erupted once again in Sudan. Forced Islamization policies of the Arab Muslim government in the north enraged the largely black animist south, and oil discovered in the southern Sudan in 1979 added to the conflict. The government also played to established rivalries between Dinka and Nuer.

> Service rendered
> means service is owed.
> EAST AFRICAN PROVERB

Large populations of refugees have fled to northern Sudan, to neighboring countries, and to places such as the United States, Europe, and Australia. Among the refugees were the so-called Lost Boys of Sudan, young Dinka men who were off guarding cattle when their families were wiped out. Banding together, they set out on a long, perilous journey. Those who survived have begun new lives vastly removed from their Dinka past.

Southern Sudan achieved self-determination in January 2005, effectively ending the north-south conflict. The terrible conflict in Darfur in western Sudan, however, still awaits resolution.

KIKUYU

Population: 5.3 million
Location: Kenya
Language family: Bantu

Largest ethnic group in Kenya, the Kikuyu live throughout modern Kenya and in parts of Tanzania and Uganda as well. The earliest Kikuyu arrived in what is now Kenya during the massive Bantu migrations of A.D. 1200 to 1600. Over the years this ethnic group has played an important and highly visible role in the country's politics.

Kikuyu legend holds that a man named Gikuyu was the group's founder. He and his wife had nine daughters, who eventually married, had their own families, and retained a dominant role in Kikuyu society. The story helps explain the Kikuyu's nine family groupings. In fact, there are ten clans, but because the number ten is taboo, the usual practice is to count nine clans (plus one).

The Kikuyu were mainly farmers during the period of English colonization, but as the city of Nairobi grew under British rule, Kikuyu migrants made their way there. Many of the migrants had been educated at mission schools and had held municipal jobs that gave them unique exposure to colonial abuses. As a consequence, the city's Kikuyu began to organize politically in the 1920s; by the 1950s, the Kikuyu protest had solidified into a nationalist movement involving all ethnic groups. The government declared a state of emergency during the Mau Mau rebellion, arresting approximately 15,000 Africans in Nairobi, many of them Kikuyu, and sending them to detention camps. With Kenyan independence in December 1963, Nairobi became the national capital, and Jomo Kenyatta, a Kikuyu, soon became the first president of the Republic of Kenya.

The British at one time banned the Kikuyu language, often called Gikuyu, but today many schools teach it to children, following a policy of teaching the local language first, then Swahili and English.

Many Kikuyu name their children after important family members, alternating between families of the father and the mother. All Kikuyu recognize a supreme deity called Ngai, who habitually dwells invisibly in the sky but periodically manifests himself within an enormous cloud on Mount Kenya. When the Kikuyu people see clouds on the mountaintop, they know that Ngai is present.

A Malagasy woman brings in her daughter for a consultation with a Western-trained doctor. Many Africans also seek the ministrations of traditional healers.

MALAGASY

Population: 17.2 million
Location: Madagascar
Language family: Malayo-Polynesian [East Barito]

The term "Malagasy" denotes the language and identity of a complex and diverse group of people who live on Madagascar, the fourth largest island in the world. As many as 20 different ethnic groups—including the Merina, Betsimisaraka, Betsileo, Sakalava, and Antandroy—occupy the island. But while the millions of members of these ethnic groups claim particular cultural affiliations, these people also tend to say they are Malagasy and to speak Malagasy, the national language. Despite their many differences, most Malagasy communities have similar religious beliefs, bilateral kinship systems, and irrigated rice-farming economies. Perhaps the most salient ethnic division is not between particular groups but between the central highlands people, mainly of Indonesian descent, and the coastal people, of black African descent. Today these two

The Genes of Our Ancestors

During the past two years the National Museums of Kenya have been hard at work renovating their flagship Nairobi Museum. Set to open its expanded halls in 2008, this East African country's permanent exhibit showcases arguably the strongest evidence of an evolutionary origin for our species. Displayed throughout the museum are the clearest links to our distant ancestors yet uncovered, a temporal continuum of hominid species stretching back four million years to the time when apes first stood upright. Headlining the collection is the 1.6-million-year-old Turkana Boy, the most complete hominid skeleton ever unearthed, a juvenile *Homo erectus* excavated less than 250 miles north of the capital city, in the heart of Africa's Rift Valley. These are Kenya's national treasures, and nowhere else on Earth can one peer through display glass and look directly into the hollow eyes of four million years of evolution.

Meet mitochondrial Eve

But it is quite a jump from the ancient bones of Turkana Boy to those of modern humans—and that jump represents a gap that paleoanthropologists have been hard-pressed to bridge. The remains of anatomically modern humans have been discovered all across Africa and the Levant. They date from as early as 195,000 years ago, and they raise important questions—without offering answers—about both the location and timing of the dawn of our species.

In 1987 Rebecca Cann and colleagues took up the cause in a revolutionary study on the mitochondrial DNA

of people from populations both African and non-African, looking at the diversity of genetic lineages around the world. What they found rang in a new era of molecular anthropology, showing that all humans today share a common ancestor, now famously known as

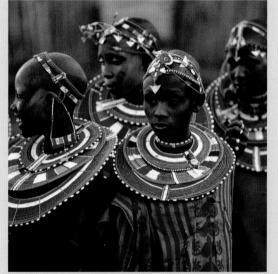

Adorned with traditional beaded accessories, Masai women gather for a ritual in Kenya.

"mitochondrial Eve," a hypothetical human being who lived in sub-Saharan Africa. Perhaps more importantly, because DNA changes at a relatively constant rate over time, Cann and her colleagues were able to use the diversity of genetic material as a sort of molecular clock, leading them to conclude that this lucky woman lived right around 200,000 years ago—a date that matches nicely with the earliest fossil evidence of our species.

Out of Africa

With an origin firmly planted in the sub-Sahara, geneticists turned their focus to

the rest of the world and found the age of human lineages outside of Africa to be far younger than those within it. If the entire world's genetic diversity was baked into a single pie, they discovered, non-African DNA would account for no more than a sliver. Dating the age of non-African lineages (again using that molecular clock), the findings indicate that from the dawn of our species, it took a very long time—over 100,000 years—before our *Homo sapiens* ancestors finally left the African cradle in their successive waves of migrations.

But if it took so long, why did they finally succeed?

First cultural revolution

Right around the time of those first successful waves out of Africa, one each to Australia and the Middle East about 50,000 years ago, something peculiar started happening in East Africa.

Evidence for complex art and refined tools—projectile points, knife blades, bone artifacts—pops up all over sites dating to this period. The Late Stone Age, as it is known, signified a cultural revolution and a great leap forward for our species. Findings suggest that by this time people were able to transmit complex ideas and work in large groups: newfound advantages that kicked off the exponential population boom that has continued ever since.

The exact location of our earliest African ancestors is still hotly debated, but it is clear from archaeological and genetic evidence that the first hunter-gatherers to leave this sub-Saharan homeland likely did so from the same East African savannahs that produced the earliest signs of human evolution.

regions are engaged in a fierce political, social, and economic competition.

Although Madagascar's native inhabitants are known to be descendants of people who came from islands off the coast of eastern Africa or from the Indonesian archipelago, the specific migrations that led to today's population have not yet been precisely identified by scholars. The Malagasy language shares many linguistic features with Indonesian tongues. French, the language of colonists who occupied Madagascar and its close neighbor Mauritius, is a secondary national language spoken by about a quarter of the population, mainly city and town dwellers.

Like other Malagasy, the large Merina ethnic group divides its society into a hierarchy of elites, commoners, and descendants of slaves. This social hierarchy is evident not only in politics, where elites hold the most power, but also in small-scale activities such as the evening meal: The youngest family members and more distant relatives from commoner or slave kinship groups always eat last.

Although the French abolished slavery on the southeastern islands of Africa in 1897, the Malagasy people retain extensive genealogical memories of slave ancestry. There is still some freedom in kinship affiliation, since people can reckon descent through either the father or the mother's brother. The results can become confusing, with people tracing their descent from different Malagasy ethnic groups as well as from Indians, Chinese, Arabs, and non-Malagasy Africans.

Perhaps the culture's most distinctive aspect—the one that has stimulated the most anthropological research—is the burial tomb. The Malagasy take great care to protect and honor the dead because they, like many other African peoples, believe that their ancestors influence their life every day. Often they build elaborate wood, stone, or concrete tombs that remain partly above the ground. Relatives can thus enter a tomb to

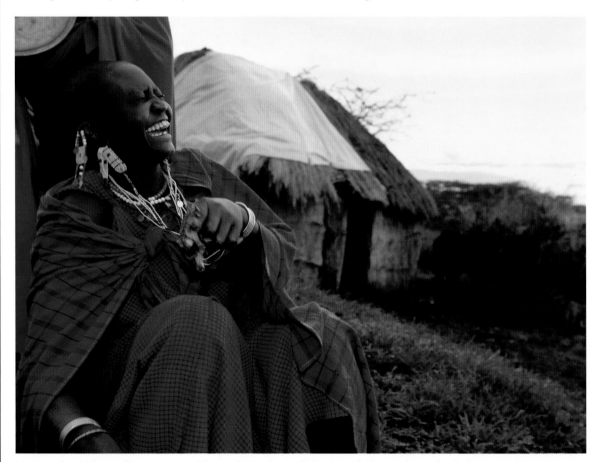

Member of a tribe known for stoic reserve while guarding cattle, an off-duty Masai finds something to laugh about. Masai sometimes profit from picture-taking by tourists on guided excursions to their homeland.

adorn it or to offer sacrifices and prayers. They may also practice what anthropologists sometimes call secondary funerals: Certain Malagasy groups in central Madagascar will place a deceased relative in a tomb, then remove the body a short time later, either for reburial in a larger tomb or to rewrap and reposition the body. Failure to properly care for the dead during and after burial, believe the Malagasy, can bring harm to the living.

MASAI

Alternate name: Maasai   Population: 883,000
Location: Kenya, Tanzania
Language family: Nilotic

The Masai pastoralists living near the Rift Valley of Kenya and Tanzania are among the most easily recognizable people in East Africa. Tall, with dark skin, Masai men wear jewelry and colorful, togalike garments, and they often carry spears as symbols of their manhood. Very few of them escape the attention of the annual swarms of tourists in East Africa. Some marketing efforts include photographs of Masai in native costumes and even offer visits to their households. Nevertheless, the people appear to have profited little from the safari business that goes on all around them.

Unlike most African pastoralists, who rely on crops as well as animals, the Masai do not practice agriculture. They depend on cattle for subsistence, consuming the milk, blood, and meat of their animals. The Masai are one of the few African societies who struggle, usually with success, to practice pastoralism exclusively, even in the context of East Africa's extensive tourist industry. Often moving their cattle to available grasslands and water, they see themselves ideally as nomadic; in the 1970s, however, they began privatizing herds into ranches, and that process has increased inequality among the people.

Each Masai settlement contains a cattle enclosure and homesteads consisting of houses made of mud and wood. Some of the residences are occupied by youths, others by warriors, and still others by elders. Among the more distinctive aspects of Masai society is the age-set kinship system, which defines relations among men and also between men and women.

Age sets are groups of people born into the same generation. Members share the same life events, such as circumcision and marriage, and remain in the same groups for life. The age sets group men into three main categories—uncircumcised, circumcised, and elders—and these are divided into smaller categories having to do with property ownership, marriage, parentage, and so on. Women, by comparison, are grouped into only two categories: circumcised and uncircumcised.

In Masai society, the elders among the men have great power, for they make most of the important decisions. They are the ones responsible for deciding on the physical layout of villages; on the production, sale, and distribution of livestock; and on marriage partnerships within the community.

The Masai of different territories employ numerous rituals to initiate men and women into age sets, and all of the rites involve recognition of changing status. They involve various sacrifices of oxen and the consuming of certain foods. In some areas, rituals incorporating a man into the set of elders may take up to 15 years to complete.

The neck of a cow cannot overtake the head.
MASAI PROVERB

One ceremony, called *e unoto,* is held years after the last member of an age set has been circumcised; it is intended to signal passage into the stage of true adulthood. Preceding e unoto is the "ox of the earplugs" ritual, in which adult men and their mothers accuse each other of incest, then slaughter oxen that the men feed to their mothers as a sign that they now can care for them. At this time, men still wear their hair in braids, but at the close of e unoto, they cut their hair to signal their new status.

SOMALI

Population: 13 million
Location: Somalia, Ethiopia
Language family: Cushitic

East Africa's entire Horn area is home to the Somali people, the majority of whom live in the country of Somalia and in the breakaway nation known as Somaliland. In 1991, after escalating civil conflict, northwestern Somalia declared independence and became Somaliland, but it still awaits diplomatic recognition from the international community. Somali are the principal inhabitants of the Ogadēn region of southeastern Ethiopia; they can also be found in Djibouti and in northeastern Kenya.

According to archaeological and historical evidence, Somali have been living in the Horn of Africa for nearly 3,000 years. In some local genealogical accounts, certain Somali clans have been traced to the Arabian Peninsula and associated with the Sharifs, the family of the Prophet Muhammad. But linguistic, cultural, and historical evidence indicates that the Somali came originally from the southern highlands of what is now Ethiopia and are a Cushite people with ties to a broad range of Cushite ethnic groups. Part of an ancient region known as Nubia, Cush gave rise to a group of languages that eventually defined numerous peoples in northern and northeastern Africa; the Somali tongue is a member of the Eastern Cushitic language family.

Claims to an Arab origin may arise not only from trade relationships and marriage alliances with Arab colonies on the Somali coast but also from a desire for stronger ties to the heart of Islam. The Somali people had accepted Islam by the 1400s, and according to some historians they may have done so as early as the 1100s. In recent years, the Ayaana religion, which emphasizes fertility and the intersection of the spirit world in the human, has been growing among the Somali. At the same time, Islamic fundamentalism has been gaining ground over the traditional Sufi mystical orders.

As with many African groups, the Somali people were never a unified or corporate political body before the arrival of various European powers. Instead of establishing a political system that encompassed all the people, they relied on clan federations that provided a broad, loose identity. Traditionally a nomadic people, they did maintain boundaries for the herding area of each clan and subclan. Somali clans resisted invasions into recognized settlements and herding areas; actual borders were somewhat vague, however, and military clashes were common among the clans themselves.

During the colonial era, the British, French, and Italians established territories, or Somalilands, roughly following the geographical areas of the clan federations. In 1960 Britain and Italy combined their territories into

Traveling light is the norm for nomadic Somali herders. Men care for prized camels, women and children for sheep and goats.

a unified, independent nation known as the Somali Democratic Republic. The French territory remained separate, and in 1977 it gained independence under the name Djibouti.

As a nomadic, pastoral people, the Somali center their economic culture around camels, raising a few cattle, goats, and sheep in the more fertile areas. The women and young children care for sheep and goats, while the young men and boys herd the highly esteemed camels. In a land where rainfall averages less than four inches a year, Somali lives are consumed with finding water and grazing land for their livestock. Their diet once consisted almost entirely of cow's milk and milk products, but for most people it now includes maize meal and rice.

SWAHILI

Population: 500,000
Location: Tanzania, Kenya
Language family: Bantu

Although the word "Swahili" usually refers to an East African lingua franca, it is also the name for a large mercantile civilization on the East African coast and on islands such as Zanzibar and Lamu. The word is widely thought to have come from the Arabic *sawahil,* meaning "coast," thus making the Swahili the "people of the coast."

Descendants of Arab and Persian traders who, over the years, intermarried with East Africans, the Swahili are merchants with a long history as brokers between East Africa and Middle Eastern, European, and central African countries. They also frequently served as middlemen between Africa and Asia during the slave trade. Today the extensive interaction between Africans and Arabs is reflected in art and architecture: Carved wooden doors, for example, are a renowned art form of the Swahili. Because Swahili art is Islamic art, the human body is never depicted. Instead, the people create elaborate carvings or paint intricate designs, and these can be seen decorating the doors as well as chests, furniture, house walls, and even boats known as dhows.

Swahili, the national language of both Tanzania and Kenya, is a mixture of Bantu grammar and Arabic vocabulary. As evidence of the Swahili's success as long-distance traders, variants of the language are spoken today throughout Uganda, Rwanda, Burundi, and the eastern portion of the Democratic Republic of the Congo. There is also an extensive literature in Swahili, dating back to the mid-17th century.

About 500,000 Swahili live on East Africa's coast and nearby islands, but some traders live on islands as far south as Mozambique and as far north as Somalia. Spread out over such a large area, they have significant cultural differences, with many groups claiming different origins. The Swahili are almost always integrated politically and socially into other communities, yet even so, those who consider themselves to be Swahili do share many beliefs, traditions, and attributes. Most of them are Muslim. They are often wealthier than their neighbors, residing in stone houses with the distinctive, carved wooden doors considered signs of wealth.

Swahili men and women both place a high value on a good physical appearance, which they believe can symbolize inner purity. Swahili men wear amulets that contain koranic verses. Swahili women use reddish henna dye to create intricate designs on their hands, and they also tend to adorn themselves with jewelry, cosmetics, interesting hairstyles, and aromatics.

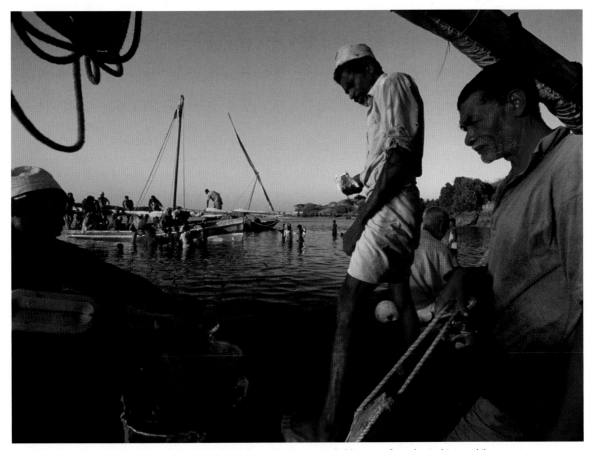

Swahili fishermen prepare breakfast on the deck of their boat. Their name probably comes from the Arabic sawahil, or coast.

When Languages Die

The world is losing its languages at an alarming rate—and with them,
we lose wisdom, diversity, culture, and knowledge.

Human languages are rapidly going extinct. If current trends continue, we will lose one tongue every two weeks for the foreseeable future. In the year 2007, at least 6,912 distinct human languages were spoken worldwide. Linguists predict that by the end of our current 21st century—by the year 2101, that is—only half of the languages in current use may still be spoken. The picture comes clear: The voices of the last speakers of small languages are now fading away, never to be heard again.

There is another side to this picture. On a global scale, a few major tongues dominate. The biggest 83 languages, including Mandarin Chinese, Spanish, English, and Hindi, account for nearly 80 percent of the world's population. Most languages have far fewer speakers. More than half of the world's languages are spoken by less than one percent of the population. Languages such as Urarina (spoken by fewer than 3,000 people in the Amazon), Halkomelem (spoken by 200, in Canada), and Tofa (spoken by no more than 25 people, in Siberia) face a precarious and uncertain future.

Small languages are being abandoned by speakers all over the world. Why is this happening? Native speakers stop using their original language for a variety of reasons. They may be favoring a different language because it is more dominant, more prestigious, or more widely known. They may be motivated by official state policies to suppress speech or by social pressure to speak differently. Many Canadian First Nations people and Native Americans who are now adults shared dismal experiences of childhoods spent at boarding schools, where they were forbidden to speak their mother tongues. Children worldwide experience both subtle and overt pressures to switch to globally dominant languages.

The global biosphere faces grave threats as animal and plant species go extinct. But linguistic extinction is happening much faster, as the ethnosphere—all the riches of human culture—collapses under the pressures of globalization. Scientists' best estimates show that since the year 1600, the planet has lost more than 1,200 plant and animal species. These numbers, while sobering, make up less than 7 percent of known species. Compared to this, the estimated 40 percent of languages now endangered is a staggering figure.

Our understanding is still quite imperfect as to how and why language death occurs. Children's decisions to learn a global language and abandon their ancestral tongues may ripple through societies to create a tidal wave of change.

We also lack a clear understanding of what exactly is being lost—is it unique, irreplaceable knowledge, or merely commonsense knowledge easily translated? Could such knowledge ever be adequately captured in books and video recordings, in the absence of any live speakers? Once it has vanished, can such knowledge reemerge spontaneously or be re-created, or is it forever extinguished?

The multiplicity of languages

How did we get so many languages in the first place? we might first begin by asking. What is the global distribution of all those languages? The natural state of human beings—harking back to our hunter-gatherer past—was to live in small bands. This is an ideal scenario for language diversity, as speech habits are free to change rapidly within a group. If one group splits into two, the pace of language change is such that within the space of just eight or ten generations, descendants of the same ancestors may already begin to have difficulty communicating. Within two

When a language is not embraced by younger generations, its demise draws nearer with the passing of each native speaker, such as this Alaskan Haida woman.

to three centuries, mutual comprehensibility can be lost: Where one language was, now there are two. At the same time, a small language family is formed. As linguists, we are able to discern similiarities between the two new languages that they inherited from their common ancestor.

It turns out that we find the greatest linguistic diversity in places with small and sparsely distributed populations. Consider the 65 inhabited islands of Vanuatu, for example: Altogether, these islands equal Connecticut in size geographically but their population is a tenth its size. Yet Vanuatu boasts 109 distinct tongues—one entire language for every 1,880 people.

Scientists today are working to get an accurate measure of global language diversity before it vanishes. A recent project, undertaken by scientists at the Living Tongues Institute for Endangered Languages, with support from the National Geographic Society, has developed a model called Language Hotspots. These zones, found around the globe in often remote and sur-

prising locations, show the greatest concentrations of endangered languages. They also have the greatest levels of unrelated language families, the highest levels of language endangerment, and the lowest levels of scientific study. The Language Hotspots map, coming out of this study, presents a radically new view of this extinction crisis, focusing our attention and resources on the most critical areas worldwide, in order to better preserve languages.

When a language dies

What exactly is lost when languages vanish? Why should we care? One answer is that we lose unique human knowledge. When ideas go extinct, we all grow poorer.

Many medicinal plants are known only to local practitioners, their healing secrets encoded in unwritten languages that distill generations of experience. Entire plant and animal species still awaiting scientific discovery in the modern sense of the word are in fact already well known, described, and classified by the indigenous peoples who recognize, gather, and use those plants in the languages they speak. Losing those languages, we lose much more.

Societies that rely on nature for survival have developed technologies to cultivate plants, domesticate animals, and sustainably exploit local resources. These knowledge systems—encoded in indigenous languages—can be even more precise than our modern scientific ways of knowing. For example, the Musqueam people of British Columbia, fisherfolk who speak Halkomelem, have always used just one word to name the fish that we call salmon and trout. At first glance, it appears to be a primitive mistake in knowledge. But in 2004, a genetic study confirmed the Musqueam classification to be more accurate genetically than our English one: Pacific trout and salmon belong to the same genus.

Much—if not most—of what humankind knows about the natural world lies completely outside of science textbooks, libraries, and databases, existing only in spoken languages. This unbroken oral tradition is always just one generation away from extinction, always in jeopardy of not being passed on. An immense knowledge base remains largely unexplored and uncatalogued. The need for traditional knowledge becomes ever more acute as we strain our planet's carrying capacity. But we can only hope to access this knowledge if the people who possess and nurture it can be encouraged to continue speaking their languages and to pass them on to their children.

There is a second answer to the question of what is lost: our common cultural heritage. A wealth of traditional wisdom is found in oral history, poetry, epic tales, creation stories, riddles, and wise sayings. These products of human ingenuity and creativity may be found in all cultures. But the vast majority of human languages, never written down, exist only in memory and are especially vulnerable to forgetting as languages go extinct.

There is nothing so sacred in a culture that it cannot be forgotten. The Tofa people of Siberia are losing their language and no longer remember the following creation myth that they once believed:

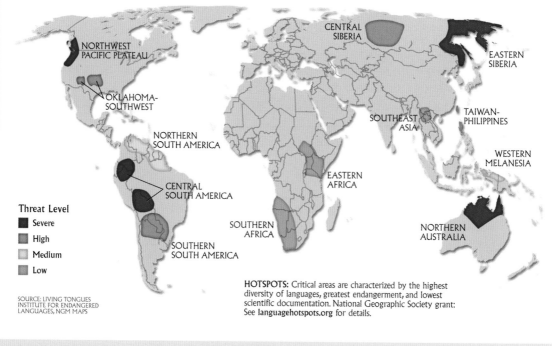

GLOBAL LANGUAGE HOTSPOTS

NORTHWEST PACIFIC PLATEAU

OKLAHOMA-SOUTHWEST

NORTHERN SOUTH AMERICA

CENTRAL SOUTH AMERICA

SOUTHERN SOUTH AMERICA

CENTRAL SIBERIA

EASTERN SIBERIA

TAIWAN-PHILIPPINES

SOUTHEAST ASIA

WESTERN MELANESIA

EASTERN AFRICA

SOUTHERN AFRICA

NORTHERN AUSTRALIA

Threat Level
- Severe
- High
- Medium
- Low

SOURCE: LIVING TONGUES INSTITUTE FOR ENDANGERED LANGUAGES, NGM MAPS

HOTSPOTS: Critical areas are characterized by the highest diversity of languages, greatest endangerment, and lowest scientific documentation. National Geographic Society grant: See languagehotspots.org for details.

Linguists have identified global language hotspots—locations where the number of native speakers of a language is dwindling and in danger soon of reaching zero—in five of the six inhabited continents of the world.

In the very beginning there were no people,
there was nothing at all.
There was only the first duck,
she was flying along.
Having settled down for the night,
the duck laid an egg.
Then, her egg broke.
The liquid poured out and formed a lake,
and the egg shell became earth.

We may be indifferent to the passing of this whimsical story, but all mythical traditions are attempts to make sense of the universe. Each one provides a piece of the puzzle of how humans understand life, creation, and the sacred. Without this Tofa duck myth, we would be missing a small piece of that puzzle.

A conservation challenge

A third answer to the question "What is lost?" is our scientific understanding of the human mind. Languages reveal the limits and potentialities of human cognition—how the mind works. Underneath our global Babel lie deep similarities in the way human brains process speech and information. As a science, linguistics seeks the deep universal properties of all human languages.

But to advance their science, linguists need to examine the oddest, quirkiest, most unusual languages and words. If we had only major world languages to study, we would be severely limited in understanding human cognition. Linguists' theories have been challenged (or flatly contradicted) by the discovery of unique language structures not previously documented.

For example, a basic feature of a language is the standard order in which subject, verb, and object occur. In English, it's usually subject, verb, and then object ("He eats rice"). The Urarina tongue, spoken in Peru's Amazon jungle, places the object first, the verb second, and the subject last ("Rice eats he"). This pattern differs not only from English but from almost every known language in the world. Without Urarina and a few other Amazonian languages, scientists might not even suspect such a pattern to be possible. The loss of even one language may forever close the door to a full understanding of human cognitive capacity.

We must safeguard and document vanishing languages, first, because our human knowledge base is

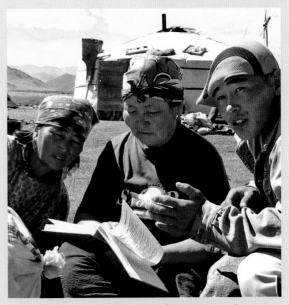

Young Monchak, traditional nomads of western Mongolia, see more advantages to speaking Mongolian than Monchak. If their preference persists, the Monchak language may soon die out.

rapidly eroding. Most of what humans have learned over the millennia about how to thrive on this planet is encapsulated in threatened languages. If we allow them to fade, we may compromise our very ability to survive as our ballooning human population strains Earth's ecosystems. Second, because our rich patrimony of human cultural heritage, including myth, history, and poetry is being forgotten. Allowing our own histories to be erased, we condemn ourselves to a cultural amnesia that may undermine our ability to live in peace with diverse peoples. Third, because the great puzzle of human cognition remains to be solved. Much of the human mind is still a black box. We cannot discern its inner workings—and we often only know them by what comes out in the form of speech. Obscure languages hold keys that may unlock the mind.

For all these reasons, and with the possibility of dire consequences for failure, documenting endangered languages while they may still be heard, and saving or revitalizing tongues that still may be viable, must be viewed as the single greatest conservation challenge of our lifetime. ∎

— *K. David Harrison*

Adapted from the book When Languages Die: The Extinction of the World's Languages and the Erosion of Human Knowledge *by K. David Harrison.*

NORTH AFRICA & THE MIDDLE EAST

NORTH AFRICA
Arabs • Berbers • Egyptians
Nubians • Tuareg

THE MIDDLE EAST
Jews • Kurds • Lebanese • Palestinians
Persians • Qashqai • Turks

Distinctive hats protect Yemeni women from the sun as they
gather clover for their cattle in Wadi Hadramaut.

The history and cultures of North Africa have long been influenced by those of the Middle East, a region rich in ethnic groups and ancient traditions. Encompassing the Near Eastern civilizations of antiquity, the Middle East was also the birthplace of Judaism, Christianity, and Islam, all of which trace their roots to the biblical Abraham. Today, religion remains a key defining factor for ethnicity, more so even than language, region of origin, or class. Still, religious differences between groups are often diminished by a shared past and similar traditions.

Around 8,000 to 10,000 years ago, the Tigris and Euphrates Rivers in Mesopotamia and the Nile in Egypt gave rise to the world's earliest agriculture. Cultivation of crops in turn helped lead to the first civilizations, in Sumeria and Egypt. But despite the presence of these major rivers and a few other fertile areas, much of the Middle East and North Africa is arid, with some of the most hostile deserts in the world. Nomadic herding has been the means of subsistence for generations, and human life has centered around oases scattered through the deserts. On the Arabian Peninsula, domestication of the camel between 3000 and 1000 B.C. offered a way to travel in these otherwise inhospitable lands, opening new routes for trade and expansion across the peninsula and the Sahara.

Cultural intersection Four major cultural groups with ancient roots still predominate in the Middle East: Arabs, Turks, Persians, and Jews. While Turks, Persians, and Jews are dominant in Turkey, Iran, and Israel, respectively, Arabs are spread throughout the region and all across North Africa.

The word "Arab" comes from the Semitic-speaking A'raab people, who by 900 to 800 B.C. had established trade and pastoral networks between Syria and the Arabian Peninsula. They are related to speakers of such other Semitic languages as Hebrew and Aramaic. Over time, some Arab groups became sedentary, while others continued as nomads. The settled Arabs called the nomadic Arabs *Bedu*, from which the word "Bedouin" comes. Today Arabs are quite diverse, with their own cultural differences, but they continue to be unified by a common language—Arabic—spoken in many dialects from Morocco into East Africa, throughout the eastern Mediterranean, and into the Persian Gulf region.

Coptic Christians pray at an ancient church in Asmara, Eritrea. About half of all Eritreans are Christian; the other half are Muslim.

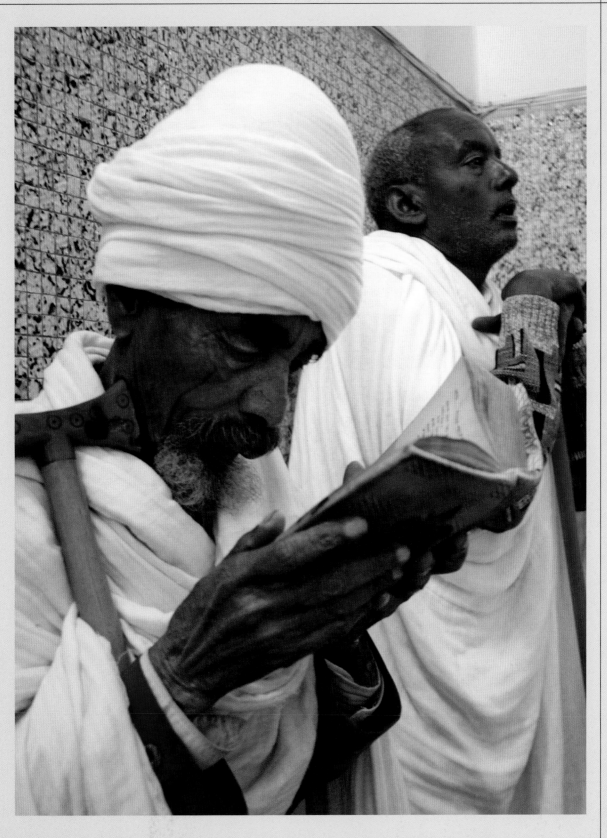

Because the Bedouin were the ancestors of modern Arabs, these people are regarded by other Arabs as true and original representatives of their culture and language. Even in the 21st century, a few Bedouin continue to travel the deserts of the Arabian Peninsula, Egypt, and Libya by camel, living in tents and tending their herds as they have for centuries. But modern pressures are redefining the Bedouin way of life, and increasingly fewer of them continue to live as nomads.

Arabic and Hebrew are Semitic languages spoken by Arabs and Jews. Although these two groups share common religious roots, relations between them have been strained to the point of war on a number of occasions since the mid-20th century, when the state of Israel was created as a Jewish nation by the partitioning of Palestine. Today Israel's population is roughly 80 percent Jewish, while Islam is the major religion of most other Middle Eastern and North African nations. Islam itself is split into two sects, the Sunnis and the Shiites, each of which holds different beliefs concerning the successor to Muhammad, the Prophet of Islam. Most Shiites reside in Iran and southern Iraq, while Sunnis predominate in the rest of the region.

Head covered but face unveiled, a Kurdish woman from Turkey displays her culture's more relaxed attitude toward female dress.

Bread is life Ancient traditions straining against modern trends introduced from the West have created friction between cultures in recent decades, resulting in the pan-Islamic movement that has swept the region. A return to orthodox practices has also been occurring in Israel. As more people have chosen to follow traditional religious customs and centuries-old habits, and as ethnic and religious pride has swelled, tensions have grown between different ethnic and religious groups. Still, common customs unite the various peoples in their day-to-day lives, even down to the foods they eat.

Central Asian and Mediterranean influences flavor the cuisine, and bread—flat or in loaves—is a staple so important that in Egypt it is called *aish*, "life" in Arabic. Rice dishes with herbs, beans, fruits, or nuts abound everywhere, except in North Africa, where couscous takes the place of rice. Yogurt salads and kebabs made of lamb, beef, or chicken are widely eaten, as are lamb or chicken stews with vegetables or fruits. *Meze*, a plate of appetizers featuring eggplant, beans, olives, and pickles, often starts a meal in the eastern Mediterranean. Rice pudding, halvah (a sesame-based confection), honey-soaked pastries, or European-style pastries frequently bring a meal to its end.

Life passages Some customs have to do with rites of passage. For example, most groups bury their recently deceased loved ones within specified periods of time; they also observe prescribed periods of mourning. Marriage, too, follows shared customs. Though "love matches" are becoming more prevalent, arranged marriages occur among all religious communities of this region, with a first-cousin marriage traditionally deemed an ideal match. Whole families are involved in the negotiations concerning bride-price (the amount of money the groom should give the bride's family); the marriage contract; the time of the marriage; and the future residence of the couple, traditionally the family home of the groom. Marriages are celebrated for several days, even a week, by Jews, Christians, and Muslims. Among Arab Muslims and Coptic Christians in Egypt, the bride and women from both sides of the family come together for a day or more to decorate their hands and feet with geometric and floral henna designs. These gatherings allow women of the joining families to become better acquainted before the marriage.

Among adherents of all three Abrahamic religions, women are expected to dress modestly. In Saudi Arabia and Iran, veiling is mandatory, but with a wide range of interpretation. A Muslim woman in Saudi Arabia must be completely covered, including her face, hands, and feet. In Iran, a scarf covering the hair and a loose coat are deemed sufficient. Most Christians and Jews in the Middle East wear Western-style clothing, though Orthodox Jewish women also cover their hair and wear long dresses.

A six-year-old Turkish boy apprehensively awaits his circumcision ritual, a rite of passage for all Muslim males.

In an area of the world where conflict and political uncertainty have been consistent realities, such long-cherished traditions and the ethnic identities that engender them offer constancy and comfort in the face of change. Commonly held customs help to keep communities intact from one generation to the next. ∎

North Africa

Containing the vast Sahara and the diverse Mediterranean coastline, the region of North Africa spans some 3,500 miles west to east. It contains the Atlas Mountains of Morocco and Algeria; the ancient cities of Tunis, Alexandria, Cairo, and Giza; and the mighty Nile River, longest in the world. The Sahara itself extends southward more than a thousand miles, terminating in the Sahel, a steppe that borders the region of West Africa. Morocco, Algeria, Tunisia, Libya, and Egypt all share a Mediterranean coastline; the Sahara stretches into Mauritania, Mali, Niger, Chad, and Sudan.

To listen to music from Algeria, Egypt, Mali, and Morocco, visit http://worldmusic.nationalgeographic.com.

ARABS

Alternate name: Bedouin   Population: 250 million
Location: North Africa and Middle East
Language family: Semitic

Until the advent of Islam, Arabs and their culture remained almost entirely on the Arabian Peninsula. But the revelations of God to the Prophet Muhammad, himself an Arab, resulted in a cultural and economic flourishing in seventh-century Arabia. This in turn led to a spectacular spreading and mixing of cultures, as Arabs traveled throughout the Middle East, North Africa, and Spain and into central and southern Asia. The result today is an incredibly diverse culture, where both nomadic Bedouin and long-time urban dwellers call themselves Arabs.

Despite their diversity, Arabs throughout the world share cultural ideas and practices, including a common faith (more than 90 percent are Muslims) and language (Arabic), traditional gender roles, male-oriented inheritance laws, and ritualized ideas of honor, hospitality, and generosity.

Classical Arabic is the sacred language of Muslims, because it is believed to be the language in which God revealed the Koran to Muhammad. Well-educated Arabs and religious scholars speak and read classical Arabic, and its use in radio and television has increased its comprehension among less educated listeners. Every Arab, however, speaks at least one of the many colloquial forms of Arabic, which may be quite different from one another. Moroccan Arabic, for example, is

ER

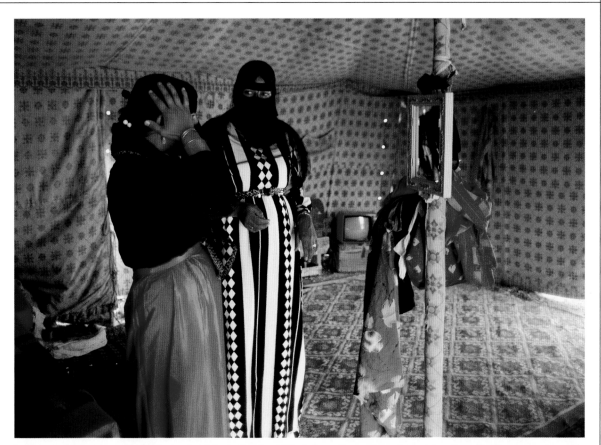

Inside a spacious and comfortable tent, a Saudi Bedouin woman adjusts her veil as a companion watches. Some Saudi women compensate for the country's conservative veiling practices by wearing colorful clothing and accessories.

almost incomprehensible to an Arab of the eastern Mediterranean or the Persian Gulf area. In recent times, movies and television soap operas, often produced in Cairo but widely distributed, have helped familiarize Arabs with other dialects.

As with all Muslims, Arab Muslims are enjoined to make the hajj, the sacred pilgrimage to Mecca, before they die. The most important rite of passage next to birth, marriage, and death, the hajj is a spiritual and religious event, a reenactment of the journey of Muhammad. Muslims believe that if they die on the pilgrimage, they will immediately go to heaven.

The Bedouin, believed to be ancestral to other Arab groups, are considered the culture's purest representatives, although they now make up less than 10 percent of the modern Arab population. Living in Libya, Egypt, Lebanon, Jordan, Syria, Israel, Iraq, and throughout the Arabian Peninsula, they are distinct from other Arabs because of their nomadic, pastoral lifestyle and their more extensive kinship networks, which provide them with community support and the basic necessities for survival. Such networks traditionally served to ensure the safety of families and to protect their property.

As contemporary Middle Eastern governments have encouraged the Bedouin to settle, large family networks and the nomadic lifestyle have been diminishing. Nevertheless, the Bedouin continue to be revered by other Arabs, especially because of their rich oral poetic tradition, their herding lifestyle, and their traditional code of honor.

While poetry and literature are very important for all Arabs, the Bedouin are masters at oral verse, an emotional and evocative form of poetry that is recited from memory in classical Arabic. These people believe displays of unchecked emotions weaken the group's solidarity, so they use poetry to express strong feelings: sadness, love, and anger. Among other Arabs, poetry is also a way to convey feelings that might be difficult to express in everyday life.

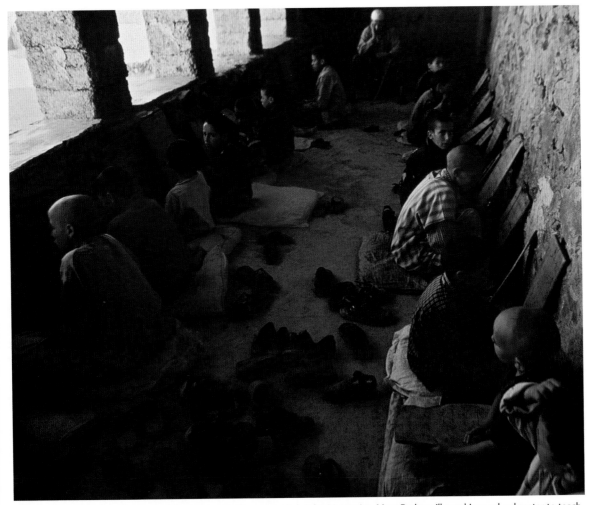

Berber boys ponder their slates at an Islamic school in Morocco's High Atlas Mountains. Most Berber villages hire a schoolmaster to teach boys to recite the Koran.

An important feature of the Arab world, a shared honor code dictates certain behaviors, especially to preserve a family's reputation and help its members in times of need. For men, honorable behavior means supporting their families economically and defending the reputations of relatives, particularly women. For women, honorable behavior translates into being loving mothers and wives, running efficient and generous households, and acting in modest and respectable ways.

Arab families are very close, and home life is seen as the reward for hard work. While the life of a family remains quite private, Arab hospitality is famous: The people are generally quick to invite strangers to join them for a meal. Their hospitality and generosity are sincerely offered; as a result, friendships are intense, with sincerity and kindness expected in return.

BERBERS

Population: 14 million
Location: Morocco, Algeria, Libya, Mali, Niger
Language family: Berber

A diverse group, Berbers comprise the indigenous peoples of northwest Africa. They include the Irifiyen, Imazighen, and Shleuh of Morocco; the Kabyles of Algeria; and the Tuareg of Algeria, Libya, Mali, and Niger. All speak dialects of Berber, a language of the Afro-Asiatic family.

Though scholars are uncertain about the Berbers' exact origins, they think members of this group probably came from the Near East and settled in northwest Africa around 3000 B.C. Over the millennia, Berber territories were invaded by Carthaginians, Romans, Vandals, Turks, Arabs, and Europeans, but against all these foreign powers the Berber culture remained distinct. The Arabs exerted the greatest influence on their culture, and in the early 8th century, Berbers were the main force behind the Arab conquest of the Iberian Peninsula. Later, in the 11th and 12th centuries, two great Berber empires arose and dominated much of Morocco, Algeria, Tunisia, and southern Spain. Berber traders once connected the Mediterranean markets to those of West Africa, and even today some Berber tribes still link trade between North and West Africa.

Most Berbers today are sedentary agriculturists who also tend small herds of goats and sheep. A few tribes, such as the Tuareg of Mali and the Imazighen of

> ## The ropes can be stretched far enough for forgiveness.
> BEDOUIN PROVERB

central Morocco, are seminomadic, herding sheep and using camels for mobility. The majority of Berbers trace their ancestry through their fathers, and men govern tribal affairs. There is a strong division of labor, with the men managing lands and herds and the women performing housework. Among the Tuareg, though, women inherit and own property, control the herds, cultivate land, and bring in the harvest. Tuareg men herd, tend the gardens, and conduct the direct activity of trade.

In urban areas, the distinction between Arabs and Berbers is diminishing, but Berber dialects, tribal customs, and traditional handicraft—handwoven carpets, silver jewelry, leather, and pottery, for example—continue to prevail in such remote areas as the mountains and valleys of Morocco's interior. A persistent custom is the local tribal council, which is composed of clan heads representing extended families.

Berber religious beliefs and practices are derived from Islam and are no different from the orthodox ones of other Sunni Muslims. There is an emphasis, however, on *baraka,* the belief in the special blessings from God, and on *marabouts,* individuals who are considered holy. Even in death, marabouts are thought to

act as spiritual intermediaries and to bestow God's blessings upon the living. These individuals once played key political, religious, and economic roles, and they are still honored at numerous shrines throughout northwestern Africa.

EGYPTIANS

Population: 79 million
Location: Egypt
Language family: Semitic

For thousands of years, Egyptians have owed their lives and livelihoods to the Nile River and its delta, part of the world's longest river system, which transforms a narrow band of the eastern Sahara into a fertile and viable nation, now home to 79 million people. In the past, the yearly flooding of the Nile, brought on by rains closer to the river's source, deposited the thick black silt that the fellahin, or peasant farmers, planted with wheat, rice, and cotton, all still valuable crops in Egypt.

The construction of the Aswan High Dam in Upper Egypt—southern Egypt, since the Nile flows, unusually, south to north—ended the annual floods, but irrigation systems maintain agricultural fields and even expand them by claiming more of the desert for cultivation. Still, less than 3 percent of Egypt's territory can support agriculture, yet it remains the largest arena of employment.

Although they are proud of their pharaonic past, Egyptians identify with their Arab Muslim present; about 90 percent of the population embraces Islam and nearly all Egyptians speak Arabic. Seventh-century Arab invasions brought about the conversion of Egypt's Coptic Christians, a major religion since Roman occupation in the first century. Egypt resonates with the everyday rhythms of Muslim life, including the calls to prayer that ring out over communities five times a day, and with the yearly cycle of fasting and feasting.

Some five million Egyptians remain Coptic Christians, descendents of Egyptians who did not convert to Islam. Copts share many cultural customs and general appearance with Egyptian Muslims, although they may tattoo a small cross on the inside of the wrist. Most reside in Cairo and in several villages in southern Egypt.

Coptic Christianity has its own patriarch, who is chosen by the community and believed to be divinely ordained. The church's sacred text and liturgy traditionally uses the Coptic language, which was based on ancient Egyptian, with a strong Greek influence. Coptic no longer is spoken, however; most Copts today speak Arabic. The Coptic community is wary of conflicts that can arise from religious differences, especially in light of clashes with ultraconservative Muslims, and in general try to keep a low profile. Recently, the government showed support of Egypt's Christians by making Christmas a national holiday.

Egypt's deserts are mostly unpopulated, except for the nomadic Bedouin who occasionally travel through them, though most Bedouin now live settled lives. They are found in Egypt's major cities, such as Cairo and Alexandria, but some prefer to live in oases, places in the desert where water trapped in rock layers rises to the surface and can support plant, animal, and human life on a year-round basis. Small groups of Bedouin are found in the Western and Eastern Deserts and on the Sinai Peninsula.

Despite programs to increase farm capacity, Egyptians continue to move to the cities. A population of some 16 million makes Cairo the largest city in Africa and the Middle East, and one of the world's most densely populated. Its population grows each year with people from the countryside who seek employment and the possibility of a better life. Reality tends to be

---

When you sleep in a house,
your thoughts are as high as the ceiling;
when you sleep outside,
they are as high as the stars.
BEDOUIN PROVERB

---

harsh, however, and many end up living in makeshift settlements in Cairo cemeteries or in shacks constructed on the roofs of high-rise buildings.

Overcrowding is only one of Cairo's modern ills. Pollution fueled by several million automobiles as well as factories and metal smelters manufactures a yellowish fog that hangs over the city. Tourists, who bring in a significant portion of Egypt's revenue, tend to make short stays in Cairo—long enough to see the pyramids and Sphinx on the city's outskirts and to visit its outstanding archaeological museum—before

heading off to the clearer air of Luxor and the pharaonic treasures of the Valley of the Kings about 400 miles south.

As an ancient center of learning in the Arab world, Egypt is a natural choice for a major modern media presence. Newspapers, radio, cinema, and television—enhanced by several Egyptian satellites launched in recent years—provide information and entertainment to Egyptians and many others in that strategic region.

NUBIANS

Population: 873,000   Location: Sudan, Egypt
Language family: Eastern Sudanic

More than 50 years ago, the pent-up waters of the Nile began to pour over the houses, shrines, graves, and palm groves along the river's banks in southern Egypt and northern Sudan, near the site of the Aswan High Dam. The dam was designed to prevent the annual flooding of the Nile, to make its waters more manageable and available to agriculture on a controlled basis—an important development for Egypt, a nation wrested from the desert that encroaches on both sides of the river. In order for this happen, a homeland and a way of life had to be obliterated: the fate that befell the Nubians.

The Nubians are a non-Arab people who traditionally lived in Nubia, an unbounded area about 180 miles long that encompasses the Nile Valley on both sides of the border between Egypt and Sudan. Descended from peoples who produced a pharaonic dynasty in the eighth century B.C. and later established the Kingdom of Meroë in Sudan, the Nubians differed from Arab Egyptians and Sudanese in a number of ways, including language. Most Nubians spoke Nobiin, a tongue from the Eastern Sudanic language family, although one of the four main groups commonly spoke Arabic. Today, Nobiin is spoken mostly by older people, while the young tend to use Arabic.

The Nubians converted to Coptic Christianity after the sixth century. But unlike ethnic Egyptians, they did not accept Islam in the first wave of Arab invasions in the 8th century A.D. They chose to pay a poll tax rather than convert. The Nubians eventually did convert, but not until the 14th or 15th century. The vast majority of Nubians today, both Sudanese and Egyptian, are Muslim.

Seeking Greener Pastures

At the top of the continent of Africa lies a thousand-mile-wide sea of sand that has stood for millennia as one of the world's most inhospitable places. While the fertile tropics and savannahs to its south nurtured the emergence of our species, North Africa's seemingly impermeable desert barrier kept most of Africa tucked safely away from the rest of the world through the early part of human evolution. The second largest desert on the planet after Antarctica and home to the world's hottest recorded temperature (136°F), the Sahara has remained off-limits to all but the most resilient migrants willing to brave its interior.

But the Sahara has not always been as it appears today. The Serengeti plains of today's Tanzania suggest a landscape not all that different from what the desert would have been like 7,000 years ago, verdant with tall grasses and acacia woodlands, a wide variety of grazing herbivores, and rain. Difficult to envision given the expanse and hostility of today's Sahara, it was a place suitable for human occupation. We know this history of the Sahara to be true because of what we have found by digging up large cores of the eastern Mediterranean seabed and looking for signs of life in those ancient layers.

Shifting Sahara

Much of Africa's climate is controlled by the intertropical convergence zone, a belt of low pressure created by the upwelling of hot, moist air above and below the Equator which eventually cools, condenses, and returns to Earth where the intertropics converge. The system produces both equatorial rainfall and incredibly arid conditions to its north and south, resulting in today's Sahara and Kalahari deserts. But the process is thrown out of whack as the Earth precesses, or wobbles, on its axis, causing the convergence zone to migrate as much as 20° in latitude northward and bringing tropical

A Berber woman displays the fading decoration of her henna-stained hand.

precipitation with it. Increased rainfall throughout the region floods into the Nile River, which dumps the water, rich with organic material, into the Eastern Mediterranean and kills the sea's normal convection current in the process. With no current to circulate the water, organic material falls to the bottom and hardens into a new seabed layer. Then, as Earth's orbit shifts back, the convection current starts over.

This cycle happens like clockwork, around every 20,000 years, and carbon-rich layers known as sapropelles are deposited by Nile River runoff on the Mediterranean seabed in patterns that look like a sedimentary bar code. By digging up cores from the eastern Mediterranean and dating the carbon layers thus deposited, scientists can glean an accurate idea of when the Sahara might have been passable.

Desert escape

The analysis of DNA from populations throughout North Africa and the Middle East confirms that when climate shifted, our ancestors headed for greener pastures. The first modern humans to migrate northward successfully along this fertile passage did so about 50,000 years ago, capitalizing on a short window of opportunity before desert conditions forced their descendants back out of the region, as the Sahara expanded once again. Humans were subsequently locked out of North Africa until the next shift in Earth's axis. Then, peoples who had been kept apart for almost 20,000 years came together from both sub-Saharan Africa and the Middle East.

The genetic lineages of these Paleolithic hunter-gatherers survive today in some North African populations, evidence that humans have learned to adapt to harsh and variable conditions, in part by depending on an underwater system of aquifers filled during the wetter periods. More recently, successive civilizations have also left their genetic stamp on the landscape of today's North Africans—descendants of the Egyptians, Phoenicians, Garamantes, and Arabs all survive—and the present gene pool reflects a genetic tapestry as complex as the environmental interactions that have shaped this timeless land.

An Egyptian man inspects ancient graffiti on an unfinished supplemental tomb for Ramses XI in the Valley of the Kings, near Luxor. Modern Egyptians are proud stewards of their pharaonic past.

Traditional Nubian villages hugged the Nile's banks in an area where the river formed cataracts, or steep rapids. The villages contained separate hamlets, usually based on familial descent, and were separated from each other by low, rocky hills. Nubian farmers had two cultivation seasons a year, harvesting grains such as wheat, barley, and millet, and vegetables. The date palm, however, was the Nubian signature crop. They carefully tended the planted palm shoots and nurtured the tree, encouraging the properties they valued in the fruits. The Nubians used every part of the date palm, including its wood and fibers.

A squeeze on agricultural land sent Nubian men to cities in search of work even before the Aswan Dam was completed. Egyptian Nubians migrated to places such as Alexandria, Cairo, and Suez, while the women of the villages carried on with the agricultural work.

As part of the Aswan Dam project, both Sudanese and Egyptian Nubians were offered relocation in villages away from the dam area. In Egypt, the new homes were only about 30 miles from the old settlements, but were 2 to 6 miles from the Nile; in Sudan, they were some 480 miles from the old settlements, along the banks of a narrower river, the Atbara. In the new settlements, houses were built in rows and were no longer were clustered by kin group. The agricultural fields were larger and had to be managed in a different way, and there were no date palms. Although the new villages bore the same names as the old, they were nothing like the traditional Nubian homeland. They had more amenities but neither the organization nor the ethos of the communities they replaced.

The displaced Sudanese and Egyptian Nubians still mourn their fate. They and various advocacy groups point out that more care was spent moving the temples of Abu Simbel and other Nubian archaeological treasures to higher ground (or, in the case of the Temple of Dendur, to the Metropolitan Museum in New York City) than was taken with the lives of the displaced Nubians. Recently, land near Aswan has been opened to settlement by poor farmers, but the displaced Nubians receive no preference. It is land inferior to what they had, some claim, and it would never recompense the life they have lost.

TUAREG

Alternate name: Touareg   Population: 1.2 million
Location: Niger, Mali   Language family: Berber

The Tuareg, their origins likely in Libya, remain one of the few Berber tribes to retain the nomadic way of life they have practiced for centuries. In the past, they led camel caravans across the Sahara to trade in gold, ivory, salt, and slaves that they captured from sub-Saharan tribes. They also absorbed and assimilated a number of different peoples into their group, with the result that the Tuareg as a whole resemble both light-skinned North Africans and the darker peoples south of the Sahara.

Tuareg men are known for the long indigo veils they wind around their heads and across their faces, earning them the names of "The Blue Men" and "People of the Veil." The turbanlike cloths keep out sun and sand and make it possible for them to ride their camels or walk alongside them for more than 12 hours a day on weeks-long journeys across the desert.

The Tuareg number about one million people, dispersed in the countries of the Sahara and the Sahel, the semiarid regions to the desert's south. They are found mainly in Libya, Algeria, Niger, Nigeria, Mali, and Burkina Faso. They speak a number of dialects of Tamasheq, a Berber language, as well as some sub-Saharan languages such as Hausa and Songhay, along with French, the lingua franca of much of West Africa.

Historically, the Tuareg society divided itself into a hierarchy of groups related to men's descent and occupations. These included nobles, vassal-like offerers of tribute, smiths and artisans, and a serflike group.

Tuareg frequently practice polygamy. As Muslims, the Tuareg are allowed four wives, as long as they can provide for them and their children equally. Large families are common—and highly desired. Children help with the many tasks of agriculture and other aspects of daily life. Tuareg women enjoy more freedom than other Muslim women in Africa, and they do not necessarily veil their faces. Traditionally, descent and inheritance are reckoned in the female line, although Islamic practices have tended to undermine this.

Some Tuareg intensively cultivate the oases of the Sahara, planting crops such as maize, millet, carrots, tomatoes, and onions, and tending orchards of oranges, lemons, pomegranates, and figs. They use their camels to pull up water from the aquifers that they then dump into channels to irrigate the fields. Some Tuareg also farm in the Sahel; some live as pastoralists, maintaining herds of sheep, goats, cattle, and camels, and moving in search of water and pasturage.

Tuareg caravans still traverse the desert, cameleers singing to pass the time, creating images that seem no different from those of centuries ago. Caravans tend to be much smaller than in the past, when thousands of camels may have stretched in a line several miles long across the sands. Most caravan trade today deals in salt.

From time to time, during the more than four decades since the West African nations of Mali and Niger achieved independence, Tuareg dissatisfaction with government policies regarding assistance and access to land has fomented violent uprisings. In addition, the dramatic acceleration of desertification as a result of severe drought has forced many Tuareg to migrate temporarily to Algeria and Libya. Tuareg people also have often been at odds with non-Tuareg farmers over issues of access and use of land.

An Algerian Tuareg woman's headdress and veil pale in comparison to Tuareg men's traditional indigo wrappings.

The Middle East

A crossroads of geography, history, and culture, the Middle East is the nexus among Europe to the northwest, Asia to the northeast, and Africa to the southwest. It stretches from the Black Sea and the Caspian Sea of Central Asia to the Red Sea, the Persian Gulf, and the Gulf of Oman. The Middle East includes the entire Arabian Peninsula and Asia Minor, or Anatolia, the peninsula containing Turkey. Much of the Arabian Peninsula is dry desert or steppe, irrigated only by wadis, or seasonal streams, while the terrain just north of it, regions of Iraq and Iran known as the Fertile Crescent, stay fecund thanks to the Tigris and Euphrates Rivers.

▣To listen to music from Iran, Iraq, Israel, Jordan, Lebanon, Syria, and Turkey, visit http://world music.nationalgeographic.com.

JEWS
Population: 5 million (in Israel)
Location: Israel
Language family: Semitic

The more than five million Jews who live in the Middle East and North Africa share the same religion and have the sacred language of Hebrew in common; even so, members of this group are as diverse as the peoples they have dwelled among for over two millennia. Until the state of Israel was formally established in 1948, almost all Jews also held in common the feeling of living in exile. Destruction of the First and Second Temples of Jerusalem—in the sixth century B.C. and first century A.D.—was followed by great dispersions of Jews from the city and the surrounding region. They went to what is now Iraq, as well as Yemen, Egypt, Ethiopia, Turkey, Iran, and Central Asia. Some diaspora Jews settled among the Berbers of northwestern Africa.

In the 20th century, tensions between Zionists and Arab nationalists, along with the realization of a homeland, led many Jews to move to Israel. As a result, the old Jewish communities of North Africa and the Middle East, once numbering in the thousands, were reduced to a few hundred as Israel's cities and towns grew to include representatives from every Jewish group in the world. These groups are often placed in two categories: Sephardim—Jews from the Middle East, North Africa, and Western Europe—and Ashkenazim—Jews from central and eastern Europe. In the United States, Orthodox Jews are usually Sephardim, while the more numerous Conservative and Reform congregations belong to the Ashkenazic tradition.

Because they have a homeland, Jews no longer suffer as exiles, but their cultural diversity has become apparent during their resettlement in Israel. The country faces the enormous task of integrating the many languages, customs, occupational classes, and religious interpretations that have developed over the centuries. All Jews follow the same religious laws and offer up their

Devout Jews pray at the Western Wall in Jerusalem. Remains of the city's Second Temple, the wall represents Judaism's most revered site.

prayers, but the words and styles may vary. The differences are especially obvious between Sephardic and Ashkenazic traditions. Given the many Jews from the Arab world, Arabic is widely spoken, along with Hebrew, Persian, Turkish, Kurdish, Russian, and other Asian languages. Some African languages are also in the mix. Jews from Eastern Europe may speak Yiddish, a hybrid of Hebrew and Medieval German. People from the eastern Mediterranean may speak Ladino, a form of Spanish retained by 15th-century Jewish refugees from Spain.

Like Muslims and Christians, many Jews believe in pilgrimages and in mystics and holy people—saints—who can intercede in earthly affairs. And in several areas of the Middle East and North Africa, Jews and Muslims make pilgrimages to the same holy sites.

Some Jewish laws also have features in common with those of the surrounding Muslim majority in the Middle East and North Africa. Laws pertaining to inheritance, residence, and marriage, for example,

have traditionally favored the father's side of the family, even though one major definition of Jewishness is birth by a Jewish mother. With immigration and urbanization, however, fewer Jews are following the practice of residing with the groom's family, and new families are setting up smaller, separate households.

KURDS

Population: 25 million
Location: Turkey, Iraq, Iran
Language family: Iranian

Residing for more than 2,000 years in contiguous mountain regions of Turkey, Syria, Iraq, Iran, and Armenia, the Kurds have remained reasonably autonomous, despite the fact that they have rarely enjoyed self-governance over the territory they call Kurdistan, "land of the Kurds." Some scholars believe these people are descended from Medes, an ancient Iranian group who settled in southwest Asia more than 2,700 years ago.

Today Kurds live in Turkey, Iraq, Iran, Syria, Europe, and the United States. Because of their long, isolated existence in mountainous areas, Kurds have been able to retain their own language—Kurdish, which is most closely related to Persian—as well as their own social organization and oral traditions. Almost all Kurds are Muslims, but a small minority known as the Yazidi practice a unique religion that blends Zoroastrianism, Manichaeanism, Nestorian Christianity, and Shiite Islam.

Though Kurdish society is patriarchal and only male siblings inherit property, Kurdish women nevertheless enjoy a more public life than do other rural women from surrounding Turkish, Arab, and Iranian societies. They have greater involvement in community decisions and more freedom of interaction with men. Women may also opt not to wear a veil, a choice that is much more difficult for women in some neighboring societies. A Kurdish woman traditionally wears a bright floral skirt, an embroidered jacket, and a turban or scarf on her head. A man's traditional attire consists of loose-fitting pants, a short-waisted jacket, a sash around the waist, and a turban similar in style to a woman's. Kurds share many culinary practices with their Turkish, Arab, and Iranian neighbors, and they are famous for their cheeses and yogurt.

Because of the Turkish, Iraqi, and Iranian policies of forced settlement, Kurds are now a settled agrarian people. Not long ago, more of them were nomadic and tribally organized, and some continue to organize themselves tribally, with loyalty building from family to lineage to clan to tribe.

Other Kurdish farmers have organized instead around village leaders, who usually own the land and lease it out to farmers in exchange for labor or a portion of the harvest. Unlike Arab nomads, whose leaders are selected, Kurdish nomadic leaders inherit their titles. Many aspects of the Kurds' social life are changing dramatically, due to warfare, political instability, and sectarian tensions in their home areas. Some Kurds have migrated to cities and now work in urban trades.

Kurdish women line up to cast their votes outside a polling place in Kirkuk, Iraq, in December, 2005. Heightened security surrounded the historic national and regional elections.

Having been controlled by many outside forces and forced to witness the deaths of numerous members of their group, including children, Kurds have adopted a rather stoic attitude over the years. Their New Year's celebration, Nowruz, is similar to the Persian holiday, except that the Kurds not only celebrate new life and new beginnings but also ritually mourn their dead.

LEBANESE

Population: 3.7 million
Location: Lebanon
Language family: Semitic

The ancient Phoenicians of Lebanon created a maritime culture that stood at the hub of the Middle Eastern interior and the Mediterranean cultures beyond. The modern Lebanese still play this role and also mediate the tension-filled distance between Syria and Israel, while trying to balance the interests of their own multicultural population.

Nearly all Lebanese are Arabs, except for a small Armenian minority, representing a number of different cultural traditions. An estimated 60 percent of Lebanon's 3.8 million people are Muslim, mainly Shia and Sunni, but also including the Druze, an Islamic offshoot who form a closed community with esoteric religious practices. Christians account for nearly all the rest, the largest group being the Maronites, the only Middle Eastern Christian group to wield considerable political power in the Arab world. Some Lebanese Christians currently reject the Arab label and refer to themselves as Phoenicians.

The smallest mainland country in the Middle East, Lebanon has accommodated its cultural diversity partly by means of geographical separation. In a space that averages only 35 miles from the Mediterranean to the eastern border, Lebanon spans a coastal plain, the Mount Lebanon range, the fertile plains of the Bekaa Valley, and another range, the Anti-Lebanon Mountains.

The Mount Lebanon range historically provided opportunities for cultural separation. The Maronites, who ultimately fall under the jurisdiction of the Roman Catholic Church while retaining their own rituals and local patriarch, occupy the northern end. Maronites have often allied themselves with the West, first with medieval crusaders and Rome and later with the French. After World War I, the French held a mandate over Lebanon and Syria. They gave considerable power to the Maronites, who continue to feel an affinity for French culture and often speak French in private life.

The central Mount Lebanon area is the traditional home of the Druze, divided religiously between the *ëuqqal,* who are initiated into the esoteric mystical teachings, and the *juhhal,* who live the Druze way but are kept ignorant of deeper knowledge. Generally known Druze beliefs encompass an omnipresent God, the return of a messiah, and reincarnation of souls into newborn Druze. Druze mountain communities usually were built toward the summits, near sacred shrines.

The southern end of the range is traditional Shiite homeland, characterized by a rural Arab lifestyle. Shiites tend to be more agricultural than Sunnis, who generally live in Lebanon's coastal cities and are

> ### Play together as brothers but conduct business as strangers.
> SYRIAN PROVERB

involved in banking, trade, tourism, and other services that form the basis of Lebanon's economy and prosperity in times of political stability.

The Bekaa Valley, Lebanon's primary agricultural region, where crops of fruit, vegetables, and tobacco are grown, is also traditionally organized into sectarian enclaves, which include Shiites, Sunnis, Druze, and some of Lebanon's Christians, such as Greek Orthodox. Nevertheless, since the mid-1900s, there has been movement of all cultural groups to coastal cities, especially to Beirut.

The last official census taken in Lebanon dates back to 1932, due to the delicate nature of sectarian affiliation. Back then, Maronite Christians and Muslims were equally represented in the Lebanese population. When the 1943 National Pact was formulated, it allowed for a Maronite president, a Sunni prime minister, and a Shia speaker of parliament.

But a higher rate of Christian emigration, along with a higher Muslim birthrate, shifted the sectarian percentages. By the 1970s, with the population expanded by hundreds of thousands of Palestinian refugees—some there previously but many of whom came following the 1967 Arab-Israeli conflict—the scene was set for the civil war that broke out in 1975. During the 16-year conflict, which also absorbed regional differences involving Israel, Syria, and the Palestinian Liberation Organization, some 100,000 people were killed and an estimated 250,000 left as refugees. Beirut and the whole Lebanese economy were in shambles. In July 2006, fighting erupted again between Israel and the Lebanon-based radical group Hezbollah, causing widespread devastation despite the conflict's short duration.

Throughout the turmoil of the past 50 years, the Lebanese have retained the customs of hospitality, cuisine, and social etiquette that link them to other Arabs, and they have maintained values that make them some of the most skilled and educated people in the Middle East. Their complex cultural and political profile, however, continues to challenge notions of Lebanese unity.

PALESTINIANS

Population: 2.8 million
Location: Palestinian Territory, Israel
Language family: Semitic

Perhaps the most highly disputed territory on Earth, Palestine exerts a sacred, symbolic, and very tangible hold on the members of the three great Abrahamic faiths. It is a name long used to describe the land between the Mediterranean Sea and the Jordan River, and it derives from the Philistines, an Aegean people who arrived there at about the same time as the Hebrews, 3,000 years ago.

After the Romans expelled the rebellious Jews, in the years A.D. 70 and 135, Palestine eventually became a Christian land. The Arabs brought Islam in the seventh century, amassing converts and intermingling with the population. Later, four centuries of Turkish domination ended with World War I, replaced by a British mandate. Promises made to both Arabs and Jews gave both strong hopes of a permanent Palestinian homeland. Diaspora Jews began to return and form settlements.

In 1947, the United Nations voted to divide Palestine into an Arab and a Jewish state. Fighting began immediately, and intensified first when the State of Israel was proclaimed in 1948, and then with the departure of more than 750,000 Palestinians from their homes, an event Palestinians call the Nakba, or Catastrophe. These events initiated the difficult situation that exists today—fueled by continual conflict and violence—with Palestinians now living in varied circumstances.

Who hawks his oil by shouting, "Poor oil"?
SYRIAN PROVERB

Some Arabs in the Jewish state were able to stay on and obtain Israeli citizenship. Others live in areas now nominally overseen by the Palestinian National Authority but mostly under Israeli control; these territories include the Gaza Strip, along the Mediterranean Sea, and the territory along the West Bank of the Jordan River.

Palestinians also inhabit Israeli-controlled East Jerusalem. Millions of Palestinians, however, are either refugees within the territories formerly occupied by Israel and in neighboring countries such as Syria, Jordan, Egypt, and the Gulf States or are émigrés in other parts of the world.

Couples sway to the beat in Beirut, Lebanon. The city boasts one of the Mediterranean's hottest nightlife scenes.

The tobacco harvest holds the promise of income for this West Bank Palestinian couple. Many other Palestinians are landless and live in refugee camps.

Despite the turmoil of their lives and the fragmentation of their population, Palestinians continue to lead the lives that have defined them as a unique Arab people who are Sunni Muslim by a large majority, but also Christian and Druze. Most speak Arabic; some speak Hebrew or English. They live amid economic circumstances ranging from abject poverty to amenity-filled comfort. Many Palestinians remain subsistence farmers, like their ancestors of long ago, and others thrive in business and trade. Refugees experience high rates of unemployment and underemployment. Although they have been torn from their land base, Palestinian families remain strong. Both Muslims and Christians continue to celebrate the holy days and festivals of their religious traditions.

For the Palestinian people, dress strongly conveys notions of ethnicity and identity. Men traditionally wear the black-and-white checked headdress known as the *kafiyyeh,* held in place by the *agal,* a black rope circlet. Often they will don a long tunic and perhaps top it with a tailored suit jacket. Traditional dress for a Palestinian woman includes a *thobe,* a long, black, robelike dress with an embroidered bodice. The design and style of embroidery vary by region: In some areas, handstitching covers every inch of the bodice, whereas in others it forms decorative accents. While traditional dress often reinforces Palestinian identity, Western dress, including suits, slacks, and blue jeans, is very common, especially in towns and cities.

Palestinian foods have much in common with the rest of the Mediterranean world and feature wheat breads and cracked wheat, chickpeas, eggplant, rice, and stuffed squash and grape leaves, along with succulent dishes of lamb and beef. At feasts such as weddings, huge spreads of food are assembled for the guests.

Despite difficult circumstances, the Palestinian population is growing. Many refugee children receive a decent education through schools supervised by the United Nations. The handful of West Bank universities have large student populations who tend to be very politicized in their views, political strife and violence

Harvests in the Fertile Crescent

In 1971, Eldridge Niles and Stephen Jay Gould presented a new theory that changed the course of evolutionary thought overnight. Sifting through millions of years of fossilized arthropods, Niles and Gould found over and again long periods of evolutionary stasis interspersed with short bursts of substantial morphological change. Known today as punctuated equilibrium, their theory explains the discovery that biological diversity tends to remain stable until something jolts the system, and in short, punctuated bursts of adaptation, new species emerge to replace the old ones.

Sprouting seeds

Their conclusions may hold true for recent human history. The Middle East has been an inhospitable habitation for a long time, and yet our ancestors have spent 50,000 years struggling to survive there. One reason for this was that, lying at the crossroads of Africa and Eurasia, the Mediterranean Sea and the Indian Ocean, it presented an inviting migration path. Another reason is that their local climate was wreaking havoc.

Genetic evidence of migrations both into and out of the region of the Middle East suggests that early humans were often on the move. Then, around 10,000 years ago, humans changed tactics.

Pope Shenouda III, patriarch of the Coptic Orthodox Church, presides at an Easter mass in Cairo's Cathedral of Saint Mark.

Hunter-gatherers living in the so-called Fertile Crescent found that seeds they were collecting (and dropping on the way back home) began sprouting up close to their camps. They started planting systematically and, when conditions forced them to abandon a traditional hunter-gatherer lifestyle in exchange for a reli-

able food source, their nascent practice of sowing seeds and cultivating their products tied them to the land.

From seed to city

This move to agriculture, often called the Neolithic Revolution, rapidly changed the course of human culture. It allowed for higher population densities, stratified societal complexes, and warfare. Seemingly overnight, the age of civilizations was born. Though DNA from some populations indigenous to the region shows ancient ties to those first migrations, the predominant gen-etic patterns of today suggest that the early farmers of the Fertile Crescent moved south into both the Levant and the Arabian Peninsula, sticking to the lush Lebanese and Zagros Mountains until around 6,000 years ago. Then, when the region turned wetter, people began leaving the highlands and established towns in lowland Mesopotamia. Urban societies quickly developed and, with the emergence of Sumerian, the earliest written language, the rise of the first great city-states was at hand.

being all they have known since birth. They wait, along with the rest of the Palestinians, for the reality of a homeland.

PERSIANS

Population: 32 million
Location: Iran, Afghanistan
Language family: Iranian

The majority population in Iran, Persians are also well represented in Afghanistan, Tajikistan, the United Arab Emirates, and Bahrain. Since the Iranian revolution of 1979, many Persians have immigrated to Western Europe and North America as well.

Persians are descended from waves of Eurasian pastoral nomads who arrived in southwestern Asia from 2000 to 1000 B.C. Ancient Persia was home to

many different tribes, but as long ago as the sixth century B.C., these tribes were united under the Persian Empire and by the Zoroastrian religion. Only in the seventh century A.D. did invading Arabs bring Islam to the region and supplant the old religion.

Despite many foreign invasions since then, Persians have continued to maintain their distinct culture, language, and group identity. Their uniqueness is in part reinforced by their religious beliefs: They represent the single largest group of Shiite Muslims in the world, in contrast to the Sunni Muslims who dominate in the rest of the Middle East. A minority of Persians still practice Zoroastrianism, and there are small communities of Jewish, Christian, and Baha'i Persians as well. Members of all faiths observe and celebrate the Persian New Year—Nowruz—an ancient

Zoroastrian rite of spring and rebirth that begins with a thorough cleaning of the house and the setting of an altar rich with items that symbolize good luck and abundance. Beginning on the first day of spring and continuing for 13 days, the holiday is a time when families visit each other. On the 13th day, families go on picnics and spend time outdoors while ridding their homes of any bad luck from the past year.

A Persian family is dominated by the father, who tends to be formal and a disciplinarian, while the mother often plays the role of peacemaker and intermediary. The nuclear family is the most important domestic group, but extended families often choose to live near one another. Drawing artistic and poetic inspiration from their past, contemporary Persians have a cultural pride that runs very deep: Mystical poetry, classical Persian music, calligraphy, and miniature painting continue to be practiced in their traditional forms, although the global pop culture also exerts an influence.

Perhaps the most dramatic differences among Persians in the Middle East are to be found between urban residents and those who reside in rural areas. Urban Persians live in a hierarchical society based on occupation and social class, while rural Persians occupy tightly knit villages and have a farming lifestyle. Whether urban or rural, Persians have formal social customs whose fluency is an important aspect of functioning correctly in their hierarchical society.

One of these customs is *taroof*, the social art of deference. Though a person may be offered much—in the form of concrete items such as gifts or abstract items such as social favors and friendship—by the subtle practice of taroof, the recipient knows how much to accept politely.

QASHQAI

Population: 1.5 million
Location: Iran
Language family: Turkic

Largely nomadic or seminomadic, the Qashqai live in southwestern Iran, their traditional territory, and are famous for political prowess. They are among the few peoples in today's Middle East to organize themselves into a tribal confederacy with influence on national and local politics. Shiite Muslims, the Qashqai trace their origins to the 18th century, when several Iranian groups united under one tribal banner.

In the 1930s, the Iranian government forced the people to settle, and other periods of repression followed. But immediately after the founding of the Islamic Republic of Iran in 1979, many Qashqai made a dramatic return to their nomadic lifestyle, herding sheep and goats across the large territory between their summer and winter pastures in the Zagros Mountains. The city of Shiraz lies in the middle of this territory, and the Qashqai people have many ties to it.

Qashqai women enjoy social equality and hold roles complementary to those of the men in the tribe. Given the demands of nomadic life, every man, woman, and child participates in breaking camp, migrating, and setting up a new camp. Because of the policies of the Islamic Republic, Qashqai women now wear the veil more than in times past. Traditionally, however, women did not veil themselves unless they were going to non-Qashqai towns or into urban centers. Women's dress still retains its traditional style of bright colors,

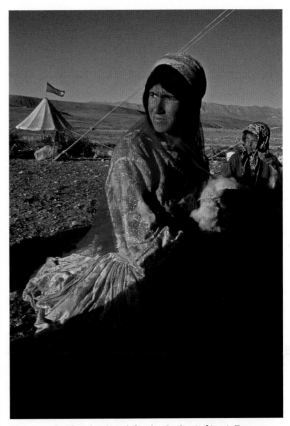

The nomadic life is hard work for the Qashqai of Iran's Zagros Mountains. The highly politicized Qashqai returned to nomadism when Iran became an Islamic Republic in 1979.

With one palm held up and the other down, Mevlevi Sufis twirl in a dance that unites heaven and earth.

multilayered skirts, tunics, and ornate scarves. Men's attire is less colorful but consists of loose-fitting trousers, a tunic and vest, and the famous felt cap with its rounded top and side earflaps. This cap has become a symbol of Qashqai political unity.

The Qashqai are also famous for woven carpets, the designs of which often depict tribal life and lands in symbolic form. As with many other ethnic groups, storytelling is a highly enjoyed and revered skill.

TURKS

Population: 62 million
Location: Turkey
Language family: Turkic

From as far away as Mongolia and China, several migratory waves of different Turkic tribes came to southwestern Asia between the 11th and the 15th centuries. Each tribe created a distinct culture, identity, and way of life. Those invaders who unified—first the Seljuk Turks, in a large part of the Middle East, and later the Ottoman Turks, in Anatolia (a portion of Turkey) and the Balkans—formed an expansive Turkish culture with a common language and historical experience. Islam was everyone's religion, and Turkish was the shared identity. Other Turkic peoples, speaking related Turkic languages, diverged and forged their own identities and cultures separate from the Anatolian Turks. These groups live in Iran, Afghanistan, China, Azerbaijan, Kazakhstan, Uzbekistan, Kyrgyzstan, and Turkmenistan.

There are more than 62 million Anatolian Turks in Turkey, with an additional 1.8 million living in Europe, especially in Germany, Cyprus, and Bulgaria. Although most Turks speak Turkish, members of the large groups of emigrants now residing and working in Europe may also speak German or other European languages. A tongue unrelated to Arabic or Persian, Turkish is from the Ural-Altaic language family of Central Asia.

From the beginning of their settlement in Turkey, Turks rose in influence in the Middle East and North Africa. They ruled many Middle Eastern peoples during the time of the Ottoman Empire and integrated these groups into their culture. At their most powerful, around A.D. 1700, Ottoman Turks governed all the lands from the Persian Gulf, through the Balkans, and across North Africa to Algeria. The Ottoman Empire ended after World War I and was met by a rise in Turkish nationalism and pride under the leadership of Mustafa Kemal, or Atatürk.

A long time has passed since Turks in Turkey were nomadic or tribally organized, and today their society is a complex mix of opposites: People see their identity as both European and Middle Eastern, as secular while still devoted to Islam, and as Western while also honoring their Eastern traditions. Turks in western Turkey tend toward more cosmopolitan attitudes and more Western-influenced industries. But many Turks in the central and eastern regions of the country are closely tied to the land; they have maintained traditional customs, such as a division of labor where the women tend fields and weave rugs and the men govern public life. Turkish family relations, which are similar to those of other Middle Eastern peoples, follow marriage and inheritance practices that emphasize the father's lineage and are in accord with Islamic law.

A Turkish Islamic mystical order—the famed Mevlevi Sufis—are popularly known in the West as the whirling dervishes. While mystical Islam is expressed

> You, who are buying cheap cuts of meat,
> when you come to the broth,
> you will regret it.
> SYRIAN PROVERB

throughout the Middle East, in Turkey the Mevlevis uphold the philosophy that all humans can gain direct experience of the divine, and they combine this belief with the physical practice of whirling. Their aim is to achieve a trance state wherein their awareness is fully concentrated on God.

Predating Islam are traditional symbols still used in Turkey's well-known rugs; they derive from ancient Central Asian peoples who were ancestral to the Turks. Traditional styles of another sort are retained in much of the classical literature and architecture—the mid-16th-century Ottoman Suleymaniye Mosque in Istanbul being a famous example. Many of today's literary and visual arts have taken on a modern tone because of reforms made by Atatürk.

A Life on the Move

Far from primitive, the pastoral nomads of today live according to highly refined bodies of knowledge about their animals and their landscapes.

Nomads, contrary to popular belief, do not wander aimlessly, and they are never lost in their home territory. Their seasonal movements are regulated like clockwork, responding to the subtle cycles of vegetation, weather, and climate as well as the need to fatten their animals and sustain themselves. Migration cycles may be very long, both in distance and in time, sometimes cycling through a series of locations over a decade before returning to the same spot again. The outward simplicity of this way of life—owning only what can be easily carried on a few pack animals—belies an astonishing set of intellectual and scientific achievements made by nomadic cultures in order to survive and thrive on grass.

Nomadism solved one of the great problems of human adaptation: How can people inhabit vast areas of land that are too poor to grow crops or forage for food? The answer lies in the many technologies of domesticating animals and migrating them across grazing lands. This advance allowed one of the greatest population expansions in human history, covering much of Central Asia and North Africa, and still persisting today. A significant human advancement, nomadism still has many things to teach us. Though it is a way of life now under threat from overcrowding and globalization, nomadism is still actively practiced in many parts of the world, from the high grassy plains of Mongolia and Tibet, to above the Arctic Circle in Finland and Russia, to the Andes of Boliva and Peru.

Nomadic technologies

Nomads have domesticated, or tamed, a very wide range of animals around the globe: sheep, goats, reindeer, camels, horses, yaks, cows, and llamas. Living in intimate and constant contact with these animals, they have developed an immense knowledge base of expertise about the life cycles, habits, mental states, lactation, and useful by-products of the animals. In many cases, nomads know more about their animals than do modern zoologists or veterinarians. Though their view is a more traditional one, we can learn much from their expertise.

For example, in Mongolia, herders of yaks and camels have developed a large repertoire of "domestication songs" and special noises that they produce while tending or milking the animals. They believe that these songs and sounds induce certain mental states in the animals that allow them to be better managed, more fertile, and more productive. In observing the calming effect of this singing on a mother yak or camel that is being trained to nurse its calf, it is impossible not to wonder at the effectiveness and genius of this sound technology.

Nomads are also pioneering geneticists, having made discoveries about animal breeding long before scientists knew about genes at all. They have learned

Solitude is a way of life for pastoral nomads such as this shepherd in Qinghai Province, China. Men often spend months away from family with herds in seasonal pastures.

A Wodaabe man of Niger gives his Mehari camel a rest. North African nomadic peoples favor the long-legged and streamlined Meharis and often race them.

to control breeding and reproduction carefully to maintain robust animals and in many cases to breed bigger and better animals. The Evenki people of eastern Siberia succeeded, through controlled breeding, in creating a bigger and hardier reindeer that could be saddled and ridden.

Early genetic engineering

The Bodi people of Somalia created an elaborate hierarchy of cow colors, markings, and patterns. By observing these outward morphological traits and using them to decide which animals to mate, they have effectively been successfully controlling genetic mutation centuries before scientists considered it.

Bodi herders give individual, descriptive names to most animals. The names may describe the coat color, pattern, horn shape, or other characteristic. And they can recite the ancestry of a particular cow, sometimes as far back as a dozen generations. The knowledge of folk genetics transmitted orally by the Bodi is astonishing: They give distinct names to more than 80

different combinations of coat color and pattern. For example, a cow that is entirely black is called *koro*. If that black cow mates with a bull that has the pattern *ludi*—all white with a black head and rump—their calf will be a *kalmi*, all black with just with a narrow white stripe around its midsection.

By observing the breeding of cows across many centuries, the Bodi have mastered a highly complex system that names and keeps track of all possible color and patterns for cows and tracks the patterns predictably produced by cross-matings. The Bodi people group certain colors and patterns together into cow clans that mirror the structure of their human clans.

Bodi involvement with cows goes far beyond mere sustenance of meat and milk. Though they are semi-nomadic—they also practice swidden farming—their entire worldview centers on their symbiotic relationship with the cow, which represents fecundity, life, and survival. They sacrifice specifically patterned cows for marriage, for birth and death rituals, or when a human or cow falls ill, when they pray for rain, or

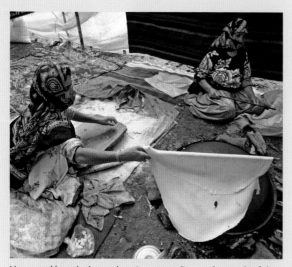

Home and hearth change locations according to the needs of the herd for these Azeri women of northwestern Iran.

when a lion is killed. Cows with certain patterns must never be sacrificed, lest plague or famine ensue.

Nomads invented veterinary medicine. They understand the health and illness of their animals. They also solve complex economic problems by using precise and time-tested formulas of mixed herding. For example, in the high Andes of Bolivia, herders combine llamas with sheep to make the most of the thin vegetation. Like the Bodi, the Aymara people of Bolivia use a complex classification system to name their alpacas and llamas according to sex, age, and fleece color or pattern. Though Andean pastoralists are now mostly sedentary, living in houses and keeping their animals in stone enclosures, the archeological evidence suggests that nomadic pastoralists raised camelids for nearly 2,000 years in the Andes alongside sedentary peoples who grew potatoes and quinoa.

Naming of the land

Nomads have an intricate knowledge of the landscape they inhabit. Typically, they will have names for every single topographic feature, at a far greater level of detail considering they may live in areas with no roads, towns, or addresses. The languages spoken by nomads often encode features of the landscape into the verbs or other parts of their grammar. For example, in Tuvan, a language spoken by yak herders in southern Siberia, in order to simply say the word "go" you must know the direction of water current in the nearest river, and you must choose one among three verbs that indicate

"upstream," "downstream," or "cross-stream." In other words, the Tuvan nomads can orient themselves precisely because their language—evolved as it has to help them survive in their ecosystem—requires them to pay attention at all times to the landscape.

The work of horses

Nomads' work is never done, and there are no vacations, because the animals never rest and must always be supplied with water and vegetation. In Mongolia, a typical horse-breeding nomad's day begins before daybreak. Horses in Mongolia are used for riding, for carrying or pulling, for milk, and sometimes for edible meat. Horse racing is a national sport, practiced by both young boys who ride bareback and men who ride with saddles, competing for glory and medals. A common herd numbers up to 30 mares, 15 foals, 20 two- and three-year-old horses, 10 geldings (castrated male horses), and 1 breeding stallion.

Horses are a source of great pride, and their care and well-being is what the nomads—the entire extended family—devote their lives to. Early in the morning, the horses must be let out of the stockade to graze, and the

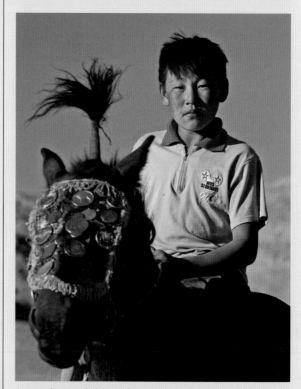

A nomadic Monchak boy of Western Mongolia proudly displays medals he won riding his horse in races.

On the move with their herd of cattle and flock of goats, Niger pastoralists transport the accoutrements of daily life—and themselves—on camels and donkeys.

foals must be let out of their separate pen. The foals will be allowed to nurse for just a few minutes, to get the mares' milk flowing. Then the foals are tied up and the mares must be milked, not once but every two hours during the daytime. The milk is processed to make a rich "white food" for young children. In three summer months, a mare can produce up to six liters of milk a day. Women and girls collect it by hand-milking.

Men work with colts to break them, train them to the bridle and saddle, and train them to carry a rider. Breeding must be carefully controlled to obtain a line of healthy offspring.

Leather must be worked by hand to make lassos, saddles, and bridles. Women collect horsehair from the tail and painstakingly twist it by hand into sturdy ropes. Hair may also be used to make stringed instruments, especially the *morin huur* (horsehead fiddle), decorated with a carved wooden horsehead and believed to embody the spirit of the horse.

Will nomadism survive our shrinking world? Even in the most remote areas of Central Asia or in the high Andes, nomads are feeling the pressures of globalization. Many areas now suffer from overgrazing, as well as periodic winter famines. As it becomes harder to fatten up the animals, young people may see herding as a dead end and prefer to migrate to the cities to work as day laborers instead.

Those who do stay in the countryside are acquiring technologies that change their way of life: solar panels, televisions, radios, tractors, motorcycles, and cellular phones are all commonly seen. Despite these imports, many thousands of people in Mongolia, Siberia, Central Asia, North Africa, and the Andes still live as their ancestors did centuries ago, listening to the sounds of wind and rain, driving the animals on to greener pastures, and tending to the rhythms of their sheep, camels, llamas, yaks, and horses. ■

— *K. David Harrison*

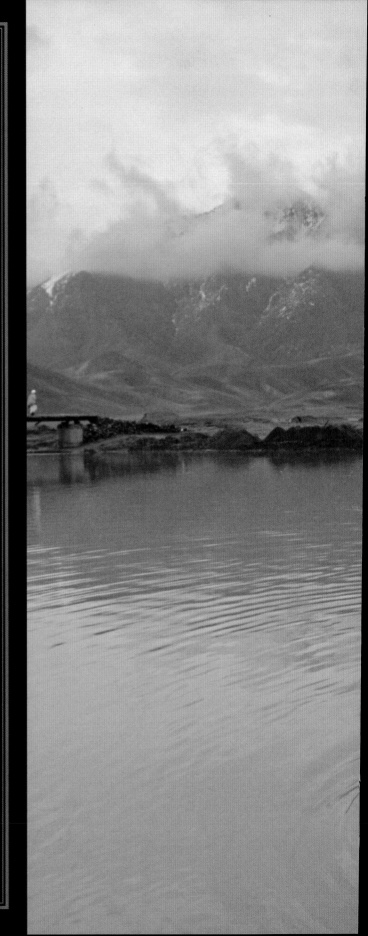

ASIA

CAUCASUS
Armenians • Azeris • Chechens & Ingush

CENTRAL ASIA
Baluchi • Burusho • Kazakhs • Kyrgyz
Pashtun • Turkmen • Uzbeks

EAST ASIA
Ainu • Bai • Dong • Han • Japanese
Koreans • Mongols • Tibetans • Uygurs

SOUTHEAST ASIA
Balinese • Dayak • Hmong • Ifugao
Javanese • Khmer • Minangkabau
Thais • Vietnamese

SOUTH ASIA
Bengalis • Gujaratis • Nagas
Nepalis • Punjabis • Sora
Sinhalese • Tamils

THE ASIAN NORTH
Chukchi & Koryak • Evenk • Nenets
Tuvans • Yakut • Yukaghir

To prepare for evening prayers, an Afghan man washes his face
in a river at the eastern edge of Kabul.

Asia's cultural makeup fully matches the geographic complexity and richness of the world's largest continent. From Japan to Georgia, from Mongolia to Malaysia, Asia is home to more ethnic groups than any other major region. These groups have evolved over a very long time. Some of them developed in isolation, while others have complex histories of interaction and sharing, either through peaceful migration or military conquest.

China, India, and Indonesia—the first, second, and fourth most populous nations of the world—are home to 40 percent of Earth's people, and in these three countries reside extraordinary numbers of ethnic groups. Language, a major measure of ethnicity, reveals in its diversity the range of a country's human wealth: Indonesia counts more than 700 languages, India over 400, and China more than 200. In China, at least 90 percent of the people consider themselves to be Han. This term is commonly used interchangeably with "Chinese" and dates from the Han dynasty, China's first long-lasting period of unification. For more than 2,000 years, smaller ethnic groups have been driven into mountains and marginal areas by the Han Chinese, whose more than one billion people now constitute the world's largest ethnic group.

China's population has tens of millions of minority members constituting hundreds of ethnic groups, yet officially the Chinese government recognizes only 55 "national minorities." Some groups have been lost through a steady acculturation, which continues to threaten Tibetans, Mongolians, and others whose lands abut heavily populated Chinese regions. One group, the Manchu, ruled China as the last imperial dynasty (until 1911) but did so at the expense of ethnic identity: By assimilating Chinese ways, the Manchu lost their own language and culture. While millions survive, their language now has as few as a hundred speakers.

Religion Throughout history, religion has given cohesion and meaning to ethnic groups, so much so that it often seems inseparable from an overall way of life. This is clearly true with Tibetan Buddhism, where belief and culture have evolved intertwined. Many parts of Asia have been touched by Islam, brought by Arabs from the seventh century onward. The religious, political, and social forces of this faith continue to dominate hundreds of millions of people every day. In Armenia, Christianity has been a foundation of society

Recalling the era of Genghis Khan, a formation of official Mongolian state horsemen opens an annual festival in Ulaanbataar.

and a balm during the long and difficult history of its people. But religion can also inflame local hatreds: Ethnic hostilities have erupted between Muslims and Hindus in India, Hindus and Buddhists in Sri Lanka, and Christians and Muslims in Indonesia.

Practicing skills that older Sherpas use as porters and guides on Everest ascents, a young girl totes a toddler-filled basket.

Buddhism developed into a world religion from Indian origins 2,500 years ago. Eventually it all but disappeared in its homeland, but by traversing the Himalaya and streaming along Silk Road trade routes, the religion reached China and from there spread to other parts of Asia. In Japan, especially, Buddhism and contacts with China's mature civilization helped shape the character of the people.

While holding fast to their indigenous traditions, the Japanese borrowed and adapted foreign ways to great benefit: Landscape gardening, flower arranging, and the art of serving tea, for example, all began in China, with Japan bringing them to full bloom. The tea ceremony involves the graceful serving of tea with simple implements in impeccable surroundings, combining aesthetic and spiritual aspects to express the Japanese love of beauty and inner calm. Despite Japan's modern ways, this ritual survives and continues to grow in popularity.

Influences Through government and architecture, painting and sculpture, science and warfare, even the use of chopsticks, Chinese institutions also influenced the cultures of Korea, Vietnam, and other areas of East and Southeast Asia. Even so, local peoples created and maintained vital, thriving cultures of their own, while sharing a common written language and elements of Confucianism, a code of conduct as much as a religion that dates back to its founder, born in China in 551 B.C. In fact, the Confucian ethical system of social relations still underlies the modern state in China, Korea, Singapore, and elsewhere.

India has left its mark, too, dramatically spreading its civilization and religions into South and Central Asia. Aspects of its culture reached into Sri Lanka, Pakistan, and Afghanistan, to name a few present-day countries, and traveled sea routes all the way to

Bali, which remains Hindu to this day. Indian scholars and priests introduced many of Asia's peoples to the classical languages of Sanskrit and Pali, which were used in early writings and historical records.

Rice One of history's most important developments remains a shared legacy and a critical component of many Asian cultures: wet-rice cultivation. For millennia, Asians from Japan southward have shared the common inheritance of rice, a staple that is central to the survival of groups large and small. People eat it every day and rely on it for a hundred other uses. Versatile rice straw, for example, supplies material for thatch, basketry, floor mats, sandals, brooms, bedding, rough cloaks, and hats; it also serves as feed for the animals.

People in all of Asia's rice-growing countries honor this grain through seasonal festivals and ceremonies. For them, rice has a sacred, even divine significance, so offerings of cooked and uncooked rice, rice cakes, rice stalks, and rice wine serve to ensure good harvests and to rejuvenate the vital forces of the Earth itself. Many Asian cultures esteem a god or goddess of rice. Among the Ifugao of the Philippines, a carved effigy of the *bulul,* or rice god, is placed in the rice granary to honor and protect the harvest.

Rice cultivation demands many hands and a spirit of cooperation to prepare fields, sow seeds, transplant shoots, maintain irrigation systems, and harvest, husk, and polish the grains that will be cooked and eaten (almost all Asians prefer polished, white rice rather than brown rice). Accompanied by pickles or chilies, or served with other dishes, a bowl of rice represents the enduring hopes and expectations of Asia's billions.

Tradition suggests a mother attending a pensive bride; in reality, mom adjusts the costume a Miss India hopeful wears to perform a classical Indian dance in the pageant's talent segment.

To grow this grain in submerged fields, farmers have reshaped entire landscapes with hand-built terraces, dikes, water channels, and carefully constructed beds stretching to the horizon. Stepped emerald fields, such as those of the Ifugao people in the mountains of central Luzon in the Philippines, stand as a lasting image of Asia. ■

Caucasus

The Caucasus region is divided into two major subregions: the North Caucasia, which is a part of Russia, and the Transcaucasia, which comprises Georgia, Armenia, and Azerbaijan. The topography here is defined by a 750-mile-long belt of mountainous land stretching from the mouth of the Kuban River, on the Black Sea, to the Apsheron peninsula, protruding into the Caspian Sea. For millennia, the Caucasus Mountains have been seen as the boundary line between Europe and Asia. It was on these heights that Zeus tied Prometheus, according to ancient Greek myth, to punish him for giving fire to humans. The region has served as the gateway linking those two continents with the Middle East. The political, cultural, and linguistic tableaus of these lands have shifted constantly through trade and travel, despite the daunting mountain range that slices though them.

ARMENIANS

Population: 7 million
Location: Armenia
Language family: Armenian

Landlocked Armenia, a mountainous country slightly smaller than Maryland, with many rivers and narrow, fertile valleys, counts some three million people within its borders. But this population represents only half of the world's Armenians; the rest—officially considered part of the nation—live in the former Soviet Union, India, the Middle East, Poland, Romania, Western Europe, and North America, where many have achieved success in business, crafts, and other occupations. Independent only since 1991, the Republic of Armenia faces major challenges: The economy is grim, many skilled workers are emigrating, and an ethnic war with Azerbaijan has killed tens of thousands.

Armenians remember a time during the Middle Ages when they were part of a major kingdom that also included what is now northeastern Turkey. Yet the greatest events in Armenia's collective memory are invasions, suppressions, and forced exiles over the past thousand years. The worst was the 1915 massacre, when Turks drove the people from eastern Anatolia; more than 600,000 died.

Among diaspora Armenians, cosmopolitan attitudes coexist with a great love of home, family, and age-old traditions. The people strongly value their distinct language; although it belongs to the large Indo-European family, it has no close linguistic relatives and stands alone with a unique 38-letter alphabet.

A distinctive brand of Christianity is the foundation that underlies the unity of all Armenians, who converted to the faith early and in the fourth century declared that Christianity was their state religion. This tie has produced an invaluable corpus of religious literature as well as remarkable art and architecture. The people are renowned for their mosaics and tiles, and the circular dome of their churches is thought to have had a strong influence on Byzantine and Ottoman buildings. On theological grounds, primarily the interpretation of Christ's divinity, the Armenian Apostolic Church stands independently and proudly next to the Roman Catholic and Orthodox Churches. It has been a pillar of Christianity and a primary force in maintaining Armenian culture.

Azeri men stand to pray in a restored mosque. The more moderate forms of Islam, as practiced in Azerbaijan, have come under pressure from hard-line Muslims in neighboring Iran.

AZERIS

Alternate name: Azerbaijanis
Population: 7.2 million   **Location:** Azerbaijan
Language family: Turkic

The seven million Azeris of Azerbaijan form the largest group in the ethnic mosaic of the Caucasus. A hundred years ago, their homeland was the world's top oil producer; today, it is again actively tapping the immense Caspian Sea reserves, with the oil industry advancing the trend toward urbanization. While most Azeris now live in cities, many are farmers and nearly all are Muslims, in contrast to neighboring Armenia and Georgia, which are Christian. According to local custom, Azeri Muslims may drink wine, and women are free to work and go unveiled.

Islam arrived with 7th-century Arab conquerors, the first of many waves that included Turks, Mongols, Persians, and Russians, who began dominating the area in the 19th century. A hybrid people, Azeris were ethnically and linguistically Turkic by the 11th century,

yet their roots go deep into ancient Caucasia and Iran. To the south lies an Iranian region also named Azerbaijan, larger in both size and population but lacking a nation's cohesiveness.

Azeris also honor Zoroaster, who lived in the 6th century B.C. and founded Zoroastrianism, a religion with a central belief in the cosmic conflict between good and evil. Today, their Islam sets them apart. Of Islam's two main branches, the Shiites began to dominate after the departure of the Sunnis, who had allied themselves with Ottoman Turks in the 19th century. Later there was reconciliation as Azeri nationalism stressed a common heritage and downplayed sectarian differences. With improved relations came a cultural flowering from the mid-1800s to the early 1900s, bringing new libraries, hospitals, schools, art academies, and charities. A spirit of emancipation spread to Turkic peoples throughout the Russian Empire and elsewhere.

The Soviet era suppressed this awakening, closing Azerbaijan's 2,000 mosques, crushing intellectuals and artists, and forcing the people to abandon Arabic and adopt a Cyrillic alphabet. Then, under glasnost and following independence in 1991, writers and historians returned to resurrect past glories. In recent years, Azeris have reopened or rebuilt their mosques. After 70 years of Soviet rule, few reminders of Russian culture remain, though broad education policies and the country's high literacy rate are by-products.

CHECHENS & INGUSH

Population: 1.2 million (Chechens); 467,000 (Ingush)
Location: Russia
Language family: Nakh

The Chechens and the Ingush together share many aspects of culture and language, as well as a remote location in the northern Caucasus Mountains, on the southern fringes of Russia. They also unfortunately share centuries of history fraught with domination, violence, and repression, which have accelerated in the decades since World War II.

The names Chechen and Ingush are actually Russian designations; the two groups refer to themselves collectively as *vaj nakh*—our people. They live in adjoining territories that were formed by the Soviets into a single autonomous republic. Chechnya declared independence in 1991, and both it and Ingushetia are now republics within the framework of the Russian Federation.

Both groups are Sunni Muslims, having embraced Islam between the 17th and early 19th centuries. Chechen and Ingush represent two distinct but closely related languages of the Nakh branch of Northeast Caucasian languages. Exposure to each other's language has allowed them to communicate easily; many Chechens and Ingush also speak Russian.

Their territory incorporates fertile, northern lowlands where farming is practiced, and high mountains and valleys where sheepherding forms the major occupation. Lowland villages tend to be larger than mountain ones, with compactly arranged one-story

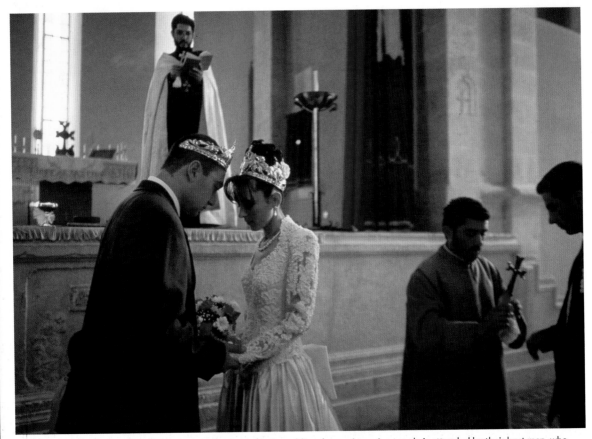

Wearing the crowns that proclaim them king and queen on their wedding day, an Armenian couple is attended by their best man, who holds a cross. Most Armenians adhere to the Armenian Apostolic faith.

wood or brick houses, while mountain villages typically feature stone buildings, including tall watchtowers that are also inhabited. People from the highlands traded their livestock and eggs for grain from lowland farmers. In more recent times, both groups participated in oil production from the nearby Caspian Sea fields.

Traditionally, men and women led largely separate lives, with extreme deference shown to men by women: Women stood when a man entered the room, they kept eyes downcast when a man spoke to them, and they ate separately, in the kitchen, after the men had eaten. Women still dress modestly but cover their heads, usually with a wool or silk scarf. More traditional Chechen and Ingush men wear tall lambswool hats.

Like other people of the Caucasus, Chechens and Ingush place a high premium on hospitality. Visitors are entertained lavishly with the best the family has to offer, both in food and accommodation. Meals tend to include lamb or mutton; vegetables such as tomatoes, eggplants, and peppers; corn or wheat flatbreads; fruits such as apples, pears, and plums; and a large number of dairy products including milk, butter, cheese, curds, yogurt, and sour cream.

Chechen and Ingush social organization is based on clans of paternally related lineages with no internal or external hierarchical relationships, other than the high esteem and respect accorded to elders and

> There is no marksman
> who does not miss,
> there is no sage who does not err.
> OLD TURKIC PROVERB

others who have earned merit. Marriages usually are contracted outside of one's clan. The egalitarian nature of Chechen and Ingush life has made it difficult for them to accept outside authority.

The Chechens, however, have demonstrated a more rebellious nature against Russia's many attempts to control the land and its access to main routes through the mountains, to eliminate the people directly or eradicate their culture by forced Russianization, and more recently, to acquire more direct access to Caspian Sea

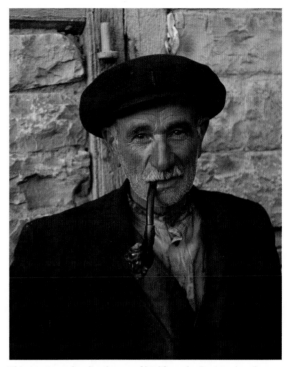

This Azeri man has lived most of his life under Soviet rule, when Azeri culture was suppressed in favor of Russianization.

oil. Chechens were fierce fighters during the 50 years of the Caucasian Wars, which ended in defeat, with many northern Caucasians killed, repressed, or forced to emigrate.

The Ingush's relative reluctance to resist has not prevented them from feeling the effects of a kind of guilt by association. Along with the Chechens, the Ingush were accused by Stalin of Nazi collaboration during World War II and exiled for 14 years to Central Asia and Siberia. The journey and the harsh conditions of exile took their toll on both populations. During the exile, Chechen and Ingush lands were resettled by Russians and Russian-speaking Cossacks.

The Chechens' declaration of independence in 1991 caused the Ingush to withdraw from their union. Ingush have tried to avoid the ongoing hostilities between the Chechens and Moscow, including a war from 1994 to 1996 and more recent occupation by Russian troops, but they have been involved in the fighting and have had to absorb many Chechen refugees. Their own territorial disputes with neighboring North Ossetia brought Russian retaliation. Ongoing violence and disorder continue in Chechnya, amid some rebuilding of its shattered infrastructure.

Central Asia

Politically, Central Asia often refers to the cluster of former Soviet republics—Kazakhstan, Kyrgyzstan, Tajikistan, Turkmenistan, and Uzbekistan—encircled by the nation giants of India, China, and Russia. Geographically, the region combines bleak flatlands, including the Russian Steppes, and nearly impenetrable mountain ranges: the Zagros of Iran, the Altay of Russia and Mongolia, and the Karakoram, in territory under dispute between China and Pakistan, which contains K2, the world's second-highest mountain. The historic Silk Road snaked through these reaches, connecting Asia, Europe, and Africa through centuries of trade and cultural exchange.

▣ To listen to music from Afghanistan, Kazakhstan, Pakistan, and Uzbekistan, visit http://worldmusic.national geographic.com.

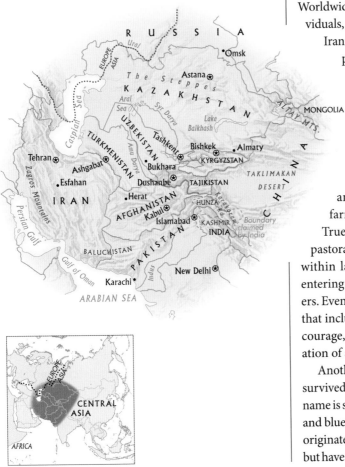

BALUCHI

Alternate name: Balochi
Population: 7 million   Location: Pakistan
Language family: Iranian

Fiercely independent seminomads whose origins may go back to Middle Eastern and Caspian Sea nomadic peoples, the Baluchi have for centuries integrated marginal groups from many cultures under their tribal name. Today, this broad ethnic group comprises dozens of tribes and occupies a vast area of Pakistan, southeastern Iran, and southwestern Afghanistan. Although arid and largely inhospitable, with dramatic landscapes and few roads, the region also encompasses green valleys, juniper forests, and lofty mountains with wildflowers, as well as irrigated gardens and orchards producing dates, apples, cherries, almonds, and cumin. Where the land meets the Arabian Sea, a 500-mile-long coastline has fine, sandy beaches.

About 7 percent of the Baluchi call Baluchistan—nearly half of Pakistan's land surface—their home. Worldwide, the group numbers some ten million individuals, including people who speak Baluchi, an Indo-Iranian language similar to Kurdish and Pashtu; people who consider themselves to be Baluchi but speak a different language, such as Urdu or Farsi; and even people whose disparate ancestors historically found solidarity among the Baluchi. Each tribal group follows a head chief, or *pir*, a Sufi mystic or Muslim holy man.

Nearly 80 percent of all Baluchi raise sheep and other livestock and rely on small-scale farming activities for part of their livelihood. True nomadism has almost disappeared, and the pastoral life has given way to cultural assimilation within larger nations. The people are increasingly entering the mainstream, frequently as migrant laborers. Even so, they retain a vibrant storytelling tradition that includes age-old songs with themes emphasizing courage, heroism, protection of the weak, and veneration of ancestors.

Another notable aspect of Baluchi culture has also survived: In Afghanistan and eastern Iran, the tribal name is still applied to intricate rugs with rich, dark reds and blues, highlighted sparingly with white. The colors originate from vegetable and fruit dyes used long ago but have in the last century been replicated synthetically.

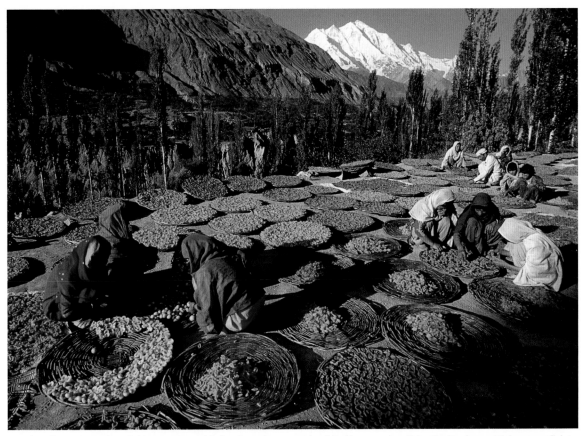

Burusho villagers in northern Pakistan sort sun-dried apricots, long a staple of the Hunza region. Using the Karakoram Highway as a link to the outside world, the people sell this fruit elsewhere in Pakistan and also in China.

BURUSHO

Alternate name: Hunzakuts   Population: 87,000
Location: Pakistan
Language family: Language isolate

The Hunza region, found within northern Pakistan's Karakoram Range, is home to the Burusho, a people who claim descent from soldiers in the fourth-century B.C. army of Alexander the Great. As fanciful as the story may be, many Burusho do appear European; some people say they look specifically Celtic. The Burushaski language is unrelated to any other world tongue.

Over the years, misconceptions about the Burusho diet and a romantic ideal held by gullible Westerners gave rise to stories about exceptional life spans in the Hunza region. While it is true the people have traditionally relied on apricots during the long winter, the stories connecting their diet to longevity are myths.

The Burusho once lived in a much larger area, but they were eventually driven into the mountains, where they established their virtually impregnable homeland. Hunza was ideally situated, allowing the Burusho to tax—or raid—caravans traveling between India and China.

Governed by the same family of *mirs* (rulers) since the 11th century, the remote outpost converted late to Islam; in 1904, it pledged loyalty to the Aga Khan and his Ismaili sect, a branch of Islam with no mosques and no imams. This sect defers, as do the Baluchi, to a pir, a religious leader who exhibits sanctity or special charismatic powers.

In 1974 Hunza became fully integrated with Pakistan, ending the long rule of the mirs, and four years later the Karakoram Highway arrived to relieve the severe isolation. Most important, the Aga Khan Foundation's programs for health, education, agriculture, transport, and small businesses have given new hope to the people. Money has slowly replaced barter, and schooling, especially for girls, is seen as the necessary way forward for Burusho society.

The Central Asian Passageway

Only a few thousand years after the second wave of humans migrating out of Africa had settled into life in the Middle East, climate shifted once again, drying out the vast plains of the Tigris and Euphrates River basins and forcing these early hunter-gatherers to pick up camp and search for a new homeland. The luckiest of these migrations headed northeast, crossing the Zagros and Taurus Mountains before moving directly into central Asia, stopping finally to settle amid the giant granite upwelling known as the Pamir Mountains.

Genetic information from today's Pamiri populations shows that their DNA has been there continuously for the past 40,000 years, almost as long as the first lineages found in the Middle East. The finding is now well accepted by population geneticists, but it initially drew some skepticism. After all, it is difficult to imagine why humans, largely accustomed to life on the lowland African savannahs, would make a move to settle in one of the world's more rugged landscapes.

There is an explanation.

On to greener lands

Around 45,000 years ago, the world was entering a dry spell, and the lush corridor that had made North Africa and the Middle East hospitable for life and fruitful for cultivation was becoming a desert.

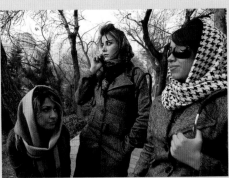

Modestly yet fashionably dressed, young Tehrani women track down a friend via cell phone.

Dependent on game and water, the few humans who had made it to the Middle East were now being evicted by climate change, forced to look elsewhere for green pastures. Fortunately for them, the mountains to their east provided a much needed refuge. In drier times, mountains act as atmospheric sponges, soaking up what little moisture is available in the air around them and providing a haven for wildlife. If the Garden of Eden had mountains, we can be fairly certain that they looked something like what central Asia did 35,000 years ago.

Staging ground

Once in central Asia, humans thrived, quickly expanding across the steppes, inhabiting the river valleys of the Pamir Mountains, and setting the stage for migrations to come.

As the climate turned again, groups began spreading out from the region, generations of rugged mountain living enabling them to inhabit all corners of the world successfully. Europe, East Asia, India, and the Americas were all populated by independent migrations originating from the Eurasian heartland over a period lasting 20,000 years.

Considering the importance of central Asia as a staging ground for human dispersal, one could say that if Africa was the cradle of humanity, central Asia was its nursery.

KAZAKHS

Alternate name: Kazaks
Population: 10 million   Location: Kazakhstan
Language family: Turkic

The motif of Kazakh history has been the struggle and interplay between Mongol and Turkic tribes across the vast stage of Central Asia, from the Gobi Desert to the Caspian Sea. Kazakhs speak a Turkic language, but some scholars consider them to be Turko-Mongols; in appearance they seem more Mongoloid than their Turkic brethren. United under the Mongols in Uzbek lands, Kazakh clan leaders in the 1460s broke away to return to coveted pastures in the east, where they prospered as nomads. At that time they became known as Kazakhs, which means "secessionists" or "independents," and their ethnic identity firmly took shape.

The arrival of Russian soldiers and traders in the 1600s spelled a slow doom for indigenous culture. From Moscow to Kazakhstan is not much farther than from Washington, D.C., to Boston, so Russian penetration came steadily. In the modern era, Kazakhstan played a main role in Soviet industrial and military development, with its northeastern region subjected to more nuclear tests than any other place on the planet.

Today, Kazakhstan's ethnic Kazakhs do not form a clear majority in their own land; nearly as many Russians live there. Two and a half million more Kazakhs reside in China, Uzbekistan, Mongolia, and Russia. The largest country in Central Asia and the ninth largest in the world, Kazakhstan is sparsely populated and three-fourths desert or semidesert. Deep in the ground, though, lie rich reserves of oil, gas, and coal.

Kazakhs in all regions can communicate fairly easily, but their language never developed a modern technical vocabulary and thus lives in the shadow of Russian, the language of education, business, and technology. The issue of language and ethnicity has come to the fore as the two official languages—Kazakh and Russian—vie for position and symbolize the deep rifts between two peoples living in entirely different spheres. Russians are skilled, technically capable, and international; Kazakhs seem unsure of the way forward as they struggle to balance the needs of a young nation, Islam, and modern mass culture.

Even in a modern state, the people find security by relying on traditional ties that go back 500 years. Each Kazakh holds allegiance to one of three ancient groups, or *zhuz* (hordes): the Lesser Horde in the west, the Middle Horde in the north and east, and the Great Horde in the south. Because clan and national politics, as well as economic decisions, depend on such affiliations, the ancient hordes remain important in the makeup and functioning of Kazakh society.

KYRGYZ

Population: 3.6 million
Location: Kyrgyzstan
Language family: Turkic

The Kyrgyz represent an amalgam of nomadic peoples that reflects their movement through Central Asia for about two thousand years and includes both Mongols and Turkic tribes. The earliest Kyrgyz state was a khanate that extended from south-central Siberia to the eastern part of present-day Kyrgyzstan, now Central Asia's second smallest nation.

Mountains dominate Kyrgyzstan's landscape. The Kyrgyz use the high pastures to raise livestock, primarily sheep, cattle, horses, and goats. They grow crops of wheat, sugar beets, potatoes, and fruit in the fertile Fergana Valley and elsewhere in the limited lowlands.

Ethnic Kyrgyz today form more than half of Kyrgyzstan's total population. They speak Kyrgyz, which belongs to the Turkic family of languages and did not appear in written form until the 1920s. The Kyrgyz converted to Islam mainly between the 8th and

The weather-worn face of a Kazakh hunter, eyes steady and cheeks aglow, displays a blend of Turkic and Mongolian features. Kazakhs fall short of forming a majority in the nation of Kazakhstan.

12th centuries. About 80 percent of Kyrgyz are Sunni Muslims, although the day-to-day expression of their faith is somewhat relaxed, and some Kyrgyz still observe practices from their culture's animist past. Relationships between men and women in Kyrgyz society also tend to be less rigid than among some neighboring Central Asian groups.

> It is better to be a slave
> in your homeland than to be
> a ruler in a foreign country.
> KAZAKH PROVERB

Under Soviet control throughout much of the 20th century, the Kyrgyz were forced to abandon their nomadic lifestyle and adapt to collectivized farming and mining. Few Kyrgyz now live mainly in yurts, circular portable homes of felt secured over a collapsible wooden framework.

Yurt interiors traditionally are divided into a men's side on the left, which includes accoutrements for hunting, fishing, and livestock, and a women's side on the right, where cooking utensils and sewing equipment are stored. A small stove used for cooking and heating sits in the center, and the bedding used at night is hung on a back wall protected by a decorative cover, forming a backdrop for the seating of an honored guest who might be served the delicacy of sliced sheep's liver and tail fat. The traditional Kyrgyz diet features dairy products, including *koumiss*—fermented mare's milk—along with mutton and vegetables.

Although yurts are no longer used as much for residences, even urban Kyrgyz may erect one on an important occasion, such as the birth of a child. So central is the structure to Kyrgyz identity that the national flag features a component of the yurt's roof at its center.

As Kyrgyzstan's mainly urban Russian population, concentrated in the capital city of Bishkek, has decreased, the population as a whole has become more rural. Now some two-thirds of Kyrgyz are involved in agriculture, including animal husbandry. Gold mining has become another important economic activity.

Proud stewards of a rich oral tradition, the Kyrgyz have maintained for a millennium an oral epic poem that is twice as long as the *Iliad* and *Odyssey* combined—and it still has not been written down in its entirety. It relates the tenth-century saga of the folk hero Manas, considered the father of the Kyrgyz people. Many Kyrgyz know portions of the saga of Manas, his son, and grandson, which also is performed by a special class of storytellers called *manaschy*.

Like many Central Asian peoples, the Kyrgyz are skilled and enthusiastic equestrians. Young children learn to ride almost at the same time as they learn to walk. The Kyrgyz play many sports and games on horseback and show off their skills at shows and festivals.

An independent Kyrgyzstan strives to retain and rebuild Kyrgyz culture and language without making the country's non-Kyrgyz residents uncomfortable. After establishing Kyrgyz as the national language in 1993, the Kyrgyz added back Russian as an official language in 2001, partly to reassure Russian speakers. Despite the predominance of Islam, the Kyrgyz also have not attempted to establish a state religion.

PASHTUN

Alternate name: Pakhtun, Pathan
Population: 27 million
Location: Pakistan, Afghanistan
Language family: Iranian

In southeastern Afghanistan and adjacent regions of Pakistan live the Pathan or, as they call themselves, the Pashtun, also spelled Pakhtun. The Persian name "Afghan" referred specifically to this group long before the word became a geographic designation. In multiethnic Afghanistan, where over 45 languages are spoken, these people form the largest ethnic group, and Pakistan is home to even more Pashtun people.

Pashtu, an eastern Iranian tongue incorporating numerous loanwords from Persian and Arabic, forms one of Afghanistan's two national languages. Written in a type of Arabic alphabet since the early 1500s, this language has inspired many poets and writers, including Ahmad Shah Durrani, 18th-century founder of the Afghan nation.

Pashtun lands have witnessed tides of invasion by Persians, Alexander the Great, Turks, Moguls, British, and, most recently, Russians, who invaded Afghanistan in 1979. Undaunted and self-assured, the people have always resisted external control and have gained fame as fierce fighters.

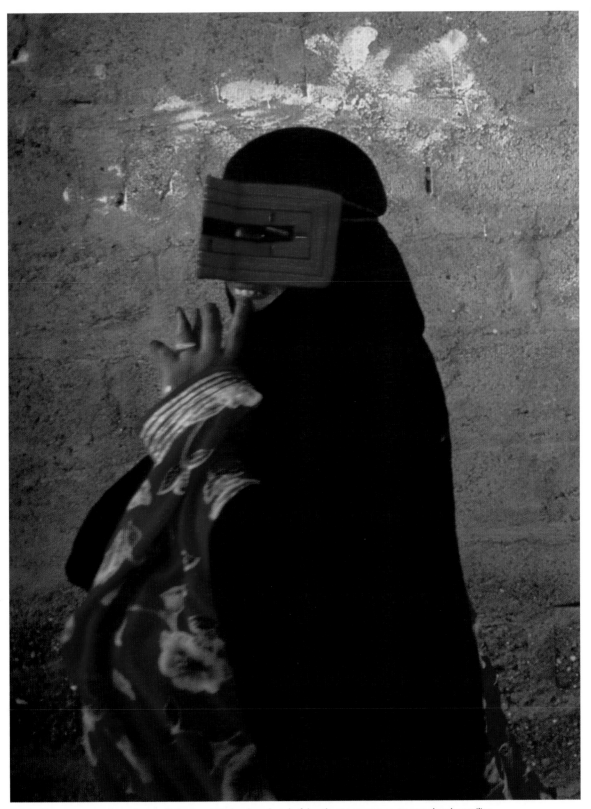

A Baluchi woman wears her culture's distinctive slitted red mask, colorful and yet anonymous, to complete her veiling.

The Pashtun make up some 60 tribes, all with separate territories, and together they form the largest tribal society in the world. Central to their lives as farmers, herders, traders, and warriors is the *pakhtunwalimale*, the Pashtun code of conduct embodying core values of pride, honor, and hospitality. The code's strict rules concern tribal property, succession, the right to speak in gatherings, and even slights.

Among the Pashtun, most of the men carry guns, and blood feuds frequently erupt over land, water, injury, and women. A severe beating or death could be the price a stranger pays for talking to a Pashtun woman. While this behavior seems severe to outsiders, such strict adherence to rules has kept Pashtun society independent and intact.

Tribal ways do erode, though, as electricity, roads, schools, and government officials steadily encroach. Above all, legitimate commerce, paralleling the age-old occupation of smuggling, is opening the Pashtun to a larger world.

TURKMEN

Population: 6 million
Location: Turkmenistan, Iran
Language family: Turkic

To be Turkmen is to claim lineage through a male Turkmen, to be a Sunni Muslim, and to speak the Turkmen language, related to modern Turkish and Azeri. In the past, Turkmen were famous as horsemen and warriors from the steppes of Central Asia. As nomads, they herded on lands that supported little besides those herd animals, and they occasionally raided settled areas. Their transient lifestyle enabled them to avoid taxes and control by larger governing powers. Today, more than four million Turkmen live in northeastern Iran, Turkmenistan, Afghanistan, Turkey, Syria, and Iraq.

Though tribal ties are very strong, fewer Turkmen are nomadic now; most are either sedentary farmers who grow wheat, barley, and cotton or seminomads who divide their economic labors between raising crops

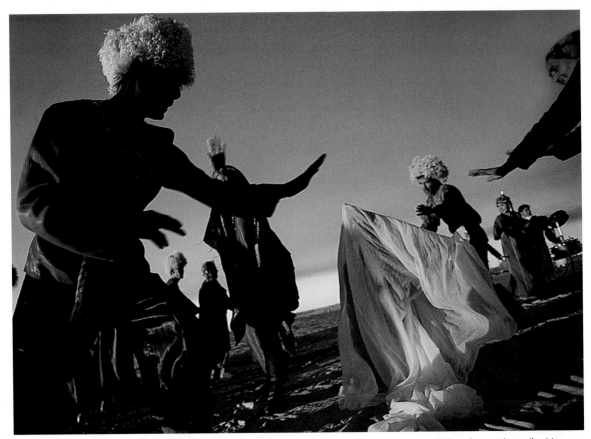

Turkmen folkdancers practice a traditional dance with dynamic jumps and gestures that were long ago believed to combat evil spirits. Among Turkmen, herders by custom hold higher status than farmers—a valuation that seems to contradict modern definitions of progress.

Pashtun shopkeepers wait out a lull in business in their shop in Pakistan. Fierce independence and strong tribal loyalty keep the Pashtun culture intact despite political upheavals.

and herding sheep, cows, goats, horses, and camels. The importance of nomadism and animal husbandry is seen in the higher status held by a *chorva* (herder) compared with the lower status of a *chomur* (farmer). It is widely held among Turkmen that a farmer is someone who does not have the wealth to remain a herder and is therefore no longer independent of larger political powers.

Using wool gathered from their own sheep—and occasionally adding silk to the weave—Turkmen women create carpets that are internationally prized for their quality, design, and colors. Their designs are geometric and make repeated use of polygonal shapes called *guls*. Each tribe has a distinctive gul that communicates the tribal affiliation of the weaver, and this design is passed from one generation to the next within the tribe. Weaving styles produce knotted carpets with a thick pile, and colors range from saturated rusty hues to deep shades of red, black, and tan. Turkmen use their many woven goods for everyday living, as can be seen in their tents, ground coverings, and saddlebags.

UZBEKS

Population: 20.2 million
Location: Uzbekistan
Language family: Turkic

The Uzbeks occupy a Central Asian land famous through the centuries for its wealth, learning centers, and culture. Two thousand years ago, the Uzbeks'

successful merchant ancestors traded along the Silk Road with Russia, China, India, and Afghanistan, creating a brilliant commercial hub whose riches inevitably attracted invaders.

Arab conquerors in the seventh century brought Islam and helped usher in a golden age, with Bukhara becoming one of the world's greatest cities. From the ninth century A.D. onward, Turks came from the northern grasslands.

Mongols arrived in the 13th century, but Turkic language and culture predominated because Genghis Khan's armies were in fact mostly Turkic soldiers, many of whom settled here and married local women. One Mongol chieftain, Öz Beg, left the legacy of his name, which survives as "Uzbek."

In the 1380s, the Turkic conqueror Timur (sometimes anglicized as Tamerlane) captured much of Asia and brought more scientists, artists, and architects to the region; he also established Turkish as a written language. But after 1501, as Tamerlane's empire was crumbling, a tribe from north of the Aral Sea invaded and became the core of people we now call Uzbeks.

In the 1900s, artificial ethnic and regional boundaries imposed by the Soviets dramatically altered Uzbek life: Until the Soviet Republic of Uzbekistan was set up in the 1920s, the people had seen themselves as members of tribes and clans, not as part of a nation. The Uzbek language, too, has only a short history as a distinct tongue. Before the 1920s, it was not considered a separate state language; instead, it was one of many Turkic dialects. All of the trappings of nationhood were achieved in 1991, when the Soviet empire ended and Uzbekistan became an independent country.

Uzbekistan's population of 25 million, the largest in Central Asia, is more than 80 percent Uzbek. Sizable Uzbek populations also reside in Afghanistan, China, and Kazakhstan.

While its geographic position and ethnic clout lend Uzbekistan some claim to being Central Asia's leader, the country is beset with economic and environmental ills. Reckless expansion of cotton-growing areas and overuse of water have led to the shrinking of the Aral Sea, which now has just one-third its volume of 40 years ago. Fierce storms throw tons of salt and sand into the air, causing severe health problems. Many people worry about the future of the Uzbeks, who once lived so gloriously on the land.

East Asia

China, a country of more than 3.5 million square miles and the most populous nation of the world, forms the heartland of East Asia. It stretches from the 12,000-foot-high Tibetan plateau through highlands and plains of the east and northeast, to the 4,000-mile coastline along the Yellow, East China, and South China Seas. Within China's borders can be found the Tibetan plateau, 12,000 feet above sea level; the Gobi Desert, 500,000 square miles; and two great rivers, the Yangtze, flowing into the East China Sea, and the Yellow, flowing into the Yellow Sea. East Asia also contains the mighty Himalayan region, including Mount Everest, at 29,035 feet above sea level the world's highest mountain; the rich and fertile Korean peninsula; and the densely populated, economically significant islands of Taiwan and Japan.

To listen to music from China and Mongolia, visit http://worldmusic.nationalgeographic.com.

AINU

Population: 25,000
Location: Japan
Language family: Language isolate

Among Asia's most enigmatic ethnic groups, the Ainu live on Japan's Hokkaido Island and on Russia's Sakhalin and Kuril Islands. For countless generations, these people led outwardly simple lives that relied on fishing, hunting, and primitive agriculture. They were once known as the "hairy Ainu," because men grew large beards and women adorned themselves with mustachelike tattoos around their mouths. Traditionally, they dressed in animal skins and beautiful robes of elm bark and feathers. Where the people came from remains a mystery.

Of the Ainu who survive today, few are considered true, or pure, Ainu. Into the 18th century, most lived on Honshu, Japan's main island, but they were so different from the rest of the population that the Japanese majority marked them for destruction. Official policy and population pressures eventually drove the Ainu people northward. Now, however, the Japanese hold their culture to be worth protecting, perhaps because of the Ainu's almost total assimilation through intermarriage and domination, especially during the past half-century.

For the Ainu, the focus of spiritual life has long been the bear-spirit ceremony, or *iyomante,* a ritual involving a sacred space and objects such as prayer sticks, carved staves, and elaborate shaved-wood animals. During the ceremony, a specially raised bear is killed, to allow its soul to return to the spirit world. This offering affirms Ainu devotion to, and respect for, nature's hidden forces. The skin and meat of the bear are treated as gifts from the gods.

Traditionally, daily life centered on the village and its immediate territory, or *iwor,* which determined the limits of the Ainu world; within it, the people were largely self-sufficient, relying on salmon, deer, and the cultivation of millet. They excelled in the construction of bows, arrows, spears, traps, and harpoons, and they retained a deep knowledge of the forests and waters of their

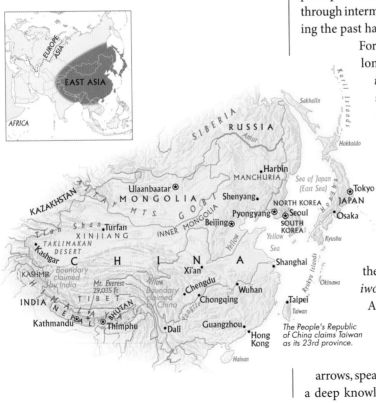

The People's Republic of China claims Taiwan as its 23rd province.

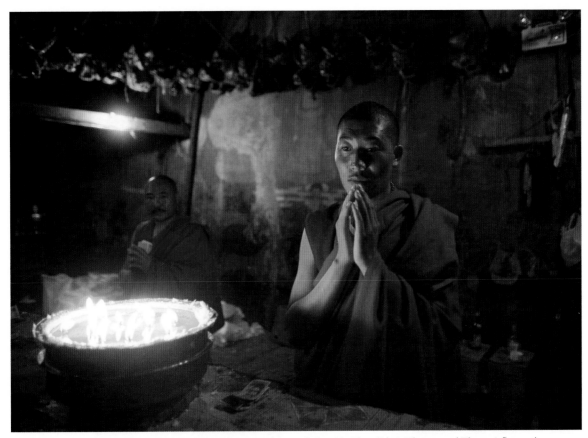

A young monk prays at Gyantse Monastery, located between Lhasa and Xigazê in Tibet. Ethnic Tibetans and Tibetan-influenced cultures inhabit an area far beyond that encompassed by China's Xizang (Tibet) Autonomous Region.

homeland. Now many Ainu work in the Japanese construction industry, and their plight clearly exemplifies the precarious survival of an ethnic group within a dominant majority.

BAI

Population: 2 million Location: People's Republic of China
Language family: Tibeto-Burman [Bai]

The 1.75 million Bai of Yunnan Province are among China's most assimilated, prosperous, and successful minorities. For centuries they have maintained close ties with the majority Han Chinese, and because they lacked a written language of their own, they have always relied on Chinese characters. While their name means "white" and they call themselves "Speakers of the White Tongue," the Bai's actual origin and language affiliation are not known for certain.

Dali, the Bai capital, is known to have once stood at the center of a kingdom that endured for nearly 500 years, separate from dynastic China until the mid-13th century. This well-documented independent history is the reason for the people's status as a recognized ethnic group.

The geography of their homeland has greatly affected the Bai, who dwell along the shores of sparkling Er Hai, beneath a range of snowcapped granite peaks. A 35-mile-long lakeside plain seems specially designed for a protected and bountiful life: Rich, productive rice fields and dazzling yellow rapeseed flowers contrast with the blue lake and red hills of the far shore, planted with peach and pear orchards. Towns and villages of weathered gray stone look across the entire plain, once covered with hundreds of pagodas standing as beacons to the Buddhist faithful. A trio of thousand-year-old pagodas still stands today as the emblem of the Bai.

In the past, horses were very important in this remote, mountainous region, and the Bai became known for the strong, small ponies that they supplied to members of various dynasties. Only with the coming of the Burma Road in the 1930s did the style of

Bai life and transport truly change, and today's airports, highways, and trains have brought the Bai people into the mainstream of modern Chinese life.

Still, the old love of horses lives on in an annual fair hosted by the Bai. The event has grown enormously, with mountain dwellers and minorities from many parts of China coming not only to trade animals and traditional medicines but also to race horses, eat and drink, and enjoy the mountain scenery.

DONG

Population: 3 million
Location: People's Republic of China
Language family: Kam-Sui

Dotting the border regions of South China's Guangxi, Hunan, and Guizhou Provinces are the fascinating villages of the Dong, an official minority of the People's Republic of China. Considered the northeasternmost extension of the greater Thai peoples, the Dong speak a language that, requiring more than 15 distinct tones, is one of the world's most difficult to learn.

In this culture, new parents commonly plant a grove of pines called "18-year trees," which will later supply their son or daughter with timber for a home. This concern for building needs extends beyond individual houses—generally two stories tall, with firewood and farm animals downstairs, belongings and sleeping quarters upstairs—to communal projects and public architecture. All major settlements proudly raise one or more drum towers, elaborate constructions up to 13 stories high, with tight, overlapping pagodalike roofs. People paint the eaves with scenes from myths, legends, and daily life: Cooking, farming, weaving, hunting, and the playing of musical instruments. Statues of beasts and birds decorate the roofs. From afar these towers resemble stylized fir trees, sacred to the Dong.

In ancient times, a huge drum suspended inside each tower helped warn of danger; now its beating calls people together for meetings, celebrations, and festivals, during which songs of praise may be sung for the towers. Dong architecture also includes "wind and rain bridges" of elegant proportions, each bridge having up to five separate pagoda structures. Originally built for shelter, these covered bridges and their special roofing now add beautiful touches to the landscape. Locals have discovered yet another use for them: Leafy vegetables are hung from the railings to dry.

A Hmong shaman attempts a cure by rubbing a machete along a woman's back. Hmong live in the mountains of Laos, Vietnam, Thailand, and southern China.

This attention to creative design can also be seen in Dong embroidery. On hot days, women may be found sitting in the shade of wind-and-rain bridges, dabbling their feet in cool streams while painstakingly adding bright stitches to bags, collars, aprons, or baby carriers.

HAN

Alternate name: Chinese Population: 1,214 million
Location: People's Republic of China
Language family: Sinitic

One in every six individuals on this planet is Han, a member of China's largest ethnic group. Today, about 1.2 billion Han share a country about the size of the United States with more than 100 million people representing 55 other ethnic groups, most of whom live at China's fringes. Han also form the majority of the population of Taiwan.

The Han descend from the people who were settled in the middle and lower basin of the Yellow River 4,000 years ago. The name "Han" came into being as a dynasty in 206 B.C., as those people took an already somewhat unified northern China and solidified it, ruling what they called the Middle Kingdom. Then the Han people moved south, spurred by warfare and famine, spreading into the area below the Yangtze River in at least three great migrations and many smaller ones.

Most Han speak a northern dialect of Chinese. Commonly known as Mandarin, it has become the *Putonghua,* or standard language of China.

Chinese writing is based on a system of some 60,000 characters known as pictographs and ideographs. Unlike hieroglyphics, Chinese characters no longer present any visual clue to their meaning. The mastery of written Chinese requires a degree of education that has not been accessible to everyone. In the 20th century, attempts were made to simplify a script, applicable to all dialects, to make it more widely available.

Since mountains, high plateaus, and deserts make up much of China's west, about 95 percent of the population crowds into the eastern third of the country. Millions live in the cities there, including more than 15 million in Beijing, the capital, but most Han still live in the countryside. Farmers in the west and north grow wheat, while rice is the staple grain in most of the country. A surplus of several hundred million agricultural workers is one of the causes of *liudong renkou,* or floating populations, that by law are not allowed to settle permanently in other locations. Some 24 percent of the Chinese work in industry; low wages, an industrious workforce, and the possibility of the cheapest unit cost of manufactured goods contribute to China's industrial explosion.

Despite China's official communist atheism, many Han still observe traditional religious traditions. The three main traditions—Daoism, Confucianism, and Buddhism—each offer a separate approach. Daoism, founded by Lao-tzu in the sixth century B.C., looks to the balance and order in nature. The teachings of Confucius of the same period extol proper workings of society through hierarchical relationships. Buddhism, a religious import, aims for enlightenment and the dissolution of earthly bonds. Many Han observe elements of all three, as well as honoring various gods and goddesses and taking measures to increase good luck.

The most important Han holiday is the lunar new year, or Spring Holiday, which usually occurs in January or February. People travel to be with family at this time, eat festive meals, and watch fireworks and parades featuring dragon- and lion-costumed dancers.

Rural Han families traditionally consist of several generations living under one roof. In the patrilineal and patriarchal Han society, women move in at marriage with their husband's family. Urban families often are nuclear and tend to enjoy a higher income and more amenities and luxuries than their rural counterparts. A growing, mostly urban, middle class widens the gap between rich and poor.

Worried about China's burgeoning population, the government enacted a one-child policy several decades ago that mostly affects Han Chinese; China's minorities, on the other hand, are exempt from this rule. The prevalence of only children among the Han has contributed to a very child-centric culture and—as boys are favored because they carry on the family line—to discrimination against girls. Some couples use ultrasound to determine fetal sex and will abort female fetuses, although this practice is condemned by the government. Others do not register female births, which causes problems for those girls in later life.

Modern multitasking crosses cultures: A young Chinese man lights sticks of incense at a Shanghai temple while keeping in touch with the secular world.

JAPANESE

Population: 125.5 million
Location: Japan Language family: Language isolate

Japan occupies four major and thousands of smaller islands spread out in a 2,000-mile-long arc in the Western Pacific. More than 125 million Japanese crowd a country the size of California. Steep mountains run through the center of the islands, leaving flat terrain only along the coasts and river valleys. More than 50 percent of the Japanese live along one 265-mile stretch from Kobe to Tokyo on southern Honshu.

Japan is one of the world's most ethnically homogeneous nations: Some 99 percent of the population is

Japanese, a group with origins mostly on the Asian mainland. The remaining minority population includes people of Korean, Chinese, and Okinawan ancestry, as well as the Ainu, an indigenous people now confined to northern Hokkaido. All speak Japanese, a language with many regional dialects and a written form derived from Chinese.

About four-fifths of all Japanese live in large conurbations, packed into tiny apartments, although many have more rural roots to which they return for family

> ## Where there is no fire, there is no smoke.
> KOREAN PROVERB

celebrations during the year. With only 15 percent of the terrain suitable for agriculture, Japanese farmers have painstakingly constructed terraced fields on sides of mountains where they grow rice, the Japanese staple, along with vegetables and fruit. Japan's large fishing fleet ranges far and wide to provide the major protein component of the Japanese diet.

Most Japanese today follow the religious traditions of Shinto, Japan's ancient animist religion, which emphasizes connections with nature, and Buddhism, imported from China. Many families blend observances: They may marry at a Shinto shrine but hold funerals at a Buddhist temple. Christianity has taken a small but significant hold in Japan, and while celebrating the Christmas season has gained popularity, it is almost entirely a secular observance.

For several centuries, until the end of the shogunate in the mid-19th century, Japan was isolated from the rest of the world—by choice. Since then, and especially since World War II, Japan has embraced Western ideas and technology and built the world's second largest economy, nearly cornering the international market in cars and consumer electronics.

From obtaining a high-paying job to marrying well, success and status in Japan revolve around the credentials a person acquires, especially those achieved through education. Japanese education is high-pressure from the earliest years on. Mothers closely oversee their

children's academic efforts—the most hands-on are known as "education mamas"—including long hours of homework, as well as additional time in *juku,* or cram schools, to improve their chances of doing well on the very competitive entrance exams to upper-level secondary schools and universities. Many firms recruit only from the most highly regarded institutions, such as Tokyo University.

On landing that first job, the Japanese worker is folded into the company ethos in a strong, familial relationship that goes way beyond the nine-to-five realm. Male employees known as "salary men" often are expected to socialize for hours over drinks after work before returning home. As a result, Japanese fathers have little time to share with their children. Women increasingly work outside the home. They hold fewer responsible positions and earn significantly less than men, however, and many will quit their jobs to raise children. Japanese men tend to spend their whole working lives with one company. The Japanese business values of loyalty, conformity, and the collective good over individual expression permeate the culture.

The Japanese live in a state of perpetual preparedness for earthquakes. Some 20 percent of all the world's earthquakes, with up to 10,000 tremors per year, occur in Japan, the result of riding the boundaries of at least three tectonic plates. Elaborate public safety plans have been devised to minimize effects of future earthquakes.

While heavily influenced by Western trends, especially those from the United States, the Japanese have made a number of contributions to worldwide popular culture, including *manga* (comic books or graphic novels) and animé (graphic animation). With a rapidly aging population and a falling birthrate, Japan may have to look outside for workers to fulfill its employment needs and hence accept the reality of more ethnic diversity in its future.

KOREANS

Population: 72 million
Location: Republic of Korea,
Democratic People's Republic of Korea
Language family: Language isolate

The robust Koreans occupy East Asia's strategic Korean Peninsula. Mountainous North Korea has more than half the land of the peninsula and yet less than half the population of neighboring South Korea. The

The sight of Japan's imperial family brings tears to the eyes of an elderly man during a New Year's public appearance in Tokyo. Although imperial divine status was renounced after World War II, many older Japanese still revere the emperor and his family.

1945 division of the peninsula along a 150-mile border led eventually to the Korean War, which raged from 1950 to 1953. Tensions remain high today.

Despite their separation, Koreans historically have had a feeling of shared identity, reinforced by geography: Water borders them on three sides; mountains are to the north. Their location between China, in the north and west, and Japan, in the east, has played a major role in shaping their national character. Early colonization by China encouraged Korea to form institutions based on Chinese models of administration, writing, and the arts, yet the Koreans never relinquished their own identity. They excelled in arts, crafts, and construction, and they have contributed significantly to the aesthetics of East Asian painting, calligraphy, sculpture, and pottery, with an artistic spirit that is natural and spontaneous. Many collectors prize the pale green porcelains known as celadon, created during the 10th- to 14th-century Koryo dynasty.

The present language evolved from the time of Korean unification in the 7th century and, like Japanese, has hierarchies of usage and a sensitivity to social position. Koreans used Chinese characters for writing into the 15th century, when they invented a script called *hangul;* its 40 symbols are extremely accurate in representing spoken sounds. This break with Chinese tradition allowed Koreans to develop their own popular literary forms to deal with life, love, humor, and even social criticism; at this time, the people began to record colorful folktales possessing funny, ribald qualities. Today Koreans enjoy one of the highest literacy rates in Asia, and South Koreans have one of the world's highest rates of university attendance.

Korean religion, diverse and complex, has roots in the old traditions of Confucianism and Buddhism, later overlaid with Christianity. The indigenous Ch'ondogyo faith, with elements of Confucianism, Buddhism, Daoism, shamanism, and Catholicism, has been joined in recent times by hundreds of new charismatic sects, such as the Unification Church of Sun Myung Moon and his millions of followers.

Diet is a point of pride for Koreans, who enjoy grilled meats and vegetable dishes such as kimchi, a fiery pickled cabbage that accompanies every meal.

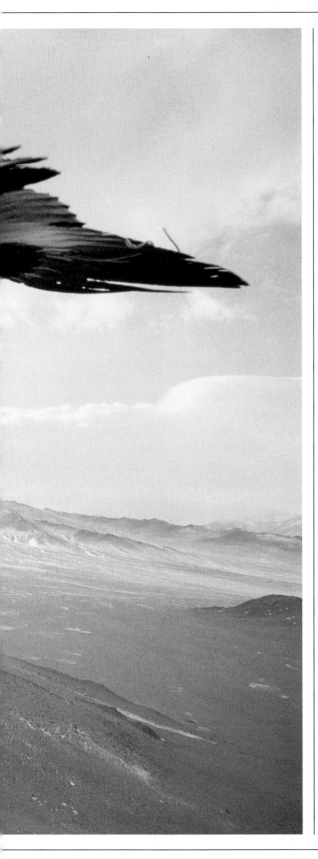

Kazakhs, long skilled in hunting with golden eagles, occupy barren lands in western Mongolia. Fierce eagles with seven-foot wingspans can swoop at one hundred miles an hour to capture fur-bearing prey, a source of income for their masters.

MONGOLS

Alternate name: Khalkhs Population: 9 million
Location: People's Republic of China, Mongolia
Language family: Mongolic

The Mongols burst onto the world scene in the 13th and 14th centuries and left a short but audacious legacy that is remembered to this day. After Genghis Khan unified diverse clans in the heart of Asia's steppe-lands, swift mounted warriors known as the Mongols went on to conquer much of Eurasia. But their empire—from the Pacific to the borders of Egypt and Western Europe—lasted only 175 years. The stereotype of cruel hordes has survived much longer, however, even though peaceful herding has been the Mongol norm ever since that time.

On the vast grasslands where they lived, Mongols found success as nomadic pastoralists, horsemen, and herders. They made their homes in circular tents (yurts, or *gers* in Mongolian) of felt and canvas, supported by wooden frames. Women and children took an active part in the pastoral life, caring for animals and collecting dung to burn for fuel.

A toughness born from their exposed, windswept life prepared the Mongols well for survival, which required the skillful handling of small horses while tending sheep, goats, cattle, camels, and yaks. Today such animals continue to support a diet made up of dairy products and meat; milk, cheese, and yogurt appear in a hundred different forms, and there is even a distilled "milk vodka" for festivities. All parts of the animals are used, with large chunks of fat considered a delicacy.

Mongol culture has been strongly influenced over the years by Buddhism, introduced from Tibet, combined with indigenous shamanism. The nomads learned to use portable altars and devotional scroll paintings that could be rolled up and easily transported. In the 16th century, the bond between Tibet and Mongolia became so strong that a Mongol khan bestowed the title of Dalai Lama, meaning "ocean of wisdom," on the Tibetan leader.

Today Mongols have their own country, in north-central Asia. Known as the Republic of Mongolia, it encompasses a high, rolling plateau nearly three times the size of France and embraces a population of 2.6 million. Even more Mongols live across the southern border, in China's Inner Mongolia and other Chinese provinces; additional clusters survive in Kazakhstan, Siberia, and the Kalmyk region of Russia's lower Volga River.

Mongolia achieved its status as a republic and as the world's second communist country, after Russia, in 1924. Antireligious revolutionaries murdered many thousands of monks and forced changes in lifestyle, limiting nomadism and setting up collectives. Most Mongols now reside in towns and settlements, though many prefer to live in gers, even in the suburbs of Ulaanbaatar, the capital.

The popular revival of wrestling, archery, folk dancing, and horse racing reveals the Mongols' deeply rooted desire to maintain their age-old traditions.

TIBETANS

Population: 5.5 million
Location: People's Republic of China
Language family: Tibeto-Burman [Tibetic]

With their numbers estimated at between five and six million, the Tibetan people inhabit an immense plateau, a high-elevation desert bordered by barren cold expanses and the world's highest mountains, the Himalaya.

Cultural Tibet is far larger than the territory within China called the Tibet Autonomous Region. This "Greater Tibet" includes Bhutan, Sikkim, northern Nepal, and sections of Kashmir in northern India. Significant parts of China's Gansu, Qinghai, Sichuan, and Yunnan Provinces are ethnically Tibetan as well.

Groups indelibly influenced by Tibetan culture are the Sherpas of Nepal, the Drukpas of Bhutan, and the Ladakhis of northern India; dozens of smaller groups speaking diverse dialects contribute to the complex Tibetan world. Within China, Mandarin Chinese has become a lingua franca for many Tibetans who otherwise could not converse with one another.

Harsh physical barriers, along with official isolation, allowed Tibetans to maintain a nearly medieval way of life into the mid-20th century. Their culture developed in the relatively well-watered southern part of the plateau, where raising barley proved possible, while in the great north, nomads living in black tents tended livestock, primarily the ubiquitous yak.

A Uygur man eyes a motorcycle in Kashgar, once a fabled stop on the Silk Road in far western China. A highway to Pakistan and a train link with eastern China have brought modern transportation, while supermarkets have begun replacing ancient bazaars.

In the seventh century, the Buddhist religion was introduced into Tibet from China. Early word of the religion was soon followed by the arrival of Buddhist missionaries from India. Spiritual and secular institutions blended together, touching all aspects of life. The land eventually supported 6,000 monasteries, which required most families to have at least one son as a monk. Although Tibetan Buddhism has several branches, the Gelukpa sect has been dominant since the 17th century, when the fifth Dalai Lama reached the apex of Tibet's theocracy.

Buddhism fostered a sophisticated civilization of advanced learning and philosophy that survives to this day, albeit in limited form. Tibet's de facto independence from 1912 to 1950 ended when China occupied the country and, in 1959, forced the exile of the Dalai Lama and 80,000 of his followers to India. Suppression of religion and destruction of monasteries followed, and a steady influx of Chinese immigrants has diluted the indigenous population.

UYGURS

Alternate name: Uighurs   Population: 8.4 million
Location: People's Republic of China
Language family: Turkic

The Uygur people of western China's Xinjiang region inhabit desert and mountain expanses that were once known as eastern Turkestan. More Uygurs live in Pakistan, Afghanistan, Saudi Arabia, Turkey, Europe, and North America.

The Uygurs' origins date from the third and fourth centuries, when Turkic tribes roamed as nomads in search of pastures and oases. In time, the people created empires extending east to the Yellow River, north to Siberia, and south to Pakistan. Positioned at the Silk Road's midpoint, Uygurs slowly abandoned their nomadic lifestyle, took up farming and trade, and enhanced their culture with religious and intellectual exchange. They became scholars, administrators, inventors of a versatile script, and creators of magnificent cave art. Their contributions to architecture, music, printing, and medicine have enriched the whole region.

Uygur life, long tied to oases, was centered in two cities: Buddhist Turfan in the northeast and Muslim Kashgar in the southwest. Both lie in today's Xinjiang region of China. The Muslims conquered their brethren to the northeast at the end of the 14th century and were able to remain independent from China until 1759, when the Qing dynasty took over. The Chinese government has determined the larger fate of the Uygurs ever since.

Although Uygurs have ostensible autonomy in their homeland, ethnic unrest is prevalent. For decades, large numbers of Han Chinese have been migrating to Xinjiang to relieve population pressures and develop the region. For the Uygurs, this has meant curtailment of their religion and dilution of their communities.

Today, the markets of Xinjiang are a mix of Arab souk, Chinese bazaar, and Central Asian trading station, filled with animals, tack shops, pungent spices, furs, carpets, brilliantly hued silk dresses, and vendors selling kebabs and huge flatbreads. Beyond the markets, farmers still irrigate their fields with an ingenious system of underground channels that bring water from the distant Tian Shan mountains.

Rising miragelike against a backdrop of high mountains, the Potala Palace in Lhasa, Tibet, offers a breathtaking vision. A rail line from Beijing to Lhasa, completed in 2006, can now bring in up to 6,000 tourists a day.

Southeast Asia

Southeast Asia includes the mainland nations of Myanmar, Thailand, Cambodia, Laos, and Vietnam, as well as the island nations of the Philippines, Malaysia, and Indonesia. East Timor, once part of Indonesia, gained independence in 2002. Other islands and cities maintain distinct cultural and political identities, such as Bali, an Indonesian island with a defining Hindu presence; Hong Kong, now part of China but still steeped in its tradition as a British-owned port of trade; and Singapore, an independent city-state and a world-class center of trade and industry.

To listen to music from Cambodia, Indonesia, and Thailand, visit http://worldmusic.nationalgeographic.com.

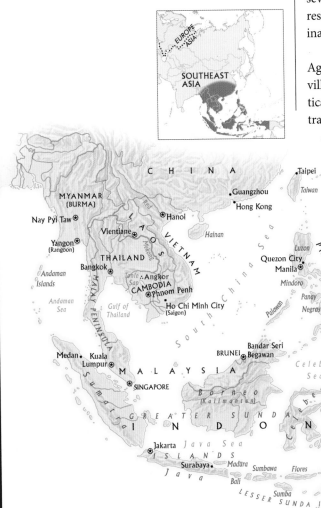

BALINESE

Population: 3 million   **Location:** Indonesia
Language family: Malayo-Polynesian [Bali-Sasak]

The tiny, volcanic island of Bali, east of Java, has long enthralled visitors and residents alike. For the three million Balinese, this tropical island is an entire world, with physical and spiritual attributes important for existence. The Balinese believe that because their cosmos is so rich, the psychic, unseen forces constantly spill over into the mundane. Daily life becomes a vibrant expression of propitiation and praise for gods and nymphs, demons and witches. Hardly a day goes by without a procession or a temple festival. At night, villages come alive with the music of gamelan percussion orchestras.

In the otherwise Muslim expanse of Indonesia, Bali has remained a Hindu holdout. Hinduism arrived with Indian traders and found such a firm foothold in the seventh and eighth centuries that Bali was later able to resist all attempts at conversion, even after Islam dominated Java and other islands in the sixteenth century.

Beneath a holy volcano known as the Gunung Agung, "navel of the world," spread the rice fields and villages forming the heart of Balinese life. Here, sophisticated artists continually create, remake, and teach their traditions. Myths, rituals, painting, carving, acting, and dancing all seem to come together, where more than 5,000 dance troupes testify to the importance of creative and religious expression.

Bali's most powerful drama revolves around the clash between two mythical creatures, Barong and Rangda. The lion-beast Barong—representing sunshine, medicine, life, and light—provides the antidote for evil. He likes to dance for sheer joy, but his playfulness is interrupted by the appearance of Rangda, hideous witch and queen of death. In a climactic struggle, trance dancers rush to Barong's aid, only to have their own

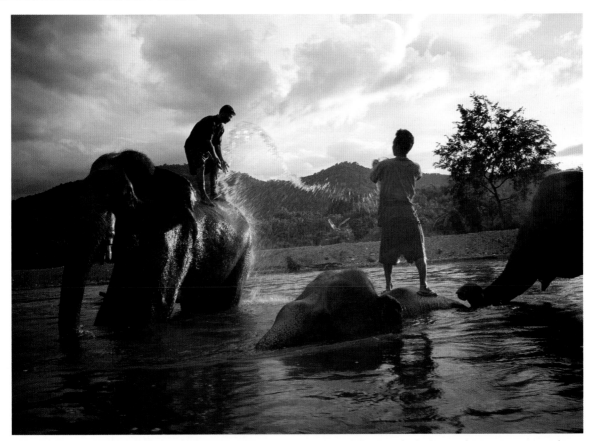

Thai mahouts bathe their elephant charges in a river at twilight. The Asian elephant, far more docile than its African counterpart, performs tasks in a number of enterprises, including logging.

daggers turned against them by Rangda's evil magic. But Barong's power prevents the daggers from piercing the flesh. Slowly, the dancers are brought out of their trances by Barong's beard, his power center. Neither creature wins this cosmic struggle; goodness gains only a temporary victory.

Since the 1930s, Bali has seen growing numbers of tourists, and now more than a million each year swarm through temples and villages. The threat of cultural breakdown and commercialization of the entire island is always present, yet Bali's dynamic, adaptable people keep a firm view of themselves and their unique culture.

DAYAK

Population: 2.2 million
Location: Indonesia, Malaysia
Language family: Malayo-Polynesian [Land Dayak]

Living along large, meandering rivers flowing through the forests of Borneo, the Dayak are a people whose name covers numerous non-Muslim ethnic groups. Most of the Dayak people live in southern and western Borneo, in both East Malaysia and Indonesian Kalimantan.

Traditionally, Dayak communities were made up of several hundred people who maintained few ties with other groups. Family clusters lived in longhouses and led a largely self-sufficient way of life that took raw materials and animals from the forest and fish from the rivers. Slightly back from the riverbanks, they practiced simple agriculture, growing dry rice for a few seasons in one field, then abandoning the site for another. Ritual warfare, including head-hunting, was also part of their lives.

In recent decades, the Dayak have been confronted with major changes. Beginning in the 1960s, the Indonesian government poured resources and people into Kalimantan in an effort to exploit the forests and relieve overcrowding elsewhere. A program called *trans-migrasi* relocated ethnic groups from other parts of the densely populated nation, especially the Madurese from Madura and East Java. The harvest of hardwood timber from

Dayak regions has paralleled the growth of farms, plantations, and towns. Placed near native Dayak animists, Muslim immigrants caused economic disparity and distrust, fueling tensions. The Dayak feared newcomers would take tribal lands and jobs.

Fighting has broken out periodically, but it became fierce in 2001. Hundreds were killed, and, during the frenzied bloodletting, head-hunting reappeared. Many Madurese left Borneo or fled to refugee camps; counterattacks in towns caused more deaths. Historic neglect and insensitivity to Dayak needs had set the stage for the misunderstandings and conflicts that have since exploded into full-scale ethnic trauma.

HMONG

Alternate name: Miao, Meo **Population:** 10 million
Location: People's Republic of China, Vietnam, Laos
Language family: Hmong-Mien

The mountains of southern China and northern Laos and Vietnam are home to the Hmong, a tribal people known for independence and self-sufficiency. In China, the Hmong are called Miao or Meo—names that mean "barbarian" and that they consider pejorative.

The Hmong language, both tonal and monosyllabic, had no written version until Christian missionaries devised a Roman-based alphabet for it. Consequently, the Hmong have a well-developed oral tradition that includes sung poetry, proverbs, and aphorisms, and combines embroidered figural cloths with storytelling.

The Hmong practice swidden agriculture. After clear-cutting an area, they burn off the rest of the vegetation before planting crops. The fields remain fertile for a few years; when they are spent, the Hmong move on. Hmong grow dry rice, corn, and vegetables. They eat their grains steamed or boiled and heavily seasoned with hot peppers. They also cultivate opium poppies for their own use and as a cash crop. They were urged to grow the poppies during the French colonial period, but current national governments discourage the practice.

Organized around patrilineal clans, the Hmong have no formal organization above that level. Their mountaintop villages consist of small, simple houses

Masked dancers take a break during a performance of the Ramayana at a Balinese temple. The Indian epic represents only one aspect of the pervasive Hinduism that did not succumb to Muslim influence, unlike elsewhere in Indonesia.

that contain few furnishings. Extended patrilineal families tend to live together, with sons bringing in their wives that they have married outside of their clan. Traditionally, Hmong marry young, in their teens. Couples may court during singing events. They form groups and sing to each other, sometimes passing a ball back and forth, hoping to kindle romantic interest.

The Hmong believe that spirits inhabit objects in nature and in the material world. Humans have multiple souls, and some Hmong rituals are attempts to call spirits back into the body. When a nonresponsive illness occurs, shamans may be called in to discern the cause from the vantage point of a trance. The spirits of ancestors also must be appeased to ensure the well-being of the living.

Beginning in 1975, many Hmong fled Laos due to the civil war that involved them either as members of the communist Pathet Lao party or as guerrilla operatives for the U.S. Central Intelligence Agency. Over the next decade or so, some 100,000 Hmong made their way as refugees to the United States. They live in large communities, mostly in Fresno and elsewhere in California, in Minnesota, Wisconsin, and Rhode Island. Some work in farming. Quite a few of the unskilled older generation are unemployed, but the young are finding success through education. Many Hmong women make decorative squares of appliquéd embroidery called *paj ntaub,* which they sell at craft fairs.

A Taiwanese bride prepares to serve tea to her new husband's parents, blending Western influences and traditional practices.

IFUGAO

Population: 192,000
Location: Philippines
Language family: Malayo-Polynesian [Northern Philippine]

High in the mountains of Luzon, the largest of the Philippine islands, stands a monument to human ingenuity. Massive stone walls, hand-built by the Ifugao people, carve the steep mountainsides into thousands of terraced fields, while sophisticated hydrological systems supply water. The graceful stone terraces—designated a UNESCO World Heritage Site—are served by a vast network of channels, pools, and aqueducts. Hardly a drop of rain falls that is not captured, controlled, and put to the service of growing rice. Boulders larger than a man and structures as small as a single leaf pinned down with twigs can serve to divert rainwater into a pond field.

The worldview of the Ifugao has traditionally revolved around rice, a crop that they have domesticated intensely, producing dozens of distinct varieties. In a myth now mostly forgotten, ancient Ifugao were first given rice and instructions for planting by unearthly beings they call "skyworld people."

Many Ifugao villagers still reside in thatched houses supported on tall posts, with an open space underneath for cooking and relaxation. After a day's labor, villagers sit under their houses drinking fermented rice beer and gazing out over their fields.

In each hamlet, once a rice field is designated as ritually important, it must be harvested first by the joint efforts of the entire community. On harvest day, the family may invite a shaman to sacrifice a chicken, drain its blood, and read the entrails for signs of an auspicious year, season, and crop. The shaman sits for hours, chanting genealogies to invoke the spirit world of deceased ancestors in support of a successful harvest. On festive occasions men may dress in traditional red loincloths, playing flutes and beating gongs to accompany dancers.

Down in the pond fields, women harvest rice by hand, using small metal blades. Out in front of the harvesters works a lone woman, the seed selector, an expert trained to identify and collect the plumpest and healthiest grains to use as seed for replanting in the coming season.

Occasionally women hum a song as they tread the rice paddies. In the past, epic chants called *hud-hud,* telling of hero-ancestors, were sung by women while harvesting rice. Hud-hud chants, designated a Masterpiece of Oral and Intangible Heritage of Humanity by UNESCO, have fallen into disuse, and are now remembered only in fragments.

The Ifugao language is still spoken vigorously by people of all ages. It includes an intricate vocabulary for rice technology, with 27 different names for pottery vessels for storing rice wine, 30 names for types of woven baskets used to carry foods, and 130 phrases describing payments for the use of rice fields. Ifugao has uniquely expressive verbs like *tiw-tiw,* meaning "to frighten animals, birds or chickens away from drying rice."

Ifugao rice knowledge—including genetics, hydrology, and the cultural belief system that fostered these technologies—is now eroding. As fertilization and genetically engineered rice varieties—promoted by international agrobusiness—gain popularity, Ifugao farmers are coming under increasing pressure to abandon traditional growing methods and strains of rice bred by their ancestors over millennia.

The Ifugao now face the challenge of nurturing their culture as they change and modernize. Many young Ifugao people have migrated to Philippine towns or foreign countries for work and education, and electricity and television have come into the villages. Few young people nowadays aspire to grow rice, and the rich traditional knowledge of the Ifugao is being forgotten as terraces erode from disuse.

JAVANESE

Population: 95 million
Location: Indonesia
Language family: Malayo-Polynesian [Javanese]

An Indonesian island smaller than Florida, Java is home to more than 100 million people, the great majority of whom are ethnic Javanese living in the central and eastern parts of the island. Beneath Java's backbone of volcanoes and crater lakes, people have engaged in agriculture for 4,500 years. Here, rich soil and abundant water have allowed industrious villagers to turn their homeland into a wet-rice miracle, able to support the dense population.

Throughout their history, the Javanese have evolved an ability to adapt and transform outside forces into a profound inheritance. Layers of cultural history, vital and varied, have created a complex and sophisticated people. Invaders, immigrants, traders, and colonists from Polynesia, India, China, Arabia, Portugal, the Netherlands, and Great Britain left their

> Sugar may be sweet,
> but barley meal is more filling.
> TIBETAN PROVERB

imprint on the culture, bringing along many of the world's main religions: Hinduism, Buddhism, Islam, and Christianity.

Indian civilization on Java culminated between A.D. 750 and 900 in a great age of temple building, the legacy of which can still be seen in Hindu and Buddhist monuments sprinkled across the countryside. Borobudur, a massive carved stupa, is Java's most magnificent structure. The refinement of court life during this era also encouraged a language hierarchy that remains to this day. With separate vocabularies reflecting the social positions of its speakers, the Javanese language displays varying levels of speech: coarse, ordinary, modestly respectful, and fully respectful.

In the 15th and 16th centuries, maritime merchants introduced Islam, but the ascendancy of this faith was less a formal conversion than an adaptation of Islam to earlier Hindu-Buddhist institutions. The Javanese also practice animism and ancestor worship, believing in the supernatural and acknowledging a world of spirits and ghosts, magic and malevolence. Their religious epics, mytho-heroic stories, and comedies—presented as plays for *wayang kulit* (shadow puppets), *wayang golek* (wooden puppets), and *wayang wong* (human actors)—find enthusiastic audiences.

In arts and crafts, the kris, a double-edged sword with a wavy blade, has an aura of holiness. Many believe krises can fly or that the original owner's soul lives in the blade. Javanese masters of batik, a wax-and-dye process on silk or cotton cloth, create masterpieces based on themes that are secular and sacred, ancient and mod-

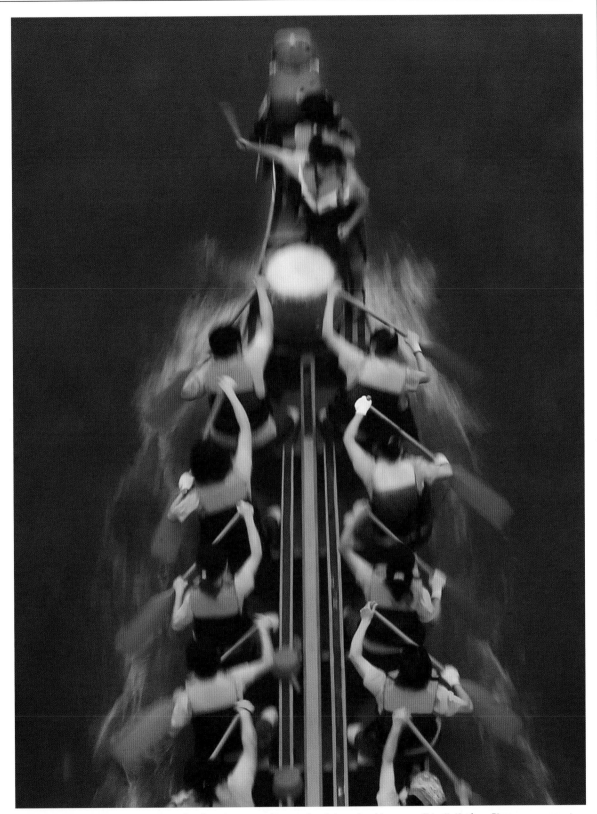

Dragon boat racers row to a coxswain's drumbeat in an annual international championship race on Taipei's Keelung River.

ern. Batik can be a fine art of subtle styles, colors, and symbols, or it may result in practical productions of shirts, sarongs, and bags.

KHMER

Population: 14 million   **Location:** Cambodia
Language family: Mon-Khmer [Khmeric]

Cambodia's Khmer live in a fertile land watered by the Mekong River and Tonlé Sap ("Great Lake"), Southeast Asia's largest lake.

For more than a thousand years, the Khmer have been animated by Buddhism—influenced by earlier Hinduism—as both a personal faith and state religion. Under a line of Buddhist kings who combined just administrations with huge building projects, the people established a civilization of profound creativity and grand accomplishments.

The carved stone complex at Angkor, not merely a temple but a city, represents the flowering of the Khmer culture from the 9th to 13th centuries. This high point focused on a courtly life of ritual and classical dance,

a slow, graceful art form that portrayed Indian epics, romances, and Buddhist themes. Temple dancers served as the earthly counterparts of celestial nymphs. Angkor's stone carvings record this tradition, which not only entertained the gods but also embodied Khmer ideals.

Incredibly, this land of beauty and refinement was transformed into a place of utter darkness between 1975 and 1979. The Khmer Rouge, a communist military and political contingent, embarked on a bloody revolution that killed more than 1.5 million people, brought the Khmer people close to cultural suicide, and almost destroyed all traces of the past. The revolution took the lives of artists, dancers, and musicians and threatened to erase the nearly thousand-year-old classical dance tradition. Every Khmer was changed by the mass death, forced labor, disease, and famine. Many fled, with nearly 150,000 finding refuge in the United States.

When the nightmare came to an end, a handful of survivors revived the classical dance and its slow, rhythmic music. Discipline and training started anew, with

A Vietnamese woman empties her baskets at a salt production area along the eastern coast. People-powered hauling and transport are still common in Vietnam and elsewhere in Southeast Asia.

children as young as eight learning how to dress in opulent, glittering costumes and bring to life the ancient court dance. In their struggle to survive, the Khmer have preserved intact the nation's great arts, the living pieces of cultural memory that provide links to the past and hope for the future.

MINANGKABAU

Population: 6 million **Location:** Indonesia
Language family: Malayo-Polynesian [Malayic]

Vigorous and successful, the Minangkabau people inhabit the western section of Sumatra, sixth largest island in the world. Their region of verdant plateaus, forests, gorges, and escarpments supports many small villages where people farm or engage in handicraft, creating articles of silver and gold filigree and fine embroidered shawls.

The Minangkabau form one of the world's largest matrilineal societies. This means that titles, property, family names, and inheritance go through the female line, even under Islam, which normally favors men. The arrangement provides a degree of social equality uncommon in Asia.

Traditionally, many families live together in a *rumah gadang* (longhouse), and every person stays through life as a member of the mother's original house. When a couple wishes to marry, the prospective bride's family usually makes the proposal, and the new husband, not the

> One parent can look after many children,
> but it takes many children
> to look after one parent.
> THAI PROVERB

wife, changes homes to enter the woman's clan house. In some rural places there is even a groom-price.

When a daughter takes a husband, an annex is added to the longhouse for the growing family. Such extensions, with swooping saddleback roofs, have hornlike adornments that rise toward the sky and symbolize the horns of a water buffalo, sacred animal of the Minangkabau. By counting longhouse extensions, visitors can guess the number of daughters with husbands and children.

Because of the strong family ties and an emphasis on education, the Minangkabau have one of the highest literacy rates in Indonesia. This group shines in the world of Indonesian letters, having produced many well-known writers over the past century.

Overpopulation and a decline in traditional ways have caused many Minangkabau men to emigrate to other parts of the island nation. Most have gone to the capital, Jakarta, and become successful shop owners, teachers, or cooks—who serve up the tasty, spicy dishes for which the Minangkabau people are famous.

THAIS

Population: 49 million **Location:** Thailand
Language family: Taic

In the daily bustle and roar of Bangkok, the capital of Thailand and one of Asia's megacities, all the elements of Thai society have been thrown together. Here coexist the four core groups making up the greater ethnic "nation": Central Thai, Thai-Lao, Northern Thai, and Southern Thai. They all share the faith of Theravada Buddhism, dialects of a common language, and a similar ethnic origin—and they all face the same summer monsoon downpours and the long, dry periods from autumn to spring.

Today's Thais descend from ancestors who came from southwestern China's Yunnan Province. From the 9th to 13th centuries, a large, non-Chinese kingdom proved to be a buffer that allowed Thais to escape Chinese assimilation. Within this kingdom, Thais held high positions and could expand and migrate steadily into Southeast Asia, even into areas that extend far beyond the present-day borders of Thailand. As a result, most Laotians are Thai by descent, as are the Shan, who make up about 10 percent of the population of Myanmar (Burma). Other Tai-speaking people live in southern China and Vietnam.

Most of the early Thais settled in the fertile zone of the Chao Phraya River, which dominates Thailand's central valley. They officially emerged as a people in 1238, when diverse groups were unified under the Sukhothai kingdom and freed from the formerly dominant Khmer. Buddhism helped to bind them, and this in turn inspired a distinct art style reflecting prosperity and self-confidence, as still seen in carved temples and giant Buddha sculptures.

Today, one of the country's most popular activities

is Thai boxing; in fact, it is a national pastime. For all its outward appearance of violence, this sport is layered with refinements and cultural meanings, which aficionados have come to recognize and admire.

Many Thais follow the lunar calendar and look forward to the predictable and joyous yearly festivals. Perhaps the most popular festival is Loy Krathong. Under a November full moon, the country's rivers, streams, lakes, and canals become sites for honoring Mae Khongkha, goddess of rivers and waterways. People of all ages prepare little boats in the shape of lotuses or miniature temples, which are then blessed and decorated with candles, incense, flowers, and coins before being set afloat. All through the night, millions of tiny lights drift and bob on the waters.

VIETNAMESE

Alternate name: Kinh   Population: 74 million
Location: Vietnam
Language family: Mon-Khmer [Viet-Muong]

After four decades of intermittent warfare against varied foes—the Japanese, the French, the Americans, the Cambodians, and the Chinese—and following the successful unification of the country in 1975, after a long civil war, the roughly 74 million Vietnamese

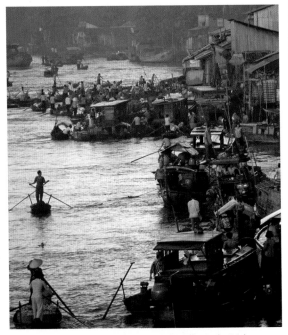

All manner of boats crowd the river at Can Tho in the Mekong Delta of Vietnam. Floating markets lure customers onto the river in this delta trade and transportation hub.

have now settled down to the task of rebuilding their ancient land.

The Vietnamese people originated in the Red River Delta region of the north, but their early roots are very hazy. Sometime between 500 and 200 B.C., they emerged as an ethnic entity from a melting pot that contained seaborne travelers from Oceania and various migrants from Asia, with northern Mongol characteristics predominating.

Once established, the Vietnamese marched slowly and steadily southward, settling plains and deltas along the way and reaching the southern Mekong region by the early 1700s. Today, their thousand-mile-long country extends like a huge, stretched letter S, reaching all the way from the Chinese border to the Gulf of Thailand and taking in an area half the size of Texas.

The Vietnamese language was deeply influenced during a millennium of domination by China, when classical Chinese stood as the official discourse of mandarins—imperial officials representing the Chinese government—and scholars. Much later, in the 17th century, European missionaries created a new script representing the Vietnamese language using the Roman alphabet, which replaced Chinese to become the common form of writing Vietnamese.

Confucianism from China held society together through interlocking relationships and duties, helping to establish four major social groups: scholar-officials, artisans, merchants, and farmers. Then as now, the peasantry cultivated rice and secured protein by fishing. Today, nearly four out of five Vietnamese continue to reside in the countryside.

Both Mahayana and Theravada Buddhism took hold in Vietnam, the northern branch from China, the southern from India. Buddhist institutions functioned freely until communism arrived in the 20th century, at which point all aspects of religious life were curtailed. Catholics, presently three million strong, flourished for a century after French colonial dominance in the mid-1800s. In the early 20th century, Vietnam saw the establishment of Cao Dai—a mix of Daoism, Buddhism, Confucianism, and Christianity—in which utopian and cosmological ideals merged with an all-inclusive theology; Cao Dai saints include Buddha, Confucius, Jesus, Muhammad, Victor Hugo, Napoleon, Einstein, Churchill, and Sun Yat-Sen.

Introgression

As early as 50,000 years ago, the first humans arrived into uninhabited Southeast Asia. Glaciers trapped water in the polar ice caps, dropping global sea levels by as much as 300 feet and exposing an overland passageway known as Sundaland. Short migrations across stretches of open water brought people to both Australia and the highlands of Papua New Guinea, which were connected at the time, and left a corridor of early human settlements along the eastward route they had followed. Encampments presumably dotted the coastline from eastern Arabia across southern Asia, but they became submerged as the global climate warmed and as water, once locked in ice, returned into the oceans. The absence of an archaeological footprint of this early migration has left many historians perplexed, but new technologies are finally allowing archaeologists to delve underwater in search of villages submerged thousands of years ago.

South Asian arrival

Genetic research among populations along the South Asian coastline has uncovered a continuous thread linking Australians with Africans. The DNA carried by native tribes living throughout the region tells the story, and genetic work with populations from the Andaman Islands, Malaysia, and Papua New Guinea has revealed clues into these early movements. Recent studies of both their maternally inherited mitochondrial DNA and paternally inherited Y chromosome gene pools indicate that these populations appear to have arrived by a route along the South Asia

coastline within a few thousand years of leaving Africa.

The effects of chance—in genetics, known as genetic drift—meant that the patterns of genetic diversity among these people are quite different from among their African relatives. There appears in these groups to be a reduced

A Khmer man dances in full peacock regalia.

Y chromosome diversity, compared with their mitochondrial gene pools, a gender bias that makes sense when one considers the traditional marriage practices of these people. Both patrilocality—the tendency for a family to live in the male's community—and polygyny—the taking of multiple wives, which increases male reproductive success—are common practices in the region and help to explain this sex-biased genetic pattern.

The genetic data suggest that these groups predominated in Southeast Asia until about 10,000 years ago, when the advent of rice farming in East Asia led to

a large population expansion. Archaeological evidence for the spread of agriculture to Japan, Taiwan, and Southeast Asia parallels the genetic patterns of the people living there. Sites in northern China show evidence for the cultivation of millet and rice beginning around 7,000 years ago; by 4,000 years ago, rice farming had reached the Indonesian islands of Borneo and Sumatra. As these Asian agriculturalists moved south, they encountered populations that had been living in the area for tens of thousands of years.

The role of agriculture

There is conflicting evidence over the degree to which agriculturalists' DNA spread as their new way of life was adopted around the globe. The process by which genes are introduced into an existing population, known as introgression, is determined by factors such as population size, duration of contact, and the survival value of features offered by the new DNA. In Southeast Asia, the impact of agriculture appears to have been significant, for the vast majority of the genetic lineages found here today (between 50 and 90 percent, depending on the population) trace their origins back to the expansion of agriculture.

Though the first Southeast Asian populations lived in an area where large farming communities were popping up throughout the countryside, dominating the landscape with terraced rice farms and high population densities, their cultural and geographic isolation kept introgression at a minimum. Today these ancient populations still hold on to both the land and the genes of their earliest ancestors.

South Asia

Rimmed by the great Himalaya to the north, South Asia stretches from Afghanistan, Pakistan, and the Indus River in the west to Bangladesh, beyond the Ganges River, to the east. The entire Indian subcontinent is contained within South Asia. Second in population only to China, and significantly less than half its size, India's landmass varies from steep mountains in the north and arable river plains in the midsection to subtropical swamps and deltas, especially in the east. Rainfall depends on annual monsoon cycles for many parts of India and the rest of South Asia.

To listen to music from India and Sri Lanka, visit http://worldmusic.nationalgeographic.com.

BENGALIS

Population: 172 million   **Location:** Bangladesh, India
Language family: Indo-Aryan

The great Brahmaputra River meets the expansive Ganges River Delta in the Bengali heartland, and here the people divide themselves into two main regions: the nation of Bangladesh and the Indian state of West Bengal. Though short on many resources, both areas have water and people in excess. Bangladesh, with nearly 126 million people, is the world's most densely populated country, while West Bengal, with 70 million, is India's densest state; the Bengali language ranks sixth in number of speakers.

In 1947 the partition of India split its Bengal Province into Indian and Pakistani sectors; eventually Bangladesh (formerly East Pakistan) declared independence and, in 1971, became a nation. The division followed religious, not ethnic, lines, for all of the people in the area speak the Bengali language and consider themselves Bengalis. India's West Bengal has always been overwhelmingly Hindu, but Bangladesh, with the world's largest concentration of Muslims, follows a form of Islam that contains pre-Islamic Hindu and Buddhist elements.

Both sectors share a common history and acknowledge common successes, such as the 19th-century revival of literature, music, and the arts. Their shared language, an Indo-European tongue, preserves a rich literary heritage. The works of Rabindranath Tagore, beloved poet and 1913 winner of the Nobel Prize for Literature, are still read and memorized by Muslim and Hindu alike. Poet and playwright Kazi Nazrul Islam, called the voice of Bengali nationalism, grew to become a champion of poor farmers; his plays and tales on political and historical themes gave hope to long-subjugated Muslims.

While many Bengalis live in huge cities such as Calcutta and Dhaka, most of the people are villagers. To the north, they inhabit the hills, but elsewhere Bengalis dwell in a largely watery realm where fishermen, traders, and farmers depend on shallow inlets, fragile islands, and shifting fingers of land. Although the annual summer flooding rejuvenates the countryside with silt, every few years great inundations kill thousands of people.

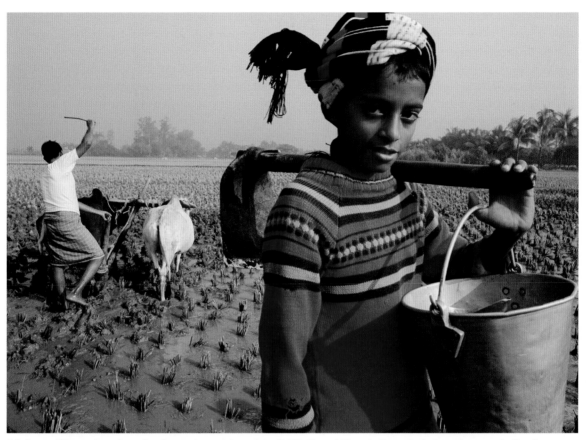

A father and his son share the tasks of preparing an irrigated rice field in Bengal. These Indian agriculturists rely on regular flooding to replenish their fields with silt, which carries essential nutrients for a recurring harvest.

GUJARATIS

Population: 46 million   Location: India
Language family: Indo-Aryan

The western Indian state of Gujarat sits at the junction of historical overland trading routes and the maritime outlets to the Indian Ocean. No wonder then that the Gujaratis have long been oriented toward trade. Their language, Gujarati, has ties both to Sanskrit, India's ancient language and the major vehicle of priestly ritual, and to Prakrit, vernacular languages.

The vast majority of Gujaratis, some 90 percent, are Hindus, but there are also a number of Muslims, Jains, and Parsis. Banias figure prominently among the Gujarati Hindu castes. In caste hierarchy they are ranked third after Brahmins (priests) and Kshatriyas (warriors), but as traditional merchants and traders, they often experience greater economic success. In fact, much of the commerce in bustling Mumbai (Bombay) in neighboring state of Maharashtra is controlled by Gujarati Banias.

In Jainism, an offshoot of Hinduism, adherents go to great pains not to injure any living being; some even sweep the streets in front of them as they walk in order to avoid stepping on any insects. Jains, as well as the Parsis, Indian Zoroastrians who came to the subcontinent from Persia more than a thousand years ago, also participate in Gujarat's large trading community.

In addition to trade, Gujarat supports a large manufacturing base as one of India's most industrialized states, producing goods such as textiles, chemicals, and plastics. Gujarati farmers grow crops of millet, sorghum, wheat, and rice, many at the subsistence level, and also crops of cotton, groundnut, sugarcane, and tobacco for export. The cutting of precious stones, especially diamonds, is a traditional Gujarati specialty.

Gujarat was the birthplace of Mohandas K. Gandhi, best known as the Mahatma, or Great Soul. The slight, bespectacled, British-trained lawyer led his country on the arduous path to independence in 1947 through the power of his charisma and the principles of self-sufficiency and nonviolence that have been adapted by leaders and causes the world over.

Many Gujaratis observe the same life-cycle rituals and celebrate most of the same festivals and holy days as they do elsewhere in Hindu India, but they emphasize some more than others. Diwali, the Festival of Lights, marks a fresh start for everyone: Merchants close out the year's books and begin new ones. Navratri honors the mother goddess with nine nights *(navratri)* of worship and celebration that include typical Gujarati dances such as the *garba,* a circular women's dance accompanied by singing and vigorous drumming.

On an international basis, Gujaratis outside India are perhaps even better known than those who reside there. Beginning in the 6th and 7th centuries, Gujarati traders traveled to Indonesia and East Asia; by the 13th century, they were in Africa. More Gujaratis came to Africa in the 19th century, when Indian labor was used to build the continent's railroads. A large number of Banias stayed on after others returned to India, and they are ubiquitous as shopkeepers and businessmen, many with the common Gujarati surname of Patel, especially in East Africa. Gujaratis also formed the vanguard of immigration to the United Kingdom and North America in the 20th century. Many who came to the United States got their economic foothold in small mom-and-pop motels on well-traveled routes. Now Gujaratis own tens of billions of dollars worth of national chain hotel properties throughout the United States.

NAGAS

Population: 1.5 million   **Location:** India
Language family: Tibeto-Burman [Kuki-Chiin-Naga]

A strip of rugged territory in northeastern India between Myanmar (Burma) and the Brahmaputra River Valley is home to the numerous tribal peoples of Nagaland. Although the Nagas are difficult to distinguish from other Assamese and Burmese ethnic groups, these people acknowledge an unmistakable shared identity. And while their customs may vary, they commonly

Commuting to work takes many forms in Bangladesh. Here a businessman in Dhaka carries a satchel and umbrella as a barefooted oarsman paddles him to work. A cell phone keeps him in touch as he crosses the swollen river

occupy small villages perched on hilly spurs. The land's jumbled isolation has allowed development of more than 50 dialects, requiring different Naga peoples to use either a pidgin form or Assamese to communicate with one another.

Historically, the Nagas obtained all they needed from the land, the forest, and minor trading. Farming and hunting, supplemented by fishing, supported them well inside their walled villages. Outside, beautiful gateways with bas-relief decorations greeted anyone approaching along the winding, sunken paths leading up to them.

A variety of local organizations distinguish the Nagas, from strong chiefs with near total power to democratic councils to gerontocracies. Throughout the Naga tribes, women have always enjoyed high status, with equality in work and at tribal meetings.

The British, by establishing control over the Naga Hill District in the 1870s, stopped ritual warfare and head-hunting—a practice that had grown out of the belief that the human head holds a vital force, or soul-power. By taking the head of an enemy, a warrior could gain status, win a bride, and bring to his village an increase in positive energy. Such acts also inspired dances and various forms of art, all with skull motifs. The last case of Naga head-hunting occurred in 1958, several years after the British had left the area. In the late 19th century, American missionaries began converting Nagas, and two-thirds are now Christian. Their religion has reinforced their identity in a region where the majority of people are Hindu.

NEPALIS

Population: 17 million
Location: Nepal
Language family: Indo-Aryan

In the 1760s, the ruler of a Himalayan principality formed a unified Nepal from a number of independent states with populations as diverse as the terrain they lived in. Today's Nepalis represent three different ethnic stocks: the Indian peoples from the south, the Tibetans from the north, and indigenous peoples, who predate the first two. Each source contributed differences in physical appearance, in culture, and in languages. Nepalis speak dozens of languages and dialects, but many can converse in Nepali, an Indo-Aryan language closely related to Hindi, which some Nepalis also speak or understand. Those Nepalis who are

highly educated and those who come into frequent contact with tourists from other countries also speak the English language.

About three-quarters of Nepalis engage in farming, mainly at the subsistence level. Nepal's terrain sorts into three distinct horizontal bands that rise to the Himalaya. The hot fertile plains of the southern Terai provide most of the country's agricultural land, where rice is grown in the monsoon season and wheat and other grains are planted after the rice. For many Nepalis, rice is a daily

> Where there is rhythm and alliteration, there lies a proverb.
> GUJARATI PROVERB

staple along with dal—a lentil dish—and vegetables.

Hills climb from the Terai into a zone of rivers and valleys and the large, ancient lakebed that forms the Kathmandu Valley, home to some 700,000 Nepalis. Here, crops grow at lower elevations and livestock grazes in pastures higher up. Above them rise more than 200 peaks over 18,000 feet high, including Sagarmatha, or Mount Everest, the world's highest at 29,035 feet. Nepal extends in places to the north of the highest ridge; the Tibetans who live on that side raise yaks and dzos, their yak-cattle hybrids.

The Indo-Aryans brought with them Hinduism, Nepal's dominant religion, embraced by four-fifths of the population. In 563 B.C. Gautama Siddhartha was born in the Nepali village of Lumbini in the Terai. He traveled to India and attained enlightenment, and then as the Buddha imparted his insights to his followers, who filtered back to Nepal and now make up about 10 percent of its population. In general, Hindus and Buddhists celebrate each other's festivals and revere each other's shrines and sacred sites, of which there are more than 2,700 in the Kathmandu Valley. The Nepali population also includes small percentages of Muslims, Christians, and other believers.

The Hindu Indo-Aryans also brought with them notions of caste, which have been widely applied across Nepal's diverse population. Until recently, caste ranking correlated fairly closely with wealth, which was based on land ownership. Now a wider range of people have opportunities in trade, tourism, and light industry. Nepal even boasts a small-scale film industry, known as Kollywood (*K* for Kathmandu).

Nepal's great scenic beauty draws many visitors as well as adventure-seekers and serious climbers who attempt ascents of Everest. They require the knowledge and skills of the Sherpas, a group that traditionally has acted as guides and porters in mountain-climbing expeditions. Another specialized group, the Gurkhas, have earned renown as soldiers and for nearly two centuries have supplied crack regiments to the British Army.

Still, Nepal is one of the world's poorest countries, with about a third of Nepalis living below the poverty level. Many of them belong to marginalized ethnic groups who have become highly politicized in a quest for greater rights and opportunities.

Centuries of deforestation to obtain firewood, building materials, crop land, and fodder is reaching crisis proportions in Nepal, causing serious problems with erosion on mountain slopes and leading to frequent landslides on the country's expanding road network. A solution gaining ground is biogas, known locally as gobargas, a fuel alternative made of cow dung, or *gobar*. Instead of climbing ever higher up the slopes to gather scraps of wood for a cooking fire, Nepali women collect gobar from the family cattle's never-ending supply and place it in a low-tech, airtight container, where it mixes with water to produce methane gas. There is even the possibility that gobargas production could yield energy credits under the Kyoto Treaty protocols.

PUNJABIS

Population: 90 million
Location: Pakistan, India
Language family: Indo-Aryan

The Punjabis, a hardy people with strong ties to the land, originated in the northwestern corner of the Indian subcontinent. Their name is tied to their region, where five *(panj)* rivers *(ab)*, tributaries of the Indus, drain fertile plains forming one of South Asia's most productive agricultural areas. The Punjab region was home to the flowering of the great Indus River civilization of the third millennium B.C., which included well-planned and administered cities such as Harappa and suffered a lengthy procession of invaders—the Turks, Persians, Huns, Greeks, Afghans, and others. All left their marks

on the present-day Punjabi people, who tend to be taller and more robust than other ethnic groups in the region.

Once a unified cultural and linguistic area accommodating members of the Hindu, Sikh, and Muslim faiths, the Punjab was divided during the partition that occurred at Indian independence in 1947, when the separate nation of Pakistan was created as a Muslim homeland. Hindus and Sikhs, who represent a distinctly Punjabi reformist movement within Hinduism with the city of Amritsar as its spiritual center, fled the

One uses a torch to look at others' feet.
VIETNAMESE PROVERB

western part of the region; most Muslims went in the opposite direction. Violent reprisals took place on both sides of the border, leading eventually to almost a million deaths.

Today the Punjabi population of Pakistan is about 97 percent Muslim, while in India, Punjabis are Sikh or Hindu, the ratio between them about three to two. Punjabi is spoken in both countries, although Pakistani Punjabis may also speak Urdu, Pakistan's official language, and those in India will also often speak Hindi.

Punjabis in both Pakistan and India engage in agriculture, either as landowners or as workers, although Pakistan's Punjabi population is much more urbanized, centered in towns and cities such as Lahore. Punjabi agriculture is carried out on a larger scale, with more mechanization and scientific advances, than elsewhere in the subcontinent, and even if a farmer provides his own subsistence, there often is a significant surplus to sell commercially. Wheat is the main food crop grown—together with lentils, vegetables, and maize in the summer—and cotton is the main cash crop. Manufacturing including food processing, other agriculture-related industries, and heavy machinery also contribute to Punjabi prosperity.

The traditional Punjabi village consisted of a tight cluster of adjoining homes surrounded by a mud-brick enclosure fronted by a *darwaza*, or immense door; fields lay outside the village walls. Contemporary villages,

In drought-prone Rajasthan, India's most arid state, advanced water management techniques improve the bounty. Now this woman can harvest grain from former desert land.

especially in the Indian Punjab, often have brick houses with running water, electricity, and other amenities.

Rural Punjabi communities center on the inter-generational family: a man, his wife, his married sons, their dependents, and any unmarried children. Punjabis marry outside their clans and villages.

Muslim, Hindu, and Sikh Punjabis observe their own religious traditions, yet they also ecumenically celebrate festivals such as Vaisakhi, commemorating the Hindu harvest and also the founding of the Khalsa, the Sikh brotherhood. In Punjab, Vaisakhi features *bhangra* dancing, in which brightly costumed and elaborately turbaned men—in the traditional version—dance vigorously to a relentless drumbeat and vocal accompaniment, while women perform their own more subdued dances.

Bhangra has taken the international pop music world by storm, and this traditionally Punjabi music now appears singly and in fusion with hip-hop, disco, and reggae.

SORA

Alternate name: Savara Population: 300,000
Location: India Language family: Munda

The Sora are an indigenous people of India. Their ancestors settled in India long before the arrival of the Aryan and Dravidian populations that now dominate and outnumber them. They are ethnically and linguistically related to various Mon-Khmer peoples, including the Cambodians, who live a considerable distance to their east. To this day the Sora, as well as other indigenous peoples of India, are referred to collectively as *adivasi*, "first" peoples. Popularly known as "tribals," they exist outside and beneath India's socially rigid caste system, lower even than the Untouchables.

The Sora were formerly hunter-gatherers but are now rice cultivators, using yoked oxen and simple wooden plows to tend pond fields. Due to the alternating wet and dry seasons, they can only grow one or two crops of rice each year, and small family plots often do not yield enough food for a family to survive. Outside of the rice growing season, the Sora work as day laborers and practice minor trades such as brick making, cashew processing, and tamarind growing.

In stark contrast to the Hinduism practiced by 81 percent of India's citizens, the Sora traditionally eschewed the worship of gods in temples, instead worshiping outdoors in nature, where some venerated stone megaliths built by their ancestors. Unlike Hindus, the Sora have no taboos against eating meat, and they used to sacrifice water buffalo ritually.

The Sora have traditionally valued communication with the spirits of recently deceased persons, for which they rely on mediums, who enter into trances and speak in the voices of the deceased. The Sora people seek advice or protection from the dead, and they also strive to console or appease them. This practice of dialoguing with the dead is now fading, however, under pressure from Christianity.

Sora women once tattooed their arms or faces and pierced and elongated their earlobes; Sora men once wore loincloths. These practices have now waned, and they may be seen only among the oldest members of rural communities.

In recent decades, many Sora have been converted to evangelical Christianity, which some now zealously practice, worshiping in elaborate churches that they have constructed. In the few small villages that have not yet been missionized, people retain more traditions. They brew palm wine, paint totemic designs on the interior walls of their mud-brick houses, and engage in ceremonial music and dancing. The vibrant sounds of musicians playing cymbals and horns can summon an entire village population out into the streets in minutes, congregating to dance frenziedly for hours at a wedding or important event.

The Sora language is one of the most important Munda languages. It has attracted the attention of linguists for its ability to build very complex verbs. A Sora verb can incorporate the subject and direct object, effectively compacting an entire complex sentence into just a single word. The main concentration of Sora speakers are located in the state of Orissa, India, but speakers are also found in adjacent Andhra Pradesh. Estimates of the total number of speakers vary between 150,000 and 300,000. In some areas with significant Sora populations, however, language shift is occurring, and members of the younger generations no longer speak Sora. While not immediately endangered, Sora, like other similarly sized and marginalized minority languages of India, may be considered threatened. Sora remains a primarily oral language, not widely read or written even by speakers who may be fully fluent and literate in Oriya, a regionally dominant language, and in English. A rich story tradition helps impart values by cautioning against greed, family strife, and vanity. Though the Sora Bible may be found as a prized household possession in some Christianized villages, it is not typically read. In many areas Sora remains a vital and thriving language; in other areas, it is being replaced by Telugu or Oriya.

The Sora people are now eager to educate their young and join India's technological revolution. Though social mobility for tribals is quite limited, and the value of their culture remains largely unacknowledged, schools for Sora and other tribal children are beginning to break down some social barriers and provide opportunities.

SINHALESE

Population: 15 million
Location: Sri Lanka
Language family: Indo-Aryan

In multiethnic Sri Lanka, a teardrop-shaped island off the southeastern tip of India, the majority Sinhalese number 15 million out of a population of 20 million. The Sinhalese have since earliest times coexisted with other ethnic groups on the island—first the Tamils, then Muslim traders, then the Portuguese, the Dutch, and the British. In recent times, though, contention with Tamils has grown into warfare because the Tamils, inhabitants of the northern and eastern reaches of the island, seek an independent homeland free of Sinhalese control. Points of division include religion, language, and ethnic identity.

Indo-Europeans (Aryans) from northern India moved to Sri Lanka about the fifth century B.C. and in time became the Sinhalese, with their own distinct language, Sinhala. As early as the third century B.C., they had fully converted to Buddhism, and their mutual faith and shared language bound the people together. Sinhalese kings played important roles as patrons of Buddhism in the early centuries of the first millennium A.D. At a time when the Buddhist religion was declining and disappearing in India, the people of the island nation felt protective toward their faith, and the Sinhalese people stressied the need to preserve their special path to enlightenment.

The Sinhalese also strongly influenced the development of Buddhism in Southeast Asia through the missionary efforts of their teachers and artists, who traveled beyond their island home and used religion and a distinct writing system to direct the flow of education, literature, Buddhist chronicles, and common aspirations. Today, the village monastery or temple still stands as the local center for culture, and to become a monk is considered a noble goal.

Throughout history, successful kingship has been marked by massive irrigation works for the growing of rice and by impressive art and architecture: A period of exceptional flowering in the 12th century produced Polonnaruwa, a magnificent royal Buddhist city in north-central Sri Lanka that achieved greatness in art, sculpture, and architecture.

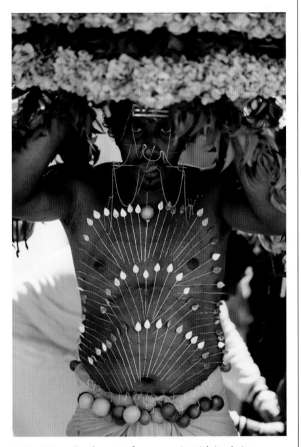

In Mauritius, a Tamil man performs a penitential rite during Cavadee, a festival honoring the god Shiva. The island, off the eastern coast of Africa, is home to many diaspora Indians.

TAMILS

Population: 57 million
Location: India
Language family: Dravidian

The Tamils largely inhabit Tamil Nadu, an Indian state created in 1956 to be a home for Tamil speakers, a group tending to be stockier and somewhat darker than northern Indians. Since before the arrival of the Aryans around 1500 B.C., these people have lived at the southeastern limit of the Indian subcontinent.

Well over 50 million Tamils define themselves as Tamil-speaking Hindus who share in a great Dravidian culture. The term "Dravidian" describes an independent family of some 22 languages and the special culture of the south of India. Except for classical Sanskrit, Tamil is the oldest written language in India: Going back nearly 2,000 years, its rich literary repository includes epics, religious and secular poetry, philosophy, and moral instructions.

Of particular interest are the verses and hymns of devotional literature dating from the sixth to ninth centuries A.D. Collectively, these works are considered to be among the great Tamil contributions to Indian civilization. Tamils believe that bhakti, meaning "devotion," elevates a devotee's personal relationship with a god to a level of ecstatic love and selfless praise. Above all, the path of bhakti leads to salvation.

Over the years, Tamils have vociferously resisted the encroachment of the Hindi language and northern cultural influences. They have done so even though they, too, are overwhelmingly Hindu, worshiping at more than 9,000 temples and celebrating a huge variety of riotous festivals.

Madras, the Tamil capital, was a weaving center when the British East India Company built a fort and trading station there in the mid-17th century. Later it became the administrative and trading capital of southern India. Because of British needs for labor elsewhere, emigration created Tamil communities as far away as Fiji, Malaysia, Singapore, South Africa, and Mauritius.

The Tamil people's presence in Sri Lanka consists of two groups: the Sri Lankan Tamils, who settled there more than 1,500 years ago, and the Indian Tamils, who came in the 19th and 20th centuries to work on tea and rubber plantations. Civil war in Sri Lanka has led Tamils to migrate to many other countries, but wherever they go, they build temples and develop strong local ties.

The Asian North

The area of the globe centering on the North Pole, the Arctic Circle is delineated by latitude 66° 30′ N. Among the Asian countries, it is Russia whose northernmost realms fall within the Arctic Circle. At its center is a large basin, the Arctic Ocean, ringed with a variety of landscapes. The Russian Arctic includes two mountain ranges, the Urals in the west and the Verkhoyansk in the east, and numerous islands in the Barents, the Kara, and the Laptev Seas. The northernmost realms of Scandinavia belong to this region, as well: Norway, Sweden, and Finland. Tundra vegetation characterizes the landscape year-round, with very cold, long winters and brief, mild summers.

♫ To listen to music from Tuva, visit http://worldmusic.nationalgeographic.com.

CHUKCHI & KORYAK
Population: 15,700 (Chukchi), 8,700 (Koryak)
Location: Russia
Language family: Chukotko-Kamchatkan

Across the Bering Strait from North America's Alaskan Eskimos live the Chukchi and Koryak, two peoples who have been in close contact over the years. The Chukchi inhabit the farthest reaches of northeastern Siberia, and the Koryak live on the Kamchatka Peninsula to the south. Both groups descend from Paleolithic hunters and fishermen and are physiologically related to the Mongoloid northern Asians. They speak mutually intelligible languages.

Originally, the Chukchi and Koryak were split into coastal groups of maritime hunters and fishers and inland groups of reindeer herders. The coastal societies had more in common with each other and nearby Eskimo groups than they did with their inland relatives. They hunted on the ice in winter and from skin boats during the summer, relying on sea mammals such as whales, seals, and walrus for food. Since Koryak territory impinged on the taiga, or boreal forest, to the south and west, the Koryak also availed themselves of plant resources and freshwater fishing.

The inland Chukchi and Koryak maintained herds of reindeer for food, transport, clothing, and shelter. The semidomesticated deer had to be recaptured and retrained each season to pull the sleds. Watching over the animals were herdsmen who lived in family encampments of four or five large skin *yaranga,* or tents, made of reindeer hides. The families kept large herds, so concepts of wealth, private property, and social stratification became well developed among these people even before the first Russian contacts in the 1640s. In both Chukchi and Koryak cultures, shamanism was highly developed, and their religious systems shared a number of beliefs and

An Evenk herder leads her domesticated reindeer to pasture in the early morning. The Evenk excel in animal husbandry, performing sophisticated procedures to maintain their herds.

associated rituals, including the sacred family fire and the concept of Raven as a major cultural hero. Complex fertility ceremonies held at annual reindeer slaughters and sea mammal feasts were intended to ensure the continued availability of game.

The Chukchi now live mostly in villages established by the Soviets during the Siberian collectivization of the 1930s; only a few villages still keep reindeer herds. Among the difficulties faced by this nomadic culture as it adjusted to settled life were the pressures of industrialization and, later, nuclear testing, all of which—until recently—contributed to very high rates of infant mortality, alcoholism, and suicide.

These same general conditions affect the contemporary Koryak people, who were also formed into a national district by the First Congress of Kamchatka Soviets in 1930. The Koryak have suffered under the same deleterious effects of modern civilization as those that have affected their northern neighbors, and their average life span is now less than 50 years.

EVENK

Alternate name: Evenki, Tungus   Population: 65,000
Location: China, Russia
Language family: Tungusic

Among the most widespread of the Siberian Arctic cultures, the Evenk people are subdivided into two parts. The Evenki group inhabits the area extending eastward from the Yenisey River to the Pacific Ocean and northward from the Amur River to the Arctic Ocean; the Even, or Lamut, group lives along the coast of the Sea of Okhotsk.

The Evenk are reindeer pastoralists who keep large herds of completely domesticated deer, which are bigger and more uniform in color than the wild variety. For these people, reindeer domestication seems to be more closely modeled on herds kept by horsemen to the south than on dogs kept by the northeastern Siberians. Evenk reindeer are milked, ridden, and used as pack animals but, owing to their value, are not eaten except on ceremonial occasions or if starvation is imminent.

The Evenk derive the bulk of their food, clothing, and shelter from hunting and trapping, the main daily activities of the men. Like the Aleut, they have a great interest in animal anatomy, not hesitating to pursue and capture unfamiliar creatures to observe their behaviors and learn about their anatomies through dissection. The Evenk's knowledge of physiology and comparative anatomy astonished early Russian ethnographers, who also noted that they performed complex surgeries.

Shamanism was more highly developed by the Evenk than by any other Siberian group—the word "shaman" has an Evenki origin. Shamans could reputedly tell the future, predict the weather, cure or cause an illness, and assure success in hunting or herding. An Evenk shaman frequently used the agaric mushroom to induce trance states. Bear ceremonialism, another frequent circumpolar practice, was also common.

In the past, the Evenk lived near the taiga in winter and then moved their herds onto the tundra in summer. Because of climatic extremes, people were widely scattered in groups of only two or three families during the long Arctic winter, which lasts about three-quarters of the year; in summer, they formed larger camps.

The people continued keeping their herds and trading furs with the Chinese and later Russian merchants. Then, in the 1930s, during the Soviet period, they and other Siberian nomads were coerced into moving to permanent villages. Today 30 to 50 percent of the population still herd and hunt for a living, while the rest of the people work in industry, education, administration, and health care or as unskilled labor.

The Evenk National Okrug (or District) was created in 1930, but its relationship with the state remains uneasy. As late as 1999, this district, by then autonomous, refused to hand over power to the governor of Krasnoyarsk, Gen. Aleksandr Ledbed, who was a former security chief and Russian presidential hopeful.

NENETS

Population: 41,000 Location: Russia
Language family: Samoyedic

Also known as the Nentsy, Samoyed, and Yurak, the Nenets inhabit northwestern Siberia, from the Kanin Peninsula on the White Sea to the Yenisey River Delta. This is a region of wet tundra underlain by permafrost, combined with tundra and taiga mosaic ecosystems to the south.

Apparently the ancestors of modern Nenets moved into this area from the south during the early centuries of the first millennium A.D., replacing or assimilating the original hunting-and-gathering population with one that relied on reindeer herding. These newcomers practiced herding techniques that seem to have been adapted from ones used by horse and cattle breeders to the south.

Like other Siberian groups, the Nenets developed a migratory lifestyle fully adjusted to tundra existence. In autumn they moved with their herds from the coast to the taiga, and in spring they went back to the tundra. The Nenets became well known as breeders of reindeer large enough to be ridden like horses, and their animals were widely sought after by other groups. By comparison, the neighboring Evenk's reindeer were so small that riders had to sit forward, above the shoulders.

Nenet contacts with the Russian Empire were hostile and fraught with uprisings, a situation that did not improve with the Sovietization of the 1930s; with a millennia-long history as successful nomadic herdsmen, they did not yield easily to collectivization. The area has since become the focus of the chemical and oil industries, and nuclear testing on Novaya Zemlya has posed grave dangers to the health of indigenous peoples. During the 1989 census, 34,665 Nenets were counted, more than 70 percent of whom still speak Samoyedic, a language related to Turkic. Their life expectancy is now reckoned at only 45 to 50 years.

TUVANS

Population: 275,000
Location: Russia   Language family: Turkic

At the geographic center of Asia lies Tuva, a secluded and mountainous land in southern Siberia, adjacent to Mongolia. As a nation, Tuva enjoyed a few brief years of independence before being annexed by the Soviet Union in 1944. Since then it has had limited autonomy within the Russian Federation.

The Tuvans are an Inner Asian Turkic people, related to the neighboring Altais and Kazakhs. They have cultivated a centuries-long, sometimes uneasy alliance with their Mongolian neighbors, sharing some physical and cultural traits though differing linguistically. Small Tuvan communities reside in the People's Republic of China and Mongolia, though they lack official recognition as ethnic groups in those countries.

Tuvans are known for their virtuoso throat-singing,

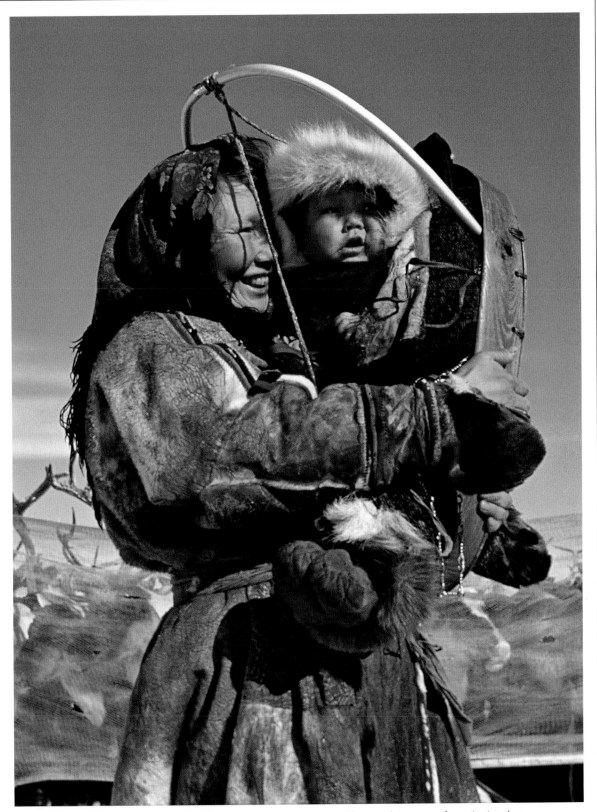

Bundled against the cold in clothing made of furs and hides, a Nenet woman and her grandson prepare for an Arctic trek.

also called overtone singing, in which performers produce multiple notes simultaneously, including high-pitched whistling and very low drones. An annual competition held in Kyzyl, the capital city, can launch the career of a young artist. Accompanying instruments may include a drum, bull's testicle rattle, bowed fiddle, goat-skin banjo, and *khomus,* a metal Jew's harp.

The Tuvan language boasts a rich oral tradition of songs, riddles, sayings, blessings, poems, and stories. Genres like the epic tale, once performed by itinerant storytellers over several evenings, are now seldom heard and in danger of being forgotten. Tuvan was first written in the 1930s, using a Latin alphabet, and later, under Russian pressure, a Cyrillic script. Many books are now available, including elementary and high school curricula. Tuvan is spoken by people of all ages, and most educated Tuvans also speak Russian.

A minority of Tuvans practice nomadism and herd camels, yaks, sheep, goats, cows, and horses. In the far north of Tuva, a small population of reindeer herders still thrives. Migrating seasonally to reach greener pastures, Tuvan nomads live, as did their ancestors, in collapsible, round felt houses. Sheep entrails and tail fat provide a favored meal on special occasions, while salty tea with milk slakes their thirst daily.

Tuvans practice a form of Buddhism adopted from Mongolia and Tibet. Buddhist practice was suppressed in Tuva under Stalinism and communism, and many temples were destroyed. After the fall of communism, Tuvans rebuilt their temples with great enthusiasm, and they continue to look for guidance to their own Buddhist leaders, headed by the Kamby Lama, as well as spiritual envoys sent by the Tibetan 14th Dalai Lama.

Most Tuvans also continue to practice animism, venerating Earth spirits and maintaining an elaborate cosmology of supernatural beings. Shamans are sometimes called upon to heal the sick or mediate with the spirit world; they may drum, chant, and burn juniper incense to undergo a trance journey to another world. Tuvans revere the landscape they inhabit, making frequent offerings at sacred springs, rock cairns, and other sites believed to be inhabited by spirits. The Tuvan language has a rich vocabulary for naming topographic features and for imitating natural ambient sounds such as rivers, winds, echoes, birds, and game animals.

Tuvans enjoy some benefits of modern technology while also being shielded by geography. They are one of the few small ethnic groups of Russia that constitutes a majority in their home territory. As a result, they have managed to hang on to much of their language, lifeways, and beliefs. It is still possible in remote Tuva to meet elderly nomads who have never ventured more than one hundred miles from their birthplace, people who are still sustained by their connection to their land and animals. At the same time, many educated Tuvans have traveled abroad or served in the Russian military, while a few have risen to influential political positions.

YAKUT

Alternate name: Sakha   Population: 275,000
Location: Russian Federation
Language family: Turkic

Although the early history of the Yakut is obscure, the people, who call themselves Sakha, emerged as a distinct ethnic group in the early 1300s, a fact that makes them the most recently arrived indigenous group in the Siberian Arctic. By the 17th century, they had peacefully assimilated with other northern peoples, particularly the Evenk, and had organized themselves into 80 independent tribes that were themselves subdivided into numerous clans.

Like the Evenk, the Yakut based their subsistence on herding, but in this case the herds were made up of horses and cattle. Because of the extreme cold, Yakut animals

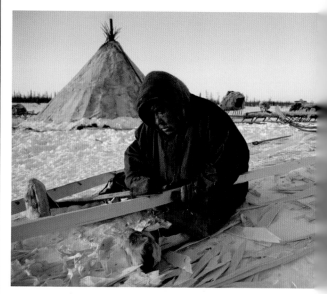

A Nenet man fashions a tent frame by carving and planing wooden poles. Covered with reindeer skins, the poles will become tents to house herder families. The Nenets are known for the large reindeer they raise, which can be ridden like horses.

tend to be hardy but rather unproductive and have to be sheltered and fed for a large part of the year.

The far northern Yakut, known as Dolgan, adapted to reindeer herding and hunting learned from neighboring peoples, often hunting from the backs of oxen or horses. The people also hunted ermine, sables, otters, and ferrets, and their culture flourished as the Russian fur trade grew. The Yakut valued reindeer hides and furs as personal property, and great wealth could be accumulated by families with hunters and large herds. The society eventually became stratified, causing the old clan system to become nonfunctional and then fall apart. Shamans among the Yakut got paid for their services, and as shamanism developed a complex hierarchy of duties, the shamans, too, accumulated enough wealth and power to become threats to the social order.

From the 17th century on, the Yakut were best known as fur traders and blacksmiths; by the early 1800s, most had joined the Russian Orthodox Church. As in the rest of Siberia, Yakut pastoralism and agriculture were collectivized between 1930 and 1950, but in a particularly brutal manner: Thousands who resisted were arrested, killed, or forcibly deported. Yakut schools, publications, and organizations were officially banned by Joseph Stalin, who promoted the development of heavy industry in the region.

Yakut nationalism reemerged in the wake of Mikhail Gorbachev's reform policies of the 1980s, and in 1990-1991 Yakutia proclaimed its sovereignty and established its own parliament. Despite political differences between Yakut and Russian leaders during the 1990s, President Boris Yeltsin in 1994 officially apologized to the people for their persecution by the Stalin regime and granted them greater control of their own resources. In 1997, with the help of the Worldwide Fund for Nature, 270,000 square miles of Yakutia's Arctic tundra were set aside as an ecological preserve. In 2000, President Putin made the Sakha (Yakut) Republic part of the Far Eastern Federal District.

YUKAGHIR

Alternate name: Odul   Population: 1,500
Location: Russia   Language family: Yukaghiric

Although the Yukaghir, or Odul as they call themselves, are among the smallest of the Eurasian Arctic populations, they are extremely important to the understanding of far northern cultures. These people probably represent most closely the ancient, original cultural adjustment to the coldest regions of Arctic Siberia. The area they occupy is generally north of the Verkhoyansk Range and is known for having the most severe winters in the world. Here, all of the water surfaces are frozen for seven or eight months of the year; the January temperature averages -70°F, as measured at the town of Verkhoyansk, and only 70 to 80 days each year are free of frost. During the short summer season, the land becomes a vast lake-studded marsh, because the meltwater from the considerable snowmass cannot percolate down into the permafrost.

The most important subsistence animals in this region are large herds of herbivores: reindeer. For generations, reindeer hunting furnished virtually all of the food, clothing, and shelter items needed by the Yukaghir, who were originally a nomadic people with an unusually large inventory of hunting methods. They used tame deer as decoys, crouching behind them to infiltrate a wild herd, and employed noose traps to catch the animals along their trails. From skin boats, they hunted deer at water crossings, using harpoons and compound bows. Elaborate, large-scale communal hunts called drives or pounds took place during calving season in the spring. At these times, men stampeded a herd into a keyhole funnel formed by waiting hunters, who then killed as many of the animals as possible.

The Yukaghir formerly lived in extended-family bands with fewer than a hundred people, occupying conical skin tents much smaller than the Chukchi's yaranga and somewhat resembling the tipi of the North American Plains Indian. Their shamans, like those of other Siberian societies, were powerful individuals, and elders and ancestors occupied places of particular prominence. At one time, the people used a pictographic writing system, the only remaining evidence of which is a love letter written on birch bark. Few today still speak their native tongue, a language related to Chukchi and Koryak.

Ethnologists knew the Yukaghir as a kind, mildmannered, and honest people exploited and abused by Cossacks, Russian settlers, and local priests, leading to the rapid assimilation of their native culture. Russianization brought the Yukaghir to the brink of extinction. In recent years, the people have adapted to life in small permanent villages with rectangular wood houses and herds of no more than 30 to 40 domesticated reindeer.

To Sail by the Wisdom of the Stars

Before global positioning systems, before sextants, even before compasses,
native peoples navigated their ways through thousands of miles of Earth's waters.

Until 1500 A.D., many European scientists believed the world was flat—yet indigenous mariners of Oceania had been sailing the nearly 20 million square miles of Oceanic seas in double-hulled canoes for more than a thousand years.

How did they accomplish such a feat? Polynesian navigators had a sophisticated technology all their own. Their specialized science, now referred to as wayfinding, was a system of observation that synthesized patterns in nature and allowed seafaring cultures to navigate with keen accuracy. The shape and sequence of waves, the rising and setting of stars, even the flight patterns of birds served as instruments for the wayfinder. Intimately wedded to his environment, the navigator employed a highly developed facility for observation, memorization, and integration. These skills required a lifetime of study and commitment. In the Hawaiian system, the training was so rigorous that few apprentices ever achieved the rank of *kahuna ho'okele*, navigator-priest.

Wayfinding was a revered science and a priestly profession that linked the cosmos, sea, and land. The initiate had to be not only a superior seafarer but also a healer, leader, and interdisciplinary scholar in subjects as diverse as astronomy and botany. Once on the sea, a full-fledged navigator outranked even the highest chiefs of the land.

The ho'okele and his counterparts across Oceania had no paper map or charts. Instead, they carried conceptual constructs of the sky. One of these was "the path of the spider," the track of the sun and the planets around the earth: the ecliptic, in Western terminology. The spider's web, like a knotted net covering a gourd, spreads out in star lines running north and south, east and west, and on the diagonal, much like a Westerner's star chart.

The Polynesian god of the ocean, Tangaroa (or Kanaloa), is represented by the octopus whose eight great arms are the sea highways between the far-flung islands. The head of the octopus is in the southern ocean, celestially represented by either the Southern Cross or Canopus, depending on one's culture. His tentacles point north, much like eight lines of longitude, and are celestially represented by star lines.

The navigator also needed to know the horizon markers. "Stone canoes," like the carved rock located at Kukaniloko on Oahu, Hawaii, and one in Kiribati, taught the navigator the location of "star pits," the points on the horizon from which a star rose in the east or into which a star fell in the west. The horizon markers served as compass points like that on a watch bezel.

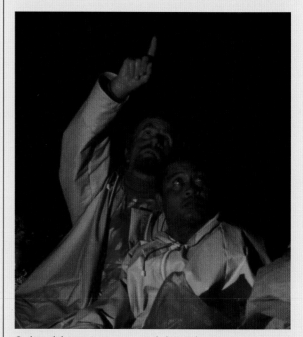

On board the outrigger canoe *Hokule'a*, Polynesian men use stars to navigate a long sea journey between Hawaii and Tahiti.

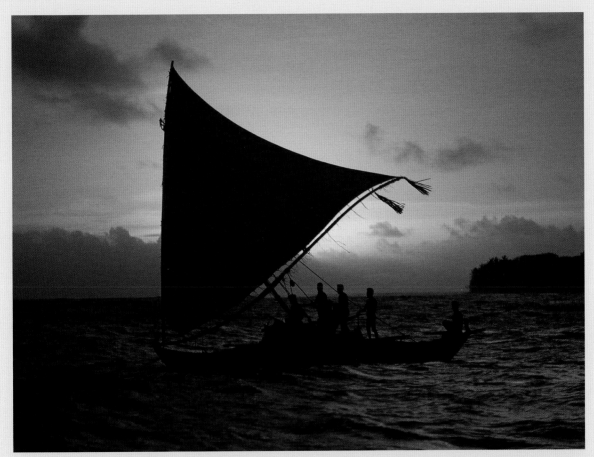

For centuries, outrigger canoes—such as this one, gliding out to sea at sunrise from the Caroline Islands of Micronesia—have been carrying the seafarers of Oceania over millions of squares miles of Pacific ocean waters.

The navigator was required to know how far along the horizon he would need to look for the star pits from one sighting to the next.

The decan, or ten-day week common throughout Polynesia, was a navigational calendar based on the rotation of the horizon. The decan week, known in Hawaii as *anahulu,* was a system that worked in concert with the solar and lunar calendars as an invaluable system of temporal orientation for the navigator.

Stars as guides

The mariners' guide stars—Polaris, Sirius, and the Southern Cross, common to nearly all maritime cultures—were also used by the navigators of Oceania. Zenith stars, which pass directly overhead, served as another reference point to land. Satawalese voyagers from the Caroline Islands referred to various storm stars throughout the year, including Canopus, Vega, and Arcturus, to predict inclement weather.

A navigator in training also learned to interpret the color of sunrises, sunsets, and clouds to determine weather conditions and proximity to land. The deep red, purple, and orange in a sunrise or sunset, coupled with certain shapes, types, and positions of clouds, forecast rain. The color of the cloud's underbelly suggested the type of land the mariner was approaching. A shining bright cloud, for example, indicated an atoll's sandy, shallow lagoon, while a greenish color reflected verdant land, and grayish blue signified open sea. There were also myriad ways of referring to directions. A conceptual compass based on prevailing winds identified 16 directions. An astral compass marked the stars' rising and setting around the horizon.

The navigator's responsibility was so immense that he would not allow himself complete rest. Instead he would lie in the hull of the canoe, much like a child in a mother's womb, where he could keenly feel the direction, rhythm, and sequence of the waves. Such methodology might be lost on Western science, dismissed as intuition or mysticism. Yet the wayfinder was gathering explicit data. His facility to determine the dominant swell of a wave was as finely calibrated as any instrument. This was one of the navigator's key methods for maintaining the canoe's proper angle, particularly important during the day and on cloudy nights, when stars were not visible.

The patterns of living creatures also informed the navigator. In the morning, seabirds go in search of food, returning to their islands late in the day. Some birds fly far out to sea; some stay closer to land. By knowing the different birds and their behaviors, the navigator deduced how close he was to shore. Certain schools of fish indicated, among other things, sea lanes, similar to the messages we receive from highway signs. The color of the water and the smells carried on the wind provided signposts to the skilled wayfinder.

The navigator had to know what foods to bring and what to leave behind. Breadfruit and banana, for example, were stored in the form of fermented paste and fruit leather. Coconuts provided water and food. Some items had to be prepared long before the voyage began—dried fish, fermented foods, and dried fruits, for instance. Other foods, like chickens or pigs, could be carried live, but they, too, needed to be fed.

And this was just the beginning of what it meant to be a navigator. It wasn't enough for him to find his way. He was also responsible for the feeding and general well-being of those on board, and, when necessary, was required to administer to the injured. Each culture had medicinal resources available from the environment. In Hawaii, for example, 'uhaloa (*Waltheria americana*) was used for chest and throat congestion. *Ko'oko'olau (Bidens pilosa)* served as a general tonic, a treatment for kidney and bladder ailments, and a blood fortifier.

Micronesian navigator Mau Piailug instructs his son and grandson on the intricacies of a star compass. The ring of stones represents stars; the band of leaves, the pattern of sea swells; and the two leaves at center, an outrigger canoe.

'Olena (*Curcuma longa*) was used to treat the common cold and other ear, nose, and throat disorders—and, most importantly, was used and continues to be used for cleansing and purification rituals.

Navigators committed themselves to regimes of physical training, similar in complexity to those of the martial arts. The *palu* of Micronesia, for example, practiced *pwaeng*, a physical discipline by which the navigator and his crew used their bodies to right a capsized canoe. During storms, palu mariners would also loosen the lashings on their vessels to accommodate conflicting stresses of winds, waves, and swells, reducing the likelihood of breakage. They had to secure themselves to the mast until the storm had passed, and then relash the canoe and continue on.

Without charts and maps on paper, ancient navigators repeated sailing chants, which taught the names of the stars, winds, rains, and key navigational reference points. Skylore and tribal mythology served as science texts among cultures where myth and legend were particularly developed.

As exceptional as these skills were, it was and still is the magic possessed by the priestly order of way-finders that is most extraordinary. These seafaring sages rely on a multifaceted system, which includes ritual, chant, myth, prayer, dreams, and visions. Polynesian cosmology takes as fundamental the interdependent relationships among humankind, the natural world, and deity. If the navigator prayed, he trusted—he knew—an answer would be revealed.

Navigating our future

Throughout the world—from Chowra, India, to Satawal, Micronesia—navigator-priests called the winds and calmed the seas by means of their magic. Such phenomena defied Western belief. Unfortunately, this mysticism was dismissed by classic science and demonized by Christianity. As native societies were conquered, decimated, and assimilated, these priests—Hawaiian kahuna, Micronesian palu, and many others—were forced to abandon or denounce their ancestral traditions or conceal their secrets. The judgments and consequent constraints imposed on native people almost destroyed their indigenous knowledge and practices. That period of history nearly sounded the death knell of native maritime science.

Fortunately, remnants of this ancient knowledge still

Master navigator Mau Piailug, known as Papa Mau, receives a hero's tribute in Hawaii for reintroducing the traditional art of navigating without instruments to Hawaiians.

exist within the vanishing clans such as the palu of Satawal, Micronesia. In March 2007, navigator Pius "Mau" Piailug, one of a handful of Satawalese sailing masters, conducted *pwo*, an initiatory ceremony, conferring 16 Micronesian and Polynesian men with the mantle of navigator—the first such ceremony in 50 years. Without Piailug's vision and dedication, wayfinding would be little more than a myth, traditional sciences shattered and forgotten, among the descendants of Satawal and other Pacific cultures.

Ancient seafarers were not unlike modern-day astronauts exploring new frontiers—their sea, our space; their canoes, our space capsules. We cannot overestimate the extent of their brilliance, their daring, and their achievements.

As we in the modern world teeter on the brink of environmental and social collapse, we are not unlike the ancient mariners who crossed uncharted waters, carrying finite resources along. Whether guided by stars, instinct, or global positioning systems, we are now the wayfinders. The success of our journey depends on everyone. As navigator Piailug says, "The canoe is our island; our island, the canoe."

The planet is our canoe; the canoe, our planet. ■

— *Elizabeth Kapu'uwailani Lindsey*

OCEANIA

AUSTRALIA
Arrernte • Australians • Cape York Peoples
Mardu • Ngarrindjeri • Noongar • Palawa
Pintubi • Tiwi • Torres Strait Islanders
Warlpiri • Wurundjeri • Yolngu

MELANESIA
Chimbu • Enga • Fijians • Marind-anim
Middle Sepik • Motu • Tannese
Tolai • Trobrianders

POLYNESIA
Hawaiians • Maori • New Zealanders
Samoans • Tahitians • Tongans

MICRONESIA
Chamorros • Chuuk Islanders • Marshallese
Palauans • Yapese

A Samoan diver explores a coral reef
in the National Park of American Samoa.

In the 19th century, European scholars recognized three broad geographical, cultural, and linguistic zones across the vast Pacific Ocean: Melanesia, immediately to the north and east of Australia; Polynesia, in the central Pacific; and Micronesia, east of the Philippines in the North Pacific. This largely artificial division, which downplays important similarities and connections among the islands, is said to have originated with French explorer Jules-Sébastien-César Dumont D'Urville (1790-1842), who based it on the mistaken notion that three separate races of people dwelled on the widely dispersed islands.

Australia, on the other hand, has always been viewed separately. Indeed, the Aboriginal languages and customs of this continent are not closely linked to those of other Pacific peoples, although archaeological evidence suggests that continuing migrations from Asia through Melanesia and onto the world's largest island began as early as 50,000 years ago.

Resistance and reconciliation In the past few centuries, the indigenous cultures of Oceania—a collective name for the Pacific islands and Australia—have been greatly affected by colonialism; at various times they were disrupted or even unified by their opposition to it. In New Zealand, for example, strong Maori resistance to settlement by Europeans resulted in an 1840 treaty establishing terms of coexistence.

Such a treaty was never contemplated with the Aborigines of Australia. The British considered Australia *terra nullius,* a "land without people," despite the fact that at the time of James Cook's 1770 expedition more than 500 tribes were living there. Because Aborigines had no recognizable system of land tenure in the eyes of British law, the British believed there was no one with whom they could conduct negotiations for the transfer of land.

Following the tragic excesses of the chaotic frontier period, Australia's policy in relation to the Aborigines ranged from protection to assimilation, integration, and finally self-determination. Not until 1992 was the terra nullius doctrine overturned by the Australian High Court. Now Aboriginal groups are reclaiming their homelands through federally enacted native title legislation, and Aboriginal reconciliation ranks high on the national agenda. Through it all, Aborigines have held on to many of their traditions,

In Papua New Guinea's Asaro Valley, a young "mudman" wears the mud-based body paint used cosmetically by the region's beauty-conscious males.

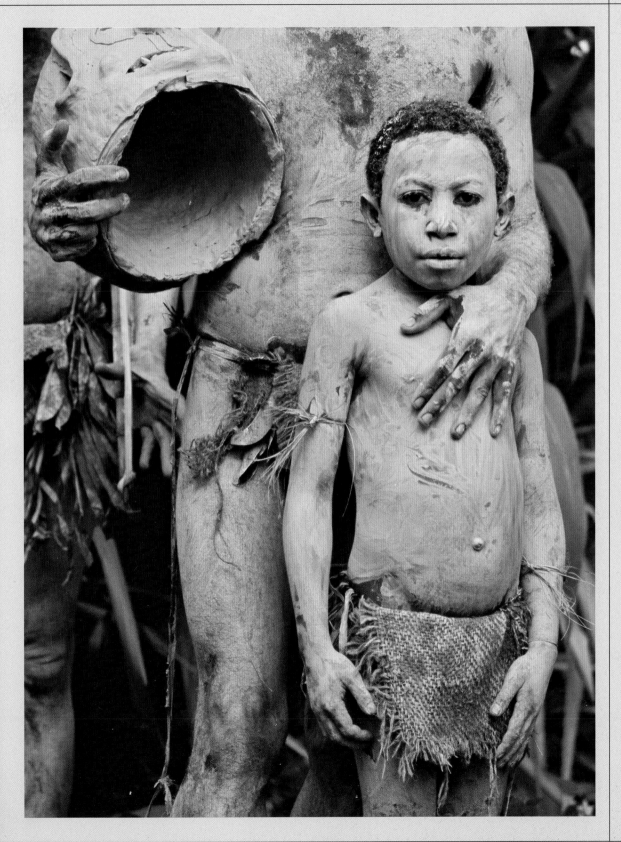

continuing to follow rituals and practices associated with the Dreaming or Dreamtime, a system of beliefs related to events at the "beginning of time."

Traditions are also important to Pacific islanders, providing links to the past and helping them maintain a sense of solidarity. Over countless generations and sometimes across great distances, islanders reached out and connected through trade and intermarriage to other Pacific peoples. Then, in the 16th century, European explorers sailed into their waters, and by the mid-1800s, most of their islands had been claimed by Germany, France, Spain, and England. The United States entered the colonial arena following the Spanish-American War of 1898, with acquisitions in the Philippines, Guam, Hawaii, and Samoa. After World War I, Japan took control of many former German territories.

Toward independence The invasiveness of colonial rule varied widely: In some cases, contact was infrequent and did not threaten the cultural integrity of local populations, while in others, the rights of self-determination were curtailed. Some groups felt compelled to develop strategies of avoidance or resistance that often grew into anticolonial and proto-nationalist movements. The most famous of these responses were the Melanesian cargo cults, which held that a supernatural "cargo" of deities and ancestors would arrive among supplies delivered to the islands, bringing about an age of plenty and a new, moral world order devoid of a ruling European presence.

Hawaiian women practice the hula on Waimanalo Beach in Oahu, part of a revival of interest in the islands' traditional Polynesian culture.

Between 1962 and 1980, most colonial territories achieved independence. But the postcolonial period for many of them has been marked by deep division and civil unrest. In Polynesia, where chiefdoms are largely determined by genealogy and seniority rather than personal prowess, island chiefs have readily made the transition to political leadership; however, the justice of their continued rule is sometimes challenged. In much of Melanesia, political organization centers on "big men" who achieve leadership through oratory skills, gift giving, and marriage alliances. While Melanesians share a common religion (Christianity), they often resist forming alliances with strangers and former enemies. Military coups in Fiji in 1987, independence movements in Bougainville and Irian Jaya, and the 1985 assassination of the president of Palau are symptoms of the difficulties Pacific islanders face as they move toward democracy.

As indigenous groups achieve freedom from foreign rule, they sometimes find that the national unity in which they are newly participating threatens their traditional cultural distinctiveness. New states, often beset by local demands for autonomy, may actively resist the notion of land rights for cultural or ethnic groups within their boundaries. Governments may promote a sense of shared identity, particularly in regard to *kastom* (custom or tradition).

Decorated to mimic birds of paradise, Huli tribesmen of Papua New Guinea await the start of a *sing-sing,* a welcoming dance.

In Melanesia, people have a long history of making and remaking kastom, creating and re-creating songs, myths, dances, and other cultural expressions associated with constituent groups. Such expressions are sources of prestige for their creators, and new variations are traded and exchanged following traditional practices—as exemplified by the Trobriand Islands' *kula* ring. Members of this trading network travel in canoes around an island group off Papua New Guinea, and as they exchange arm rings, necklaces, and other items, they affirm ties between ring partners and their communities.

In some Oceanian states, population growth rates are among the world's highest; even so, survival of many groups is threatened by large-scale plantation agriculture, mining activities, migration and transmigration, and uncontrolled fishing and logging. Forced dislocation and illnesses stemming from atomic testing have been major problems in Micronesia, where many people are kept from their former homes by alarming levels of radioactivity. Traditional small villages with a strongly hierarchical social order remain, however, together with a deep sense of attachment to homes and ancient customs—a feeling shared by many Oceanians. ■

Australia

A continent and a country, Australia lies between the Indian and the Pacific Oceans, a landmass of nearly three million square miles that is by and large flat and dry. Its southwest corner collects moisture enough to be verdant and fertile, and its northeast corner, the Cape York Peninsula, supports a tropical rain forest. Much of the continent, however, is covered by desert. To the northeast, Australia's coastline is fringed by the Great Barrier Reef, the world's largest. Two major rivers, the Murray and the Darling, join and flow west into the Indian Ocean. The country is divided into five states—Queensland, New South Wales, Victoria, South Australia, and Western Australia—and includes several external territories. The island state of Tasmania, to the southeast and separated from the mainland by the Bass Strait, is also part of Australia.

♫ To listen to music from Australia, visit http://worldmusic.nationalgeographic.com.

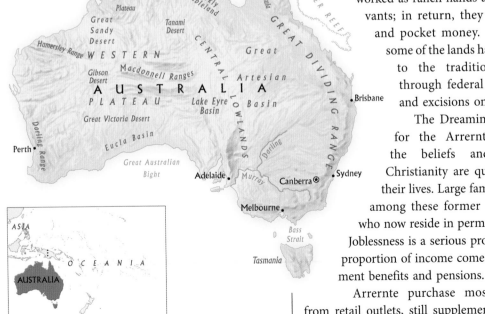

ARRERNTE

Alternate name: Aranda, Arunta
Population: 3,800
Location: Australia
Language family: Pama-Nyungan

Central Australia's Arrernte are perhaps the most famous Aboriginal Australians, thanks in part to the writings of such distinguished European social scientists as Sigmund Freud (1856-1939) and Émile Durkheim (1858-1917). Their works were classic ethnographic studies focusing on the concept and meaning of the Dreaming or Dreamtime—the traditional land-based Aboriginal religion—and on the Arrernte kinship system, within which a man marries his mother's mother's brother's daughter's daughter (his second cousin).

In fact, the Arrernte are a collection of peoples from the well-watered Macdonnell Ranges region in the vicinity of Alice Springs. These peoples include the Alyawarre, Anmatyerre, and Western Arrernte. All suffered gravely after contact with Europeans, experiencing high mortality rates, physical and emotional dislocation, and ethnocide. Some groups became extinct.

In the 1860s, after 20,000 years of living in this region, the Arrernte first encountered non-Aborigines. With colonization, their lands were converted into grazing lands, where they worked as ranch hands and domestic servants; in return, they received rations and pocket money. Since the 1970s, some of the lands have been returned to the traditional landowners through federal land rights laws and excisions on ranches.

The Dreaming is still relevant for the Arrernte, even though the beliefs and practices of Christianity are quite prominent in their lives. Large families are common among these former hunter-gatherers, who now reside in permanent settlements. Joblessness is a serious problem, and a large proportion of income comes from unemployment benefits and pensions.

Arrernte purchase most of their food from retail outlets, still supplementing with kanga-

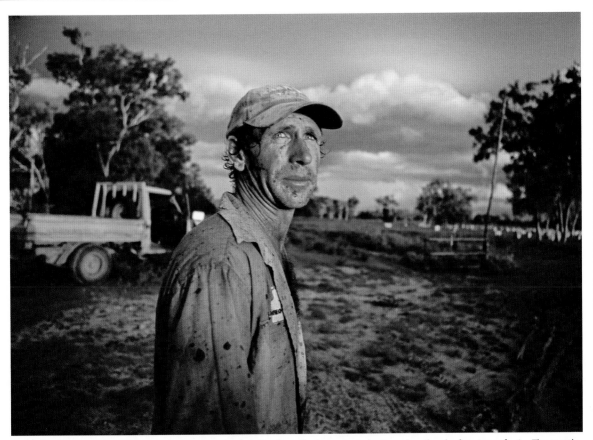

On a remote station, or ranch, near Darwin in Australia's Northern Territory, a rancher searches the sky for signs of rain. The mostly desert and semiarid Australian interior pushed the bulk of European settlement to the coasts.

roos, emus, bush turkeys, goannas (a monitor lizard), rabbits, honey ants, grubs, and bush fruits that they hunt and gather.

AUSTRALIANS

Population: 18.7 million
Location: Australia
Language family: Germanic

Although Australia's indigenous peoples arrived on the island continent more than 40,000 years ago, the forerunners of its current non-native population date only to the end of the 18th century. In 1788 the first ship of British settlers, many of them convicts, landed at Sydney on the southeastern coast. Soon, free British immigrated voluntarily, and in the mid-19th century, the discovery of gold accelerated the process. Over time, people of many countries would make the long journey, but Australia was to retain its British-based character, as seen in aspects of its government, laws, system of education, and many customs and traditions. Today, 18.7 million Australians, of whom only 2 percent are Aborigines, live in an area the size of the contiguous United States, making Australia the least densely populated country in the world.

Alarmed by the rising Asian migration spurred by the gold rush, Australia passed an Immigration Restriction Act in 1901 promoting a "White Australia Policy" that was not totally dismantled until 1973. During this time British immigrants received top preference, followed by northern Europeans, and then southern Europeans; others were admitted as these sources dwindled. Australians now strive to be inclusive and supportive of the 200 different nationalities who call Australia home, but there has been conflict, nevertheless. They also are attempting reconciliation with the Aborigines, who for so long were marginalized and mistreated.

Encouragement of immigration in general did not work as hoped—newcomers still tended to settle in coastal cities, where some 90 percent of the population lives. Few have chosen the nearly empty interior, with its mainly arid conditions, as their destination. Australia's cities tend to have compact centers fringed by far-reaching suburbs of single-family homes that contribute to one of the highest rates of home ownership in the world. The great majority of Australians—some 70 percent—now work in the service sector.

Australian English is based on British English, but with differences in pronunciation and a vocabulary that reflects Australia's unique contexts, such as the rugged bush life of the outback. As Australia's population of non-English origin has grown, so too have the number of languages heard routinely, especially in Melbourne, the country's most multiracial city, where Italian, Greek, Serbo-Croatian, Arabic, German, Vietnamese, and other languages are spoken.

There were many more men than women in the early days of Australian settlement, a situation that brought about a culture of "mateship." The hard life of remote sheep and cattle stations, coal and gold mines, and later the military fostered mutual reliance between and among men that has endured despite correction of the country's gender imbalance. Mateship also evolved with the Australian obsession with sports—as both participants and spectators. Nowadays, girls and women also are referred to as mates, but the concept generally describes institutionalized male camaraderie, with beer drinking often the common denominator.

Since Christmas falls in the Southern Hemisphere's summer, many Australians celebrate it as a beach day. At home they may have a traditional Christmas meal—or a barbeque instead. Some counter the hot weather by observing "Christmas in July," feasting on turkey, ham, and Christmas pudding in more seasonal weather. Australians also observe the British

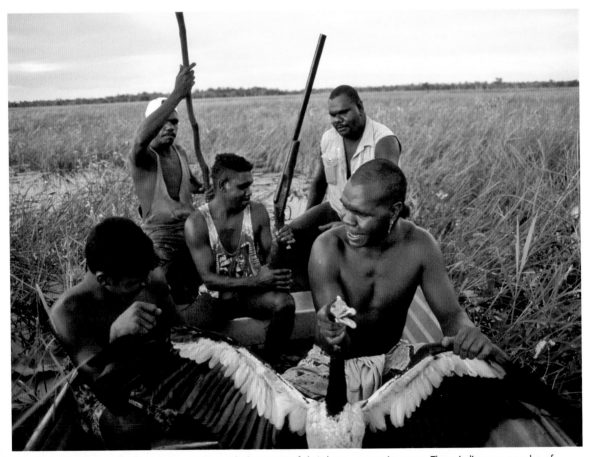

Cape York Aborigines glide through the marshes with the quarry of their hunt—a magpie goose. These indigenous peoples of northeastern Australia are among the continent's most disadvantaged.

custom of Boxing Day on December 26, taking advantage of more time for the beach.

The national holiday, Australia Day, inspires parades, picnics, and fireworks. ANZAC (Australian and New Zealand Army Corps) Day on April 25 honors the contributions of all war veterans, especially those who fought at Gallipoli in World War I, a military campaign that galvanized Australians and drew them closer to their New Zealand neighbors.

It appears that Australia's days as a member of the British Commonwealth may be numbered. In 1999 the population came close to a majority vote on a referendum, possibly paving the way for an Australian republic. In 1984 Australians changed their national anthem from "God Save the Queen" to "Advance Australia Fair," putting more distance between them and their colonial past.

CAPE YORK PEOPLES

Population: 6,000   Location: Australia
Language family: Pama-Nyungan

Exhibiting considerable social, cultural, and linguistic diversity, as of 2001 the Aborigines living in Cape York made up 35 percent of the cape's population and owned 20 percent of the land. Most of them dwell in Aboriginal-controlled townships and outstations. According to archaeological evidence, Cape York Aborigines at one time tried farming activities, but the benefits of agriculture did not outweigh the costs in terms of labor. A migratory lifestyle provided much more time for leisure activities, rituals, and the forging and maintenance of inter- and intra-clan alliances.

The Wik of the central west coast may be the best known Cape Aborigines. Their participation in the momentous legal movement of the 1990s helped end the long fiction of *terra nullius,* "land without people," the policy that had facilitated dispossession of Aboriginal lands.

In the early 1990s the Cape York Land Council was formed to pursue Aboriginal property rights on the cape. The council has embarked on a number of novel and groundbreaking regional co-management schemes, connecting conservationists, pastoralists, and miners. Even so, Cape York Aborigines continue to endure poor health standards and have a life expectancy that is among the lowest in the country.

MARDU

Alternate name: Martu   Population: 720
Location: Australia
Language family: Pama-Nyungan

Australia's western desert, one of Earth's most inhospitable landscapes, is devoid of permanent streams or lakes. For this reason, the Mardu homelands were long considered undesirable by non-Aborigines, and they remained unsettled until well into the 1960s, thus enabling desert-dwellers to survive European contact with their cultures intact.

Before contact, the Mardu—a collective term for the Giyadjarra, Mandjildjarra, and Budidjarra language groups—led a nomadic life in the desert. They moved from place to place, taking advantage of changing weather patterns and using stone, bone, and wood tools to provide for themselves. Population density was low, averaging only one person in 75 square miles.

Like other Aborigines, the Mardu believe that the continued existence of both the world and their people depends on the maintenance of their relationship with all-powerful Dreaming entities, the objects of their religious life. These entities are said to have emerged from the flat, featureless void that

Those who lose dreaming are lost.
AUSTRALIAN PROVERB

was Earth at the beginning of time. With the outward appearance of either humans or animals, they moved across the landscape, shaping the territories of the Mardu as they traveled.

These totemic beings performed rituals to be emulated by the people, and they imbued the landscape with the spirit that animates humans and all other living things. In addition, they instituted laws and procedures that were blueprints for social interaction, hunting, performing circumcision and subincision, and more. Eventually the entities transformed themselves into features of the landscape, which serve as eternal reminders of the sacred laws followed by all Mardu. Today, Mardu men still spend much of their time discussing spiritual matters, crafting sacred objects, and performing age-old rituals at sacred sites known as *jabiya.*

NGARRINDJERI

Population: 3,000
Location: Australia
Language family: Pama-Nyungan

The Ngarrindjeri of South Australia's lower Murray River were once best known for the near-equality of their men and women, something unique in Aboriginal Australia. Sacred rituals were the province of men, but Ngarrindjeri women also played important roles in the ceremonial life of the tribe.

Encompassing five different lowland zones, the tribe's rich environment was particularly attractive to colonists, and so the Ngarrindjeri became predominantly of mixed descent by 1900. Less than half a century later, few people retained knowledge of traditional ways and customs. This situation grew worse as the government increased pressure on the people to assimilate into the dominant culture.

Currently, the Ngarrindjeri are perhaps more socioeconomically integrated than other Aboriginal groups. Nevertheless, they embrace their Aboriginality and actively attempt to revive traditions and beliefs. They also hope to remedy problems associated with alcohol abuse and economic disadvantage.

One of their chief means of reinvigorating tradition is the clanwide, ongoing opposition to the destruction of sacred sites by developers, particularly in the vicinity of Hindmarsh Island. Led by Ngarrindjeri women, the protest has brought worldwide attention to the plight of this marginalized group and forced debate on a great national concern: Has the tide of history washed away not only knowledge of ancestral beliefs and practices but also traditional attachments and rights to the land?

NOONGAR

Alternate names: Nyungah, Nyoongah
Population: 8,000 Location: Australia
Language family: Pama-Nyungan

For at least 40,000 years, the Noongar and their ancestors have occupied the Swan River area in the vicinity of Perth. The name of their language group, Nyungah, forms part of the collective label for a body of languages: the Pama-Nyungan language family, spoken by 80 percent of Aborigines, from the tip of Cape York to the southwest corner of the continent.

Until 1829, when the British established a colony in the Noongar's Western Australia homelands, the people had led a seminomadic life; they moved freely from one area to another, depending on available water, fish, game, fruit, and root vegetables. But colonization struck the Aboriginal economy at its core. Depleted or destroyed were the Noongar's traditional food resources, and the people soon became dependent on introduced goods. The first few decades of the settlement at Swan River saw large numbers of Aborigines dying after contracting measles, influenza, and other introduced illnesses.

Despite their violent 19th-century clashes with soldiers, convicts, and free settlers—and subsequent harassment by 20th-century bureaucrats—the Noongar have maintained a sense of themselves as a distinct cultural entity. As an urban Aboriginal collective, they face immense problems, not the least of which is how to reinvigorate a land-based culture when areas of greatest significance are covered by asphalt and concrete.

Aboriginality in Australia is a matter of self-ascription, but recognition from the state requires two things: proof of descent and membership in a community of Aborigines. In the case of the Noongar, various territorial and linguistic bands merged in the late 1800s, and new communities evolved that could claim descent from earlier groupings. Noongar associations now provide a collective voice for speaking out on topics of common concern.

PALAWA

Population: 16,700
Location: Australia
Language family: Pama-Nyungan

Aborigines have occupied Tasmania for as long as 32,000 years. Known as the Palawa, these people thrived during the last ice age as one of the world's southernmost human populations. Then, as the ice age came to a close around 10,000 B.C., rising seas separated Tasmania and its people from the rest of Australia. The population would live in

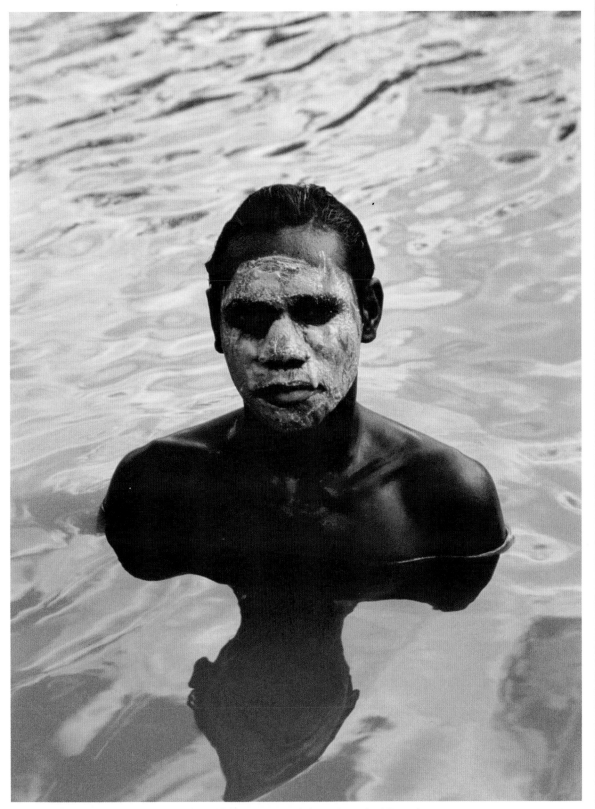

A mud-masked Cape York youth cools off in a billabong, or water hole, in Queensland, Australia.

Australian Arrival

In 2005 a team of Genographic scientists undertook an ambitious expedition to Chad, in North Africa, in search of genetic evidence for the earliest Saharan migrants. It was the first foreign expedition into the remote Tibesti Mountains in over 40 years, and the team relied on the expertise of local guides to shepherd them safely through scorching sands to the provincial capital of Faya-Largeau, an oasis town near the country's northern border with Libya.

On the third night the team sought protection from summer winds at the base of a large dune and bedded down for a crystal clear moonrise in the cold desert night. The following morning they awoke to find sleeping bags, tents, research equipment, and food all covered in several inches of fine sand. Overnight, the sheltering dune itself had migrated as a result of the same winds they were trying to escape.

In the sand

Shifting sands like those in the Sahara can both cover up and expose evidence of human occupation, and in 1974 such sands revealed an ancient fossil lying near Lake Mungo, one of several dry lakes in southern Australia's Willandra Lakes region. The modern human skeleton, named Lake Mungo 3, was found to be at least 40,000 years old. With evidence from other similarly dated sites in the region, it quickly became apparent that humans had been on the continent for quite some time.

These findings added fuel to a long-standing debate over human origins. Some anthropologists, citing morphological similarities between peoples today and extinct hominid species from similar geographic regions, argued a theory of multiregionalism, which proposed that humans descended from a number of ancestral lines of independent evolutionary origin. The implication of Lake Mungo 3, they argued, was that Australian aborigines could be at least as old as African populations, if not older.

Genetic research has since answered

As Australia redresses wrongs toward Aborigines, there is hope for younger generations.

the question of origin resoundingly, showing that the DNA of all living humans directly descends from Africa; that Africa's indigenous populations are genetically older than others; and that they possess mutations ancestral to those found elsewhere. But Lake Mungo 3's antiquity did present a difficult question: If they originated in Africa, how did modern humans make it to Australia, over 10,000 miles away, so long ago?

The first modern humans to leave Africa 60,000 years ago likely did so by exploiting a combination of terrestrial and marine resources, following the Nile River and Indian Ocean coastline northward until, unbeknownst to them, they had left Africa and arrived on the doorstep to the rest of the world. This period marked a global dry spell, when much of the world's water was locked in the polar ice caps, and continental Southeast Asia was connected to the nearby Indonesian and Malaysian islands as a single landmass called Sundaland, while Australia and New Guinea were similarly connected as a single landmass called Sahul.

The lower sea levels during this period meant that a continuous overland migration, with only a few minor open-water crossings, would have been possible from Africa to Australia. By traveling along the coasts of southern Asia at a rate of only two miles a year, people would have made it to within a boat ride of Australia in less than 5,000 years.

The fires of Australia

Australia was then a lush landscape of lakes and rivers, full of large marsupials now extinct, like the buffalo-sized *Zygomaturus* and a 450-pound short-faced kangaroo, *Procoptodon*. Evidence suggests that humans changed Australia's ecosystem by setting massive fires, and they transformed the region from forests and grassland to today's landscape of fire-adapted shrubs. The purpose of these fires remains a mystery. Nevertheless, roughly 60 species of the continent's large mammals went extinct soon after humans arrived, forcing them to maintain the mobile hunter-gatherer lifestyle that brought them to the continent.

Many of today's indigenous Australian people still practice the traditional way of life, and Lake Mungo 3 is a good example of this: The body was found sprinkled with red ochre in a burial ritual similar to that practiced by many of today's Aboriginals.

isolation until Dutch, French, and English explorers arrived, beginning in the 17th century.

The Palawa were divided into 70 to 85 bands of 30 to 80 people, with each band occupying a territory of around 200 to 300 square miles. These Tasmanians were grouped into nine larger social units or tribes that shared a common culture and language. Very little is known of their religious beliefs and practices, apart from the fact that 3,500 years ago, for unknown reasons, fish ceased to be part of their diet; instead, shellfish, crustaceans, and penguins became their nutritional mainstays.

In 1803, the English established a convict settlement at Hobart. At that time, the massacre of local Aborigines began. Martial law was declared in 1828, culminating in a huge military operation, or "Black Line," which was designed to corral all surviving Aborigines onto offshore islands and into remote enclaves. By 1838, there were only 82 survivors from the original population; the last "full blood" Palawa—a woman named Truganini—died in 1876.

Today, thousands of people claim Palawa ancestry, rationalizing the claim through the knowledge that they descend from Aboriginal women and non-Aboriginal sealers and whalers. Through their mothers, the Palawa of today have learned about the importance of their native heritage and about the strength of the Aboriginal spirit, and they continue to use kinship, oral history, and traditions to keep the culture alive. In Aboriginal schools, old languages are again being spoken, and sacred sites are being honored.

PINTUBI

Population: 1,500 to 2,000
Location: Australia
Language family: Pama-Nyungan

By 1965, the government of Australia's Northern Territory had removed the so-called lost tribe of Gibson Desert Pintubi Aborigines from their homeland and settled them hundreds of miles to the east, in Papunya. About 150 miles west of Alice Springs, the settlement was one of the last Aboriginal communities to be established. It was intended as a place for "re-educating" people, to ensure their assimilation into mainstream society, but the Aborigines who were taken there managed to retain their tradi-

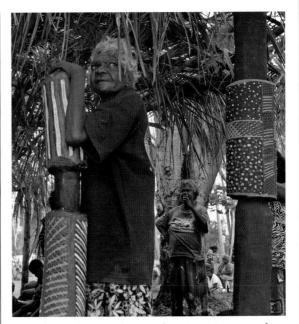

A Tiwi family plants a *pukamani* pole at a gravesite, part of their many duties at a funeral. The carved-and-painted pole proclaims the clan membership of the deceased.

tional language and culture. The Papunya community, now one of the best known autonomous Aboriginal settlements, instead became the focus of an extraordinary 20th-century success story. Ceremonial sand designs, as well as designs inscribed or painted on the body during sacred and secret Pintubi rituals, became the centerpiece of a local arts movement that eventually spread throughout Australia. One of the most successful businesses owned and directed by the Aborigines is Papunya Tula Artists, a cooperative that began in 1971. Its art has done very well internationally, sometimes selling for record prices in New York and Paris.

The increasing prominence of Pintubi designs has had a dramatic impact on art and craft production throughout Australia's center. To meet tourists' growing demand for the art, other Aborigines have been motivated to learn more about their Dreaming stories and designs and to seek out elders who could teach them, leading to a widespread cultural renaissance. Artists insist they are not selling their heritage; rather, they want the world to know about their culture. They keep the sacred knowledge for themselves, to be passed on to their children. Style may have changed, but the sacred message has not.

Since 1981, artists have established outstations at

Warlungurra and Kiwirrkura, near the Northern Territory's border with Western Australia, and both are flourishing settlements. Kiwirrkura was the scene of a remarkable development in 1984, when first contact was made with perhaps the last of the traditional or "bush" Pintubi. Neither Aborigines nor non-Aborigines had believed that there were such desert-dwellers, who still followed a traditional lifestyle, and the reuniting of the nine bush Pintubi with family members—who had lost touch with them more than 25 years before—attracted international media attention.

TIWI

Population: 1,900
Location: Australia   Language family: Tiwian

The Tiwi of northern Australia's Melville and Bathurst Islands experienced their first recorded exposure to Europeans in the 18th century; it was an encounter that would be followed by many more over the years. After a false start in the 1820s, European settlement of the Tiwi islands finally began in earnest in the early 20th century. Since that time, however, the Aboriginal Land Rights (Northern Territory) Act of 1976 has been passed, and the Tiwi have regained full control of their islands.

Today, most Tiwi live in three townships: Nguiu, the former Catholic mission; Pularumpi, which had been a school for part-Aboriginal children; and Milikapi, the former government settlement. Some of the people here go on weekend excursions, hunting kangaroos and turtles, but rather than paddling their traditional dugout canoes and carrying spears, they now steer outboard motorboats and wield shotguns.

The Tiwi's concept of Dreaming distinguishes them from other Aborigines. Divided into *murukupupuni,* or individual Tiwi "countries," their islands are "spirit-child" centers in which membership is determined by the burial place of one's father. Tiwi believe that when a new clan member is conceived, a spirit-child is transferred through a dream from a father to a mother of the same clan.

Celebrating the Tiwi culture, Nguiu's Tiwi Design Aboriginal Corporation is the base of operations for Tiwi Design, a collective of about a hundred artists involved in textile design, weaving, painting, print-making, wood carving, and ceramics. Many consider it a good model for other Aboriginal art enterprises.

TORRES STRAIT ISLANDERS

Population: 30,000   Location: Australia
Language family: English-based Creole

Where once there was a land bridge, 90 miles of sea now separate Australia's Cape York Peninsula from Papua New Guinea. More than a hundred named islands and many thousands of islets, reefs, and sandbanks dot the Torres Strait, home to an indigenous population quite distinct from the original inhabitants of mainland Australia.

Combining cultural and genetic influences from both Australia and Melanesia, the 30,000 Torres Strait Islanders trace their ancestry to 14 island groups in the South Pacific. Today these people claim rights of ownership to the lands and waters where their ancestors have dwelled for more than 4,000 years.

Before colonization by Europeans, the Torres Strait's eastern and northern islands, such as Mer and Saibai, were home to permanent villages of bamboo-and-thatch huts. Elsewhere, settlements were transitory and populated according to the seasonal availability of resources.

In their large double-outrigger canoes, the Torres Strait Islanders engaged in extensive trading relationships not only with each other but also with Papuans to the north and Aborigines to the south.

> ### Where there is kindness, there is life.
> MARSHALLESE PROVERB

They carried out pearl-shell harpoons, ornaments, and human heads, and in return they received sago, yams, coconuts, tobacco, bird of paradise feathers, and outrigger canoes. Subsistence came from both the sea and horticulture: Positioned on platforms constructed in shallow waters, islanders fished or hunted turtles and dugongs (a type of manatee); families also relied on defined garden plots, which they inherited from their ancestors along the

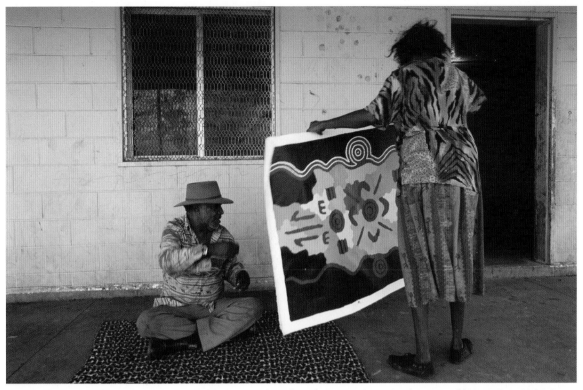

Renowned Warlpiri artist Michael Jagamara Nelson instructs his wife and assistant, Marjorie, about one of his paintings. Nelson's works of traditional Aboriginal subjects such as the Dreaming are in the Sydney Opera House and Australian parliament building.

male line. If they wished, the owners could transfer or lend their lands to others for gardening and foraging purposes.

Unlike inhabitants of the Australian mainland, Torres Strait Islanders have been able to maintain their traditional production, exchange, and subsistence practices. Today, the strait is largely an autonomous zone, a political configuration unique in indigenous Australia. Islanders manage their own affairs through the Torres Strait Regional Authority, the Island Coordinating Council, and the Torres Strait Council. In addition, each one of the 17 most abundantly populated islands has a council that performs local government responsibilities.

Major issues include a significant out-migration to the mainland, poor health, relatively low education levels, and overcrowding in the limited available housing. Ties to coastal New Guinea communities, once strong, are now in decline or have been terminated: The international boundary limits communications, and there is growing disparity in wealth among the former trading partners.

WARLPIRI

Population: 3,000 Location: Australia
Language family: Pama-Nyungan

Among the most populous Aboriginal groups in Australia's Northern Territory, the Warlpiri were traditionally hunter-gatherers living in small groups of up to 30 people. They led a hydrocentric existence in the Tanami Desert, their movements around water sources characterizing life in their vast, arid homeland.

Regular contact with Europeans commenced in 1911 with the establishment of the Tanami goldfields. Later, in the Coniston Massacre of 1928, as many as a hundred Warlpiri were killed by government forces; others fled northward from home territories to escape further depredations. Survivors were forced to settle in the 1940s, and today they and their descendants inhabit the small communities of Yuendumu, Lajamanu, Warrabri, Willowra, and Nyirrpi, as well as outstations.

Following the 1976 enactment of federal land rights legislation, almost all of the country the

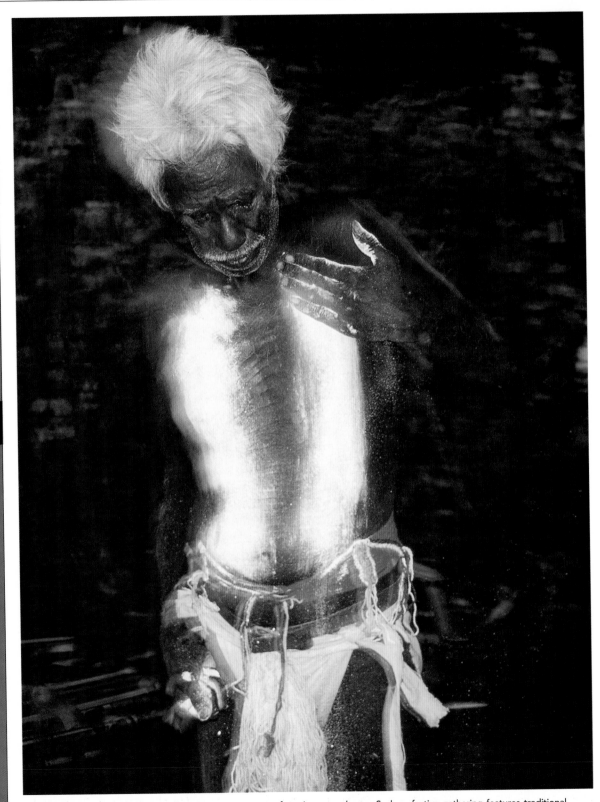

Applying pigment to his body, an Aborigine prepares to perform in a *corroboree*. Such a festive gathering features traditional Aboriginal songs and dances.

Warlpiri owned prior to contact was returned to them. This has not restored the independence they once enjoyed, however. Most of the people are unemployed and getting by on various forms of government support, minimally supplemented by mining royalties and art sales.

The Warlpiri are known for their "dot paintings," which illustrate visions of their *Jukurrpa* (Dreaming) narratives. Artists re-create individual and collective Dreamings and associated places in the landscape, using customary U-shapes, concentric circles, and journey lines. With this art, the Warlpiri artists assert their rights and obligations to the land.

WURUNDJERI

Population: Undetermined   Location: Australia
Language family: Pama-Nyungan

Koorie is the popular name among Aborigines for the indigenous people of southeastern Australia. The Wurundjeri, a Koorie group, live on the Yarra River plains, now encompassed by Melbourne, Australia's second-largest city, after Sydney.

In the first decade of contact between English colonists and the Wurundjeri people, diseases decimated local populations. Survivors watched as their hunting grounds were cleared and drained and their sites of cultural significance were destroyed. Within 10 years, only 300 to 400 Wurundjeri people remained, and they soon became totally dependent on the newcomers.

Very little is known about the Wurundjeri's traditional religious and spiritual life, except that clan members belonged to one of two intermarrying moieties, or halves, called Eagle Hawk and Crow. The Wurundjeri also were part of a confederacy of clans known as Kulin; today, though, social life centers on the extended family. The Wurundjeri still maintain spiritual and cultural ties to the land, asserting their role as traditional caretakers of the territory created by the Dreaming entity known as Bunjil.

In response to the situation of urban Aborigines, the federal government established the Indigenous Land Council, which has since helped the Wurundjeri purchase the old mission site of Coranderrk and the surrounding 200 acres—a small portion of their former tribal lands. The Wurundjeri have also established a heritage walking trail and a bush-food trail in Melbourne to raise awareness among the general population about the region's history and its significance to the Koorie. Downtown Melbourne was built atop Aboriginal burial sites, resource extraction areas, ceremonial and sacred areas, and former campsites. Markers placed along the trails describe the old Aboriginal way of life.

YOLNGU

Population: 4,500   Location: Australia
Language family: Pama-Nyungan

The Aboriginal people of Arnhem Land, in Australia's Northern Territory, refer to themselves as Yolngu. They are well known for the richness of their cultural heritage, as expressed in traditional feathered ornaments and paintings on eucalyptus tree bark, and for their Christian beliefs.

The Yolngu community of Galiwin'ku, which was the setting for the landmark Adjustment Movement in Arnhem Land, is especially noteworthy for the innovative ways people have incorporated Christianity into their worldview without compromising the sanctity of the Dreaming. Affirming their belief in both traditional religion and Christianity, residents publicly state that neither would receive preference in their lives. Galiwin'ku is also the base of the touring Aboriginal Black Crusade, whose aim is to re-Christianize Australia's non-Aborigines.

From the late 1600s to the early 1900s, the Yolngu traded with Indonesian fisherfolk who were seeking access to fisheries and trade beyond Europe's control. Together they gathered trepang, a sea cucumber prepared as food in China and Indonesia. Thus Australia's first international industry was established. These precolonial contacts probably enabled the Yolngu to better deal with the missionaries, miners, and bureaucrats who arrived later.

In the early 1960s, the Yolngu mounted a protest against bauxite mining by a multinational company. They presented a bark petition—a typed manuscript combined with a traditional bark painting. They did not win the case, but their efforts set into motion an inquiry into how land rights could be delivered to Aboriginal Australians and led to the proclamation of the Aboriginal Land Rights Act of 1976, which mandated that land in the Northern Territory be returned to Aborigines.

Melanesia

Melanesia is one of three divisions of the Pacific islands to the north and east of Australia. The name means "black island," although its origins are not clear: Perhaps the name applies to the rock of the islands, perhaps the dark skin of the people who live there. Melanesia is the westernmost of the three South Pacific island clusters, lying closest to Australia. It includes Papua New Guinea, at the east end of the Indonesian archipelago; the Bismarck Archipelago, a volcanic island group dominated by New Britain; the Solomon Islands, a chain that includes the historically significant Guadalcanal; Vanuatu, a double-chain of about 80 islands; and Fiji, an island grouping that may number as many as 800, 150 of which are inhabited. Most of the islands of Melanesia are ancient volcanoes, ringed with coral reefs and containing tropical forests on their windward slopes and mangrove swamps on their leeward stretches. Occasional hot springs give evidence of their volcanic past.

To listen to music from Papua New Guinea, visit http://worldmusic.nationalgeographic.com.

CHIMBU

Alternate name: Simbu   **Population:** 80,000
Location: Papua New Guinea
Language family: East New Guinea Highlands

Inhabiting the Wahgi and Chimbu River Valleys of the eastern highlands, the Chimbu are one of Papua New Guinea's largest populations. They were first contacted by Jim Taylor and Michael and Dan Leahy, Australian explorers and gold prospectors, on their patrol into the New Guinea highlands in 1933, when the region was controlled by Australia.

Soon after contact, the Chimbu were missionized by Lutherans and Catholics. They also experienced rapid cultural change in the post–World War II period, when Australia placed the Territory of Papua and the Trust Territory of New Guinea under a single administration. In 1975, Papua New Guinea became independent.

Originally part of the Eastern Highlands District (now a province), the Chimbu broke away and their lands later became the Simbu Province. Today, they and other eastern highlanders are successful coffee growers and a dynamic force in the economy and on the national political scene.

Along with western highlanders, the Chimbu were transformed by the agricultural revolution that introduced sweet potatoes into New Guinea almost 300 years ago. This crop, which allowed intensive cultivation, not only spurred growth of the human population but also supported a large domestic pig population. The Chimbu subsequently developed an elaborate ceremonial system based on the exchange of pigs, shell valuables, feathers, and other items.

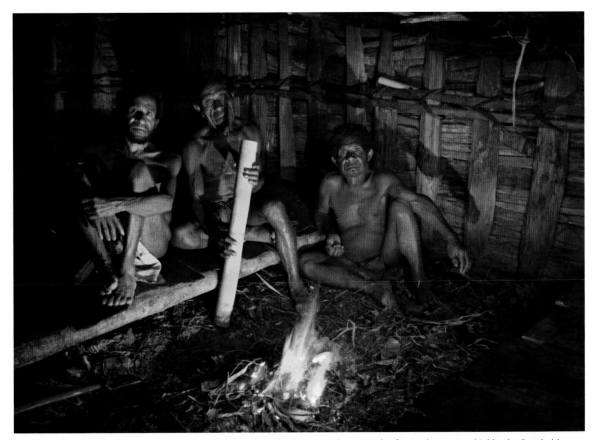

Members of a notably egalitarian Papua New Guinea tribe, Chimbu men relax around a fire in the eastern highlands. One holds a hollow bamboo section used for carrying water.

Because of their expanding population, these people became chronically short of land. Early in the 1960s, in some parts of Chimbu territory, population densities reached as high as 500 inhabitants per square mile. This led to endemic warfare, and the Chimbu expanded into less densely populated, lower-elevation areas south of their original home.

Like the western highlanders, the Chimbu have no hereditary positions of authority. They are very egalitarian, with men exerting authority on the basis of personal characteristics such as strength, bravery, and generosity.

ENGA
Population: 230,000
Location: Papua New Guinea
Language family: East New Guinea Highlands

The Enga are one of the most numerous peoples of the western highlands of Papua New Guinea. As is the case with the Chimbu of the eastern highlands, the Enga have their own province, Enga Province, with its capital at Wapenamanda. They survive on intensive sweet potato cultivation, which in turn supports vast pig herds. Other garden foods, including greens, sugarcane, bananas, and introduced vegetables, supplement the sweet potato.

The Enga do not include pork in their daily diet; instead, they use the pigs in a regional exchange cycle called the *tee*, which also involves trading ceremonial crescent pearl shells. The pigs are periodically slaughtered at highly ceremonialized events that are part of the tee.

Before Australian colonial pacification in the 1950s, warfare was endemic among Enga groups. Casualties claimed a quarter of Enga males between 1900 and 1955. The acquisition and competitive display of shell wealth and pigs during the tee is a peaceful substitute for warfare, and the ceremony has become enhanced and more important in local political life since the advent of the Pax Australiana.

White hats are all the fashion for a church service in Fiji. Missionaries—most of them Methodist—converted ethnic Fijians to Christianity in the 19th century.

The Enga are known for their strict separation of men and women. Like their Huli neighbors, Enga men feared contamination by women's menstrual blood and other sexual fluids. Cohabitation was not permitted, and women were not allowed to enter the men's space in the village during their menstrual periods. Feminine fertility, on the other hand, figured centrally in the Enga's precontact male cults, a general characteristic of groups in the western highlands.

Hereditary chiefs and other formal leadership positions are not part of Enga culture or, for that matter, part of the societies of most other large horticultural groups who make their homes in the New Guinea highlands. Male leadership is acquired through prowess in warfare, through success in the various aspects of the tee exchange, through skill in oratory and magic, and through management of ceremonial wealth. Enga politics are thus mutable and dynamic, and in many ways they reflect an egalitarian society.

FIJIANS

Population: 503,000
Location: Fiji
Language family: Malayo-Polynesian

A cluster of more than 300 volcanic islands in the South Pacific, Fiji is home to the Fijians, a people of mixed Melanesian and Polynesian ancestry who have inhabited the islands for some 3,500 years. Since the late 19th century, Fiji has also absorbed an influx of East Indians, who came initially and involuntarily as indentured workers for British-run sugarcane plantations and later—voluntarily—as merchants and traders. Fiji's population is represented also by small numbers of Europeans, Australians, New Zealanders, Chinese, and other Pacific islanders, as well as people of mixed European and Fijian ancestry.

Native Fijians insist on exclusive entitlement to designation as Fijian, for which they also use the term Taukei; currently, they make up some 60 percent of the total Fijian population of about 800,000. At the same time, the Indo-Fijian population has formed an Indian diaspora community that intersects with ethnic Fijians, mostly in commercial and political spheres.

Ethnic Fijians inhabit only about a hundred of the Fijian islands, which they call Viti, a word that

---

Each bay, its wind.
FIJIAN PROVERB

---

means "east" or "sunrise" to the Fijians. Most live on the two largest islands, Viti Levu and Vanua Levu, which account for about 86 percent of Fiji's territory. In rural areas they form villages occupied by members of one or several patrilineal lineages or subclans headed by a hereditary chief.

When the British took control of the islands in the 19th century, they acknowledged the power and importance of the traditional chiefdoms and incorporated them into the administrative structure. They also allowed the Fijian system of communal land tenure to continue. Fiji has been independent since 1970 and a republic since 1987. The Council of Chiefs still meets at least yearly; it also appoints Fiji's president (a largely ceremonial position), vice president, and nearly half of the Fijian Senate. Fiji's government officially uses English, but Fijian and Fijian Hindi also are formally recognized.

Fijian villagers typically fish and cultivate taro, cassava, and other crops that meet their own food needs as well as providing some surplus to sell. Sugar production is still the largest export; the fields, worked mainly by Indo-Fijians, are on leased land.

Over the years Fijians have been moving from rural areas to the cities, so that 40 percent of them are now urban. Many ethnic Fijians work in the services tied to tourism, a major source of revenue. Every year thousands of cruise ships stop in Fiji, disembarking tens of thousands of tourists, who also arrive by air, especially from Australia and New Zealand. Fijian women also work for low wages in the textile industry.

European missionaries, predominantly Methodists who created a writing system for Fijian in order to translate the Bible, successfully converted most Fijians to Christianity. Although churches have replaced native temples and Fijians embrace Christian practices, animistic beliefs live on, especially those concerning ancestral spirits

Some of the central practices of traditional Fijian life also persist and have been modified for presentation to tourists. One is the drinking of kava, also known as *yaqona*, an intoxicating beverage made from the root of a pepper plant that has been the focus of a Fijian ritual for centuries. Formal etiquette traditionally surrounds the preparation and consumption of yaqona, but it is also drunk socially—known as "having a grog"—and tends to loosen the tongue and encourage storytelling.

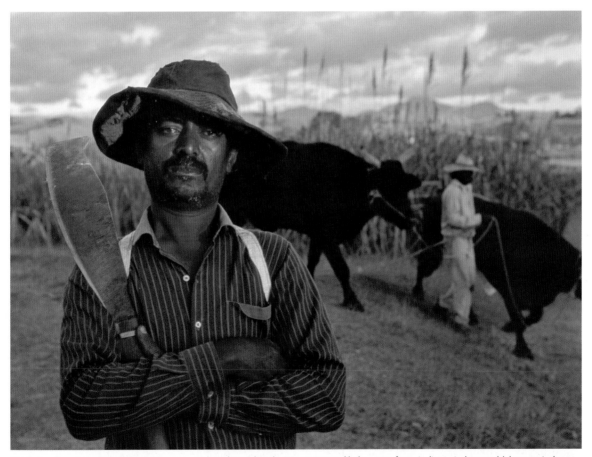

Machete at rest, an Indo-Fijian sugarcane cutter takes a break. His ancestors likely came from India as indentured laborers; Indo-Fijians now comprise about 40 percent of Fiji's population.

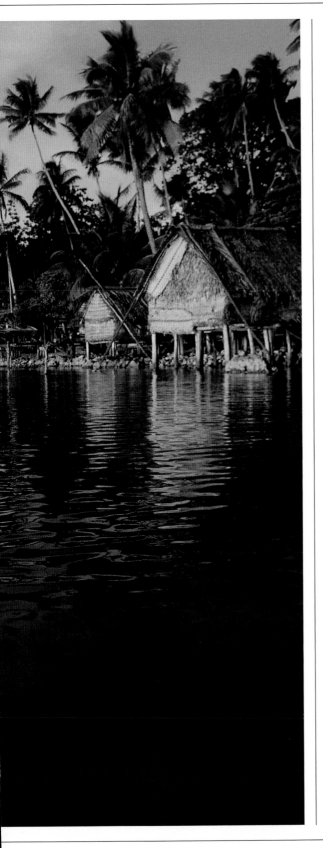

A number of recent military coups in response to growing racial tension and political conflict between ethnic Fijians and Indo-Fijians have caused thousands of Indo-Fijians to flee the country. Some worry that the political instability could further disrupt the tourist economy on which Fiji now depends.

MARIND-ANIM

Population: 10,000
Location: Papua New Guinea
Language family: Marind

Traditional inhabitants of New Guinea's southern coast, the Marind-anim lived in Irian Jaya, an Indonesian province that recently declared itself to be independent West Papua. They were a flamboyant society known for head-hunting raids, often far afield, and for elaborate ceremonies and mythology. Their sexual practices drew the attention of many anthropologists and medical specialists.

The Marind-anim were divided into two groups, as were most of the south coast peoples; each group had its own mythology and specific ceremonial responsibilities toward the other group. Each boy was appointed a *binahor* father from the opposite group, and the man would undertake to inseminate the boy anally on regular occasions until the boy attained physical maturity. In this culture, semen was considered the source of male growth, life, and fertility in general; its regular ingestion was thought to benefit both men and women, fortifying them and increasing fecundity.

The Marind-anim believed that the semen of a man's entire patrilineal lineage was needed for conception. As a result, a woman was obliged to copulate with her husband and his male kinsmen on a regular basis; she also did so on occasions when semen was needed by men for medicinal or ritual purposes. According to early 20th-century studies by a Dutch medical team, this custom led to a high incidence of genital tract infection and consequent sterility in women. The Marind-anim thus suffered from a very low birthrate, which they made up for by capturing children during head-hunting raids on neighboring tribes.

Two young girls bathe in the warm tropical waters of the Trobriands, a coral archipelago off the coast of Papua New Guinea.

The ceremony, mythology, and sexual practices of the Marind-anim, as well as their cults of warfare and head-hunting, were brought to an end by the Dutch colonial presence and subsequent Indonesian dominance over Irian Jaya (since 1962). With their traditional culture severely repressed by colonial authorities, the Marind-anim embraced Christianity and were assimilated into Indonesian society.

MIDDLE SEPIK

Population: 123,000
Location: Papua New Guinea
Language family: Several language families

Because of their highly developed art and architectural styles, the Middle Sepik River peoples are probably among the best known groups in New Guinea. Their now famous *haus tambaran* (spirit house), a ceremonial longhouse with a high, overhanging roof, was the model for the Papua New Guinea High Commission building in Canberra, Australia.

The peoples of the Middle Sepik—Kwoma, Arapesh, Manambu, and Iatmul—share many cultural similarities, including a totemic clan system organized into larger groups and an elaborate system of initiation for boys, organized around sacred bamboo flutes. Secrecy is a major dimension of public life along the Sepik River, and as men grow older, they attain greater knowledge of mythological names and significances. Iatmul and Manambu men debate in public, challenging each other's knowledge of secret totemic names. Among the Iatmul, the journeys of ancestral creators are depicted by a knotted cord, each knot representing a place where an ancestor stopped; knowledge of these creators is a mark of ritual prominence.

Among the Kwoma and other lowland Sepik River peoples, the staple yam is the focus of fertility ceremonies. In recent times, these ceremonies and the boys' initiations have taken on new forms—nonsacred versions performed for the many tourists who visit every year. Art, too, has become important for the tourist market and is an integral part of the local economy. Sepik carvers are renowned for their masks and depictions of local animals and birds.

East Sepik Province has long provided prominent leaders for the nation of Papua New Guinea, includ-

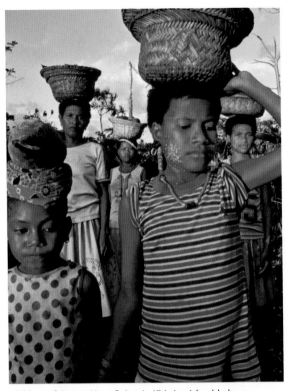

Children of Papua New Guinea's Kiriwina Island balance baskets atop their heads, carrying yams to their village after harvest.

ing Michael Somare, who in 1975 was inaugurated as the first prime minister. The province was also one of the first in the country to incorporate traditional landowning clans, allowing them to become modern business organizations suited to the demands of commercial development.

MOTU

Population: 14,000
Location: Papua New Guinea
Language family: Malayo-Polynesian [Papuan Tip]

Indigenous people of the coastal area around Port Moresby, in southeastern Papua New Guinea, the Motu inhabit a tropical savannah that changes dramatically between dry and wet seasons. Traditionally, the people have been potters, traders, and fishermen, with gardening and hunting as supplementary activities. They have lived closely with the Koita people, who depend on horticulture, and have intermarried extensively with them, exchanging pottery and fish for the Koitans' garden produce.

The Motu became most famous for *hiri*, their

annual trading voyages along the Papuan Gulf coast in outrigger canoes. Under the leadership of a man who had claimed a vision in a dream told him to organize such a journey, as many as 600 men would sail forth on a voyage. They took pots made by Motu women to Elema and the home of the Namau people. There they exchanged the pots for sago and for timber they would make into canoes.

When the traders got back home, the Motu held a *koriko* feast, during which the return gifts were ceremonially distributed. As a result of these voyages, Motuan became a trade language along the south coast and today serves as the other indigenous lingua franca of Papua New Guinea. Tok Pisin, a mixture of Tolai, German, and English, remains the country's dominant language.

One of the central ideas in the Motu religion is *irutahuna*, which can refer to the center of a house, an individual's heart or mind, the central part between two masts of an outrigger, or the base of a single-masted vessel. Clearly, the core or center of an important architectural or organic entity is a space of great sacredness for the Motu. This concept reflects a widespread preoccupation among Melanesians with the vital, germinal core of all things.

TANNESE

Population: 20,000
Location: Vanuatu
Language family: Malayo-Polynesian [South Vanuatu]

The island of Tanna, in the southern part of the Vanuatu archipelago (formerly the New Hebrides), has a fascinating history as well as a rich ceremonial culture. As is the case with villages elsewhere in Vanuatu, a dancing ground called the *nakamal* is situated near each small group of huts. This site is where ceremonies, rituals, and social events occur, including gatherings of men who come

Checking out his face paint, a Tannese man prepares for a ceremony on Tanna Island in Vanuatu.

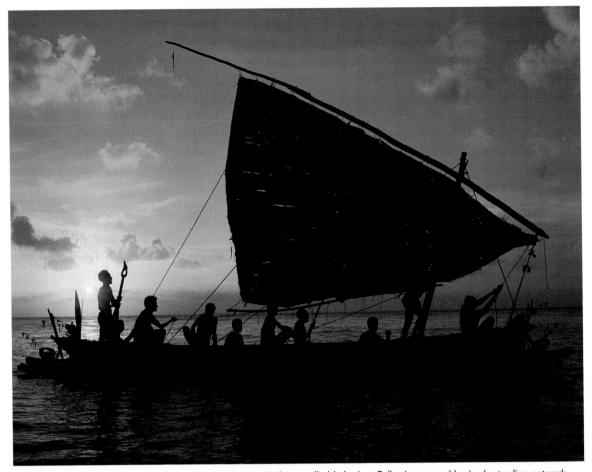

Trobrianders set off in their outrigger canoe to participate in the so-called kula ring. Following a roughly circular trading network, they ceremonially exchange shell ornaments while reinforcing alliances between islands.

to drink kava at the end of the day. The core of men who meet this way is called a "canoe," the local term for a small group related through the male line.

Because the Tannese have a long history of contact with the European world, their culture has in many respects evolved as a reaction to, and an incorporation of, colonial encounters. Among the most important encounters were the notorious "blackbirding" expeditions mounted in the late 1800s by seagoing Australian merchants. These expeditions transported thousands of Tannese—as well as indigenous Melanesian men from eastern New Guinea, the Solomon Islands, and other nearby areas—to Australia, where they were put to work in the cane fields of northern and central Queensland. During this period, more than 100,000 Melanesians were brought to Australia and to plantations and mines on Fiji, New Caledonia, and Samoa, leaving many of their home islands depopulated and their cultures weakened. The name "Tanna" survives as a common surname among descendants of the original laborers.

Tannese efforts to preserve their heritage and maintain distinctiveness in the face of dominant outside forces can be summed up in the term *kastom* (custom), from the Bislama pidgin of Vanuatu. Used throughout the archipelago, the word describes a fusion of old, rediscovered traditions with new or re-created traditions.

The island of Tanna was home to the famous cargo cult started by John Frum. In the 1930s and '40s, Frum preached the return of traditional political power to the Tannese and prayed for the departure of the Europeans. The British acted decisively to crush the movement in 1941, but the legend of John Frum and the influence of his followers continue to this day.

TOLAI

Population: 61,000
Location: Papua New Guinea
Language family: Malayo-Polynesian [New Ireland]

The Tolai inhabit the Gazelle Peninsula at the eastern edge of New Britain Island—site of Rabaul, the most important town in Papua New Guinea and the location for a major Japanese naval base during World War II. This group experienced colonization relatively early in Melanesian terms: Before the Japanese, there were Germans who came in 1884 and Australians who arrived after World War I. As a result, the Tolai became one of the most literate, sophisticated, and vocal groups in all of Papua New Guinea, and they are a dominant force on the national scene today.

Tolai society is organized into groups called *vunatarai,* a term that can refer either to clans—descendants of a particular ancestor associated with a particular everyday leader—or to groups into which the clans are placed. Members of vunatarai hold land, property, and ceremonial objects in common.

Because of the early plantation activity on New Britain, cash cropping has long been a primary component of the village economy, with copra and cocoa the most important crops. The people are famous for the use of shell money known as *tambu,* which consists of nassa shells sewn into plaits about six feet long. A true local currency, tambu is used to purchase food and implements and is exchanged for ceremonial purposes such as bridewealth and mortuary payments.

Art created by the Tolai includes elaborate effigies and masks representing the female spirits of the *tubuan,* entities owned by the clans and considered the incarnation of ritual and sociopolitical power.

TROBRIANDERS

Population: 20,000
Location: Papua New Guinea
Language family: Malayo-Polynesian [Papuan Tip]

Inhabiting Kiriwina and a number of smaller islands off the east coast of Milne Bay Province, Trobriand Islanders are probably among Papua New Guinea's most famous groups—thanks in large part to anthropologist Bronislaw Malinowski, who did pioneering fieldwork on them early in the 20th century. As he discovered and subsequently reported, Trobriand men and women engage in relatively uninhibited sexual activity from an early age. Sexuality is prized and admired as a desirable trait, with both men and women devoting time, attention, and resources to obtaining love and beauty magic.

The Trobrianders also are noted for their involvement in a regional inter-island trading network called the *kula,* which encompasses all the coral and larger islands in the Massim group, off the east coast of Papua New Guinea. In the kula, valuable arm shells and shell necklaces are circulated among the islands by traders who travel in opposite directions around the island group in seagoing canoes. This trading arrangement, essentially a competition for prestige, is not limited to the valuable shell objects: Many islands also contribute specialty items such as clay pots to the trade.

Like most Massim area people, the Trobrianders are organized into clans based on descent through their mothers. But fathers also bequeath important property rights to their children, and these are from their own matrilineal connections.

In recent years, Trobriander artists have become internationally known for their traditional carving of canoe prow boards, figures, and masks, an art form that has caught the attention of the tourist trade.

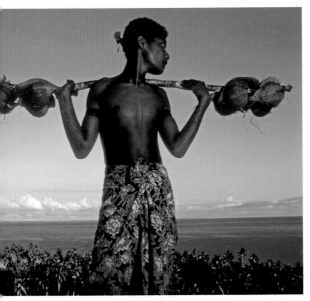

Balancing half a dozen across his shoulders, a young Trobriand man carries coconuts—a staple of the Trobriand Islanders' diet—back to his village.

Polynesia

Largest of the three divisions of Pacific islands, Polynesia's boundaries are roughly drawn as a triangle including Midway and the Hawaiian Islands at the north point, Pitcairn Island and French Polynesia at the east point, and New Zealand at the south point. Contained within that large boundary are numerous other islands and island groups, including Tonga, Tuvalu, Samoa and American Samoa, and Kiribati, a republic that includes the former Christmas Island. The well-known island of Tahiti is part of French Polynesia.

To listen to music from Hawaii, New Zealand, and Tahiti, visit http://worldmusic.nationalgeographic.com.

HAWAIIANS

Population: 80,000
Location: United States
Language family: Germanic (English), Malayo-Polynesian [East-Fijian Polynesian] (Hawaiian)

Native Hawaiians are the descendants of intrepid voyagers whose canoes reached one of the most isolated island groups in the world. Though scholars debate the details, the original Hawaiians probably arrived from the Marquesas Islands at least 1,700 years ago. There may have been a subsequent migration from Tahiti as well, long before Capt. James Cook's 1778 "discovery" of the islands put them on maps made in Europe.

When Cook arrived, he encountered the most highly developed political system in all of Polynesia. Like other Pacific islanders, Hawaiians lacked metal technology, but even without metal tools, their agricultural system produced enough food to support a population conservatively estimated at 300,000. There was an array of chiefs, priests, and craft specialists, whose lifestyles set them apart from the rest of society. Thought to be descended from the gods, Hawaiian chiefs, or *ali'i*, theoretically inherited their positions as the firstborn in a male line. In practice, however, ability—particularly in making war—was a potent factor in establishing and expanding a chiefdom. Women, too, could enjoy ali'i status.

A Hawaiian chief controlled land, especially irrigated fields, together with the labor of commoners. The complex system of chiefdoms was supported by an ideology of supernatural power: Kamehameha I, for example, inherited a war god's title. He used his own skills and European weaponry to unite all the islands by 1810, an unprecedented feat in Hawaii. After the chief's death in 1819, his widow, Ka'ahumanu, became a powerful figure in her own right.

American Protestant missionaries arrived in the islands in 1820. Even before that time, native Hawaiians had begun to suffer severe population losses from measles, influenza, and other introduced diseases for which they had no immunity; by 1854, their numbers

A drummer accompanies young dancers performing against the spectacular backdrop of Waipo'o Falls in Waimea Canyon State Park on the Hawaiian island of Kauai.

had been reduced by at least 75 percent. When foreigners began to establish sugar plantations, they found it necessary to import labor from Asia. These same commercial interests, as well as missionary descendants, began assuming power in the Hawaiian kingdom. In 1893, the last Hawaiian monarch, Queen Liliuokalani, was deposed by a group of mostly American businessmen, who then established a republic in 1894. The United States annexed the islands as a territory in 1898, and in 1959 Hawaii became the 50th state.

Native Hawaiians, now mostly of mixed ancestry, began to increase in number in the 20th century; generally, however, they remained socially inferior not only to "white" Americans but also to the descendants of Asian laborers, who moved into higher economic and political positions after statehood.

In the past half century, though, a new sense of Hawaiian identity has emerged. Hawaiians have self-consciously revived their language and customs such as hula and traditional healing. In 1976, the sailing canoe *Hokule'a* was built according to traditional style. With the help of a navigator from the Caroline Islands, a crew sailed the vessel to Tahiti using only stars, wind, and waves to guide them. Subsequently, *Hokule'a* has voyaged to all the major islands in the Polynesian triangle, inspiring young Hawaiians as well as Tahitians and other Pacific islanders to assert their ethnic pride.

MAORI

Population: 526,000
Location: New Zealand
Language family: Malayo-Polynesian [East-Fijian Polynesian]

The Maori people were the last major group of Polynesians to settle their islands. Legend has it that Kupe, a fisherman and navigator, left his eastern Polynesia homeland of Hawaiki to pursue a huge octopus that had been stealing his bait. He caught up with the creature and killed it; then he began exploring what is now New Zealand. Kupe later sailed home to tell others of uninhabited land available for settlement. Regardless of this story's accuracy, modern scholars agree that Maori began settling in New Zealand about 1,200 years ago, after they had made the longest and last voyage of settlement in Polynesian history.

The new settlers, having come from a warmer climate, faced challenges in adapting to a different environment. In the early days, they depended in part

---

At planting time one labors alone; at harvest, friends are all around.

MAORI PROVERB

---

on the moa, a large flightless bird that Maori hunters eventually destroyed. The people subsisted by fishing, cultivating sweet potatoes, and gathering forest products. Between sweet potato harvests, foraged plant foods such as fern roots provided an important part of the diet.

The largest social unit in traditional Maori life was the *iwi,* often translated as "tribe." Each iwi occupied a distinct territory and was ideally based on descent through males or females from a founding ancestor. Within each iwi were several *hapu,* or sections, whose members also claimed common kinship. Because the Maori could claim descent through either sex, individuals potentially could belong to more than one hapu. Actual membership depended primarily on one's residence and cooperation in group activities.

Each hapu had its own chief, and the chief of the most senior hapu was the paramount chief of the entire iwi. Ideally, the tribal chief was succeeded by his eldest son, but in some groups a senior daughter received special recognition. Conflict was frequent, even within the same iwi. When Europeans eventually reached New Zealand, the Maori quickly gained a reputation for ferocity. Maori tribes were known for enslaving their defeated enemies or perhaps even eating them as a final humiliation.

Like other Polynesians, Maori traditionally believed in an elaborate pantheon of supernatural beings, from which the highest ranking individuals were thought to derive their power. Chiefs presided over major ceremonies, but a specially trained priesthood also existed. Most public rites were celebrated on special open-air platforms that were associated with a particular hapu or iwi.

Europeans were drawn to New Zealand at the end of the 1700s, when they decided to exploit the rich sealing and whaling grounds off the North Island. Protestant missionaries arrived in 1814, and soon other Europeans and Australians followed. In 1840, many Maori chiefs signed the Treaty of Waitangi, which gave sovereignty to England. But from 1860 to 1865—sometimes called the period of the Maori Wars—battles were fought over land rights and questions of sovereignty. These issues remain controversial; now, however, Maori struggles to obtain rights are usually played out in courtrooms.

People identifying themselves as Maori number about 525,000, or between 10 and 15 percent of New Zealand's population. Although they are a more cohesive and visible ethnic group than their Hawaiian relatives, they have followed some of the same strategies for cultural survival. Exhibits of traditional arts and crafts have toured overseas with success, while younger artists are making their own statements about ethnic identity. Maori language schools have provided models for those in Hawaii.

NEW ZEALANDERS

Population: 2.9 million
Location: New Zealand
Language family: Germanic

While the indigenous Maori have populated New Zealand, with its two main islands and some 140 smaller ones, for at least a millennium, settlers of European origin began to arrive in significant numbers only since the mid-1800s. They now represent about 80 percent of the nation's population.

New Zealand was first sighted by Dutch explorer Abel Tasman in 1642. Under attack from Maori, he got only a quick glimpse before sailing off. Other Dutch explorers got a better look and named the islands Nieuw Zeeland, for the Zeeland province of the Netherlands. Within a hundred years, European and American seal hunters and whalers were stopping there, until both the seal and whale populations were depleted.

About the time of an 1840 treaty between the British and Maori, the first groups of British and Australian settlers came to the North Island, where 76 percent of New Zealand's population lives today. They began to farm and herd sheep, starting immense flocks that by the late 20th century had grown so large, the sheep in New Zealand outnumbered the humans, twelve to one. With refrigerated shipping, New Zealanders began exporting meat as well as wool, adding to their economic success.

Anglican missionaries settled the South Island and gave it the unabashedly British feel it still has today, with its fine homes, gardens, and the elegant neo-Gothic cathedral in the city of Christchurch. The South Island's population sorted itself into a mainly English northern end and a Scottish south-

Traditional tattoos cover the face of a Maori man. A cloak made from feathers of the kiwi—a New Zealand symbol—covers his shoulders.

ern one, as clearly witnessed in the place names: Dunedin and Invercargill are the principal southern cities. Today, Anglicans represent almost half of the 40 percent of New Zealand's Protestants, including Presbyterians and Methodists. Some 13 percent of New Zealanders are Roman Catholic.

Other immigrants came to New Zealand—Polish, Lebanese, and Chinese, who flocked there during the gold rush of the 1860s. In recent decades new immigrants have arrived mostly from South Asia as well as other South Pacific islands. All New Zealanders, including Maori, share the nickname "Kiwi," after the round, brown, flightless bird that has become the emblem of the nation. When the New Zealanders developed the Chinese gooseberry into a fuzzy-skinned fruit now popular worldwide, they naturally gave it their favorite name.

New Zealanders revel in their diverse landscape and take to its hills, glacier-carved mountains, rivers, lakes, volcanic thermal springs, and beaches as often as possible. Hiking—or, as Kiwis call it, tramping—is a favorite pastime, especially along the South Island's famous Milford and Routeburn Tracks. On weekends many people spend time in beach houses called "cribs" on the South Island and "bachs" on the North Island.

As the demand for wool has declined, so has the raising of sheep, and New Zealanders now focus more on lumbering and the export of dairy products. They also encourage adventure tourism, which brings in thousands of tourists each year, not only for the more staid possibilities, such as trekking, but for the bigger thrills such as skydiving and bungee jumping off dramatic cliffs. New Zealand's spectacular scenery also draws filmmakers, providing the backdrop for recent Hollywood productions such as *King Kong, The Chronicles of Narnia,* and the *Lord of the Rings,* as well as the country's own burgeoning film industry.

New Zealanders celebrate many holidays with the same traditions as the British, and their cuisine follows a number of British preferences, with the Sunday roast typically being lamb, not beef. ANZAC Day, an important national holiday, commemorates the sacrifices of Australian and New Zealand armed forces at the Battle of Gallipoli in World War I, in which New Zealand's casualties were higher per capita than any other country's.

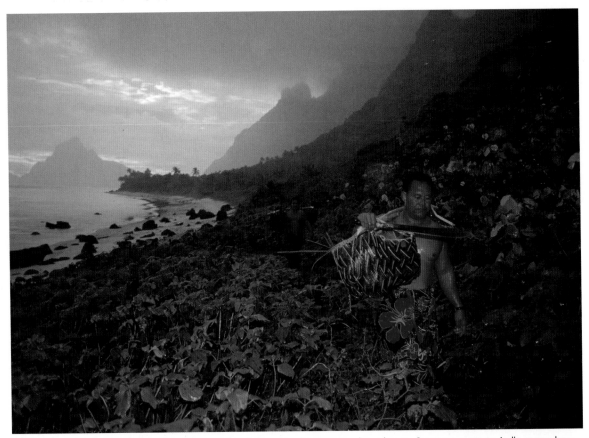

A Samoan trudges home, carrying his machete and baskets made of woven pandanus leaves. Samoan women typically weave baskets and mats, which are exchanged ceremonially.

SAMOANS

Population: 370,000
Location: Samoa
Language family: Malayo-Polynesian [East-Fijian Polynesian]

Since 1900, Samoans have been divided into two polities. Eastern Samoa is a territory of the United States, while the western islands—ruled first by Germany, and then by New Zealand until 1962—are independent. Samoans settled here more than 3,000 years ago, and for centuries the people have regularly interacted with Tongans and Fijians. Today their islands are home to the world's second largest concentration of full-blooded Polynesians: more than 60,000 in American Samoa and some 165,000 in independent (formerly Western) Samoa.

Traditional Samoan life was based on horticulture, with taro and breadfruit considered the primary crops. Men carried out more strenuous tasks, including clearing and planting the land, fishing beyond the reefs, and even cooking food. Women collected wild plants and gathered small sea creatures in the lagoons and reefs. They also wove mats, and these continue to be important exchange items on ceremonial occasions such as weddings.

Samoans typically lived in self-contained communities made up of a number of kin groups that were related through descent from either male or female ancestors, or by adoption or marriage. Still basic to the Samoan social structure is the *matai* system, in which chiefly titles are assumed on the basis of birth, ability, or a combination of the two factors. Titles are of two kinds, *ali'i* (head chiefs) and *tulafale* (orators), and are ranked within the village and in wider political contexts. The degree of authority exercised by titleholders varies according to rank; for example, a council of matai exercises supreme authority over village affairs.

When Samoa became independent, only titleholders were allowed to vote and to be candidates in general elections. This changed in 1990, when a referendum created universal suffrage; only matai can be candidates for most of the parliamentary seats, however.

During aboriginal times, matai also served as religious practitioners, and they were responsible for the worship of family gods. But teachers from the London Missionary Society eventually began their work in Samoa, and today about half the people of independent Samoa are affiliated with the Congregational Church. About one-quarter are Catholics, and the rest are Methodists, Mormons, and members of other faiths.

Today Samoans have become noteworthy for the way they have spread through the English-speaking world: More people live away from their home islands than on them. In New Zealand, there are more than 100,000 Samoans, and about the same number live in Hawaii and the 49 other states. Several Samoans are, or have been, members of professional football teams. But no matter where Samoans live, they maintain ethnic identity through their own church congregations. They have also revived the practice of elaborate tattooing, which is done by using traditional instruments, such as toothed combs and mallets, to tap pigments into the skin.

TAHITIANS

Population: 131,000
Location: French Polynesia
Language family: Malayo-Polynesian [East-Fijian Polynesian]

Many romantic images of the South Seas were created when French and English explorers first met Tahitians in the late 18th century. Before these early encounters, there may have been as many as 30,000 islanders; afterward, the population declined for a time. (In 1999, estimates exceeded 100,000, though, including a number of people with mixed ancestry.) Like other speakers of Polynesian languages, the early Tahitians settled their homeland after making long canoe voyages from Southeast Asia. These voyagers passed through Tonga and Samoa before arriving in what are now called the Society Islands.

Traditionally, Tahitians divided their society into three classes: nobility (ari'i), commoners, and servants. Nobles inherited their rank from their fathers. Usually, the firstborn male would become the heir, though women might also enjoy high status.

Because people at the highest level of society claimed descent from the gods, the culture was a complex mixture of religion, status, and power. Chiefs received tribute from lower ranks, but competition among those who were claiming power in different parts of the island group meant that no ruler could rise above all of the others. That situation changed when Europeans arrived and introduced new weapons and different political ideas to the islands.

> **Ferocious is the centipede, but scared of the chicken.**
> SAMOAN PROVERB

Though Tahitians were among the first Polynesians to be converted to Christianity, they originally recognized a ranked series of gods. Some of these deities were worshiped by an entire region, while others received the devotions of families or individuals. Drawn from the ranks of the ari'i were the priests who officiated at major ceremonies involving whole districts; many of them were thought to have the power to practice sorcery.

People believed that divine anger could cause untimely death, but they also recognized death through aging as a normal occurrence. Funeral rituals depended on the deceased's social status: For example, the body of a high-ranking Tahitian was exposed on a covered platform, or ghost house, before burial, and lengthy and elaborate expressions of mourning were a high chief's prerogative.

Tahitians used to support themselves by gardening and fishing. The men fished, did construction work, and made tools, weapons, and canoes. Women made bark cloth, a very important item for trade, formal gift-giving, and clothing. They also wove mats, hats, and baskets from the leaves of the pandanus plant.

Both sexes shared the gardening chores, raising a variety of crops that included yams and sweet potatoes. The numerous coconut trees provided not only food but also craft materials. Today Tahitians participate in modern economic activities including tourism and the cultivation of black pearls. Traditional dancing, featuring rapid hip movements accompanied by frenetic drumming, has become a staple of Pacific island tourist performances and a potent symbol of identity.

Tahiti has long been tied to France, which made it part of a protectorate in 1842 and today includes it within the Overseas Territory of French Polynesia. In recent decades, France was criticized for carrying out nuclear tests in other parts of the Society Islands. The tests ended in 1996, and now funds for compensation and other French government subsidies provide much of the income for Tahitians. For more than 70 years, the people of Tahiti have pressed France for greater freedom, and they have recently achieved some increase in local autonomy.

TONGANS

Population: 100,000
Location: Tonga
Language family: Malayo-Polynesian
[East-Fijian Polynesian]

In all of Polynesia, only Tongans can boast that their islands were never ruled by a foreign power. Settled some 3,000 years ago—like Samoa, whose chiefs Tongan nobility once married—the Tongan archipelago is the largest group at the western end of the Polynesian triangle of islands. Of the Tongans there today, almost 70 percent of them live on the main island of Tongatapu.

Tongan society seems always to have been extremely centralized and stratified. Traditionally, the supreme ruler held the title of Tu'i Tonga; he claimed descent from the gods and had power that was originally both sacred and secular. As the population grew, however, the Tu'i Tonga delegated more responsibility to his close relatives, who became chiefs in their own areas.

The political instability that ensued led to a separation of powers, with the Tu'i Tonga remaining sacred ruler and someone else becoming secular leader. Later, the secular leader delegated authority to his son, creating a new royal lineage and title. The Tu'i Tonga's sister—Tu'i Tonga Fefine—was also a powerful figure, but her oldest daughter—the Tamaha—was the most sacred being of all. Theoretically all Tongans, including the reigning monarch, trace their kinship affiliations and relative social rank from one of these four chiefly titleholders.

A significant feature of Tongan life was the superiority of women as sisters over men as brothers, meaning that brothers were expected to defer to their sisters and sisters' children. The higher status had a material basis, in that women created valuable property such as mats, baskets, and bark cloth, to be exchanged at important events. They also prepared the pepper plant–based kava drink featured on social and political occasions.

Christian missionaries brought major changes to traditional Tongan life, including an increase in the political instability that was created by newly arriving European commercial interests. In 1826, a Wesleyan Methodist mission was established, and by 1845, a Tongan newly converted to Protestantism had brought political defeat to the Tu'i Tonga, who was supported by Catholic missionaries.

Proclaimed King George Tupou I and guided by Methodist missionaries, he modeled his rule after British constitutional monarchy. A constitution was created in 1875, giving the sovereign ownership of all the land while designating a class of hereditary nobles as trustees and guaranteeing all adult males a farm and village allotment.

Today, the independent Kingdom of Tonga remains centralized and traditional. The present king, fourth in the Tupou dynasty, appoints a cabinet that is the highest governing body. Although a pro-

> A fair wind blowing
> on a tattered sail.
> TONGAN PROVERB

democracy movement emerged in 1994, the monarchy and its associated nobility appear firmly in control. Tonga relies heavily on foreign aid and on income that is earned elsewhere but sent back by Tongans who migrated; more than 30,000 of them now reside in New Zealand. A number of migrant men have achieved prominence in sports, including rugby and boxing.

Fast Train or Slow Boat?

Over 3,000 years before Capt. James Cook first encountered the Polynesian islands, a remarkable group of seafaring explorers landed on their uninhabited shores, completing the greatest migration in human history. These proto-Polynesians had learned to harness the Pacific winds and currents to power their exploration, and they did so without European navigation technologies like the compass, astrolabe, and sextant. But while these open-water voyages landed humans on the shores of paradise, the conditions forcing their migrations were anything but.

Calibrated radiocarbon dating from early Holocene human encampments in continental East Asia shows that by 9,000 years ago people had begun domesticating a few wild types of a tall grass found throughout the region. Over the next few millennia, the practice grew and rice spread through South and East Asia.

Agricultural intensity led to a surplus of rice, and new domesticates led to denser populations. This was not much of a problem as long as these early farmers were able to expand through peninsular Southeast Asia and the nearby islands of Indonesia, the Philippines, and Taiwan. Eventually, however, expansion became a problem: Fertile land was at a premium. Humans had effectively invented the notion of real estate.

Space race

The competition for space fueled intense rivalries. Rather than going to war, some turned their gaze east toward the Pacific, emboldened by a novel double-hulled outrigger canoe that had been perfected

sailing through island Southeast Asia. Packing every known plant and animal domesticate into their newly invented vessels, these daring agriculturalists set off to colonize islands they didn't yet know existed. Along with breadfruit, taro, and banana, the tropical farmers brought with them breeding pairs of pigs, dogs, and

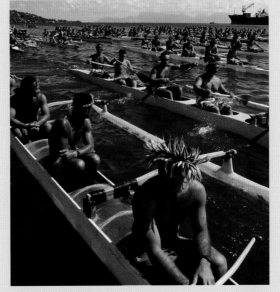

Tahitians await the start of an outrigger canoe race in French Polynesia.

rats, fast-reproducing food sources capable of thriving in unknown conditions.

The exact route of those first migrations is still hotly debated, and historians tend to fall into one of two camps. The "express train" theory proposes that the Polynesian ancestors left from Taiwan speaking Austronesian languages and rapidly colonized the South Pacific in a straight migration eastward, depositing their people and culture along the way. The "slow boat" theory argues that the expansion originated in Asia and proceeded slowly through Melanesia before continuing to Polynesia.

Trade networks widen

It is fairly certain that around 3,500 years ago the first settlers came into the region: a people known as the Lapita, distinguished by a pottery style first discovered in the 1950s. Using Fiji as a home base, the Lapita people systematically colonized the Tongan and Samoan islands, the Marshalls, and much of Micronesia, depositing their characteristic pottery style across western Oceania. The oral histories of people living today throughout the region largely corroborate this account and serve as a good instance of the genetic and archaeological data supporting ancestral storylines.

The Lapita seafarers established a trade network. Some of the best evidence for this comes from obsidian, a naturally occurring glass formed by the rapid cooling of volcanic lava, which can be pinpointed to its original source based on geochemical analysis. Obsidian, widely used in Oceania for tool construction, has been found on some coral atolls and determined to have been imported from islands hundreds of miles away.

People certainly continued east, extending the Melanesian trade networks to distances greater than ever in human history. They colonized the remote Marquesas, Hawaiian, and Easter Islands, and they probably established contact with coastal South America, bringing its sweet potato back with them. The Lapita made it as far east as Tonga and Samoa—but suddenly, in what remains one of the great mysteries of the Polynesian expansion, they disappeared. None of their famous pottery can be found in the more remote archipelagos of the region of Oceania.

Micronesia

Lying primarily north of the Equator, Micronesia spreads to the northwest among the three divisions of Pacific islands. It includes the Caroline Islands, the Marshall Islands, the Mariana Islands, the Gilbert Islands, Palau, and Nauru. Some of these islands—the Carolines, without Palau—have formed the Federated States of Micronesia, which has "free association status" with the United States, bringing U.S. investments. Kosrae, Pohnpei, Chuuk, and Yap are the four states within the federation. Deposits of bauxite, iron, and phosphate represent the mineral riches of these islands, especially the Carolines. Nauru, an island republic within Micronesia, also holds significant phosphate deposits. The Marshall Islands have less economic potential; they are coral islands and atolls from which the major exports are fish and coconut products. Bikini Atoll, part of the Marshall Islands, was used by the United States for more than 20 atomic bomb tests during the 1940s and 1950s. Efforts to repopulate the island began in the 1970s, but as of today no one lives there yet.

CHAMORROS

Population: 83,000
Location: Guam, Northern Mariana Islands
Language family: Malayo-Polynesian [Chamorro]

The Pacific people having the longest history of contact with the Western world are the Chamorros of Guam and the Mariana Islands. In 1521, Ferdinand Magellan landed on their islands while in command of the first expedition to circumnavigate the world. Spain claimed the islands in 1565 but established settlements there only in 1668. Three decades of war and disease followed, and by 1710 fewer than 4,000 Chamorros remained. Today, an estimated 150,000 people live on Guam, while 72,000 reside in the Commonwealth of the Northern Marianas. Many are of mixed ancestry, with forebears who may have been Spanish, Filipino, American, Asian, or perhaps Micronesian (from the Caroline Islands). Regardless of their ancestry, though, Chamorros are linked by a language believed to be related to ones spoken in the Philippines.

The original Chamorros wore very little clothing, and early European observers were impressed with their physiques. They were fishers and gardeners, as well as the only Pacific islanders who, when first contacted, cultivated rice as a staple crop. Men did most of the gardening and some of the fishing,

Yapese women perform a ceremonial dance on the Yap Islands in the Federated States of Micronesia. In traditional Yapese culture, men and women perform highly segmented roles.

built houses and canoes, and created stone structures. Women made pottery, cooked, gathered food in the jungle, and fished with hand nets on the reefs. They were particularly skilled at working with pandanus fiber to create fine mats, sails, hats, baskets, and boxes, some of which were traded in places as far away as the Caroline Islands. The betel nut, chewed with pepper plant and lime, was the Chamorros' preferred stimulant.

Traditional Chamorro society was based on clans whose membership was inherited through females. These clans were ranked to form separate social classes, with women of the upper class holding high positions in society. Within the clans themselves, rank was determined by seniority, and the senior member of each group would use clan property for the benefit of all.

Today Chamorros are overwhelmingly Christians; the majority are Catholics, reflecting 17th-century Spanish missionization. A form of ancestor worship seems to have prevailed originally, and at that time some individuals were thought to have been professional sorcerers.

Chamorro history has taken many turns since Europeans first made contact. Under early Spanish rule, the Marianas population was moved to Guam and not returned until 1815, when other Micronesians were also settled on the islands. After the Spanish-American War, the United States took over Guam, and Germany purchased other Mariana Islands. After World War I, Japan ruled Germany's old possessions as a League of Nations mandate. World War II brought bloody fighting to all the islands. Today Guam is an unincorporated territory of the United States, while the Northern Marianas have been an independent commonwealth in association with the U.S. since 1986. Hence the Chamorros operate in a modern political and economic world, while their language links them to the lives they once led.

CHUUK ISLANDERS

Alternate name: Trukese
Population: 50,000
Location: Federated States of Micronesia
Language family: Malayo-Polynesian [Micronesian]

Chuuk (formerly Truk) Islanders live on a group of islands surrounded by coral reefs enclosing a large lagoon. After sailing there in outrigger canoes, their ancestors settled these islands by the beginning of the Christian era. They eventually established and maintained trade relationships with nearby atolls, obtaining pandanus mats and sennit cord made from plant fiber and occasionally receiving canoes built to order. In return, they supplied the atolls with a plant dye used as a cosmetic.

Chuuk was divided into small districts, within which households spread out to form loose neighborhoods. These households were made up of extended families formed by a group of related women; husbands generally lived on their wives' land. Clans and smaller kin groups, such as lineages, were also based on descent through females. In each district, certain lineages claimed the right to particular lands, and for each district this claim was the basis for chieftainship. Though lineages were based on descent through women, the senior male in the line of senior women usually served as chief. The oldest man in the lineage generally acted as a kind of symbolic chief, receiving gifts of food as his right. Conflict often occurred over just which lineage member had the right to succeed as chief and thereby control land and other resources.

While coconuts provided food, drink, and fiber for cord, breadfruit was the traditional staple food, preserved by fermentation in pits. Gardens also included taro, plants for cosmetic dye, and sugarcane. Men gardened, prepared food in bulk, fished in deep waters, engaged in war and political affairs, built canoes and houses, and worked with wood, shells, and stone. Women wove with hibiscus and banana fibers on looms, and they plaited mats and baskets. They also prepared routine meals, did inshore fishing, and took the main responsibility for child care.

Since the middle of the 20th century, the people have been either Protestant or Catholic Christians, but Chuuk Islanders traditionally believed in a wide

Marshallese offload their possessions from boats on their return to Bikini Atoll. U.S. nuclear testing there in 1946 caused contamination.

variety of spirits, some of whom lived in the sky and were especially important. Chiefly clans derived part of their power from association with these spirits and the magic lore they controlled. There were spirits who controlled particular crafts and others who brought illness. Sickness was commonly believed to be caused by malevolent spirits, who might be invoked by a sorcerer to harm the infirm. Every person was thought to possess two souls—one good, the other bad—and at death, the good soul went to the sky world, while the bad one became a potentially dangerous ghost.

Like many other Micronesians, Chuuk Islanders became the subjects of successive colonial regimes. Between the First and Second World Wars, Japan administered Chuuk as a League of Nations mandate and developed the islands as a military base. United States troops mounted an invasion in World War II, bringing much suffering and loss of life; Chuuk later became part of the Trust Territory of the Pacific Islands, administered by the United States for the United Nations. After two decades of negotiation, in 1986 the Federated States of Micronesia (FSM) became self-governing in free association with the United States. Chuuk is one of the four states making up the FSM; its population of more than 50,000 includes people living on nearby atolls. Because "free association" means that the islanders can easily immigrate to the United States, many have done just that. Today a number of Chuuk communities are found in Hawaii and California.

MARSHALLESE

Population: 60,000
Location: Marshall Islands
Language family: Malayo-Polynesian [Micronesian]

The people of the Marshall Islands became best known to the wider world in 1946, when the United States began a series of nuclear tests on tiny Bikini Atoll. They are descendants of seafarers who came to these islands almost 2,000 years ago. They speak a language that is most closely related to those of Fiji, Nauru, and the nearby Caroline Islands.

Five small islands, 29 atolls, and hundreds of reefs form the islands' double chain, with those in the south having a more favorable, reliable climate. Gardening, fishing, and reef diving traditionally provided sustenance for the Marshallese. On northern atolls, arrowroot, pandanus, and coconut were cultivated, along with some breadfruit. Southern atolls enjoyed larger breadfruit yields, together with some taro.

Marshallese men always looked to the sea, where they fished from canoes that they had made. Women dominated activities on the land, making mats, baskets, and clothing from pandanus and coconut fronds. Marshallese women also prepared meals, cared for children, fished occasionally, and collected seafood from the reefs.

On such small islands, land was inevitably a key factor in social life. On larger isles with more resources, the control of land permitted chiefs to exercise considerable power over those who depended on them for access. Links through females were basic to social organization—rights to land were inherited through women—but the paramount chiefs, who claimed descent from ancient gods, were male.

Generally, social arrangements were flexible enough to provide people with what they needed for their livelihoods; residence and cooperation in socially valued activities could give individuals claim to resources that they might not have received through descent alone.

The Marshallese formerly believed in many kinds of spiritual beings, both male and female. Major deities were associated with constellations, while others were believed to inhabit specific local sites. Most people believed that ancestor spirits were able to exert a direct effect on their daily lives. The Marshallese were first missionized by American Protestants, and today almost all adhere to some form of Christianity.

After living under different colonial powers and surviving the trials of World War II, the Marshallese were included in the U.S.-administered Trust Territory of the Pacific Islands in 1947. A Compact of Free Association with the U.S. became effective in 1986, creating the Republic of the Marshall Islands (RMI). The United States pays for the use of a missile testing base at Kwajalein. The United States also continues to compensate the Marshallese for the health and social problems that have resulted from past nuclear testing.

PALAUANS

Population: 15.000
Location: Palau
Language family: Malayo-Polynesian [Palauan]

The westernmost Caroline Islands are home to the Palauans, whose proximity to Asia has strongly influenced their culture over the years. The first Palauans are thought to have arrived in these islands more than 2,000 years ago; they were voyagers who perhaps came directly from Southeast Asia and chose to settle here rather than venture farther east. Today, the people speak an Austronesian language that is more closely related to those of western Indonesia and the Philippines than to those of islands to the east. They have also marked out a political path separate from other Micronesians by establishing themselves as a self-governing nation: the Republic of Palau, or Belau.

In the prehistoric past, Palauans built inland villages on elaborate stone foundations. The village meetinghouse, or *bai*, was the center of the basic social unit, which not only controlled land for homes and taro patches but also had responsibilities regarding chiefly titles, certain valuables, and ceremonial functions. Members were related either through maternal or, less often, paternal ties, and adoption was common within this extended kin group. Rank governed relations among siblings, among houses within a village, between titles in a political council, and among villages in the largest political grouping. Chiefly titles were ranked according to the social value of local land holdings, and titleholders assigned land to families according to their needs.

Fishing and taro cultivation provided the basis for traditional subsistence, with fishing symbolizing male virtue and taro cultivation serving as the emblem of female productivity. This division was paralleled by the control of valuables: Women exchanged hammered turtle-shell trays, while men used beads of foreign origin. Other items exchanged between districts depended on local resources and included canoe sails, pottery, and wooden tools.

Like the rest of the Caroline Islanders, Palauans lived under a succession of colonial rulers: Spanish, Germans, Japanese, and finally Americans, who administered the Trust Territory of the Pacific Islands under the auspices of the United Nations.

> You don't know if a coconut contains milk until you open it.
> PALAUAN PROVERB

Because of its location, the Palauan archipelago was especially subject to Japanese influence during the period between the World Wars. Japanese men sometimes married Palauan women, and even today Japanese is spoken on Angaur Island, in addition to the local language. During World War II, Japan used the archipelago as a base from which to stage its attack on the Philippines.

Palau was the last of the four political units to emerge from what had been the Trust Territory of the Pacific Islands; the others were the Northern Marianas, the Federated States of Micronesia, and the Republic of the Marshall Islands. Negotiations were delayed because the Palauans, in 1981, adopted a constitution declaring their islands a nuclear-free zone—a sticking point for the United States, which hoped to maintain a strategic presence in the area. In 1994, the impasse was broken, and from that year on Palauans assumed a new national identity as citizens of a republic.

YAPESE

Population: 6,000
Location: Federated States of Micronesia
Language family: Malayo-Polynesian [Yapese Oceanic]

The Yapese ranged widely as sailors in outrigger canoes from their base in the western Carolines, where they live on four islands surrounded by a coral reef, now part of the Federated States of Micronesia. Despite historically close contact with a number of other groups, the Yapese differ from most of their Micronesian neighbors in both their language and social organization.

Yapese is an Malayo-Polynesian language that some linguists tie to those spoken in the Melanesian Islands of Vanuatu far to the southwest. The Yapese today also speak English, the state's official language. Unlike most other Micronesians, the Yapese reckon descent patrilineally for the purposes of land ownership, which traditionally has determined status and rank within and between Yapese village communities. Through their mother's line, though, Yapese belong to clans to which they can turn for emotional support and for refuge should they have a falling-out with their patrilineal kin.

In other respects, the Yapese practiced the same subsistence activities organized by gender as other Micronesians, with the men responsible for providing fish and the women cultivating taro and yams. Like the nearby Palauns, the Yapese constructed their villages using large amounts of stone for foundations, pathways, seating areas, piers, and retaining walls. Yapese men also routinely sailed to Palau and Guam for the arduous and hazardous task of quarrying and transporting the large coral stone discs used as a kind of money in ritual exchanges on Yap, although they had no value for trade with other peoples.

The basic Yapese social unit is the family, or

tabinaw, defined as a group who eats together. Typically, this group includes a married couple and their children, and it can include the wives and children of married sons before they establish their own households. Traditionally, rank and status operated within the family and was manifest in the use of restricted cooking (and eating) pots for different family members, although this practice is fading.

The Yapese shared the area-wide experiences of Spanish and German colonization, Catholic missionizing, and Japanese and U.S. occupation in the 20th century—as well as U.S. bombing during World War II—culminating in the writing of a constitution for the Federated States of Micronesia in 1978, with sovereignty finalized in 1986. Many Yapese are now Roman Catholic, but the people persist in animistic beliefs linking female spirits to the sea and male spirits to the land, where they pose threats to the subsistence activities of humans of the opposite sex.

A number of changes in recent decades have combined to erode certain traditional structures of Yapese life. With about half of Yapese men working for wages, it becomes difficult for them to keep up with their contribution of fish, and they have had to resort to buying canned fish and meat for family meals, lowering their traditional status. Yapese youth spend less time learning cultural traditions from older men in the village men's house and more time with peers, sometimes with undesirable consequences. And young men and women are more likely to meet a future spouse on the school bus traveling to the central high school than they are within family-approved villages.

Yapese men carry the heavy stone disks often used in ceremonial exchanges on their islands. Larger disks may be left in place, even when they change ownership.

Notes on the World's Scales

In something as simple as a sequence of notes to form a musical scale, a culture expresses its unique identity and its relation to others around the world.

The neck of a guitar provides opportunities to make a limitless number of notes. Place your finger anywhere along the string, pluck the string, and you hear a pitch. But the pitch you find along the string might not sound like any note you've heard before. Beginning guitar players learn quickly that the right notes lie only in a few places on the instrument. But what about all the space—and all the possible notes—in between?

Musical traditions around the world vary in many ways: in their melodies, instruments, rhythms, and even in what notes they use. Western music uses only a certain set of notes, which splits an octave into twelve half-steps. Our word "octave" is based on the Latin root *octo*, eight, because of the seven whole steps within an octave and the next note up, the eighth, that finishes the scale. The word "octave" can, however, be used to talk about scale systems with any number of notes.

The pentatonic scale

One of the most common ways of splitting an octave into a scale is to use only five notes in each octave. Pentatonic (five-note) scales are used in traditions from folk music in the United States to percussion ensembles in Indonesia. Playing the five adjacent black keys on a piano produces one pentatonic scale, and there are many other varieties.

The sound of a pentatonic scale often makes Western listeners think of Asia, and not without reason. Musical traditions throughout Asia rely on pentatonic scales: the Indonesian gamelan, for example. A gamelan is a musical ensemble based primarily on a set of metal and wood percussion instruments. Percussion instruments are the core of the ensemble: The word "gamelan" comes from the Javanese word

for "striking with a hammer," and the melodic instruments of the gamelan are metallophones, made of metal bars laid in a single row and struck with hammers. Gamelan music may also include voices, strings and wind instruments, and it is often used in religious ceremonies or to accompany dance or shadow puppet performances.

Gamelan music uses a few different scale systems. Each percussion instrument is tuned when it is made and can only play the notes of a particular scale. Instruments from one ensemble, then, cannot necessarily play with instruments of a different group, and even within one gamelan some instruments will never be played at the same time.

One of the two most common gamelan tuning systems is *slendro*, a pentatonic scale. The five notes in slendro are spaced roughly evenly in the octave; this means that the notes do not follow the whole and half steps used in Western music. The other common scale system is called *pelog*, which is a system of seven notes, only five of which are used in any given piece of music. Pelog splits the notes of one octave into seven approximately even intervals. Any five-note subset of pelog, then, will sound different from the five-note scale of slendro, because the pitches of the notes in the two systems are different. The two tuning systems are associated with different moods in gamelan music, with slendro used for more melancholy pieces than pelog.

While guitarists have to determine the intonation of the notes they play, tuning their strings and then putting their left-hand fingers down in the proper place, gamelan players are more like pianists, with the instrument determining what pitches they produce. Unlike pianists, though, gamelan musicians never play alone.

A Mongol girl dances the traditional "wild horse" on a Mongolian steppe, accompanied by stringed instruments with necks shaped like the heads of horses. Horses play a central role in Mongol culture, and even young children train for summer races.

A note produced by only one instrument is considered incomplete in gamelan music. To play a complete note, two performers must play the same note on a pair of nearly identical instruments. When gamelan instruments are made, they are crafted in pairs, with the two instruments of a pair tuned to slightly different notes. Played simultaneously, the two instruments produce nearly identical sound waves, which interfere with each other to create a characteristic shimmery sound.

Microtones and bent notes

The notes that gamelan musicians can use are limited by the instruments they play; once the instruments of an ensemble are made, the pitches are set. Other musical traditions value the ability to adjust pitches delicately. The basic structure of composition in Indian classical music, for example, uses microtones (pitches more closely spaced than half steps, the smallest interval in Western music) and bent notes (notes with contoured pitch).

A distinction is often made in Indian classical music between Carnatic, southern Indian, and Hindustani, or northern Indian. The traditions are very different, but they share some basic concepts, including the role of the scale system in compositions. Like Western music, Indian classical music uses seven named notes, or *swara*. Certain swara can be sharp or flat, to create a twelve-tone scale like the Western scale.

Indian classical music is based on a raga, which has a function somewhere between a scale and a melody. The raga specifies what notes will be used in a piece, to some extent what order they should be used in, and the intonation of the notes. One particular raga can call for an extra-flat or an extra-sharp note, or it can call for a note that begins at one pitch, veers down, and then comes back to the starting pitch.

These precise intonation requirements mean that an instrument with fixed pitches, like an Indonesian metallophone or a piano, is not ideal for playing

Indian classical music. Traditionally, an Indian ensemble includes three musicians: one playing a tabla drum or other percussion instruments, one playing a drone, and one playing or singing a melody. The percussion maintains an underlying rhythmic structure, while the drone establishes the pitch to which all the notes of the melody relate.

The melody instrument or vocalist must be able to produce very carefully controlled pitches. A traditional Indian melody instrument is the sitar, a lute with a very long neck. Violins, introduced by Westerners, are quite common and accepted melody instruments, and more recently Indian musicians have adapted slide guitars to play traditional music.

Creating a national instrument

Like all parts of musical traditions, the notes and scales of a musical style change over time. The music of Zimbabwe illustrates this. The Shona are the largest ethnic group of Zimbabwe; their folk music is centered on the *mbira,* or thumb piano, which is tuned differently according to each performer and each situation.

The mbira is made of 22 to 28 metal keys mounted on a wooden sounding board. To amplify the instrument, mbira players place the instrument inside a gourd; to create a buzzing sound, they attach metal beads or shells to the bottom of the sounding board. In modern times, the metal keys have been made of sofa springs, bicycle spokes, or any other source of steel, and the buzzing beads and shells have been replaced by bottle caps. A performer uses the thumbs of both hands and the right forefinger to pluck the metal keys of the mbira. Tuning is a matter of personal preference, both in the pitch of any note and in the intervals between notes. The mbira is rarely played on its own; more commonly it is played in pairs or with other instruments, so performers playing together must agree on tuning.

Another major instrument in Zimbabwe is the marimba, a wooden xylophone, which is tuned with equally spaced intervals, using the same pitches as

Members of a Balinese gamelan accompany a dance performance. Gamelan includes instruments such as gongs, bamboo flutes, metallophones, drums, and strings, tuned to play as an ensemble and sometimes incorporating solo or choral vocals.

Western music. The mbira, found throughout southern Africa, is closely identified with tribal cultures, while the marimba has no traditional roots in Zimbabwe—which is precisely why it is now the national instrument there.

In 1960, the area that would become Zimbabwe was still under the rule of the British government, and the black majority of the country wanted white minority rule to end. One political initiative was to create a national instrument, taking inspiration from the marimbas from Central America and other parts of Africa and adding buzzer membranes, like the beads and shells of the mbira. The creators of this instrument wanted to make an instrument that could play both African and Western music, and therefore they tuned it to a Western C-major scale, with the addition of an F-sharp, which is not part of the traditional Western scale. The Zimbabwean marimba has been fully accepted as a national instrument, despite its foreign tuning system and untraditional birth.

Hearing the world in music

The range of world music is astounding. Cultures around the world have developed their own instruments from local materials, their own melodies and lyrics, and their own ways of using music in daily and ritual life. The scale systems of the world are extremely diverse and are closely linked to the notes available on traditional instruments as well as to the cultural importance of music. In South America, tuning systems range from the paired panpipes of Aymara speakers in Peru, which must be played together to include all the notes of a melody, to the practice among the Suyá of Brazil, who listen for the amount a pitch rises rather than any fixed pitch. The Otomí of Mexico similarly assign specific healing qualities to intervals between pitches but place little importance on individual notes.

In contrast to the uniformity of its classical music, the folk music of Europe is extremely varied. The folk songs of Georgia, for example, are almost always performed by an ensemble singing in harmony, with a number of complex tuning systems including the whole-tone pentatonic scale (which you hear when you play the adjacent black keys on a piano). Norwegian traditional music centers around the

Amid some of the many fine flutes he has made, a Bolivian master craftsman, Don Fortunato, plays a panpipe melody.

hardanger fiddle, which plays intervals somewhere between a half step and a whole step. Music played on this instrument involves unusual harmonic effects created by using all the strings as drones throughout a piece and by having extra sympathetic strings, which are never played but which resonate with the notes of the played melody. Traditional music in the United States includes various tunings, such as the blues scale, which is a pentatonic scale with the additional "blue note"—a very flat diminished fifth above the first note of the scale (the first interval in the song "Maria" from *West Side Story* is a diminished fifth).

Today we can witness the interaction of unrelated musical traditions: performers like Krakatau, an Indonesian ensemble that combines elements of pop and jazz with traditional gamelan music, or the Jaipur Kawa Brass Band, which plays jazz inspired by classical Indian music. Despite diversity, there are constants. Musical traditions worldwide include the concept of a scale that determines the relationships of pitches. The notes used in scale systems are the music of this sphere. ■

— *Miranda Weinberg*

EUROPE

EASTERN EUROPE
Kalmyks • Lithuanians • Roma
Romanians & Moldovans • Russians • Ukrainians

CENTRAL EUROPE
Bosnian Muslims • Croats • Czechs • Magyars
Poles • Serbs • Slovaks • Slovenes

SOUTHERN EUROPE
Albanians • Greeks • Italians

WESTERN EUROPE
Basques • Bretons • Catalans • Dutch & Frisians
French • Germans • Portuguese • Spanish

NORTHERN EUROPE
Cornish • Danes • English • Faroese • Finns
Icelanders • Irish • Norwegians • Sami
Scots • Swedes • Welsh

Each December 13, Swedish girls don white gowns and candle
crowns to serenade family members on St. Lucia Day.

Europe has witnessed, over the course of many millennia, an astonishing florescence of settlement and cultural development. From an area that—including the European part of Russia—is less than half the size of North America, streams of influential ideas, technologies, political and legal structures, works of art, literature, music, and other history-making products of human endeavor have poured forth into the rest of the world. Europe and its remarkably diverse peoples have engendered and nurtured many of the ideals that inform and inspire modern society and culture.

Today some geographers question whether Europe should even be considered a continent, attached as it is to Asia in the fashion of a large peninsula. Nevertheless, the traditional division that separates the two is a line that runs south along the Ural Mountains and the Ural River to the Caspian Sea before jogging west along the Caucasus Mountains to the Black Sea. More bodies of water provide other boundaries, and within them are a number of major islands, including Great Britain, Ireland, and Iceland.

Early Europe After Asia, Europe has the world's largest and densest population of any traditionally considered continent: Here, on just 7 percent of Earth's land, live more than three-quarters of a billion people, representing hundreds of distinct ethnic groups and speaking at least 164 different languages.

Europe's peopling by modern humans began only about 40,000 years ago, nearly 200,000 years after the continent's occupation by Neandertals and perhaps 700,000 years after the arrival of *Homo erectus,* who may have been the ancestor of both groups. Neandertals disappeared mysteriously about 30,000 years ago, and all subsequent populations in Europe have belonged to the subspecies *Homo sapiens sapiens.*

During Europe's Ice Age, Cro-Magnon hunters of western Europe gathered regularly for ceremonial purposes, bringing with them an increasingly advanced tool technology and an aesthetic sense represented by shell and amber ornaments and by small, exquisite carvings of people and animals. On the walls of their caves in northern Spain and southern France, they rendered dramatic and graceful images of horses, bulls, reindeer, and other animals that figured prominently in their Stone Age culture.

A lifetime of hard work and experience etch the face of this Csángó man from Romania.

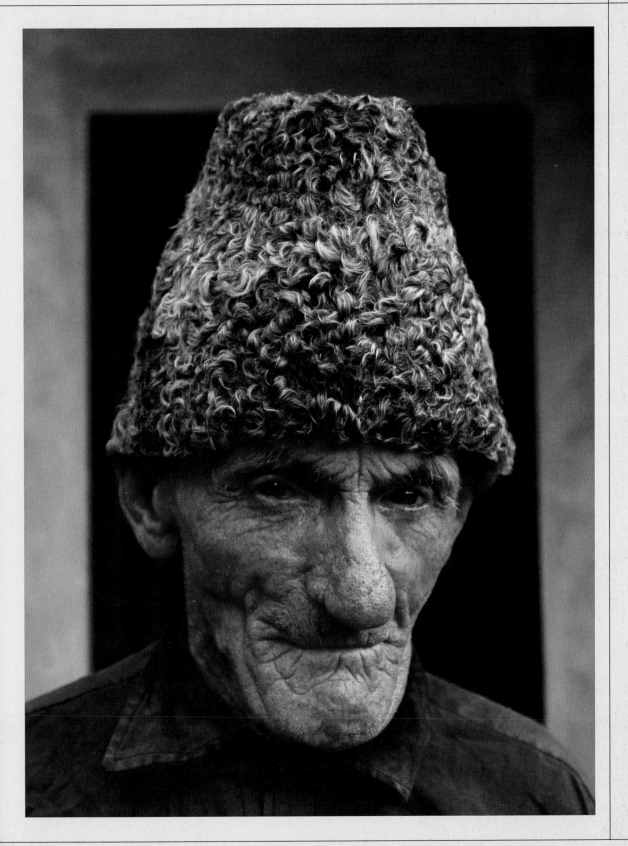

The migrations that gave way to most European ethnic groups of today are believed to have begun some 5,000 years ago with Indo-European pastoralists from Central Asia. They carried with them the beginnings of the Indo-European language family, which in Europe survives in eight main branches, ranging from the Italic family—including modern Italian, French, Spanish, Portuguese, and Romanian—to the Thraco-Illyrian, with Albanian the lone modern representative.

Not all European languages are Indo-European, however. Finnish, Hungarian, and Estonian fall into the Uralic family, originating in the area of the Ural Mountains, while the Basque language of the Pyrenees is related to no other language known in the world and is believed to predate the Indo-Europeans.

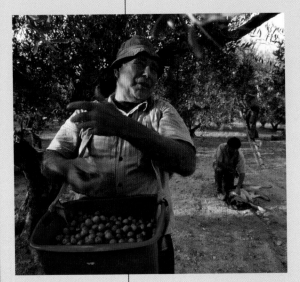

Careful tending of his olive groves yields a good harvest for a Sicilian farmer.

Hunter-gatherers had already made the transition to agriculture when peoples from the Middle East and Egypt arrived on the island of Crete. Accomplished seafarers, they spread the influence of the Minoan civilization through the Mediterranean world. But by 1450 B.C., the balance of power had shifted to mainland Greece and the Mycenaeans. The ancient Greeks, especially those of the fifth century B.C., left a legacy of excellence in art and architecture, mathematics and scientific achievement, and philosophical and political thought, bequeathing the democratic ideals that still shape European thinking.

Christianity Romans helped filter this legacy through their widespread empire, which in the second century A.D. stretched from the British Isles to Iran. By the fourth century, the Roman people had adopted Christianity as their state religion, and the empire's decline did not end the faith's influence.

As ethnic groups moved into areas that would become their homelands, leaders often embraced Christianity on behalf of their people. A split in the 11th century resulted in the distinction between Roman Catholicism and Eastern Orthodoxy that persists today, with southern and western Europe generally following the former and Orthodoxy taking hold in eastern Europe.

The effects of the Reformation of the 16th century endure in the Protestantism of most northern European groups. Between the 12th and 20th centuries, Ottoman Turks conquered and controlled parts of Europe, and wholesale conversions to Islam took place; today, however, Islam survives on the continent mainly in Albania, among Bosnia's Muslims, and in the small European nub of Turkey. Followers of Judaism once formed significant populations throughout Europe, but their numbers were reduced tragically during the Holocaust.

Nationalism As Europe began to move from the feudal model of the Middle Ages to that of centralized authority in the second millennium, the concept of nationalism began to replace provincial allegiances. Nationalism became imbued with the notion of a common language and religion and thus helped create the modern states that formed toward the end of the millennium.

Nationalism also led to the spread of empires around the globe, as rising powers emphasized their own cultures and promoted their own interests over those of other peoples. The dawn of the industrial revolution in the 18th century further aided Europe's domination of the world economy while it turned Europeans into urban workers. In the 20th century, industrial might and nationalistic fervor fueled two World Wars and other upheavals. Borders were redrawn and millions of people were forced to relocate. Massive migrations occurred as people sought to avoid conflict, escape persecution, or find better economic opportunities.

The current trend toward unity and cooperation, typified by the European Union formed in 1993, demonstrates the pragmatic nature of cultures and nationalities to work past divisions that have separated them. At the same time, Europeans are indicating renewed interest in languages, music, and other aspects of cultural identity. Religion, seemingly less important in a secular world, still holds the ability to divide, as seen in the cases of Northern Ireland and the former Yugoslavia. ■

Czech musicians in a Prague pub let loose with a tune that mocks the era of Austrian domination.

Eastern Europe

Although proximity to the sea characterizes most of Europe's territory, this eastern region contains many of the continent's landlocked nations. It is the region of contact between Europe and Asia, a boundary across which stretch the Ural Mountains and the Central Upland of Russia. Through this region flow legendary rivers: the Dniester and the Dnieper, the Don and the Volga, all emptying into the Black Sea, Earth's second largest inland body of water. Eastern Europe also includes the northerly reaches where lake-studded Finland meets Russia's northwestern corner.

♫ To listen to music from Bulgaria and Romania, visit http://worldmusic.nationalgeographic.com.

KALMYKS

Population: 174,000
Location: Russian Federation
Language family: Mongolic

The Kalmyks originally were a western Mongolian people, known as the Oirat. Nomadic herders, they moved seasonally between camps on their traditional grazing lands in Mongolia, southern Siberia, and China, while tending their flocks of sheep, goats, cattle, camels, donkeys, and horses. When it was time to shift to another location, they disassembled their large, circular felt tents called yurts or *gers* and moved on.

In the 13th century, the Oirat became involved in the infighting among Mongol tribes, starting out on the side of Genghis Khan and ending up affiliated with the khanate of his grandson, Kublai, after a stint with the opposition—Kublai's brother, Ariq Boke. It was at this juncture that they adopted the religious orientation of Tibetan Buddhism and became involved in Tibetan politics and the protection of the Dalai Lama.

In the mid-17th century, a large group of Oirats, perhaps as many as 50,000 households, continued to move west to the steppes between the Volga and Don Rivers on the northwestern shore of the Caspian Sea. Theirs was the last major westward migration of peoples from the steppes of Central Asia. Some time before this period, the name "Kalmyk," which probably originated with a Turkish word meaning "remnant," became associated with these Oirats.

Now living in Europe, the Kalmyks continued their lives as nomadic herders. They maintained their language—a western branch of Mongolian—and their practice of Tibetan Buddhism, which made them Europe's only Buddhist people. They operated in the region as an autonomous khanate that was absorbed, as the Kalmyks lost their influence, into Russia's empire under Catherine the Great.

Then began the first of several attempts to Russianize the Kalmyks, getting them to abandon the nomadic lifestyle and settle into houses, and attempting to convert them to Russian Orthodox Christianity. Under communist rule, the Kalmyks resisted attempts to collectivize their efforts and deny their religion. About a third of them were slaughtered in the 1920s. Later their religion was prohibited, their monasteries destroyed.

The situation worsened under Stalin: In one sweeping action, he deported all the Kalmyks to Siberia in

Fifty years of wedded bliss reside in the kiss of a Crimean couple, who celebrate their golden anniversary in the city of Sevastopol, Ukraine. Residents of the Crimea, a large Black Sea peninsula, include Russian pensioners who revel in the region's pleasant climate.

1943. Almost half died immediately. The survivors spent 14 years in exile, until they were brought back to Kalmykia by Nikita Khrushchev in 1957.

Returning Kalmyks found their land settled by Russians and Ukrainians, their houses lost, and their livelihoods stolen from them. Some resumed the nomadic way of living. But they retained few artifacts from their former lives, and their language came perilously close to extinction.

In the meantime, a group of 2,000 Kalmyks who had come under Allied control at the end of World War II had nowhere to go. Their kinsmen languished in Siberia, and returning to Kalmykia was tantamount to a death sentence. The United States took them in. Initial resettlement in New Mexico proved untenable, but the next stop—New Jersey—worked out. Eventually, one of their spiritual leaders immigrated, giving the expatriate Kalmyks in the United States more of a sense of community. This population recently celebrated its 50th anniversary.

Some 174,000 Kalmyks live in their autonomous republic in the Russian Federation, facing the challenges of the post-Soviet economy. But now Kalmyk culture appears revitalized: Their practice of Tibetan Buddhism has been re-established, and children learn Kalmyk in school, now written in a modified Mongolian script developed in the 17th century instead of Russian's Cyrillic alphabet.

LITHUANIANS

Population: 2.9 million
Location: Lithuania
Language family: Baltic

Lithuania, the largest and southernmost of the Baltic states, may have first been occupied by peoples who came from Asia some 4,000 to 10,000 years ago. The Lithuanians experienced a heyday from the 14th to 18th centuries, which included a period of union with Poland as Lithuania's power began to decline. Yet for much of their more recent existence,

Lithuanians have tried to maintain their culture in the face of formidable challenges—German, tsarist, and Soviet control, and now a period of rebuilding in the post-Soviet era.

Today 80 percent of the country's population is ethnic Lithuanian; the remaining 20 percent is mostly Russian or Polish. Most speak Lithuanian, though, which along with Latvian belongs to the Eastern Baltic group of Indo-European languages. Lithuanian was an underground language during a period of Russian domination in the late 19th and early 20th centuries, when the language was banned and other attempts were made to thwart Lithuanian identity.

About 80 percent of Lithuanians today are Roman Catholic. Nearly all of Lithuania's Jews—some 240,000—perished during World War II. The strength of Lithuanian Catholicism often is credited with the culture's endurance. Yet this staunch Catholic faith was built on a pervasive animistic past. Lithuanians held sacred the forests and fires and worshiped gods who presided over the natural world. Ongoing regard for nature is seen in a number of popular names, such as Ausra (dawn), Giedrius (dew), and Ruta (rue). It also persists in celebrations, such as the practice of dashing into the forest on Midsummer's Eve in search of a "fern blossom" which, though imaginary, brings good luck.

Lithuanians traditionally stretched the observance of Christmas and Easter to two days or more. Christmas Eve dinner, the most important meal of the year, featured 12 courses. Everyday meals included dairy products, especially sour cream and curds; potatoes; root vegetables; and meats such as pork and beef. Easter celebrations included roving groups of young men who went house to house, singing carols and begging for *marguciai,* or decorated Easter eggs.

In the secular realm, Lithuanians observe their independence in modern times, recalling post–World War I liberation from the Germans, the declaration of independence from the Soviets in 1990, and a standoff against Soviet tanks at the Vilnius television tower in January 1991, when 13 people died. A source of great national and ethnic pride is the folk music festival held in Vilnius every five years, which draws tens of thousands of performers.

The Lithuanians came through the era of Soviet control with a strong sense of purpose but with a crumbling infrastructure and an economy that was

Kalmyks pray at a Buddhist center in Elitsa, Kalmykia. Soviet domination and long years of exile did not extinguish the faith of Europe's only Buddhist people.

limited by price controls and quotas. The outlook was rather bleak in the first years of independence, but the Lithuanians have made great strides toward establishing a strong market economy. Reward for their efforts came in 2004 with entrance into both the European Union and NATO.

Today about 20 percent of the people are involved in agriculture and 30 percent work in industries such as machinery, textiles, clothing, and fertilizer; the rest are employed in services. While basketball is not an official export, the Lithuanians produce and send out a significant number of very skilled players, many of whom have ended up on college and professional teams in the United States.

ROMA

Alternate name: Romani, Gypsies
Population: 8-10 million
Location: most European countries
Language family: Indo-Iranian

The Roma are known by a number of names, many of which—"Gitanes" in France, "Czigany" in Hungary, and "Zigeuner" in Germany—are variations of "Gypsy," a term that erroneously ascribed their origins to Egypt. In fact, the Roma have been linguistically traced to northwest India: They speak Romany, an Indic language from which comes the word *roma,* meaning "man" or "people." One theory ties the group's 11th-century diaspora from India to their recruitment as troops who drove out Islamic invaders and pursued them for centuries into the Byzantine Empire and southeastern Europe.

Today the Roma are a minority in every country in Europe. Exact population figures are unknown for one reason: A long history of discrimination has made them reluctant to admit their heritage. Targeted by Nazis, more than half a million died in World War II. Communist regimes also suppressed their culture, but the collapse of communism did not stop the repression. A rise in nationalism led to more violence. In 1971 the first World Romani Congress established a much needed forum through which the people can address their struggle against racism and loss of cultural identity.

The Roma have long existed at the margins of other societies, partly to avoid discrimination and partly because of their migratory lifestyle. For centuries, families traveled in brightly painted, horse-drawn caravans, plying trades consistent with this kind of nomadism. They were horse traders, peddlers, metalsmiths, musicians, fortune-tellers, and carnival workers. In recent decades, some countries encouraged or forced permanent settlement, especially in Eastern Europe, where the Roma were put to work in state-run industries. With the fall of socialism, many settled Roma have lost their livelihoods.

Over the years, the people have embraced a number of faiths, often depending on the dominant local tradition. But while they observe rituals of mainstream religion, they sometimes add their own practices. For example, followers of Roman Catholicism gather near France's Rhône Delta each May to honor Black Sarah, their patron saint, even though she is not recognized by the church. Recently, many Roma have been drawn to Pentecostalism.

The Roma are organized into clans that are usually based on occupation, each with a chief or head. Clan

Roma girls dance away a summer afternoon in their home in Slovakia. Despite a centuries-old tradition of movement among these people, most European governments encourage the peripatetic Roma to become settled.

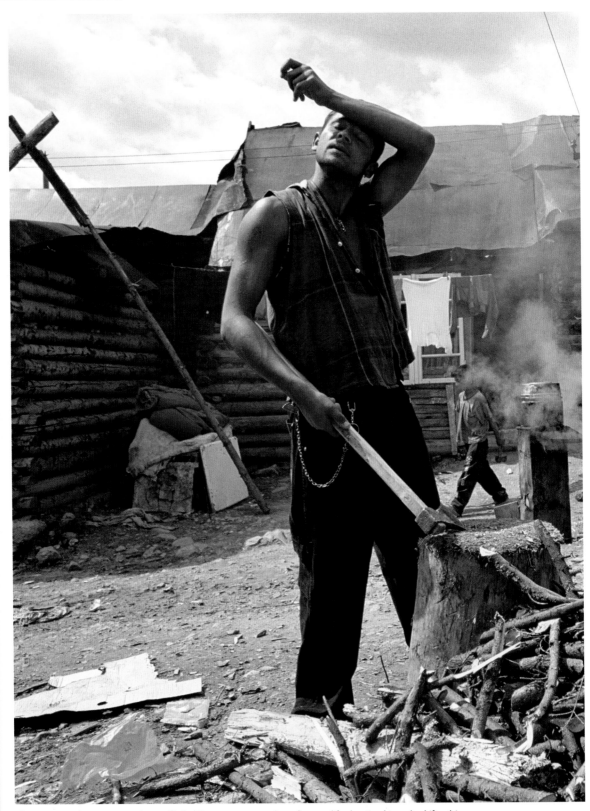

Chopping up whatever scraps he can find, a Roma man accumulates firewood for heating his makeshift cabin.

members, or large groups of Roma in general, will travel long distances together, but now they frequently do so in mobile homes and RVs. Music and dance are integral parts of their culture and have influenced aspects of other European cultures. In recent years, Roma musical rhythms have enjoyed a surge of worldwide popularity.

Marimé, the Roma code of ritual purity, is a remnant of the people's origins in India incorporating a number of taboos regarding social relationships and food. As a result, traditional Roma society is a closed one, shunning out-of-group marriages and other contacts with *gadjés,* non-Roma peoples who, as a group, are deemed unpure. Ideally, marriages were arranged and occurred at an early age, but such arrangements are becoming less common.

While birthrates for other European ethnic groups are declining, the Roma one is rising dramatically. Some demographers even speculate that by the year 2060, Slovakia's Roma population will outnumber the country's Slovaks.

ROMANIANS & MOLDOVANS

Population: 2.2 million
Location: Romania, Moldova
Language family: Italic

When the Romans invaded what is now Romania in the first century A.D., they encountered the strong and prosperous Dacians, who had established a kingdom along the Danube, on the central plateau, and in the Carpathian Mountains. The Dacians fought a good fight but succumbed to Roman troops and occupation. The introduction of Latin led to the development of the Romanian language and to influences that would last long after the Romans' retreat in 271. For the next 1,600 years, the Romanians saw invaders come and go—barbarians, Ottoman Turks, and Hungarian Magyars among them. The latter populated the western province of Transylvania, which has changed hands between Romania and Hungary a number of times. Communist control after World War II ended with the toppling of dictator Nicolae Ceausescu in 1989.

Today ethnic Romanians make up about 90 percent of the country's population of 22 million, and about 70 percent of them follow the Romanian Orthodox faith, a branch of Eastern Orthodoxy. Roman and Uniate

(Greek) Catholics and Protestants make up the remainder of the country's religious affiliation. Most of Romania's 400,000 Jews perished in the Holocaust, and many of those who survived immigrated to Israel.

Although religious expression was suppressed under communism, Romanians continued to practice their faith, which includes the veneration of icons in

A slip of the foot is
not nearly so dangerous
as a slip of the tongue.
BULGARIAN PROVERB

both churches and homes. These images, usually reverse paintings on glass, are believed to embody the physical presence of Christ, the angels, the saints, and other religious figures depicted on them. On entering a home, visitors acknowledge the family icon by bowing and making the sign of the cross before greeting their hosts. Each church holds numerous icons, which receive special veneration on feast days and by bridal couples during weddings.

Much of Romania's social life, especially in rural areas, traditionally centers around church activities such as parties and dances. The seasons leading to Christmas and Easter are elaborately observed, and at Christmas the Romanian love of music has given birth to an extensive repertoire of Christmas carols.

Pre-Christian practices survive in Romania as well, especially in rural areas. Belief in spirits in nature, witches, and the spirits of the undead still lead to precautions to thwart malevolent actions. The legend of Dracula is based on a number of elements in Romanian culture, including the historical figure of Vlad Tepes, a 15th-century local prince who fought ruthlessly against all who opposed him, earning the nickname Vlad the Impaler. Today Romanians often reluctantly—but lucratively—promote Dracula tourism in Transylvania, which has visitors flocking to its mountains to listen for the cry of wolves as they tour ruins of Dracula's purported castle fortress.

The Romanians endured communist control for more than 40 years, until severe food and fuel shortages and the growing dissent in Eastern Europe led to the ouster and death of Ceausescu. Today the country is still recovering from the privations of the communist regime and the mismanagement that followed. Most Romanians are poor by European standards and inflation has cut sharply into their incomes. Housing is scarce, especially in cities, and accommodations are cramped. Roughly a third of Romanians work in agriculture, and in recent years they have been able to reclaim land taken from their families as far back as four generations, leading to increased agricultural production. Another third have jobs in industry, and almost as many work in the service sector.

Everyday Romanian cuisine features stews and soups, including borscht made from cabbage; pork and sausages; and *mammaglia,* a cornmeal mush considered the national dish. Lamb often appears on the table at holidays. Common beverages include local wines and a strong plum brandy called *tuica.*

Romanian identity extends to the Moldovans, residents of the republic to the east of Romania. A high percentage of the Moldovans consider themselves ethnic Romanians. The Moldovan language is a sub-dialect of Romanian, with many borrowings from Russian and Ukrainian. Like Romanians, most Moldovans are Orthodox Christians, but they follow Russian, not Romanian, Orthodoxy.

Many of the inhabitants of the eastern part of Moldova, called Bessarabia, have a more mixed ethnic background. In the 1990s the Moldovans considered unification with Romania but ultimately rejected it, choosing political independence over cultural unity.

Wine makes an ordinary meal seem festive for a rural family in western Russia. Multigenerational households often reflect Russia's ongoing housing shortage.

RUSSIANS

Population: 140 million
Location: Russia
Language family: Slavic

The largest ethnic group in Europe, the Russians developed from ancient Slavic tribes who had settled in the area north of the Black Sea by the first millennium A.D. By the ninth century, when Vikings established a dynasty in the state of Kievan Rus, a number of tribes inhabited the area from the Black Sea to the Baltic.

Official conversion to Eastern Orthodox Christianity occurred in A.D. 988, linking Russians to the Byzantine Empire. Mongol occupation from the mid-13th to the late 15th centuries, however, sealed off the people from the cultural changes coming to Western Europe. These would not be felt until the early 18th century, when Tsar Peter the Great modernized and westernized the culture and enlarged Russia's territory, a trend that continued under Catherine the Great.

As the tsars expanded Russia's boundaries, the original Slavic tribes assimilated groups with Finnish, Turkish, Siberian, and Baltic origins to form the present-day Russian people, who number about 140 million. In the post-Soviet era, ethnic strife has led to violence in some parts of Russia, notably in Chechnya, a region in the Caucasus Mountains.

The Russian language belongs to the East Slavic group of Indo-European tongues. An old form of Russian known as Old Church Slavonic survives through the Russian Orthodox Church. Up until the tenth century, Russian did not have a written form, but then disciples of the monks Cyril and Methodius constructed a hybrid alphabet from the Latin, Greek, and Hebrew alphabets. Today, a number of other Slavic languages also use the Cyrillic alphabet that the two monks devised.

Though officially condemned during the Soviet era, when perhaps up to 85 percent of churches were closed and their property confiscated, the Russian

Orthodox Church survived and has been experiencing a resurgence of participation and elevation of status as a cherished cultural institution. Western proselytizers have also had significant influence in present-day Russia, as evidenced by the growing numbers of Baptists, Jehovah's Witnesses, and Seventh-Day Adventists in the region.

Russians have traditionally been rural people. For centuries, many of them were serfs, but even after their emancipation in 1861, serfs saw little improvement in their condition. During the Soviet era from 1917 to 1991, the central government endeavored to hold all property and organized large collective and state farms. This did not deter food production on private plots, though, and people sold their surplus produce to alleviate shortages caused by a poor distribution system.

As the society and economy continue to adjust to the post-Soviet era, some situations have changed dramatically while at the same time others remain virtually the same. A warm, effusive people by nature, Russians of the Soviet era had become guarded in their public lives, and thus they tended to lead a dual existence, a situation which has since eased.

Shoppers' lives have also eased, as the long lines for food and consumer goods have disappeared. One aspect that has not changed, however, is the housing shortage. After marriage, a young couple typically resides with the groom's parents until housing becomes available—sometimes a very long wait. Children continue to be highly valued, and parents will commit much of a family's time and resources to them. Unfortunately, the standard of living for most people is austere, and alcoholism and domestic abuse remain serious social issues.

Russians have a rich folk culture, often expressed in music and the decorative arts. *Byliny* are traditional epic songs, some dating back more than a thousand years. Songs are frequently sung to accompaniments played on the balalaika, a three-stringed, triangular guitar. Also popular among all levels of Russian society are classical music, literature, and chess.

A typical Russian meal has four courses and often includes borscht, a red beet-and-meat soup served with sour cream. Among other traditional fare are *ikra* (caviar) and blini (small filled pancakes). Sweetened hot tea, vodka, and brandy are typical beverages.

Russian friends and family members congregate to celebrate the feast days of the Orthodox liturgical year as well as life-cycle rituals, including weddings and school graduations.

UKRAINIANS

Population: 37 million
Location: Ukraine   Language family: Slavic

Ukrainians are an amalgam of Slavic tribes who settled the vast grassy plains, or steppelands, west of the Black Sea. By medieval times, the area around Kiev in the north had gained supremacy, and a union known as Kievan Rus dominated the region between the 9th and 13th centuries. At that time, the people were known as Ruthens. A Ukrainian republic did not exist until the fall of tsarist Russia in 1918; it was short-lived, however, and another was not formed until the end of the First World War, when Soviet leaders made Ukraine a socialist state. In 1991, Ukraine became an independent nation.

Today, approximately 37 million Ukrainians make up about three-fourths of the country's population. They speak Ukrainian, a language that belongs to the East Slavic group and is written in the Cyrillic alphabet. Since the end of the Soviet era, this language, along with other aspects of Ukrainians' ethnic identity, has flourished, while Russian influences and language use have declined.

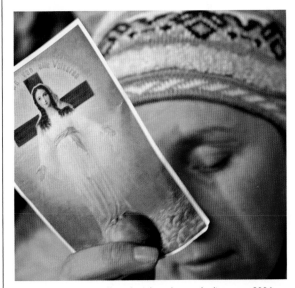

A Ukrainian woman collects her thoughts as she listens to 2004 presidential candidate Victor Yushchenko addressing the public about the recent election fraud and an imminent revote.

Blessed with rich soils, Ukraine was regarded as the "bread basket of Europe" until the 1986 nuclear meltdown at Chernobyl rendered some of the region's agricultural lands radioactive for many years to come. People continue to farm on lands that were unaffected, growing grains, fruits, and vegetables and raising livestock. Ukrainian farmers live in villages that tend to be large, often holding more than a thousand residents. Until the 18th century, it was not uncommon for three generations to live together; since then, however, the nuclear family has been the norm in both rural and urban areas, which contain about two-thirds of the country's people. Industry, centered in the east, includes the mining of coal and mineral resources.

Most people follow a branch of the Eastern Orthodox faith. Because of their proximity to the Near East, Ukrainians became Christians early on, although the prince of Kievan Rus did not officially adopt the religion on behalf of the state until A.D. 988. Of the many Christian holy days celebrated by Ukrainians, Easter remains foremost, surpassing Christmas in importance. Pre-Christian beliefs continue to influence observances of life passages, especially death, but weddings exhibit the fullest expression of Ukrainian life-cycle recognition.

Ukrainians are an effusive people who often greet others exuberantly with hugs, vigorous handshakes, or triple kisses. They entertain readily, frequently turning routine events into parties, at which toasting is a common form of recognition. In Ukrainian rituals, food plays an important role, as can be seen in the variety of breads used to commemorate different occasions. Traditionally, a dinner is not considered complete unless borscht is served.

At least one form of Ukrainian folk art elicits worldwide recognition: *pysanky,* the Ukrainian name for an intricate hot-wax-removal technique for coloring Easter eggs, which results in delicate lines and brilliant colors. The art dates back to pre-Christian times but readily became infused with Christian symbols and meanings. Elaborate embroidery applied to clothing and everyday textiles is another typical folk art. Ukrainians are also enthusiastic dancers and singers, known especially for their unique New Year's carols.

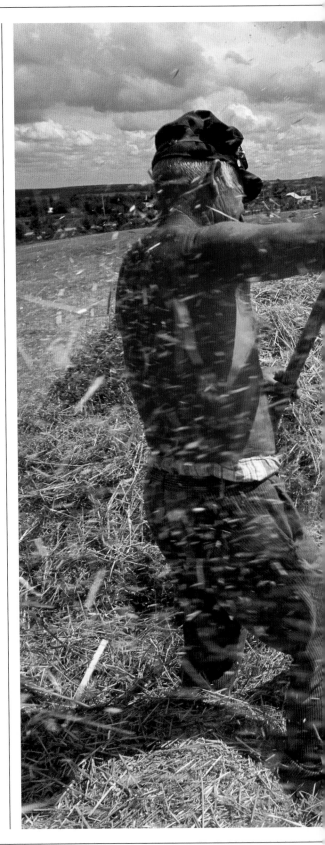

Ukrainian men rake straw onto a lift after the wheat harvest, made bountiful due to Ukraine's rich black-earth soil.

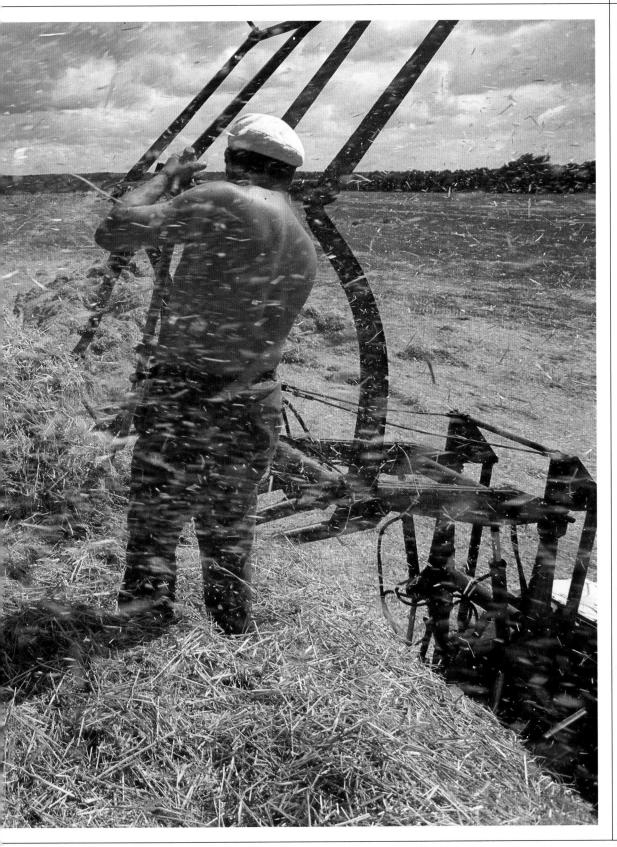

Central Europe

Stretching from the Baltic Sea in the north to the Adriatic Sea in the south, the region of Central Europe represents a wide band of lands and cultures. Rivers begin in the Carpathian Mountains, curving through the heart of these lands, and flow in all directions. The greatest of the rivers in Central Europe is the Danube, 1,770 miles long, which begins at two headwaters in Germany and flows through Central Europe, forming several national boundaries, and finally emptying into the Black Sea.

To listen to music from the Czech Republic, Hungary, Montenegro, and Serbia, visit http://worldmusic.national geographic.com.

BOSNIAN MUSLIMS

Alternate name: Bosniaks   Population: 1.8 million
Location: Bosnia and Herzegovina
Language family: Slavic

Of all the countries that once formed Yugoslavia, Bosnia and Herzegovina (or simply Bosnia) is probably the most unusual. Distinctions there tend to be made on the basis of religion and culture, not ethnicity. About 40 percent of the total population are Muslims, 34 percent are Serbs who follow the Eastern Orthodox religion, and 15 percent are Roman Catholic Croats. All speak what was known before the breakup of Yugoslavia as a Serbo-Croatian language.

By the seventh century A.D., south Slavic peoples populated the area that is now Bosnia. During the long occupation by Ottoman Turks, from 1328 to 1878, many Bosnians converted to Islam from Christianity (in particular from a heretical sect called the Bogomils), because doing so was often a way to obtain economic or social advantage with Turkish officials. Bosnian Muslims were landowners and merchants then but tend to be urban dwellers now. The Turks strongly influenced other aspects of Bosnian culture, including architecture, cuisine, music, poetry, and dance.

Typically forgoing orthodoxy or fundamentalism, Bosnian Muslims mostly follow the Sunni form of Islam, although Sufism, or Islamic mysticism, is also practiced. Muslims observe the month-long fast of Ramadan, which ends with a three-day feast known as Bajram (Id al-Fitr elsewhere). Bosnian Muslim women do not wear the all-enveloping coverings called *chadors,* but some wear raincoats and scarves for public occasions.

During the oil shortages of the 1970s, Yugoslav President Josip Broz Tito highlighted the religion of Bosnia's Muslims to obtain favorable terms from Saudi Arabia and other oil-producing countries; then, as fundamentalism took hold in the Middle East, Tito backed away from this approach, fearing its potential divisiveness in Yugoslavia.

With the breakup of the former Yugoslav federation in 1991, a great deal of religious and ethnic hatred has been released, much of it directed toward Bosnian Muslims. War broke out in 1992, as Serbs vigorously pursued a policy of "ethnic cleansing"—raping and murdering Muslims and forcing them from their towns—with the goal of forming a "greater Serbia."

Cossacks pose during a celebration commemorating their heyday as the warrior defenders of Russia. Poet Alexander Pushkin viewed the Cossacks as "eternally on horseback, eternally ready to fight, eternally on guard."

Intervention by the UN and NATO, along with the Dayton Peace Accords signed in 1995, has brought about some semblance of stability, but in general much of Bosnia remains in ruins. In the once beautiful city of Sarajevo, where many people were rendered homeless, residents are trying to rebuild their lives and their city. The Muslims have been effectively isolated, though, by a Croat alliance with Croatia and a Serb alliance with Serbia. At least 40 percent of the population is unemployed, and many young Bosnians of all faiths have left their war-torn homeland in pursuit of a better future.

CROATS

Population: 4.6 million
Location: Croatia
Language family: Slavic

In the seventh century a south Slavic group known as the Croats settled in the Dalmatian region of the Adriatic coast, in the northern area of present-day Croatia, and in parts of Bosnia and Herzegovina. A Croatian state began to form in the 9th century and endured until the early 12th century. Strategically situated at a crossroads for Western and Eastern Europe and for Western and Eastern Christianity, the Croats sustained years of domination by Hungarians, Austrians, Italians, French, and the Turks; they were, however, more successful in containing the expansion of the Turks than others whose territories fell to the invaders. In the 19th and early 20th centuries, Croats resisted joining forces with other south Slavs, preferring their independence, and only reluctantly did they decide to become part of the newly created Yugoslavia following World War I—all the while remaining suspicious of Serbian expansion and control.

During the era of President Josip Broz Tito, Croatian nationalism was thwarted. But after Tito died in 1980 and communism began to wane, Croats voted for independence in 1991; they did so despite aggression from Serbs, who controlled the government and the army, even though they made up only about 12 percent of Croatia's population. After years of fighting, peace has been restored. Nevertheless, the country must contend with unemployment, now around 14 percent but as high as 20 percent in the last decade.

The Croatian language, which is spoken by the vast majority of people inside Croatia and by many outside as well, has three major dialects. It is written in the Roman alphabet and contains a number of loanwords, mainly from Latin and German.

Almost 88 percent of Croatia's people are members of the Roman Catholic Church, and about 5 percent are members of the Eastern Orthodox Church, also adhering to the teachings of the pope. Catholicism has largely defined the country's culture, as it has in other parts of the former Yugoslavia, although the religion was suppressed during the communist era. While Carnival and Easter are important religious holidays, Croatians also look forward to the celebration of Badnjak, or Christmas Eve, and their tradition of lighting the yule log.

The country of Croatia is made up of a total of 115 communes (općina)—carryovers from socialism. Each commune comprises several villages and its own local government. A majority of the Croat people work in the service sector; about 35 percent work in industry; significantly fewer work in agriculture. Croatians build their lives around family and a gregarious café-type culture, with much socializing in public places and homes.

CZECHS

Population: 9.2 million
Location: Czech Republic
Language family: Slavic

In describing the modern Czech people, it is inevitable that they be compared with Slovaks, the ethnic group with whom they were politically united from 1918 to 1993 (except during World War II). Ethnically, the Czechs are an amalgam of Celtic, Germanic, and Slavic peoples who accepted Christianity in the 9th century. In the year 1085 they formed the

A Czech women polishes the intricate patterns she has engraved into a crystal vase in a factory in Podebrady. Czechs have exported cut glassware for centuries.

kingdom of Bohemia, which was centered in Prague. By the 14th century, this kingdom oversaw the greatest expression of political and cultural development in central Europe. In 1526, a vacant Bohemian throne was filled by an Austrian Habsburg, whose house continued to control the kingdom until the end of World War I, when the Czechoslovak Republic was created.

Adolph Hitler annexed the republic's provinces of Bohemia and Moravia 20 years later, and Slovakia became a Nazi puppet state. After World War II, communists controlled a reunited Czechoslovakia until the "Velvet Revolution" under dissident playwright and political activist Václav Havel ushered in democracy. Leaders among the Czechs and the Slovaks disbanded the union in 1993, and since then Czechs have fared better than Slovaks at effecting economic and social progress.

In general, the Czechs have made a rapid transition to a market economy, with a long history of industrialization translating into highly regarded ceramics, glassware, and textiles. Agriculture is also heavily mechanized, and farms are very productive. The Plzen area, 50 miles southwest of Prague, is known worldwide for its beer production.

Over the years, Czechs have been far more urbanized than Slovaks, and today many live in small towns and in the largest cities, Prague and Brno. People may also have *chaty*, or country homes, which they visit

> ### Youth is the gift of nature, but age is a work of art.
> **POLISH PROVERB**

on weekends and holidays. About 27 percent of the population is Roman Catholic, and adherence to Catholic practice often tends to be quite relaxed. Evangelical Lutherans make up about 20 percent of the Czech population.

Most Czechs are part of small nuclear families, which may expand at some point as adult children assume the care of their aged parents. Many families make time in the middle of the day to enjoy their main meal, traditionally heavy in meats, game, and the characteristic *knedliky*, or dumplings. Current trends, however, seem to indicate that people are trying to consume lighter, healthier meals. Traditional folk costumes of embroidered shirts, pants, and vests for the men and embroidered blouses, skirts, and aprons for the women are worn mostly in the more rural southern areas.

The Czech language, like Slovak, is part of a cluster of Slavic tongues written in the Roman rather than the Cyrillic alphabet. Though Czech and Slovak are mutually intelligible, they are actually two distinct languages. Czech makes a distinction between formal or written communication and everyday speech.

According to a common saying, "Every Czech is a musician." While folk songs and classical music remain popular, rock has entrenched itself in the Czech culture—especially in Prague—and continues to be the medium of political protest.

MAGYARS

Alternate name: Hungarians
Population: 15 million   Location: Hungary
Language family: Ugric

Hungary's Magyars stand out amid the mostly Slavic peoples who live around them. As a result of population shifts occurring after World War II, Magyars now make up about 90 percent of the population of Hungary, establishing their country as one of the most ethnically homogeneous in the area.

Magyars first settled the Carpathian basin in the ninth century. They descended from a tribal people with origins in the forests between the Volga River and Ural Mountains. Their language, also called Magyar, is today spoken by some 15 million people; it belongs to the Ugric branch of the Finno-Ugric family and is distantly related to Finnish and Estonian. Used interchangeably with Magyar, the name "Hungarian" probably derives from the Turkic words *on ogur*, or "ten arrows," a reference perhaps to the number of Magyar tribes.

In A.D. 1000, pagan Magyars embraced Christianity under King Stephen I, who gained legitimacy for a Hungarian monarchy. About 52 percent of Hungary's people are now Roman Catholic and 25 percent are Protestant. Centuries of invasion and domination by the Turks—who conducted massive conversions to

Islam—and by the Austrian Habsburgs ended in the late 1800s, when Hungary entered a joint monarchy with Austria. World War I undid that alliance and greatly reduced Hungary's territory. The post–World War II era saw the development of a communist state, which in 1956 crushed a popular pro-democracy revolution quickly and harshly, causing hundreds of thousands of Magyars to leave the country. The communist regime ended with the declaration of a republic in 1989, although some socioeconomic changes had begun in the 1970s.

In the past 50 years, the Hungarian population has shifted from rural to urban, and even in areas where agriculture is predominant, many households derive income from both industry and farming. More than three-fourths of the women work outside their homes, and one in four workers of both sexes commutes a considerable distance. Holding down more than one job is not unusual here, as people try to make ends meet or to afford a more comfortable lifestyle. Families tend to be smaller than in the past, and many Hungarian couples eventually opt for divorce. A quarter of all families live below the poverty line, and the suicide rate is one of the highest in the world.

Although Magyars are becoming more secular, they continue to celebrate significant days of the liturgical year as well as benchmarks in the agricultural calendar. As with other expressions of traditional culture, the distinctive Hungarian folk music, based on a pentatonic (five-note) scale, is in decline. Composers Béla Bartók and Zoltán Kodály preserved the best examples of this music form in the early 20th century. Hand kissing, a formal gesture still practiced by older men, has been replaced by the younger generation with the verbal greeting, "*Csókolom*—I kiss it."

POLES

Population: 43 million   Location: Poland
Language family: Slavic

Poland's physical geography—a low-lying plain open at both the eastern and western ends—has worked against its security for millennia: It is a region

Young people in Budapest, Hungary, play a challenging game on stilts in the city's Millenaris Park, a former electrical factory and grounds that have been redesigned as a cultural and recreational center for plays, concerts, art exhibitions, and outdoor fun.

too easy for others to enter and exit. The earliest Slavic settlers most likely came through the eastern portal, although they left no evidence of when or from where they came. They have been an established presence in the region now called Poland since the eighth century. Embracing Christianity in the tenth century, the Polanie, or "people of the plain," eventually created a nation. In their lives and culture, Polish ethnicity and Roman Catholic Christianity have become inextricably linked. Poles prefer to consider themselves Western Europeans, not Eastern, and they do share a Western orientation.

Today, 98 percent of Poland's people are ethnic Poles; some 90 percent of them are Catholic. Poland's Jews, about 3 million strong before the Holocaust, now number only about 10,000. Other ethnic minorities include Lithuanians, Belarusans, Ukrainians, and Germans—cultural groups representing Poland's neighboring countries.

The strong moral authority and political clout of the Catholic Church provided the support needed to carry the Poles through the difficult periods of their history. The Poles have undergone periods of Austrian, Prussian, and Russian domination from the 18th through early 20th centuries and then moved into an era of Soviet control following World War II.

Polish is a western Slavic language written in the Roman alphabet, with diacritical marks and characters used to represent unique sounds. There are a number of dialect groups, although education, migration, and the influence of the media have produced a standardized written and spoken Polish language.

Etiquette and polite formality are hallmarks of Polish social behavior. Close friends often greet each other with a triple kiss, and men may kiss women's hands at meeting and leave-taking. Such deference does not extend to home life, however. Even though about half of all Polish women work outside the home, Polish men tend to avoid any involvement in housework or child care.

Farmers, gentry, workers, intelligentsia, and, recently, the upwardly mobile Soviet-era *nomenclatura*, or new class, form the broad categories of class among the Poles. In the late 20th century, the first four of these groups, along with the Catholic Church, came together to form the formidable union *Solidarnosc* (Solidarity). Outlawed through the 1980s, Solidarity

A rural Magyar father and daughter share a tender moment. Since World War II, Hungary's population in general has become more urban.

nevertheless won a majority in the 1989 election. A year later Solidarity's leader, Lech Walesa, became president, and he initiated a plan to impose a sort of shock therapy to jolt Poland into a market economy. The plan failed, however, and resulted in inflation and high unemployment.

Today industries employ about 40 percent of all Poles. Largely privatized, they are helping the Polish economy make new strides forward. During the era of Soviet control, farmers managed to avoid collectivization, and farms mostly remained in private hands. Holdings still tend to be small, and farms provide a livelihood for about 28 percent of the population.

The Poles' strong Catholic devotion inspires regular church attendance, at a rate estimated at about 75 percent of the total population—perhaps the highest rate of observance of any Catholic country in Europe. The Poles hold the Virgin Mary in special regard as their patron, honoring her with many feast days and making pilgrimages to Marian shrines such as that of the Black Madonna at Czestochowa.

The church calendar guides Polish holiday celebrations, with Christmas and Easter the most important of the year. Christmas Eve dinner is a sedate event featuring an odd number of meatless dishes as well as a thin white wafer known as angel bread. The Easter meal often includes a festive roasted suckling pig served with a dyed red egg in its mouth.

Everyday Polish meals incorporate bread, meat, and plenty of potatoes—Poles consume an average of 300 pounds of potatoes per person each year. Potatoes also go into the manufacture of vodka, which Poles often claim as their own invention.

Some 13 million Poles live outside of Poland, with large groups in the United States, Canada, and the United Kingdom. By comparison with the expatriates, Poles in Poland have a modest standard of living. Many still don't own automobiles, although public transportation opportunites are extensive.

SERBS

Population: 7.8 million
Location: Serbia and Montenegro
Language family: Slavic

About 6.5 million Serbs form the ethnic majority in Serbia, one of the two republics that constitute the new, self-proclaimed Federal Republic of Yugoslavia; the other is Montenegro, also primarily a Serb country. In addition, there are Serb minorities in Croatia and in Bosnia and Herzegovina. Serbs speak Serbian, a South Slavic language related to Croatian but written in the Cyrillic alphabet.

Most people belong to the Serbian Orthodox Church, a self-governing body that has wielded a great deal of political power throughout the republic's history. In recent ethnic conflicts in the region, Serbian Orthodoxy has been drawn even further into the cause of Serbian nationalism.

During the sixth century A.D., Serbs and their flocks moved from the Carpathian Mountains into the Balkan Peninsula and occupied an area that stood to the east of the territory of the Croats, another South Slavic people. Within three centuries, the Serbs had established a state that would expand into a powerful kingdom by the mid-1300s. Internal struggles so weakened Serbia that Ottoman Turks were able to conquer the region and hold it for more than 400 years. Many Serbs fled west into the Dinaric Alps. A strong sense of nationalism prevailed, leading to several revolts by rival Serbian families and eventually forcing the Turks to grant autonomy to the Serbs in the early 19th century. Interfamily rivalries remained a theme of Serbian history into the 20th century.

Following World War I, the Serbs believed they had an opportunity to create a greater Serb kingdom, but what came about was a more inclusive state—the former Yugoslavia—uniting the South Slavs. The country became communist at the end of the Second World War, but under Josip Broz Tito, Yugoslavia withdrew from the Soviet alliance and forged a brand of communism that allowed more worker control and a greater degree of prosperity. President Tito's death in 1980 and communism's decline set the stage for the dissolution of the Yugoslav federation in the last decade of the 20th century.

Serbian nationalism and long-harbored animosities against other groups, such as the Croats and the Muslims, engendered aggression in Croatia and Bosnia. In Serbia, violence ensued against Albanian Muslims who formed the majority population in the autonomous province of Kosovo. The conflicts took tens of thousands of lives, led to large-scale movements of peoples, and brought worldwide sanctions against the Serbs and their leader Slobodan Milošević. His ouster in 2000 and the presence of UN and NATO overseers offered some hope of less conflict for the Serbs, their compatriots, and their neighbors.

Before World War II, most Serbs made a living through agriculture, but today many families have a mixed economic base involving farming and industry.

Couples twirl in a Slovak folk dance. Slovaks frequently wear traditional dress at cultural festivals and also at weddings.

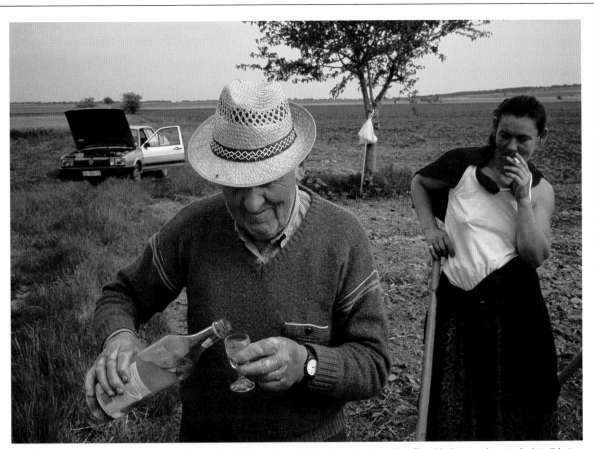

Break time for a Serb refugee worker from Kosovo includes a glass of *slivovitz*, or plum brandy, offered by her employer in Serbia. Ethnic Serbs fled Kosovo during the fighting there with Albanian Muslims.

As a result, some of the tasks once performed just by men have been taken over by women. The *zadruga*—extended family household composed of several generations in the male line—continues to survive in Serbia, though not in most other south Slavic communities; it is seen more often in rural areas than in urban ones.

Also important is the *vamilija*, or lineage traced from a common male ancestor. Vamilija members share a last name and venerate the same patron saint, whose annual feast day is one of the most important celebrations for the family. In this strongly male-dominated society, being heirless in the male line is considered a tragedy. A man without an heir can bring in a son-in-law to inherit his land and possessions, but such a step is almost always regarded as an unfortunate compromise.

Serbs have long been known for their grand tradition of oral epic poetry, which is often accompanied in recital by a single-stringed instrument called a *gusle*. The people like to socialize outside the home, and in cities and towns they frequent sidewalk cafés for coffee and conversation. On a daily basis, their diet generally consists of bread and a hearty stew made with a lard base. Lamb appears on festive occasions such as Easter.

SLOVAKS

Population: 4.8 million
Location: Slovakia Language family: Slavic

A Slavic people, Slovaks first inhabited the area between the Carpathian Mountains and the Danube River around the fifth century A.D. As residents of the former Czechoslovakia, they occupied the easternmost third of the country. The Slovak language—like Czech, a closely related tongue—belongs to the West Slavic group and is distinctive for its inflection and large number of vowel-less words.

After a period of hegemony by the Moravian Empire, named for the Morava River Valley, the

As the day comes to a close, a group of Slovenes follows a snowy path to a hilltop church in Ljubljana. Roman Catholicism remained strong during the communist era in the former Yugoslavia.

Slovaks endured a series of invasions by the Magyars, or Hungarians, who controlled Slovakia from A.D. 907 to the end of World War I. The Magyars themselves were incorporated into the Austro-Hungarian Empire in the 16th century. Through a "Magyarization" program, the empire tried to suppress Slovak language and culture and, as a result, Slovak expatriates joined with their Czech counterparts at the end of World War I to press for the creation of Czechoslovakia. Except for the years from 1939 to 1945, this union persisted, albeit under communist control following World War II. In 1989, the so-called Velvet Revolution led by Václav Havel overthrew the communist regime, and about four years later the Czech and Slovak republics became separate entities.

Slovaks traditionally have been a more rural people than the Czechs. Their hamlets and villages still have many of the simple one- and two-room homesteads that, slightly expanded, would often house three generations of a Slovak family. Rural families typically farmed, growing rye, wheat, corn, potatoes, sugar beets, and wine grapes. The steel, chemical, and aluminum industries established during the communist years have declined following the dismantling of the Soviet Union.

Much socializing takes place along gender lines, with men gathering in bars at night and women visiting at home. This is especially common in rural areas, as is adherence to pre-Christian beliefs and to superstitions about such things as the giving of flowers; cut flowers, for example, should be presented to one's host in an odd number; even-numbered bouquets are only appropriate at funerals. About 69 percent of Slovaks are Roman Catholics, who practice a much more observant form of Catholicism than their Czech neighbors, while about 11 percent are Protestants. A once sizable Jewish population was annihilated during the Holocaust.

Slovaks are a rather formal people, with ritualized greetings that include using a person's professional credentials in a form of address. Like Czechs, many are avid musicians who enjoy both vocal and instrumental forms of folk music. Folk dancing is a favorite activity as well. It is quite common to see traditional folk dress at festivals and on occasions such as marriage. For men, this means dark woolen suits, blouses, and knitted caps; for women, full skirts, aprons, and scarves. Celebrations are also good times for enjoying the traditional *bryndzové halusky,* potato dumplings served with sheep's cheese.

SLOVENES

Population: 2 million
Location: Slovenia
Language family: Slavic

Together with the Croats, the Slovenes provided a catalyst for the independence movement leading to the 1991 dissolution of the former Yugoslavia. In many respects, the Slovenes have emerged from the country's breakup in a stronger position than the other ethnic groups who lived there. These people have long had a Western orientation and a higher standard of living, and since independence, that difference has only been enhanced.

Almost two million Slovenes inhabit the northwestern corner of the former Yugoslavia. Their new nation, Slovenia, is quite hilly and contains a sizable area of limestone karst; both geologic realities make the country unsuitable for large-scale agriculture and to some extent reliant on grain imports. Nevertheless, wheat, rye, oats, barley, and potatoes are grown and livestock is raised. Forestry, industry, and tourism are also major economic activities. Today, about 50 percent of the Slovenes live in urban areas. The largest and most populated of their cities is Ljubljana, the capital of Slovenia.

Slovenes are a Slavic people who have inhabited the area for more than 13 centuries. They speak Slovene, an old South Slavic language that has many dialects and subdialects.

After joining a Slavic union in the seventh century, the Slovenes came under Frankish rule in the late eighth and early ninth centuries and were heavily converted to Christianity. For much of Slovenia's history, though, the people were under German control and influence, then Austrian and Austro-Hungarian rule until World War I, when Yugoslavia—"land of the south Slavs"—was created. Communists took over after World War II, but Yugoslavia managed to forge significant regional autonomy.

During the communist era, the Roman Catholic Church fared better in Slovenia than it did in other areas of Yugoslavia. Today its members make up more than half of the population, while a small proportion of the country's people are Orthodox or Protestant. For centuries, Catholicism has been inextricably intertwined with Slovenian culture. While regular attendance at Mass has dropped off, the church continues to influence cultural and life-cycle celebrations. Slovenes enthusiastically celebrate the pre-Lenten Carnival season, which they call *pust,* and combine Christian and pre-Christian elements in their festivities. Both children and adults don costumes at this time, and children go door-to-door in search of treats from their neighbors.

Music and dancing—both folk and modern—play a very large role in Slovene culture. Choral music is quite popular and is supported by hundreds of different singing groups. For many Slovene people, entertainment involves family activities and the visiting of friends, and it is not unusual for city dwellers to spend

A tree leans on a tree,
a man on a man.
SLOVENE PROVERB

weekends out in the country, helping relatives with their agricultural chores and relaxing together afterward. Many urban families also have small country cottages of their own.

Potatoes are frequently featured in Slovenian cuisine, as are breads and pastries. *Potica,* a festive bread made with either a sweet or salty filling, appears during holidays, especially at Christmas and Easter. So, too, do copious amounts of alcoholic beverages. In recent years, alcohol consumption has risen by 25 percent, and alcohol abuse is a recognized problem for many Slovenes, regardless of age or gender.

Southern Europe

Southern Europe, considered the cradle of ancient Western civilizations, includes Italy, Greece, and Turkey, together with Serbia, Montenegro, Albania, Macedonia, and Bulgaria. This is a region defined by water, its intricate coastlines outlining the Tyrrhenian, Adriatic, Ionian, and Aegean Seas, as well as the northern span of the Mediterranean. Thousands of islands populate these waters, from those with histories and cultures all their own—Malta, Sicily, and Crete—to tiny, uninhabited rock outcroppings. Greece alone contains nearly 10,000 square miles of islands, some—like Samothrace, Lesbos, and Ithaki—enjoying colorful histories as part of Greece's mythical past. Craggy mountains rise up from the shore of both landmasses, Italy and the Balkan Peninsula. Montenegro, Serbia, Albania, Macedonia, and Bulgaria all have distinct histories, even though their current boundaries have been recently drawn.

🎵 To listen to music from Greece and Italy, visit http://worldmusic.nationalgeographic.com.

SOUTHERN EUROPE

AFRICA

Population: 5 million
Location: Albania
Language family: Albanian

For some ethnic groups, religious identity is paramount; Albanians, however, are fond of saying that they are, above all else, Albanian. Ethnically, they are a homogeneous group, probably descended from ancient Illyrians who controlled the Balkan area and parts of Greece in the 13th century B.C. Conquered by Romans a thousand years later, Albania was part of the Roman and Byzantine Empires before Ottoman Turks took control in the 14th century. Russia defeated the Turks in the late 19th century, and as the weakened empire came apart, Albania lost most of its territory to neighboring countries. Now, almost as many Albanians live in Bosnia, Macedonia, and Greece as live in present-day Albania, whose population stands closer to five million.

The Albanian language, one of the nine original Indo-European languages, is written in the Latin alphabet. Although Albanian was proscribed during Ottoman rule, it has made a strong comeback since the late 19th century. Its speakers make up two groups—Ghegs in the north and Tosks in the south—and the main distinction between them has to do with certain aspects of pronunciation.

The religious lives of Albanians are difficult to discern at the present time. Before the communist takeover in 1946, about 70 percent of the people were Muslim (a reflection of Ottoman rule); 20 percent were Eastern Orthodox; and the rest were Catholic. From 1967 until independence in 1990, Albania was officially an atheist state. Today many Albanian people are drawn to evangelical Christian groups; there is also the suggestion of a resurgence of Catholicism. Historically, Albanians have been tolerant of other religions, and in the era before communism the Albanian clergy, in short supply nationwide, were respected and consulted by many individuals, no matter what their belief system. During World War II, Albania not only sheltered its own Jews but also took in those of neighboring countries, meaning that at war's end its Jewish population was larger than the one it had at the beginning.

An Albanian shepherd watches over his town in northern Macedonia. Driven by poor economic prospects in their homeland, thousands of Albanians have emigrated to neighboring countries.

Albanians are a very polite and formal people with extremely elaborate habits of greeting and social interaction. Great respect is shown for elders, especially older men, to the point that boys and young men will kiss their hands. A person's pledged word is his bond, and a pledge sealed with a handshake or embrace is the most binding of contracts. Traditionally, slights to a family's honor and transgressions such as theft and murder were answered with a blood feud. Since World War II and the communist era, women have gained status in this male-oriented country.

About 35 percent of Albanians live in urban areas, 65 percent in rural. Despite valuable mineral resources and strong agriculture, Albania's transition to a market economy has been very shaky, though not for lack of effort by its residents. Political repression continues to occur, even in the wake of democratic elections. Outside Albania, in the Kosovo region of Serbia, Muslim Albanians have been persecuted, killed, or forced out of their communities.

In cuisine, as in other aspects of Albanian life, the Turkish influence is strong. Bread is the main staple; lamb is the main meat. A Greek influence is seen in a multilayered stuffed pastry called *lakror*. The Mediterranean climate in the southern reaches of the country assures an abundant supply of fruits and nuts. One of the most prized products is a three-star brandy named for George Kastrioti, a national folk hero from the 15th century, popularly known as Skanderbeg.

GREEKS

Population: 10.5 million
Location: Greece, Cyprus   Language family: Greek

The more than ten million people of Greece occupy the mountainous southern tip of the Balkan Peninsula and many of the myriad islands off its convoluted coastline. There their ancestors established the basis for Western civilization some 2,500 years ago, including the ideals of democracy. Conquest by the Macedonians in the 4th century B.C. ushered in

a long era of foreign domination. Greece won official independence in 1832, although European royals still ruled. A bitter civil war between Greek royalists and communists occurred in the mid-20th century. Culturally, however, a unified Greek spirit prevails.

About 98 percent of Greece's population speaks Greek, an Indo-European language more than 3,000 years old. Ancient Greek spread throughout Greece's colonies, even supplanting Latin as the language of the Eastern Roman Empire. Although there are two major forms of Greek in general use—*demotic,* or the every-

> Women make the house,
> and then they destroy it.
> GREEK PROVERB

day language of conversation, and *katharevousa,* the language of government and media—the current trend favors the use of demotic in most contexts. A third form, *koine,* the Greek of the New Testament, is the language of church liturgy. Small numbers of Greeks speak other languages of the Balkans, as well as Turkish, and Greek children learn English beginning in the early grades.

The Greek Orthodox religion is a cornerstone of Greek culture, and it is the official religion of the nation. Services tend to be long, three hours or more, and it is not uncommon for people to wander in and out during a service. Maintaining Greece's many churches falls to parishioners, especially the women, who clean the buildings and often bake the bread to be served for communion.

The Greeks are a warm, effusive people who value relaxed socializing. They gather both privately and publicly for meals, coffee, and drinks. Conviviality often includes heated debate worthy of the ancient Greek philosophers as well as dancing. Ouzo, an anise-flavored beverage, and retsina, a resinated wine, may flow freely amid calls of "*Yiassas!*— Here's to health!"

Duet at the meat counter: Greek musicians entertain the butcher and his customers at the Central Market in Athens.

Typical Greek foods include many lamb and seafood dishes, as well as dolmades—stuffed grape leaves—and moussaka, a casserole made with eggplant and lamb. The Greeks avidly consume many dairy products, including feta cheese and yogurt.

Annual celebrations follow the calendar of the Greek Orthodox Church, with Holy Week and Easter the most important. Greek Easter usually begins at midnight on Saturday with a candlelight vigil and service, followed by parties and a meal featuring roasted

---

One who loves does not smell the odor of garlic.

SICILIAN PROVERB

---

lamb. Instead of celebrating their own birthdays, Greeks mostly observe the day honoring the saint for whom they are named.

Greek social organization revolves around family, extended kin, and patronage relationships, with godparents and wedding sponsors playing important roles in an individual's life. Family inheritance passes to both males and females, and women traditionally receive their portion at marriage in the form of large and lavish dowries. A law passed in the 1980s tried, rather unsuccessfully, to limit the extravagances of this marriage practice. Newlyweds may live with the groom's family until they can afford their own home. Greeks consider owning a home, whether a hand-built, whitewashed house in a village or an apartment in Athens, the ultimate goal.

The Greek family will close ranks against other families if there is a dispute or if the family honor is violated. The concept of *philotino*, or love of honor, permeates Greek culture in both bold and subtle ways, guiding behavior, defining responsibilities, and contributing to an individual's or family's esteem or status. If breached, it can lead to longlasting feuds and, on occasion, to violence.

Many Greek businesses, large and small, are family enterprises. Fewer than 30 percent of Greeks farm, and they have moved from subsistence agriculture to growing cash crops, selling products such as grain and

fruits, including olives and grapes. Greece remains relatively unindustrialized compared to other parts of Europe, although it supports a world-class shipping industry. Many Greeks have emigrated to northern Europe, North America, South Africa, and Australia in search of better prospects.

Ethnic Greeks form the majority—some 80 percent—of the population on the island nation of Cyprus, which lies in the Mediterranean south of Turkey. The rest of the population are mostly Muslim Turkish Cypriots, who have claimed an unrecognized independence for the northern third of the island. As a result of conflicting claims, Cyprus has been a hotbed of civil strife and violence in recent times. Greek Cypriots share the language, religion, and other aspects of mainland Greek culture. They are mostly agriculturalists, and most live inland. Cyprus has few coastal settlements, due to poor fishing and a history of pirate attacks.

ITALIANS

Population: 60 million
Location: Italy
Language family: Italic

The Italians inhabit one of the most recognizable landforms on the planet, a boot-shaped peninsula that juts into the Mediterranean Sea. Etruscans, Germanic peoples, Greeks, North Africans, and Phoenicians all contributed to the Italian heritage. A topography consisting of 80 percent mountains or hills encouraged the development of regional cultures. These eventually became the city-states ruled by powerful individuals or families that would unite under the impetus of 19th-century nationalism to become the kingdom of Italy in 1861.

Italy's population numbers more than 55 million; nearly all of them speak Italian, a Romance language derived from Latin, albeit in a number of regional dialects. Over time the Tuscan dialect has become the national standard. Along the borders with France, Austria, and Slovenia live populations that speak French, German, and Slovene, as well as pockets of Albanian speakers in the south.

Italians tend to be warm and engaging, fixing the steadiness of their gaze on conversation partners and punctuating their phrases with touches and gestures. Family provides the anchor of their social life.

Although kinship is reckoned equally on both sides of the family, there is commonly more attachment with the mother's kin, and newlyweds may live for a time with the bride's family. In recent decades birth rates have fallen sharply, leading to predictions of a dramatic drop in population—perhaps by a third—in the next half century.

In general, northern Italy is more prosperous and has a longer history of industrialization than the south. The north boasts the fertile Po Valley and also the industrial triangle of Milan, Turin, and Genoa, which, in addition to being Italy's major ship-building and financial and commercial center, turns out textiles, clothing, iron, steel, furniture, cars, airplanes, and motorcycles. Italian farms produce wheat, vegetables, olives, and grapes; Italy's wine production ranks near the top worldwide.

With Rome as the epicenter of world Catholicism, it is to be expected that some 90 percent of Italians would be Roman Catholic. What may seem surprising is that about 2 percent of Italians are Jews, a population that has endured since the days of the Roman republic. There are also small numbers of Muslims and Orthodox Christians.

Most Italians will boast of the superiority of their regional cuisine, more specifically of their home town's, and above all of their own mother's, cooking. While pizza and pasta have entered the international vernacular as Italian foods, these items do not begin to represent the culture's everyday cuisine, although in most parts of Italy some kind of pasta dish appears at the day's main meal, which may also include soup, bread, and fish or meat. A family's status can be determined in part by how much meat they can afford.

Italian holidays call for festive meals and special food traditions. In addition to the numerous preparations for Christmas and Easter, holiday traditions include special bread for the feast of St. Joseph and various foods shaped like eyes in honor of the martyr St. Lucy. Family life revolves around these special occasions, although any visitor to an Italian home will be offered the hospitality of food and drink.

Italians live among some of the most splendid works of art and architecture of three millennia, starting with the frescoes of the Etruscans, continuing through the glories of Rome—exemplified by the Pantheon and the Colosseum—and by no means ending with the Renaissance wonders of Michelangelo, Leonardo da Vinci, and Gian Lorenzo Bernini.

Italy's population includes the five million inhabitants of Sicily, the Mediterranean's largest and most populous island. The Sicilians are an amalgamation of the island's invaders: Greeks, Romans, Carthaginians, Byzantine Greeks, North African Muslims, Normans, Angevin French, and Spanish. Some linguists classify the Sicilian language as a dialect of southern Italy, although it is not mutually intelligible with standard Italian. Most young Sicilians speak Italian as well.

Sicilians of the interior are mainly farmers, while those on the coast fish and also work in industry and services. A notorious fact of Sicilian life is the existence and power of the Mafia, known locally as Cosa Nostra, meaning "our thing." Rising from lawless conditions centuries ago, families of organized crime are involved in the international drug trade as well as bogus government contracts and extortion. It remains difficult to convict Mafiosi because their members observe a strict code of silence.

Emotions, including love, run high among Italians like this cuddling couple in Tuscany.

Western Europe

Powerhouse nations through history—Portugal, Spain, France, Germany, Austria, Switzerland, Belgium, and the Netherlands—join as members of the region of Western Europe. An intricate coastline wraps around the region, edging the Mediterranean Sea, the Atlantic Ocean, and the North Sea. Mountain ranges punctuate the landscape and form natural boundary lines. France and Spain meet in the Pyrenees; France, Germany, Switzerland, and Italy share the Alps. Great rivers run north, south, east, and west, notably Germany's Rhine; France's Seine, Loire, and Rhône; and Italy's Po. Geophysically Europe is an extension of the landmass of Asia, and it is as much because of its history and economic significance as because of its geographic character that it is called a continent.

▣ To listen to music from France, Portugal, and Spain, visit http://worldmusic.nationalgeographic.com.

BASQUES

Population: 2.5 million
Location: Spain, France
Language family: Language isolate

I n their Pyrenees stronghold straddling the border between France and Spain, the Basques developed one of the most enigmatic cultures in Europe. Many scholars consider them the oldest ethnic group on the continent, saying that they lived in the area before Indo-European peoples arrived more than 3,000 years ago. Some suggest they are descendants of Upper Paleolithic Cro-Magnons who occupied the region about 30,000 years ago.

The Basque language, Euskera, occupies its own family and is not related to any other language spoken in Europe; scholars have even looked for its roots in the Russian Caucasus and in North Africa as well. It is an extremely complex tongue, and a Basque tradition holds that the devil spent seven years trying to learn it but finally gave up. Nevertheless, Euskera has lent itself to a vast oral tradition kept alive by storytellers and by spontaneous versifiers called *bertsolariak*. Most Basques are bilingual, speaking French or Spanish and sometimes both.

Although the overwhelming majority of Basque people are Roman Catholics, a millennium has passed since the Basques inhabited a unified community. Today, they occupy three provinces in France and four in Spain—a homeland that includes the Pyrenees Mountains, the foothills of the Pyrenees, and the coastal plain along the Bay of Biscay.

An intensely independent people, the Basques have long managed to maintain some autonomy even when dominated by foreign powers. Under the 1939-1975 regime of Spain's Francisco Franco, however, Basque language and culture were vigorously suppressed, giving rise to the ETA— *Euskadi ta Askatasuna*, Basque Fatherland and Freedom—a strong, sometimes violent independence movement that has endorsed terrorist acts.

Traditionally, Basques worked as fishermen, farmers, and shepherds. Noted mariners, some even

Basque men lug stones through the streets in preparation for a competition testing strength—and manliness. The challenge evolved from rock-clearing chores on farms in the Basque regions of France and Spain.

crewed for Columbus and Magellan. Many Basque people now work in the area's large industrial sector, and while only 20 percent of Basques continue to farm, the *baserria,* or farmstead, remains a fixture in the rural areas inhabited by the Basque people.

Large three-story stone dwellings provide room for livestock on the bottom floor, living quarters for an extended family on the middle level, and storage for hay on the top.

One child within each baserria is designated the heir, the one who will receive the landholding at the time of his or her marriage. Males are favored, but females may also inherit. In the past, other siblings typically left the farm, sometimes settling for a religious life, and many also emigrated to other parts of Europe and beyond. A Basque village comprises 10 or 12 farmsteads, a church, a school, taverns, a town hall, and a handball court, often an extension of the church wall. A number of fast-paced ball games, including jai alai, originated in Basque country.

BRETONS

Population: 4 million
Location: France
Language family: Celtic

Just a look at a map showing Brittany, a peninsula jutting into the English Channel and the Atlantic Ocean, gives a hint that this region's population stands apart from other ethnic groups in France.

The Bretons are a Celtic people, with ties to the British Isles dating back to migrations that occurred between the 3rd and 5th centuries A.D. Over the years, numerous invasions thwarted their attempts to remain independent, and in the early 16th century their land was annexed to France. Provisions for some autonomy, however, and distance from the state administration in Paris served to isolate and insulate the Bretons, preventing their assimilation into the French nation until well into the 19th century.

With some 2,100 miles of coastline, including islands, Brittany has a distinct maritime orientation

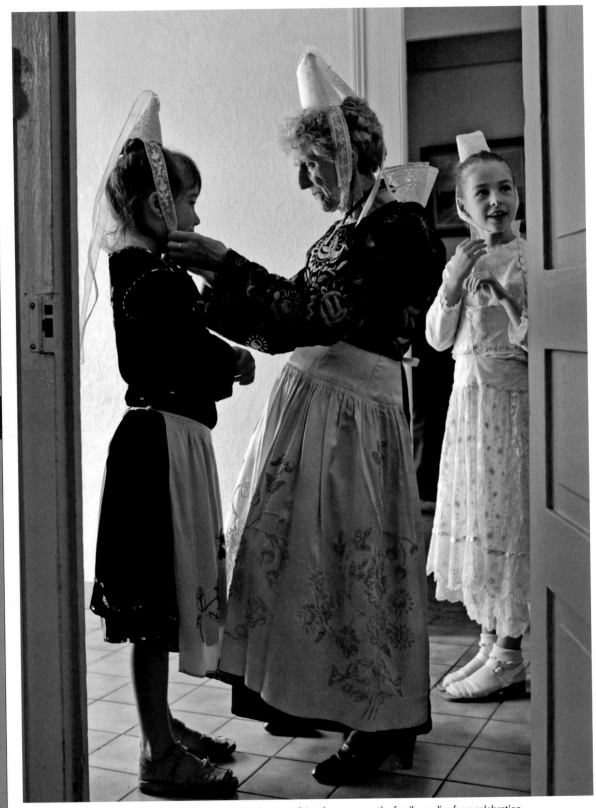

A Breton woman adjusts the headpiece of her granddaughter's traditional costume as the family readies for a celebration.

and a regional cuisine in which various seafoods figure prominently. The economy has long been based on fish and crustaceans and, until recently, algae gathering. Brittany also relies on its strong agricultural base. For generations, Bretons have worked the lands of the interior, planting vegetable crops and raising livestock on farmsteads marked by dense hedges. Today, mechanization of farming has made Brittany the premier agricultural region of France, complemented by large food processing and agricultural machinery industries.

The traditional rural scene of Brittany was composed of scattered homesteads—rectangular granite buildings with roofs of thatch or slate and chimneys at their gabled ends—as well as small villages and larger settlements called *plous*. The largest plous were subdivided into *treviou*. Vestiges of this system survive in the many place names beginning with *Plou-* or *Tre-*, especially in northwestern Brittany.

The Breton tongue, today spoken by just over half a million residents, belongs to the Brythonic branch of Celtic languages, making it closely related to Welsh and the now extinct Cornish tongue. Despite the decline in their spoken language, Bretons avidly foster their Celtic heritage and enjoy its many traditions, particularly folk music—which features a small bagpipe called a *biniou*—and folk dance. They routinely invite Celts from the British Isles to participate in their festivals.

Most Bretons are Roman Catholics, with their regional celebrations tending to be religious in nature. They show much devotion to hundreds of local saints, make pilgrimages to the region's nine cathedrals, and participate in festivals called *pardons*. These feature large processions, as well as traditional music and dancing, and they take on a secular atmosphere once religious devotions have been completed.

CATALANS

Population: 7 million
Location: Spain
Language family: Italic

Like their Basque neighbors to the west, Catalans retain a strong sense of identity and autonomy despite their longstanding incorporation into the national structures of France and Spain. These people reside in the Països Catalans, the "Catalan Countries," which historically included the Catalonia region of northeastern Spain, as well as Valencia, the Balearic Islands, the independent state of Andorra, and the French province of Pyrénées-Orientales. These people speak Catalan, a Romance language with ties to the Provençal language of southern France.

Spanish Catalonia has for a long time been an area of strategic importance. Union with Aragon in the 12th century and with Castile and León in the 15th

> ### He who hunts after bargains will scratch his head.
> CATALAN PROVERB

century widened the region's political sphere but subjugated Catalan interests. The people later experienced repression of their language and culture under Francisco Franco's dictatorship, lasting from 1939 to 1975. Finally, in 1979, regional autonomy for Catalonia was established and the Catalan language was allowed to flourish again, fueling the cultural pride that has led to a renaissance of Catalan music and literature, especially poetry.

Catalans are overwhelmingly Roman Catholic, with the cycles of the church year defining cultural observances. Each village and town honors its patron saint at an annual festival, during which processions typically feature huge papier-mâché representations of ritual figures: *capgrosses* ("bigheads") and giants, some 15 feet tall. All of Catalonia reveres Sant Jordi (St. George). On his feast day in April, which is also the official opening of the book publishing season, Catalans distribute his symbols of roses and books to their loved ones. Another feature of these Catalan celebrations is the *sardana*, the traditional dance whose stately cadences reflect the highly regarded concept of *seny*, a kind of refined good sense and self-realization at the heart of the Catalan self-image.

Economically, the region depends on a strong base of industry and tourism—seen at such places as Costa Brava, where hundreds of thousands of Europeans, including Catalan families, vacation each year. Despite a pastoral past, only 10 percent of the approximately seven million Spanish Catalans currently farm, while 25 percent reside and work in cosmopolitan Barcelona, the Catalonian capital.

DUTCH & FRISIANS

Population: 14 million
Location: Netherlands
Language family: Germanic

Some 14 million Dutch inhabit the Netherlands, or "lowlands," at the southeastern edge of the North Sea. These people are descendants of German, Frisian, and Frankish tribes who entered the area in pre-Roman times. Long tied to the fortunes of the Frankish and Habsburg empires, the Netherlands came into its own with the development of cities and subsequent involvement in commerce, trade, and colonial expansion. In the 17th century, the Netherlands entered a golden age of wealth and culture splendidly documented in the paintings of Rembrandt, Vermeer, and Frans Hals.

The Dutch language belongs to the Germanic family of Indo-European languages and is therefore related to English. Although regional dialects abound, they are mutually understood, their differences tempered by media influence. Dutch schoolchildren learn English as well, and many people, especially young urbanites, speak it fluently.

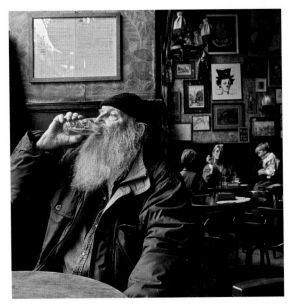

Polishing off his beer, a Dutch man enjoys the respite of Amsterdam's Brown Café, a city landmark named for its tobacco-stained interior.

The Dutch are vigilant stewards of the land, much of which has been reclaimed from a former North Sea inlet, the Zuider Zee (now the IJsselmeer). Despite their renown for growing tulips and for other kinds of horticulture and agriculture, only 4 percent of the Dutch still farm. Many now work in services and in industries such as food processing, petrochemicals, and electronics.

Modest and reserved in public, the Dutch place much emphasis on a *gezellig*, or cozy, family life. The nuclear family *(gezin)* has long been the ideal, with families tending to be small and children generally receiving much care and attention. People take fierce pride in their homes and gardens, and an evening stroll reveals the old practice of *schmeren:* Household curtains are open to let passersby get a lingering glimpse of the respectable gezellig gezin within. The ubiquitous bicycle serves many transportation needs in a country that boasts 6,200 miles of bike trails.

Though noted for their racial and ethnic tolerance and for neutrality in war, the Dutch traditionally divide along lines of religion. Currently more than a third of the people are Roman Catholic, and about a quarter are Protestants, spread among six groups, the largest being the Dutch Reformed Church.

Religious affiliation forms the basis of *verzuiling,* a "pillarization" or segmenting of Dutch society into separate groups, all with their own schools, newspapers, political parties, labor unions, and other organizations. While divisions have weakened—and were always moderated by the Dutch emphasis on mutual respect—verzuiling still significantly influences rural communities.

The Frisians, contributors to the original mixture of populations who became the Dutch, also maintained their own culture in Friesland, a small region on the coast of the upper North Sea that includes several barrier islands.

Since the early days of settlement there, around 400 B.C., the Frisians have battled the sea, constructing and continuously maintaining the "golden hoop," a system of dikes designed for protection against frequent storms and flooding. Laws specific to Frisian life were codified by Charlemagne into the Lex Frisionum, recorded in the early ninth century A.D. Among them is *bourrereplicht,* or "neighbor's duty," requiring that neighbors assist one another in a crisis.

Raging bulls scatter costumed participants during the annual festival of San Fermín in Pamplona. The running of the bulls there occurs every morning for a week in July.

Historically, trade was important in Friesland. Today many Frisians participate in agriculture by growing crops or dairying, as well as by breeding their prized milk cows. The typical "head-neck-body" house, a fixture in the Frisian countryside, consists of living quarters attached to a large barn by a passage that contains a kitchen, milk cellar, and churning area.

The Frisian language is related to Dutch, and the region's 700,000 Frisians speak it mostly at home. With its 11 cities, Friesland has remained fairly independent of the rest of the Netherlands; among the Frisians, a modern independence movement persists.

FRENCH

Population: 63 million
Location: France
Language family: Italic

Descendents of Celts, Romans, and Franks, the French inhabit Western Europe's largest country, one of its oldest, having become a unified kingdom in the 15th century. The French language derives from Latin; it originated in and around Paris. It now is spoken by virtually the entire population of France, as well as by hundreds of millions of people worldwide, in countries as diverse as Senegal, Canada, and India.

Shortly after the French Revolution, regional languages and dialects were suppressed and a mandate given that standard French be taught in all schools. Today, the Académie Française guards the purity of the language against outside influences, especially those of English. Nevertheless, the French still speak of *le parking* and *le weekend,* and the language of the Internet further erodes the purity of standard French.

Although about 80 percent of the French are Roman Catholic, attendance at Mass is quite low on any given Sunday. About 2 percent of the French are Protestant, mainly Lutheran and Calvinist.

Following World War II, large numbers of immigrants from former North African colonies began to arrive in France. Although these immigrants spoke

French, their Muslim religious affiliation and their distinctions in dress and other customs caused some conflicts in a larger culture that generally prizes conformity. Today, about two million French people are Muslim, more than half a million are Jewish, and a significant number are Buddhist, primarily immigrants from Vietnam.

Though regional and individual differences certainly exist, the French tend to be a formal people. They have a strong sense of correct behavior and procedures that they expect others to share. They also maintain distinctions of class based on occupation and education. Carrying formality into their home lives, they entertain guests in their public rooms while all other rooms remain off-limits, behind closed doors.

Since World War II, French families have become significantly smaller. To encourage population growth, the government offers subsidies for pregnant women and for children from birth until young adulthood,

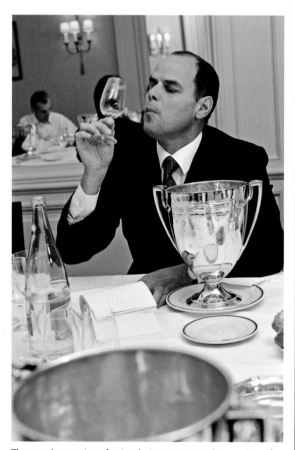

The nose knows: A professional wine taster samples a variety of champagnes at a Paris event. The French claim superiority in most gustatory matters.

regardless of a family's financial worth. French towns and cities offer preschools—*écoles maternelles*—and nearly all children attend full-time from age two on.

Much of French culture is geared toward food—its purchase, preparation, and consumption. French cuisine, with all of its regional nuances, benefits from France's fertile farmland, still abundant forests, and

> One should not let the grass grow
> on friendship's road.
> FRENCH PROVERB

wide access to the bounties of the sea. Daily meals unfold in a ritualized way that usually includes soup or another starter, meat and vegetables, salad, cheese, and dessert, along with wine. On weekends, the main meal usually occurs at midday and can last for hours.

Many holidays, such as Christmas and Easter, are marked with a further elaboration of foods, wines, and other spirits. The French national holiday, *Le quatorze juillet* (The Fourteenth of July), also known as Bastille Day, commemorates the storming of the Bastille in Paris during the French Revolution and the overthrow of the monarchy. Bastille Day is celebrated with parades, dances, fireworks, and other festivities.

The French symbolize their republic as an idealized woman, called Marianne. In recent times she has been depicted in statuary modeled after various famous women, including the actresses Brigitte Bardot and Catherine Deneuve.

Although France is self-sufficient agriculturally, only 3 percent of the people are involved in farming; this corresponds to a trend that now finds four-fifths of the population living in cities and suburbs. But that 3 percent produce some 60 varieties of grapes, mostly used in winemaking, and 400 types of cheese.

About one-third of the French work in industry, and the majority—more than 70 percent—work in the service sector. The French workday tends to be long, due in part to a lengthy lunch break, and so weekends tend to become very important. Many urban French escape as often as they can to second homes that they own or rent in the countryside.

Mothers of Invention

When DNA from participants of the Genographic Project is analyzed in the laboratory, the goal is to place each lineage on a specific branch of the human family tree. Generally speaking, this is done through the analysis of genetic mutations, or markers, which when shared by people unite them into an ancestral clan called a "haplogroup." By analyzing both the geographic distribution and genetic diversity of markers within each haplogroup, geneticists are able to trace back to the group's most recent common ancestor, allowing us to pinpoint where their predecessors came from, and when.

Around 30,000 years ago the Eurasian steppelands extended from present-day Germany, and possibly France, to Korea and China. The climate fostered a land rich in resources and opened a window into Europe. During this period a new mutation in the DNA of a Central Asian man was carried by his descendants into Europe during the first major wave of modern humans to colonize the region. This man's DNA, and specifically the genetic marker carried during that fateful migration, is now found in over 70 percent of all Western European men and as much as 90 percent in some populations. Because the first groups into Western Europe were part of a broad migration, it would seem unlikely that a single haplogroup should reach such high frequencies across a wide geographic range, and several factors contributed to its success.

The European chapter

The emergence of modern humans in Western Europe marked the appearance and spread of what archaeologists call the Aurignacian, a culture distinguished by significant innovations in tool manufacturing such as end-scrapers for preparing animal skins and tools for woodworking. These inventive early humans, named the Cro-Magnon after the cave where the first specimens were

Some Dutch women, like this smiling elder, still choose to wear distinctive regional dress and hairstyles.

found in southwest France, also used bone, ivory, antler, and shells as part of their tool kit. The large number of archaeological sites found in Europe from around 30,000 years ago indicates that they were experiencing a population expansion, and jewelry found at several of the sites—often an indication of status—suggests a more complex social organization was beginning to develop.

The Cro-Magnon are responsible for the famous cave paintings found in southern France that depict animals like bison, deer, and horses in colors far more intricate than anything seen prior to this period, providing evidence for a sudden blossoming of artistic skills as they moved into Europe. Their emergence heralded an end to the era of the Neandertals, a hominid species that inhabited Europe and parts of western Asia from about 250,000 to 25,000 years ago, and it is thought that the better communication skills, weapons, and resourcefulness of the Cro-Magnon probably allowed them to outcompete Neandertals for scarce resources.

Ice effects

But these early Europeans were hardly in the clear, and around 20,000 years ago the climate window that had allowed their rapid diffusion from Central Asia slammed shut, expanding ice sheets forcing people to move south. During the glacial maximum all of Northern Europe, almost all of Canada, and the northern half of the West Siberian Plain were covered by huge ice sheets, and for a period of about 2,000 years humans were restricted to isolated refuge regions in southern Iberia and the Balkans, areas close to the more temperate Mediterranean Sea.

Through these bitter cold times, human populations dwindled. The reduction in population size also reduced the group's genetic diversity. Once temperatures warmed and the ice retreated, beginning about 12,000 years ago, people emerging from the southern regions had a better shot at passing their DNA on to subsequent generations. Migrations northward allowed people to recolonize areas that had been vacated during the Ice Age. Much of Western Europe's current gene pool descends directly from these early survivors.

German soccer fans resort to prayer during a penalty-kick shoot-out at the 2006 World Cup quarterfinals. Staged in Berlin, the match drew home-team fans, who thrilled to see their team enter the semifinals, only to lose to Italy, the international champion.

The French revere education. The whole country closely follows the yearly back-to-school transition, called *La rentrée,* which is chronicled on the nightly news with a countdown to opening day. The national government sets school curricula as well as the questions for the month-long *baccalauréat,* the nation's secondary school exit exams. Results of this stressful ordeal determine eligibility for a university education, which is free for French students. Higher scores qualify students for enrollment at that nation's more prestigious universities.

GERMANS

Population: 75.4 million
Location: Germany
Language family: Germanic

The reunion of East and West Germany following the dismantling of the Berlin Wall in 1989 brought all 82 million Germans together in a single nation for only the second time in almost 120 years. German-speaking peoples had occupied the land east of the Rhine River from the first century B.C., eventually becoming incorporated into the Holy Roman Empire. In 1871, amid strong stirrings of nationalism, Prussian Chancellor Otto von Bismarck united independent German cities and provinces in a nation-state. Following the German defeat in World War II, the Federal Republic of Germany was formed, and the eastern part of the country became the Soviet-controlled German Democratic Republic. In the years that followed, East Germans fled to West Germany by the thousands, a diaspora that was thwarted by a wall erected in the divided city of Berlin, beginning in 1961.

The German language is closely related to English and Dutch. Dialects of German fall into two broad groups: the High German spoken in the southern

German highlands and the Low German spoken in the northern lowlands. Religious affiliation follows a similar geographic trend, with a mainly Protestant north and a largely Catholic south and Rhineland. Germany's Jewish population, about half a million before the genocide of the Holocaust, now numbers significantly less than 100,000.

The Christian religious calendar sets many annual celebrations, including Karneval or Fastnacht before Lent, as well as Easter and Christmas. Many towns sponsor a yearly Weihnachtsmarkt, a Christmas mar-

---

God is a good worker but loves to be helped.
BASQUE PROVERB

---

ket, at which people can buy seasonal foods and holiday trimmings. A new secular holiday on October 3 commemorates German reunification.

German cuisine incorporates a wide variety of starches, including bread, potatoes, and noodles, along with root vegetables. The favored meat is pork, often made into tasty sausages. World-famous German beers have been made according to the same laws of purity since the 16th century, which allow the use of only grain, hops, yeast, and water. Today Germans can choose their libations from more than 1,200 breweries in their country alone.

Germans typically prepare themselves for a career by seeking extensive education and training, whether the goal is to become a physicist or a plumber. A highly skilled labor force, respect for precision, and attention to detail contribute to German success in science and engineering, represented by the highly valued automobiles that roll out of German factories. The German industrial force contributes to the world's second largest export economy.

Although less than 3 percent of the population is engaged in farming, almost half of Germany's land is under cultivation, and the nation produces some 85 percent of its own food. Overall, Germans are well compensated for their work and enjoy a high standard of living that includes ample vacation time.

Gastarbeiter, or guest workers, coming from Turkey, the Balkans, and other countries, supplement the German work force.

For centuries, the bucolic and impeccably maintained German countryside has stood in contrast to the country's highly organized and bustling cities, where commerce and trade flourished. Today the central areas of many cities have been transformed into pedestrian-only zones where people can stroll, shop, and perhaps take in a concert in the city square. Germans also put a great deal of care and attention into their homes, and they relish family time, especially on the weekends. Many of them also join clubs and other interest-based groups in their local communities and, on a larger scale, they join unions and other advocacy organizations

Many Germans remain self-conscious about the horrifying events that occurred during the Nazi period of the 1930s and 1940s. As a nation and a people, Germans have spent the intervening decades trying to come to terms with the factors that allowed the Third Reich to take form and eliminating aspects of the regretted past—display of the *Hakenkreuz,* or swastika, is now forbidden, and measures are in place to assure that the media cannot be co-opted for propaganda purposes.

German reunification has come with its own set of concerns. There is still economic disparity, with higher unemployment and housing shortages in the East, and there are social implications as well. Germans still frequently differentiate between *Wessi* (Westerners) and *Ossi* (Easterners) in conversation, and some maintain that their diverse experiences on either side of the physical wall contribute to different mindsets, a result of the *Mauer in den Kopfen,* or "wall in the mind."

PORTUGUESE

Population: 10.5 million
Location: Portugal, Brazil
Language family: Italic

The Portuguese occupy about a sixth of the Iberian Peninsula, clustered mainly in towns and cities and in rural settlements in river valleys and along the coast. They also inhabit the Azores and Madeira, islands in the Atlantic off the coast of Western Africa.

The Portuguese people have descended from Iberian groups who entered the area in the third millennium B.C. and, later, Celtic peoples who entered the area after 900 B.C. The establishment of boundaries as they exist today occurred in the 13th century and solidified the Portuguese ethnic identity. These people displayed their maritime prowess several centuries later, as explorers and colonizers of an empire that formed rapidly.

A fairly strong north-south distinction characterizes many aspects of Portuguese life. Northerners tend to be more traditional in outlook than the people living in the south, a region known as the Algarve. Foods grown in the north include corn, potatoes, wine grapes, and vegetables. Southern cash crops include wheat, olives, and cork. People along the coast fish, and *bacalhau*, or salt cod, is the national dish. Portugal also maintains a large fish canning industry.

Virtually the entire population speaks Portuguese, a Romance language based on Latin. On the whole, Portuguese is spoken by almost 200 million people, including those living in regions in Africa, Asia, and South America formerly colonized by Portugal. At home, the Portuguese respond with polite dismay when visitors assume that Spanish can be spoken there as a lingua franca.

Portuguese society is less formal and hierarchical than it was in the past. Status still permeates social relationships as well as businesses and other organizations. A great deal of time is spent cultivating appropriate relationships, as loyalties are forged between individuals, not companies.

About 94 percent of the Portuguese are Roman Catholic. A tradition of *romarias*, pilgrimages to sites associated with particular saints, combines with *festas*, local festival days. Portugal has gone through several periods of anticlericalism in which the status of the clergy was challenged to the point of shutting down convents and monasteries. Currently, priests receive tempered respect, acknowledged for both their spiritual leadership and their human fallibility.

Catholicism coexists with strong beliefs in magic, sorcery, and witchcraft. The Portuguese also fear the malevolent effects of *inveja*, or envy, and practice measures to avoid the evil eye. Christian and pre-Christian beliefs surround death. Brotherhoods

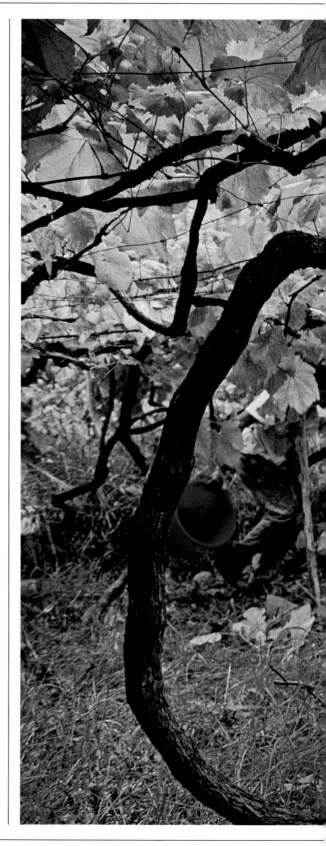

Amid a labyrinth of vines, women collect grapes destined to become one of Portugal's fine wines. Women provide much of the workforce in Portuguese viticulture.

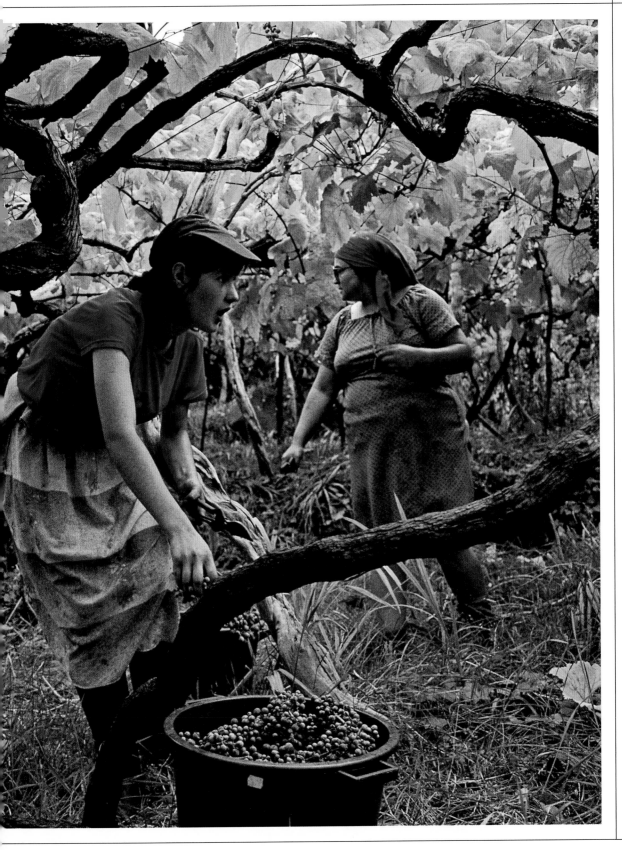

called *confrerias* help arrange funerals, assist with funeral expenses, and provide Masses of remembrance, which take place for years after the death of a loved one. Mourning practices may continue for years; widows usually wear black clothing for the rest of their lives.

Like most Europeans, the Portuguese are avid soccer fans. Their traditions in the sport of bullfighting differ from those in neighboring Spain in that much of the contest takes place with *cavaleiros* on horseback, and the bull is worked over but not killed in public at the end.

Portuguese musical forms include the complex and stylized vocal tradition known as fado (from the word for "fate") performed by men or women, but more often female *fadistas*. Accompanied by two guitars, a fado vocalist performs poignant narratives that embody the quintessential Portuguese concept of *saudade*, a pervasive and ineffable longing.

SPANISH

Population: 30 million
Location: Spain
Language family: Italic

The Spanish people inhabit the bulk of the Iberian peninsula as well as the Canary and Balearic Islands, making Western Europe's second largest country one of its less densely populated. Roman conquest of indigenous tribes in 200 B.C. brought Latin to the peninsula, giving rise to Spanish as well as the Catalan and Galician languages, but not supplanting Basque, a pre-Roman language of the Pyrenees. In the fifth century the Visigoths invaded, followed by the Moors three centuries later. The Moors finally were driven out in 1492, when their last ruler fled from his stronghold in Granada. In the modern era, a bloody civil war from 1936 to 1939 set the scene for the long dictatorship of Francisco Franco. At his death in 1975, a constitutional monarchy was reinstated.

Members of La Resurrección brotherhood assemble prior to the annual Easter Sunday procession in Seville. Religiously based brotherhoods play important roles in Spanish communities.

Geographic diversity characterizes the Spanish landscape. Mountains, rolling hills, valleys, coastal plains, and the vast tableland that forms Spain's interior promote regional variations in culture, although regional dialects of Spanish are mutually intelligible with Castilian, the country's official language.

Spain is 95 percent Catholic, and although the church wields far less influence than in the past, the religion permeates the culture and the landscape. Beautiful churches and cathedrals draw visitors even as weekly attendance at Mass declines. People celebrate the feast days of saints, especially that of Santiago (St. James), the country's patron saint. Other holidays include October 12, the Dia de Hispanidad, commemorating colonization of the New World.

Spanish families value togetherness, often organizing their workdays around the afternoon meal. Many businesses, shops, and schools close between 1 and 2 p.m. so that people can return home for what most consider the main meal of the day. It may consist of a stew or perhaps paella, saffron-infused rice with vegetables and seafood or meat that is associated with the Valencia region but has become a national dish. A siesta may follow the meal, and people return to work and school by four or five o'clock. The evening meal, usually less elaborate, may be eaten as late as 10 p.m. Weekend meals expand in social importance, offering opportunities for relatives or friends (known as *cuadrillas* or *peñas*) to share a leisurely repast.

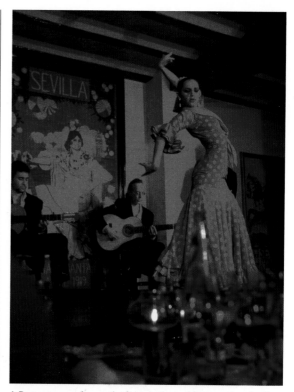

A Roma woman dances the fiery rhythms of flamenco in a Seville nightclub. Flamenco has roots in the Islamic, Sephardic, and Gypsy cultures of southern Andalusia.

> ## To a dog once scalded, cold water seems hot.
> ITALIAN PROVERB

Spanish homes usually are built to maximize a family's privacy, often by means of an interior patio, while public spaces let people see and be seen. Housing tends to be tightly clustered, and people spend a great deal of time outside of the home, going for *paseos,* or walks, in the street or plazas, visiting friends, shopping, or stopping for a beverage and snacks called tapas.

The Spanish live mostly in nuclear families. At marriage, a couple usually establishes a household. In rural areas, the child expecting to take over the family farm may stay on at the farmstead after marriage. Class differences matter less than in the past, and now more people can achieve higher status through education or professional achievement.

Until the mid-20th century, the Spanish worked predominantly in agriculture. Typical crops are wheat, rice, grapes, citrus fruits, and vegetables, along with cured hams, Spanish wines, and sherry, a fortified wine named for its origins in Jerez de la Frontera. Industrialization came later to Spain than to more northern countries, but it is now well established, the major industries being arms and munitions, machinery, and automobiles. Today, tourism and related services provide the largest number of jobs.

Although a controversial entertainment in these times, the bullfight remains a Spanish national symbol. The event unfolds in three highly ritualized stages, ending with the killing of the bull by the matador. The Spanish also identify with the iconic figure of Don Quixote, from the 1605 novel by Cervantes, whose ingenuous optimism endears readers worldwide.

Northern Europe

The region of Northern Europe comprises the peninsulas and island nations in the northwestern stretch of the European continent. The British Isles—Ireland and Northern Ireland, Scotland, Wales, and England—while forming a closeknit geographical unit, have been joined together and split asunder politically in a variety of combinations over the centuries. Demanding landscapes and rugged lifestyles of the nations of Scandinavia—Denmark, Norway, Sweden, and Finland—give grounds for a common regional identity. Out on its own in the Norwegian Sea, the volcanic island of Iceland stakes a claim in world literary history.

To listen to music from Ireland, Norway, Sweden, and the United Kingdom, visit http://worldmusic.national geographic.com.

CORNISH

Population: 500,000
Location: United Kingdom
Language family: Celtic

Descendants of one of three Brythonic kingdoms (the others were Wales and Strathclyde, now southern Scotland), the Cornish reside in Cornwall, at the southwestern tip of Great Britain. For generations, they spoke a language that was closely related to Welsh and a cousin to Irish and other Gaelic languages; today, however, they speak English almost exclusively, while retaining certain words and phrases that mark the distinct Cornish English dialect.

At present, about 500,000 people live in Cornwall, but because the British government does not officially recognize the Cornish as an ethnic group, no one knows for certain how many residents claim specific Cornish ancestry.

Recent developments in a solidarity movement have pushed the identity issue forward, and many people are now asserting the uniqueness of their culture and history. They hope that Cornwall will eventually see the establishment of its own regional government—somewhat like Scotland and Wales, each of which have independent parliaments and yet are part of Great Britain.

Cornwall has long been known not only for the skill of its miners but also for a ubiquitous meat-stuffed pastry dubbed the Cornish pasty. In fact, the histories of the two are deeply intertwined: Pasties were convenient food for miners to carry to work with them, and the miners are said to have offered corners of the pasty to the "knockers," mine-spirits who could prove troublesome. Cornish miners emigrating to the American West brought this tradition with them, and around mines from Colorado to Montana it is still common to hear stories about the "tommyknockers."

The last Cornish tin mine closed in 1998, yet stories and traditions associated with mining persist.

Inextricably linked with northern Europe's Sami, reindeer herding provides a full-time livelihood for only 10 percent of the population.

DANES

Population: 5 million
Location: Denmark
Language family: Germanic

The Danish people originated in southern Sweden, crossing the narrow sound to the Jutland Peninsula—the northern extension of the West European Plain—and the several hundred islands that surround it. For centuries their rural agricultural communities practiced a communalism of open fields and pooled livestock herds, a tradition that has carried over into the agricultural cooperatives of Denmark today. Aversion to conflict and confrontation are Danish traits fostered by the communal spirit. Children are taught to suppress aggression and work things out through dialogue and compromise.

Danes universally speak Danish, a Germanic language known for dialectal variations and related to the other Scandinavian languages and to English, German, and Dutch. Danes also typically speak a second language, either German or English—sometimes both.

At birth, a Dane automatically is considered a member of the Evangelical Lutheran state church, although actual church affiliation includes other denominations such as Danish Baptist and Roman Catholic. Lutheran confirmation remains an important rite of passage, but modern Danes otherwise spend little time in church, except perhaps at holidays. For the pre-Lenten observance of *fastelavn*, costumed children visit door-to-door, singing songs and asking for treats. Bonfires light the night sky on Saint Hans Day at the summer solstice, when an effigy of a witch is burned in the blaze.

Holiday meals tend to be festive and include a wider range of foods than the traditional daily fare of open-faced sandwiches, boiled potatoes and vegetables, and fried meats with gravy. Special seasonal Danish beers complement holiday foods.

There is an economy of scale to almost every physical feature in Denmark, natural and built. The land itself has little elevation, all from gently rolling hills. Houses, both old-fashioned and newly built, are low, rarely rising more than a single story. Few commercial buildings are taller than four or five stories.

The Danes excel at design and have inspired several generations of manufacturers worldwide with their sleek, functional, and easily assembled furniture. The small, interlocking blocks called Lego also have Danish roots, and visitors to the Legoland theme park in Billund can see their possibilities carried to the most fanciful extremes.

About two-thirds of the Danish landscape is cultivated, and Danish farmers grow much more food than the population needs. Cooperatives produce dairy products such as milk, butter, and cheese. The yields of commercial fishing and livestock raising are consumed locally as well as exported. Industries and services now employ many more Danes than agriculture, and a very high proportion of women—some 80 percent—are found in the workforce.

Danish family life is based on a privacy that usually admits only family and close friends. Currently, though, nuclear families consisting of married parents and children make up fewer than half of all households. Elderly parents once were automatically cared for by the family of the eldest son, but now extensive Danish social services, which include universal health care and free higher education, provide elder care as well.

ENGLISH

Population: 45 million
Location: United Kingdom, United States, Canada
Language family: Germanic

Eingland had been settled for thousands of years by Celtic tribes when the Romans occupied and unified it, beginning in the middle of the first century B.C. The Germanic tribes of Angles, Saxons, and Jutes who followed brought the basis for the English language (the Angles supplying the root of the name), with further additions from the Vikings and especially from the Norman French.

Today English is spoken by 49 million English and by hundreds of millions of others worldwide. In England, the language exhibits strong regional and class differences. Standard English is based on pronunciation in southeastern England and is the version spoken by most media announcers. It is often called "BBC English," after the national broadcasting network.

Two Englishmen share the pleasure of a country outing, pausing for a nip at the Blencathra Foxhounds Club in Cumbria.

Although churchgoing has declined dramatically, the Church of England still serves as a defining institution of English culture. Its *Book of Common Prayer,* first published in 1549, has served as a rich source of expression in the English language, together with the plays of Shakespeare. Today about half the English are Anglican; the rest of England's Protestants are mostly Methodists and Baptists. About 10 percent of the English are Roman Catholic and the country includes sizable numbers of Jews, Hindus, Sikhs, and Muslims, most of whom represent England's large immigrant populations.

Criticized by some as anachronistic, the monarchy also remains an enduring English symbol. The escapades of younger royals may fill the tabloids, but the English still expect to see their Queen in familiar roles and places—opening Parliament, inspecting her troops, and broadcasting a Christmas Day message.

The English value reserve, civility, and a sense of fair play. The habit of "queuing," or lining up in an orderly fashion at bus stops and other venues, expresses all of these qualities. They also highly value the varied landscapes of their small country, including the built environment, and work to preserve them. Extensive walking trails throughout the island nation offer a chance to explore the countryside, and by law it is the duty of private landowners to allow access to the paths that run through their property.

English cuisine endures a worldwide reputation of being bland, based on traditional fare of well-cooked meats, boiled vegetables, and fried foods such as fish and chips. Tea is the national drink, and the English consume about a third of the world's production. Afternoon tea—the beverage plus dainty sandwiches and cakes—traditionally was an upper-class habit. Working people, who often ate their main meal at lunchtime, took "high tea" in the evening, and the food included more hardy fare. Workers and businesspeople both often stop in at their local pub (short for "public house") for a pint of ale or lager after work. In the past few decades, the English have broadened their culinary horizons, as witnessed by the proliferation of internationally trendy restaurants and celebrity chefs.

Avid sports fans, the English enthusiastically follow the fortunes of their favorite teams, whether the game is football (soccer), rugby, or cricket—all English inventions. It is legal to gamble on sports in England, and many people frequent betting shops to play the odds, as they also do on horse racing.

For centuries, gardening has been a favorite English pastime. An English home almost invariably includes a garden, yet even a city window box is apt to receive considerable time and attention. With the popularity of home improvement programs on British television, DIY (do-it-yourself) now rivals gardening as a week-end passion.

Most English—about 90 percent—live in urban or suburban areas. Despite the popular notion of bucolic rural England, few people actually farm, and as the industrial north of England has declined, the number of people employed in the service economy, especially in the southeast, has risen dramatically.

In the 17th and 18th centuries, thousands of English sailed to the New World and established settlements there. They became the foundation of the non-native populations of Canada and the United States. Since Canada has remained in England's fold as a member of the Commonwealth, its population of English descent remains closer in many ways to the country of origin. Americans are a somewhat different story, and it has been said facetiously that England and the United States are "two countries separated by a common language." Although the American Revolution broke the political connection, language and the legal system reveal America's deep English roots.

FAROESE

Population: 48,000
Location: Faroe Islands
Language family: Germanic

The Faroese way of life centers on small villages spread out among the North Atlantic's 18 Faroe Islands. Intensely proud of their beautiful homeland, the people are primarily fishermen who exploit rich Gulf Stream waters surrounding their archipelago. The Faroese have enormous boating skills, and these are frequently exhibited at festivals where wooden boats are raced. The events recall a time when large groups worked together to hunt whales from such vessels. But the sea is not the only focus here: Sheep herding is also a feature of Faroese life, with twice as many sheep as people occupying the islands.

The Faroese are scattered across the islands, dwelling in and among towns that may have as few as 500 inhabitants. People often gather for the religious holidays observed by the Lutheran Church, which

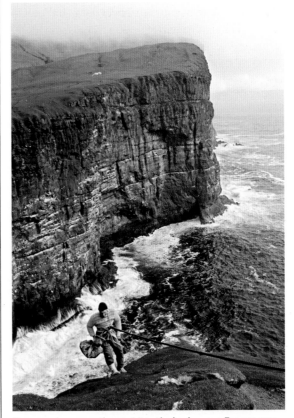

Far more dangerous than a visit to the henhouse, a Faroese man scales cliffs to collect the eggs of the guillemot, an abundant seabird on the Danish-administered islands.

continues to be an active force in the culture. Chain dances where people form circles, hold hands, and sing catchy, rhyming songs were first known in the Middle Ages and are still popular here, even among residents who drive modern vehicles and carry cellular phones. Because of their geographic isolation and small numbers, the people are untroubled by most urban problems, but the collapse of the fishing industry in the 1990s created a recession and encouraged emigration. Though the Faroese have recovered, their dependence on fishing leaves them vulnerable.

With a history much like that of Iceland—these islands were settled in the ninth century by Norwegian Vikings and people of Celtic origin—the Faroe Islanders speak a language very similar to Icelandic. But unlike Iceland, the Faroe Islands are part of the Danish kingdom. A movement to break free of Denmark continues to grow in popularity, mostly because of differing attitudes toward European unity; Denmark is a member of the European Union, while the islands are not. The Faroese, however, already enjoy a high degree of autonomy, and they would find it difficult to survive without financial subsidies from Denmark.

FINNS

Population: 5 million
Location: Finland
Language family: Finno-Permic

Until 1809, Finland was part of the kingdom of Sweden and had been for more than 500 years, causing some people to think of it as a Scandinavian country. Further, about 20 percent of the population in southern Finland, especially in the Åland Islands, is of Swedish descent. But while Finns may resemble Scandinavians, with light skin, hair, and eyes, their culture is actually very distinct from that of Scandinavia.

The people speak a Finno-Ugric language, which has more in common with Hungarian than with Swedish—suggesting that they may have originated in eastern Europe or Siberia. The *Kalevala,* an epic poem about a mythical hero who not only brings music and prosperity to Finland but also rescues the sun and moon, is considered the national story. It has elements that are thought to be more than 3,000 years old. Composed in Finnish, the poem is sung and performed on national holidays as a way of celebrating the distinct Finnish identity. It was based on folktales collected in

Karelia, an eastern part of Finland where the tradition of singing complex poems lasted well into the 19th century. A large section of this region now lies within Russia's borders, and its people follow the Russian Orthodox religion.

Politically, Finland was annexed by tsarist Russia in 1809 and was for many years influenced by Russian culture, architecture, and political thought. Even so, it became an independent republic in 1917 and later observed strict neutrality during the Cold War. Today's Finns see themselves bridging the cultures of Western

> ## You cannot catch fish until you wet your feet.
> SAMI PROVERB

and Eastern Europe; some adhere to Eastern Orthodoxy, but more than 90 percent practice evangelical Lutheranism, the dominant faith in Scandinavia.

Though Finns are typically known for their reserved personal style, they are today's number one users of cellular phones, and their main recreational activities are mambo dancing, winter sports, *pesäpallo* (a form of baseball), and relaxing in saunas, which they invented. Several Finnish designers and architects enjoy world renown, and the design style often associated with Scandinavia actually finds it origin in Finnish aesthetics of austerity, beauty, and practicality.

ICELANDERS

Population: 250,000
Location: Iceland
Language family: Germanic

Little more than a quarter of a million people live on the volcanic island of Iceland, first settled by Norwegian Vikings in A.D. 874 and included in the Scandinavian kingdoms until its people declared independence in 1944.

Because of that long connection, Icelanders are similar to Scandinavians in more ways than just physical type: They enjoy a high standard of living, have socialized health care, eat the same kinds of food, and are Lutheran. A number of early settlers, however, were

Lost Songlines

Northern Europe encompasses a geographic range where local populations speak languages belonging to completely different families, practice ways of life from reindeer herding to whale hunting to farming, and have cultural histories that range in age from 40,000 years old to as recent as a few hundred. And yet, beginning with the European age of exploration and continuing with the rapid periods of industrialization and globalization that have characterized these past two centuries, its people and their culture have now arrived on every continent, and they have forever changed our planet's genetic landscape.

At the turn of the 20th century, Europeans arrived by the scores to Ellis Island, the main entry facility in New York for immigrants entering the United States. Hoping to make a fresh start, they adopted new names and moved to towns they had never heard of before, breaking with their cultural past in hopes of a better life. More than 12 million people, many from Northern Europe, entered their names in Ellis Island's official ledger over a 60-year period, and today more than 100 million Americans can trace their ancestry to those people, the first immigrants to walk through its golden door.

Hunting and gathering

This pattern of recent migration has been mirrored around the world, and so today people are for the first time in history confronted with the difficult reality of not knowing exactly where their own ancestors come from, what cultural traditions they practiced, and which languages their people spoke.

Because many people now live in places where everybody comes from somewhere else, we no longer have the oral histories or ancient songlines to educate us about our distant past.

Surprisingly, genetic research is now allowing people to reconstruct the birthplace of those long lost migrations.

A Northern Irish bartender pulls pints in a Belfast pub.

DNA markers take a long time to become historically informative, which is why they are traditionally used to help answer questions of anthropological interest. While mutations occur in every generation, it typically requires hundreds, if not thousands, of years before they can be used as windows back into the distant past, signposts on the human trail that tell us something about the people that have come before us. But if we accumulate enough genetic information from enough people around the world, our own genetic sequences may reveal details of the smaller, more recent branches of that trail. It may be difficult to say anything about the history of these subgroups, but they can reveal the distribution of other people alive today who are more closely related to us, helping to fill in events that have occurred as recently as the past few hundred years. It is a useful way to help bridge the anthropology of population genetics with the popular study of genealogy, to which we are all accustomed.

Ancestral gene pools

Public interest in genealogy has become a global phenomenon, and people are now turning to DNA to pinpoint the origins of their ancestors' first migrations. As these databases grow and people from around the world sign up to have their own DNA anonymously tested, scientists are beginning to recognize a real value in numbers.

A recent survey for Scandinavian ancestry in one such database revealed that some lineages characteristic of this Northern European region were showing up in people from the British Isles. When the team looked more closely, they found that the villages where these people lived were predominantly sites of known Viking influence, suggesting an entire scenario of travel and cultural interaction that happened many centuries ago.

These realizations provide some of the first evidence for the impact these seafaring traders and warriors had on the gene pool of places they had raided. Research that was initially intended to address questions of great antiquity is now helping to solve the genetic riddles still puzzling the past few dozen human generations.

Like huge volcanic hot tubs, the geothermal pools of Iceland's Blue Lagoon make a year-round spa. In a landscape of remarkable natural phenomena, including live volcanoes, Icelanders make the most of their free time outdoors.

Celtic slaves who had been captured in Scotland and Ireland, and their contribution to the gene pool means Icelanders are as likely to be brown-haired as blond. After a thousand years of intermarriage, Scandinavians and Celts have become one people—a tightly knit culture in which almost everyone is related to everyone else by blood, if only distantly, and family names do not exist.

The language of Iceland, related to archaic Norwegian, is very different from the ones of modern Scandinavia. It is considered a main distinguishing ethnic marker, with the government pursuing an aggressive policy of language purity and even maintaining a list of approved names for newborns. Iceland's people are also distinguished by a love of writing and storytelling that led to their creation of the Icelandic sagas, a medieval body of literature that continues to be read and cherished. One of the most literate peoples in the world, Icelanders most often give books as birthday and Christmas presents.

While rooted in the past, the nation of Iceland is also very modern. More than half of the Icelandic population resides in Reykjavík, the capital city, where advanced technology, tourism, music, and fashion have overtaken fishing and farming as the most common occupations. Living on a geologically active volcanic island, where natural hot springs abut huge glaciers, Icelanders have pioneered the use of geothermal energy to produce electricity for industry and to provide heat and light for their homes.

Although they have high-quality public education through the university level, Icelanders often go abroad for specialized education, which also contributes to the international influences on the country's population. Wherever they go, though, Icelanders remain attached to their "little nation." Today, Iceland's cultural influences come primarily from Europe and the Americas, befitting a nation that sits astride the Mid-Atlantic Ridge, where the European and North American tectonic plates meet.

IRISH

Population: 4.1 million
Location: Ireland
Language family: Celtic (Irish Gaelic), Germanic (English)

In the Republic of Ireland, the Irish people number a little over four million, but it is impossible to know just how many Irish live and work throughout the British Isles and abroad. In terms of global Irish culture, it is probably equally impossible to quantify how many people worldwide claim some degree of Irish ancestry.

In the modern era, after a long period as a colony of England, Ireland asserted its independence with the Easter Rebellion of 1916. This movement eventually led to the creation of the Irish Free State, in 1921. Ratification of the Free State meant an independent Ireland, but it also ensured British sovereignty in Northern Ireland. In 1949, the Republic of Ireland that we know today was born.

Following the tragic potato famine of 1846-51, some two million Irish emigrated to England and America to seek employment. Even in more recent years Irish workers have continued to emigrate and pursue their fortunes abroad, but today many expatriates have come home to participate in the country's wide-ranging economic revival. Growth in computers, telecommunications, and other technology industries has increased the opportunities in Ireland for professional employment. In addition, Ireland's expanding infrastructure, spurred by its inclusion in the European Union, has brought about a marked increase in work for skilled tradesmen.

Ireland's cultural traditions remain firmly ensconced in its people, more than 90 percent of whom are Roman Catholic, with minority populations of various Protestant denominations. The Irish, and the rest of the world, revere the legacy of intellectual centers such as Trinity College in Dublin, where the most famous medieval Gospel book, the *Book of Kells,* resides. Literature, music, and theater are staples of Irish life, along with soccer, Gaelic football, and hurling—an exuberant relative of field hockey.

Like their English neighbors, the Irish have an appreciation for life in the public house. At the pub, friends gather for snooker, darts, and other games while debating James Joyce or the finer points of Irish politics—all, of course, accompanied by a pint of Guinness or Murphy's stout.

The principal language of Ireland is English, but Irish is still very important in the contemporary culture. Irish, or Irish Gaelic, is spoken by a large part of the population, especially in the north and west, and cities, towns, and roads bear Irish names, as do many organizations and businesses. Learned either traditionally or in schools, the Irish Gaelic language is used professionally, informally, and artistically.

The wool of the feral Norwegian sheep called villsau is not sheared, but pulled by hand. It makes a fabric fine enough to be used in making sails for Viking ship replicas. Villsau are related to sheep bred by Vikings some thousand years ago.

NORWEGIANS

Population: 4.6 million
Location: Norway
Language family: Germanic

With only four and a half million of them in a more than thousand-mile-long country, the Norwegians find themselves with plenty of room to stretch out—in fact, they have the lowest population density in northern Europe. Mountains and water are defining features of their land, in the form of a long chain that runs Norway's length and numerous rivers, lakes, and fjords, as well as a long, rugged coastline.

Norwegians descend from the Vikings who unified the territory in A.D. 900 under Harald Fairhair, whose moniker still describes a great many of the people. They became Christians a century later and, as the

Reformation became entrenched in northern Europe, adopted evangelical Lutheranism as the state religion in 1814, upon the dissolution of a 400-year union under Danish kings. A merger with Sweden ended this brief period of independence.

By 1905 Norway was free again, but without a monarch, so a Danish prince was appropriated and made Håkon VII, King of Norway. By this point the Norwegians had begun in earnest to stress their Norwegian heritage, to distinguish themselves from their neighbors and create links to their Viking past— a process of reinvention that continues to this day.

The Norwegian language is closely related to other Scandinavian languages and exists in many spoken dialects and two literary forms: *Bokmål,* "book language," a Danish-oriented version from eastern Norway, and *Nynorsk,* "new Norwegian," consciously forged in the 19th century from peasant dialects and tied directly to Old Norse. Norwegians today utilize both, or may simply write their own dialect as spoken.

More than a third of Norway stretches beyond the Arctic Circle. The country's extreme northern location means long days in summer. On the longest, Midsummer's Eve at the summer solstice in June, Norwegians celebrate all night with bonfires, feasting, and dancing. They also emphasize Christmas, which they treat as a season lasting into January, and observe with candles, greens, carols, and traditional foods including lutefisk, dried cod soaked in lye.

The main secular feast is Constitution Day, on May 17, and is celebrated with parades and public ceremonies followed by gatherings of family and friends at home. In keeping with their reverence for the rural Norwegian past, many individuals own complete folk costumes that they wear at celebrations or on formal occasions.

The discovery of offshore oil and natural gas in the 1960s has turned Norway into a very prosperous country and has made it the second largest exporter of these fuels. Norway's farming and fishing base involves only about 5 percent of the people, industry employs some 23 percent, and services the rest. Well paid and well covered by socialized health care and other state-run programs, Norwegians on the whole enjoy a very high standard of living.

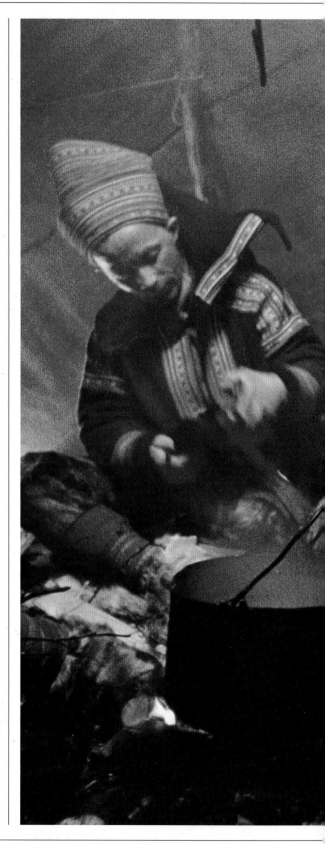

In the cold, harsh reaches of northern Norway, a Sami family prepares a meal in their tent.

Although they are known as a nation of readers—supporting more daily newspapers than many larger populations—Norwegians spend much of their leisure time out of doors, often gathering together in little huts or cabins in the mountains for weekends and in the summer. Skiing in all its forms is the national sport, and even for residents of Oslo the ski trails are only a tram ride away.

SAMI

Alternate name: Saami, Lapps   Population: 60,000
Location: Norway, Sweden, Finland
Language family: Sami

Most likely those who have lived the longest on the Scandinavian peninsula, the Sami are a non-Germanic ethnic group living in northern Norway and Sweden as well as in northern Finland and northwestern Russia (the Kola Peninsula, in particular). The Sami were traditionally nomadic pastoralists and occasional hunters, heavily dependent on their reindeer herds—which are likely the inspiration for the reindeer that accompany the cultural icon, Santa Claus. The Sami practiced a shamanistic religion and saw power in natural features such as rocks and mountains. But because of their nomadic way of life, they were discriminated against by Scandinavians, who called them Lapps, a derogatory name.

The Sami are well adapted for living in the north. To get from place to place, for example, they rely on skis—which they invented as a means for accompanying their sleds. Traditionally, they used every part of a reindeer for survival; animal skins were made into clothing or draped around poles to create a transportable dwelling similar to a tipi. Their brightly colored ceremonial costumes, worn with upturned boots, include jackets, skirts, and hats that are ornately decorated with strips of colored material.

Although they follow a way of life that shares customs with Arctic groups, the Sami are genetically different. Some researchers place their origin in the Alps, while others say ancient Siberia. In any case, they most likely came to northern Europe thousands of years ago, following reindeer herds as the polar ice cap receded. The people speak a Finno-Ugric language like Finnish, but the two tongues are not mutually intelligible. In fact, there are three main dialects of Sami, and these developed probably through the isolation of the different bands in the hard-to-cross terrain of the northern reaches of Scandinavia. Today, Sami is a vibrant, living language that continues to be taught in schools, and it is a distinguishing ethnic marker of the people who speak it. The vocabulary reflects a particular way of life, and at least one word—tundra—is used worldwide.

More than a thousand years of close cultural ties with Scandinavians and other Europeans have created considerable variation within the Sami. A good half of today's Sami people still herd reindeer, and many subsist as farmers and fishermen or live in villages, working as miners and loggers. But changes in their traditional lifestyle have not weakened the Sami's sense of who they are, and today this group is reasserting its unique identity.

Sweden, Norway, and Finland once tried to limit claims of Sami identity to the people who still practice reindeer herding. But all of the people who speak the Sami language or who had Sami parents and grandparents, regardless of occupation, consider themselves to be Sami. They also are demanding political autonomy for northern areas of the Scandinavian peninsula that have traditionally been their home. To secure their rights and ensure the continuance of their culture, the Sami have organized a representative body—the Sami Parliament—in Norway, Sweden, and Finland.

SCOTS

Population: 4.8 million
Location: United Kingdom
Language family: Germanic

Scotland's population is largely concentrated in major urban centers such as Edinburgh, Glasgow, Dundee, and Aberdeen. Scots are also found beyond the Scottish border, living and working elsewhere in the United Kingdom and in many other parts of the world. Most people are members of the Church of Scotland, which is Presbyterian.

For much of its history, Scotland has been viewed by its English neighbors as a rugged, untamed land filled with rugged, untamed people. And like widely held views of the American West, this conception has some measure of truth and a goodly portion of fancy. The latter stems from English prejudice against Scotland's warring clans. These groups wore tartans, woolen clothing of variously colored plaid patterns

While more Irish people are found outside of the country than within it, this father and son call County Kerry, an area of superlative natural beauty in western Ireland, their home.

that served the political function of identifying one's clan affiliation. Worn less and less frequently, though still preferred for formal wear, kilts continue to be symbols of Scottish ethnicity and the time of independence before 1707, when England and Scotland were united under one king.

Known as the birthplace of golf, Scotland is perhaps equally famous for its poets, its military heroes, its whisky, and its national dish, called haggis, a pudding made from a mixture of organ meats and oatmeal, stuffed and boiled within a sheep's stomach. Haggis originated in Scotland's agrarian past, when the herding of sheep was a mainstay of the economy.

While many Scots continue to ranch and farm, the modern economy increasingly revolves around such high-technology endeavors as semiconductor production, software design, genetics, and environmental science. The birth of the world's first cloned sheep, called Dolly, at the Roslin Institute in Edinburgh bears ample testimony to Scotland's ability to blend cutting-edge science with traditional occupations. New industries coexist with longstanding work in petroleum production, shipbuilding, and the making of malt whisky, known to the world as Scotch.

But if Scotch is a drink, the name "Scots" means a people and their language. Scots English, known from the 18th century as Broad Scots, is a Germanic dialect akin to English. Although it was the language of the great Scottish poet Robert Burns (1759-96), it was largely abandoned in the latter part of the 19th century—banned in schools and discouraged everywhere else—so that Scots could compete in the dominant English economy. Scots English enjoys only limited use today and is principally observed in dialects such as Glasgow Patter and the Broad Buchan of the northeast coastal region.

Scots Gaelic, a Celtic language that had nearly disappeared by 1970, has recently experienced a resurgence. There are now Scots Gaelic development programs, theater groups, and television programs, and the language is taught in some schools. The new popularity of bagpipe music, played by an instrument perfected in 18th-century Scotland, is another sign of the survival of Scottish ethnicity.

Scotland's greatest heroes—William Wallace, Robert the Bruce, and Bonnie Prince Charlie—all fought for independence. Today, after the 1997 referendum to convene a new parliament, a measure of that independence has been realized. The Scottish Parliament first met in 1999 and maintains administrative authority over internal finance, education, transportation, the environment, and other important areas.

SWEDES

Population: 9 million
Location: Sweden
Language family: Germanic

The Roman historian Tacitus wrote in the first century A.D. of the Sviones, a people "mighty in ships and arms," indicating that they traded with the Roman Empire. Some seven centuries later, Viking longboats were setting out for trading voyages to Western Europe and Russia, and the Swedes were soon to become a unified—and Christian—kingdom. They also began to struggle politically with their Scandinavian neighbors: Sweden controlled Finland for almost 800 years and was united with Norway for almost a century, until 1905.

Today, some nine million Swedes live in a country the size of California, mostly clustered around three major cities in the south. Their nation boasts 100,000 lakes, and about 70 percent of their land is forested. Climate varies dramatically, from the cold and snowy north above the Arctic Circle to milder, relatively

Throughout highland Scotland, annual games challenge local men with feats of strength and stamina. In the Scottish hammer throw, a 20-pound metal ball attached to a wooden pole is twirled and flung over the contestant's shoulder.

snowless regions in the south, which experience little more than one snowy month each year.

All Swedes speak Swedish, a Germanic language related to Danish and Norwegian. This is true of the Sami people, who live in the far north, and also of Sweden's Finnish population. Until recently, Swedes automatically became members of the state Lutheran church at birth, but the 21st century brought a separation of church and state. Still, some 90 percent of Swedes are Lutherans, with the rest mainly Jews, Roman Catholics, Muslims, and Greek Orthodox.

In modern times the Swedes have chosen to keep a neutral position in international conflicts. During World War II, Sweden took in large numbers of refugees and gave many political asylum, as they have in recent years, along with many immigrant workers. Sweden also awards the annual Nobel Prizes, bequeathed by Swedish dynamite inventor Alfred Nobel before his death in 1896. These prizes honor significant advances in the sciences and literature, and they also include the all-important award given to a person or persons who have made noteworthy contributions toward achieving world peace.

The Swedes enthusiastically spend a great deal of time outdoors in all seasons. Many of them make frequent use of vacation homes—often abandoned farmhouses, of which there are more than a half million in the countryside. Boating, skiing, bicycling, and tennis are popular sports. Many of their holidays celebrate aspects of nature and ties to Sweden's rural past. The coming of spring is celebrated, as is the summer solstice.

Like other Scandinavians, Swedes relish open-faced sandwiches and smoked, marinated, and cured fish, especially salmon, whitefish, herring, and eel. Hot meals may include small meatballs, or *köttbulla,* served with lingonberry jam.

Swedes enjoy one of the world's highest standards of living. High taxes mean comprehensive social services, including child care, parental leave, and other assistance, allowing more than 80 percent of Swedish women to work outside of the home, often in upper-level positions.

Within the past few decades, the number of marriages in Sweden has declined considerably, and more couples are opting to live together. In Swedish this situation is called *sambo,* and legislation enacted in 1988 entitles the partners to a number of legal rights. Many sambo couples end up marrying, before or after children arrive.

The majority of Swedes are employed in services and industry; only 2 percent farm. About 85 percent of Swedish workers belong to unions. The Swedish system stresses dialogue and negotiation between workers and employers, and the government, since a general strike in 1909, has generally been able to keep strikes at bay. A strong desire to prevent the escalation of disputes led the Swedish to develop the concept of the ombudsman—a representative who investigates complaints against a corporation, government, or other organization—which has spread to many parts of the world.

The Swedes were latecomers to the European Union, joining in 1995, although they opted out of using the Euro as currency and have declined membership in NATO. In 1980 the Swedes voted to get rid of all nuclear energy plants and are following a plan for systematic decommissioning.

Sweden's immigrant population has grown to about 10 percent of the total, dramatically changing its demographic landscape. As a result, some Swedes no longer support the country's welcoming and inclusive immigration policies.

WELSH

Population: 2.7 million
Location: United Kingdom
Language family: Germanic (English), Celtic (Welsh)

The population in Wales currently stands at nearly three million, but countless Welsh and people of Welsh descent live throughout the world. Ever since the decline in the coal and steel industries after World War II, the majority of citizens in Wales have lived in or near urban centers such as Cardiff, the capital. Nearly all are Protestants, with Methodism foremost.

Although many people now enjoy city ways, life in smaller villages remains an important touchstone to cultural identity. Nowhere is this more apparent than in the annual *eisteddfodau,* or "chairing" festivals, where towns choose poetry champions who are crowned and raised aloft on chairs or thrones. These festivals have expanded in recent years to cover the breadth of Welsh cultural life and now include music in all forms, as well as dancing, drama, arts, and crafts. Winners hope to compete in the Royal National Eisteddfod of Wales, Europe's largest folk festival, and no other language but Welsh may be spoken on the poetry stage.

> The spender will get what he will spend and the saver won't get what he will save.
> HIGHLAND SCOTS PROVERB

Currently Welsh is spoken by at least half a million people in Wales alone. Contrary to popular belief, Welsh is not a Gaelic language, like Irish, but a language of British origin. A living tongue, Welsh is learned at home and in schools, and it is used in any circumstance, whether professional, artistic, or informal. "Wales" itself is not a Welsh word; in fact, it comes from the Anglo-Saxon *wœl,* meaning "foreigner" or "slave." The country's name in Welsh is Cymru (KUM-ree), from which Cambria, another name for Wales, survives in English usage today. For most Welsh people, English is the language of everyday use.

Issues of language use have become more prominent since 1998, when the Government of Wales Act was passed by the British Parliament. This act established the National Assembly for Wales, which exercises administrative authority over such important concerns as transportation, education, housing, and the environment. Wales still retains representation in the British Parliament as well.

The advent of the National Assembly has accompanied a gradual transformation in the Welsh economy. While Wales maintains an agrarian base—it is Europe's most important sheep raising center—its modern economy revolves around many high-technology enterprises. These include software design, precision manufacturing in aerospace and hydrodynamics, and the development of sustainable environmental strategies, all of which contribute to a Wales at ease with its past and its future.

Written Word, Oral World

Since long before the printed word, stories, wisdom, history, and knowledge were collected, remembered, and shared as part of a worldwide oral tradition, still alive today.

We live in a world inundated with written words. On paper and on the screen, in trashy novels and in great works of literature, in chat rooms, field guides, instruction manuals, and emails—we transmit and receive much of our knowledge through writing.

This was not always the case. For thousands of years, millions of people have existed in a purely oral world, where information is conveyed without the aid of scripts. In our literate world, it's difficult to conceive that most of human knowledge, for most of human history, existed entirely in memory. Oral traditions range from one-word names to epic adventures that take weeks to tell. They have been shaped by, and they have shaped, human cognition. Oral traditions have been a vital tool for human education, expression, and survival. Though oral cultures are speedily being transformed by literacy today, some persist.

Teller of tales

In a felt-covered yurt in Mongolia, a *toolju* prepares to begin his tale. He arrived in the afternoon, and now as the sun sets and the last chores are finished, the herders settle in to listen. The storyteller has donned a special robe and made a tea offering to the spirits, and he begins to sing.

The toolju has performed this tale before, as have the bard he learned it from and countless others across the steppes. There are as many variations of the story as there are tellings, but the core remains the same. This time, the audience reacts vocally as they hear of a sister's quest to bring her brother back to life, contests of strength, disguises, an evil king, a talking horse, a beautiful princess—and a happy ending.

Although the enthralled listeners here are Tuvan nomads, a similar scene could be taking place in many other places in the world: an Irish pub, an Australian desert, the rain forest of America's Pacific Northwest.

Oral traditions and knowledge

The study of oral traditions in the 20th century started with epic tales like these—and particularly in scholars' attempts to understand the oral roots of classic epics like Homer's *Iliad* and *Odyssey*. We only remember those stories, echoes of a tradition long past, because they were transcribed into text, but epics elsewhere survive, never written down but still passed from teller to teller.

In the mountains of Kyrgyzstan, the epic tale of the hero Manas has been passed down orally for a thousand years. When transcribed, the tales of how Manas and his companions united the tribes can exceed 500,000 lines, more than the *Iliad* and the *Odyssey* combined. Still a living epic tradition, it is told today by Manas-tellers, all of whom learned the stories by ear.

But epics do not represent the entirety of oral traditions. In a completely oral society, everything is preserved by memory—not just the imaginative folktales, epic histories, riddles, creation myths, jokes, and bawdy stories, but also factual information, the oral equivalents of field guides and instruction manuals.

An oral tradition can convey information simply—by naming a poisonous plant "baneberry," for example—or with dizzyingly complex symbols. The Hai‖om people of Namibia (‖ represents a click sound), long famed for their pathfinding skills, employ an almost constant back and forth of "topographical gossip" on their travels, an intricate system of landscape feature names they use to orient themselves.

Elements of the mythic and the immediately practical are often one and the same. A creation myth from the Chehalis people of Washington State describes the

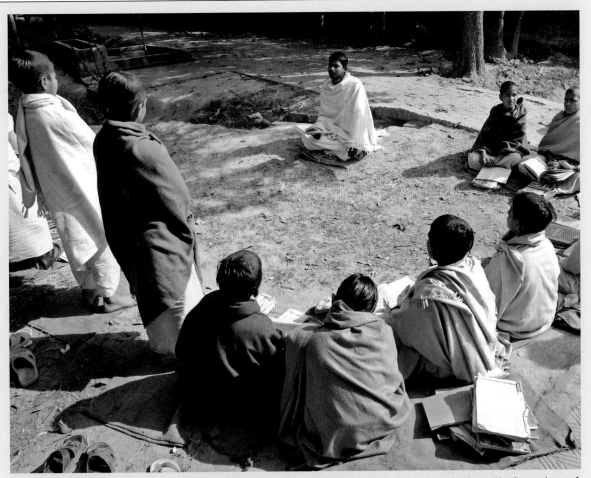

Indian students learn to read and recite the ancient Sanskrit language at the Gurukul Prabhat in Meerut, India. Some 40 miles northeast of New Delhi, the Gurukul is an ashram established in 1939 to encourage the study of the Vedas, Hinduism's sacred texts.

travels of Honné, the primordial spirit, and his magical transformations. As the tale progresses, Honné carefully assigns a dozen varieties of salmon their color, season, place and manner of spawning, and life span. To recall and retell that story is to pass on significant zoological information.

The Wayampi people of Brazil tell creation stories featuring the golden-tailed japu bird whose snot, spread over the jungle as it sobs, became vines and creepers. This may not seem at first glance to include practical information, but when a Wayampi man sings at the japu festival, he transmits as much detailed information about this culturally important bird's habitat, nest, mating rituals, foraging behavior, preferred foods, and flight patterns as any field guide. The narrative matrix used to deliver information is itself a mnemonic device that enables greater retention than if the information was presented as a bare list of facts.

Persistence of memory

Many Americans remember the school game in which a whispered phrase is passed down a line of children and emerges at the end completely transformed. It gives a simple, modern analogy for the way great bodies of knowledge have remained intact for thousands of years in a purely oral milieu.

Some scholars draw a parallel with evolutionary selection. As information is passed down, what is memorable survives. What remains after dozens of generations is well adapted to fit its niche—namely, the human memory. The irrelevant falls away and the core elements remain. Just as memory and transmission shape information, thinking in memorable ways shapes the cognitive strategies available to oral cultures.

Certain similarities emerge in oral traditions formed by this process. Successful strategies in this cognitive environment include rhyme, alliteration, rhythmic stress patterns, and a full vocabulary of memorable phrases, characters, themes, and episodes that a teller may draw upon.

Structural constraints can function as mnemonic mechanisms that greatly aid memory. The most familiar poetic device in English is rhyme, but rhyme is fairly rare worldwide. For the toolju, rhyme would be pointless. Tuvan, like many languages, makes heavy use of suffixes, making rhymes both trivially easy and useless as an error-checking or mnemonic device. More common worldwide are rhythmic stress patterns and the regular repetition of certain sounds, by alliteration or assonance.

An existing vocabulary of formulaic characters—the clever young woman, the magical companion, the evil king—and events—setting out on a quest, reviving the dead, feats of strength—occurs in every narrative tradition and aids the bard's task of memorization and composition. These general motifs combine with specific characters (the wise Odysseus, perhaps, or the mighty Manas) and episodes in those characters' lives that the teller can stitch together, depending on the particular occasion.

Change and tradition

Despite all of these strategies for remembering, oral traditions are organic systems, and forgetting also has its place. When the tales of Ndwera Jakpa, the founder of the Gonja state in Ghana, were first transcribed by the British, they featured the seven sons of the founder, each credited with beginning one of the seven divisions of Gonja. Sixty years later, after boundaries had shifted and only five divisions remained, bards sang of the five sons of Ndwera Jakpa.

The adaptivity of oral transmission is also evident in non-narrative traditions. The Natchez tribe, who lived along the lower Mississippi, named their lunar months after important foods gathered. Their eighth month was "Turkey Month," their ninth "Corn Month." By the 1750s, their calendar included "Watermelon

A Bedouin storyteller entertains his companions after the evening meal in the Sinai Desert. Oral forms help keep cultural ties vital and record human history even among people who never write their memories down.

Month" and "Peach Month"—two foods introduced by European settlers. Contrast the modern English calendar, which has existed in a literate context for hundreds of years and preserves a jumble of meaningless month names in Latin, a dead language.

Even when oral traditions are not responsively changing their core elements, there is constant low-level change. The Tuvan toolju's tale is unique—different every time he tells it. Although bards may claim to be repeating a tale exactly as it was told to them, and although their memories are exceptional by literate standards, all of these strategies produce an oral performance that falls somewhere between a recitation and an improvisation.

Certain other elements are shared by oral traditions. As with the toolju's tea offering, ritual often surrounds tales, providing a necessary cultural context. Ritual can extend from a special hat to the trance-like state of a Manas-like storyteller channeling the epic. As live performance, the words are accompanied by gestures—subtle or full-body, idiosyncratic or stylized. Driven by its purely sequential nature (you can't glance back at the preceding line), oral expression is often highly redundant, both for the sake of the bard's memory and the audience's comprehension.

Oral to literate

India, one of the most populous and linguistically diverse countries in the world, is also one with an ancient history of writing. In the perhaps four thousand years that India has had some form of writing, more than a dozen scripts have been used. But throughout that time, India has remained home to primarily oral cultures. Among other great oral traditions, India is home to Vedic oratory, remarkable for its antiquity, size, and attention to accuracy (to such a degree that practitioners train in singing complex variations, forward and backward, in an effort to retain the exact order of the words).

India's long history of oral traditions is rapidly changing, however. In the 50 years between 1951 and 2001, India's literacy increased from less than 20 percent to 65 percent. This and similar increases worldwide during the last century are perhaps laudable, but something is clearly lost when oral traditions fall silent. Devoid of ritual, participation, gesture, tone, organic fecundity, and disembodied from their human source, even those

Storytellers draw on voice, gesture, and performance to link the present to the past, as shown by this Koryak woman of Siberia.

oral traditions that are transcribed and preserved are no longer living, but petrified. The *Odyssey*, frozen in type, is not the Manas, still told from memory.

This is not a new observation. More than a thousand years ago, ambivalence toward a wholescale shift to literacy can be seen in early written English. Images of fire and bookworms haunt the books of Anglo-Saxon riddles, reflecting their authors' anxiety at relegating their oral culture to paper. In some ways, memory is the more durable medium. Stories told by Australian Aborigines may date back 20,000 years, while no written sources even approach such antiquity.

What might be lost

At a fundamental level, all of language is an oral tradition, and it all shares the same fragility, more petrified than preserved by written records in the absence of person-to-person transmission. We are currently in the throes of a massive extinction of the world's languages, as speakers abandon indigenous tongues for global megalanguages. Global language extinction threatens to disrupt oral traditions as never before, risking the wholesale loss of an enormous and ancient accretion of knowledge, preserved for centuries in the world's oral traditions. ■

— *Robert E. Hart*

Adapted in part from When Languages Die: The Extinction of the World's Languages and the Erosion of Human Knowldge *by K. David Harrison.*

NORTH AMERICA

THE AMERICAN ARCTIC
Alaskan Eskimos • Aleut • Inuit

NORTHWEST COAST
Kwakiutl • Tlingit

SOUTHWEST AND FAR WEST
Apache • Havasupai • Hopi • Navajo
Pomo • Tohono O'odham

PLAINS
Blackfeet • Cheyenne • Crow • Dakota • Mandan

PLATEAU AND GREAT BASIN
Klamath • Nez Percé • Northern Paiute

NORTHEAST
Amish • Chippewa • Cree and Métis • Iroquois

SOUTHEAST
Cajuns • Cherokee • Creek & Seminole
Lumbee • Gullah

Against the dramatic backdrop of Monument Valley,
Navajo herders make their camp.

In 1491, the year before Christopher Columbus set foot in the Western Hemisphere, millions of people of great cultural, linguistic, and ethnic diversity were already living in North America. They spoke hundreds of languages and had a range of political systems, family structures, art forms, spiritual beliefs, and adaptations to local environments. The marked variation of physical traits bespoke many peoples, many ethnicities.

In the southeastern and midwestern regions of what is now the United States, streams teemed with fish, forests held abundant game, and the climate provided the long growing season needed for agriculture. Out of these favorable conditions arose the most highly developed Native American civilization north of Mexico: the prehistoric Mississippian tradition. This very complex, class-structured society featured populous towns with temple mounds where elaborate ceremonies were held.

To the north, Iroquoian speakers of the Saint Lawrence lowlands dwelled in fortified villages supported by intensive horticulture, fishing, and hunting. The more severe climate of northern Algonquian speakers generally precluded farming—they hunted, gathered, and fished—but it was perfect for white birch trees, from which people built wigwams and highly maneuverable canoes.

Early migrations In the vast boreal forest of the Alaskan and Canadian subarctic lived a number of related tribes who spoke languages of the Northern Athabaskan family. They were probably descendants of Paleo-Indians who crossed the Bering land bridge and began spreading south and east perhaps 20,000 years ago. Unlike their Inuit and Eskimo neighbors, groups such as the Koyukon and Kutchin, or Gwich'in, saw their extreme environment as a dark and dangerous place, so they developed taboos and rituals to appease numerous forest spirits. Northern Athapaskans were also very adaptable, and their cultures easily incorporated useful customs from other groups. Thus, the Sarsi and Sekani absorbed the horse culture of the Great Plains and became almost indistinguishable from the neighboring Blackfeet, while the Eyak took on the appearance of a northwest coast tribe. Still other groups wandered thousands of miles into the American Southwest.

Athapaskans migrated from Canada sometime before European arrival, adapted to a new landscape and new neighbors, and became the Navajo and six Apache tribes.

Some Mexicans trace their ancestry back to Black Seminole Indians—descendants of runaway slaves who joined forces with the southeastern tribe, fled south to escape slave raiders, and then settled there.

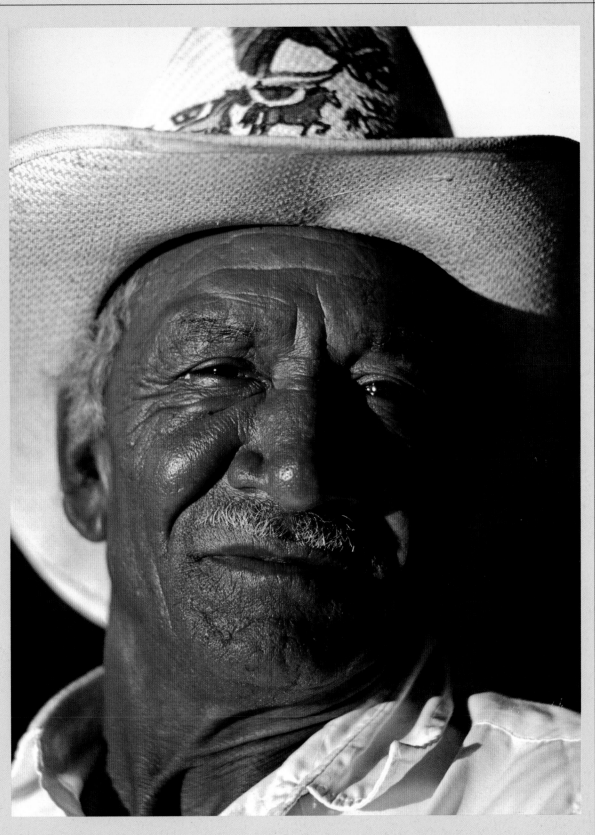

The Kiowa-Apache and other groups mingled with Plains tribes, living in tipis and sharing their customs, while the Navajo and Western Apache incorporated farming and ceremonies from the Pueblo. Named by the Spanish, for their compact villages of multistoried houses, Puebloan peoples have been living in the Southwest since 500 B.C. On the Great Plains, drought and population pressures caused significant population shifts long before white settlers began displacing tribes. Around A.D. 1300, the agricultural Pawnee moved into Nebraska from east Texas; by 1400, the Mandan had left eastern prairies for the upper Missouri Valley. Both groups lived in villages made possible by agriculture near rivers, while groups such as the Siouan tribes were bison-hunting nomads who carried their belongings on dog-pulled travois. Horses would transform their lives: The Lakota and other Sioux got their first horses between 1750 and 1770, after which they reached the height of their powers, riding freely across vast grasslands.

Far from the grasslands are the lush cedar forests and salmon-streaked waters of the continent's northwest coast, a region whose rich resource base enabled people to develop complex societies and elaborate ceremonies. California, south along the coast, offered a benign climate and a plentiful supply of wild foods. Home to the greatest concentration of divergent and unrelated languages, California was probably settled over a long period by peoples who spoke different languages and who, over generations, developed a wide array of dialects that distinguished their home villages and ethnicity.

The simple pleasures of family life delight these Mennonites of the Missouri Ozarks.

Preserving their heritage By the late 19th century, most tribes in the United States had been isolated on reservations. Children were often removed from communities to hasten assimilation into white culture; forced to attend boarding schools, they were forbidden to speak their own languages, a situation that led to the loss of most Native American tongues. Canadian Indians, designated "First Nations," did not experience such wholesale removals and great reductions in tribal land because competition for resources was not as intense at the time. Established in 1876, the Canadian reserve system—so called because Native American land was "reserved" as hunting grounds—continues to administer Indian affairs, but today the First Nations are beginning to confront economic pressures to exploit the oil and mineral resources found on their lands.

In 1990, more than half the Native Americans in the U.S. were living in urban areas. The government has recognized 562 Indian tribes, and more than 200 groups are petitioning for federal recognition. Contemporary Native Americans are not only preserving their cultures but also reshaping them in ways that make them more meaningful to their peoples. Groups such as the Makah of Washington State, who recently conducted their first whale hunt in generations, are re-creating their cultural heritage, while tribes such as the Hopi maintain ceremonies in an unbroken tradition. In 1978, Native Americans in the Southwest created the American Indian Language Development Institute,

Gullah children take pride in dressing up for the community's annual Heritage Days on Saint Helena Island, South Carolina. The unique Gullah culture developed among isolated Sea Islands slaves.

a major force for the continuing vitality of tribal languages. Many Plains tribes have revived the Sun Dance, an elaborate ritual in which dancers endure physical suffering to ensure blessings for their people. Today Native Americans are still under considerable pressure to assimilate, yet they continue to celebrate individual tribal identities and their pan-tribal ethnic identity as American Indians.

Many immigrants or their progeny also hold fast to beliefs and traditions brought from other continents. Among the millions of arrivals over the years were Amish from Switzerland, France, and Germany; Hutterites from Moravia; and Old Believers from Russia—groups who sought separate ethnic identities based on religious beliefs. Descendants of these pacifistic, agrarian peoples still favor plain garb and reject "worldly" practices, eschewing electric lights and mechanized vehicles. During the slave trade, more than nine million Africans were brought to the New World against their will; many of their descendants are rediscovering their ancestral cultures. Between 1820 and 1924, many Asians came to work on railroads and farms in the West, followed later by large groups from the Philippines, India, and Korea. Recent decades have seen the arrival of millions more from Asia, Eastern Europe, and elsewhere in the Americas, almost all of them drawn to North America, a land that is still home to many peoples, many ethnicities. ■

The American Arctic

Roughly the northern one-third of the state of Alaska lies above the Arctic Circle—north of the 66°30' latitude line—together with Canada's Arctic Archipelago, a group of about 50 large islands in Nunavut and the Northwest Territories. Tundra and permanent ice characterize this mountainous region. Its landforms include the Brooks Range, which runs inland along the northern coast of Alaska, giving way via the North Slope to the Beaufort Sea and the Arctic Ocean. On the west side of the Brooks Range, the De Long Mountains and the Baird Mountains form the Noatak National Preserve; to the east, the Endicott Mountains are the main feature of the Gates of the Arctic National Park and Preserve. The Dalton Highway—the only major road through the American Arctic—runs straight north to Prudhoe Bay on the Beaufort Sea.

ALASKAN ESKIMOS

Population: 54,800
Location: United States
Language family: Eskimo

Of all the Eskimo populations today, the Alaskans are the most numerous and most diverse, dwelling in a variety of environments from the Arctic tundra of the North Slope to the forested seacoasts of the south. Several thousand years ago, Alaska's Eskimos split into the northern Inupiat and the southern Yupiat, or Yupik, peoples.

In the north, the interior Eskimos were mainly caribou hunters, while the coastal groups had diverse economies alternating between sea-mammal hunting, fishing, and inland hunting. Because of these seasonal subsistence activities, social organization was flexible, often bilateral, with ties relating individuals to the families of both their mothers and fathers, maximizing territorial connections. The nuclear family—father, mother, children, and perhaps an older relative—was the basic social unit during most of the year. The larger, extended family band met and lived together during times of abundance in the spring or fall.

Non-kin extensions of social ties, such as wife exchanges and trading partnerships, were also important. Belying the notions of popular fiction, wife exchange was considered an economic necessity: The tasks of both men and women were essential for survival, and men often had to be away hunting for weeks at a time. Partnerships established between interior and coastal villages were beneficial in that they assured fairness in trading, access to each other's territory in times of need, and availability of products not found in one's own home environment.

Infanticide (abandonment of newborns, especially females) and senilicide (voluntary suicide by the elderly) were practiced by all Eskimo groups in times of extreme hardship; such acts were never common, however, and they were always

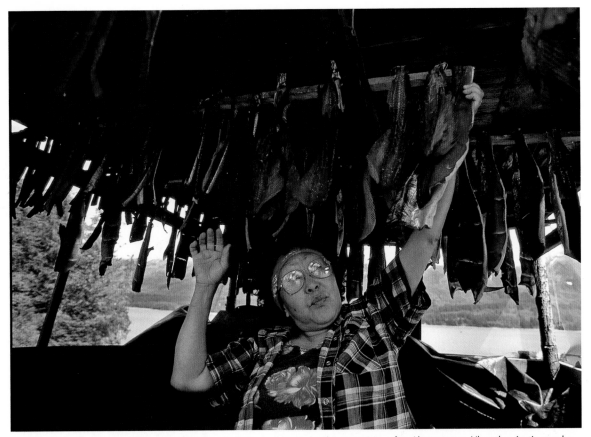

Food for the long winter months, a bountiful harvest of salmon dries under the supervision of an Aleut woman. Like other Arctic peoples, the Aleuts have a diet rich in protein.

occasions of great sadness. The elderly were much valued for their wealth of life experiences, and children were cherished, as shown by the frequency of adoption and the complete lack of social stigma attached to an adopted child.

As culturally diverse as the Inupiat in the north, the Yupik-speaking Eskimos have long lived south of Norton Sound, scattered along the coasts of the Bering Sea and Pacific Ocean; some dwell on Siberian shores, including those of Russia's Kamchatka Peninsula, west of the Bering Strait. Because they have had access to an abundance of sea mammals and fish, Eskimo settlements and populations on Kodiak Island and elsewhere in southern Alaska have been among the largest in the circumpolar Arctic.

Today, Alaskan Eskimos are not entirely dependent on hunting and fishing. Most lead relatively settled lives in villages, where they operate their own businesses or work for wages, and if they go hunting, they may take snowmobiles instead of dogsleds, and they may carry rifles rather than harpoons. Sometimes they supplement their incomes with sales of local art, such as soapstone and fossil-ivory carvings of animals; the Nunamiut at Anaktuvuk Pass are particularly famous for their skin masks.

In 1971 the Alaska Native Claims Settlement Act authorized a grant of 44 million acres and a payment of 962 million dollars to Alaska natives. Village and regional corporations were established, and these entities have functioned more or less successfully to encourage economic growth.

ALEUT

Population: 17,000
Location: United States
Language family: Aleut

The hardy, seafaring Aleut originally occupied the 1,100-mile-long Aleutian archipelago, more than 70 volcanic islands stretching between North America and the Asian mainland, with the Bering Sea on the north and the North Pacific to the south. Until two centuries ago, the Aleut maintained a population of perhaps 20,000, but because of exploitation and introduced diseases, the population since then has been steadily declining. Often relocated by the United States government, the people live in scattered villages, sometimes not even in the Aleutians.

Compared with northern Alaska, the Aleutian Islands enjoy a relatively temperate climate, made less harsh by the warming influence of the Pacific's Kuroshio (Japan) Current flowing from the west. Even so, the islands receive their fair share of extreme weather. They are often lashed by violent winter storms, soaked by summer squalls, and blanketed by heavy fog. The continually windy and wet climate has naturally had a profound effect on the Aleut way of life. People settled in fairly permanent villages with large multifamily houses. Because staying dry was as important as staying warm, the Aleut developed highly sophisticated rain parkas made of bird skin, fish skin, and sea-mammal intestine.

The Bering Strait region contains Earth's greatest concentration of animal protein, but the sources of all this protein are usually deep in the water or under the ice. To get at them, the Aleut became some of the world's most capable hunters of seals, sea lions, walrus, and whales. They excelled as builders of seaworthy skin boats (called *baidarka* by Russians) and as seamen and navigators, and it was not uncommon for hunters to paddle for days on end in search of sea mammals, covering hundreds of miles in often turbulent waters.

The Aleut used nearly every part of the animals they caught—skin, bones, organs, sinews, even whiskers—for food, clothing, fuel, and tools. Excellent weavers, they made basketry items from tundra grasses and whale baleen. They also were very knowledgeable about animal and human anatomy and the principles

Spear in hand, an Inuit hunter waits by a hole in the ice, practicing the patience needed to catch an emerging seal. Global warming has affected traditional Arctic pursuits, changing the landscape and thus stressing animals adapted to these frigid terrains.

of physiology, even practicing mummification; they wrapped corpses in woven mats and placed them in caves facing the sea.

The Aleut's extraordinary seamanship, combined with a wealth of sealskin and furs in the region, made their first contact with Russian explorers and traders,

> ### The wind is not a river; at some point, it stops.
> ALEUT PROVERB

in 1741, an unmitigated disaster. In the 18th and 19th centuries, the area was plundered by Russian hunters, adventurers, thieves, and princes, some of whom commissioned Aleuts to build two-, three-, and four-hole baidarka to transport missionaries and traders. The Russians wiped out many villages, and diseases further decimated the population.

During World War II, key battles protecting American territory from Japanese aggression disrupted the dwindling Aleut population, now concentrated in only a few seaside towns. One such town is Unalaska. Its population of 150 is about three-quarters Aleut, and although the people no longer hunt sea mammals, they have recently renewed their tradition of crafting boats made from animal skins.

INUIT

Population: 80,000
Location: Greenland, Canada
Language family: Eskimo

The earliest recognizable Eskimo peoples came into the Bering Strait area around 6,000 years ago and over the next 2,000 years moved east toward Greenland. After about A.D. 1000, these earliest cultures began to be absorbed or replaced by groups rapidly migrating into the region from the west—sea-mammal hunters who were the ancestors of today's Inuit. The term "Inuit" encompasses not only the Greenlanders but also the Polar Eskimos and the Central Eskimos (Caribou, Iglulik, Netsilik, and Copper Eskimos).

Around A.D. 1500 the climate began to change, initiating what some scientists call the little ice age and

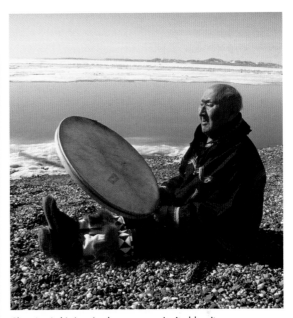

Chanting in his Inupiaq language, an Inuit elder sits on a pebble-strewn shore at Kotzebue, Alaska.

hastening the Norse abandonment of Greenland. It also forced the Central Eskimos of what is now northern Canada to give up semipermanent coastal villages for a new lifestyle: In summer, they fished and hunted caribou; in winter, they hunted sea mammals out on the ice. For winter encampments, they built snow houses, while their Greenland cousins—able to maintain the stable coastal subsistence of former times—still lived in partly subterranean houses constructed of sod, driftwood, and stone. The Greenlanders also continued to hunt from their single-cockpit skin kayaks and larger open *umiaks*.

Skin boats were used by most Eskimo and Siberian groups. The Polar Eskimos remained an exception. This small, isolated Inuit group, whose culture inspired the popular, legendary image of Eskimo life, inhabited the northernmost reaches of western Greenland and Ellesmere Island, where the polar seas were frozen all year, rendering boats useless. Dogsleds, with the animals harnessed in a fan shape by the Inuit and in tandem by the Alaskans, were also used by almost every group. The Aleut were an exception and did not have dogsleds because the warmer climate of the Aleutians did not make the use of dogsleds practical.

Inuit cosmology was similar to that of other Eskimo societies: It was directly linked to hunting and fishing, with the most common religious practices related to taboos about subsistence. Religion was animistic; that is, all things—human, animal, and inanimate—had souls, and all were related to each other. Fantastic ivory carvings dating from A.D. 1000 to 1300 attest to the rich spiritual life.

A shaman, or *angakok,* served as a direct link to animal spirits, and he could prophesy and cure illness by sucking out objects that had intruded into souls. In Alaska, the shaman's job also included retrieving lost souls in an elaborate villagewide ritual. Although successful shamans could accrue a good deal of power, community leaders were chosen because of their abilities as providers. Social control was generally informal; leaders were usually followed by consensus.

The Inuit finally were accorded full Canadian citizenship around 1960. Their politial clout increased in the 1970s when ten assembly seats were allocated to the Northwest Territories for Inuit territory. In 1979 the first Inuit was elected to the National House of Commons. The people of the Northwest Territories later voted in 1982 to create a new territory called Nunavut. Eleven years later the Nunavut Act was passed. The legislation set aside nearly 750,000 square miles for the Inuit people and authorized the government to pay them 1.1 billion dollars between 1993 and 2007. In a historic step toward self-determination, the election for the First Nunavut Legislative Assembly was held in 1999.

The Inuit story is different in Greenland, which became part of Denmark in 1953. Although complete home rule was ultimately achieved in 1979, most key administrative positions in the government are still held by Danes.

Today, hunting and fishing remain important activities, but they are now abetted by modern equipment such as rifles and snowmobiles. A number of Inuit communities—such as Baffin Island's Cape Dorset, for example—have established arts cooperatives that attract much international interest.

At Point Barrow, Alaska, Eskimo subsistence hunters butcher a bowhead whale on the beach. Typically, the whole community will share in the distribution.

Into the Americas

Nowhere on Earth is the human capacity to adapt more evident than inside the Arctic Circle. In an area where the annual average temperature is less than 20°F, it is no surprise that a region comprising nearly 10 percent of the planet's landmass harbors only 0.2 percent of its human population. To put this into perspective: South Asia packs roughly one thousand people into every square mile, the Arctic not even one. The major reason: Humans are a hairless species of tropical primate. Our morphology developed on the African savannahs, where it tended toward taller stature and longer extremities, both favorable for animals needing to dissipate heat in an equatorial climate. But head to the Far North—even with warm clothing—and increased surface area is the last thing we want. The cold weather instead makes larger body mass and a more compact stature—think of the polar bear—the best configuration for generating and maintaining body heat. In short, humans were not built to live here.

Adapting

And yet a select few thrive. Around 35,000 years ago, migrations originating in and around the fertile Altai Mountains of southern Siberia brought people to the inhospitable reaches of the Arctic. These intrepid people were the end result of a long, difficult struggle for survival, a tug-of-war between resilient Man and an unrelenting Mother Nature, and over time our biology responded to the new environment. Shorter, stockier frames better equipped for the frigid weather became the norm and are retained in today's Arctic populations,

many whom have average heights of around 5'4".

But biology is not the only mechanism of adaptation, and an important innovation tens of thousands of years ago finally made life here feasible. The earliest groups into the region relied heavily on reindeer, bison, and mammoth herds,

Long years in a harsh environment accentuate the age of an Alaskan Eskimo.

following them from Central Asia into the cold beyond. They hunted with complex group coordination honed on the African savannahs of yesteryear, but as their hunts led them onward, they encountered cold their African ancestors could never have imagined. It's debated exactly when and where people began exploiting the skins of their prey for clothing and shelter, and because the materials used by these primitive tailors were organic and therefore quickly degraded, there remains no direct evidence for this important cultural adaptation prior to the last 10,000 years. Regardless, the advent of footwear and

other warm clothing meant that humans could follow reindeer across the Arctic tundra. In doing so, people walked into a world never before seen by humans.

Linguistic clues

The timing, number, and location of migrations into the Americas remain among the most hotly disputed topics in anthropology. Linguistic work in recent years on the structure of languages spoken by populations from both sides of the migration route has played a pivotal role in moving the debate forward.

Languages indigenous to the Americas, linked by descent from their common proto-language, fall into one of three primary language families: Eskimo-Aleut, found widespread in the Arctic; Na-Dene, spoken throughout Alaska and in isolated parts of southwestern North America; and Amerind, spoken everywhere else in the Americas.

In 1986 Joseph Greenberg and his colleagues presented a seminal, though controversial, paper showing that each of these language clusters more closely with a set of languages spoken in Eurasia than they do with each other, suggesting that they could not have come as one homogeneous migration.

The earliest of these groups likely came across the Bering land bridge that had been created during the last glacial maximum, around 16,000 years ago. Then, around 14,000 years ago, the ice sheets parted briefly and allowed small groups of hunter-gatherers, adapted to life inside the Arctic Circle, to cross through the narrow, passable corridor and enter the rest of the Americas—a new era in a new world.

Northwest Coast

The mountainous, lush swath of coastline running from the Yukon down the west coasts of British Columbia and Washington State is dominated by the Coast Mountains through British Columbia and the Coast and Cascade Ranges in Washington State. The Rocky Mountains form the eastern boundary of this heavily forested region, where more than 80 inches of rain falls each year. Though there are some major urban areas such as Vancouver and Seattle, some areas of this region are vast, uninterrupted woodland and mountains. The Coast Mountains are very sparsely populated; fewer than nine people live in each square mile, on average. Major industry in this region includes fishing, forestry and manufacturing.

KWAKIUTL

Alternate name: Kwakwaka'wakw
Population: 5,000   Location: Canada
Language family: Wakashan

The 30 or so Kwakiutl tribes occupying the area around the Queen Charlotte Strait in British Columbia exploited a shore environment so rich in marine life that they were able to follow a settled village lifestyle usually enjoyed only by agriculturalists.

Residing in their permanent villages, the Kwakiutl developed an extensive ceremonial and artistic life that included the carving of totem poles to represent clan figures. The poles had become a well-established art form long before Europeans arrived on the Pacific coast, but they were much easier to carve—and began to increase in number—after the Kwakiutl acquired the iron and steel blades introduced by the newcomers.

Members of the Kwakiutl aristocracy demonstrated the degree of their greatness by the amount of wealth they gave away at potlatches. These events, which included much singing, speech-giving, and dancing, validated a person's social status as he or she distributed extensive property to vast numbers of guests. Because potlatches were required for membership in secret religious societies, wealthy people were also initiates who learned to conduct the societies' enthralling dance-dramas. Commoners composed most of the audiences for these dramas and were usually spellbound by the performers' apparent ability to influence supernatural powers; such magic, in turn, reinforced the status of the aristocrats.

The most terrifying ceremonial performance was the Hamatsa, or Cannibal Dance. For the Kwakiutl, who avoided contact with the dead, the concept of eating human flesh was both disgusting and awe-inspiring. The bodies of the dancers supposedly were inhabited by cannibal spirits, and as the performers flung themselves around in a frenzy, they screamed and pretended to eat human flesh. Hidden attendants made strange howling sounds just offstage, and carved bird monsters swooped over the anxious audience. Eventually, certain rites pacified the cannibal spirits, and the dancers vanished in puffs of smoke.

The Kwakiutl once built specialized canoes for whaling, sealing, fishing, freight

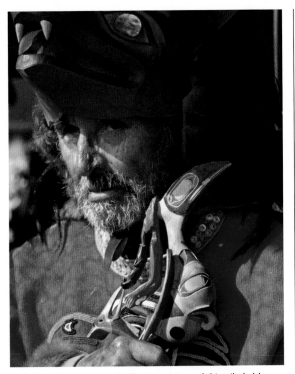

Seniority and rank matter in Tlingit society, and this tribal elder has both. His traditional wolf headdress and the carvings he holds display Tlingit mastery of the craft.

transport, river travel, racing, and war; by 1900, however, canoemaking and seagoing travel were all but forgotten. Then, in the 1980s, a Haida Indian carved a 50-foot-long canoe. His craft inspired the Kwakiutl to make similar canoes and organize paddling events, such as the 1989 "Paddle to Seattle," which included participants from several groups along the northwest coast. Bringing back the great canoes led to the revival of potlatches and the songs, dances, and prayers associated with them, instilling a sense of cultural pride.

TLINGIT

Population: 12,000
Location: United States, Canada
Language family: Athabaskan-Eyak-Tlingit

Sharing customs and a common language, various Tlingit tribes dwell on reservations and reserves in British Columbia, the Yukon Territory, and Alaska's southeastern panhandle. Here, mountains rise almost directly from the sea, isolating the mist-shrouded land. The 80-mile-wide archipelago off the fjord-carved coast is also mountainous, and its islands, like the mainland, are covered by dense forests.

In the past, when the fishing season had ended and stores of salmon and other food had been set aside for winter, families moved from their summer fishing camps to permanent winter villages. Plentiful resources from the ocean, rivers, and land—sea mammals, shellfish, fish, deer, bears, sheep, and mountain goats—enabled people to obtain enough food to last through winter, the time for potlatching. If a person had amassed enough wealth to validate an inherited

> When the tide is low,
> the table is set.
> TLINGIT PROVERB

clan leader position, he or she hosted a potlatch, a massive feast and giveaway for another clan. The size of the gathering and the value of the gifts were thought to reflect the clan leader's status. By accepting gifts, guests confirmed the host's right to the inherited privileges and tacitly agreed to reciprocate. Potlatches not only served to circulate material wealth but also helped to establish alliances between clans.

The Tlingit developed complex ceremonies within their class-conscious society that was headed by high-ranking individuals. Commoners made up the majority of the people, while slaves, usually women and children captured from other tribes, were forced to perform menial labor for their masters. Each clan had several crests that members displayed on totem poles, canoes, dishes, hats, and Chilkat blankets worn by high-ranking individuals.

Today, Tlingit women still weave Chilkat blankets from cedar bark and mountain goat's wool, with designs based on clan crests that men painted on wooden boards. Recently, weavers resurrected the technique for making raven's tail robes, an ancient art that had been replaced by the curvilinear designs of Chilkat weaving. Woodcarving has also experienced a revitalization in the form of bas reliefs, transformation masks, portrait masks, house posts, and totem poles. Although artists sell much of their work, many of them dedicate a significant part of their time to carving items for ceremonial use in their villages.

Southwest and Far West

From the sunny west coast of southern California to the remote, desertlike regions of western Texas, the Southwest and Far West of North America forms a dry and arid landscape. The temperate year-round climate of southern California's heavily irrigated coastal region turns searing east of the Coast Ranges. Temperatures in Death Valley soar consistently into the hundreds. Western Texas's dry plains give way northward to the cool peaks of the Rocky Mountains and Rio Grande in New Mexico. In northwest Arizona, one of North America's most remarkable natural formations, the Grand Canyon, has been cut through the landscape by the erosive action of the Colorado River over thousands of years. The region has a number of striking natural formations, such as mesas and buttes.

APACHE
Population: 97,000
Location: United States
Language family: Athabaskan

The six main tribes known as Apache have their origins among the Athabaskan-speaking peoples of Canada, who also are the ancestors of the Navajo. Migrating southward, the Apache arrived in the Southwest around 1400 and fanned out into varied environments there. The kinds of cultural and economic pursuits they developed depended on their surroundings and on relationships with other peoples in the area such as the Navajo, the settled farmers of the Pueblos, or the bison-hunting Plains Indians.

Regardless of their economic orientation, most Apache took up raiding when they acquired horses. They would descend upon other Indian groups—including their trading partners—and take food and whatever material objects they wanted. This activity differed significantly from warfare, which was intended to avenge the deaths of individuals.

The Western Apache covered nearly all but the northwesternmost quarter of Arizona and farmed on a fairly large scale. They shared many similarities in culture and language with the Navajo, making the Western Apache a likely late offshoot of that group. The Jicarilla of northern New Mexico also farmed, but culturally were similar to the Plains Indians and hunted bison. The Jicarilla probably gave rise to the wide-ranging Lipan of eastern New Mexico and western Texas, who were driven down into Mexico by the Comanche. The Mescalero of south-central New Mexico displayed some Plains traits and mostly hunted and gathered.

The Chiricahua also were hunters and gatherers and lived in southern Arizona, western New Mexico, and northern Mexico. They also hold the distinction of being the last Indians in the United States to lay down their arms. They surrendered in 1886, and for the next 27 years were treated as prisoners of war and shuffled between prison sites in Florida, Alabama, and Oklahoma. When they finally were freed in 1913, most chose to join the Mescalero and Lipan Apache on their reservation in south-central New Mexico. They are represented by

In ceremonial dress, a Havasupai storyteller works the atmosphere of a blazing campfire, telling tales that link life today with ways of life in centuries past. Peaceful ways historically characterize this Grand Canyon–based tribe.

the Chiricahua Apache Prisoners-of-War Descendants today, whose ancestors include Cochise, Geronimo, and warriors who rode with the famous chiefs.

The Kiowa-Apache, also known as the Plains Apache, followed a trajectory different from the five other tribes. When those groups were pushing farther into the Southwest, the Kiowa-Apache stayed on the plains and became associated with the Kiowa, a typical Plains tribe, eventually functioning as a Kiowa band, although they retained their Apache language. Together with the Kiowa they obtained horses early on and used them to hunt bison. Today, they have no particular economic base but are known as superb musicians, dancers, and artists. Other Apache tribes currently experience a wide range of cultural and economic circumstances on their reservations. Apache horsemanship has turned some descendants of fierce raiders into skilled cowboys.

Many Apache ritual traditions continue to the present day. Wearing painted wooden-slat headdresses and holding wooden swords aloft, Crown Dancers embody mountain spirits known as *ga'an*. Along with a medicine man, singers, and drummers, they evoke supernatural power to cure and protect. Some Apache also perform the Sunrise Ceremony for girls reaching puberty, infusing them with the White-Painted Woman's powers to ensure long life, vitality, prosperity, and a good disposition. During the elaborate four-day ritual, singers recount tribal history from the creation of the universe to the present.

HAVASUPAI

Population: 600
Location: United States
Language family: Yuman

For nearly a millennium, the Havasupai have dwelt amid one of the planet's most spectacular landscapes: the Grand Canyon. Unusually for a post-contact Indian tribe, they continue to inhabit the same land where their ancestors lived. The Havasupai are an

Traditionally, Hopi girls undergo coming-of-age rituals. The adoption of a squash-blossom, or butterfly, hairstyle indicates eligibility for marriage.

Upland Yuman people, related to the Yavapai and also the Walapai (Hualapi), who probably were their ancestors and with whom they still intermarry. The language of the Havasupai, whose name means "People of the Blue-Green Water," is mutually intelligible with other Upland Yuman languages and remains strong, spoken by young and old. A written language was created toward the end of the 20th century. Most Havasupai also speak and are literate in English.

The Havasupai and other groups were part of the southwestern Desert Culture of hunters and gatherers who lived lightly on the land and developed a simple material and ritual culture. They constructed dome-shaped huts of branches covered with bark or thatch. Contact with the pueblo-dwelling Hopi inspired them to enrich their economic and cultural pursuits.

Under Hopi tutelage, the Havasupai planted corn, beans, and squash, as well as tobacco and cotton, on the floor of Cataract Canyon, a side branch of the Grand Canyon about 3,000 feet below the rim, and learned to irrigate the crops with water from Cataract Creek. As novice agriculturalists the Havasupai also adopted Hopi

rituals aimed at ensuring success, such as prayers at the time of corn planting and the Rain Dance.

After the fall harvest the Havasupai would ascend the narrow trails to the canyon rim and resume hunting and gathering on the plateau. The women collected pine nuts, mesquite pods, berries, and honey, while the men hunted rabbits, deer, pronghorn, and other game. Then they returned to the canyon floor to start the agricultural cycle.

The Havasupai led a calm and peaceful existence in their out-of-the-way canyon and were recognized by other tribes for their noncombative nature. They lived in family groups under the leadership of a head chief. Disputes within the group often were worked out by the men during sessions in the sweat lodge.

In the 1880s the Havasupai were stripped of most of their land and granted only 518 acres within the canyon as the Havasu Creek Reservation. They also were prevented from hunting and gathering on the plateau, and so they began more intense cultivation in the canyon, adding peaches to their crops and a peach festival to their annual celebrations. In 1912 they began to raise cattle.

Since then, agriculture has been mostly replaced with wage labor and federal employment tied to tourism. The Havasupai act as mule guides for tourists who want to visit the canyon floor, maintaining the mule herds as well as operating a lodge and other services and selling crafts such as baskets. In 1975 the government restored 185,000 acres to the tribe.

Havasupai children attend the local school until eighth grade, when many are sent to boarding school in California. But they remain part of the community and the peach festival has moved in the calendar so that they can participate.

HOPI

Population: 15,300
Location: United States
Language family: Uto-Aztecan

For the Hopi people occupying 13 villages on and around three mesas in northern Arizona, each year centers around the arrival and departure of the *katsinam,* spirit beings who carry prayers to Hopi deities. The people believe that katsinam live among them from roughly January to June and then for the next six months dwell in the spirit world atop San Francisco

Mountain. These beings are not worshiped but are instead respected as powerful spirits who bring rain and other blessings.

The word *katsina* refers to the incorporeal spirit and to the dancer who brings this spirit to life. As a baby, a Hopi girl receives the first of many katsina carvings representing spirits as real beings who will bestow upon her the gift of reproduction. Such carvings are sacred and made exclusively for the Hopi—as opposed to the carved kachina figures that went on sale to the public in the 1930s.

The Hopi are also known for their distinctive basketry, jewelry, and pottery. The art of pottery-making was revived around 1900 when a woman named Nampeyo, a Hopi-Tewa, began to copy fine prehistoric ware that had been found at nearby Sikyatki, an abandoned Anasazi pueblo. Developing a style based on the ancient pottery as well as Hopi-Tewa ceramic traditions, Nampeyo painted stylized birds and katsina beings in black, orange, and white designs on cream, white, or dark red backgrounds.

In the Hopi world, corn is life and is tended with almost the same depth of care that people give to their children. To grow this crop in such an arid environment (it receives just a few inches of rain or snow each year) is an act of faith requiring deep commitment—and the help of katsinam. These beings are considered masters of the art of raising corn and other plants, and songs and ceremonies with katsina dancers evoke the reverential attitude that the Hopi believe is necessary for growing corn. The rituals renew the people's faith, as well as their aspiration and commitment to the ideals of compassion and cooperation.

Today, the Hopi continue their ceremonies, including the well-known Snake Dance, and tourists from around the world come to watch. Although most outsiders are respectful, some push aside members of the Hopi audience, disregard signs that prohibit photography, and dress inappropriately. The Hopi, who believe that every person can contribute spiritual energy and heartfelt prayers, are struggling with whether to exclude visitors from rituals.

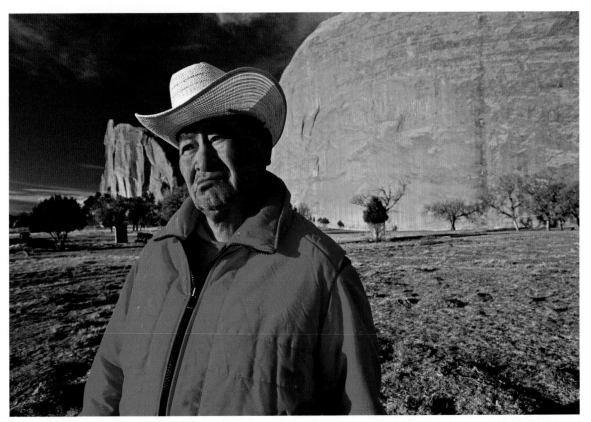

At Arizona's Window Rock, a Navajo man surveys reservation land that spans part of three states. After the forced Long Walk to Bosque Redondo, New Mexico, beginning in 1863, Navajo returned to the Four Corners area.

NAVAJO

Alternate name: Diné Population: 298,000
Location: United States
Language family: Athabaskan

Sprawling across parts of Arizona, New Mexico, and Utah, the Navajo reservation is home to a group of people who speak an Athabaskan language, like their Apache cousins and distant relatives in northwestern Canada. By A.D. 1400, small bands of Athapaskans had begun to arrive in the Southwest, and sometime later, the Navajo separated from the rest, moving into the Four Corners area and settling on land that could not support the agricultural towns of their Pueblo neighbors.

The Navajo thrived, however, and by the early 1800s they counted their wealth in horses and flocks of sheep. As pastoralists and farmers, they lived in isolated family groups surrounded by grazing land, and they built earth-covered, domed dwellings known as hogans. Most Navajo live in houses today, but some still dwell in hogans, which are also settings for ceremonies.

Navajo ceremonies often focus on the physical, mental, and spiritual healing of persons who become ill after failing to maintain proper relations with supernatural powers. The many songs, prayers, rites, and sandpaintings in a ceremony must be precisely replicated for it to be effective. Each chant, or ceremony, is a ritual drama that tells the story of a person who overcame great obstacles to receive healing. For some ceremonies, the chanter and his helpers make a sandpainting from 12 to 20 feet in diameter on a hogan floor. After completion, the painting is blessed, and the patient sits on it to absorb healing power. The power of the Holy People, who created the ceremony with its sandpainting designs, penetrates the person's body and restores a state of harmony and health. Unlike the sandpaintings that are applied to a board and sold as art, ceremonial works are sacred and ephemeral and can include crushed flowers, pollen, and cornmeal.

Today, a major part of Navajo ethnic identity centers on the Long Walk, an event people still talk about as if it had happened yesterday. In 1863, after burning Navajo fields and property, the military forced nearly everyone to walk to Bosque Redondo, New Mexico, where many died of starvation and disease. Five years passed before the Navajo signed a treaty that established a reservation and allowed them to go home.

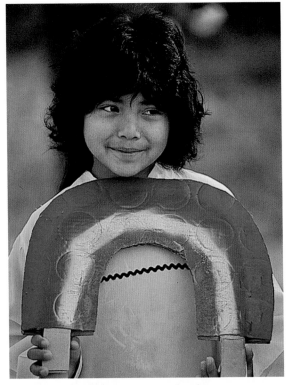

A Tohono O'odham child holds a painted rainbow in a contemporary dance. Traditional tribal culture revolves around the harvest and use of saguaro cactus fruit.

Long before trading posts were built in the late 1800s, Navajo women had created a market far beyond the Southwest for their magnificent blankets. Then, in an effort to increase the commercial value of Navajo weaving, traders introduced non-Navajo designs, such as geometric motifs from Plains beadwork and hooked elements from Persian rugs. Today women no longer weave rugs as a career, but most practice the art because weaving is a vital part of Navajo culture.

In 1969 the Navajo opened the first tribal college in the United States. Now known as Diné Community College (from the Navajo name for themselves, which means "the people"), it integrates typical college classes with Navajo culture and language courses.

POMO

Population: 7,900
Location: United States
Language family: Pomoan

When the Spanish came to California in 1769, some 300,000 native people were already living there and speaking scores of mutually unintelligible languages that differentiated into an unknown number of dialects. Although there are other language hotspots in the world where many languages are spoken within a small geographical area, California is one of only a few places in North America where this level of diversity is known to have occurred.

As different ethnic groups moved into the area, they discovered an abundance of natural resources and a relatively mild climate. Each group found its own territory, and with time, isolation from each other led to variations in speech and dialect. The Pomo, for example, speak seven distinct and mutually unintelligible languages of the Hokan language stock—more appropriately called the Pomoan family of languages. The most divergent of these differ more from one another than English does from Icelandic.

The Northern Pomo lived north of San Francisco in the Russian River Valley area where their territory had 22 miles of coastline. As did other California Indians,

> If you want to see what your body
> will look like tomorrow,
> look at your thoughts today.
> NAVAJO PROVERB

they formed tribelets, small autonomous groups occupying a territory that was recognized by neighboring communities. The rocky coast provided crustaceans, sea mammals, and fish, while streams held plenty of trout and salmon. In summer and fall, the Pomo relied on temporary shelters when they were gathering wild plants and hunting game, but the dependability of their food supply allowed them to live in permanent camps with substantial houses for the rest of the year. Acorns, which they ground into flour to make gruel or bread, were a staple of their diet.

Known for weaving baskets that are considered to be among the finest in the world, California Indians have revitalized this once dying art as an essential part of their tribal identities. Learning to weave also means learning the songs and cultural knowledge related to the making and use of baskets. Traditionally, Pomo women made feathered, twined, and coiled baskets— some of them as small as pearls—while men wove

bird traps, fishing weirs, and the baby baskets that were begun immediately after the birth of a child. Basket-making requires dedication, the same trait California Indians are using to revitalize their cultures.

TOHONO O'ODHAM

Population: 21,000
Location: United States
Language family: Uto-Aztecan

In the Sonoran Desert of southern Arizona and northern Mexico, where drought is a constant threat, the Tohono O'odham once divided the year between summer villages near their fields and winter villages near permanent springs in mountain foothills. Their reliance on mesquite beans led the Spanish to call them Papago (Bean People), but in 1986 they became officially known as the Tohono O'odham (Desert People) Nation, their name for themselves. Today they dwell on three southern Arizona reservations.

In the intense summer heat, these people harvest the crimson fruit of the giant saguaro cactus, such a symbol of their culture that its harvest traditionally marks the start of the year. Resembling kiwi fruit in taste, the saguaro fruit is boiled into syrup, candy, and jam. The Keeper of the Smoke, who is the village headman and ceremonial leader, oversees the fermentation of the juice produced from the fruit, a three-day process that occurs in the "rain house."

At night, while the juice ferments, men and women dance to the singing of rain songs, and on the third day, the headman partakes of the wine as he recites ritual orations describing the desolation of the desert without rain. The ceremony is intended to bring rains up from the Gulf of California, thus ensuring the well-being of crops planted after the festival. By saturating his body with saguaro wine, the headman simulates the rain's saturation of cracked and dusty land.

Today, the Tohono O'odham are a contemporary people who are using income generated by their casinos to build and staff their own college, as well as a nursing home where tribal elders can be cared for by those who speak their own language. Casino profits have also provided scholarships for higher education. The work of tribal members helps to revitalize and preserve the O'odham language—one of only a handful of Native American languages predicted to survive into future generations.

Plains

A high plateau stretches throughout the central region of North America, roughly from the Rocky Mountains on the west to the Mississippi River on the east, and from the Rio Grande in the south to the Arctic Ocean's Mackenzie River delta in the north. The region includes part or all of ten U.S. states—North Dakota, South Dakota, Montana, Wyoming, Nebraska, Kansas, Colorado, Oklahoma, Texas, and New Mexico—as well as two Canadian provinces—Saskatchewan and Manitoba with parts of Alberta and the Northwest Territories. Major rivers running through this area include the two longest rivers in the U.S., the Missouri and the Mississippi. The climate in this region consists of cold, possibly snowy winters and warm, mostly dry summers.

BLACKFEET

Population: 88,500
Location: United States
Language family: Algonquian

Among the westernmost Algonquian-speaking peoples are the Blackfeet tribes: The Southern Piegan have a reservation in northern Montana, and the Northern Piegan, Blood, and Blackfeet proper live on reserves in southern Alberta. Once dependent on the bison for food, shelter, and tools, the Blackfeet saw their way of life transformed after acquiring horses in the mid-1700s. Families following bison had used dogs to carry belongings, but the dogs could carry only about 75 pounds, which meant women had to carry large loads and the old and the infirm who could not walk had to be left behind. After they obtained horses and guns, the Blackfeet became fierce warriors who were known for raids far from home. Extending their hunting and raiding territory, they eventually forced the Shoshoni, who lacked guns, southward and westward into the Rocky Mountains, and they drove the Kutenai westward across the Canadian Rockies.

Today, like many other tribes, the Blackfeet are sharing their land through "edu-tourism." In the form of tribally run tours, edu-tourism allows visitors to see some of the most beautiful wilderness in the West, and it may also help bring down the extremely high unemployment rates found on reservations. Such programs enable people to work as guides near their homes, telling tourists what they want them to know about their cultures. In Montana, Blackfeet Historical Site tours take visitors to centuries-old places, teaching them about the significance of sacred sites and how to travel with a spirit of respect. The Blackfeet themselves still smudge their bodies with sweet grass and pine boughs for purification before going into the mountains, and they leave tobacco offerings to the trees and animals that they find along their way. They also continue to hold an annual Sun Dance, take ritual sweat baths, and maintain sacred medicine bundles.

CHEYENNE

Population: 18,200
Location: United States
Language family: Algonquian

Around A.D. 1700, the ancestors of the Algonquian-speaking Cheyenne moved onto the northern

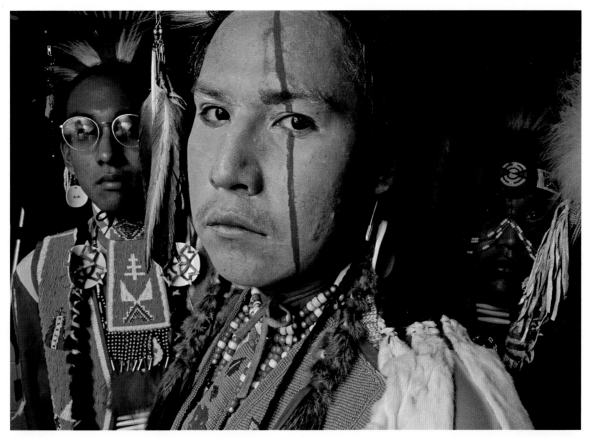

Powwow dancers get ready in Oklahoma, a state that has fostered so many styles of powwow singing, dancing, and costumes that people often call it "the cradle of powwowing."

prairies from the eastern woodlands, where they had long been gatherers of wild rice. By 1800, they had moved farther west onto the Great Plains, becoming nomadic bison hunters who depended on animals they killed during the summer to sustain them through the long winter.

Cheyenne warrior societies, such as the Dog Soldiers, enforced strict control over hunters and, together with the Council of Forty-four, provided order for the physical and spiritual survival of their people. The council head was the Sweet Medicine chief, who protected the sacred sweet-grass bundle; just below him were four subchiefs representing supernatural beings. The next level of power was vested in 39 chiefs known for both generosity and wisdom in settling disputes. If, for example, the council decided that a case of murder threatened tribal welfare, they banished the accused person, along with those who chose to accompany him or her, for at least five years. While their decisions today may often conflict with those of the officially

recognized tribal government, the Southern and Northern Cheyenne chiefs, the religious leaders, and the military society members continue to operate as the traditional tribal government authority.

The Northern Cheyenne Reservation is in southeastern Montana. The Oklahoma reservation of the Southern Cheyenne was eradicated by the U.S. federal government, but this people formed the Cheyenne-Arapaho Tribes of Oklahoma, an organization with its own tribally elected business council and president. Both the Northern and Southern Cheyenne teach their language and culture in their schools, and many continue to perform traditional ceremonies, some of which have been revived—the Sacred Arrows and Sun Dances, for example. Women participate in the War Mothers Association, honoring Cheyenne veterans from all wars. For those skilled at working with porcupine quills, there is the Quillwork Society, whose members have sacred rights to use particular quill and beadwork designs.

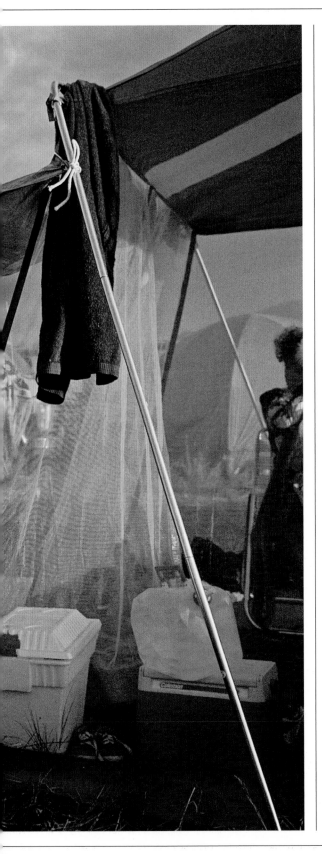

Today the Northern Cheyenne and 50 other tribes participate in the InterTribal Bison Cooperative. By purchasing bison, which are indigenous to the plains, and learning to manage their herds, the tribes are helping to restore the ecological balance that was disturbed when cattle ranching led to overgrazing; they are also gaining needed income from bison meat, a leaner source of protein than beef. Restoring bison to the plains helps accomplish two other important goals: reestablishing connections to the Creator and reviving ancient traditions.

CROW

Population: 13,400
Location: United States
Language family: Siouan

In the struggle for control of the northern plains, the Crow were such fierce enemies of the Lakota Sioux that they served as scouts for Lt. Col. George Custer in his 1876 campaign against Sitting Bull on Crow lands near the Little Bighorn River in Montana. Even so, the Sioux defeated Custer, whose name was subsequently used in the battlefield designation. In 1991, following lengthy Congressional hearings, the site was renamed Little Bighorn Battlefield National Monument, and a memorial for Indian warriors was commissioned to correct a one-sided view of history and commemorate the efforts of those who had fallen there. After two centuries of animosity, people from both native nations met in 1995 for reconciliation ceremonies at the battlefield, along with other tribes and representatives of the Seventh Cavalry.

Historic accounts of the Crow record their tall, striking appearance, noble bearing, and horsemanship. The men placed elaborately ornamented blankets and saddles on the backs of their horses, and women used beadwork on trade cloth to create collars that adorned the animals' necks and chests. Women also painted designs on the hide coverings of tipis, cone-shaped dwellings that they made even larger after they acquired horses to carry heavier loads.

Today's Crow, whose reservation is in south-central Montana, retain their unique vision of themselves. They continue to perform the traditional Sun Dance in

In the Montana Rockies, a Dakota man prepares his costume for the Traditional Dance. Known for their air of dignity, traditional dancers represent a distinct style of powwow dance and dress.

summer, medicine men conduct healing ceremonies throughout the year, and a majority of children and adults still speak the ancestral language. At the Crow Fair each August, people renew their kinship and social ties while celebrating with parades, feasts, rodeos, giveaways, and powwow singing and dancing. For competitions, Crow artists use vivid colors and both geometric and flower designs to decorate horse-riding gear and dance clothing. Also called "the Tipi Capital of the World," the fair boasts as many as 1,500 tipis pitched near the banks of the Little Bighorn.

DAKOTA

Alternate name: Sioux Population: 153,000
Location: United States
Language family: Siouan

For many, the image of a Dakota warrior galloping across the Great Plains still captivates, as it appears to represent a time-honored Indian way of life. In fact, the nomadic horse culture was a comparitively short-lived phase in the Dakota tradition. Not until the 1750s or so did the Dakota acquire, through raiding or trading, the horses that allowed them to hunt bison more efficiently and gave them greater freedom in their other endeavors.

"Dakota" is an umbrella term, recognized by the tribe members themselves, encompassing the groups that are more popularly known as Sioux—the Dakota, the Nakota, and the Lakota. The word "Sioux" itself has multiple linguistic origins; the term is a shortened French corruption of a Chippewa (Ojibwa) word meaning "lesser adder," denoting an enemy. Dakota, Nakota, and Lakota dialects belong to the language family known as Siouan—the blanket term Dakota does not apply in this case.

The Dakota, the Nakota, and the Lakota, also known as the Santee, Yankton, and Teton, respectively, represent eastern, central, and western distributions of an Indian population with some cultural variations, in addition to distinct dialects. These Indians perhaps started out in the area of the lower Mississippi River centuries ago and then moved to the Ohio Valley, before ending up in the upper Mississippi region.

As eastern Indian tribes began a general westward movement, away from white settlers, they displaced other native groups in a domino effect. By the late 1700s, Lakota tribes had moved from the prairies onto the western High Plains. The Nakota also were soon on the move; the Dakota were the last to leave the prairies. Out on the plains, all the Dakota Sioux used strategy and horsemanship to develop warfare into an art.

Horses also transformed the bison hunt, because men no longer had to stampede entire herds over cliffs; instead, riders could bring down several bison with rifles or bows and arrows. The Dakota considered the bison a sacred gift from the Creator, and through the Sun Dance, their annual ritual of sacrifice and thanksgiving, they honored the bison for the food, shelter, tools, and fuel it provided. By 1875 the bison was nearing extinction because of overhunting by white settlers, who often took the animals' hides but left their carcasses to rot. A popular pasttime for those on frontier hunting trips was to shoot the animals en masse from moving trains as they passed.

Extermination was encouraged by the military, who believed the end of the bison would help to bring

> ## A people without history is like wind on the buffalo grass.
> ### PLAINS INDIAN PROVERB

the Indians under their control. They continued pursuing the Dakota until 1876, when these Indians, led by Lakota Chiefs Crazy Horse and Sitting Bull, and their Cheyenne allies, defeated Custer at the Battle of the Little Bighorn, the greatest Indian victory, but a sad step toward the finish and a losing war.

Now numbering about 150,000 and living on reservations in Minnesota, North and South Dakota, Nebraska, and Montana, the Dakota tribes today are grouped into the three divisions of Dakota, Lakota, and Nakota. For all of these tribes, pipe smoking remains an essential marker of their Dakota identity and culture. In Pipestone, Minnesota, both Dakota and Ojibwa artists continue to fashion the dusty-red catlinite stone into the traditional T-shaped calumets. Highly prized, these pipes are then smoked to bring a spiritual dimension to human interactions, for as the smoke rises from the pipe, it carries the smoker's prayers to the spirit world.

Palpable scars mark the places where skewers pierced this Dakota man's chest during the annual Sun Dance ritual. The pain of mutilation brings spiritual benefits to the participants.

Today mounted Dakota warriors embody pan-Indian identity for all Native Americans, many of whom travel great distances to participate in annual powwows featuring Plains-style dancers. In reality, the nomadic hunters have been replaced by workers in a multitude of occupations, although unemployment plagues many Dakota tribes. On many reservations the Dakota own and operate bingo halls and casinos, and some are involved in the development of natural resources, including oil, on tribal lands.

MANDAN

Population: 1,300
Location: United States
Language family: Siouan

Not all Plains people became nomadic after they had acquired horses. The Mandan of the upper Missouri River are an example of a path that turned in another direction: They continued to live in fixed settlements and did not change their way of life to follow bison by horseback. They retained the agricultural lifestyle of their forebears and simply went on seasonal bison hunts, every summer and every autumn, in the neighboring countryside.

Mandan villages therefore developed more intricate topographies. Each Mandan village featured a formal town plan with a central plaza, where ceremonies and competitive games were held. Surrounding the plaza were dome-shaped earth lodges for families. Partly subterranean, lodges were both snug in winter and cool in summer; their slightly flattened roofs also served as porches and proved an ideal place for relaxing at the end of the day. In addition, Mandan women were able to use the roofs as a place to dry corn and to store goods.

In the rich soil near the Missouri River, women raised corn, tobacco, sunflowers, pumpkins, beans, and squashes. But rich soil was not all that was needed for growing crops; the Mandan also regularly invoked divine assistance through elaborate agricultural rituals. Playing important roles in ceremonies of renewal were sacred ceremonial bundles of crops. Each one was considered vital to the people's continued existence. The owner of the sacred corn bundle, for example, was responsible for calling the spirits of the corn back from the south before seeds could be distributed to women for planting.

Traditional Mandan culture was illustrated in paintings by 19th-century artists George Catlin and Karl Bodmer. They were also described in the journals of explorers Meriwether Lewis and William Clark, who spent the winter of 1804–05 with the Mandan. As portrayed in these works, the Mandan people lived in settled villages, and this tradition left them especially susceptible to European-introduced diseases such as smallpox, which killed more than 800 of their people in 1837.

Today, the Mandan share North Dakota's Fort Berthold Indian Reservation with the Arikara and Hidatsa; known as the Three Affiliated Tribes, all look to a single tribal government, although each tribe maintains its separate, distinct ethnic identity. The Mandan strive to keep their culture alive with language classes and with traditional religious ceremonies, beadwork and quillwork, and powwows.

Plateau and Great Basin

Rare rainfall and snowmelt in the mountains of Nevada and western Utah drain into valleys but go no farther, earning this area the name of Great Basin. Treacherous north-south mountain ranges thwarted many westward settlers. Even if they managed to make it over the Wasatch Range on the eastern side, they had to contend with peaks of up to 9,000 feet and long desert valleys before encountering the Sierra Nevada mountains at the western end. The area is bordered by the Mojave Desert and the Grand Canyon's Colorado Plateau to the south, and the Columbia Plateau to the north.

KLAMATH
Population: Fewer than 5,000
Location: United States
Language family: Klamath-Modoc (Penutian)

The Klamath traditionally lived at the southern edge of the Plateau region in southern Oregon and northern California. They were not a large, unified tribe but a series of tribelets that set up winter camps along the upland lakes, marshes, and streams that form the headwaters of the Klamath River. In the summer they roamed the area, catching freshwater fish, hunting waterfowl and game, and gathering wild foods such as roots, berries, and *wokas*—water lily seeds that they ground into flour. All individual Klamath were encouraged to be industrious and to amass enough food to sustain them through the long winters.

At their winter camps the Klamath constructed large, circular, semi-subterranean lodges that had wooden posts for support and earth-covered logs for a roof. A single family typically lived in a small lodge; several families could fit into a larger one. Entry was gained through a hole in the roof. In the summer the Klamath erected smaller wooden structures covered with mats.

Klamath culture bore elements of the aboriginal Plateau culture combined with later elements added from the Northwest Coast tribes, such as conspicuous accumulations of wealth, and also the Plains peoples, especially after the introduction of horses. Individuals were encouraged to stockpile shells, skins, and weapons. Klamath tribelets did not come together cooperatively, but they did join forces to wage war, which they did fiercely and frequently, taking slaves from the vanquished tribes.

Klamath shamans acquired powers through prayer, fasting, and visions, and they used their powers to stage dramatic healings among their people. Individual Klamath also went off by themselves to acquire spiritual insight. Adolescent boys were sent on five-day coming-of-age vision quests. Currently they practice a religion that is a synthesis of traditional and Christian beliefs.

In 1864, following years of hostilities, the Klamath ceded more than 13 million square miles of land to the U.S. government and began reservation life, joined by the Modoc and Yahooskin to become the Klamath

An Idaho Nez Percé mother leads her children on an Appaloosa, the breed favored by the tribe known for their superb horsemanship. Nez Percé women traditionally made saddles, collars, and bridles for the horses.

Tribes. They channeled their industriousness into new economic ventures such as cattle raising, freight hauling, and timber production. Tribe members took advantage of training opportunities and were able to find skilled local jobs.

In 1954, the government terminated recognition of the Klamath, sending into rapid decline one of the most successful and self-sufficient Indian tribes in the country. Almost immediately Klamath individual and collective economic fortunes plummeted, and within a few decades more than 70 percent of the Klamath lived below the poverty level. But the tribe's traditional work ethic did not disappear with its recognition, and the Klamath organized legal efforts to regain it. They prevailed in the 1970s, when hunting and fishing rights were recognized, although no land was returned. In 1986, their tribal status was restored, but again without a land base. Today the Klamath, with only a few thousand enrolled members, continue to press their claims and in the meantime have created many programs to benefit their people and the population of Klamath County, Oregon.

NEZ PERCÉ

Population: 6,500
Location: United States
Language family: Plateau Penutian

Now residing on a reservation in north-central Idaho, the Nez Percé are best known for a leader named Chief Joseph, whose valiant attempt to lead 200 to 300 warriors and their families to sanctuary in Canada is one of the most heroic—and tragic—feats of American history. Forced to relocate in 1855, when Oregon settlers wanted their land, the Nez Percé again were pressured to move eight years later, after gold was discovered on their reservation. Tempers flared dramatically in 1877, but when the Army refused to negotiate with Chief Joseph, he and his people pushed north in a 15-week, 1,700-mile trek over the steep Bitterroot Range. Seeing his people cold and starving, Joseph

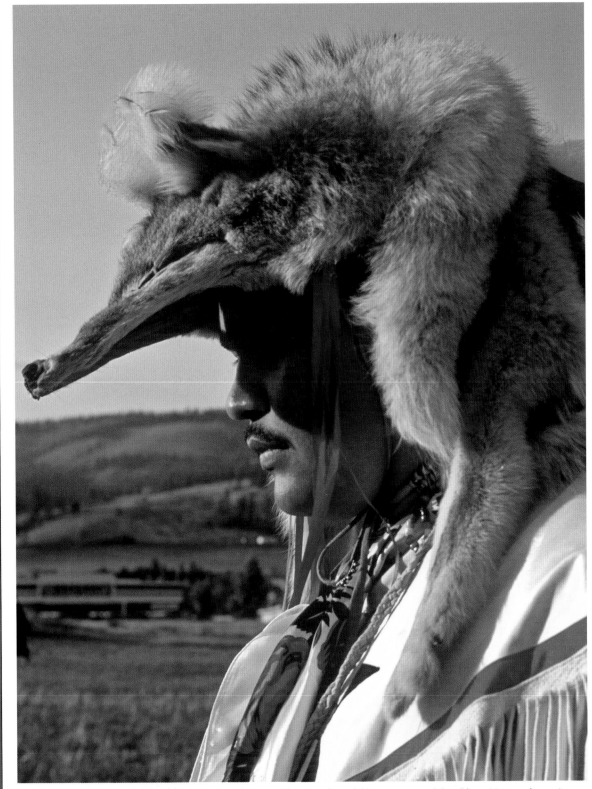

While some tribes favor carved representations, this Nez Percé man wears the real thing: a coyote-pelt headdress. He attends a spring powwow on the Kamiah Reservation in Idaho.

stopped and delivered his legendary surrender pronouncement: "My heart is sick and sad. From where the sun now stands, I will fight no more forever."

The Nez Percé homeland—where the borders of Washington, Oregon, and Idaho meet and the Clearwater, Salmon, and Snake Rivers flow—provided the people with grassy valleys and forested mountains. In the spring, summer, and autumn, men hunted and fished while women gathered camas bulbs, roots, and berries. After the autumn bison hunt on Montana's eastern plains, the Nez Percé would return to winter camps in the sheltered valleys of their homeland.

The most renowned horsemen of their area, the Nez Percé carefully worked to improve the bloodlines of their herds. Men prized Appaloosas for their endurance and distinctive speckled markings, and women fashioned elaborately beaded horse trappings such as collars, bridles, and saddles. Although the people were forced to give up their 1,100 horses when they surrendered in 1877, today's tribe now has a few Appaloosas; they were a gift from a New Mexico Appaloosa breeder who donated ten mares to the tribally sponsored Chief Joseph Foundation in 1991.

The Nez Percé are very proud of their heritage. In 1988, they began the Cultural Resources Program as a means of preserving their language, history, and arts, and every July descendants of Chief Joseph's band travel to Oregon to celebrate Chief Joseph Days in a town named for the chief.

NORTHERN PAIUTE

Population: 13,500
Location: United States
Language family: Uto-Aztecan

The homeland of the Northern Paiute once encompassed more than 70,000 square miles of Nevada, southern Oregon, western Idaho, and eastern California. It was part of the Great Basin, the only area in North America where nearly all groups spoke languages from the same language family; such uniformity came about probably because this resource-poor region never attracted a large, diverse population.

Today, Northern Paiute tribes have reservations in Nevada, California, and Oregon. Descendants of a cultural tradition that stretches back more than 10,000 years, the Northern Paiute have survived by developing an intimate knowledge of their environment. With limited precipitation and no rivers that drain to the ocean, the Great Basin forced its early inhabitants to establish and maintain an even more delicate balance with their surroundings than did people in more hospitable areas. Resources and terrain still vary widely here, from the freshwater marshland of western Nevada to the deserts and salt flats that make up the majority of the region.

The rugged environment supported small groups who could survive on intermittent harvests of roots, seeds, and berries. Seminomadic family groups endured by gathering a wide variety of plants that ripened at different times of year and by supplementing this activity with hunting and fishing. Groups with relatively richer, more specialized environments were able to remain for a season or part of a season in one location, while other groups had to follow a more nomadic or generalized seasonal routine, relying on an immense range of plants and animals. Each family belonged to a flexible camp group, which expanded and contracted according to the changing seasons and availability of resources. In autumn, groups came together to harvest piñon seeds and to undertake communal activities such as rabbit and antelope hunts.

Although each tribe has its own government today, not all groups have been able to develop viable tribal businesses. Some individuals raise cattle and grow hay and grain, while others make a living through wage work in a variety of jobs. In the 1980s, to preserve an important part of their heritage, some Northern Paiute tribes began conducting classes in traditional basketmaking, a highly developed art form that had been necessary for survival.

Most of the people now participate in some branch of Christianity; even so, some individuals retain aspects of their heritage through Paiute songs, stories, and prayers, and a few traditional healers continue to practice. The Ghost Dance Movement, which originated with two late-19th-century prophets who envisioned a revival of native culture, has come and gone. But since the 1930s, people have adopted a number of other tribes' religious movements and activities: the Native American Church, the Sweat Lodge, and the Sun Dance, for example. Because so few of their own traditions have survived, many young Northern Paiute join in these pan-Indian rituals as a way to establish their ethnic identity.

Northeast

The northeastern region of North America runs roughly from eastern Illinois in the United States up to Labrador and Newfoundland on the northeastern coast of Canada. States included in this region are Illinois, Indiana, Ohio, Pennsylvania, New Jersey, New York, Vermont, New Hampshire, Massachusetts, Connecticut, Rhode Island, and Maine; Canadian provinces are Ontario, Quebec, Newfoundland and Labrador, New Brunswick, Nova Scotia, and Prince Edward Island. Running from southwest to northeast like a crooked backbone through this entire region is the Appalachian Mountain range, which takes in smaller ranges, including the Alleghenies and the Catskills. Much of this area enjoys four distinct seasons, with cold, snowy winters, verdant springs, warm summers, and colorful autumns. Annual rainfall varies from more than 80 inches in Newfoundland to as little as 20 annually in Ohio and Indiana.

AMISH

Alternate name: Amish Mennonite **Population:** 81,000
Location: United States
Language family: Germanic

The Amish get their name from Jakob Ammann, a 16th-century Alsatian reformer who led a breakaway group of Mennonites, or Anabaptists, into a stricter interpretation of that radical European Reformation tradition. Anabaptists, found in Switzerland, Germany, and France, were persecuted for rebaptizing adults, believing that a mature confession of faith should precede baptism. In search of religious freedom, the Amish immigrated to North America in the 18th and 19th centuries; the European communities eventually died out. Today there are 200 Amish settlements in 22 states and Ontario, Canada. The largest clusters are in Pennsylvania, Ohio, New York, Indiana, and Illinois.

The Amish way of life is tied to *Gelassenheit,* or submission to a higher authority. Their code of conduct requires plain living, humility, obedience, community spirit, and suppression of individual ambitions. The Amish live apart in farm communities of some 20 to 35 families who make up congregations. They usually meet for services in homes or barns, led by a bishop, two preachers, and deacons. Those who disobey the *Ordnung,* or law, may end up being shunned by the entire community.

The Amish are perhaps better known as the Pennsylvania Dutch, which is a misnomer from the word for German—Deutsch—or the name they call themselves, Deitsch. All Amish speak a German dialect, and they also speak English and often standard German.

Though the Amish dress plainly, they allow themselves to wear colors—green, blue, and lavender shirts and dresses are common—but not patterns. Men wear dark pants, vests, and hats and grow full beards, but they keep the upper lip clean-shaven. Women wear dresses with aprons and caps or bonnets. No makeup or jewelry is worn—not even wedding rings.

Old Order Amish ban the use of electricity, telephones, cars, and many other modern technologies and amenities. Travel and transport occur by horse and

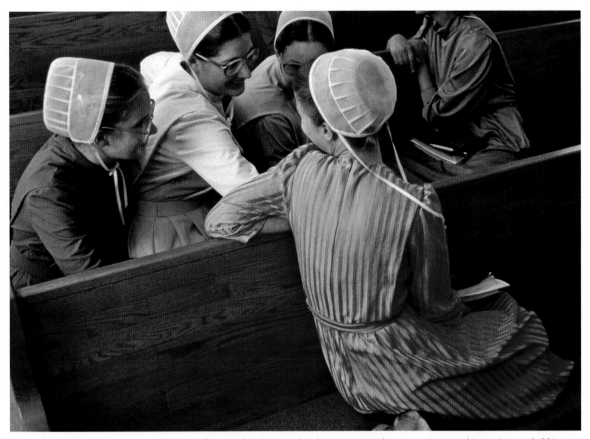

Amish girls catch up on the news in the pews of a Partridge, Kansas, church. In many Amish communities, worship services are held in private homes. Whether in homes or sanctuaries, the church provides a community center and lasting identity for the Amish people.

buggy, although Amish may ride as passengers in cars. New Order Amish may use phones installed in rural areas and draw electricity off 12-volt batteries; some use tractors. Variations in what is allowed can occur among different communities in the same region.

The Amish operate their own one-room schools that mostly advance only to the eighth grade, a practice that was upheld by the U.S. Supreme Court. They hire their own teachers from within the community. Secondary and higher education are deemed unnecessary for Amish life and unwise for the temptations they may pose to Amish adolescents.

Nevertheless, Amish young people are given a culturally sanctioned opportunity called *Rumspringen,* or running around, to explore forbidden activities such as driving, dating, drinking, and unsupervised travel, beginning at age 16. Some of their exploits now even end up on the Internet. Despite the taste of freedom, six out of every seven return home and opt for full incorporation into the Amish community.

The Amish tend to marry young and to select their own spouses. Most marriages occur on Tuesdays or Thursdays during the post-harvest wedding season, which lasts from October through December. Weddings often involve the whole community. The couple's parents may give furniture, farm equipment, and other substantial gifts to help the new couple begin their married life together.

Large families are common among the Amish—on average they have seven children—and houses are correspondingly large. The family usually sits down to eat meals together. During the school year the main meal is taken in the evening; it shifts to midday in summer. The Amish eat plainly but not blandly, and pickled vegetables are a favorite food. They use seasonal ingredients, putting up the surplus for use in the winter.

The Amish celebrate Christian holidays but without the secular trimmings. In addition to religious observances, Christmas involves festive meals and some gift giving, but no Chrismas tree or Santa Claus.

The Amish work hard, but they also like to have fun—a capella singalongs are a popular pastime. They also play softball and volleyball and go hiking, fishing, swimming, skating, and sledding. Amish travel to visit relatives and attend weddings, and some even escape to Florida for a few weeks in winter to stay in the Amish village in Sarasota.

Land pressures have made it harder for the Amish to stay in farming, and so they have turned to cottage industries such as furniture making, shed building, and shopkeeping. New ventures mean new situations that often take the Amish a bit further from their traditions.

CHIPPEWA

Alternate name: Ojibwa Population: 175,000
Location: United States
Language family: Algonquian

One of North America's largest Indian groups, the Chippewa live on reservations or reserves in Michigan, Wisconsin, Minnesota, North Dakota, Montana, and the Canadian provinces of Ontario, Manitoba, and Saskatchewan. They once spoke an Algonquian language and dwelled in dome-shaped wigwams covered with birch bark. Because wild plants and game in their region did not support large villages, they formed widely scattered, autonomous bands of approximately one hundred or so people. In the fall, hunters traveled as far as a hundred miles to track moose, woodland caribou, and bears—animals with which people also sought, through prayer and ceremonies, to establish spiritual connections central to their religion.

Joining other families in maple groves near rivers and lakes, the Chippewa marked the end of winter with sugar-making activities. From there, they proceeded to summer villages, where they spent the warm months tanning hides and building the birch-bark canoes for which they became famous. At summer's end, families

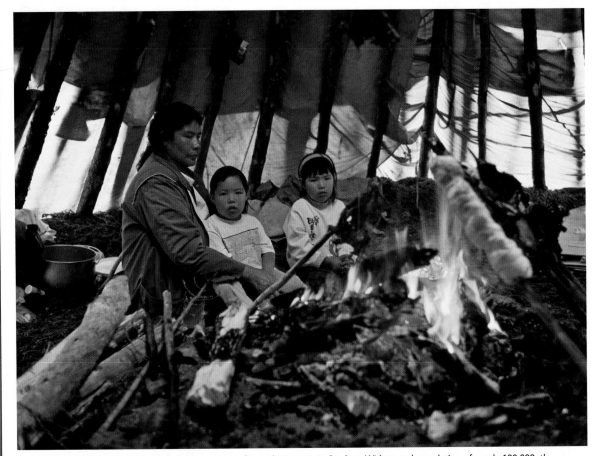

The members of a Cree family cook their dinner over a fire in their tepee in Quebec. With a total population of nearly 100,000, the Cree are Canada's largest First Nations people.

harvested corn, squash, and perhaps wild rice, a seed-bearing grass that grows along the muddy shores of some streams and marshes. Wild rice often made survival possible in regions where a short growing season made agriculture unreliable.

The Chippewa performed the ceremonies of the *Midewiwin* (Great Medicine Society), a secret group of men and women healers whose primary purpose during the rituals was healing the sick and initiating new members who had served long, demanding apprenticeships. Today the Chippewa continue to carry out the two- to five-day ceremonies, as well as traditional forms of hunting, fishing, sugar mapling, wild-rice gathering, and beadworking—all very important markers of their ethnicity.

CREE & MÉTIS

Population: 90,000
Location: Canada   Language family: Algonquian

The Cree were a widely dispersed people who at one time ranged from Labrador in eastern Canada all the way to Alberta in the west and as far north as the Northern Territories and south into North Dakota and Montana. Their territory encompassed the northern boreal forest, the tundra, and part of the northern plains. It was a harsh environment, with short summers and long, very cold winters followed by strong melts and flooding.

The name Cree probably comes from Kristeneaux, which is a French corruption of the name of a particular Cree tribe. The Cree language belongs to the central Algonquian group and today is spoken by tens of thousands of people.

Cree men were very skilled at hunting and trapping both large and small game. The hunters roamed together in small bands, which formed larger communities in the summer. In addition to fishing, these groups of men hunted moose, elk, caribou, deer, and bear. Cree women contributed to the food supply by gathering roots, berries, tubers, and eggs.

The Cree also kept domesticated dogs that they used as pack animals and for hauling. The dogs could carry parts of dismantled housing, with long poles strapped across their chests. When the travois, a kind of runnerless sled, was introduced in the area, dogs were harnessed up to pull loads.

The Cree way of life began to change irrevocably

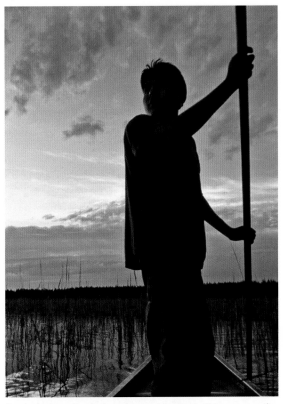

On the lookout for ducks to hunt, a Minnesota Chippewa youth poles his canoe through Nett Lake, following the practices of his ancestors. Ducks seek out the lake's wild rice.

when French and English trappers and traders arrived in their territory. The Cree were often pressed into service as guides for the new arrivals. They also worked as trappers and middlemen. They traded pelts for desirable items the Europeans could provide, including household items, tools, and especially firearms, which aided in expanding their territory. Cree communities sprang up around the trading posts and tribe members became dependent not only on the goods they received but on alcohol, which along with disease took a heavy toll on the population.

The Cree succumbed dramatically to the major outbreaks of smallpox in the 18th century, as well as to subsequent epidemics of influenza and tuberculosis in the 20th century. Each time disease struck, their population plummeted. Today, all the different groups of Cree join together to represent one of Canada's largest groups of indigenous people. Most now live in Ontario and Quebec.

As some Cree began to acquire horses in the 18th century, they took on elements of Plains Indian culture,

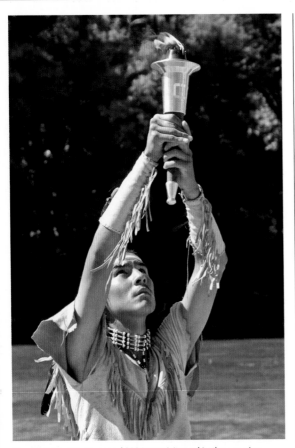

Canada's First Nations and Métis participated in the opening events of the Pan American Games in Manitoba in 1999. Participants carried the torch by canoe on the Assiniboine River.

including hunting bison, the use of horses, and large scale intertribal warfare with scalp taking.

Traditionally the Cree people were animists, and they believed that spirits inhabit all living beings as well as some nonliving objects. Their belief in the manitou, or a singular Great Spirit, may have developed after the influence of European contact, which introduced Christianity and monotheism. Cree individuals by tradition sought to enhance their own power through visions in which they tapped into powerful spirits. In times of misfortune or illness they consulted shamans who used their own enhanced powers for divination and healing. The Cree were heavily missionized through their trading relationships with the French and the British, and most became at least nominally Roman Catholic or Anglican.

In the 19th and 20th centuries, the Cree in both Canada and the United States were collected into reserves and reservations. Some halfhearted attempts were made to adapt their lifestyle to farming, and if a number of Cree did succeed it was through their own efforts. As they lost their traditional way of life. the Cree shared the problems that plagued other native groups, including rampant unemployment and alcoholism. These issues continue to confront the Cree to the present day. Their way of life also faces

> ## It is good to tell one's heart.
> CHIPPEWA PROVERB

problems from the effects of oil drilling and the consequences to bodies of water of local hydroelectric projects, both of which threaten to further erode their quality of life.

Intermarriages occurred from the beginning of Cree contact with Europeans; white fur trappers and traders took wives from among the Cree people and also the Chippewa and Athabaskan people, with whom they interacted. Offspring from such unions became known as Métis, from the French word for "mixed," and they remain a distinct group. In Canada they mostly live in Manitoba and are counted with Indians and Inuit as First Nations, although as people of mixed race they have not been able to obtain official recognition or benefits. In Montana the Métis live mostly in Chippewa communities.

IROQUOIS

Population: 80,800
Location: United States
Language family: Iroquoian

Now living on reservations and reserves in upstate New York and Canada, the Iroquois people are best known for the powerful league formed by five Iroquoian-speaking tribes to peacefully resolve conflicts. The league, which gave fair representation to each group, was established sometime between A.D. 1400 and 1600, after a long history of bloody intertribal feuding. Within the member tribes—Mohawk, Oneida, Onondaga, Cayuga, and Seneca (and later, the Tuscarora)—clan mothers chose sachems to represent their family lineages on the basis of their integrity, wisdom, vision, and oratorical ability. The 49 sachems composed the governing council of the league, also served on their separate tribal councils, and settled disputes through diplomacy and ceremonies.

Inspired by the Iroquois model that put values of unity, democracy, and liberty into action, Benjamin Franklin and other leaders of the American colonies sought the help of the Iroquois in establishing a fair and democratic colonial union. Their meeting in 1754 produced the Albany Plan of Union, a precursor of the Articles of Confederation. Today, ideals espoused by the Iroquois League continue to guide such organizations as the United Nations.

The Iroquois call themselves the Haudenosaunee —People of the Longhouse—in reference to their traditional homes. Accommodating as many as a dozen families, each bark-covered dwelling was as long as 200 feet, with a width of 25 feet; families had separate apartments but shared a fire with others. Iroquois settlements held between 30 to 150 longhouses and were protected by palisades.

Large numbers of Iroquois men and women now pursue urban lifestyles, holding jobs in industry, education, and other fields, but they continue returning to the reservations for ceremonies. They also still play lacrosse. The Iroquois version of this Native American game was the basis for today's sport, and it is a mainstay of ethnic identity, promoting the health, strength, and community spirit that binds Iroquois nations together.

To control land claims, to counter environmental pollution, and to keep their traditions alive, the people have revitalized the Six Nations Iroquois Confederacy, as it is known today. The present-day confederacy actively participates in international forums related to the rights of indigenous peoples and even issues its own passports, which are honored by many nations.

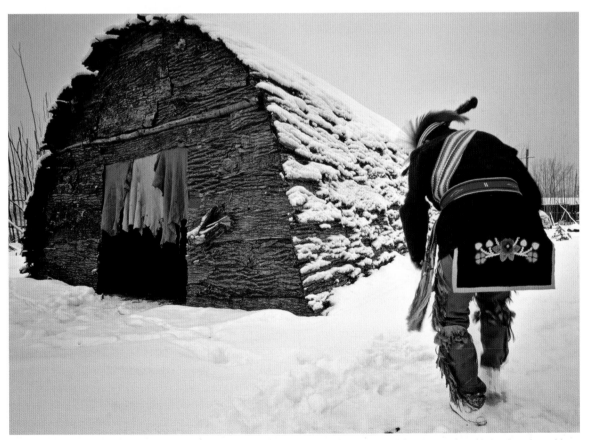

Outside a reconstructed longhouse, an Iroquois in upper New York State dances and chants in the snow. In the past, longhouses could reach 200 feet in length and accommodate a dozen families.

Southeast

Known for its summertime heat and humidity, the Southeast includes Maryland, Delaware, Virginia, West Virginia, North Carolina, South Carolina, Kentucky, Tennessee, Georgia, Florida, Mississippi, and part of Louisiana. The region also contains Washington, D.C. Florida, jutting southeast from the mainland between the Atlantic Ocean and the Gulf of Mexico, has a subtropic climate and is highly vulnerable to hurricanes and tropical storms, as are the coastal regions of the other Gulf Coast States. Coastline along the Atlantic in this region features wide, sandy beaches, mild waters, and tame surf. The largest mountain range in this region, and one of the oldest in the United States, is the Appalachian Mountains, which run from Maine to Georgia.

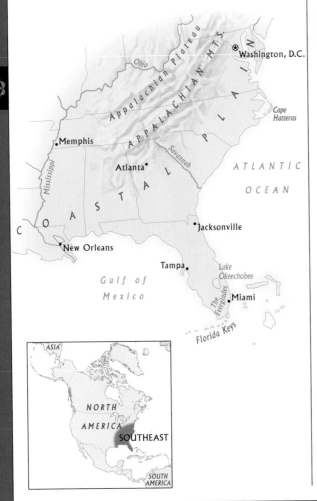

CAJUNS
Alternate name: Acadians   Population: 600,000
Location: United States
Language family: Italic

In order to understand the Cajuns it is necessary to know their backstory, the long journey that brought them to southern Louisiana. The French had first settled in Acadie (present-day Nova Scotia) in 1604 and became a colony of farmers, trappers, and fishermen whose settlements resembled those of their northern French homes.

But in 1755, after the British had won France's Canadian possessions and were themselves becoming established there, they abruptly exiled the Acadians, an event known as the *Grand Dérangement*, or Great Displacement. Some 8,000 were rounded up and loaded onto ships, with no attempt made to keep families together, and sent on their way to destinations on the Atlantic Coast. Those who made it all the way to Louisiana, sometimes after a lapse of 20 years, received a warm welcome from the French government there. The Acadians (whose name eventually was corrupted to Cajuns) were given land and guidance on settling it.

Some of the Acadians became farmers, concentrated on the banks of the Mississippi River, the Bayou Teche, and Bayou Lafourche, and on the prairies to the west, where they also raised cattle. Those who settled in the swamps and marshes and along the coast became hunters, trappers, and fishermen. They plied the waters in small boats called pirogues, which they dug out from single cypress logs or planks. The French, Spanish, and Creoles the Acadians encountered in Louisiana were of a higher class than the newcomers, but intermarriages occurred, as they did also with local Indians. In general, though, Cajun communities tended to be isolated and also insular, because people were encouraged to marry within them.

Cajun French is a somewhat archaic form of French with a simplified grammar, combined with contributions from English, Spanish, and Indian and African languages. Beginning in 1921, the speaking of Cajun French was outlawed for a time in Louisiana and English made compulsory. Cajun French is spoken less often now, especially by the younger generation. Most Cajuns also speak and use English regularly.

The Cajuns are largely Roman Catholic, a fact that differentiated them from many other Louisiana settlers.

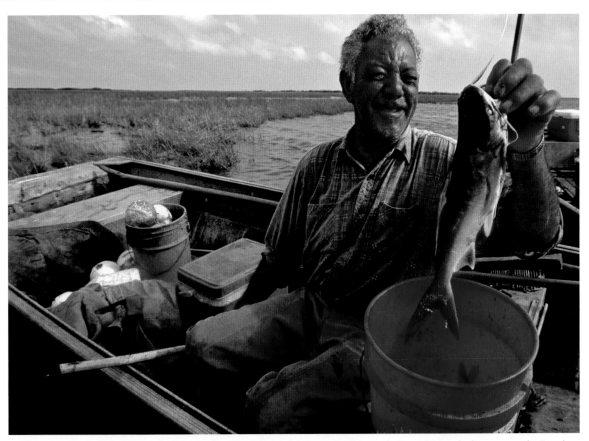

The marshes of southern Louisiana yield a catfish for a Cajun Indian fisherman. Much interethnic marriage took place among the French Acadians, Spanish, Creoles, and Indians in the early years of settlement there.

Religious observance has played an important role in Cajun communities, tempered with a sanctioned joie de vivre, expressed in the saying *"Laissez les bons temps rouler!*—Let the good times roll!" Most Cajun life events call for elaborate celebration, usually with music and dancing. The highlight of the annual calendar is still Mardi Gras (Fat Tuesday), a days-long festival prior to the beginning of Lent.

The Acadians brought to Louisiana a musical tradition that included *complaintes*, long unaccompanied songs describing the trials and tribulations of life. They took up the fiddle, creating spirited accompaniment. The accordion joined the mix in the early 19th century, and eventually other percussion instruments were added, such as the washboard and triangle. Dancing was and is synonymous with Cajun music, especially the two-step and waltz. Most Cajun communities held a weekly late-night dance called a *fais do-do*—literally, "go to sleep"—because children were put to bed there. These dances offered opportunities for supervised courtship, with the young male attendees sometimes held in a pen called *une cage aux chiens*, "a dogs' cage," unless they were actually dancing.

Cajun food fuses Acadian French with local cultures and local ingredients, such as bountiful shrimp and crayfish. Many Cajun dishes start with a roux— butter, lard, or other fat mixed with flour. Typical dishes include gumbo (from an African word for okra), a spicy mixture of meats and vegetables that often includes ground sassafras filé for seasoning, and jambalaya, a rice-based dish similar to paella that may include ham, sausage, and poultry as well as seafood.

Today, Louisiana's Cajuns operate in all social and economic spheres. Many are employed in commercial fisheries and in offshore oil and gas drilling and exploration. Cajun landholdings have declined over time; much of their former land is now owned by large corporations. Mostly spared by Hurricane Katrina in August 2005, Cajun Country was hit by flooding from Hurricane Rita less than a month later.

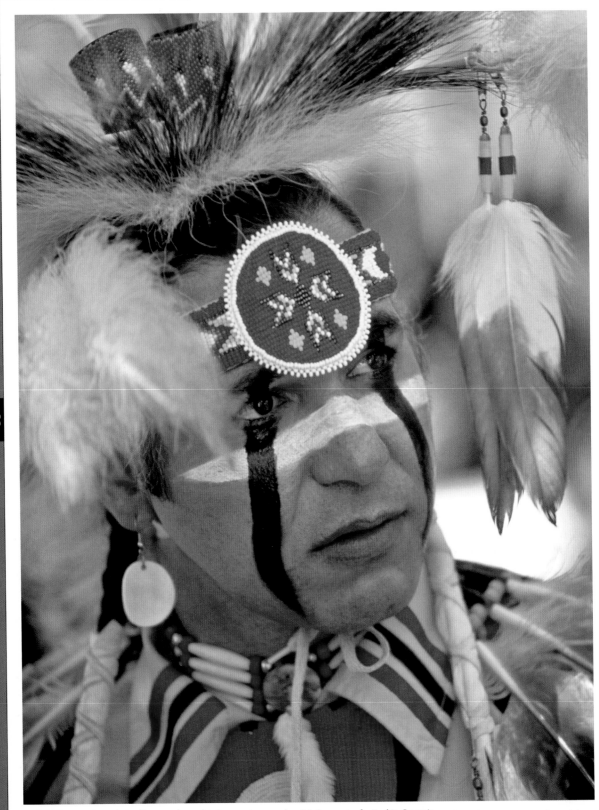

A Cherokee from North Carolina prepares to take part in a ceremonial dance at a festival in Georgia.

CHEROKEE

Population: 730,000
Location: United States
Language family: Iroquoian

For centuries the Appalachian highlands in North Carolina and Tennessee were home to the Cherokee, largest tribe in the southeastern United States. Then white settlers pushed across the Appalachians, taking over the fertile farmland of the Cherokee and other Indian groups in the region and forcing their removal to Indian Territory (now Oklahoma).

The Cherokee, who with the Chickasaw, Choctaw, Creek, and Seminole were known as the Five Civilized Tribes, had adapted to white culture and owned houses, farms, livestock, and slaves. By the 1820s, thousands of the people had learned to read and write their own language, using a syllabary devised by a Cherokee named Sequoyah, the only man in history known to have created a writing system single-handedly. His phonetic system comprised 85 symbols, each of which signified a sound in the Cherokee language. Tribal doctors recorded their medical beliefs and practices with Sequoyah's invention, and as a result much is known today about traditional Cherokee medicine.

In 1838 President Andrew Jackson enforced the Indian Removal Act of 1830, evicting 18,000 Cherokee from their homes in the southeast, even though the law had said the people must give their consent—and the Supreme Court had affirmed their rights to remain. Under conditions so brutal that 4,000 died, the Cherokee were marched westward; over the next decade, 60,000 Native Americans would walk the Trail of Tears to Oklahoma.

Some Cherokee managed to elude capture by hiding in North Carolina's mountains, and eventually their right to remain in the East was recognized by both the federal and state governments. In 1889 they became known as the Eastern Band of Cherokee Indians. Members of this band still tell the story today of Cherokee removal in their revered outdoor drama, *Unto These Hills.*

When the majority of Cherokee arrived in Oklahoma in 1839, they adopted a new constitution and began to establish schools, churches, and businesses. They also started to print their own newspaper and periodical. Soon, the Cherokee had a higher literacy rate than their white neighbors did.

In 1984 the Eastern Band of North Carolina and the Cherokee Nation of Oklahoma met in council for the first time in nearly 150 years; since then, they have met every two years. Both groups have elected women as principal chiefs, evidence that women play important roles in Cherokee society. Both have also striven to keep their culture strong through the continued use of their own language and by participation in such age-old activities as the stickball game. Traditional basketmaking, long a vital part of the identity of Cherokee women, is still carried out in North Carolina, where, in 1996, the Eastern Band used their casino profits to buy farmland encompassing Kituhwa, the Cherokee origin place and sacred burial ground.

CREEK & SEMINOLE

Population: 71,300 (Creek), 27,400 (Seminole)
Location: United States
Language family: Muskogean

The Creek of Alabama and eastern Georgia probably were descendants of prehistoric Mississippian temple mound builders who had migrated eastward. They maintained a complex and loose confederacy of both Creek and non-Creek tribes, anchored by the core Creek group, the Muskogee.

Creek towns tended to be large—from 100 to 1,000 residents—headed by a *miko,* or chief. The miko presided over tribal council meetings (which began with participants ingesting a heavily caffeinated "black drink") where decision-making was based on consensus. Within the towns were family compounds of one to four buildings, depending upon the owner's wealth. The Creek led a very active ritual life, including a number of traditional "stomp" dances performed on the community's stomp ground.

In colonial times, the Creek became allies of the English, although they were not above playing Europeans off each other. In the 1700s, after the English and Creek had all but destroyed the Apalachee and Timucua tribes of Spanish-held northern Florida, some Creek began moving into that region. They then became known as the Seminole, from the Muskogee word *simanóli,* meaning "runaway" or, more appropriately, "pioneer," which refers to the tribe's move to a new homeland, away from encroaching planters.

Border friction between white slaveholders and the Seminole intensified, though, because the latter treated

African Americans as equals, giving haven to runaway slaves, intermarrying with them, and heeding their advice in council. By the 1830s, when President Andrew Jackson signed an act to relocate the Seminole into Oklahoma, small bands were waging fierce guerrilla warfare in what came to be considered the longest and least successful Indian war in United States history.

Determined to preserve their freedom, the Seminole managed to carry on even after Osceola, their most famous leader, was captured under a flag of truce in 1837 and died in captivity the following year. From 3,000 to 4,000 Seminole, along with the remaining Creek in their home territory and other tribes, were forcibly marched to Oklahoma along the Trail of Tears. A few hundred Seminole managed to escape by fleeing south into the Everglades, eluding pursuers who in time gave up looking for them.

By the early 1900s, Florida's Seminole were trading alligator hides and egret feathers to non-Indians for cotton cloth, pots, and metal tools. In 1928 they started selling their crafts along the recently built Tamiami Trail, which linked Tampa to Miami via the Everglades. Over the next three decades, as increasing numbers of tourists began to flock to Miami, non-Indian entrepreneurs invited the tribe to create and work in Seminole "villages." Alligator wrestling, popularized at this time, and the machine-sewn patchwork clothing women began to make around 1900 have continued to promote a strong sense of tribal identity.

In 1957 the Seminole Tribe of Florida received federal recognition. Four years later, the Miccosukee, a tribe long incorporated into the Seminole, broke away from them. More conservative in social and religious values, the Miccosukee continue to follow the political leadership of their medicine men and council. Today, both tribes attract European and American visitors to their re-created villages, where museums tell the history of their people. They also operate successful eco-tourism enterprises that take visitors through the Everglades in airboats and swamp buggies. In contrast, most Oklahoma Seminole rely on jobs in the oil industry or in construction, manufacturing, and agriculture. Oklahoma Creek reside mostly on reservations and in tribal towns, and hold tribal jobs or work in bingo halls or on farms. Oklahoma Seminole and Creek maintain some of their traditions, including dances, on tribal stomp grounds there.

LUMBEE

Population: 58,000
Location: United States
Language family: Algonquian (extinct)

When European settlers in North Carolina first came face to face with the Lumbee, sometime around 1730, they found a people who looked like members of the other Indian tribes they knew, yet they spoke only English. Moreover, the Lumbee were settled farmers without any vestige of an Indian lifestyle whose appearance also showed both Anglo and African features.

The detailed facts of Lumbee origin remain a mystery to the Lumbee and to those who have studied them. One popular explanation tied the Lumbee to the original English settlers of Sir Walter Raleigh's Lost Colony of Roanoke Island who vanished some time between 1587 and 1590; it has been pointed out that the Lumbee share about 20 surnames with those settlers. More recent scholarship suggests that Lumbee ancestry incorporates remnants of Cherewan and other Siouan tribes who once lived in the area; some Cherokee, Tuscarora, and Croatoan Indians; and some Algonquian and Iroquoian speakers as well. Clearly there were also white and African contributions to Lumbee population genetics.

For nearly three centuries, the Lumbee have had an ongoing presence in the former marshland of the southeastern corner where North and South Carolina meet. The area is watered by the Pee Dee River and the Lumber (formerly Lumbee) River, from which the Lumbee get their name. Most Lumbee land is now in Robeson and surrounding counties. There are also a few scattered Lumbee populations elsewhere in the Southeast and in Baltimore, Philadelphia, and Detroit.

The Lumbee lived an isolated yet parallel existence as Protestant farmers with the English, Highland Scots, and Scots-Irish settlers, until land competition began to draw attention to their status. In 1835 the state of North Carolina took away the voting rights of all "free persons of color," including the Lumbee.

The now-disenfranchised Lumbee endured further oppression during the Civil War. After conscription into forced labor, they were starved and mistreated while building fortifications near Wilmington. This abuse created a fired-up Lumbee avenger: Henry Berry Lowry, who had also watched the North Carolina

Early in the Americas

L ife-forms are made up of organic matter, all their molecules containing carbon. Two stable, non-radioactive states, or isotopes, of carbon occur throughout the natural world: carbon 12 and carbon 13, so named for the combined number of protons and neutrons in each atom.

Fortunately for archaeologists, a third isotope, carbon 14, differs from the others in that it is unstable and, over time, decays into a different atom entirely. Carbon 14 results when cosmic rays bombard Earth at 30,000 to 50,000 feet above sea level and force nitrogen in the atmosphere to undergo a nuclear reaction.

Like other carbon atoms, the resulting carbon 14 can combine with oxygen to form carbon dioxide and then enter plants through the process of photosynthesis. Plants, and the animals that eat plants, ingest minute amounts of this harmless unstable isotope—and thereby incorporate into their bodies a timekeeper that will keep going tens of thousands of years after their bodies expire.

Carbon 14 atoms decay at a known constant rate into stable, non-radioactive nitrogen 14. Because their life cycle follows a predictable pattern, the proportional amounts of carbon 14 and nitrogen 14 that can be found in decayed life-forms can be measured and used to infer how much time has passed since the organism was living.

Telltale atoms

Although the stone tools used by humans are inorganic, they tend to accumulate in places where humans congregated—places where we eat, cook, hunt and are buried. These are the areas where archaeologists can find abundant organic deposits, such fire hearths scattered with charred seeds or hunting grounds replete with animal bones and spear points. If the sites are not too old, then the organic material left behind, analyzed with radiocarbon dating techniques, can help

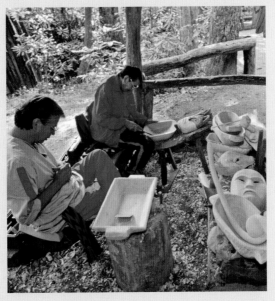

Cherokee demonstrate traditional crafts at a re-created village in North Carolina.

anthropologists date human activity at a given location.

In 1908 a deadly storm known as the Folsom Flood swept across southwestern North America, killing 17 people and causing property damage that took months to repair. That year a cowboy mending a fence on his New Mexico ranch noticed a few bones protruding from the exposed soil below. Having seen his fair share of bones from years on the range, George McJunkin quickly deduced that these were much larger and older than what he typically came across, and conjectured (correctly) that

they belonged to an extinct species of bison. He also discovered an arrowhead, about 13 feet down. Owing to the depth of the find, he believed both bones and point must have been quite old.

For decades, that arrowhead remained on McJunkin's mantle. Then a number of similar findings from New Mexico increased interest in the Clovis region. Dating the sites sent shockwaves through the anthropological community: Results showed that humans had been in New Mexico for at least 11,000 years. The spearheads from these sites came to characterize a prehistoric Native American culture known as Clovis, named for the town in New Mexico where the first site was systematically excavated.

Doubts

Clovis sites have since been identified throughout the contiguous United States, Mexico, and Central America, leading to the presumption that all indigenous cultures of North and South America descended from the Clovis people. New doubts have since arisen. Sites such as Monte Verde in southern Chile have been dated to 12,500 years old, indicating that humans arrived there far earlier than the first Clovis emergence.

Though the Clovis debate lives on, the Southwest's importance in Native American history is undisputed. The region saw several later cultures flourish, including that of the Ancient Pueblo or Anasazi people, who lived along on the Colorado Plateau before climate change in the 12th and 13th centuries turned the landscape dry and forced a people that had thrived for over 2,000 years to quickly abandon their settlements.

Home Guard shoot his father and brother. He and his tri-racial followers took 18 lives during an eight-year spree, which made Lowry a man wanted by every conceivable branch of law enforcement. He was caught and escaped a number of times until finally, in 1872, he disappeared and was never seen again. Lumbee today acknowledge Lowry as a tribal hero.

What the Lumbee lack in specific details about their distant Indian origins they make up for with detailed knowledge of their personal genealogies. Family is a cornerstone of contemporary Lumbee life, and extended family members keep in constant contact with each other. Lumbee marry other Lumbee at a rate of some 70 percent and most tribe members in Robeson County attend one of 130 Lumbee churches there, mainly Methodist and Baptist, which also serve as community resource centers. Children attend many Lumbee-majority schools, and higher education needs are met in part at the University of North Carolina at Pembroke, once a Lumbee teacher-training college. The Lumbee annual homecoming each summer brings thousands of Lumbee to Robeson County for parades, cookouts, competitions, and informal get-togethers.

Contemporary Lumbee have entered almost all areas of the local economy, although some still farm. As a tribe with more than 40,000 registered members, they zealously pursue both the Lumbee cause and a

> Seek wisdom, not knowledge.
> Knowledge is of the past.
> Wisdom is of the future.
> LUMBEE PROVERB

pan-Indian identity. For more than a century they have tried to gain full federal recognition as an Indian tribe. In 1987 the Lumbee submitted to the Bureau of Indian Affairs an exhaustive, three-volume petition believed to cover all the criteria required for complete recognition by the federal government. They were then surprised to learn that a loophole in the 1956 act giving them partial recognition prevented the petition from even being heard. The Lumbee continue forward with their cause and have lobbied for the legislative change necessary for the petition to be considered.

GULLAH

Alternate name: Sea Islanders   Population: 250,000
Location: United States
Language family: English and African-based Creole

The barrier islands and tidewater area from the Carolinas through Georgia into northern Florida is the traditional home of the Gullah. Also known as the Geechee and the Sea Islanders, the Gullah descend from freed slaves who formerly worked the rice fields and cotton plantations in this low-lying region.

The Gullah first arrived in the Southeast as slaves in the 1700s. Linguistic and other research has determined that they most likely came from Sierra Leone and nearby countries in West Africa. Some spent time in Barbados before reaching the Carolinas, where many entered through St. Helena Island near the port of Charleston, South Carolina.

Sierra Leone lies on the "Rice Coast" of Africa, and experience with that difficult and labor-intensive crop meant that slaves from the region were highly prized by low-country plantation owners. These West Africans also possessed a high tolerance to diseases rife in the semitropical coastal areas, such as malaria. When the owners fled inland to escape the heat, humidity, and bugs, as they often did from April to October and sometimes permanently, the Gullah remained in charge and alone, giving them a degree of freedom unknown to slaves elsewhere.

At the end of the Civil War, the Gullah were freed and offered the chance to buy island land in parcels rarely larger than ten acres. The ability to farm their own plots allowed them to escape the fate of other freed slaves, many of whom became sharecroppers. Still isolated by the rivers, swamps, and marshes separating them from the mainland, the Gullah have been able to retain more aspects of their traditional culture than any other former American slave population.

The Gullah language, which has drawn scholars to the islands since the mid-20th century, shares vocabulary and syntax with Krio—an English-based Creole—spoken in Sierra Leone. It also contains elements of English as it was spoken in the colonies in the 17th and 18th centuries and some Barbadian influences. In addition, Gullah oral traditions include songs and fragments of tales passed down from non-Creole West African tribal languages, notably Mende and Vai. (Probably the names "Gullah" and "Geechee" are

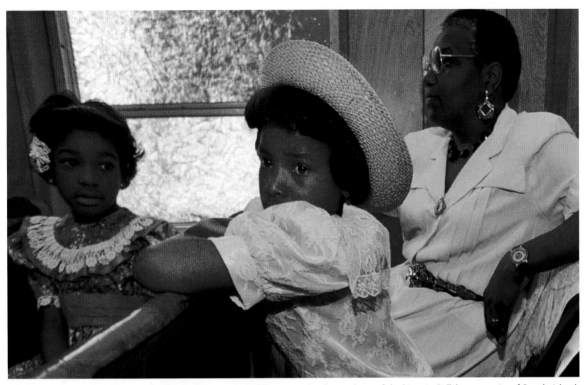

Sunday church services serve as a focal point for community life among the descendants of the historic Gullah community of Sapelo Island. Gullah inhabited the Sea Islands from the Carolinas through Georgia.

corruptions of West African tribal names.) A 1979 survey identified 100,000 speakers of Gullah, 10 percent speaking only Gullah. Although Gullah remained an unwritten language until recently, the colorful animal characters of its folktales, such as Br'er Rabbit and Br'er Fox, were immortalized in the 19th-century Uncle Remus stories written by Joel Chandler Harris.

While continuing to work as farmers, the Gullah have practiced traditional crafts and sold their ware to outsiders. Gullah women weave fine, circular sea-grass baskets that are identical to those found in Sierra Leone. Gullah men traditionally carve, making grave monuments, human figures, and walking sticks.

The Gullah are Christians who nevertheless tend to regard the individual as possessing a body, soul, and a separate spirit that may linger in the earthly realm after death. Gullah traditionally placed eating utensils and other practical items on graves to meet the spirits' needs. Both voudou and hoodoo are part of the Gullah tradition; good and evil spirits are summoned for divination, retribution, or curing. The Gullah practice folk medicine that incorporates the use of herbs and other natural remedies.

Gullah build their meals around the rice they have traditionally grown. The grain often is consumed for breakfast, lunch, and dinner, although grits also make an appearance at the first meal of the day. Rice combined with chicken and okra is a favorite dish, as is Frogmore stew (named for the Frogmore plantation), which contains a combination of small beef sausages, crabs, shrimp, and corn.

Gullah communities typically are kin-based clusters of homes built on family lands. The Gullah tend to hold their property communally, without division for inheritance, and over the generations this has created many stakeholders in the land, not all of them local— a situation exploited recently by resort developers. They often convince a few of the heirs to force a division sale and then grab the property for development.

The plight of the Gullah and their culture in the face of aggressive development and natural attrition—as younger Gullah leave for education and employment opportunities—has engendered programs to preserve and protect Gullah culture and interests. The former mission school on St. Helena, stronghold of Gullah culture, serves as the center of these efforts.

Making a Space to Live in

Not only the natural landscape but also the shape, materials, and character of the homes that people build define their worldview.

What do you need to build a house? Bricks, mortar, glass, and wood are commonly used in modern architecture. But looking around the world, we find people who have built or are still building traditional houses made of clay, straw, reeds, felt, animal hides, snow, and pits dug into the ground. Shelter is a basic need, but humans thrive in vastly different climates, eco-zones, and altitudes. Our species has always applied ingenuity to design shelters, including some of the more unusual and imaginative houses we explore here.

A house does so much more than provide shelter. Its shape reflects deep cultural values of social hierarchy, aesthetics, and the proper organization of space, a notion perhaps best known by the Chinese term "feng shui." Long before "green buildings" were fashionable and architecture became an art form, indigenous peoples used invention and artistry to build abodes of all types from many materials. Modernity has not yet swept aside this architectural legacy. Dung dwellings may still be found in India, felt houses in Mongolia, reed cottages on the floating islands of Peru's Lake Titicaca, tree houses in Papua New Guinea, goatskin tents in the Sahara, tipis in Siberia, and igloos in the Arctic North.

Traditional dwellings, along with some modern updates to them, showcase the genius of indigenous architecture. Houses may not be the pinnacle of human building arts: Societies of the past have also erected monumental tombs, public buildings, roads, cities, and pyramids for the gods. Other societies left behind nothing of the sort, because they used impermanent materials to build, perhaps, or directed their creative energies elsewhere. Regardless of their architectural prowess or grandeur, all human societies constructed dwellings for people. Traditional housing styles are now in decline worldwide as indigenous ways of life vanish and modern materials become more widely available. Unique building styles such as the Asmat longhouse, the Xingu *maloca* (a long oval house), the Evenki deerskin tipi, or the Inuit igloo vanish into the past. As they fade, we lose insight into human values and cultural traditions.

Mobile homes

Those traditional housing styles that do survive today have much to teach us about culture. Visiting the nomads of Mongolia or Kyrgyzstan, you will find them living in ergonomic round structures of felt overlain on wood lattices. Called yurts in Central Asia or gers in Mongolia, these ingenious houses manage to keep out the elements, keep in warmth, and let smoke escape through an opening in the roof.

Constructing a new yurt requires intensive labor, usually by a prospective groom in preparation for his marriage. Great bundles of wool must first be collected by shearing sheep. The wool is then beaten by hand with metal rods to form thick felt. Roof poles and collapsible wall lattices are painstakingly planed by hand and painted bright reds and yellows. Ropes of horsehair are plaited by hand to gird the entire structure. No nails or glues are used; each joint is bored through and secured by a leather thong. The doorway is then decorated with intricate geometric patterns.

When the nomads need to move, these yurts can be rapidly disassembled, packed into a truck or onto a camel's back, and transported to a new place. Because nomads must migrate to find new grass for their animals, the yurt architecture perfectly fits their lifestyle. But the yurt is also a complex space that reflects social values. Stooping to enter through the low yurt door, you find yourself in a dim interior space with light

Houses on stilts hug the coast on Jolo Island in the southwestern Philippines. The elevated structures withstand everyday fluctuations in the tides, but remain vulnerable in severe storms.

coming through the round roof opening. Immediately in front of you is a stove. The women's space is to the right and includes the stove front, cooking area, flour storage, utensils, space for processing milk and sheep entrails, and the main bed. The men's space, taking up the left half, is where food is served and guests seated. It is used for saddles and lassos, cuts of meat, a family shrine, clothing chests, and a bed for guests or children. Though the line separating the men's and women's spaces is invisible, it is keenly perceived and governs how people comport themselves inside the yurt. A guest who sits in the wrong place may be gently scolded or even asked to move. If a blind person walked into any one of many thousands of nomadic yurts in Mongolia, he could immediately locate most objects and furnishings, so regular is the interior layout. The door of the yurt must face south, and the proximity to neighboring yurts may indicate how closely the family is related.

Far away in the Sahara, the Tuareg people of Niger also move frequently to herd camels. Espousing mobile architecture, they spend their lives living in goatskin tents in the desert. Tents are the focus of their social interaction, beginning with ritual greetings outside the tent. Within a tent, the Tuareg are able to enjoy a protected space to conceal food, wealth, or information from prying eyes.

The sturdy tents, supported on curved sticks, reveal Tuareg ideas about gender roles. Built and owned by a woman, a tent is brought by her to the marriage as dowry and retained if the couple divorces. Nuptial tents are constructed for a young bride by old women, who may ritually rebuild and take down the tent for seven successive days during her wedding ceremony. The wedding tent is greeted by ceremonial songs and drumming, and there are special protocols for how the bride and groom must enter it. During a wedding, young people play a game of casting sticks across the divide between the left (female) and right (male) sides of the tent. A Tuareg women maintains control over her tent and the use of space within it; for example, she may orient the tent doors and sleeping spaces differently depending on whether her husband is present or away traveling.

Tent life also extends to some of the northernmost peoples on Earth. The Evenki reindeer herders continue to live for much of the year in canvas or deerskin-covered tipis, as did their ancestors, deep in the Siberian forest. They construct a conical frame of birch poles and cover it with deerskins, lining the interior floor with deerskins for sleeping. Mobile architecture in the form of conical lodges made of animal skins was also practiced by the Sami people of Norway but is now a vanishing art. Tipis built by the Lakota, Crow, Nez Percé, and other Native American tribes once graced America's northwest plains by the thousands. Highly practical, tipis in both Siberia and native North America provided warmth in the cold, cool in the heat, a sheltered space to cook and sleep, and mobility. American tipis may now be seen in modern forms at tribal powwows, where they help reconnect Plains peoples to their past.

Housing that is immobile can still be light, ecological, and ergonomic. The Kombai and Korowai people, hunter-gatherers of Papua New Guinea, may live as high as a hundred feet off the ground in treehouses made of wood lashed together with vines. The houses are so solid that their residents can haul small domestic animals up narrow ladders, light fires, cook, sleep, and eat—all high in the sky. Separate living spaces are maintained for men and women, another example of gender roles expressed in architecture. Primarily for protection from neighboring hostile tribes, the tree houses also shield from mosquitoes and provide a lookout point. When one deteriorates, a new one is quickly built from locally plentiful plant material.

Adaptive architecture

Perhaps the most famed example of adaptive architecture is the igloo, historically built by Inuit peoples across a large swath of Canada and Greenland. Though it begins as a house of snow blocks, melting and condensation cause snow to become ice after a few days of residence. The igloo is thus perhaps the only house that beneficially changes its substance over time. Neighboring igloos can be joined by tunnels, creating a complex of domed structures, with sunken entryways and raised sleeping platforms inside. The ingenious helix method for stacking the snow blocks produces

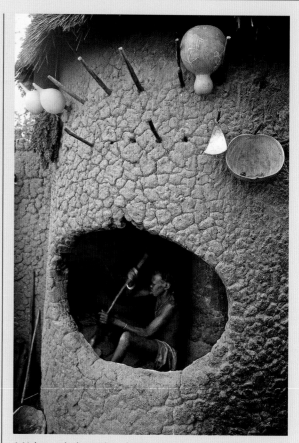

A Nuba tends the cooking fire in the kitchen of a mud-walled dwelling in the mountains of central Sudan. The off-the-ground entrance keeps out cattle and rats.

a structure of enough strength to support a grown man standing on top. Though the Inuit no longer live in igloos, some still know how to build them and can demonstrate the technology. The Inuit, now settled in modern houses, preserve the art of the snow house as part of their repertoire of survival techniques. There is considerable nostalgia for this icon of survival in harsh climes, and there is even an igloo-inspired hotel in Greenland with aluminum igloos for guests.

Going from arctic snows to high-altitude lakes, we find the Uros people of Peru's Lake Titicaca living on floating artificial islands made of Tortora reeds. Once a way of life based on birding and fishing, artificial-island dwelling has now become a magnet for tourists. The Uros build elegant boats and simple houses from this humble material. The abundant reeds are collected and processed to obtain bundles of uniform thickness and length. They are dried, then bound into bundles to form the walls and sewn into mats for the roofs. Reed houses are both disposable and renewable. They can be updated with new technologies: Tin roofs have become common, and some reed houses now have solar panels, electricity, and televisions.

Local materials

Most local building materials can be obtained for free, and the Dogon of Mali use mud as their main material. Dogon houses, towers of dried mud, are tightly clustered into geometrically complex arrangements. They may be round or quadratic, multistoried, and sometimes topped with peaked straw cones that resemble hats. Mud as a building material is constantly renewable, so any cracks can be repaired with a few handfuls of earth. As layers are added over the years, the structures take on fanciful, sand-castle shapes. Entire clusters of Dogon houses may be nestled in a rock crevice or on a cliff face, where they provide a natural fortress.

Elaborate and symbolic mahogany doors may protect a home, granary, or women's quarters. Bearing bas-relief images of crocodiles, snakes, turtles, and mythical beings, these portals serve as symbolic shields to ward off evil influences and protect people and possessions. Dogon doors have also become a valued commodity on the global art market.

Houses in traditional indigenous cultures may teach us something. Often fully biodegradable and made of local materials, their value lies more in the design and labor than the stuff of which they are made. Often mobile, lightweight, and readily replaceable, their worth lies more in their proximity to kin, grazing lands, water, and protective landscapes than in any ownership of fixed real estate. Often porous or unlockable to outsiders, their protective power lies in their ability to strengthen the social network, enfolding kin and cotribals into a private and intimate space.

And finally, with their infinite variety of design, material, geometry, and functionality, many indigenous housing styles represent the best ways people have yet devised to live in a low-impact manner in challenging environments. ▪

— *K. David Harrison*

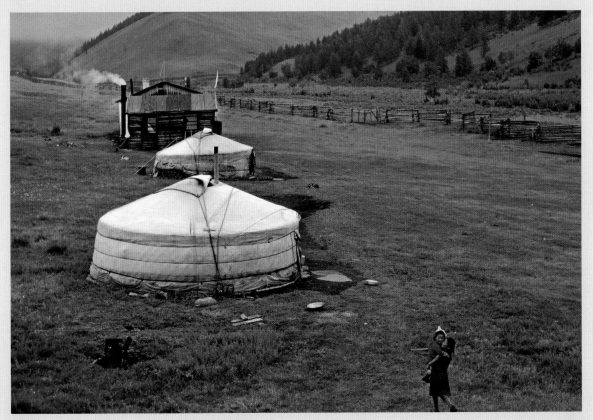

Portability is the key feature of a Mongolian yurt, also known as a ger. Nomadic herders can disassemble, transport, and reassemble the felt-covered dwellings as they move their herds to different pastures.

CENTRAL & SOUTH AMERICA

THE CARIBBEAN
African Caribbeans • Amerindians • East Indians
Euro-Caribbeans • Haitians • Jamaicans • Kogi

MESOAMERICA
Garifuna • Highland Maya • Lowland Maya
Huichol • Mixtec • Nahua • Otomí
Tarascans • Zapotec

AMAZON AND ORINOCO BASINS
Amahuaca • Bororo • Brazilians • Caribs
Desana • Kuikuru • Mundurucú • Nukak
Saramaka • Shuar • Tapirapé • Warao
Xikrín • Yanomamí

ANDES
Aymara • Kallawaya • Mapuche
Otavaleños • Q'eros • Quechua

CENTRAL SOUTH AMERICA
Guaraní • Kadiwéu • Mataco • Tupinambá

PATAGONIA
Argentines • Fuegians

Bolivian flute players entertain at a yearly carnival in Oruro,
center of the country's folkloric traditions.

Mesoamerica, the Caribbean, and South America are geographical neighbors, with each region sharing at least part of its history and culture with the other. Each area, however, has also experienced a long, complex past quite separate from the other, and this has resulted in fundamental differences between them.

Anthropologists recognize Mesoamerica as a distinct region whose peoples, although ethnically diverse, have shared significant cultural characteristics across varied terrains and a broad expanse of time. Beginning in the semidesert landscapes of north-central Mexico, the region of Mesoamerica reaches south and east toward the tropical terrain of upper Central America, where it then stretches through Guatemala, Belize, and portions of Honduras, El Salvador, and Nicaragua.

In the late 15th century, when Europeans began arriving in the Western Hemisphere, Mesoamerica was dominated by the vast empire of the Aztec. But within decades of the European arrival, Spanish conquistadores had overwhelmed that powerful people and all other major groups. Native Aztec, Zapotec, Mixtec, and others were congregated into European-style villages and towns and forcibly converted to Roman Catholicism. They were introduced to new farming methods and were taught how to create new products of fiber and metal. In short, they were forced to conform to a new economic system.

To meet their growing labor needs, the Spanish and later colonial powers also turned to Africans, who were forcibly brought to the New World to work on fruit plantations along the Caribbean coastal plain. Today, many people in both Mesoamerica and along the Caribbean are of mixed background—mostly European-Amerindian, European-African, or Amerindian-African. Spanish is the dominant language in much of the region Many indigenous peoples speak only their own language.

Cuisine, religion, festivals, and arts also reflect the European influence on indigenous cultures. Beans, maize, chilies, and other local staples are augmented by wheat, fruits, pork, and chicken introduced from Europe. In religion, the phenomenon of "folk Catholicism" fuses traditional native cosmology with Christian practices.

To the east, extending through the Caribbean Sea from the northern coast of South America to the southern tip of Florida, are the islands called the West Indies, including the Lesser Antilles, the Greater Antilles, and the Bahamas. The Spanish controlled all

A Venezuelan man and his donkey ponder the ridges of the Andes, home to many highland South American cultures.

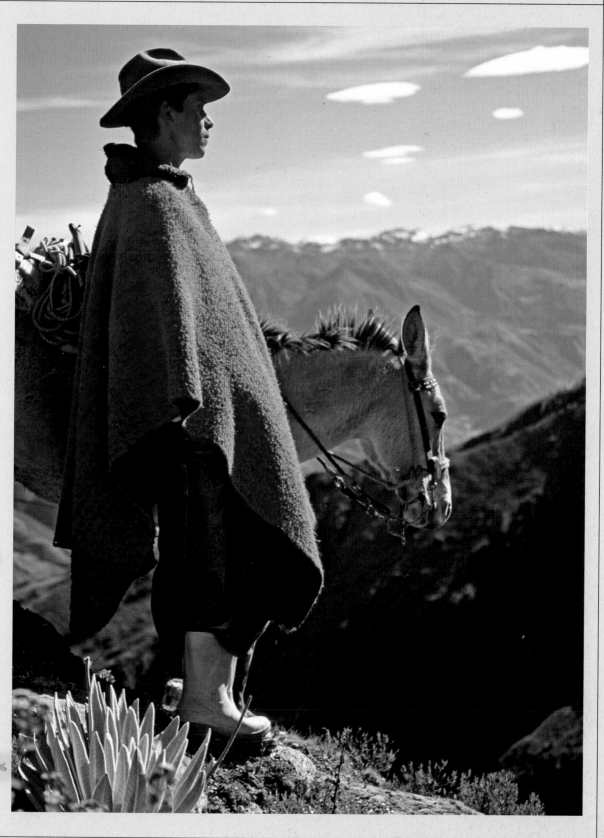

these islands from 1492, when Columbus arrived, until the 1620s, when northern Europeans established permanent settlements. Here the plantation economy took hold, and millions of Africans were brought across the Atlantic in bondage. For much of the 17th and 18th centuries, these islands witnessed wars and piracy carried out by the dominant colonial powers. The 19th century brought emancipation to the slave population, and soon immigrant labor arrived from India and elsewhere.

The ethnic composition of the West Indies is difficult to describe, because culture, ethnicity, class, and race have combined through the generations. Whites and blacks are about equal in number; a slightly smaller percentage is of mixed ancestry. The linguistically diverse West Indian region includes colonial languages, tongues brought by waves of immigration, and Creole forms such as Haitian Kreyol and Aruban Papiamento. Throughout the Caribbean, Roman Catholicism, Protestantism, Hinduism, Islam, and syncretic religions like Santeria, Voudou, Orisha, and Spiritual Baptism all thrive. So does music, such as calypso and reggae, which blends European, African, and native traditions and instruments.

Paloitos, or little sticks, pierce the cheeks of a Yanomamí girl in Brazil, and leaves, feathers, and flowers adorn her ears.

South America The South American continent is a land of dramatic environmental contrasts, with a remarkable diversity of indigenous human populations to match. In the north, a wide coastal plain borders the Caribbean Sea and is backed by a branch of the Andes mountain range, the backbone of the continent for almost 5,000 miles. The celebrated Altiplano, or high plain, surrounds Lake Titicaca, on the border of Bolivia and Peru. East of the Andes, humid tropical forest stretches across the enormous Amazon Basin. Along the Pacific coast, west of the mountains, lie some of Earth's driest deserts.

In the central part of South America, the Amazon Basin gives way to the Brazilian Highlands. Here is the huge sandstone plateau of the Mato Grosso region. Southwest of the Mato Grosso is the Gran Chaco, a series of arid plateaus descending from the Andes. To the south lie the vast grasslands of the Pampas, which stretch to the arid plateaus of Patagonia. A mountainous landscape of islands, fjords, glaciers, and densely forested valleys lies to the west and extends into Tierra del Fuego. Here, at the remote southern end of the continent, human groups arrived more than 8,000 years ago.

South America's environmental diversity led to a wide range of human societies, which adapted brilliantly to their surroundings by developing an intimate knowledge of them. For example, at the time of the Spanish conquest in the 16th century, Andean peoples were cultivating 70 indigenous plant species—including the staple, potato—a number nearly equal to all the cultivars of Europe and Asia combined at the time. In addition, hallucinogenic plants then figured—and still do figure—centrally in many religious beliefs and rituals of peoples in South America. Shamans fulfilled essential spiritual needs in many communities.

The Andes hosted the rise of a great ancient civilization, culminating in the Inca Empire of the 15th century A.D., centered in Cuzco, Peru. The empire eventually fell apart in the face of civil war and the arrival of rapacious conquistadores, beginning with Francisco Pizarro in 1532. Still, many people continued their traditional lifeways in remote valleys and desert communities.

At the time of the Spanish conquest, many South Americans made their living by hunting and gathering or by simple subsistence farming. Much of the diversity of indigenous life was destroyed by Spanish colonization, which brought not only European farming methods and technology but also horses and the pervasive influence of Catholicism. Thousands died from infectious diseases, maltreatment, and forced labor. Today, many once powerful Indian peoples eke out an existence in city slums or peasant communities. A surprising number maintain

A vendor weighs tomatoes at an open-air market in Guatemala. Market days bring communities together and help people keep up with local news.

their traditional ways, despite the arrivals of land-hungry prospectors, multinational corporations, and modern technology.

One can transform a society's technology, but the people will still prize their own deep-felt beliefs and rituals in the face of pressures from outside. From the remarkable Aymara farmers to the skilled Otavaleño weavers, much remains to admire and enjoy—and South American society is immeasurably richer as a result. ∎

The Caribbean

A narrow string of hundreds of islands, the Caribbean arches more than 2,500 miles around the Caribbean Sea. The arch starts off the southeast coast of Florida and runs to roughly the northeast coast of Venezuela in South America. The climate is tropical and subtropical, cooled by tradewinds, making it a highly desirable vacation, sailing, and scuba-diving destination. Major islands of the Caribbean include Cuba, Jamaica, the Cayman Islands, Turks and Caicos, Hispaniola (containing Haiti and the Dominican Republic), Puerto Rico, Virgin Islands, Leeward Islands, Windward Islands, Barbados, Grenada, Trinidad, and Tobago.

⏏To listen to music from Colombia, Cuba, the Dominican Republic, French Antilles, Haiti, Jamaica, Puerto Rico, Belize, Trinidad and Tobago, and Venezuela, visit http://worldmusic.nationalgeographic.com.

AFRICAN CARIBBEANS

Alternate name: Black Caribbeans Population: 15 million
Location: Caribbean island nations
Language family: Many languages spoken

Africans have had a significant impact on shaping the Caribbean ever since the 16th century. From across vast stretches of the African continent, slavers brought millions of people with diverse backgrounds to the New World. That experience, as well as contact with other African peoples and with Europeans, has created a unique culture in the West Indies. To be sure, there are numerous variations among islands: Jamaicans, for example, differ in many ways from Guadeloupeans. Nevertheless, a unique and coherent African-American Caribbean culture transcends national boundaries in important ways.

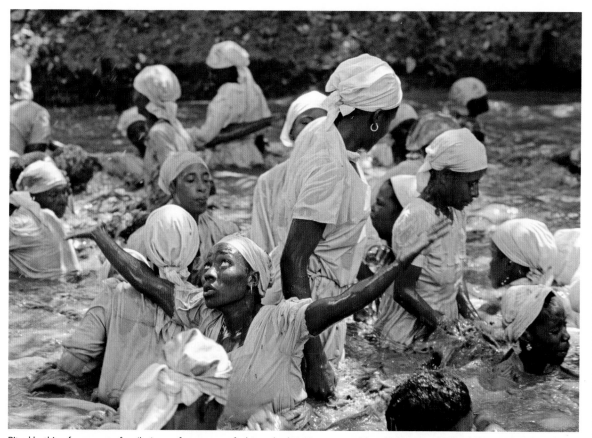

Ritual bathing forms part of a pilgrimage for a group of white-robed Haitian women. Many Haitian people blend Christian beliefs with the practices of voudou.

Approximately 36 million people live in the Caribbean region, and more than half of them have some African ancestry. They descend from people who either brought with them or later developed unique family structures, religions, cuisines, musical forms, dances, and festivals. They even had credit associations known as *susus*—revolving credit arrangements whereby participants pooled their money and then withdrew individual lump sums when needed. African peoples also adopted and transformed traditions that they encountered in the New World, thereby producing new forms of culture. Among their contributions are the syncretic religions of Voudou, Santeria, and Rastafarianism; musical forms including calypso, reggae, rumba, and zouk; and festivals such as Carnival, Jonkanoo, and Crop-Over.

In almost every part of the Caribbean, Africans rebelled against their enslavement. In some cases, communities of escaped slaves, called "Maroons," established themselves in difficult landscapes and held off repeated attempts by the colonial forces to root them out. In other cases, organized rebellions were attempted; the most notable success was the 1804 overthrow of the French in Haiti.

In Maroon societies, and in other parts of the Caribbean, aspects of African languages were preserved to greater or lesser degrees. Much of what is spoken in the Caribbean today, whether it is the Kreyol of Haiti, the patois of Jamaica, or the Papiamento language of the Dutch Antilles, owes some portion of its vocabulary and syntax to African languages such as Yoruba and KiKongo.

AMERINDIANS

Population: 25,000
Location: Caribbean island nations
Language family: English, primarily

When Columbus arrived in the New World, he encountered three distinct native peoples: The Ciboney, or Siboney, had settlements on Cuba and

Hispaniola; the Arawak controlled the Bahamas, Trinidad, and much of the Greater Antilles; and the Caribs were settled mostly in the Virgin Islands and along the Lesser Antilles. Some Carib groups lived on the South American mainland, from the Amazon River northward to the Guianas and the sea that would be named for them.

The Caribs occupied small autonomous settlements, grew staple foods such as cassava and other root crops, and hunted in nearby areas with their blowguns or bows and arrows. Although much of their history has been lost, the people were reputedly fierce warriors whose numbers were decimated by war, disease, and the brutal conditions of slavery in the early decades of European colonization. For the most part, divisions between the Carib groups ran along linguistic lines, but the languages they spoke seem to have been mutually understandable.

The Arawak, often described by the Spanish as gentle and hospitable, lived a life that was technologically simple yet ingenious. They and the Caribs both practiced *conuco,* a kind of ecologically sound farming method that involved burning a small patch of land to enrich the soil. Farmers then formed mounds of earth where they planted manioc and other crops that had high yields but a low environmental impact. Because they lived in a tropical climate, the Arawak usually felt the need to construct only simple shelters. The people also were known for creating elaborate stone sculptures, painting their bodies, and making jewelry.

According to accounts of contemporaries, both the Arawak and the Caribs were more centrally organized than the Ciboney. The Arawak had complex, intertwining forms of religion and government: Shamans were responsible for controlling *zemis,* good and evil spirits that they sometimes captured and housed in icons made of gold; caciques, or local chiefs, ruled semiautonomous provinces within the larger territory of an island. Carib organization was less centralized, with villages remaining largely independent of one

A free-for-all with pastel dyes produced this colorful scene during Phagwa, a spring festival in San Juan, Puerto Rico. Both Hinduism and Islam remain important to Caribbean people of Indian descent.

another. Although European settlers considered Caribs to be savages who ate human flesh, most scholars today say that this image was exaggerated to justify the people's conquest. This is not to say that cannibalism played no part in the culture; it was very likely practiced in ritual situations following battles. The bravest enemy warriors were tortured and killed, and parts of their bodies were ceremonially consumed.

While no "pure" native populations are left, several Caribbean communities preserve their age-old traditions and celebrate native ancestry in such venues as the Santa Rosa Carib Festival in northern Trinidad. A concerted effort is also under way to remember contributions to Caribbean life made by people such as the Taino, a subgroup of the Arawak in Puerto Rico.

EAST INDIANS

Population: 35,000
Location: Caribbean island nations
Language family: English, primarily

In 1838, slavery ended in the British West Indies. But the plantation economy still required workers, and planters were often unwilling or unable to pay fair wages to former slaves, the islands' only source of manpower. Besides, many Africans were understandably loath to work for their former masters. In an attempt to undercut African labor power, planters asked the colonial government to help find cheap labor in other parts of the empire. Various solutions were tried—including the importation of European workers, free Africans, and Chinese laborers—before the English found their greatest success in indentured workers from India.

Between 1838 and 1917, more than half a million people were brought from the Indian subcontinent to colonies in South America and the Caribbean. The vast majority came to settle in Guyana (formerly British Guiana) and Trinidad, with many others going to Guadeloupe, Jamaica, Suriname, Martinique, French Guiana, and Grenada. Smaller numbers landed in Belize, St. Vincent, St. Kitts, and St. Croix. Today descendants of those people from India and its former lands still make up a significant portion of the Caribbean population.

The Indian presence has had a profound impact on the local Caribbean culture, with cuisine, dance, music, festivals, politics, enterprise, art, and religion in many Caribbean regions all possessing elements of Indian

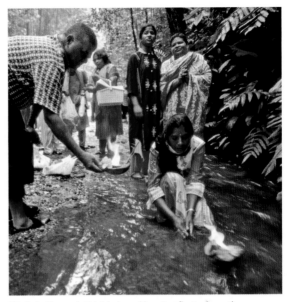

Hindu believers in Trinidad send burning floats down the Marianne River, echoing practices observed thousands of miles away on India's Ganges River.

culture These forms, though, are not "purely" Indian: Through the years a "creolization" has occurred, resulting in something unique to the region. A fine example of Caribbean Indian culture can be found in Trinidad's annual Hosay Festival, which commemorates the deaths of the Prophet Muhammad's grandsons Hassan and Husain. Called the Muharram Festival by Shiite Muslims, in Trinidad this event is celebrated with a colorful parade of large floats, or *taziya,* in the shape of elaborate mosques. The floats are accompanied by *tassa* drummers—groups of men with sticks, beating drums slung over their shoulders.

Indo-Caribbean culture has also produced "chutney" music,—a fast-tempo, modernized version of folk tunes—and other musical forms; it has itself become mixed with African-derived calypso and soca (soul meeting calypso) to produce a highly popular dance music called soca-chutney.

Finally, Indian cooking has greatly influenced the cuisines of Trinidad and Guyana with such mainstays as roti: flat bread filled with a stew of curried potatoes, chickpeas, and shrimp, goat, or chicken; "doubles": curried chickpeas served between two pieces of flat bread; and *pholouri*: deep-fried balls of yellow split-pea batter served with a mango chutney—just to name a few. Hindi words pepper the local languages, especially when it comes to food: Spinach is *bhaji,* potato is *aloo,* long string beans are *bodi,* and chickpeas are *channa.* Sometimes overlooked when considering Caribbean culture, Indian culture has evolved into a major element of the region's ethnic mix.

EURO-CARIBBEANS

Alternate name: White Caribbeans
Population: 9 million   Location: Caribbean island nations
Language family: Germanic

The permanent European presence in the Caribbean began with the arrival of Columbus in 1492 and continued as the Spanish Empire sent colonists to extract mineral wealth from the region. Because islands without precious metals were of little interest, early colonists moved fairly rapidly from one place to another in search of riches, all the while enslaving local populations and unknowingly exposing them to diseases brought from Europe.

With the arrival of other European powers through the 16th and 17th centuries, and the subsequent growth of plantation economies, additional labor was needed. But landowners did not turn immediately to African slavery as the solution; instead, they looked to European sources for workers. For a while, they relied on indentured servants: Some had been kidnapped and brought to the New World, while many others left their homelands to escape religious persecution, war,

> One hand washes the other;
> both get clean.
> CURAÇAOAN PROVERB

or even prison sentences. These early white laborers often suffered harsh treatment, succumbed to disease, and were eventually replaced by Africans.

As African slavery began to dominate the islands, white servitude declined. Even so, poor whites were not viewed kindly, and for a time local governments considered many of them to be persona non grata: idlers, thieves, and ne'er-do-wells. Owners and overseers, on the other hand, continued to do well.

Through the years, both the elite and far-from-elite classes of Europeans have had a significant effect on

the Caribbean region. They brought holidays and festivals—New Year's and Carnival, for example—as well as masked balls and various cuisines, musical forms, and dances. Like the people who brought them, many of these customs, activities, and traditions have been radically transformed over time to emerge as uniquely Caribbean.

HAITIANS

Population: 8.7 million
Location: Haiti
Language family: French-based Creole

Two hundred years ago, escaped black slaves known as Maroons staged a forceful and persistent rebellion against French colonial planters and imperial powers in Haiti, the western one-third of the island of Hispaniola in the Caribbean Sea. Their success in 1804 resulted in the establishment of the first independent black republic in the modern world.

Since then, Haiti's fortunes mostly have followed a downward spiral. Today more than eight million Haitians find themselves the poorest people in the Western Hemisphere, with high infant mortality and a life expectancy of only 52 years. Their mostly mountainous island has been stripped of its forests for building, farming, and to make charcoal for fuel. The island also presents double natural perils: an earthquake-producing tectonic fault running through the center and a prime location in the Caribbean hurricane belt.

Nearly all Haitians descend from Africans, although five percent of the population is mulatto or white. French was Haiti's official language until the constitution of 1987, when it was pushed into second place by Kreyol, a local language with French pronunciation and vocabulary but syntax similar to other Caribbean Creoles. The country's elite still speak French, and higher status accrues to those who are fluent in it.

Haitians may be poor, but nearly all of them own a little land, much of which is not very suitable for agriculture. Nevertheless, most Haitian homesteads have gardens planted by the male head of the family. They produce food for the household but, more importantly, a surplus that the women sell on the streets and in local markets, an important source of family income.

Visitors to a family compound announce their arrival in the yard by calling out *"Onè—*Honor," which is answered by the host with *"Respè—*Respect." It

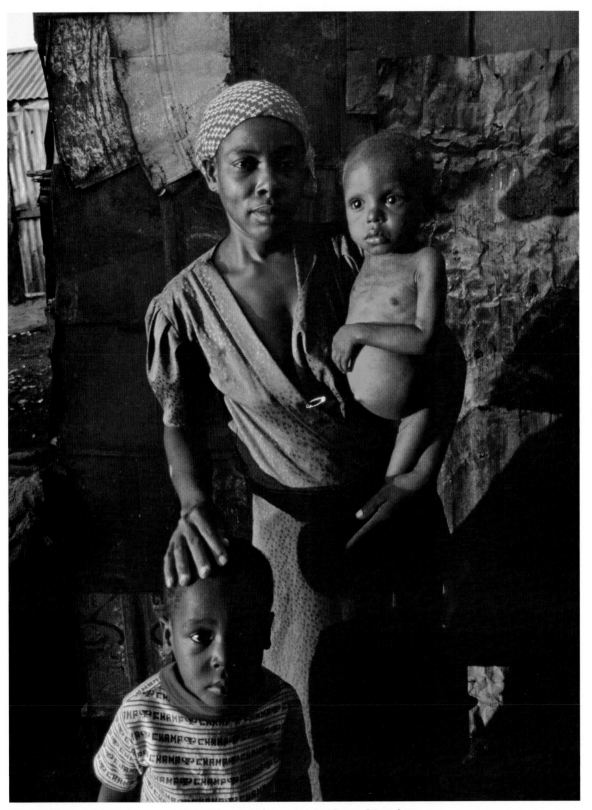

Poorest of the poor, a Haitian woman and her children struggle to survive in a Port-au-Prince slum.

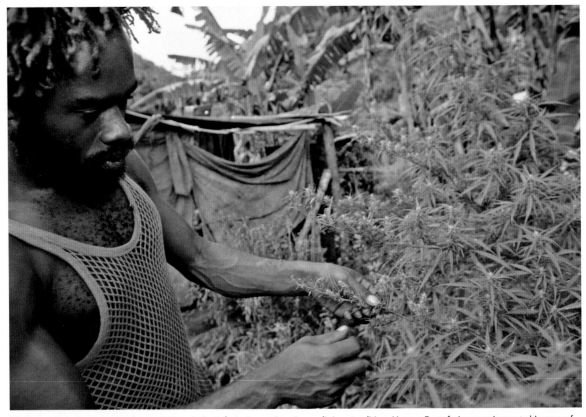

Marijuana use takes on sacred connotations in Rastafarianism, a Jamaican religious tradition. Here, a Rastafarian man inspects his crop of cannabis, considering its readiness for harvest.

would be unthinkable not to offer something to drink and perhaps eat—or, if nothing is available, a profound apology. Rice and beans appear at the main meal of the day, along with yams, sweet potatoes, manioc, plantain, corn, and sometimes chicken. Mangoes and other fruits are eaten as snacks.

Haiti at one time was an overwhelmingly Catholic country—some 90 percent—another legacy of French colonialism. In the last few decades, Catholicism has lost ground to widespread Protestant missionizing, which has captured the religious affiliation of perhaps 20 percent of the population. These Haitian Protestants refer to their faith as *levanjil,* or evangelism. At the same time, the practice of Voudou has declined somewhat. Voudou is a syncretic tradition fusing West African and Catholic beliefs and rituals. In Haiti, it can concern itself as much or more with healing as it does with causing harm to one's perceived enemies, and it involves the use of a number of different specialists, which can be either men or women.

As if to make up for the relentless hardships of their lives, Haitians spend a good deal of time and many resources planning their funerals, which are elaborate events involving days of socializing, feasting, and processions. When death occurs, relatives gather at the home of the deceased and settle in for several days. The trend currently favors above-ground burial in a *kav,* a kind of multioccupant tomb that costs a great deal to build—often more than the average home. Many Haitians think of the afterlife as going to *lafrik gine,* or Guinea Africa.

Haitians in general believe in *lwa,* a constellation of spirits who must be served in order to obtain their favor. Baron Samedi, for example, guards the crossroads where souls pass to the other side; believers offer him his symbols of a top hat, sunglasses, and cigar. Christians still usually acknowledge the lwa, although more mainstream Catholic and Protestant adherents may drop the custom.

The political instability of the past decades has shattered an already fragile Haitian economy, and the country's crumbling infrastructure likely makes Haiti's overall situation worse than it was a century ago. Several million Haitians have left the country, many as "boat people" headed to the United States. Roughly two-thirds of the population is formally unemployed, and export production has dwindled down to a few items—mainly coffee, cocoa, mangoes, and essential oils used in cosmetics.

JAMAICANS

Population: 2.6 million
Location: Jamaica
Language family: English-based Creole

Some 2.6 million people inhabit Jamaica, the third largest island in the Caribbean. It has a mountainous interior and flat coastal area that supports large urban settlements such as Kingston, the capital, on the south, and trendy, tropical playground resorts on the north. More than 90 percent of the people in Jamaica are of African ancestry; the rest include small numbers of East Indians, Chinese, and whites. Wealth is unevenly distributed in Jamaica, with a wide gap between rich and poor.

Originally the homeland of Arawak Indians, who were decimated upon contact with Europeans, here as elsewhere in the Caribbean, Jamaica endured more than 450 years of Spanish and British domination before obtaining independence in 1962. English is Jamaica's official language and has retained some Elizabethan influences. Upon leaving a friend, a person might say, "Peradventure I will see you tomorrow." Most Jamaicans also regularly speak a patois, or Creole language combining English with elements of French and Spanish that, when paired with a laid-back demeanor, serves to differentiate Jamaican identity from European authority.

Family life in Jamaica takes different forms depending on class. The middle and upper classes usually aspire to formalized, monogamous marriages and nuclear families. The poor tend to enter informal relationships that may eventually be legally sanctioned, often after the birth of several children and the attainment of financial stability. Often, though, a woman will reside in a household with her children from different relationships, her mother, and perhaps other kin on her mother's side. The bonds of kinship reckoned through women are frequently the relationships that count most among the poor. In hard times children may be passed from relative to relative to be cared for until circumstances improve. Regardless of class, child-rearing stresses politeness and courtesy in children. Elders are to be respected at all times. Children, and especially girls, acquire responsibility at an early age, often taking charge of younger siblings.

Religion permeates Jamaican life, taking myriad fluid forms. Mainstream Protestant denominations, notably Anglican, Baptist, and Methodist, made early inroads in Jamaica. In recent decades Pentacostalism has flourished; its emphasis on the power of the Holy Spirit against devils and demons resonates with the African-based belief in *obeah,* or sorcery, which many Jamaicans regard as the root cause of most misfortunes. "Obeah men" are thought to commandeer the spirits of the dead, turning them into "duppies" who perform malevolent acts. As a result, funeral rites take on great significance, as they are geared toward appeasing spirits of the dead.

Jamaicans also participate in a number of syncretic African-Caribbean movements such as Zion Revivalism and Rastafarianism. The latter venerates the late

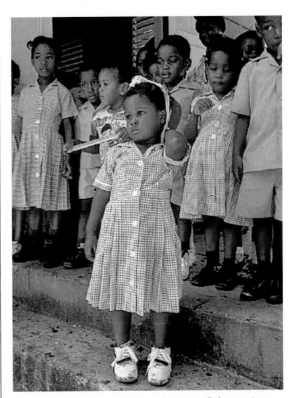

Crisp uniforms and an emphasis on decorum still characterize Jamaican schools, although a culturally relevant curriculum has replaced the colonial-era British model.

Ethiopian ruler Haile Selassie, incorporates ritual marijuana use, and worships Jah, a god within each individual. Rastafarians often wear the red, green, and gold of the Ethiopian flag; the men frequently grow dreadlocks. Reggae musician Bob Marley embraced Rastafarianism, bringing it global recognition.

Jamaican celebrations include Festival, a multiweek event that leads up to Independence Day on August 6 and features performances and competitions. Jonkanoo (John Canoe) occurs at Christmas time, when people don elaborate costumes and masks to parade and dance in the streets. Most ceremonial occasions include rice in some form, often served with goat curry. Jamaicans also eat tropical fruits and tubers—bananas, plantains, breadfruit, sweet potatoes, yams, and cassava—along with salted fish and jerk chicken or jerk pork, highly spiced and roasted over a wood fire.

About a quarter of Jamaicans are engaged in agriculture, growing coffee, sugarcane, tropical fruits, cacao, spices, and other products. Some labor in the country's valuable bauxite mines, extracting the mineral that goes into aluminum manufacture. Thousands of women called "higglers" traditionally buy produce and inexpensive imported goods for resale at local markets. Although some fear an increase of crime may jeopardize business, tourism has for years brought foreign exchange and provided many jobs for Jamaicans.

KOGI

Population: 11,000
Location: Colombia
Language family: Aruak

Colombia's Kogi people live in an environment of striking contrasts: Within a distance of only 22 miles, the land rises from sea level to peaks more than 18,000 feet high in the Sierra Nevada de Santa Marta. Here, land suitable for cultivation occurs in small pockets up to 11,500 feet, so the Kogi live vertically, traveling up and down among the hot, temperate, and colder zones of their environment. They cultivate bananas and manioc in the tropical lowlands, bananas

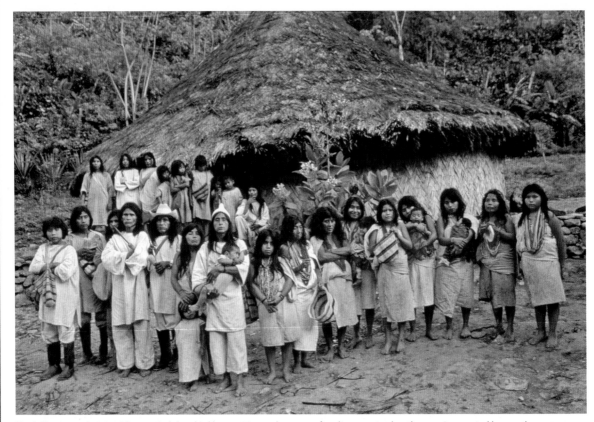

Kogi villagers gather outside a conical thatched house. Men and women often live separately—the men in a central house, the women and children in their own separate family dwellings.

and beans up to 8,200 feet, potatoes and onions in the temperate zone. No one zone can meet all their dietary needs. In earlier times, they staved off malnutrition by also eating fish from the Caribbean, but this resource became scarcer as the European population rose.

Ironically, the Kogi would fare much better if they could cultivate maize in the fertile, terraced fields left by their prehistoric predecessors, the Tairona. But their ritual leaders, or *mámas,* forbid it because they believe evil spirits occupy these lands. The Kogi's belief system thus limits their agricultural productivity and diet— despite their reputation as people who make full use of their environment, an image they cherish in their dealings with the outside world. This image is in jeopardy, for their homeland's plains and slopes are eroded and degraded after centuries of slash-and-burn agriculture, and the people now fear that their environment will not feed them adequately.

To sustain themselves during hard work and arduous climbing, Kogi men rely heavily on coca leaves, chewed with lime to release narcotic alkaloids. They eat only small amounts of food. Women and children, on the other hand, seem to be well fed and do not munch coca. Their diet is always uncertain, though, because insufficient rains and the degraded soils often lead to poor harvests. In good years, people move frequently from one zone to another, with a preference for

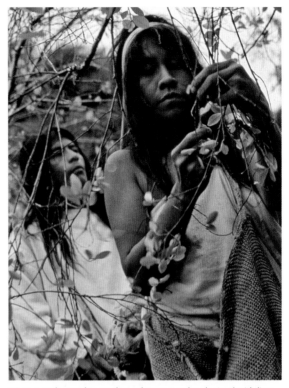

Women pick coca leaves that, when toasted and mixed with lime, provide a stimulant for Kogi men, who trudge up and down mountain slopes regularly.

When the character of a man
is not clear to you,
look at his friends.
HAITIAN PROVERB

lower, more productive elevations. At these times, the Kogi trade with mestizos and others on the coast. During hungry periods, the people move up the mountains and shift little from one elevation to another.

The largest settlements lie at different elevations, most of them between about 3,000 and 6,000 feet above sea level, but they are occupied only a few days a week when families come in from the fields. Village dwellings are circular, with thatched, conical roofs, and are scattered around a central building where the men usually reside. Women and children reside in family

dwellings. Every family also has three or four field houses at different elevations, and these are used seasonally. Typically, two dwellings face each other across an open area, the husband and adolescent boys living in one, the wife and younger children in the other. In hard times, the Kogi tend to settle close to ritual centers, near the leaders who can provide them with spiritual guidance.

Kogi society is divided into two main groups, with one comprising all the men and the other all the women, a pattern reflected in their housing arrangements. There are smaller kin groups, too, resulting in marriage arrangements that are so complex only mámas can decipher them. After marriage, a son-in-law works for his in-laws until he is deemed capable of starting fields on his own.

About 2,000 Kogi lived in an area of about 386 square miles in the 1940s, when their society was closely studied. Now that European settlement has blocked their access to the coast, many are becoming peasant farmers or laborers as their traditional lifestyle becomes less productive.

Mesoamerica

Also called Central America, this region forms the narrow connection between North and South America. Mesoamerica coasts the Gulf of Mexico and the Caribbean Sea to the east and the Pacific Ocean to the west. Countries in this region include Mexico, Guatemala, Belize, El Salvador, Honduras, Nicaragua, Costa Rica, and Panama. Temperatures in this region are fairly consistent throughout the year: For example, the average temperature in Managua, Nicaragua, is 79°F in January and 89°F in July. Annual rainfall throughout much of the region is significant, especially in some of the low-lying areas, which receive more than 80 inches a year. In height Mesoamerica reaches from long stretches of swampland along the Mosquito Coast of Nicaragua and Honduras to the Guatemalan highlands, peaking at 13,845 feet above sea level in its highest mountain, Tajumulco, an inactive volcano.

To listen to music from Belize and Mexico, visit http://worldmusic.nationalgeographic.com.

GARIFUNA

Alternate name: Black Caribs   Population: 200,000
Location: Honduras, Belize, Guatemala
Language family: Arawakan

The Garifuna people are descended from African slaves and the Carib Indians, who once gave escaped slaves refuge on St. Vincent Island in the Lesser Antilles. This group is now spread throughout parts of Mesoamerica (primarily Belize, Honduras, Guatemala, and Nicaragua), and a significant population resides in the United States.

The genesis of the Black Carib population can be traced to French and English policy in the 17th and 18th centuries. Initially, the island of St. Vincent was set aside as a refuge for Carib Indians, who later sold land to French settlers in exchange for arms. The Caribs also were joined by Maroons, African slaves who had escaped from neighboring islands or been shipwrecked, and these two groups intermarried.

In 1763, the Treaty of Paris transferred control of St. Vincent from the French to the English, without recognizing Carib land rights, and more settlers moved in. The island switched hands again, and then again. As the English sought more land for sugar plantations, local resistance grew until both sides were engaged in war. The Black Caribs won the war in the sense that their lands were preserved by the terms of a 1773 treaty with the English.

Highland Maya prepare land for the planting of corn, using a traditional slash-and-burn method. These people tend to live isolated lives and are marginalized by non-Indian Mexicans.

But that treaty also acknowledged the King of England as the people's ruler and was later used to justify their deportation. In 1795, another outbreak of hostilities led to the demise of Black Carib sovereignty and to the group's removal to Roatán Island off the Honduran coast. From there, they settled in mainland areas of Central America, where they came to be known as the Garifuna.

Today, the Garifuna thrive mainly in small towns and villages, but many have migrated to large U.S. cities. Their language is a derivation of several Indian, African, and European languages, including Arawak, Yoruba, Swahili, Bantu, Spanish, English, and French. It is distinct from others in Central America in that many words are gender specific, with men and women using different words for the same things.

Over the years, the Garifuna have developed a unique musical style that owes much to the group's various roots. The music builds from a foundation of two or three *garaon* drums: The *primera* (first) or heart drum improvises against the counter-rhythmic *segunda* (second) or shadow drum; a steady bass drum called the *tercera* (third) holds the ensemble together. Sometimes several guitar strings or wires (snares) are stretched across a drumhead to create the buzzing sound traditional in some West African music. Turtle-shells, claves (hardwood sticks), bottles, and a variety of shakers and scrapers are also used for percussion.

HIGHLAND MAYA

Population: 5 million
Location: Mexico, Guatemala
Language family: Cholan-Tzeltalan; Quichean-Mamean; Kanjobalan-Chujean

The Tzotzil, Quiché, and Cakchiquel, along with 15 or so other highland Maya groups, occupy their ancestral lands in southeastern Mexico and adjacent Guatemala. Each of these groups may be defined by its own distinctive version of the greater Mayan language family, made up of some 30 related tongues used in both the highlands and the lowlands. From the lofty, volcano-studded mountain ranges along the Pacific coast to the shores of the Yucatán Peninsula, five million Maya speak at least one of these languages.

The highland Maya known as the Tzotzil (literally, "people of the bat") live with their neighbors in Chamula, Zinacantan, Tenejapa, Oxchuc, and other towns lying in a region centered by the colonial city of San Cristóbal de Las Casas—the commercial focus of Ladino, or non-Indian, culture in Mexico's Chiapas state. Primarily maize farmers, these Maya maintain a relatively isolated existence that warily mixes the demands of national bureaucracy with an adherence to traditional customs and beliefs dating back 2,000 years or more. Their cosmology is dominated by sacred geography, with features such as mountains and water bodies receiving special devotion, and their rituals may be a blend of Maya and Christian religious practices.

Highland Maya women of Chiapas and Guatemala are particularly noted for their traditional weavings, skillfully made with back-strap looms; distinct from town to town, weaving patterns often incorporate ancient Maya concepts of time and the cosmos. A written account of creation and the gods and heroes of sacred myth is incorporated in the famed *Popol Vuh,* or *Book of Council.* Produced by ancestors of today's Quiché people, near the Guatemalan town of Chichicastenango, it is perhaps the most notable surviving work of ancient American literature.

Generations of highland Maya have been scorned by the local Ladinos as barriers to development and commerce, and they have suffered unusual degrees of oppression and negligence by their national governments. In recent decades, military repression of the Guatemalan Maya, punctuated by torture and executions, fostered mass movements of refugees to camps in Mexico. But many people have since returned under a truce—a situation resulting in part from the leadership of Rigoberta Menchú, a Quiché woman who in 1992 received the Nobel Peace Prize.

In Mexico, the Zapatista revolutionary movement, which began in San Cristóbal de Las Casas, has spread

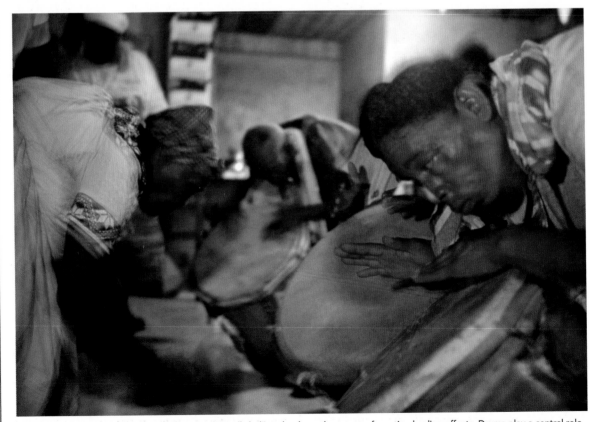

Garifuna women play at a ceremonial dance traditionally believed to have the power of creating healing effects. Drums play a central role in Garifuna music-making and rituals.

During the Classic period, from A.D. 250 to 900, Maya architects designed great stone palaces, temples, and public buildings. They were part of a cosmopolitan society also known for painting, sculpture, astronomy, and a complex writing system. Many traditions of lowland Maya life have survived, from house types to ancestral beliefs in the significance of the cardinal directions and in supernatural figures connected to landscapes and rain. The lowland groups associate numbers with gender: four for male, representing the corners of the milpa, or corn field; three for female, the number of stones in the traditional hearth. Towns usually feature a mix of dwellings, including rounded rectangular houses with walls of stone or bound poles sealed with mud and topped with palm thatch. In addition, they may have *mamposteria,* flat-roofed cement structures topped with tanks for conserving rainwater.

In 1847, the northern Maya began a general uprising against mestizos and whites. Known as the Caste War of Yucatán, this sporadic conflict was later spurred by a local religious movement. Hostilities finally ended in 1902, when the Mexican army occupied Chan-Santa Cruz, the Maya capital of the rebellion.

Modern times have seen important changes in the lives of the northern Maya. In the mid-20th century, for example, collapse of the international demand for Yucatán's sisal fiber eliminated an important source of local employment and income. This, in turn, prompted even more movement of rural people to the urban centers of Mérida, Campeche, and the coastal resorts, dominated by Cancún, where age-old cultural traditions are fast disappearing.

A shaman from southeastern Mexico represents local religion; today, traditional Highland Maya beliefs blend with Christianity.

to many of the Maya towns. It demands immediate action by the local and national governments to alleviate poverty and end the long-standing indifference toward the Maya, whose traditional culture has endured to a remarkable degree.

LOWLAND MAYA

Population: 1 million
Location: Mexico, Guatemala
Language family: Yucatecan; Cholan-Tzeltalan

The lands occupied by the Yucatec, Lacandon, and other speakers of lowland Maya languages reach from Mexico's state of Tabasco east to the Caribbean Sea, and from the highlands and piedmont of Guatemala to the northern shores of the Yucatán Peninsula. Except for the Yucatán's Puuc, or hill area, and Belize's Maya Mountains, the northern Maya lowlands consist of a vast slab of limestone, which is still emerging from the sea.

Lowland Maya mainly speak Yucatec or closely related languages such as Lacandon or Itzá, often mixed to varying degrees with Spanish. For subsistence, the people depend largely on the raising of maize, beans, squash, and chili peppers in milpas, fields selectively cleared, burned, and planted when the rainy season begins each year in early June.

HUICHOL

Population: 20,000
Location: Mexico
Language family: Uto-Aztecan

The traditional home of the Huichol lies in the Sierra Madre Occidental, a rugged landscape where the Mexican states of Nayarit, Jalisco, Zacatecas, and Durango come together. Partly because of their relative isolation from the colonial Spanish capital and other main European settlements of the central plateau, the Huichol and their immediate neighbors—among them the Tepehuans and Cora—have succeeded more than most in resisting changes that came in the wake of the Spanish conquest.

In fundamental ways, the modern Huichol culture differs very little from its pre-Hispanic form; this is particularly true in terms of worldview and religion, despite the introduction of Catholicism by the Europeans. The leaders of family lineages customarily lead rites held in family shrines, while native priests, officiating from sacred seats, customarily oversee community rituals on special occasions. These rites and rituals involve the nearly one hundred supernaturals in the complex Huichol pantheon, among them the messenger god who takes the form of a winged deer and acts as an intermediary between people in the physical world and beings in the supernatural realm.

The Huichol may be best known for religious objects: Some items include featherwork, beads, and woven string; others are made from painted stone disks and gourds. "Prayer arrows," dangling feathers affixed to shafts, help shamans send messages to the gods. *Ojos de Dios,* or "eyes of God," are made of colored yarn stretched between cruciform sticks, and these items are used to keep away the souls of the dead and ward off malevolent spirits. Perhaps the most remarkable form of Huichol art are the *tablas,* "paintings" made by pressing colored yarn into beeswax coating on boards. Tablas range from geometrical to pictorial and depict supernatural animals and other beings.

The creativity exhibited in religious art extends to Huichol handicraft and clothing, including men's trousers, shirts, and capes, as well as shoulder bags, earrings, and other adornments. Each item displays an intricate geometry of subtle forms and colors.

MIXTEC

Population: 300,000
Location: Mexico
Language family: Mixtecan

In the Nahuatl language of the Aztec, Mixtec means "cloud people," an apt description, for most of the Mixtec live in the mountains of Mexico's western state of Oaxaca; others occupy lower areas such as the hot, humid coastal region to the south. To the east, centered in the valley of Oaxaca, live the Zapotec, the other great people of the region. The intertwined histories of the Zapotec and Mixtec peoples reach deep into the

Women prepare and cook tortillas at a Oaxacan market. Throughout Mexico, the rising price of corn—the country's staple—has led to economic hardship.

past, particularly at the famed archaeological site of Monte Albán, the ancient mountaintop capital and ceremonial center.

Archaeological evidence indicates that the Zapotec flourished at Monte Albán from about A.D. 250 to 750, when the neighboring Mixtec invaded the valley and took over the city. In the centuries before the Spanish conquest, the Mixtec achieved greatness through art and craftsmanship—mainly gold jewelry, turquoise-inlay work, and deerskin codices (books). These books held pictographic histories and royal genealogies, particularly relative to the life and exploits of the king and culture hero Eight Deer Jaguar Claw.

Modern Mixtec still occupy the lands where their ancestors once dwelled—highland and coastal regions in western Oaxaca and adjacent areas of Guerrero and Puebla. Their lives, like those of other traditional Mesoamerican peoples, revolve around the cultivation of maize, chilies, beans, and squash, as well as the raising of livestock.

The Mixtec and Zapotec vary somewhat in terms of their language, culture, and crafts. Stylistic differences are evident primarily in their pottery, basketry, and woven or embroidered *huipils,* the traditional blouses or tunics worn by women in the region.

NAHUA

Population: 1.5 million
Location: Mexico
Language family: Uto-Aztecan

The Nahua of Mexico's central highlands are defined mainly by languages that are closely related dialects descended from Nahuatl, which was spoken by the Mexica, or Aztec, when Spanish conquistador Hernán Cortés entered their imperial capital, Tenochtitlán (now Mexico City), in 1519. Nahuatl speakers may also converse in Spanish, but use of this language varies greatly according to location in rural and urban areas. Today's 1.5 million Nahua live in and around Mexico City and throughout most of the central plateau, an area more or less equal to the main part of the Aztec Empire under Moctezuma II.

The various groups of Nahua share the fundamental Mesoamerican subsistence pattern of cultivating maize, beans, chili peppers, tomatoes, and squash in the rich volcanic soils of their heartland, but to do this, they rely on the European-style plow drawn by draft animals. In steep mountain areas where the soil can be poor, farmers burn the fields before planting. They also rotate maize and bean crops to help increase fertility. Other major crops include maguey (which is the source of the fermented drink known as pulque), sugarcane, rice, and coffee.

A grain at a time,
the hen fills her craw.
MEXICAN PROVERB

A church and a plaza sit at the center of a typical Nahua town, The plaza often serves as a site for the local market. The church also functions as the center point for dividing the settlement into four parts, or barrios, each of which bears a Nahuatl name—a settlement pattern that dates to before the Spanish conquest. A good example of this ancient pattern can be seen in the town plan of Milpa Alta, just south of Mexico City.

Perhaps the best known of all Nahua population centers, the Milpa Alta area is famed for its geometrical weavings of *quexquemitls* (triangular capes) and other garments made on Aztec back-strap looms. Additional household industries and crafts include adobe bricks; maguey-fiber ropes; and numerous items fashioned for the tourist trade. Among the most popular Nahua objects are pottery, copies of ancient figurines, and the remarkable lacquered boxes, chests, and gourds from the town of Olinalá, in Guerrero.

OTOMÍ

Population: 228,000
Location: Mexico
Language family: Otomian

A group known as the Otomí occupy an area of central Mexico lying just to the northwest of Nahua lands. Like most of their close neighbors, the Otomí are highland people who seldom dwell in an area having an elevation of less than 3,000 feet above mean sea level. The language they speak is distinct from Nahuatl and other Uto-Aztecan tongues used in adjacent areas, and is more closely related to those of the Mixtec and Zapotec peoples living to the south.

Peopling the Americas

Once the first villages became established in the Arctic North-west of North America, their inhabitants quickly adapted to life in a foreign land, spreading to all corners of the Americas in a few thousand years. How they did so along the corridor from present-day Alaska to the southern tip of Tierra del Fuego— a passageway spanning 12,000 miles and covering a vast longitudinal and ecological spectrum—remains one of the great mysteries of human migration.

East-west corridors like the Eurasian Steppe, a homoge-neous grassland connecting the vast plains of Central Asia and Eastern Europe, are thought to have given people a jump start in the rapid development of advanced technologies. Climate tends to remain the same along longitude, making it easier to find new resources. Cotton and silk produced in the east can be traded for iron and bronze smelt in the west, both areas able to develop more quickly than pop-ulations living in isolation.

Introducing maize
But such geography is not compulsory fare for advancing societies. While major ancient civilizations developing in the Indus Valley, the Tigris-Euphrates basin and along the Yellow River in China all benefited from this geographic advan-tage, surprisingly the fifth and arguably largest grew directly along the Ameri-can corridor.

And it all could have started with a gust of wind. Nine thousand years ago there existed in and around Mexico a number of species of large grasses, teosinte, five of which survive today. These plants' numerous branches produce small bunches of flowers, which then mature to form tiny clusters of seeds encased by a hard shell. Each species exhibits a unique combination of genetic and physical characteristics which could be mixed into a cocktail of functional types ideal for plant domestication. While the exact evolutionary process that

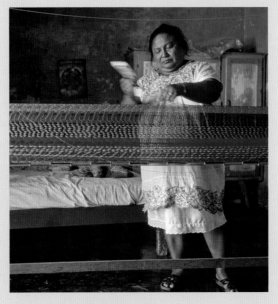

A Lowland Maya woman weaves a hammock in Yucatán, Mexico.

produced maize is still debated—in fact the role of teosinte itself is in dispute— genetic studies show that some degree of hybridization between wild species, mixing perhaps in the winds of the Mesoamerican highlands, produced off-spring more attractive to humans.

By 6,000 years ago, groups of migrants along the north-south passage had taken the biggest and best of these maize hybrids and begun growing them in lowland Mesoamerica, choosing new ear and kernel forms and plants showing the best yield potential. The diversity of these crossbreeds made them adaptable to new environments and enabled humans to bring seeds from southern Mexico to surrounding areas for the first time. With maize as a staple, pre-Columbian societies flourished.

Settlers quickly established small communities, and over the next several thousand years independent, complex societies began popping up throughout the region. But the agricultural intensity was initially minimal, and a flyover of south-ern Mexico 4,000 years ago would have shown a landscape largely unchanged by humans.

Pyramids rise up
In 1200 B.C. the isolated cities between Jalisco and Oa-xaca coalesced into the first Mesoamerican civilization, the Olmec, whose pyramids and walled cities soon dominated the landscape. The culture flour-ished for 800 years, producing jade and clay figurines and the earliest form of writing in the Americas, until it suddenly broke apart, the ruling class unable to maintain its grip on the empire.

People added squash, beans, and peppers to their diet. Soon larger, more powerful civilizations replaced the frag-mented Olmec. The Maya, and later the Aztec to the north, burst onto the scene with sophisticated mathematical systems and written languages, which enabled the construction of monumental architec-ture, dwarfing the pyramids that already dotted the Mesoamerican landscape. The cultures expanded and at their zenith could boast the largest urban populations anywhere on Earth. Despite Spanish col-onization, the Aztec and Maya never fully disappeared. Many of today's Meso-american populations directly descend from these earliest settlers.

The ways of Otomí farmers vary among populations. The more acculturated groups grow wheat, barley, and coffee, while more traditional farmers mix crops of maize, beans, and squash in the same field, often using the ancient Mesoamerican digging stick—or a modern version tipped with iron—for planting. Otomí settlements range from compact towns to dispersed settlements. House types include plank constructions thatched with grass or maguey leaves and adobe houses with flat or slanted roofs.

Well known for creating a variety of items sold to both locals and tourists, Otomí craftspeople produce pottery, stone metates (maize grinders), baskets, and woven clothing and bags. Some Otomí, particularly women in the town of San Pablito, in the state of Puebla, are noted for their manufacture of *amate,* paper made from the bark of the fig tree *(amatl);* the tradition dates back more than a thousand years. In pre-Hispanic times, amate was used in rituals or sometimes as the pages of screenfold books called codices, which were filled with hieroglyphic texts and illustrations to record important events and divination practices. Some modern Otomí cut supernatural figures from this special paper and include them in rituals connected with water and agricultural fertility. Dark paper cutouts of Otomí deities, mounted on lighter background sheets, have become a popular form of folk art in central Mexico.

TARASCANS

Alternate name: Purépecha
Population: 120,000   Location: Mexico
Language family: Tarascan

A highland region in western Mexico is home to the Tarascan people, most of whom live in the state of Michoacán. Often called a "land of fire and water" because of its volcanoes and lakes, Michoacán is the location of the Paricutín volcano. From deep crevices in a farmer's field, Paricutín quickly grew a 400-foot-high cone and destroyed two villages with its lava flows in 1943.

The Tarascan language, relatively homogeneous over the people's territory, is apparently unrelated to other linguistic groups in Mesoamerica. But it may

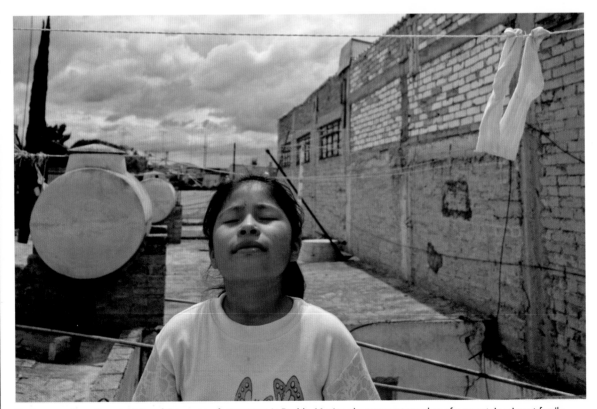

Having come from the mountains of Oaxaca to a factory town in Puebla, Mexico, the youngest member of a mountain migrant family seeks the sun on the roof of her apartment building.

have tenuous ties to language families in both North and South America, which suggests a very early presence on the Mesoamerican landscape. While modern Tarascans generally share in the traditional Mesoamerican ways of maize farming, pottery making, and weaving, other circumstances attending their possible origins and cultural history make them unique.

The story of Tarascan culture in pre-Hispanic times derives mainly from the archaeology of Tzintzuntzan, the ancient regional capital on the shores of Lake Pátzcuaro and from various chronicles set down during the time of the Spanish conquest. After studying illustrations of the unusual clothing used in the Tarascan area around that time, art historian Patricia Anawalt suggests that the people originated in the south, near present-day Ecuador, and migrated north along a well-known ancient trade route along the Pacific coast.

Today, each Tarascan village specializes in one or two kinds of handicraft, a practice that may have begun in the mid-16th century with Vasco de Quiroga, first bishop of Michoacán. The bishop not only organized social and religious life in the villages but also strengthened the occupational specialization so common in pre-Hispanic times by introducing new products and techniques. Among the distinctive output of present-day Tarascan craftspeople, one finds featherwork "paintings," guitars, and lacquerwork gourd and wood products, including elaborate masks worn during the traditional dances that form an essential part of native Mesoamerican religion. Tarascans are also notable for their work with copper, bronze, and other alloys—a tradition that appears to date back to at least A.D. 1000, when knowledge of metallurgy first appeared in the region.

ZAPOTEC

Population: 423,000
Location: Mexico
Language family: Zapotecan

Today's Zapotec population, the largest indigenous group in Mexico's Oaxaca, occupies most of the eastern portion of that state, as well as parts of neighboring ones. The varied lands of this region range from the drier, flat landscapes of the Isthmus of Tehuantepec to the high ridges and deep canyons of the Sierra Madre del Sur; the major valleys of Oaxaca—Zaachila, Tlacolula, and Etla—lie within the Sierra Madre.

Dressed in traditional clothing, two Zapotec women from Oaxaca, Mexico, enjoy their time at an evening festival.

During the Classic period, between about A.D. 250 and 900, ancestors of the modern-day Zapotec built some of the largest and most important regional centers of ancient Mesoamerica. The greatest of these, Monte Albán, occupies an artificially flattened mountaintop overlooking today's city of Oaxaca. There, a grand series of palaces, plazas, pyramid-temples, and other structures, including a great pentagonal observatory, were constructed over the ruins left by settlers who had occupied the site as far back as 1000 B.C.

Modern Zapotec share the belief systems of many of their Mesoamerican neighbors: They practice Catholicism while continuing to acknowledge a pantheon of supernatural beings associated with sacred geography and natural phenomena. They have also maintained their ancient belief in animal guardians, companion spirits that individuals acquire at birth.

Through the years, economic activities have included the Zapotec's traditional weavings and ceramics, with different settlements' wares having distinctive shapes and colors. They are also known for music, as well as for cultivating the language arts, which has given rise to a group of locally famous speechmakers.

Amazon and Orinoco Basins

The Amazon may not be the world's longest river, but more water flows through its system than the combined total of the next ten most voluminous rivers. The world's highest waterfall, Angel Falls, plunges 3,212 feet in the Orinoco region. The mouth of the Amazon lies in north-central Brazil, and its tributaries spider throughout the country, plus Colombia, Peru, and Bolivia. The Orinoco River area encompasses the top part of South America, north of the Amazon. Starting in the Guiana Highlands, the Orinoco runs 1,700 miles—mostly through Venezuela—to the Atlantic Ocean.

To listen to music from Brazil, visit http://worldmusic.nationalgeographic.com.

AMAHUACA

Population: 500
Location: Peru, Brazil
Language family: Panoan

Hunters of peccaries and rodents and farmers of maize and manioc, the Amahuaca are a remote group who live in tiny settlements of thatched dwellings in the border region of southeastern Peru and western Brazil. Their rugged homeland in the tropical forest is difficult to access, so even today they have only occasional contact with the outside world. The Amahuaca would prefer to continue their traditional ways, but international logging interests and prospectors threaten their homeland and their very simple material culture. Before steel axes and adzes arrived in the late 19th century, the people relied on stone axes, digging sticks, and tortoiseshell hatchets.

As in other forest groups, the boundaries between the physical and spiritual worlds are blurred, with shamans acting as intermediaries between them. To induce trances during group sessions, the Amahuaca use hallucinogens, especially ayahuasca—a narcotic beverage made from the yagé vine—which produces vertigo and visions. The people believe that the partker's soul leaves the body to question spirits who appear.

This group is also remarkable for having practiced endocannibalism—consuming the flesh of their own kind. In 1960, anthropologist Gertrude Dole witnessed the death of an Amahuaca infant during the night. The body was buried under the house, then disinterred, and burned in a pot. The baby's mother carefully removed the bones from the ashes and, after several days of grieving, ground maize and made gruel, which she mixed with bone powder and drank. Her period of mourning was intended to appease the deceased's spirit, just in case it had lingered. Once the mother had consumed all the bones, she reportedly became voluble and happy.

BORORO

Population: Fewer than 1,000
Location: Brazil
Language family: Bororo

In the mid-20th century, French anthropologist Claude Lévi-Strauss studied the Bororo of the southern Brazilian Highlands and found them to be a group

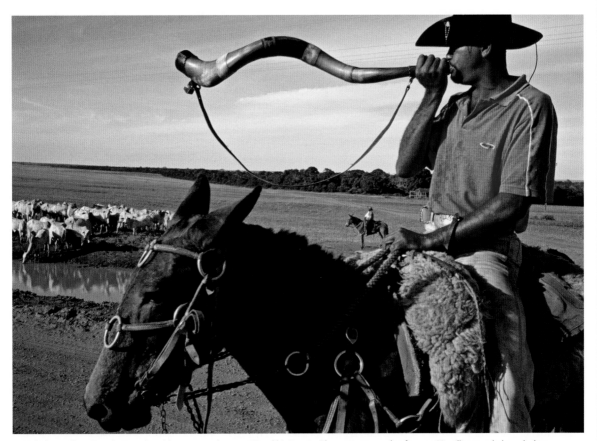

Astride his mule, a Brazilian cowboy blows a cow horn to signal his intent. The pasture needs of some 60 million cattle have led to deforestation in Brazil.

with a highly complex social life. During the more productive times of year, the people came together into a large settlement, but during the drier months they dispersed in small groups, searching for food.

In his work, Lévi-Strauss focused on 140 Bororo living in the riverside village of Kejara. A line running parallel to the river divided the village into halves known as Tugaré and Cera; another line divided the community into upstream and downstream halves, with further subdivisions into clans and groups of rich and poor, each with its own religious symbols. The Tugaré half honored mythical heroes responsible for water, rivers, vegetation, fish, and human artifacts. The Cera heroes dated from the time of the creation, when they brought order to the living world. According to the natural hierarchy of things, at least in Bororo terms, the Tugaré were closer to the physical universe and therefore "strong," whereas the Cera were closer to the human world and "weak."

To Lévi-Strauss, the Bororo seemed to delight in making the affairs of a small-scale society extremely complex. Today, both halves of society are still intricately engaged: They bury each other's dead, exchange women in marriage, and live, as it were, one for the other. Paraphrasing Lévi-Strauss, one could say that Bororo life is an escutcheon with symmetry and asymmetry in equilibrium. The people delight in social complexity, for it preserves the social order and ensures that they stay in tune with their vision of the cosmos.

BRAZILIANS

Population: 190 million
Location: Brazil
Language family: Italic

The lone Portuguese-speaking country of South America, Brazil has for the better part of 500 years represented a vast frontier of opportunities and potential. Soon after the Portuguese claimed Brazil in 1500, they began exploiting its resources by exporting hardwood. Within a few years the plantation economy was established with sugarcane, using indigenous peoples as labor until the first African slaves were imported. One by one Brazil's natural resources were tapped: gold, gems, rubber; growing terrain ideal for coffee, rice, and cocoa; and vast, grassy expanses suitable for raising cattle. The Portuguese continued to arrive, along with waves of other Europeans, Middle Easterners, and Asians.

The European settlers encountered indigenous peoples representing at least four different language families. Those living near the coast have had the most influence on Brazilian culture. Words from the Tupi-

> I shall sing the sun up, once the stars have been washed from the sky.
> SURINAMESE PROVERB

Guarani languages for flora, fauna, and place-names contribute to Brazilian Portuguese, which is spoken by nearly the entire population, although the literacy rate lags behind at some 86 percent. Today, more than 250 individual Indian groups live mainly on reserves established by the government.

Racial mixing occurred early in Brazil's colonial history. Single Portuguese men looked for women among the Indians and slaves—the more than two million Africans contributed to a Brazilian population now of at least 45 percent African descent, the largest outside Africa. Recent DNA studies demonstrate even more of a mixture in the general population than expected.

While most Brazilians are nominally Roman Catholic, the church vies for influence with African traditions, particularly Candomblé, Macumba, and Umbanda. Other diverse faiths contribute to the religious landscape, including the growing popularity of Pentacostalism and Charismatic Catholicism, both of which appeal to the Brazilians' emotive nature.

While many Brazilians point with pride to their "racial democracy," the situation on the ground shows the struggles of people of color and the widening gap between rich and poor, a situation out of sync with the high ranking overall of the Brazilian economy. Although each locality has its own economic divide, the country as a whole is differentiated between the economically disadvantaged north and the more prosperous south, with similar distinctions separating the interior from the coast. Former slaves, emancipated in 1888, became the foundation of the favelas, or shantytowns, that sprang up at the edge of Rio and other cities. Municipal governments have not succeeded in eliminating these makeshift communities and in some cases have provided them with amenities such as water, sewers, and electricity.

Some 80 percent of Brazilians live within 200 miles of the ocean, with about 18 million clustered in the coastal cities of São Paolo, Rio de Janeiro, and Salvador. Brazilians flock to their beautiful beaches where minimalist swimwear is the rule even if the wearer is deep into middle age or carries more than a few extra pounds. New Year's Eve, which occurs during Brazilian summer, also draws people to the beaches. At midnight they walk to the sea and toss in white flowers as offerings to the African goddess of the sea, Yemanjá, with hopeful prayers for the new year.

Brazilians come together for Carnival, the days-long pre-Lenten national holiday marked by parades, extravagant costumes, dancing, and musical competitions between samba schools—favela organizations. Social and economic distinctions become blurred and even reversed during Carnival, taking people, especially the poor, out of the routines of their daily lives. *Futebol* (soccer) also unites the Brazilians; World Cup play typically overtakes the entire country.

Parentela—the extended group of all maternal and paternal relatives, including in-laws—represents the core of many Brazilians' social world. Brazilians prefer to live near their kin and to socialize with them on a regular basis. Young adults tend to stay at home until they marry and not to stray too far from the family base when they do. Combined with *compadrio*, or godparenthood, the parentela provides nearly all the social support an individual needs.

CARIBS

Population: 10,000
Location: Venezuela
Language family: Cariban

Expert canoe navigators and warriors, the Carib Indians of the Caribbean's Lesser Antilles drove out the indigenous Arawak about a century before Columbus and settled on the northern and northwestern

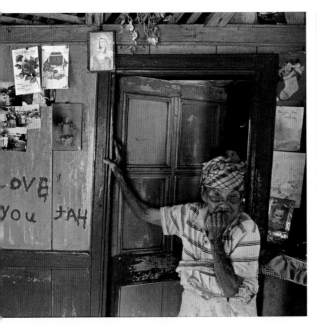

A Carib woman of the Lesser Antilles lives on a reserve there. Some of her ancestors settled on the northern shores of South America, after driving out the indigenous Arawak.

shores of South America. They were originally known as Galibi, a word corrupted by the Spaniards to "cannibal"; hence, they were thought to be eaters of human flesh. If the Caribs were cannibals, their consumption of enemies may have had purely ritual significance. Decimated by Europeans fighting for control of the Caribbean, these people survive only in small enclaves today, notably in Venezuela and Guyana.

For all their reputed ferocity, Caribs were, and still are, expert fisherfolk. They built dugout canoes, equipped them with sails, and ventured far offshore. Blowguns as well as bows and arrows provided them with forest game, and they farmed maize, cassava, yams, and squash. Today, coastal Caribs live in spacious thatched houses close to river banks. The largest Carib settlement, Galibi, is a fishing town in Suriname; a cooperative there sells fish locally to help the community remain self-supporting.

The Barama Caribs of Guyana live in small farming communities of thatched, timber houses near the Barama River and along forest trails. They are hunters, fisherfolk, and subsistence farmers whose lands are now threatened by mineral prospectors and international logging companies. For centuries, they have relied on simple, traditional methods for catching fish, but they have not hesitated to use European

fishhooks and nets when they could obtain them through trade. Much of the time, though, they resort to their ancient strategies: Men stand on large rocks and try to spear fish or shoot them with bows and arrows. Barama Caribs also set fishing lines, using hooks made from thorn trees or even bent domestic pins, but their most effective method involves a poison made from haiari roots. Although the Guyana government forbids the poisoning of the country's streams, this method is still commonplace. Almost every creek has a wickerwork fence lying across its mouth, placed there to catch the dead or stupefied fish that float downstream. Waiting women and children kill the sluggish fish as they float to the surface.

The Caribs are now Catholics. Until recently, however, shamans played an important role in Carib rituals after serving long apprenticeships. They used tight ropes to master the movements of their souls: Hands bound, they swung through the air and induced vertigo as a way of transporting themselves to the supernatural realm.

DESANA

Population: 1,800
Location: Brazil, Colombia
Language family: Tucanoan

The rain forest of Colombia's southeastern lowlands is home to the Desana, hunters and fisherfolk who also obtain much of their diet from manioc. Each household has to fend for itself and get food from a carefully delineated area surrounded by the territories of other groups. Because fish and game animals are such important foods, people try not to take too many fish from the rivers or to overhunt their prey. They also try to manage the size of their families by limiting the frequency of sexual relations.

The Desana live in local kin groups. Their dwellings are long, rectangular houses composed of wood and thatch and occupied by four to eight related families. Each family practices strict birth control, relying on oral contraceptives made from herbs and on sexual abstinence, especially before and during a hunt. For the Desana, the consequences of sex can present grave threats to their survival: People and animals share homelands with finite resources, they say, and thus both are limited in their reproductive potential. If the human population were to increase too much, then the animals and supernatural Master of Animals would grow envious of the humans' misuse of the limited sexual energy available to all. In this culture, men who sire more children than the norm are regarded with scorn, and their families are considered little more than those of dogs. The strong social controls, reinforced by the Desana's rebuke of those who ignore them, are a way to keep people in equilibrium with their food supplies.

KUIKURU

Population: 500
Location: Brazil
Language family: Cariban

The Kuikuru survive in a single group near the Kuluene River, a tributary of the Xingu in central Brazil's rain forest. They are famous for slash-and-burn, shifting agriculture, practiced amid a large forest tract near their one village. Before 1900 and the coming of iron tools, Kuikuru farmers cleared their gardens with stone axes and the sharp-toothed jaws of piranhas. Their material culture was marked by skill in making feather ornaments and baskets. Like other Brazilian groups, they clustered their thatched houses in a circle, with the men's house a major center of ceremonial activity.

Now, as then, Kuikuru farmers begin clearing land at the end of the rainy season. They let felled trees and other vegetation dry for a while; then, just before the rains come, they fire the debris in piles atop the fields. As rain falls, wood ash washes into the soil and fertilizes it. The Kuikuru plant at least 11 varieties of manioc, a tropical root crop that is poisonous unless pounded and boiled before being eaten. Although they harvest about four or five tons of manioc per acre, they lose more than half the crop to peccaries and ants.

Most other slash-and-burn farmers must move their villages regularly, but the Kuikuru have so much land within a comfortable four-mile walking radius that they never have to leave their long-established traditional settlement. Under ideal conditions, each man spends only about three and a half hours a day working to feed his family; about two hours go to farming and an hour or so to fishing. Kuikuru men spend the rest of the day dancing, wrestling, and gossiping. Today, with modern agricultural methods and fertilizers slowly coming into use, many people are choosing to leave the traditional village and settle on small family holdings nearby. Nevertheless, the Kuikuru have shown that the simplest methods of manioc cultivation can provide enough food for people to remain in the same village permanently.

Over time, social tensions and factions develop in the community, but the Kuikuru find strength in traditional religious beliefs. They seek the help of their shamans, who play important roles in a society where secular and spiritual worlds are deeply intertwined. The shamans defuse quarrels that could lead to violence. They also investigate accusations of sorcery, attempting to identify the perpetrator of evil spells so they can neutralize the magic. The Kuikuru believe in a creation god—Kanassa—and he is said to have trapped a king vulture, the master of fire, and thereby brought fire and life to the people.

MUNDURUCÚ

Population: 7,000
Location: Brazil
Language family: Munduruku

In 1770 a Mundurucú war party traveled more than 400 miles from the group's homeland on Brazil's upper Tapajós River to attack Portuguese settlements along the Amazon. Afterward, the Portuguese promptly engaged their services as mercenaries to help them fight other hostile Indians. At home, the Mundurucú lived on gently rolling grasslands away from the river. But by 1920 many of them had moved closer to the riverside forest, where they tapped rubber trees during the slack months of the agricultural year to satisfy a burgeoning demand from the distant industrial world.

Today, the Mundurucú number only about 7,000, their earlier population reduced by disease, maltreatment, and the abuses of gold and rubber hunters. They are mainly subsistence farmers and rubber traders. Between September and late May, the people cultivate manioc and other crops, but both hunting and fishing are important throughout the year in a climate where dried fish lasts just two weeks.

Traditionally, Mundurucú warriors lived in the village men's house and were responsible for guarding their community. Their society was a violent one that made raids on enemies during the dry summer months, primarily for the purpose of obtaining trophy heads. Although hostile in their behavior toward

A Maku woman of northwestern Brazil weaves plant fibers into a hammock, using hand movements repeated through the ages.

Ultimate Biodiversity

Most segments of our genome neither code for a gene nor control how active, or expressed, a gene might be. These segments are said to be selectively "neutral," meaning they are impervious to the Darwinian effects of natural selection. Though off the hook in the struggle for survival of the fittest, our non-functional DNA is at the mercy of a potentially more powerful random process that can cause drastic changes over time. Fortunately, the principles are straightforward.

In math class we are taught through a basic experiment that though the probability of flipping a coin ten times should give equal numbers of heads and tails, it is not uncommon to see the numbers skew to one side, say with eight heads and two tails. Though not conducive to a 50-minute class period, if a student were to take the time to flip a coin one million times—putting probability theory to the test and likely flunking out of school in the process—the tally would almost always come to around 500,000 for each side. There may certainly be long runs in either direction, but even the runs themselves would tend to even out over time. This same effect that can drastically influence different frequencies of heads versus tails also plays a role in determining the frequency of various lineages in neutral segments of our DNA, a process known as genetic drift.

Chancing migration

Initial migrations into the Americas were made up of perhaps only a few hundred individuals, and of these, only a fraction left the Arctic Northwest to head south. Small populations are more susceptible

to the effects of drift, much the way coins are, and perhaps nowhere on Earth has this played a bigger role in shaping genetic diversity than in the varied Amazon and Orinoco basins of South America. The region may have been populated by one or multiple waves of early migrants from North America—a question that

A Cuna woman muses; her people inhabit the San Blas archipelago off Panama.

remains unanswered—but in either case its first inhabitants quickly spread out into small, isolated pockets, allowing genetic drift to reign supreme. Once there, the jungle kept it that way.

Amazonia is roughly defined as the equatorial region east of the Andes between the Guiana and Brazilian highlands, and, though people tend to think of Brazil, it actually stretches across parts of Guyana, Venezuela, French Guiana, Suriname, Colombia, Peru, Ecuador, and Bolivia. Despite accounting for less than 2 percent of global landmass, it is presently home to over half of Earth's rain

forests and more than a third of its species. But while the area's high biodiversity makes for fascinating research, it doesn't do a very good job supporting large groups of humans. In fact the very canopy that sustains this biodiversity robs its soil of practically all useful nutrients, relegating the ground to serve as little more than anchor for the canopy's root system.

Human species drift

While small hunter-gatherer communities exploit the jungle, agriculturalists here are handcuffed by an uncooperative terra firma, since crops do very poorly in the low-light, nutrient-poor environment. Because Amazonian soil is productive for only a short period of time before nutrients are leached from the soil, farmers must constantly work new tracts of land.

This exigency kept human populations small, giving their founders a huge say in the development of a wide range of cultural practices and unique belief systems. Their descendants adopted words to describe a new surrounding and with no written tradition to keep the linguistic changes in check, the spoken word quickly changed course branching into many different directions.

A great indication of this force of cultural drift as it acts on these populations is the fact that in a bit over 12,000 years of human occupation, more than one thousand unique languages developed in tropical South America—the region's rich biological diversity seemingly matched by the cultural and linguistic diversity of its indigenous populations.

Apparently the human genome wasn't the only thing affected by the Amazon's poor soil.

outsiders, the Mundurucú repressed aggressions closer to home; they placed a high premium on cooperation and social harmony between neighboring villages for joint hunting and fishing expeditions.

The people have a simple material culture, making much use of cotton thread, basketry, and poor-quality clay vessels. To hunt, they rely on bows, reed arrows, and wooden spears, and for generations they used war clubs in raids against their enemies. The Mundurucú are famous for their featherwork, which includes aprons, capes, armbands, and other ornaments made by attaching tropical bird feathers to netting. They are

---

You can hide your grandmother, but you can't prevent her from coughing.
SURINAMESE PROVERB

---

also known for body tattoos and for painting lines on their faces that give the appearance of wings spread across their countenances.

Every village has one or two male shamans who are believed to have had supernatural powers since birth. These men cure sick people by blowing tobacco smoke on the skin, then massaging the skin while looking for the magical darts thought to have caused the illness. Shamans are feared for their powers, for they are also believed capable of causing sickness and misfortune. In extreme cases, when they are suspected of causing evil to descend on an individual or a community, they are executed. Although raids and head-hunting have ended, the Mundurucú still form an aggressive and male-dominated society in which violence is sometimes accepted social behavior—especially against women and sorcerers.

NUKAK
Population: 700 to 1,000
Location: Colombia
Language family: Maku

Not until 1988 did the Nukak of eastern Colombia come into sustained contact with Western civilization. The results of this contact were multiple influenza epidemics and massacres at the hands of growing numbers of colonists. Between 1991 and 1997, intense pressure by Survival, an indigenous people's advocacy group, led to the establishment of a tribal reserve for the remaining Indians. Now, 700 to 1,000 Nukak occupy a territory about 110 miles long by 38 miles across. They are hunters and foragers who take monkeys, peccaries, and birds, as well as insects, plant foods, and fish from the rain forest. At the same time, they manage such wild plant species as chontaduro palms, achiote, and plantains, growing them in small garden plots established some distance from their settlements. Because of the influence of missionaries and frontier farmers, the Nukak have started farming more systematically in recent years.

After centuries of building campsites in the forest, the Nukak have modified the rain-forest environment to their considerable advantage. Every five or six days, the people move to a different area and construct a new campsite, and each time they do this, they disturb the ground and leave behind seeds from plants they collect and consume. Those seeds eventually sprout and grow.

The Nukak live in a well-defined world. Like other groups, including Fuegians in the far south, they identify three geographic and social domains of their world: the area habitually used by each band; a carefully delineated wider area around their homeland; and both areas in relation to those of other indigenous people in the region.

SARAMAKA
Population: 26,000
Location: Suriname
Language family: English-based Creole

Descendants of escaped African slaves, the Saramaka live deep in the forests of Suriname. They are one of several such groups who survived not only the era of slavery but also armed aggression and other efforts to root them out of territory ceded by England to the Netherlands in 1667. Effective raiders of European-owned slave plantations, their numbers grew as other escaped slaves sought sanctuary among them.

Saramaka society, since its very foundation, has been dependent on manufactured goods and food staples brought from Europe, a situation that was addressed by an 18th-century agreement with the Dutch. In 1762 a treaty granted unconditional

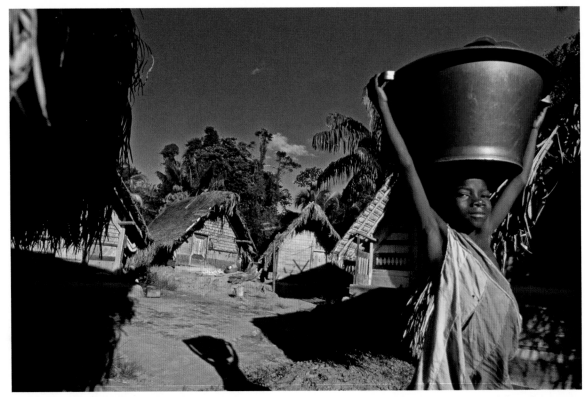

A Saramaka child totes a load in a village in central Suriname, on the northeastern shoulder of South America. Escaped slaves, known as Maroons, formed the basis of this ethnic group.

freedom to the people and required the Dutch crown to pay them tribute every year. Representatives of the crown subsequently brought boats up the winding rivers into Saramaka territory, carrying axes, pots, guns, thread, needles, cloth, and other manufactured items needed by the people. In return, the Saramaka stopped making raids on the Dutch plantations along the coast.

In 1863, after all the slaves on the coast had been emancipated, the Dutch ceased sending tribute upriver and allowed Saramaka men to venture freely into areas controlled by Europeans. Saramaka also traveled to neighboring French Guiana, where they were able to find work and earn money to buy goods that they eventually took back to their villages.

In the 19th century, nearly every able-bodied man spent about half his adulthood living and working outside of Saramaka territory, either in Suriname or French Guiana. Men worked for periods that could last as long as several years, and this form of migrant labor helped the Saramaka and their villages to remain semiautonomous. Today, the tradition continues, but

the sought-after goods now include outboard motors, gasoline, chain saws, and a wide variety of foods.

When men eventually return to their home villages, they usually give about half their wealth to their wives, children, aunts, sisters, and various other dependents. The other half is kept in storage to be used during periods of unemployment or in times of special need. If a dependent becomes ill or marries, for example, the accumulated goods pay for the associated expenses.

The Saramaka supplement their economy through swidden horticulture, with the men responsible for cutting and burning trees to clear fields and the women having the tasks of planting and harvesting. Most local food items come from the women's gardens, where they plant rice and other staple foods. Men also engage in hunting and fishing, and when a man kills an animal or makes a large catch of fish, his kill or catch is always redistributed along kinship lines within the village.

Because Saramaka society is matrilineal, each person receives his or her identity through the mother's line. Fathers play significant roles in childrearing, but legally the most important connections are on the mother's side of the family; these include her sisters, parents, and grandparents. At the same time, polygamy is widely practiced, so men may have several wives. Every man and every woman has a separate house. People have houses in their own villages, which means their mothers' villages, and often women have houses in their husbands' villages as well.

In a legal sense, matrilineal groups strongly resemble corporations. If a man commits a crime, for example, his relatives are held responsible, too. If that crime involves murder, the matrilineal descendants of the murderer are thought to be visited forever by the vengeance-seeking ghost of the victim.

Over the years, the Saramaka have developed a rich polytheistic religious tradition involving sky, earth, water, and forest gods. They also believe in the Akaa, a person's most important spirit. The Saramaka say that when an individual is born, the Akaa comes from the world of the ancestors to accompany the person throughout life; later, it travels with him or her to the land of the dead. There are two kinds of Akaas—good and bad. The "bad" one, as in much of the New World African theology, is not all bad, however. For one thing, it helps protect a person's body from other evil spirits that may try to take up residence there. It also causes the individual to have dreams—which may end in a nightmare if the spirit suddenly leaves the body. The good Akaa, on the other hand, is loyal and requires beauty and purity. But it is very timid: At the first sign of a problem, the good Akaa departs, possibly causing sickness. If a person's Akaas are out of balance, he or she is sure to become ill.

SHUAR

Alternate name: Jívaro **Population:** 50,000
Location: Ecuador
Language family: Jivaroan

The southern lowlands and lower uplands of eastern Ecuador and neighboring Peru are home to the Shuar, or Jívaro. The 20,000 Untsuri Shuar are the most numerous group, and they live across the Macuma River from their traditional enemies, the Achuar.

Killing, warfare, and other violence permeated all aspects of traditional Shuar society, which placed a high premium on acquiring individual power. From youth, every Shuar was prepared to face conflict. Everyone had potential enemies, with the more successful individuals linked to higher potentials for violence. Their objectives were simple: Kill all the members of an enemy household and decapitate them to make *tsantsas,* shrunken heads. The grim trophies not only proved that revenge had been taken but also provided the victor with powerful magic, thereby preventing the dead man's soul from wreaking vengeance in this life or the next.

Today, most Shuar killings involve feuds between members of the same group, and these usually arise from accusations of sorcery, competition over women, or quarrels over crop damage caused by pigs. First, a member of a neighbor's family is assassinated. Then a blood feud begins, resulting in another killing. Feuds can last for generations.

Until recently, these hunters and root-crop cultivators lived in small, autonomous groups that were in a constant state of political disequilibrium from all the feuding, shifting alliances, and warfare. Political power lay in the hands of talented individuals who were expert hunters, good warriors, or shamans.

Shuar aggressiveness that once led to much violent feuding now channels into political participation. This Shuar woman demonstrates in Quito, Ecuador's capital.

Qualities of physical strength and supernatural knowledge, the courage to protect and avenge family members, and the ability to endure the hardships of war were highly valued in this bellicose society. Lacking a formal political structure, the culture counted personal power and influence above everything else. Kinship ties held society together in loose, fluid alliances that gave people the moral obligation to avenge the death of a relative. Revenge has long been a driving force in Shuar society.

> ### Hide today's anger until tomorrow.
> SARAMAKA PROVERB

Contact with European colonists, missionaries, and the Ecuadoran government led the Shuar to form a federation that would help them protect their land and their rights against government-sponsored white colonists. Since 1961, the federation has set up permanent centers and associations with communal ownership of the surrounding land. It also gives these entities loans to start cattle cooperatives. The people now govern themselves with a complex mix of traditional and modern political organization.

Head-hunting has long since been outlawed by the government, and although Shuar culture still places a premium on power and revenge, killing is not as widespread as it used to be. Now, nonviolent means such as "strong speaking" are often used to resolve conflicts.

TAPIRAPÉ

Population: 350
Location: Brazil
Language family: Tupi-Guarani

Until the early 20th century, the Tapirapé of central Brazil had virtually no contact with Europeans. They were forest farmers living in isolated villages between the Araguaia and Xingu Rivers, and their fate offers an interesting example of the impact of exotic diseases on such communities.

Around 1900, there were five Tapirapé villages, each with a population of 200 to 300 people. Within a decade, one village had disbanded after enemy raids and another had been depopulated by an epidemic, possibly malaria. The first Brazilians arrived in 1910. Although the Tapirapé had only sporadic contact with outsiders in the next few decades, many of them succumbed to new diseases such as influenza, smallpox, and yellow fever. By 1932, another village had been abandoned, and seven years later the last two merged into a single settlement that still survives.

In the 1940s, Dominican friars began meeting families at a Tapirapé River port during the annual dry season, when the people worked the river for turtles and fish. The Dominicans would bestow gifts of salt, tools, and other exotic goods. Eventually, Catholic missionaries settled among the Tapirapé, helping the few who remained to preserve their customs and ceremonies; even so, the society was changing profoundly.

Today, there is an oversupply of men, which means that many men have no women to perform tasks that women have traditionally done for them. To solve this problem, men make convenient social marriages with very young girls, whose mothers then do all the domestic work. The Tapirapé now sell some crops for cash and are slowly being integrated into Brazilian society, but they live at the margins of a rapidly industrializing state. Families in cities and towns survive under conditions of extreme poverty.

WARAO

Alternate name: Warrau
Population: 32,000   Location: Venezuela
Language family: Warao

The Orinoco Delta along the northern coast of Venezuela and Guyana is home to the Warao, a group of traditional fishermen, hunters, and gatherers who occupy the marshes, swamplands, and riverbanks in the vast, watery region. The name Warao is one the people use themselves and has been translated as "owners of canoes"; they also are known as Guaraúnos. The different Warao groups speak mutually intelligible varieties of Warao, which many linguists consider a language isolate, but some believe is related to the Chibcha language family of the northern Andes.

Warao have had outside contact from the beginning of the colonial period, when Europeans entered the delta region to gain access to lands farther upriver, which they believed would turn out to be the fabled El

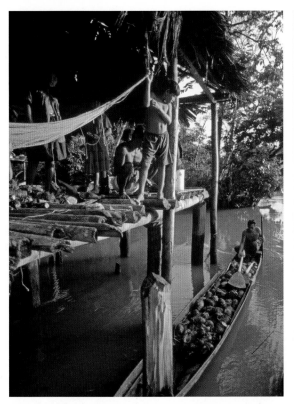

Warao build their homes on stilts to escape rising waters in the Orinoco Delta of Venezuela.

The versatile moriche also provides a source of starch in the Warao diet. However, this has been supplanted to a large extent by the Chinese ocumo, similar to taro, which they now cultivate along with a few other crops such as bananas and sugarcane. The Warao continue the long tradition of outside work, laboring in sawmills, palmetto factories, and commercial rice and fishing operations.

Catholic missionaries came to the area almost 200 years ago and converted a number of Warao, as have evangelical Protestants more recently. Most Warao still follow traditional ritual and belief systems, which are tied to a very complex cosmology and include a strong cult of ancestor worship. Spirits animate almost all natural phenomena, living and nonliving, some of which can metamorphose into jaguars. The Warao also believe in a world parallel to theirs that exists in the depths of the river. The two worlds intersect at times, as when a river being mates with a Warao woman, producing a monster. Three different kinds of shamans mediate the many connections between the Warao and the supernatural world, which receives blame for all illness and misfortune.

Warao culture is today threatened by ever widening involvement in the regional Venezuelan economy and the popularity of adventure tourism, which brings in groups to the area to sample the Warao way of life for a few days. There is also concern for the future from the high rate of tuberculosis infection in the Warao population, which has received much attention from the international medical community.

Dorado. While remaining closely tethered to their base in the swamps and marshes, the Warao worked for and traded with the Spanish and Dutch. Then, as now, the Warao plied the delta waters in their low-slung dugout canoes, crafted by men who specialize in the task.

A Warao settlement can consist of a single, large extended family or a multifamily community of some 250 people. After marriage a Warao man will go to live with his wife's family, where the couple resides in a household of sisters and their families under the ultimate authority of their father.

To build their traditional houses, or *palafitos,* the Warao use parts of the moriche palm, related to the sago, which has played an extensive role in their material culture and economy for centuries. Warao construct their homes on stilts to keep them above the rising tides and build elevated walkways between them. The wall-less dwellings have floors of moriche branches and thatched roofs of the palm's fronds. Warao women also weave moriche fibers into durable hammocks for sleeping that they sell outside the community, along with their baskets.

XIKRÍN

Alternate name: Kayapó
Population: Fewer than 500   Location: Brazil
Language family: Gê-Kaingang

Few Brazilian groups still follow their traditional lifeways, for the expanding frontier of industrial civilization has spread deep into the Amazonian rain forest. The Xikrín are among the ones who do. The northernmost group of Kayapó Indians, the Xikrín are farmers, hunters, and foragers living along the Rio Cateté in a homeland rich with Brazil nuts. Their material culture is very simple, except for featherwork and basketry, and the people wear few clothes—the men a penis cover; the women, short skirts. The people cultivate manioc and maize within a day's journey of settlements made up of thatched houses set in a circle around a central open space. Men and boys hunt and search for land turtles while the women gather wild plants, including the heart of the babassú palm. The most important house in a settlement is the men's dwelling: Inside, young boys receive instruction, and preparations take place for major ceremonies that may, for example, celebrate the first maize harvest or honor fish poisons. Only single men reside there; the married men live with their wives' families.

At night, Xikrín communities often gather for orations and discourses, which are important as a way to deliver instructions for the next day, to air and resolve disputes, and to enhance individual prestige. Little is known of Xikrín traditional religion, but shamans play a major role in mediating between the living and supernatural worlds, as they do in many other native South American societies.

Throughout the first half of the 20th century, contacts with Brazilian rubber interests, nut gatherers, and mahogany loggers were sporadic and hostile. But in the early 1960s, younger members of the tribe elected to live near the mouth of the Rio Cateté in the hope of becoming more closely integrated into Brazilian society. The rest of the community moved farther upriver to keep clear of the intruders. Since then, Xikrín society has been under siege: The downriver village became a rest stop for nut collectors, who used the threat of firearms to obtain women and to get help in their search for nut trees; also, infectious diseases decimated the Indian population.

After years of being exploited, the downstream Xikrín realized the true market value of both their resources and their labor, as well as the extent of their exploitation. They reunited with the traditional group back at the original upstream village and welcomed a Catholic mission among them, which has helped control social and commercial relationships with outsiders. In 1998, the Xikrín entered into an agreement with the Brazilian government and the World Bank

The Yanomamí, long the victims of developers and fortune seekers who have exploited and degraded their lands, now face the scourge of frenzied gold prospectors.

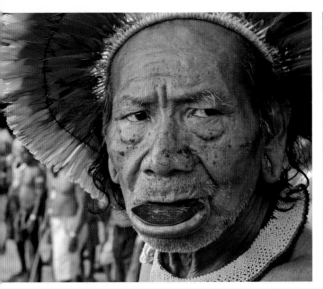

The Kayapó, who include the Xikrín, live deep in the Brazilian rain forest. They have learned to protect their interests in the face of competition for local resources.

for a sustainable mahogany-logging project. But their traditional culture remains under threat from the inexorable forces of the global economy.

YANOMAMÍ

Population: 32,000
Location: Venezuela, Brazil
Language family: Yanomam

Of all the surviving indigenous South American groups, the Yanomamí are among the most numerous. They occupy an area of rain forest in the upper Orinoco highlands of southeastern Venezuela and north-central Brazil. They are also one of the best known groups, thanks to many years of anthropological research.

The studies of anthropologist Napoleon Chagnon, in particular, have made the Yanomamí famous for their alleged fierceness and violent behavior. Recently, however, academic controversy has engulfed the research of Chagnon and other anthropologists who have worked alongside him. Critics have accused them of inciting violence among the people and using inappropriate research methods to form their conclusions. While the extent of violence among the Yanomamí may be exaggerated, there is no question that aggressive, violent behaviors—from wife abuse to raiding—are commonplace in this society. Only carefully controlled, ethical field research will establish whether the people are as violent as a generation of college students has been led to believe.

The Yanomamí are farmers, subsisting on plantains, sweet potatoes, and other carbohydrate-rich crops, as well as game and wild plant foods. Each village is some distance from its neighbors, and each specializes in different products, such as hallucinogenic drugs, arrow points, or cotton hammocks. Communities are not self-sufficient, meaning that they must depend on one another, mingling to trade and to feast. Still, there is widespread mistrust in this volatile environment where the eruption of violence and warfare is always a possibility. It is largely up to the village headmen to not allow matters to get out of control.

Many disputes are settled by aggressive chest-pounding duels or by slapping one's sides. Two or more men may engage in club fights, or there can be a formal war between neighboring villages. The ultimate level of violence involves trickery. On rare occasions, a village may invite its enemies over for a friendly feast, and then try to kill them as soon as they have let their guard down. Only by resisting ferociously or moving away as far as possible can a weaker community without allies protect itself against enemies.

In villages occupying the lower-lying areas, where populations are larger and fertile land is in shorter supply, behavior is especially aggressive and violence more frequent. Headmen in these communities must be very astute, as well as expert at persuading people to help prepare for feasts and other communal activities. Above all, they must be willing to intervene in the volatile interpersonal disputes and attempt to control the outcomes. Leadership in such an egalitarian society of aggressive individuals only comes from respect and bravery in war.

Sometimes headmen are also shamans, expert in the summoning of *hekura* spirits that cure and cause evil. The hekura arrive in the hallucinogenic snuff ingested by nearly all men in many villages, but shamans have a particular ability to dispatch evil hekura darts against their enemies. As a result, many men go through the long period of fasting and rigorous training to become shamans. In this society, where males dominate and there is a shortage of women, origin myths proclaim that fierce, warlike men arrived on Earth before women. Thus, the men are superior to them.

Andes

Longest mountain chain in the world and second highest only to the Himalaya, the Andes form a distinctive swath running practically the entire length of the continent of South America. More than 45 of the peaks in this mountain range stand more than 20,000 feet above sea level. Between the Andes and the Pacific Ocean to the west lies a narrow strip of coastal plain where can be found the Atacama Desert, the world's driest place. This landscape of extremes is shared by six countries: Colombia, Ecuador, Peru, Bolivia, Chile, and Argentina.

To listen to music from Chile and Peru, visit http://worldmusic.nationalgeographic.com.

AYMARA

Population: 3 million
Location: Bolivia, Peru
Language family: Aymaran

Six centuries ago, the Aymara paid tribute to the Inca Empire as they farmed along the shores of Lake Titicaca in highland Bolivia. They grew staple foods such as potatoes, maize, and quinoa. They also herded llamas on the semiarid Altiplano, or high plain, that surrounds the lake. Skilled fisherfolk, the Aymara developed totora-reed canoes and rafts for use on Lake Titicaca. The people are famous for these craft, which are still in use, and for distinctive homespun clothing that echoes colonial Spanish garments. Men wear conical woolen hats with earflaps, the women derby hats with wool wimples for cold days.

After the Spanish conquest, most Aymara were put to work on large estates and held in virtual serfdom. Finally, in 1953, agrarian reform laws abolished labor without pay and provided for land distribution among former estate workers. Most Aymara communities now have difficulty achieving self-sufficiency because of overpopulation, poor soils, and a harsh climate.

A thousand years ago, many of the villages around Lake Titicaca grew potatoes in raised, irrigated fields; these fields were highly productive because the water in them provided some measure of protection against frost damage. But the fields fell into disuse some centuries ago, and farmers began to depend more and more on dry-agriculture methods practiced on exposed hillsides. Evidence for the huge raised field systems has been discovered by archaeologists working at the site of the ancient city of Tiwanaku, the capital of a great Andean empire that predated the Inca and may have been founded by the Aymara's ancestors. With the cooperation of local communities, teams of scholars working on both the Bolivian and Peruvian sides of Lake Titicaca have re-created the raised fields and cut canals. While crop yields do fluctuate because of frosts, the surrounding canal water serves as a heat sink, retaining solar radiation.

The experiment has proved that this farming method is quite effective and that such fields can be created and maintained by a small group of people. Much modern agriculture on the Altiplano operates on an industrial scale, but the Aymara and their neighbors do not possess the capital to support large operations.

Aymara women wear layers of sweaters, shawls, and blankets to keep out the cold in the Andean highlands of Bolivia and Peru. Distinctive wool derbies keep heads warm.

Now that some land has been turned over to them, the Aymara are again turning to ancient, and frequently ignored, indigenous agricultural methods to regain their self-sufficiency.

KALLAWAYA

Population: Fewer than 1,000
Location: Bolivia
Language family: Mixed language (Quechua-Puquina)

Living in the Peruvian Andes northwest of Lake Titicaca, the Kallawaya are highland village farmers who cultivate maize, potatoes, quinoa, and other crops in a series of environments "stacked" one above the other on the slopes of Mount Kaata.

The Kallawaya's *ayllu,* an ancient social unit based on kinship and communal ownership of land, is so deeply tied to Mount Kaata that it treats the peak as a metaphorical human body, whose parts are kept in order by the continued existence of ayllu members. The diviners of Ayllu Kaata are responsible for ritually

pumping energy into the 13 earth shrines distributed up the mountain. In this way, the mountain "eats" produce from every climatic zone and is thus able to feed its inhabitants in turn. Kallawaya medicine men who also act as diviners obtain their powers from ancestors whose mummified remains were once paraded around the fields during fertility rituals.

The Kallawaya are renowned for their curing powers and abilities as coca diviners. At least a fifth of village men and women are involved in divination, serving visitors who come from hundreds of miles around to seek help. The most powerful diviner is also responsible for the New Earth ceremony. During this important rite, blood and fat are poured into the earth shrines, nourishing Mount Kaata so that it will continue making its resources available.

Like many other Andean groups, the Kallawaya rely on their rituals to sustain them and bring order to their lives. For these people, rituals help maintain and regulate everything that is part of human existence, including the environment, subsistence activities, and interpersonal and intercommunity relations.

MAPUCHE

Population: 1.5 million
Location: Chile
Language family: Araucanian

"People of the land," the Mapuche are one of the surviving groups of Araucanian Indians who once occupied the fertile valleys and coastal areas of central and southern Chile. Araucanians spoke a common language and fiercely resisted the Spaniards, but the Mapuche resisted the most strongly and were never completely subdued. Many retreated to isolated settlements when newcomers tried to force them to work on large estates.

Today, more than 1.5 million Mapuche live in southern Chile, inhabiting rural villages and towns or major urban centers like Santiago, where many are impoverished. For much of the year, rural Mapuche still dwell in comparative isolation in small communities, coming together now and then for formal gatherings in which they honor returning travelers, debate important affairs,

or simply enjoy a fiesta. These events are always marked by feasting, drinking, oratory, and, above all, singing.

Mapuche singing has profound social meaning, with every song bearing a message and subtle nuances. Some are prayers and supplications; others air grievances or woo a mate. Chiefs and shamans have their own more formal compositions, while other singers may improvise in their efforts to convey a message or let off steam. Women, in particular, use songs to express their feelings, even to air marital problems, since this method is socially acceptable. This tradition also fills a vital educational role in a society where skills are passed orally from one generation to the next. The songs often have a high poetic quality and help develop the personalities of young and old alike.

OTAVALEÑOS

Population: 300,000
Location: Ecuador
Language family: Quechuan

The volcano-surrounded homeland of the Otavaleños lies two hours north of Quito in highland Ecuador. In 1455, Inca armies entered the region, bringing with them the llama and the Quechua language, and before long the Otavaleños, who had woven cotton for generations, were also weaving wool and speaking the new tongue.

Otavaleño weavers traditionally used back-strap looms that required them to lean backward to create the necessary tension. When the Spanish came into contact with Otavaleño regions in the mid-16th century, they introduced treadle looms and sheep's wool, and they encouraged the raising of cash crops, which supplanted the cultivation of maize, potatoes, and quinoa by digging stick and foot plow. Otavaleño weavers prospered until the 19th century, when the industrial revolution introduced cheap mass-produced textiles. Even then, the people persisted with their ancient hand-weaving methods and became famous throughout Ecuador for fine workmanship. The Otavaleños also kept their traditional values and culture, as well as a strong ethnic identity. Although they are now Catholics, they have maintained many traditional religious beliefs that are closely tied to agriculture and the seasons.

Because of their famous textiles, the Otavaleños of today are among the most prosperous of all Indian

Among the Mapuche of central and southern Chile, women often wear traditional dress, including multiple ribbons.

The Rise of Mesoamerican Empires

Two hundred million years ago, during the middle of the Mesozoic Era—a period of enormous evolutionary change when dinosaurs rose to prominence, flowering plants first appeared, and small mammals emerged in the wake of the dinosaurs' rapid extinction—Earth's landmass was connected as a single supercontinent known as Pangea. For tens of millions of years this single continent harbored all terrestrial life, and then our planet's crust and upper mantle started breaking apart, causing a series of rifts that divided Pangea into several smaller plates. As the continents separated, South America headed west while Australia drifted east, a process of plate tectonics that set the Earth's crust on a collision course halfway around the world. Though it moved at about the same speed at which human nails grow, eventually the enormous Pacific plate slammed the smaller Nasca plate into South America. The Nasca plate slid underground, and its subduction, as this mantle downwelling is called, resulted in a north-south corridor of intense volcanic and earthquake activity. These forces created South America's longest mountain range and the Western Hemisphere's tallest point.

Mountainous extremes

The Andes run for over 4,400 miles along South America's western coast and host an area of inland drainage, the Altiplano, that constitutes one of the world's highest plateaus, with an average height of around 11,000 feet. The easterly winds of South America collect abundant moisture over the Amazon rain forest, but they dump almost all of it atop the frozen corridor of peaks, a process so absolute that it creates the driest place on earth, the Atacama Desert in eastern Chile. With most of the region's precipitation therefore coming from condensation of Pacific fog rather than rainfall, early human migrants encountered a landscape particularly harsh for continual habitation.

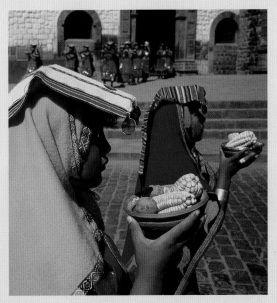

Celebrants in Cuzco, Peru, reenact the Inca sun festival, offering thanks for the harvest and prayers for future bounty.

The llama and the chinchilla were the only animals abundant there.

But those same mountains preserved a vast frozen reservoir that seasonally opened its floodgates to the Norte Chico valleys below. Spring runoff sends enormous quantities of water through this semiarid landscape, and at least 5,000 years ago people began to exploit this resource in an organized fashion. Archaeological evidence from north-central coastal Peru indicates that at around the same time, as many as 25 different communities began terracing the countryside, practicing complex irrigation to transform the barren slopes into productive farming zones.

Abundance

Growing populations moved inland across the Andean plateau to cultivate squash, beans, cotton, and potatoes, reshaping the landscape by terracing and establishing farming communities. Various civilizations rose and fell over the next few millennia, each developing its unique form of worship and government administration. In the 13th century, a central power from the Peruvian highlands rose to become the largest empire in pre-Columbian America. Employing a variety of methods, from brutal conquest to peaceful assimilation, the Inca incorporated almost a million square miles of western South America into a kingdom that was ruled by a single figure believed to descend directly from the sun.

By establishing a system of provincial governments, the Inca used a decentralized power structure to maintain command over great distances, providing security and commerce to communities in its farthest reaches, at times tearing down roads and rebuilding them simply to keep civilians employed. The Inca produced monumental architecture—the city of Machu Picchu found high in the Andes perhaps the best example—and developed complex mathematical, astronomical, and warfare systems before they ultimately fell to the Spanish conquistadors in the 16th century. Though the empire dissolved, the Inca people lived on and today the major languages of the Inca, namely Quechua and Aymara, are still spoken throughout the Andes.

groups in South America. On Poncho Plaza in the town of Otavalo, the handicraft market developed by the Indians in the 1960s and 1970s is a popular and colorful destination for tourists.

Many Otavaleños still dress in traditional costumes. Men put on fedora hats, ponchos, white shirts, and calf-length cotton pants, and they wear their hair in a long braid, or *shimba,* that reaches to the waist. The braid is never cut off and is such a strong cultural tradition that men serving in the Ecuadoran army are permitted to retain it. Women wear white blouses, blue skirts, shawls, and jewelry, including gold and coral necklaces. Proud and traditional, as well as entrepreneurial, Otavaleños value their clothing as an important symbol of their ethnic identity.

Q'EROS

Population: Fewer than 1,000
Location: Peru
Language family: Quechuan

Among the most isolated of all Andean groups, the Q'eros of Peru live on the eastern, Amazon side of the mountains. There, the terrain is so rugged that roads cannot penetrate the region. The people spend much of each year living in small hamlets of thatched houses, tucked in the upper gorges that extend down from high pastures.

Some 2,600 feet below—about a three-hour walk—lies their ceremonial center. Its houses, deserted most of the year, all have doors facing toward the rising sun. A Catholic chapel and a schoolhouse also form part of this complex, for the Q'eros' traditional beliefs are now melded with Catholic doctrine.

The homeland of the Q'eros climbs from wooded foothills at 6,000 feet above sea level to a dry, tundra-like landscape at 15,500 feet. Within about 20 square miles, these people exploit the entire range of Andean mountain environments. They offer a classic example of how highland farmers live vertically rather than horizontally. At the highest elevations, people herd alpacas and llamas, whose wool is used in the making of textiles. Operating their traditional back-strap looms, weavers fashion woolen hats, ponchos, and skirts for members of their community.

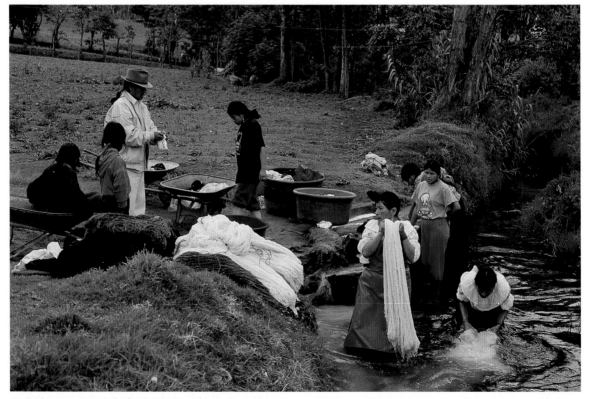

Otavaleño women wash the family laundry and long skeins of wool in a mountain stream. With the washed wool, they will weave blankets and ponchos to sell locally and to tourists.

Below the highest elevations, some locations allow the cultivation of potatoes, ullucu, and other tubers. At 8,700 feet and lower, the Q'eros combine the growing of tubers with more temperate crops such as maize, squash, chili peppers, and sweet potatoes. Until they could obtain European farming implements, people cultivated with the *chaquitaclla,* which was essentially a digging stick that a farmer drove into the soil with one of his feet. Far below all the fields lies the *sacha-sacha,* a place where the Q'eros never venture. It is the land of endless trees: the Amazonian rain forest.

Life is hard for the Q'eros, who have developed a deep distrust of outsiders over the years. For centuries they were exploited by the powerful, far-reaching Inca state. Then the Spanish arrived in their homeland, establishing several haciendas (now abandoned) and treating the people poorly. For many generations, the Q'eros have traded llama wool and potatoes with the Lake Titicaca region to the south, dealing with itinerant merchants known as *runa,* trusted people from the outside world. Today, the Q'eros continue to welcome the merchants, who bring iron tools and additional industrial commodities, but they greet other foreigners with evasion and suspicion.

QUECHUA

Population: 13 to 16 million
Location: Peru, Bolivia, Argentina, Ecuador
Language family: Quechuan

Highland Peru's Quechua lived under Spanish rule from the 1500s to the 1800s. In the pre-Spanish times, the Inca Empire imposed a degree of cultural uniformity and the Quechua language on the Andean highlands. But after the Spanish conquest, the Quechuan-speaking peoples broke up into many small groups, which were distinguished as much by their locations as by cultural differences. Today, they still share a common language—it is the most widely spoken native language in South America—and they are predominantly peasant farmers or workers on large haciendas and industrial farms. Many villagers have moved to larger highland towns, looking for work and living in poverty.

In Peru's highlands, the practice of agriculture has long been limited to mountain valleys and steep hillsides: Maize and quinoa are raised at lower elevations; potatoes are cultivated in terraced gardens higher up.

Plows are now common, but farmers in many communities continue to use the traditional foot plow to prepare their small fields. All Quechua groups are also expert weavers who still use back-strap looms and a simple weaving technology to produce the blankets, ponchos, and other garments worn by men and women in the cold mountain environment. Many

The skinny dog gets all the fleas.
COSTA RICAN PROVERB

Quechua dwell on small farmsteads or in village settlements, often grouped around a plaza and a Catholic church. Their houses are often built of mud brick or timber, with thatched roofs.

While the Quechua have adopted Catholicism, Peru's official religion, they maintain strong traditional spiritual beliefs that govern their view of the world. They envisage the cosmos as a layered entity. An upper world—often called Hanaqpacha—is a place of abundance where the spirits of people who led exemplary lives dwell, along with the pantheon of Quechua spirits, the Christian God, and Christ. Next is Kaypacha, the world of the living, and it comprises the Earth, humans, plants, animals, and the spirits of good and evil. Then there is Ukhupacha, the Inner World inhabited by diminutive people.

In Quechua belief, gods and the lives of humans are intertwined. The former intervene constantly in daily life, meting out reward and punishment in the guise of fortune and misfortune. The greatest of these is the creator-god Roal, once known as Viracocha; from his mountain home, he keeps an eye on humanity while governing the forces of nature and keeping them in balance. Pachamama is a female deity who resides deep in the Earth. She presides over agriculture: Her greatest ceremonies come at the time of planting in August and September, when she receives the seed that will become the next harvest. In a society where agriculture permeates every part of life, it is not surprising that traditional beliefs still flourish despite four centuries of vigorous missionization.

Central South America

This central region on the east cost of the South American continent includes parts of Brazil, Argentina, and Bolivia and all of Paraguay and Uruguay. Outside of this region's major cities, such as Rio de Janeiro and Buenos Aires, there are less than one hundred people per square mile, and sometimes fewer than ten, especially in the arid lowland of Chaco Boreal in eastern Bolivia and northwestern Paraguay, the two landlocked nations of the continent. Topography here ranges from those lowlands to Brazilian highlands which, in contrast, average a height of 3,300 feet. Mountain ranges in this region include the Serra do Espinhaço, Serra da Mantiqueira, and Serra do Roncador.

♫ To listen to music from Brazil, visit http://worldmusic.nationalgeographic.com.

GUARANÍ

Population: 5 million
Location: Paraguay
Language family: Tupí-Guaraní

In pre-Spanish times, the Guaraní peoples migrated into what is now Paraguay, arriving as part of the series of great population movements that took people speaking a common Tupí-Guaraní language southward from the lower Amazon region.

These former tropical farmers migrated in search of the Land of the Grandfather, a mythic sky god. They had sporadic contacts with the Inca civilization of the Andes and were subjugated by the Spanish, who hoped to find silver and gold on their lands. In time, Guaraní shamans spearheaded a strong revivalist movement based on Christian belief in the Redeemer, inciting the people to rise against their oppressors before traveling to a "land without evil."

Revivalism is just a memory now, but the Guaraní legacy is still powerful in Paraguay: Today, more than a million Paraguayans speak Guaraní, most of them living around Asunción, the capital.

Nevertheless, while cultural nationalism glorifies the Guaraní language and heritage, no Paraguayan peasants retain the traditional culture of their ancestors. They do build thatched houses in their ancient cultural manner, and they do grow maté, a Paraguayan tea that was a major product of their remote predecessors—but, in essence, they were Hispanicized centuries ago.

In the countryside, people continue to be largely self-sufficient, growing a few cash crops and living at the subsistence level. Such cash as they are able to generate is used to finance community fiestas, which here, as elsewhere in Spanish-settled South America, play an important role in rural life and the acquisition of individual prestige.

KADIWÉU

Population: 1,200
Location: Brazil
Language family: Guaicuruan

The Kadiwéu are the only surviving group of the lordly Mbayá peoples, who once dominated an area extending from Paraguay into the Mato Grosso, a western state of Brazil characterized by plateaus—and even farther afield. These people believed that

A young Guaraní girl sits in her family home in Brazil's Mato Grosso. Unlike their counterparts in Paraguay, the Guaraní people who live in Brazil currently face displacement from their territory.

they had a divine right to raid and enslave their neighbors—not only the Indian communities but also Portuguese and Spanish ones. Primarily hunters and foragers, the Kadiwéu demanded tribute in agricultural produce from their victims.

Kadiwéu hunting relied heavily on bolas, two or three balls attached to thongs and used to ensnare guanacos and other game. Always on the move, the people had a simple, portable material culture that had little use for textiles. They clothed themselves in hides, with featherwork and tattoos distinguishing between different kin groups.

The Kadiwéu remained a male-dominated society, which—because sons were preferred—widely practiced infanticide as late as the 1930s. Many newborn daughters were killed by asphyxiation or by breaking their necks and then buried under the beds where their parents slept. They also practiced abortion, for which they used a concoction of bitter roots or pounded on the mother's belly until the fetus died.

Today, the Kadiwéu are peaceful farmers, having reached an accommodation with the authorities, but their social organization still reflects an ethnic division between masters and slaves, the latter being individuals captured from other groups and their descendants. Despite frequent protests, the "slaves" still submit to their "masters" and are expected to provide economic services and food for no compensation; as the generations pass, however, the gap between slaver and enslaved continues to narrow.

MATACO

Alternate name: Wichí Population: 40,000
Location: Argentina, Bolivia
Language family: Mataco

Since 1628 the Mataco Indians of northwest Argentina's arid Gran Chaco strip of land, on the western edge of South America, have been in contact with Europeans. Because they resisted attempts at colonization and conversion, a large number of them were

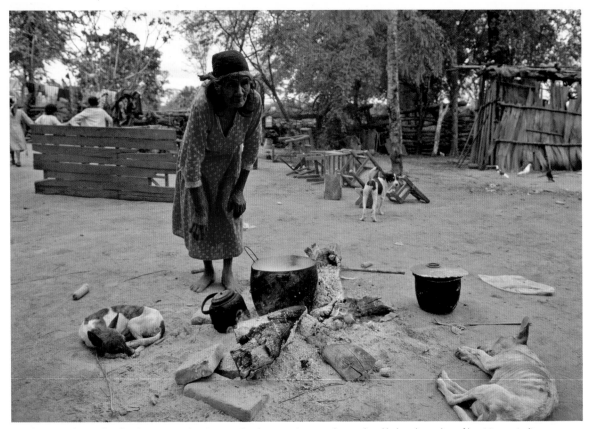

Her dress may be modern but her stance—leaning over kettles steaming atop hot rocks—likely echoes that of her Mataco Indian ancestors. This woman lives in a settlement near Tartagal in Argentina's Salta Province, to the north.

massacred, and others of their people were forced onto reservations. Today the Mataco people, much Hispanicized, survive. Many of them can be found working in the lumber business or serving as migrant laborers on large sugar plantations.

The traditional Mataco culture combined the cultivation of maize and beans with the gathering of cactus fruit and other wild plants in the thorny brush of their arid landscape. Men hunted guanacos, an ungulate like a llama, and they also took large numbers of river fish during their rivers' seasonal runs.

Reflecting their mobile lifestyle, most Mataco groups lived in simple brush huts; now, however, many people have become sedentary farmers, living in wattle-and-daub houses on small individual holdings. Today, even though Catholicism is widespread, shamans continue to be important in the more traditional communities: For many people, they are still essential intermediaries for the spirits.

The Mataco try as much as possible to remain isolated from larger society. They place a high premium on social values and reciprocity, as seen in the frequent sharing of food that goes on throughout their community and in their justice system, which punishes offenses committed against the social order.

Theft of field crops, especially tobacco, is treated as an offense against everyone. In small villages, people know each other so well that they can even recognize an individual's footprints, which can offer clues to the identity of any thief. When caught, offenders usually are punished by being expected to pay for what was taken. The punishment suits the crime, and it also serves as a lesson in communal ethics.

Instances of homicide may result from jealousy and marital disputes. If someone commits murder, the relatives of the deceased don war paint and visit the killer in his village, threatening him with their spears and gripping his chest as the women and children take to the forest. Usually, the punishment is once again economic, requiring payment in, say, goats, which are then distributed among the relatives of the victim. In addition to avenging killings by asking for "blood money," the deceased's relatives may begin a formal feud, thereby widening the conflict, or take a scalp from a member of a hostile tribe. In every case, homicide is seen as an offense against the community as a whole.

Even as the Mataco people are slowly being assimilated into wider Argentine society, they strive to maintain their own traditional values. Their distinctive legal practices offer a measure of protection against a rapidly changing world and its modern ethos, in which the individual matters more than the community at large.

TUPINAMBÁ

Population: Fewer than 8,000
Location: Brazil   Language family: Tupí-Guaraní

When the Portuguese arrived in Brazil in the early 16th century, the Tupinambá occupied more than 2,000 miles of the coast, from Ceará in the north to Porto Alegre in the south. This group had settled in their homeland some centuries earlier, after a messianic migration from the north in search of the idyllic Land of the Grandfather, the term they used to identify their mythical sky god.

What has ears but cannot hear?
Fire.

LACANDON (MEXICAN) PROVERB

The Tupinambá people dwelled in large palisaded villages, supporting themselves by cultivating five varieties of manioc, a starchy root vegetable, and by fishing in the waters of both the rivers and the coastal areas nearby.

Each Tupinambá group waged wars against its neighbors in a constant ebb and flow of blood feuds and revenge killings. Among the Portuguese, the Tupinambá soon acquired a reputation as fierce warriors, headhunters, and cannibals, when in fact, the people placed a high premium on social harmony within their own communities.

Following years of wars with the Portuguese, many Tupinambá captives were placed on colonialists' sugar plantations and forced to do work they considered beneath their dignity as warriors. Still, even though they were subdued, the Tupinambá held on to their traditional culture.

In the 17th century, under the strain of domination, another powerful messianic movement arose, again causing them to believe that when they reached the Land of the Grandfather, they would achieve immortality, regain their youth, and live at ease.

But this time the Tupinambá did not migrate from their villages. In many communities, they simply stopped working, holding the magical belief that the digging sticks they had traditionally used to cultivate fields would continue to do the agricultural work by themselves. This rich array of spiritual beliefs has now been submerged into the practice of Catholicism, and the surviving Tupinambá of Brazil have become peasant farmers.

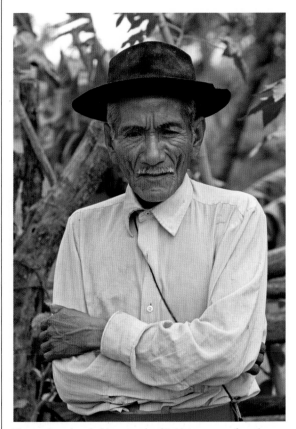

The modern-day clothing worn by this Mataco man of north-western Argentina in the arid Gran Chaco displays elements of the widespread Hispanicization of his culture.

Patagonia

Covering most of the southern half of Argentina is a semiarid plateau known as Patagonia. Covering about 260,000 square miles between the Patagonian Andes, the Colorado River, the Atlantic Ocean, and the Strait of Magellan, this nearly treeless tableland reaches an elevation of 5,000 feet. Only a few streams run continuously through the region from the Andes to the Atlantic Ocean, including the Colorado, Chubut, and Santa Cruz. Others run when there is rainfall, a rare occurrence: Patagonia receives less than ten inches of rain a year. The average monthly temperature in the city of Comodoro Rivadavia, on the eastern coast of Argentina and in the middle of in the Patagonian region, is 66°F in January and about 44°F in July. At the extreme southern tip of the continent of South America stretches the archipelago of rocky islands known as Tierra del Fuego, the land of fire: one large island and numerous smaller ones.

♫To listen to music from Argentina, visit http://worldmusic.nationalgeographic.com.

ARGENTINES

Population: 40 million
Location: Argentina
Language family: Italic

From its northern reaches in the subtropics to its southern tip in Tierra del Fuego, Argentina stretches some 2,100 miles. The Andes form its western border and a vast, flat grassland, known as the pampas, covers its central area. With fertile soil for growing grain and nutritious graze for cattle, the pampas became the lifeblood of the country's settlement.

The Spanish colonized Argentina in the 16th century and gave the country its name, derived from the Latin word for the silver they hoped to find there. Although parts of the country were in touch with other colonial centers in Latin America, most early contact and influence came directly from Spain—giving Argentina its European focus from the beginning. Spanish and Italians formed the largest waves of initial settlers; the roster would grow to include Germans, French, English, Welsh, Scots, Lebanese, Polish, and Eastern Europeans and what would become the largest settlement of Jews in South America.

Each arrival reinforced the cosmopolitan nature of Argentina. Castilian Spanish became the national language, which the Argentines have made their own with some distinct pronunciations. Italian also is widely understood and many Italian words have entered Argentine Spanish. About 70 percent of the people in Argentina are Roman Catholic and about 10 percent are Protestant, a number that continues to grow.

The country's indigenous populations, now greatly diminished, were dominated by the Spanish and ultimately pressed into forced labor. Few descendants remain of African slaves imported by the Spanish in the colonial era. One theory suggested that most succumbed in the yellow fever epidemic of 1871. The gaucho, or mestizo cowboy, who was indispensable to the success of cattle ranching, now mostly exists as an enduring cultural icon.

Despite the size of the country, Argentine life and much of its livelihood centers on the pampas and the capital of Buenos Aires. Some 70 percent of Argentines live in this area, more than 30 percent in

Poverty-ridden barrios in Buenos Aires, Argentina, bred the alluring strains of the tango. The popular vocal and dance music combined the rhythms of South American Indians and African slaves with the music of Spanish colonists.

metropolitan Buenos Aires. Porteños—as citizens of the port city are called—remain aware of life in the countryside: Each year country and city merge as people flock to the Exposición Rural, a national agricultural exhibit held in Buenos Aires featuring champion livestock, equestrian competitions, and the latest in farm machinery and other necessities of rural life.

The gregarious Argentines love to talk and make many opportunities to do so. European-style café life is vibrant, and late nights are the norm. In general, Argentines have a strong sense of themselves as individuals, which may often make collaboration difficult, as people seek to have their contributions recognized—and admired. This focus on oneself and one's thoughts and feelings routinely takes an unusually large number of Argentines into psychotherapy, a widely accepted practice.

When it comes to Argentine cuisine, it's almost all about the meat, especially beef. The *asado,* or barbeque, is an Argentine culinary and social tradition that involves grilling large quantities of various cuts of meats. Men typically do both the shopping and the grilling for an asado. Various Italian pasta dishes also are eaten regularly. For dessert, Argentines opt for confections containing *dulce de leche,* a spread made by boiling down sweetened milk. It appears at breakfast as well, as a topping on toast or pancakes.

Maté drinking is a widespread social ritual that has its roots in Argentina's Indian cultures and was adopted by the gauchos. Maté is an infusion of the leaves of the yerba maté plant, a variety of holly. It usually is sipped from a decorated gourd or silver cup through a special metal straw, and it is often passed around a group of friends. A mild stimulant, maté enabled the gauchos to keep going in the saddle without stopping for rest or food.

Few traditions are as evocative of a place as the tango is of Argentina. Tango represents both dance and song. It originated in the back streets of Buenos Aires and was at first eschewed by the upper classes.

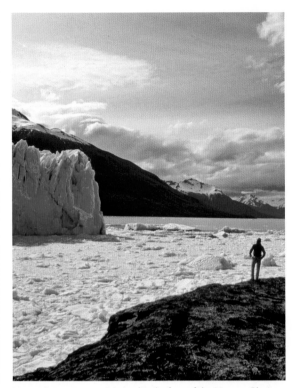

Human interests are minimized in the face of the Moreno Glacier, amid the mountains of Patagonia, in southern Argentina.

Tango partners hold each other closely and glide in long, languorous steps, pausing often for dramatic effect. Tango music is plaintive and melancholy and its best interpreters have become national celebrities.

Argentina currently is recovering from an economic downturn that thrust many of the middle class into poverty. Years of political conflict, government corruption, and inflation have held Argentina back from the economic rank it should hold due to its abundance of natural and human resources.

FUEGIANS

Population: Fewer than 100   Location: Chile, Argentina
Language family: Nearly extinct, language isolate (Yámana);
Chon (Ona)

Spanish explorer Ferdinand Magellan first encountered the Fuegian natives in 1520, when he passed through the strait later named after him and observed numerous campfires on the beaches at night—from whence came "the land of fire" (Tierra del Fuego). Botanist Charles Darwin immortalized the people as "wretched savages" in his account of the 19th-century voyage of H.M.S. *Beagle*. The Yámana of the coast, and

eventually the Ona of the interior, two of the Fuegian groups, came into sustained contact with Christian missionaries after 1875 but were not studied by anthropologists until the 1920s.

The Ona lived in western Tierra del Fuego. In the more open areas, they hunted small burrowing rodents known as cururos, llama-like guanacos, and wild fowl. They also took guanacos in forested regions and

> The one who loves you
> will make you weep.
> ARGENTINIAN PROVERB

captured sea mammals along the coast. To support their needs, Ona groups required large hunting territories, within which people were constantly on the move, living in smoke-filled shelters made from timber poles and guanaco skins. The groups were very sensitive about territorial encroachments, so much so that incursions sometimes led to fighting and blood feuds. In matters of life and death, the people looked to their shamans, who controlled health and disease, weather and war; they could even predict the discovery of stranded whales, an ability that engendered great respect and fear.

Yámana groups inhabited the windswept archipelago along the Beagle Channel and traveled long distances in search of food. They effectively lived in bark canoes, which the women paddled fearlessly over open water. Women collected mussels and fished, while the men took sea mammals. Unlike the relatively tall Selknam, the Yámana were short of stature, the men standing just over five feet. For protection against the constant cold and wet, people smeared their bodies with fish oil, wearing almost no clothing year-round.

The traditional Fuegian cultures began to disappear as people perished from smallpox and other diseases, from malnutrition, and even from bounty-hunting European settlers. Of those who managed to survive, many married Spanish immigrants. Today, a few native Ona can be found working as ranch hands and laborers, but full-blooded Yámana are, to all intents and purposes, extinct.

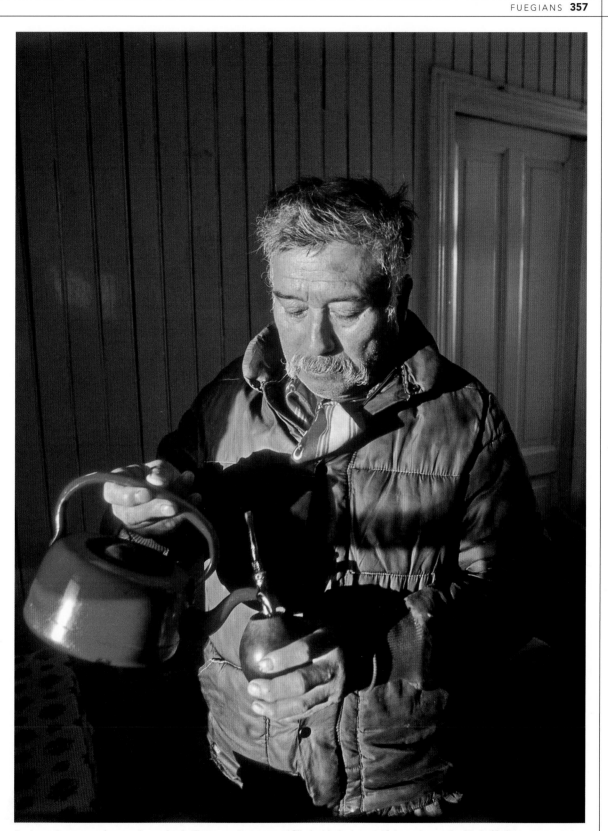

An Argentine man makes maté, pouring boiling water into a gourd filled with the leaves of the yerba maté, a kind of holly.

Ethnic Groups of the World

How many ethnic groups are there in the world? A complete list of them all would have well over 10,000 entries, and perhaps many more. The exact number is unknown and ever changing. Ethnicity itself remains an elusive concept, and there is no solid, universally accepted definition of what constitutes an ethnic group.

In typical usage, the term denotes a group of people who strongly identify themselves (or are identified by others, even against their will) as belonging together based on specific common traits they share. Such traits are largely involuntary: for example, skin color, clan or tribe membership, perceived or actual common ancestry, shared history, language, disability (e.g., deafness), or sexual orientation.

Other traits that group people into ethnicities may be chosen, abandoned, learned, or changed. These include culture, religion or sect, age, caste or social status, speech dialect, place or means of habitation, way of life, marriage into a group, immigration and naturalization—and on and on. Throughout history, people have imagined and formed communities in order to survive, to thrive, to have social support, and to realize their full potential. Many such communities are viewed and defined as ethnic groups.

Language is perhaps the most salient and typical marker of ethnicity, but there are exceptions. The Baraguyu people of Kenya speak the Masai language, but they consider themselves to be a separate ethnic group from the Masai. Many speakers of Chinese cannot understand each other at all, yet they may feel that they all belong to the Han Chinese ethnic group.

The name people call themselves in their own language may be completely different from what outsiders or neighbors use: Albanians call themselves Shqiptarët, Germans say Deutsche. Naming preferences inside or outside a group may evolve over time: The label "Eskimo," which once applied to Inuit peoples of Canada and Greenland, is no longer accepted by them—but the Yupik people of Alaska, also Inuits, still prefer it. Groups may have multiple alternate names or alternate spellings of names, depending on historical period or contemporary context. The Tuvan people who live in Russia and Mongolia are also referred to as Tuvinian, Tuvin, Urjankhay, Monchak, and Todzhan.

As we move toward a deeper appreciation of human diversity, we embrace more flexible and less rigid notions of ethnicity. Many people have come to appreciate their mixed or multiethnic status as an asset, not a disadvantage, and resist being assigned to a single ethnic category. People all around the world can legitimately identify as a member of more than one ethnic group, depending on the context.

For example, a Swahili-speaking Arab native to the island of Zanzibar may self-identify or be identified by others as being African, African-American, Muslim, Ismaili, Swahili, Tanzanian, Arab, Zanzibari—or some combination of these affiliations. Each of these labels is recognized in some context as denoting an ethnic-like grouping, though each highlights different traits. Many North Americans now embrace hyphenated ethnicities, such as Polish-American or Welsh-Canadian. American Deaf (written with a capital D) self-identify as an ethnic group because their unique shared language and culture differ radically from the hearing culture within which they live.

This book presents a sample of ethnic groups of the world. Here we list the names of more than 5,000 additional ethnic groups—and even this list represents only a small percentage of the total. The names listed are those most commonly used for each group, with some alternates added parenthetically. Slashes are used to indicate initial click sounds in African languages, but diacritics have been omitted from all group names.

Though we may be moving toward a more flexible notion of ethnicity, dark forces such as nationalism, ethnic chauvinism, and even ethnic cleansing work to reinforce rigid barriers that divide ethnicities. Ethnicity in itself is neither good nor bad. It can be a source of comfort, pride, and belonging. We encourage the reader to start from this book, and this list, and continue to explore the ethnosphere and the many more ethnic groups, names, and identities that make up our human community.

— *K. David Harrison*

A
Abanyanda *C Africa*
Abau M Abanyanda *C Africa*
Abau *Melanesia*
Abaydat *N Africa*
Abegweit *Northeast NA*
Abelam *Melanesia*
Abenaki *Northeast NA*
Abida *Middle East*
Abipon *Central SA*
Abitibiwinni *Northeast NA*
Abkhazians *Caucasus*
Abor (Adi) *S Asia*
Aboure *W Africa*
Abriwi *W Africa*
Abron *W Africa*
Absentee Shawnee *Plains NA*
Abukaya *C Africa*

Abung *SE Asia*
Aburra *Caribbean Coast SA*
Abutia *W Africa*
Acadia *Northeast NA*
Acatec (Aguatec, Awakateko) *Mesoamerica*
Acaxee *Mesoamerica*
Acehnese *SE Asia*
Achagua (Achawa) *Amazon Basin*
Achang *E Asia*
Achawa (Achagua) *Amazon Basin*
Ache (Guayaki) *Andes*
Achi *Mesoamerica*
Achikouya *C Africa*
Acho Dene Koe *Subarctic*
Acholi *E Africa*
Achomawi *Far West NA*

Achuale *Amazon Basin*
Achuar *Amazon Basin*
Acoma Pueblo *Southwest NA*
Acuera *Southeast NA*
Ada *W Africa*
Adamaua *W Africa*
Adangbe *W Africa*
Adi (Abor) *S Asia*
Adivasis *S Asia*
Adja *W Africa*
Adjarians (Ajarians) *Caucasus*
Adyumba *C Africa*
Afar (Danakil) *E Africa*
Afawa *W Africa*
Afo *W Africa*
African Caribbean *Caribbean*
Afrikaners (Boers) *S Africa*
Afshar *C Asia*

Afusare *W Africa*
Agaria *S Asia*
Aghuls *Caucasus*
Agiryama *E Africa*
Agmiut *Arctic*
Agni *W Africa*
Agoi *W Africa*
Agta *SE Asia*
Agto *Arctic*
Aguacadibe *Caribbean*
Aguano *Andes*
Aguaruna *Andes*
Aguatec (Acatec, Awakateko) *Mesoamerica*
Agusan *SE Asia*
Ahiariut *Northeast NA*
Ahir *S Asia*
Ahousaht *Northwest Coast NA*
Ahtahkakoop

Plains NA
Ahtena *Subarctic*
Ahtna *Northwest Coast NA*
Aiga *Melanesia*
Aimaq *C Asia*
Aini *E Asia*
Ainu *E Asia*
Air *W Africa*
Airiman *Australia*
Airitumiut *Northeast NA*
Ais *Southeast NA*
Aishihik *Subarctic*
Ait Atta *N Africa*
Ait Idrassen *N Africa*
Ait Khebache *N Africa*
Ait Oumalou *N Africa*
Ait Walnzgit *N Africa*
Ait Yafelman *N Africa*
Aivillirmiut *Arctic*
Aizo *W Africa*
Aja *W Africa*

Ajabakan *Australia*
Ajabatha *Australia*
Ajarians (Adjarians) *Caucasus*
Ajie *Melanesia*
Ak Posso *W Africa*
Aka *C Africa*
Akan *W Africa*
Akansa (Quapaw) *Plains NA*
Akawaio *Orinoco Basin*
Akha (Kaw, Ko) *SE Asia*
Akie *E Africa*
Aklanon *SE Asia*
Aklavik *Arctic*
Akokisa *Plains NA*
Akoko *W Africa*
Akosa *S Africa*
Akudnirmiut *Arctic*
Akuliarmiut *Arctic*
Akuna *Melanesia*

C=Central   E=East   N=North   S=South   W=West | NA=North America   SA=South America

Akurio *Orinoco Basin*
Akwa'ala (Paipai) *Mesoamerica*
Akwe *Amazon Basin*
Akwesasne Mohawks *Northeast NA*
Akyem *W Africa*
Al Haraba *N Africa*
Al Hawaashib *Middle East*
Al Hibab *Middle East*
Al Majaabra *N Africa*
Al Muraikhat *Middle East*
Al Murra *Middle East*
Al Shalawah *Middle East*
Ala *E Africa*
Ala'ngan *SE Asia*
Alaba *E Africa*
Alabama *SE NA*
Alabama Coushatta *Plains NA*
Alabama Quassarte *Plains NA*
Alacaluf (Halakwulup) *Patagonia*
Alak *SE Asia*
Alamamra *N Africa*
Aland Islanders *N Europe*
Alas *SE Asia*
Alaskan Eskimos *Arctic*
Alawa *Australia*
Alawites *Middle East*
Albanians *S Europe*
Ale *S Asia*
Aleiqat *Middle East*
Aleut *Arctic*
Algonkin *NE NA*
Ali Bin Morrah *Middle East*
Alleghenny *NE NA*
Allentiac *Andes*
Aloene *SE Asia*
Alorese *SE Asia*
Alsatians *W Europe*
Alsea *Northwest Coast NA*
Altaians *E Asia*
Aluku *Orinoco Basin*
Alur *E Africa*
Alura *Australia*
Alutiiq (Pacific Eskimos) *Arctic*
Alyawarre *Australia*
Amahuaca *Amazon Basin*
Amahumbu *S Africa*
Amaleh *C Africa*
Amanaye *Amazon Basin*
Amangu *Australia*
Amarak *Australia*
Amarakaeri *Andes*
Amarar *N Africa*
Amarken *Melanesia*
Amasili *S Africa*
Amba *E Africa*
Ambae *Melanesia*
Amberbaken *Melanesia*
Ambo (Ovambo) *S Africa*
Ambonese *SE Asia*

Ambuella *S Africa*
Amdo *C Asia*
Ameralik *Arctic*
Amerindians (Amerindino) *Caribbean*
Amerindino (Amerindians) *Caribbean*
Ameyao *Caribbean*
Amhara *E Africa*
Ami *E Asia*
Amijangal *Australia*
Amis *E Asia*
Amish *Northeast NA*
Ammassalimiut *Arctic*
Amniape *Amazon Basin*
Amoipira *Central SA*
Amr *Middle East*
Amraal *S Africa*
Amuesha *Andes*
Amurag *Australia*
Amuzgo *Mesoamerica*
Amyu *Melanesia*
Anadyr Eskimo *Arctic*
Anaiwan *Australia*
Anakamuti *Australia*
Anakazza *N Africa*
Anambe *Amazon Basin*
Anang *W Africa*
Anarkat *Arctic*
Anatolian Turks *Middle East*
Ancash *Andes*
Andakerebina *Australia*
Andalusians *W Europe*
Andamanese *SE Asia*
Andhras *S Asia*
Andingari *Australia*
Andis *Caucasus*
Andoa *Amazon Basin*
Andoke *Amazon Basin*
Angaite *Central SA*
Angara *Andes*
Angku *E Asia*
Angmagsqlik *N Europe*
Angolars *W Africa*
Angoni *E Africa*
Angoon *Northwest Coast NA*
Angu *Melanesia*
Ania *E Africa*
‖Anikhoe *S Africa*
Anishinabe *Plains NA*
Anizah *Middle East*
Ankaza *N Africa*
Ankole (Banyankole, Nkole) *E Africa*
Anlo *W Africa*
Anmatjera *Australia*
Anmatyerr *Australia*
Anoufo *W Africa*
Antaimoro *E Africa*
Antaisaka *E Africa*
Antakirinja *Australia*
Antandroy *E Africa*
Antipa *Amazon Basin*

Anuak *E Africa*
Anum Boso *W Africa*
Anuta Islanders *Melanesia*
Apa tani *S Asia*
Apache *SW NA*
Apalachee *SE NA*
Apalai *Amazon Basin*
Apanyekra *Amazon Basin*
Apapocuva *Central SA*
Apayao *SE Asia*
Apiaka *Amazon Basin*
Apinaye *Amazon Basin*
Apolista *Amazon Basin*
Aquitaine *W Europe*
Araba *Australia*
Arabama *Australia*
Arabs *Middle East, N Africa*
Arachane *Central SA*
Arafah *N Africa*
Arago *W Africa*
Arakanese (Rohingya) *SE Asia*
Arake *Amazon Basin*
Aralwa *Australia*
Aramda *Australia*
Arana *Central SA*
Aranda (Arrernte, Arunta) *Australia*
Araona *Amazon Basin*
Arapaho Plains *Plains NA*
Arapesh *Melanesia*
Arapium *Amazon Basin*
Araraibos *Amazon Basin*
Arauaki *Amazon Basin*
Aravcanian (Pehuenche) *Andes*
Arawak *Orinoco Basin*
Arawete *Orinoco Basin*
Arecuna *Orinoco Basin*
Arequipa *Andes*
Argobba *E Africa*
Arguni *Melanesia*
Arhuaco *Caribbean Coast SA*
Arica *Andes*
Aricobi *Amazon Basin*
Arikara Plains *Plains NA*
Arikem *Amazon Basin*
Arinagoto *Orinoco Basin*
ArMenians *Caucasus*
Arna *N Africa*
Arnga *Australia*
Aroland *Northeast NA*
Aroma *Melanesia*
Aroostook Micmac *Northeast NA*
Arrernte (Aranda, Arunta) *Australia*
Arsuk *Arctic*
Aru Islanders

Melanesia
Arua *Amazon Basin*
Arunta (Aranda, Arrernte) *Australia*
Arusha *E Africa*
Arusi *E Africa*
Arviqurmiut *Arctic*
Asante (Ashanti) *W Africa*
Ashan *Middle East*
Ashaninka *Amazon Basin*
Ashanti (Asante) *W Africa*
Ashkenazic Jews *Europe*
Ashluslay *Central SA*
Asiagmiut *Arctic*
Asmat *Melanesia*
Assamese *S Asia*
Assiniboin Plains *Plains NA*
Asua *C Africa*
Asurini *Orinoco Basin*
Ata Sikka *SE Asia*
Ata Tana 'Ai *SE Asia*
Atacama *Andes*
Atahun Shoshone *Great Basin NA*
Atayal *E Asia*
Athabasca Chipewyan Plains *Plains NA*
Atie *W Africa*
Atikameg Plains *Plains NA*
Atjehnese *SE Asia*
Atjinuri *Amazon Basin*
Atlin *Subarctic*
Atmanika *Caucasus*
Atna *Arctic*
Atoni *SE Asia*
Atorai *Orinoco Basin*
Atroari *Amazon Basin*
Atsahuaca *Amazon Basin*
Atsi *E Asia*
Atsina *Northeast NA*
Atsugewi *Far West NA*
Attawapiskat *Northeast NA*
Attikamek *Northeast NA*
Atuence *E Asia*
Auanbura *Australia*
Auca (Huaorani, Wao, Waorani) *Amazon Basin*
//Au//ei (Auen) *S Africa*
Auen (//Au//ei) *S Africa*
Aueti *Amazon Basin*
Augu *Melanesia*
Augustine *Far West NA*
Auk *Northwest Coast NA*
Aulad Soliman *N Africa*
Aulliminden *W Africa*
Aush *Patagonia*
Aushi *C Africa*
Australian Aborigines *Australia*
Austrians *C Europe*
Auvergnats

W Europe
Auyana *Melanesia*
Ava *Central SA*
Avars *Caucasus*
Ave *W Africa*
Averiano *Orinoco Basin*
Aveyronnais *W Europe*
Avil *Middle East*
Avukaya *C Africa*
Awa *Melanesia*
Awa Kwaiker (Koakir) *Andes*
Awabakal *Australia*
Awai *Melanesia*
Awakateko (Acatec, Aguatec) *Mesoamerica*
Awamir *Middle East*
Awaqir *N Africa*
Awarai *Australia*
Awazim *Middle East*
Awe *W Africa*
Aweer (Kilii, Somali Boni) *E Africa*
Aweikoma *Central SA*
Awi *E Africa*
Awin *Melanesia*
Awinmul *Australia*
Awishiri *Amazon Basin*
Awlad'Ali *N Africa*
Awyu *Melanesia*
Ayacucho *Andes*
Ayaida *N Africa*
Ayamaro *Melanesia*
Ayisenga *S Africa*
Aymara *Andes*
Ayoreo (Moro) *Central SA*
Azande (Zande) *C Africa*
Azerbaijanis (Azeris) *Caucasus*
Azeris (Azerbaijanis) *Caucasus*
Azoreans *W Europe*

B
Ba Mbenzele *C Africa*
Baada *Australia*
Baba *Melanesia*
Baba Chinese *SE Asia*
Babenzele *C Africa*
Babobo *SE Asia*
Baboute *C Africa*
Badaga *S Asia*
Badi *Australia*
Badimaia *Australia*
Badjalang *Australia*
Badjiri *Australia*
Badui *SE Asia*
Badutu *E Asia*
Baffin Islanders *Arctic*
Bafia *W Africa*
Baga *W Africa*
Baganda *E Africa*
Bagarra *W Africa*
Bagaz *Mesoamerica*
Baggara Arabs *N Africa*
Bagirmi *W Africa*
Bagisu (Gisu) *E Africa*
Bagobo *SE Asia*
Bagu *Australia*

Bahar Lu *Middle East*
Bahinemo *Melanesia*
Bahnar *SE Asia*
Bahwetig Mackinac *Northeast NA*
Bahwetig Ojibwa *Northeast NA*
Bai (Baizu) *E Asia*
Baia *C Africa*
Baiali *Australia*
Baiga *S Asia*
Baijungu *Australia*
Bailgu *Australia*
Bainoa *Caribbean*
Bainouk *W Africa*
Bait Imani *Middle East*
Bait Kathir *Middle East*
Baizu (Bai) *E Asia*
Bajau *SE Asia*
Baka *C Africa*
Bakairi *Amazon Basin*
Bakalahari *S Africa*
Bakamba *C Africa*
Bakanambia *Australia*
Bakele *C Africa*
Bakhtiari *Middle East*
Bakil *Middle East*
Bako *E Africa*
Bakongo *C Africa*
Bakovi *Melanesia*
Bakwe *W Africa*
Balala *S Africa*
Balali *C Africa*
Balantak *SE Asia*
Balante *W Africa*
Balardong *Australia*
Bale *E Africa*
Balearics *W Europe*
Balese Ndake *C Africa*
Balgarn *Middle East*
Bali *W Africa*
Bali Aga *SE Asia*
Balinese *SE Asia*
Balkars *Caucasus*
Ballouk *W Africa*
Baloulou (Mongo) *C Africa*
Baloundou *C Africa*
Balti *S Asia*
Balua *C Africa*
Baluchi *C Asia*
Bamakoma (Makoma) *S Africa*
Bamars (Burman) *SE Asia*
Bambara *W Africa*
Bambuti (Mbuti) *C Africa*
Bamileke *W Africa*
Bamoun *W Africa*
Bamu *Melanesia*
Banabans *Micronesia*
Banagal *C Africa*
Banaro *Melanesia*
Banbai *Australia*
Banda *C Africa*
Bandi *W Africa*
Bandjin *Australia*
Bandza *C Africa*
Banen *W Africa*
Bangala *C Africa*
Banggai *SE Asia*
Banggala *Australia*

Bangu *C Africa*
Banhun *W Africa*
Bani *Caribbean*
Bani Hajir *Middle East*
Bani Hilal *Middle East*
Bani Khalid *Middle East*
Bani Kitab *Middle East*
Bani Shahr *Middle East*
Bani Yam *Middle East*
Bania *S Asia*
Baniva *Orinoco Basin*
Banjara *S Asia*
Banka *SE Asia*
Banks Islanders *Melanesia*
Bannock *Great Basin NA*
Bantu *S Africa*
Banyak *SE Asia*
Banyankole (Ankole, Nkole) *E Africa*
Banyoro *E Africa*
Banyua *W Africa*
Banziri *C Africa*
Baoule *W Africa*
Bapoto *C Africa*
Baqum *Middle East*
Bara *Amazon Basin*
Bara *E Africa*
Baraba Baraba *Australia*
Barabaig *E Africa*
Barada *Australia*
Barama River Caribs *Orinoco Basin*
Baranbinja *Australia*
Baranzai *Middle East*
Baraparapa *Australia*
Barara *Australia*
Barasana *Amazon Basin*
Barbacoa *Caribbean*
Barbaram *Australia*
Barbocoa *Andes*
Bare *Amazon Basin*
Bari *Caribbean Coast*
Bari (Beri) *E Africa*
Bariba *W Africa*
Barimaia *Australia*
Barindji *Australia*
Bariyah *Middle East*
Barkindji *Australia*
Barlamomo *Australia*
Barna *Australia*
Barok *Melanesia*
Barona *Far West NA*
Barrumbinya *Australia*
Bartangs *C Asia*
Barunga *Australia*
Barunggam *Australia*
Barungguan *Australia*
Baruya *Melanesia*
Basakomo *W Africa*
Basarwa (Bushmen, San) *S Africa*
Bashilange *C Africa*
Bashilele (Lele)

C Africa
Bashkirs *E Europe*
Basiri *C Africa*
Basketo *E Africa*
Basoga *E Africa*
Basotho *S Africa*
Basques *W Europe*
Basrai *W Africa*
Bassa *C Africa*
Bassari *W Africa*
Basseri *Middle East*
Basua *C Africa*
Batahin *N Africa*
Batak *SE Asia*
Batatela *C Africa*
Batek *SE Asia*
Batjala *Australia*
Batjan *SE Asia*
Batlaro *S Africa*
Batlokwa *S Africa*
Batoro *E Africa*
Baul *S Asia*
Baule *W Africa*
Baure *Amazon Basin*
Bavarians *W Europe*
Bawaki *Melanesia*
Baweanese *SE Asia*
Baya (Gbaya) *C Africa*
Bayaka *C Africa*
Bayamo *Caribbean*
Bayaquitiri *Caribbean*
Bayei *S Africa*
Bayot *W Africa*
Be *W Africa*
Beafada *W Africa*
Bearspaw *Plains NA*
Beausoleil Chippewa *Northeast NA*
Beaver *Subarctic*
Bederiat *C Africa*
Bedik *W Africa*
Bedouin Arabs *Middle East*
Bega *E Africa*
Beheria *N Africa*
Beico de Pau *Amazon Basin*
Beir *E Africa*
Beja (Beni Amer) *N Africa*
Belandas *SE Asia*
Belarusians (White Russians) *E Europe*
Belau *Micronesia*
Belgians *W Europe*
Bella Bella *Northwest Coast NA*
Bella Coola *Northwest Coast NA*
Belle *W Africa*
Bellikan *Caucasus*
Belubba *E Africa*
Bemba *E Africa*
Bembe *C Africa*
Ben Guil *N Africa*
Bena *E Africa*
Benabena *Melanesia*
Bende *E Africa*
Bene Israel *Middle East, S Asia*
Bengalis *S Asia*
Benglong (Deang) *E Asia*
Beni Amer (Beja) *N Africa*

Beni Atiyah *Middle East*
Beni Hajar *Middle East*
Beni Sakhr Bedu *Middle East*
Beni Suef *N Africa*
Beothuk *Northeast NA*
Berabiche *W Africa*
Berberi *C Africa*
Berbers (Imazighen) *N Africa*
Bergamasco *W Europe*
Bergdama *S Africa*
Beri (Bari) *E Africa*
Beriquruk *Australia*
Berriait *Australia*
Berseba *S Africa*
Bersimis *Northeast NA*
Berta *E Africa*
Besorube *W Africa*
Beta Israel (Falasha) *E Africa*
Bete *W Africa*
Bethanie *S Africa*
Betoi *Amazon Basin*
Betsiamites *Northeast NA*
Betsileo *E Africa*
Betsimisaraka *E Africa*
Bettakurumbas *S Asia*
Bezanozano *E Africa*
Bhaca *S Africa*
Bhil *S Asia*
Bhilala *S Asia*
Bhota (Ngalop) *S Asia*
Bhottada *S Asia*
Bhuiya *S Asia*
Bhutanese *S Asia*
Bhutia *S Asia*
Biagai *Melanesia*
Biak *Melanesia*
Biat *SE Asia*
Bibelmen *Australia*
Bicolano *SE Asia*
Bidawal *Australia*
Bidayuh *SE Asia*
Bidia *Australia*
Bidjandjara *Australia*
Bidoon *Middle East*
Bigambul *Australia*
Bihari *S Asia*
Bikalbura *Australia*
Bikini *Micronesia*
Bikol *SE Asia*
Bilaan *SE Asia*
Bilen *E Africa*
Bilingara *Australia*
Billi *Middle East*
Billiton *SE Asia*
Biloxi *Southeast NA*
Bimanese *SE Asia*
Binandere *Melanesia*
Binbinga *Australia*
Bindal *Australia*
Bindjareb *Australia*
Bindubi *Australia*
Binga *C Africa*
Bingabura *Australia*

Bingongina *Australia*
Bini *W Africa*
Binigura *Australia*
Binji *C Africa*
Bintukua *Caribbean Coast SA*
Binumarien *Melanesia*
Bira *E Africa*
Birdi *Middle East*
Birhor *S Asia*
Biri *C Africa*
Biria *Australia*
Birifor *W Africa*
Birom *W Africa*
Birpai *Australia*
Bisa *E Africa*
Bisayah *SE Asia*
Bisis *Melanesia*
Bissa *W Africa*
Bissago *W Africa*
Bit *SE Asia*
Bitjara *Australia*
Black Thai (Tai Dam) *SE Asia*
Blackfeet *Plains NA*
Blang *E Asia*
Blood *Plains NA*
Bloodvein *Plains NA*
Boanbura *Australia*
Boardji *Melanesia*
Boazi *Melanesia*
Bobo *W Africa*
Boers (Afrikaners) *S Africa*
Bofi *C Africa*
Bohane *Central SA*
Boholano *SE Asia*
Bohra *S Asia*
Boiken *Melanesia*
Bokar *S Asia*
Bolaang Mongondow *SE Asia*
Bolewa *W Africa*
Boli *Melanesia*
Boma *C Africa*
Bombesa *C Africa*
Bomvana *S Africa*
Bonan *E Asia*
Bonari *Orinoco Basin*
Bonbarabua *Australia*
Bondei *E Africa*
Bondo *S Asia*
Bonerate *SE Asia*
Bonga *C Africa*
Bongo (Bungu) *C Africa*
Bongue *C Africa*
Boni (Aweer) *E Africa*
Bono *W Africa*
Bontok *SE Asia*
Boothroyd *Northwest Coast NA*
Bora *Amazon Basin*
Boran *E Africa*
Boro *Amazon Basin*
Boro *S Asia*
Bororo *Amazon Basin*
Boruca *Mesoamerica*
Boskien *Melanesia*
Bosnian Muslims *C Europe*
Bosyeba *C Africa*
Botocudo *Central SA*
Boubangi (Mboshi)

C Africa
Bougainville Islanders *Melanesia*
Boun *Australia*
Bouyei *E Asia*
Boyaca *Caribbean*
Boyks *E Europe*
Bozo *W Africa*
Brabralung *Australia*
Brahui *C Asia*
Braiakaulung *Australia*
Brao *SE Asia*
Braoya *N Africa*
Bratauolung *Australia*
Bretons *W Europe*
Bribri *Mesoamerica*
Brokenhead Ojibway *Plains NA*
Brotherton *Northeast NA*
Bru *SE Asia*
Btsisi *SE Asia*
Bubi *C Africa*
Buctouche *NE NA*
Budidjara *Australia*
Budu *C Africa*
Budugs *Caucasus*
Buduma *W Africa*
Bugakhoe *S Africa*
Bugakwe *S Africa*
Buganda *E Africa*
Bugis *SE Asia*
Bugle *Mesoamerica*
Bugulmara *Australia*
Bugusu (Lhuya, Luyia) *E Africa*
Buha *E Africa*
Bukidnon *SE Asia*
Bukitan *SE Asia*
Buksa *S Asia*
Bukuli *E Africa*
Bulalli *Australia*
Bulgarians *E Europe*
Bullom *W Africa*
Bulusu *SE Asia*
Buluwai *Australia*
Bumba *C Africa*
Bumbu *W Africa*
Bumiputra (Malay) *SE Asia*
Bunaba *Australia*
Bunda *C Africa*
Bundi *Melanesia*
Bunganditj *Australia*
Bungu (Bongo) *C Africa*
Buntamurra *Australia*
Bunun *E Asia*
Bunurong *Australia*
Bunyole *E Africa*
Bunyoro (Kitara, Nyoro) *E Africa*
Burakumin (Eta) *E Asia*
Burgher *S Asia*
Burgundians *W Europe*
Buriats *E Asia*
Burkinabe *W Africa*
Burman (Bamars) *SE Asia*
Burmese *SE Asia*

Buru *SE Asia*
Buruli *E Africa*
Buruna *Australia*
Burungi *E Africa*
Burushaski *S Asia*
Burusho (Hunzakuts) *C Asia*
Busansi *W Africa*
Bushmen (Basarwa, San) *S Africa*
Butlikh *Caucasus*
Butonese *SE Asia*
Butung *SE Asia*
Buwallah *Middle East*
Buyi *E Asia*
Bviri *C Africa*
Bwa *W Africa*
Bwaidoga *Melanesia*
Bwaka *C Africa*
Bwe *SE Asia*
Bwile *C Africa*

C

Caapor *Amazon Basin*
Cabazon *Far West NA*
Cabecar *Mesoamerica*
Cabo *Mesoamerica*
Cabre *Orinoco Basin*
Cachil DeHe Wintun *Far West NA*
Caddo *Plains NA*
Caddo Adais *Southeast NA*
Caete *Central SA*
Caga *E Africa*
Cagaba (Kogi) *Caribbean Coast SA*
Cahibo *Caribbean*
Cahto *Far West NA*
Cahuilla *Far West NA*
Caingua *Central SA*
Cairi *Central SA*
Caizcimu *Caribbean*
Cajamarca *Andes*
Cajatambo *Andes*
Cakchiquel (Kaqchikel) *Mesoamerica*
Calabar *W Africa*
Calabrese *S Europe*
Calapuya *Northwest Coast NA*
Calaveras Miwok *Far West NA*
Calayua *Orinoco Basin*
Calista *Subarctic*
Callahuaya *Andes*
Calusa *Caribbean*
Camacan *Central SA*
Camana *Andes*
Campa *Amazon Basin*
Campo (Tipai) *Far West NA*
Cana *Andes*
Canamari *Amazon Basin*
Canari *Andes*
Canchi *Andes*
Candoshi *Amazon Basin*

Canela
(Ramkokamekra)
Amazon Basin
Canelos Quichua
Andes
Canichana Amazon
Basin
Cantonese E Asia
Canyon Costanoan
Far West NA
Capanahua Amazon
Basin
Cape Verdeans
W Europe
Cape York Peoples
Australia
Capitan Grande Far
West NA
Caquetio Caribbean
Coast SA
Cara Andes
Caraca Caribbean
Coast SA
Carahyaby Amazon
Basin
Caranga Andes
Caravaya Andes
Cari'a Orinoco Basin
Caribou Eskimos
Arctic
Caribs (Galibi)
Caribbean, Orinoco
Basin
Cariguano Orinoco
Basin
Carijo Central SA
Carijona Amazon
Basin
Carina Orinoco Basin
Caripuna Amazon
Basin
Cariri Amazon Basin
Carmel Far West NA
Caroline Islanders
Micronesia
Carpatho Rusyns
E Europe
Carpatho Ukrainians
(Lemkos)
C Europe
Carrier Subarctic
Cascade Northwest
Coast NA
Cashibo Andes
Cashinahua Amazon
Basin
Cashite E Africa
Casma Andes
Castilians W Europe
Cataba Plains NA
Catalans W Europe
Catawba Southeast
NA
Catio Andes
Catukina Amazon
Basin
Cauatambo Andes
Cauduveo Central SA
Cavina Amazon Basin
Cavinena Amazon
Basin
Cawahib Amazon
Basin
Cayabi Amazon Basin
Cayaguayo
Caribbean

Cayapa Andes
Cayoose Creek
Northwest Coast
NA
Cayuga Northeast NA
Cayuishana Amazon
Basin
Cayuse Plateau NA
Cayuvava Amazon
Basin
Cazcan Mesoamerica
Cebaun SE Asia
Cebu SE Asia
Central Eskimos
Arctic
Central Miwok Far
West NA
Central Thai SE Asia
Ceram SE Asia
Ch'orti' Mesoamerica
Chaamba N Africa
Chabeans Caribbean
Chachapoya Andes
Chacobo Amazon
Basin
Chagga E Africa
Chaima Caribbean
Coast SA
Chakchiuma
Southeast NA
Chakmas (Changma)
SE Asia
Chaldeans C Asia
Cham SE Asia
Chama Amazon Basin
Chamacoco Central
SA
Chamars S Asia
Chamba W Africa
Chambri Melanesia
Chami Amazon Basin
Chamorros
Micronesia
Champagne Subarctic
Chamula Mesoamerica
Chana Central SA
Chane Central SA
Changma (Chakmas)
SE Asia
Chaobon SE Asia
Chaouia N Africa
Chapakura Amazon
Basin
Chara E Africa
Charca Amazon Basin
Chariguriqua
S Africa
Charrua Central SA
Chastacosta
Northwest Coast
NA
Chatino Mesoamerica
Chatot Southeast NA
Chaubunagunga-
maug Nipmuck
Northeast NA
Chaudhri S Asia
Chavchyvs Arctic
Chawai W Africa
Chayahuita Andes
Che Wong SE Asia
Chechehet Central
SA
Chechen Caucasus
Chehalis Northwest
Coast NA

Chelan Plateau NA
Chemainus Northwest
Coast NA
Chemawawin Plains
NA
Chemehuevi Great
Basin NA
Cheng SE Asia
Chepara Australia
Cheremis (Maris)
E Europe
Chero S Asia
Cherokee Plains,
Southeast NA
Cheslatta Carrier
NW Coast NA
Chetco Northwest
Coast NA
Chewa E Africa
Cheyenne Plains NA
Cheyenne Arapaho
Plains NA
Chibcha Andes
Chicha Amazon Basin
Chickahominy
Southeast NA
Chickamogee Chero-
kee Southeast NA
Chickasaw Plains NA
Chicora Sioux
Southeast NA
Chicoutimi Northeast
NA
Chikunda E Africa
Chilcotin Northwest
Coast NA
Chilkat Subarctic
Chilula Far West NA
Chimakum Northwest
Coast NA
Chimane Amazon
Basin
Chimariko Far West
NA
Chimbu Melanesia
Chimila Caribbean
Coast SA
Chimo Northeast NA
Chimu Andes
Chin S Asia
Chinantec
Mesoamerica
Chincha Andes
Chinchaycocha Andes
Ching E Asia
Chingali Australia
Chiniki Plains NA
Chinook Northwest
Coast NA
Chipaya (Uru) Andes
Chipewyan Subarctic
Chipewyan Prairie
Plains NA
Chippewa (Ojibwa)
Northeast NA
Chippewa Cree Plains
NA
Chiquitano Central SA
Chiquito Amazon
Basin
Chiquiyami Andes
Chiricahua Apache
Southwest NA
Chiriguano (Guarayo)
Andes

Chiripa Central SA
Chirma Melanesia
Chisasibi Northeast
NA
Chishinga C Africa
Chisos Plains NA
Chitimacha Southeast
NA
Chli (Try) SE Asia
Choco Andes
Choctaw Plains,
Southeast NA
Choctaw Apache
Southeast NA
Choiah C Asia
Choinumni Yokuts
Far West NA
Choiseul Islanders
Melanesia
Chokwe C Africa
Chol Mesoamerica
Cholon Andes
Chona E Asia
Chong SE Asia
Chono Patagonia
Chontal Mesoamerica

Chonyi E Africa
Chopi S Africa
Choque Orinoco
Basin
Chorote Central SA
Chorti Mesoamerica
Chrau SE Asia
Christmas Islanders
(Kiritimati Islanders)
Polynesia
Chru SE Asia
Chuabo E Africa
Chuang E Asia
Chuckbukmiut
Northeast NA
Chugach Arctic
Chuj Mesoamerica
Chukchansi Yokut
Far West NA
Chukchi Arctic
Chukotka Arctic
Chulupi Central SA
Chumash Far West
NA
Chupayachu Andes
Chuuk Islanders
(Trukese)
Micronesia
Chuvantsy Arctic
Chuvash E Europe
Cinta Larga Amazon
Basin
Cipungu S Africa
Circassians Caucasus,
Middle East

Cisama C Africa
Cisanji S Africa
Clackamas Northwest
Coast NA
Clatskanie Northwest
Coast NA
Clatsop Northwest
Coast NA
Co Sung (Kuy, Lahu)
SE Asia
Coahuiltecan
Mesoamerica
Coaiquer Amazon
Coani Orinoco Basin
Coastal Chumash
Far West NA
Coastal Miwok Far
West NA
Coastal Salish
North-west Coast
NA
Coastal Tsimshian
Northwest Coast
NA
Coastal Yuki Far West
NA

Cocama Amazon
Basin
Cocamilla Amazon
Basin
Cochapampa
Amazon Basin
Cochimi
Mesoamerica
Cochiti Pueblo
Southwest NA
Coconuco Andes
Cocopah Southwest
NA
Coeur d'Alenes
Plateau NA
Cofan Amazon Basin
Coharie Southeast
NA
Colla Andes
Collagua Andes
Collo (Shilluk) C Africa
Colorado (Tsatchela)
Andes
Columbia Plateau NA
Colville Northwest
Coast NA
Comanche Plains NA
Comorians E Africa
Comox Northwest
Coast NA
Concho Mesoamerica
Conchuco Andes
Conhaque W Africa
Conibo Andes
Conoy Northeast NA

Cook Islanders
Polynesia
Coorg S Asia
Coos Northwest
Coast NA
Copalis Northwest
Coast NA
Copper Eskimos
Arctic
Copts N Africa
Coquille Northwest
Coast NA
Cora Mesoamerica
Coree Southeast NA
Cornish N Europe
Coroado Central SA
Corsicans S Europe
Cortina Wintun Far
West NA
Costanoan (Mutsun)
Far West NA
Costanoan Esselen
Far West NA
Cotabato Manobo
SE Asia
Cote Plains NA

Coto (Orejon)
Amazon Basin
Cotopaxi Quichua
Andes
Couchiching
Northeast NA
Coushatta Southeast
NA
Coussari Orinoco
Basin
Cowessess Plains NA
Cowichan (Halkome-
lem) Northwest
Coast NA
Cowlitz Northwest
Coast NA
Coyaima Amazon
Basin
Cree Plains NA
Creek Plains NA
Creoles Southeast NA
Cretans S Europe
Crimean Tatars
C Asia, E Europe
Croats C Europe
Crow Plains NA
Cua SE Asia
Cuauhcomeca
Mesoamerica
Cubanacan
Caribbean
Cubeo (Kobewa)
Amazon Basin
Cuciba Caribbean
Cuicatec Mesoamerica

> ## Cattle of different colors are beautiful; a person of many moods is bad.
>
> TUVAN PROVERB

Cuitlatec (Teco) *Mesoamerica*
Cuiva *Orinoco Basin*
Culina *Amazon Basin*
Cumana *Caribbean Coast SA*
Cumanagoto *Caribbean Coast SA*
Cuna (Kuna) *Mesoamerica*
Cuniba *Amazon Basin*
Cupaca *Andes*
Cupeno *Far West NA*
Curripaco *Orinoco Basin*
Curuminaca *Amazon Basin*
Cusco *Andes*
Cuyapaipe *Far West NA*
Cyclades *S Europe*
Cymry (Welsh) *N Europe*
Cypriots *C Europe*
Czechs *C Europe*

D
Daarood *E Africa*
Daba *W Africa*
Dafla *S Asia*
Dagaba (Dagarti) *W Africa*
Dagada *SE Asia*
Dagamba (Dagomba) *W Africa*
Dagara (Dogara) *W Africa*
Dagarti (Dagaba) *W Africa*
Dagestani *Caucasus*
Dagomba (Dagbamba) *W Africa*
Daguru *E Africa*
Dahalo *E Africa*
Dahm *Middle East*
Dahomey (Fon) *W Africa*
Dai *E Asia*
Daii *Australia*
Dailu *E Asia*
Daina *E Asia*
Dainggati *Australia*
Daiomoni *Melanesia*
Dakota *Plains NA*
Dakota Tipi *Plains NA*
Dakwa *C Africa*
Dal *S Asia*
Dalabon *Australia*
Dalla *Australia*
Dalleburra *Australia*
Dalles (Ochiicha-gwe'babigo'ining) *Northeast NA*
Dalmatians *C Europe*
Dama *S Africa*
Damani *Middle East*
Damara (Herero) *S Africa*
Dambara *W Africa*
Damergu *N Africa*

Damura *Melanesia*
Dan *W Africa*
Danakil (Afar) *E Africa*
Danda *S Africa*
Danes *N Europe*
Dangani *Australia*
Dangbon *Australia*
Danggali *Australia*
Dangu *Australia*
Dani *Melanesia*
Dani *Amazon Basin*
Danisan *S Africa*
Darab Khani *Middle East*
Darambal *Australia*
Darasa *E Africa*
Darawa *Amazon Basin*
Darazi *Middle East*
Dard *C Asia*
Dargin *Caucasus*
Daria *Mesoamerica*
Daribi *Melanesia*
Darkinjang *Australia*
Darrehshuri *C Asia*
Dars *N Africa*
Daru *Middle East*
Daruk *Australia*
Darusar *Middle East*
Darwa *N Africa*
Darwin *Australia*
Datab *W Africa*
Daur *E Asia*
Dayak *SE Asia*
Daza *N Africa*
De *W Africa*
Dea *Melanesia*
Deang (Benglong) *E Asia*
Decherda *N Africa*
Dehi Hazaras *C Asia*
Dehwar *Middle East*
Delaware *Plains NA*
Delaware Muncie *Plains NA*
Denca *Polynesia*
Dendi *W Africa*
Dene *Subarctic*
Dene Tha' *Plains NA*
Deori *S Asia*
Deresa *E Africa*
Dern *Melanesia*
Derong *E Asia*
Dersimili *Caucasus*
Desana *Amazon Basin*
Deti *S Asia*
Dewa *Melanesia*
Dey *W Africa*
Dhakar *S Asia*
Dhanka *S Asia*
Dhodia *S Asia*
Dhurwa *S Asia*
Diaguita *Andes*
Diakui *Australia*
Dialonke *W Africa*
Dianbo *E Asia*
Diankhanke *W Africa*
Dibeyat *N Africa*
Dida *W Africa*
Didi *Caucasus*
Didinga *E Africa*
Diegueno *Far West NA*

Dieri *Australia*
Dietko *W Africa*
Digil *E Africa*
Digiri *E Africa*
Digo *E Africa*
Digueno *Mesoamerica*
Dikgale *S Africa*
Dimasa *S Asia*
Dine (Navajo) *SW NA*
Dinka *E Africa*
Diola (Jola) *W Africa*
Dioula *W Africa*
Dir *E Africa*
Dirityangura *Australia*
Disko *Arctic*
Divehi *S Asia*
Djaberadjabera *Australia*
Djagada *N Africa*
Djagaraga *Australia*
Djakunda *Australia*
Djalakuru *Australia*
Djalendi *Australia*
Djamindjung *Australia*
Djangu *Australia*
Djankun *Australia*
Djara *Australia*
Djargudi *Australia*
Djaru *Australia*
Djauan *Australia*
Djaui *Australia*
Djerait *Australia*
Djerimanga *Australia*
Djerma *W Africa*
Djilamatang *Australia*
Djinang *Australia*
Djinba *Australia*
Djiringanj *Australia*
Djiru *Australia*
Djirubal *Australia*
Djiwali *Australia*
Djowei *Australia*
Djuka *Orinoco Basin*
Djungun *Australia*
Dobu *Melanesia*
Dodos (Dodoth) *E Africa*
Dodoth (Dodos) *E Africa*
Dogara (Dagara) *W Africa*
Doglas *Caribbean*
Dogon *W Africa*
Dogorda *N Africa*
Dogrib *Subarctic*
Dokis *Northeast NA*
Doko *C Africa*
Dolgan *Arctic*
Doma (Mvura, VaDema) *S Africa*
Domu *Melanesia*
Dondo *C Africa*
Dong *E Asia*
Dongo *E Africa*
Dongxiang *E Asia*
Dorazai *Middle East*
Dorla Gond *S Asia*
Dorobo (Okiek) *E Africa*
Dorobura *Australia*
Doromba *W Africa*

Dou Menia *N Africa*
Doubla *S Asia*
Doukhobors *Northwest Coast NA*
Doura *Melanesia*
Dravidian *S Asia*
Drukpas *S Asia*
Drung *E Asia*
Druze *Middle East*
Duala *C Africa*
Duan *SE Asia*
Duane *SE Asia*
Dubla *S Asia*
Ducie *Polynesia*
Duduroa *Australia*
Dukkala *N Africa*
Dulong (Qui) *E Asia*
Duma *C, S Africa*
Dumu *Melanesia*
Duna *Melanesia*
Dungans *C Asia*
Durrani *C Asia*
Duruma *E Africa*
Dusun *SE Asia*
Dutch *W Europe*
Duulngari *Australia*
Duwala *Australia*
Duwamish *Northwest Coast NA*
Duwasir *Middle East*
Duzdgah *Middle East*
Dxeriku *S Africa*
Dyula *W Africa*
Dzayul *C Asia*
Dzheks *Caucasus*

E
E'napa (Panare) *Orinoco Basin*
Eabametoong *Northeast NA*
East Greenlanders *Arctic*
East Hupa *Far West NA*
East Indians *Caribbean*
East Shoshoni *Plains NA*
Easter Islanders (Rapa Nui) *Polynesia*
Eastern Cherokee *Southeast NA*
Eastern Chickahominy *Southeast NA*
Eastern Lamoot *Arctic*
Eastern Penan *SE Asia*
Eastern Pequot *Northeast NA*
Eastern Shawnee *Plains NA*
Ebidoso *Central SA*
Echota Cherokee *Southeast NA*
Edisto *Southeast NA*
Edo *W Africa*
Efe *C Africa*
Efik *W Africa*
Egba *W Africa*
Egedesminde *Arctic*
Ehatteshaht

Northwest Coast NA
Eipo *Melanesia*
Ekagi *Melanesia*
Ekoi (Yako) *W Africa*
Ekonda *C Africa*
El Arbaa *N Africa*
Elato *Micronesia*
Elem Pomo *Far West NA*
Eliptamin *Melanesia*
Elko Te Moak *Great Basin NA*
Elmolo *E Africa*
Ely Shoshone *Great Basin NA*
Embera *Mesoamerica*
Embu *E Africa*
Emerillon *Amazon Basin*
Emon *Australia*
Encabellado *Amazon Basin*
Endenese *SE Asia*
Endo (Keiyo) *E Africa*
Enets *Arctic*
Enga *Melanesia*
Engganese *SE Asia*
English *N Europe*
Enoch Cree *Plains NA*
Entiat *Northwest Coast NA*
Eora *Australia*
Erawirung *Australia*
Erema *Melanesia*
Eri *Australia*
Erigpactsa *Amazon Basin*
Ermineskin *Plains NA*
Erukala *S Asia*
Escoumains *Northeast NA*
Esele *C Africa*
Eshira *C Africa*
Eskasoni *NE NA*
Eskimo *Arctic*
Esmeralda *Andes*
Esquimalt *Northwest Coast NA*
Esselen *Far West NA*
Essipit *Northeast NA*
Estonians *E Europe*
Eta (Burakumin) *E Asia*
Etchaottine *Northwest Coast NA*
Eton *C Africa*
Etoro *Melanesia*
Etowah Cherokee *Southeast NA*
Etsako *W Africa*
Eudeve *Mesoamerica*
Euro Caribbean *Caribbean*
Even (Lamut) *Arctic*
Evenk (Tungus) *Arctic*
Evenki (Northern Tungus) *Arctic, E Asia*
Ewamin *Australia*
Ewe *W Africa*
Ewenki *E Asia*
Eyak *Arctic*
Eyle *E Africa*

F
Fajelu *E Africa*
Fakfak *Melanesia*
Falasha (Beta Israel) *E Africa*
Fali *W Africa*
Fang *C, W Africa*
Fante *W Africa*
Fanti *W Africa*
FaEroese *N Europe*
Farsi Madan *C Asia*
Farsiwan *C Asia*
Fasu *Melanesia*
Faur *Melanesia*
Fausa *W Africa*
Fawakhir *N Africa*
Fawayid *N Africa*
Feramin *Melanesia*
Fergusson Islanders *Melanesia*
Fezzan *N Africa*
Fijians *Melanesia*
Filipinos *SE Asia*
Fingo *S Africa*
Finns *N Europe*
Fipa *E Africa*
Flathead *Plateau NA*
Flemish *W Europe*
Foi *Melanesia*
Fokeng *S Africa*
Foll *Melanesia*
Fon (Dahomey) *W Africa*
Fore *Melanesia*
Formosans (Hakka, Min) *E Asia*
Fox *Plains NA*
French *W Europe*
Frisians *W Europe*
Friulians *S Europe*
Fuegians *Patagonia*
Fugon *W Africa*
Fukiens *E Asia*
Fulani (Fulbe, Peul) *W Africa*
Fulbe (Fulani, Peul) *W Africa*
Fulnio *Amazon Basin*
Fumbu *C Africa*
Fur *N Africa*
Furiiru *C Africa*
Futunans *Polynesia*
Fuyughe *Melanesia*

G
G//ana *S Africa*
G/wi *S Africa*
Ga *W Africa*
Ga Mashpie *W Africa*
Gaari *Australia*
Gabadi *Melanesia*
Gabbra *E Africa*
Gabou *C Africa*
Gabrieleno *Far West NA*
Gabrielino Tongvah *Far West NA*
Gadaba *S Asia*
Gadaboursis *E Africa*
Gaddang *SE Asia*
Gade *W Africa*
Gadjalivia *Australia*
Gadjerong *Australia*
Gadoa *N Africa*
Gadsup *Melanesia*

Gadudjara *Australia*
Gaelic Scots
N Europe
Gaels *N Europe*
Gaferut *Micronesia*
Gagadju *Australia*
Gagauz *E Europe*
Gagu *W Africa*
Gahukugama
Melanesia
Gaidemoe *Melanesia*
Gainj *Melanesia*
Gaiwa *Melanesia*
Galago *Australia*
Galeva *Melanesia*
Galibi (Caribs)
Orinoco Basin
Galicians *W Europe*
Galla (Oromo)
E Africa
Gambalang *Australia*
Gambier Islanders
Polynesia
Gamit *S Asia*
Gammatti *Australia*
Gamo *E Africa*
Gamta *S Asia*
Gananwa
(Mmalebogo) *S
Africa*
Ganda *E Africa*
Gandangara
Australia
Gandju *Australia*
Ganeang *Australia*
Gangulu *Australia*
Gaosazhu (Yuan-
zhumin) *E Asia*
Gaoshan *E Asia*
Garadjeri *Australia*
Garasia *S Asia*
Garia *Melanesia*
Garia *S Asia*
Garifuna
Mesoamerica
Garo *S Asia*
Gasim *Middle East*
Gaspe *Northeast NA*
Gaurna *Australia*
Gavioes *Amazon
Basin*
Gawa *Melanesia*
Gawari *S Asia*
Gayo *SE Asia*
Gayon *Orinoco Basin*
Gbande *W Africa*
Gbari *W Africa*
Gbaya (Baya) *C Africa*
Gbugble *W Africa*
Gcoika *S Africa*
Ge *W Africa*
Geawegal *Australia*
Gebusi *Melanesia*
Gelamai *Australia*
Gelao (Gelo) *E Asia*
Gelo (Gelao) *E Asia*
Gen *W Africa*
Gende *Melanesia*
Georgians *Caucasus*
German Swiss
W Europe
Germans *W Europe*
Gesgapegiag
Northeast NA
Ghalji *C Asia*

Ghamid *Middle East*
Ghanzi *S Africa*
Ghegs *S Europe*
Ghorbat *C Asia*
Ghurghusht Pathans
C Asia
Gia *Australia*
Giabal *Australia*
Giai (Nung, Whang)
SE Asia
Gibe *E Africa*
Gien *W Africa*
Gikuyu *E Africa*
Gilaki *C Asia*
Gilambabura *Australia*
Gilbert Islanders
(Kiribati) *Micronesia*
Giliu *W Africa*
Gimi *Melanesia*
Gimira *E Africa*
Gimr *N Africa*
Ginoogaming
Northeast NA
Gio *W Africa*
Giravaru *S Asia*
Giriama *E Africa*
Gishu *E Africa*
Gisu (Bagisu) *E Africa*
Gitanmaax *Northwest
Coast NA*
Gitksan *Northwest
Coast NA*
Gitlakdamix
*Northwest Coast
NA*
Gitsegukla *Northwest
Coast NA*
Gitwangak *Northwest
Coast NA*
Gitwinksihlkw
*Northwest Coast
NA*
Gitxsan *Northwest
Coast NA*
Gjelli *C Africa*
Glen Vowell
*Northwest Coast
NA*
Gnau *Melanesia*
Goa *Australia*
Goan *S Asia*
Goat *Subarctic*
Godthiaab *Arctic*
Goeng *Australia*
Gofa *E Africa*
Gog *Melanesia*
Gogada *Australia*
Gogo *E Africa*
Gogodala *Melanesia*
Goklen Turkomen *C
Asia*
Gola *W Africa*
Gond *S Asia*
Gonja *W Africa*
Goodenough Islanders
Melanesia
Gooniyandi *Australia*
Goreng *Australia*
Gorindji *Australia*
Goroka *Melanesia*
Gorontalense
(Gorontalo) *SE Asia*
Gorontalo (Gorontal-
ense) *SE Asia*
Gorotire *Amazon
Basin*

Gorowa *E Africa*
Goshute (Gosiute)
Great Basin NA
Gosiute (Goshute)
Great Basin NA
Goto *Caribbean
Coast SA*
Gounda *N Africa*
Gourmantche
W Africa
Gouro *W Africa*
Gouroa *N Africa*
Gowa *S Africa*
Grasia *S Asia*
Grebo *W Africa*
Greek Cypriots
S Europe
Greeks *S Europe*
Greenlanders *Arctic*
Grigua *S Africa*
Gringai *Australia*
Gros Ventre *Plains
NA*
Grusi *W Africa*
Gu *W Africa*
Guachichile
Mesoamerica
Guadalcanal Islanders
(Kaoka) *Melanesia*
Guaharibo *Orinoco
Basin*
Guahibo *Orinoco
Basin*
Guaica *Orinoco Basin*
Guaimaro *Caribbean*
Guaipuave *Orinoco
Basin*
Guaiqueri *Caribbean
Coast SA*
Guaitaca *Central SA*
Guaja *Amazon Basin*
Guajajara *Amazon
Basin*
Guajiro (Wayuu)
*Caribbean Coast
SA*
Guamahaya
Caribbean
Guamar *Mesoamerica*
Guambiano *Andes*
Guan *W Africa*
Guana *Central SA*
Guanachahibe
Caribbean
Guanacoa *Andes*
Guanebucan *Carib-
bean Coast SA*
Guaniguanico
Caribbean
Guarani *Central SA*
Guarategaya
Amazon Basin
Guarayo (Chiriguano)
Andes
Guarequena *Orinoco
Basin*
Guariba (Nadobo)
Amazon Basin
Guarijio *Mesoamerica*
Guarine (Palenque)
Orinoco Basin
Guarini *Central SA*
Guarna *Australia*
Guasave
Mesoamerica

Guato *Central SA*
Guaya *Amazon Basin*
Guayabero *Orinoco
Basin*
Guayaki (Ache) *Andes*
Guayana *Central SA*
Guayape *Amazon
Basin*
Guaymi (Ngawbe)
Mesoamerica
Guaytaca *Central SA*
Guennakin (Puelche)
Central SA
Guenoa *Central SA*
Guerandi *Central SA*
Guere *W Africa*
Gueren *Amazon
Basin*
Guerno *Australia*
Guetare
Mesoamerica
Guidar *W Africa*
Guiziga *W Africa*
Gujar *S Asia*
Gujarati *S Asia*
Gulay *C Africa*
Gulngai *Australia*
Gumuz *E Africa*
Gunavidji *Australia*
Gunditjmara
Australia
Gungorogone
Australia
Guni *Melanesia*
Gunwinggu *Australia*
Gurage *E Africa*
Gurama *Australia*
Gurindji *Australia*
Gurkha *S Asia*
Gurma *W Africa*
Gurmanche *W Africa*
Guro *W Africa*
Guru *E Africa*
Gurung *S Asia*
Gurunsi *W Africa*
Gururumba
Melanesia
Gusii *E Africa*
Gutsuls *E Europe*
Gwandara *W Africa*
Gwe *E Africa*
Gwich'in *Subarctic*
Gwini *Australia*
/Gwoachu *S Africa*
Gypsies (Roma)
Europe

H
Hre (Hre) *SE Asia*
Ha *E Africa*
Ha Nhy (Ha nhi)
SE Asia
Ha nhi (Ha Nhy)
SE Asia
Hadya *E Africa*
Hadza (Hadzabe)
E Africa
Hadzabe (Hadza)
E Africa
Hadzapi *E Africa*
Hagwilget *Northwest
Coast NA*
Hai//om *S Africa*
Haida *Northwest
Coast NA*

Hainna *SE Asia*
Haisla *Northwest
Coast NA*
Hakavona *S Africa*
Hakka (Formosans,
Min) *E Asia*
Halakwulup (Alacaluf)
Patagonia
Halalt *Northwest
Coast NA*
Halang Doan
SE Asia
Haliwa *Southeast NA*
Haliwa Saponi
Southeast NA
Halkomelem
(Cowichan)
*Northwest Coast
NA*
Halmahera *SE Asia*
Hamar *N Africa*
Hambukushu *S Africa*
Hamiyan *N Africa*
Han *Subarctic*
Han *E Asia*
Hanamana *Caribbean*
Hananwa *S Africa*
Haneragmiut *Arctic*
Hani *E Asia*
Haningayogmiut
Arctic
Hanunoo *SE Asia*
Hanya *S Africa*
Harabi *N Africa*
Harado *Melanesia*
Harari *E Africa*
Harasis *Middle East*
Harb *Middle East*
Hare *Subarctic*
Harvaqtormiut
Arctic
Hasa *Middle East*
Hashid *Middle East*
Hasinai *Southeast NA*
Hassaluru *S Asia*
Hassanamisco
Nipmuc *Northeast
NA*
Hassananli
Caucasus
Hattadare *Southeast
NA*
Hatteras Tuscarora
Southeast NA
Haudenosaunee
(Iroquois) *Northeast
NA*
Haue *Orinoco Basin*
Hausa *W Africa*
Haush *Patagonia*
Haut *C Africa*
Havana *Caribbean*
Havasupai *Southwest
NA*
Haw (Ho) *SE Asia*
Hawaiians (Kanaka
Maoli) *Polynesia*
Hawawir *N Africa*
Haweitat *N Africa*
Hawiye *E Africa*
Haya *E Africa*
Hazara *C Asia*
Hehe *E Africa*
Heiltsuk *Northwest
Coast NA*

Helong *SE Asia*
Hemba *C Africa*
Henga *E Africa*
Henkison *Polynesia*
Henya *Northwest
Coast NA*
Herero (Damara)
S Africa
Hesquiaht *Northwest
Coast NA*
Hesseque *S Africa*
Heta (Xeta) *Central
SA*
Hevero (Jebero)
Amazon Basin
Hewa *Melanesia*
Hezhen *E Asia*
Hiawatha Ojibway
Northeast NA
Hibito *Andes*
Hidatsa *Plains NA*
Hiechware *S Africa*
Highland Maya
Mesoamerica
Highland Scots
N Europe
Hijra *S Asia*
Hiligaynon *SE Asia*
Hill Veedan *S Asia*
Hilleri *Australia*
Hima *E Africa*
Himba *S Africa*
Hitnu *Orinoco Basin*
Hiwi *Orinoco Basin*
Hixkaryana *Amazon
Basin*
Hlengwe *S Africa*
Hlubi *S Africa*
Hmar *S Asia*
Hmong (Meo, Miao,
Mong, Tai) *S, SE
Asia*
Ho *W Africa*
Ho (Haw) *SE Asia*
Hoanya *SE Asia*
Hodh *W Africa*
Hoh *Northwest Coast
NA*
Hokkien *E Asia*
Holikachuk
Subarctic
Holoholo *C Africa*
Holsteins Borg
Arctic
Honibo *Melanesia*
Hoonah *Northwest
Coast NA*
Hopewell *Northeast
NA*
Hopi *Southwest NA*
Hopi Tewa *Southwest
NA*
Hornepayne
Northeast NA
Hoti *Orinoco Basin*
Hottentots (Khoi,
Khokhoi) *S Africa*
Houlton Maliseet
Northeast NA
Houma *Southeast NA*
Hozayl *Middle East*
Hre (H. Re) *SE Asia*
Hroy *S Africa*
Htin (T'in, Thin) *SE
Asia*

Hu *E Asia*
‡Hua *S Africa*
Hua *Melanesia*
Huacho *Andes*
Hualapai *Southwest NA*
Huambisa *Amazon Basin*
Huambo *Andes*
Huanca *Andes*
Huancabamba *Andes*
Huancavilca *Andes*
Huanuco *Andes*
Huaorani (Auca, Wao, Waorani) *Amazon Basin*
Huarayo *Amazon Basin*
Huarpe *Andes*
Huastec (Wasteko) *Mesoamerica*
Huave *Mesoamerica*
Huaylas *Andes*
Hubabo *Caribbean*
Huchnom *Far West NA*
Huddan *Middle East*
Huereo *Caribbean*
Hui *E Asia*
Huichol *Mesoamerica*
Huilliche *Andes*
Huitoto (Witoto) *Amazon Basin*
Hukwe *S Africa*
Hula *Melanesia*
Huli *Melanesia*
Humptulips *Northwest Coast NA*
Humr *C Africa*
Humum *Middle East*
Hungarians (Magyars) *C Europe*
Hungaros *W Europe*
Hunzakuts (Burusho) *C Asia*
Hupa *Far West NA*
Hupda *Amazon Basin*
Huran Potawatomi *Northeast NA*
Huron *Northeast NA*
Hurons Wendat *Northeast NA*
Huruthse *S Africa*
Hutaim *Middle East*
Hutterites *Northwest, Plains NA*
Hutu *C, E Africa*
Huu ay aht *Northwest Coast NA*
Hwaduba *S Africa*

I

Iadino *Mesoamerica*
Iatmul *Melanesia*
Ibaloi *SE Asia*
Iban *SE Asia*
Ibanag *SE Asia*
Ibenama *Amazon Basin*
Ibibio *W Africa*
Ibn Amir *Middle East*
Ica *Caribbean Coast SA*
Icelanders *N Europe*
Ichkilik *C Asia*

Idindji *Australia*
Idoma *W Africa*
Ife Ilesha *W Africa*
Ifugao *SE Asia*
Ifuluk *Micronesia*
Igara *W Africa*
Igbira *W Africa*
Igbo (Ibo) *W Africa*
Igidlorssuit *Arctic*
Iglulik Eskimos *Arctic*
Ignaciano *Amazon Basin*
Igneri *Caribbean Coast SA*
Igorot (Kankanay) *SE Asia*
Ijaw *W Africa*
Ijebu *W Africa*
Ijo *W Africa*
Ik *E Africa*

Ika *W Africa*
Ikung *S Africa*
Ila *S Africa*
Ilanon *SE Asia*
Ilba *Australia*
Ildawongga *Australia*
Iliaura *Australia*
Illinois *Northeast NA*
Ilocano *SE Asia*
Ilongo *SE Asia*
Ilongot *SE Asia*
Ilsaven (Shahsevan) *Caucasus*
Imaklimuit *Arctic*
Imazighen (Berbers) *N Africa*
Imraguen *N Africa*
Inahukwa *Amazon Basin*
Inaja *Far West NA*
Inan Iu *Middle East*
Inawongga *Australia*
Indjibandi *Australia*
Ingalik *Subarctic*
Ingano *Amazon Basin*
Inggarda *Australia*
Ingilos *Caucasus*
Inguklimiut *Arctic*
Ingurua *Australia*
Ingush *Caucasus*
Iningai *Australia*
Injibandi *Australia*
Inkjinandi *Australia*
Innu *Subarctic*
Innu Mamit Innuat *Northeast NA*
Inqua *S Africa*
Inuit *Arctic*
Inupiat *Arctic*

Inuvialuit *Arctic*
Ione Miwok *Far West NA*
Iowa *Plains NA*
Ipai *Far West NA*
Ipeca *Amazon Basin*
Ipili *Melanesia*
Ipurina *Amazon Basin*
Iquito *Amazon Basin*
Iramba *E Africa*
Irangi *E Africa*
Iranxe *Amazon Basin*
Iraqw *E Africa*
Iraya *SE Asia*
Irianese *SE Asia*
Irifiyen *N Africa*
Irish *N Europe*
Iroquois (Haudenosaunee) *Northeast NA*
Irukandii *Australia*

Irula (Irulu) *S Asia*
Irular *S Asia*
Irulu (Irula) *S Asia*
Isaaq *E Africa*
Isconahua *Amazon Basin*
Isertormeeq *Arctic*
Ishan *W Africa*
Ishinde *S Africa*
Ishkashimi *C Asia*
Isinay *SE Asia*
Iskut *Northwest Coast NA*
Iskutewizaagegan *Northeast NA*
Island Tlingit *Subarctic*
Isleta *Plains NA*
Isleta Pueblo *Southwest NA*
Islington (Wabasseemoong) *Northeast NA*
Ismailis *Middle East*
Isneg *SE Asia*
Isobei *Melanesia*
Issaks *E Africa*
Issas *E Africa*
Isukha *E Africa*
Ita Eskimo *Arctic*
Italian Swiss *W Europe*
Italians *S Europe*
Itelmen *Subarctic*
Itene (More) *Amazon Basin*
Itenm'i *Arctic*
Iteseo *E Africa*
Iteso *E Africa*

Ithu *Australia*
Itivimiut *Arctic*
Itneg *SE Asia*
Itogapuk *Amazon Basin*
Itonama *Amazon Basin*
Itsekiri *W Africa*
Ittu *E Africa*
Itza *Mesoamerica*
Iukagir *Arctic*
Ivori *Melanesia*
Iwa *E Africa*
Iwaidja *Australia*
Ixil *Mesoamerica*
Izhmi *N Europe*
Izoceno *Central SA*

J

Jaadwa *Australia*
Jaako *Australia*

Jaara *Australia*
Jaburara *Australia*
Jacaltec *Mesoamerica*
Jacobshavn *Arctic*
Jadgal *Middle East*
Jadira *Australia*
Jadliaura *Australia*
Jagalingu *Australia*
Jagara *Australia*
Jagua *Caribbean*
Jah Hut *SE Asia*
Jahai *SE Asia*
Jahanka *W Africa*
Jain *S Asia*
Jaitmathang *Australia*
Jakalteko *Mesoamerica*
Jakun *SE Asia*
Jalanga *Australia*
Jaluit *Micronesia*
Jama *SE Asia*
Jama Mapun *SE Asia*
Jambina *Australia*
Jaminawa *Amazon Basin*
Jamshidi *C Asia*
Jamul *Far West NA*
Janambre *Mesoamerica*
Janda *Australia*
Jandruwanta *Australia*
Jangaa *Australia*
Jangga *Australia*
Janggal *Australia*
Jangizai Maid *Middle East*
Jangman *Australia*

Jani Kahn *Middle East*
Janjero *E Africa*
Janjula *Australia*
Jankundjara *Australia*
Jano *Plains NA*
Japanese *E Asia*
Jarai *SE Asia*
Jaraldi *Australia*
Jarijari *Australia*
Jarildekald *Australia*
Jaroinga *Australia*
Jarowair *Australia*
Jarso *E Africa*
Jaru *Amazon Basin*
Jarwas *S Asia*
Jat *C Asia*
Jat *C, S Asia*
Jatav *S Asia*
Jathaikana *Australia*
Jauapery *Orinoco Basin*
Jaudjibaia *Australia*
Jauf *Middle East*
Jaunsari *S Asia*
Jauraworka *Australia*
Javahe (Karaja) *Amazon Basin*
Javanese *SE Asia*
Jawabis *N Africa*
Jawony *Australia*
Jawuru *Australia*
Jebero (Hevero) *Amazon Basin*
Jeidji *Australia*
Jeithi *Australia*
Jekri *W Africa*
Jeliendi *Australia*
Jemez Pueblo *Southwest NA*
Jena Choctaw *Southeast NA*
Jenu *S Asia*
Jerawa *W Africa*
Jeteneru *Australia*
Jetimarala *Australia*
Jiarong *E Asia*
Jibana *E Africa*
Jibranli *Caucasus*
Jicaque (Tolupan, Torrupanes) *Mesoamerica*
Jicarilla Apache *Southwest NA*
Jie *E Africa*
Jiegera *Australia*
Jiji *E Africa*
Jilngali *Australia*
Jiman *Australia*
Jing *E Asia*
Jingpo (Kachin) *E, S, SE Asia*
Jinigudira *Australia*
Jino *E Asia*
Jinwum *Australia*
Jirajara *Caribbean Coast SA*
Jirandali *Australia*
Jirjoront *Australia*
Jita *E Africa*
Jitajita *Australia*
Jivaro (Shuar) *Amazon Basin*

Jocome *Plains NA*
Jogula *Australia*
Jokula *Australia*
Jola (Diola) *W Africa*
Jongga *Australia*
Jongn *E Africa*
Jopadhola *E Africa*
Jotijota *Australia*
Jova *Mesoamerica*
Ju/'hoansi (Kung) *S Africa*
Juaneno *Far West NA*
Juang *S Asia*
Juat *Australia*
Juhainah *Middle East*
Juipera *Australia*
Jukambal *Australia*
Jukambe *Australia*
Jukul *Australia*
Jukun *W Africa*
Julaolinja *Australia*
Julianehaab *Arctic*
Jumanos *Mesoamerica*
Jumu *Australia*
Junggor *Australia*
Jungkurara *Australia*
Junin *Andes*
Junuba *Middle East*
Jupagalk *Australia*
Jupangati *Australia*
Jur *C Africa*
Jurassians *W Europe*
Juru *Australia*
Juruna *Amazon Basin*
Juula *W Africa*

K

K'iche' (Quiche) *Mesoamerica*
Ka'wiari *Amazon Basin*
Kaapor (Urubu) *Amazon Basin*
Kaba *C Africa*
Kababish *N Africa*
Kabalbara *Australia*
Kabardin *Caucasus*
Kabikabi *Australia*
Kabishi *Amazon Basin*
Kabora *Amazon Basin*
Kabre *W Africa*
Kabui *S Asia*
Kabula *E Africa*
Kabyles *N Africa*
Kachari *S Asia*
Kachi *S Asia*
Kachin (Jingpo) *E, S, SE Asia*
Kadar *S Asia*
Kadazan *SE Asia*
Kadiweu *Central SA*
Kadjerong *Australia*
Kadohadacho *Plains NA*
Kadu *E Asia*
Kafa *E Africa*
Kafima *S Africa*
Kafiri *S Asia*
Kagwahiv *Amazon Basin*
Kah Bay Kah Nong (Warroad

> ### Men singe termites and lizards get rich.
>
> ZANDE PROVERB, CENTRAL AFRICA

Chippewa) *Plains NA*
Kahkewistahaw *Plains NA*
Kahnawake *Northeast NA*
Kai *Melanesia*
Kaiabara *Australia*
Kaiadilt *Australia*
Kaiba Paiute *Great Basin NA*
Kaigani *Northwest Coast NA*
Kaimbi *Melanesia*
Kaingang *Central SA*
Kaiowa *Central SA*
Kairi *Australia*
Kaititia *Australia*
Kajang *SE Asia*
Kajars *C Asia*
Kaka *C Africa*
Kakadu *Australia*
Kakhetians *Caucasus*
Kakoli *Melanesia*
Kakwa *C Africa*
Kalaako *Australia*
Kalaallit *Arctic*
Kalabari *W Africa*
Kalabra *Melanesia*
Kalagan *SE Asia*
Kalakuts *E Europe*
Kalali *Australia*
Kalamaia *Australia*
Kalanga *S Africa*
Kalanke *W Africa*
Kalapalo *Amazon Basin*
Kalasha *C Asia*
Kalenjin *E Africa*
Kalibal *Australia*
Kalibamu *Australia*
Kalibugan *SE Asia*
Kalinga *SE Asia*
Kalispel *Plateau NA*
Kalkadunga *Australia*
Kallawaya *Andes*
Kalmyks (Western Mongols) *C Asia*
Kalo *SE Asia*
Kaluli *Melanesia*
Kam Mou (Kammu, Khmu, Kmhmu) *SE Asia*
Kamabe *E Africa*
Kamanga *E Africa*
Kamayura *Amazon Basin*
Kamba *E Africa*
Kambata *E Africa*
Kambure *Australia*
Kambuwal *Australia*
Kameraigal *Australia*
Kamilaroi *Australia*
Kamloops *Northwest Coast NA*
Kammu (Kam Mou, Khmu, Kmhmu) *SE Asia*
Kamor *Australia*
Kamoro *Melanesia*
Kamsa *Andes*
Kamse *Middle East*
Kamtanga *E Africa*
Kana *W Africa*

Kanaka Maoli (Hawaiians) *Polynesia*
Kanaks *Melanesia*
Kanarese *S Asia*
Kanbi *S Asia*
Kandju *Australia*
Kandyans *S Asia*
Kaneang *Australia*
Kanembou *W Africa*
Kanesatake *NE NA*
Kang *E Asia*
Kangalas *Arctic*
Kangamiut *Arctic*
Kangatsiak *Arctic*
Kangerd *Arctic*
Kanghiryuarmiut *Arctic*
Kanghiryuatjiagmiut *Arctic*
Kangulu *Australia*
Kanichana *Andes*
Kanidji *Australia*
Kaniok *C Africa*
Kanithlua *Northeast NA*
Kanjar *S Asia*
Kanjobal (Q'anjob'al) *Mesoamerica*
Kankanay (Igorot) *SE Asia*
Kannada *S Asia*
Kanolu *Australia*
Kansa *Plains NA*
Kanum *W Africa*
Kanum Anim *Melanesia*
Kanuri *W Africa*
Kaoka (Guadalcanal Islanders) *Melanesia*
Kapau *Melanesia*
Kapauku *Melanesia*
Kapawe'no *Plains NA*
Kapchepkendi *E Africa*
Kapechene *Amazon Basin*
Kapingamarangi *Micronesia*
Kaplelach *E Africa*
Kapore *Melanesia*
Kapsiki *W Africa*
Kapu *S Asia*
Kaqchikel (Cakchiquel) *Mesoamerica*
Karabi *Middle East*
Karachai *Caucasus*
Karadjeri *Australia*
Karago *W Africa*
Karaites *E Europe*
Karaja (Javahe) *Amazon Basin*
Karajak *Arctic*
Karakalpaks *C Asia*
Karakatchans *E Europe*
Karaman *Australia*
Karamojong *E Africa*
Karanga *S Africa*
Karanguru *Australia*
Karanja *Australia*
Karankawa *Mesoamerica*

Karawa *Australia*
Kare *C Africa*
Kareldi *Australia*
Karelian Izhars *Arctic*
Karen *SE Asia*
Karendala *Australia*
Karenggapa *Australia*
Kariara *Australia*
Karihona *Orinoco Basin*
Karina *Orinoco Basin*
Karingbal *Australia*
Karinni *SE Asia*
Karipuna *Amazon Basin*
Karmali *S Asia*
Karok *Northwest Coast NA*
Karranga *N Africa*
Karretijie *S Africa*
Karthians *Caucasus*
Kartudjara *Australia*
Karunbura *Australia*
Karuwali *Australia*
Kashechewan *Northeast NA*
Kashia Pomo *Far West NA*
Kashinawa *Amazon Basin*
Kashmiri *S Asia*
Kashubians *C Europe*
Kaska *Subarctic*
Kaskaskia *Northeast NA*
Kaskinampo *Southeast NA*
Kasseng *SE Asia*
Kassonke *W Africa*
Kasua *Melanesia*
Kasuiana *Orinoco Basin*
Kataligamut *Arctic*
Kate *Melanesia*
Kathlamet *Northwest Coast NA*
Kathodi *S Asia*
Kati *Melanesia*
Kato *Far West NA*
Kattang *SE Asia*
Kattunaickens *S Asia*
Katu *SE Asia*
Katubanut *Australia*
Kauma *E Africa*
Kaurareg *Australia*
Kaurna *Australia*
Kavango *S Africa*
Kaviagmut *Arctic*
Kavinenya *Andes*
Kavirondo *E Africa*
Kaw *Plains NA*
Kaw (Aka, Ko) *SE Asia*
Kawacatoose *Plains NA*
Kawadji *Australia*
Kawahiwa *Orinoco Basin*
Kawahla *N Africa*
Kawaib *Amazon Basin*
Kawaiisu *Far West NA*
Kawambarai *Australia*
Kawchottine *Arctic*

Kaweah *SE NA*
Kaxuyana *Amazon Basin*
Kayabi *Amazon Basin*
Kayah (Red Karen) *SE Asia*
Kayakhs *SE Asia*
Kayan *SE Asia*
Kayapo (Xikrin) *Amazon Basin*
Kayong *SE Asia*
Kayuvava *Amazon Basin*
KazakhS (Qazaq) *C, E Asia*
Kazanis *E Europe*
Kedang *SE Asia*
Kedayan *SE Asia*
Kede *S Africa*
Kederu *E Africa*
Kee Way Win *Northeast NA*
Keechi *Plains NA*
Keeseekoose *Plains NA*
Keeseekoowenin *Plains NA*
Keetoowah Cherokee *Plains NA*
Kefa *E Africa*
Kehewin Cree *Plains NA*
Kei Islands *Melanesia*
Keiadjara *Australia*
Keinjan *Australia*
Keiyo (Endo) *E Africa*
Kekchi (Q'eqchi) *Mesoamerica*
Kel Air *N Africa*
Kela *Melanesia*
Kelabit *SE Asia*
Kele *C Africa*
Keliko *C Africa*
Kembata *E Africa*
Kenai *Arctic*
Kenoy *SE Asia*
Kensia *SE Asia*
Kensiu *SE Asia*
Kenyah *SE Asia*
Kepkiriwat *Amazon Basin*
Kerabi *Melanesia*
Keraki *Melanesia*
Keramai *Australia*
Keres *Plains NA*
Keres Pueblo *Southwest NA*
Kerewe *E Africa*
Kerintji *SE Asia*
Ketagalan *SE Asia*
Kete *C Africa*
Kewa *Melanesia*
Key *Plains NA*
Kgakga *S Africa*
Kgalagadi *S Africa*
Kgatla *S Africa*
Kha Me (Khmer) *SE Asia*
Khabyls *N Africa*
Khakasi *C Asia*
Khalka *E Asia*
Khamseh *Middle East*
Khan *C Asia*
Khanty *Subarctic*

!Khara *S Africa*
Kharia *S Asia*
Khasi *S Asia*
Khawar *S Asia*
Khawlan Al Akiya *Middle East*
Khazara *C Asia*
Kheni *S Africa*
Khevsur *Caucasus*
Khinalughs *Caucasus*
Khirgis *C Asia*
Khitar *Middle East*
Khmer (Kha Me) *SE Asia*
Khmer Loeu *SE Asia*
Khmu (Kam Mou, Kammu, Kmhmu) *SE Asia*
Khoi (Hottentots, Khokhoi) *S Africa*
Khoja *C, S Asia*
Khokhoi (Hottentots, Khoi) *S Africa*
Khond *S Asia*
Khorin *E Asia*
Khowari *S Asia*
Khua *SE Asia*
Khumi *Middle East*
Khuze *S Africa*
Kialegee Creek *Plains NA*
Kibenel *Melanesia*
Kickapoo *Plains NA*
Kieltai *Plains NA*
Kiga *E Africa*
Kigiktagmiut *Arctic*
Kikapu *Mesoamerica*
Kikitarmiut *Arctic*
Kikuyu *E Africa*
Kil *SE Asia*
Kilenge *Melanesia*
Kilii (Aweer, Somali Boni) *E Africa*
Kiliwa (Quiligua) *Mesoamerica*
Killinermiut *Arctic*
Killtinhunmiut *Northeast NA*
Kilusiktogmiut *Arctic*
Kimbu *E Africa*
Kinaraya *SE Asia*
Kincolith *Northwest Coast NA*
Kinda *Middle East*
Kinga *E Africa*
Kingnaitmiut *Arctic*
Kinistin *Plains NA*
Kiniyen *Australia*
Kinka *C Africa*
Kintag *SE Asia*
Kinugumint *Arctic*
Kiowa *Plains NA*
Kiowa Apache (Plains Apache) *Plains NA*
Kiowiai *Melanesia*
Kipawa *Northeast NA*
Kipchornwonek *E Africa*
Kipsang'any' *E Africa*
Kipsigis *E Africa*
Kiratis *S Asia*
Kirdi *W Africa*
Kirgiz (Qyrghyz) *E Asia*

Kiribati (Gilbert Islanders) *Micronesia*
Kiritimati Islanders (Christmas Islanders) *Polynesia*
Kirm *W Africa*
Kirrae *Australia*
Kisar *SE Asia*
Kispiox *Northwest Coast NA*
Kissi *W Africa*
Kita *Melanesia*
Kitabal *Australia*
Kitamaat *Northwest Coast NA*
Kitanemuk *Far West NA*
Kitara (Bunyoro, Nyoro) *E Africa*
Kitcisakik *Northeast NA*
Kitigan Zibi Anishinabeg *Northeast NA*
Kitja *Australia*
Kitselas *Northwest Coast NA*
Kitsua *Andes*
Kitsumkalum *Northwest Coast NA*
Kiwai *Melanesia*
Klallam *Northwest Coast NA*
Klamantan *SE Asia*
Klamath *Plateau NA*
Kluane *Arctic*
Kmhmu (Kam Mou, Kammu, Khmu) *SE Asia*
!Ko (!Xoo) *S Africa*
Ko (Aka, Kaw) *SE Asia*
Koa *Australia*
Koaka *Melanesia*
Koakir (Awa Kwaiker) *Andes*
Koamu *Australia*
Koara *Australia*
Koaratira *Amazon Basin*
Koasati *Southeast NA*
Kobewa (Cubeo) *Amazon Basin*
Kodi *SE Asia*
Koenpal *Australia*
Kofan *Amazon Basin*
Kofyar *W Africa*
Kogi (Cagaba) *Caribbean Coast SA*
Kogluktogmiut *Arctic*
Kohistani *C Asia*
Koho *SE Asia*
Koiari *Melanesia*
Koinjmal *Australia*
Koita *Melanesia*
Kokama *Amazon Basin*
Kokangol *Australia*
Kokatja *Australia*
Koki *E Africa*
Kokna *S Asia*
Koko *Australia*
Kokobididji *Australia*

Kokobujundji *Australia*
Kokoimudji *Australia*
Kokojawa *Australia*
Kokojekodi *Australia*
Kokojelandji *Australia*
Kokokulunggur *Australia*
Kokomini *Australia*
Kokopatun *Australia*
Kokoperia *Australia*
Kokorda *N Africa*
Kokowalandja *Australia*
Kokowara *Australia*
Kokraimoro *Amazon Basin*
Koksoakuiut *Northeast NA*
Kol *S Asia*
Kola *C Africa*
Kolakngat *Australia*
Kolam *S Asia*
Kole *W Africa*
Koli *S Asia*
Kolisuch'ok *E Asia*
Kom *C, W Africa*
Kombaingheri *Australia*
Kombe *C Africa*
Kombobura *Australia*
Komi *E Europe*
Komolom *Melanesia*
Konai *Melanesia*
Kond *S Asia*
Konda *Melanesia*
Kone *S Africa*
Konejandi *Australia*
Kongabula *Australia*
Kongalu *Australia*
Kongkandji *Australia*
Kongo *C Africa*
Koniagui *W Africa*
Konith Lushuamiut *Northeast NA*
Konjo *E Africa*
Konkan *S Asia*
Konkomba *W Africa*
Konkow *Far West NA*
Konkubura *Australia*
Kono *W Africa*
Konso *E Africa*
Konyak (Nagas) *S Asia*
Koobe *Melanesia*
Koochiching *Northeast NA*
Koorie *Australia*
Kootenai (Kutenai) *NW Coast NA*
Kopar *Melanesia*
Kora *Melanesia*
Korana *S Africa*
Koranko *W Africa*
Koreans *E Asia*
Korekore *S Africa*
Koreng *Australia*
Korenggoreng *Australia*
Korewahe *Andes*
Koriki *Melanesia*
Korindji *Australia*
Korku *S Asia*

Koro *W Africa*
Korwa *S Asia*
Koryak *Arctic*
Kosrae Islanders *Micronesia*
Kota *C Africa*
Kota *S Asia*
Kotandji *Australia*
Kougni *C Africa*
Kounta *W Africa*
Kouyou *C Africa*
Koya *S Asia*
Koyukon *Subarctic*
Kpando *W Africa*
Kpe *C Africa*
Kpelle *W Africa*
Krahn *W Africa*
Kraho *Amazon Basin*
Kramo *Melanesia*
Kran *W Africa*
Krauatungalung *Australia*
Kreda *N Africa*
Kreenakaroke *Amazon Basin*
Kreish *C Africa*
Krene *Orinoco Basin*
Kriashen Tatars *E Europe*
Krikati *Amazon Basin*
Krim *W Africa*
Krjashen *E Europe*
Krobob *W Africa*
Krou *W Africa*
Kru *W Africa*
Kruan *W Africa*
Krung *SE Asia*
Kry *SE Asia*
Kua *S Africa*
Kuba *C Africa*
Kubachins *Caucasus*
Kubenkrankein *Amazon Basin*
Kubor *Melanesia*
Kubu *SE Asia*
Kueretu *Amazon Basin*
Kuhgalu *C Asia*
Kui *SE Asia*
KuikurA *Amazon Basin*
Kuinmurbura *Australia*
Kuitsh *Northwest Coast NA*
Kujai *Australia*
Kukabrak (Narrinyeri, Ngarrindjeri, Yaraldi) *Australia*
Kukatja *Australia*
Kukparungmiut *Arctic*
Kuku *C Africa*
Kukuruku *W Africa*
Kula *Australia*
Kulaman *SE Asia*
Kulin *Australia*
Kulumali *Australia*
Kuma *Melanesia*
Kuman *E Africa*
Kumbainggiri *Australia*
Kumbu *W Africa*
Kumeyaay *Far West NA*

Kumyk *Caucasus*
Kuna (Cuna) *Mesoamerica*
Kunaguasaya *Caribbean Coast SA*
Kunama *E Africa*
Kunbi *S Asia*
Kunfel *E Africa*
Kung (Ju/'hoansi) *S Africa*
Kungadutji *Australia*
Kungarakan *Australia*
Kunggara *Australia*
Kunggari *Australia*
Kungkalenja *Australia*
Kunimaipa *Melanesia*
Kunindiri *Australia*
Kunini *Melanesia*
Kunja *Australia*
Kupangese *SE Asia*
Kupchaks *C Asia*
Kurama *C Asia*
Kurds *Middle East*
Kureinji *Australia*
Kuria *E Africa*
Kurnai *Australia*
Kurnandaburi *Australia*
Kurripako *Orinoco Basin*
Kurtatchi *Melanesia*
Kurumbas *S Asia*
Kurung *Australia*
Kuruya *Orinoco Basin*
Kusase *W Africa*
Kusso *Southeast NA*
Kutchin *Subarctic*
Kutenai (Kootenai) *Northwest Coast NA*
Kutial *Australia*
Kutjala *Australia*
Kutswe *S Africa*
Kutu *E Africa*
Kutzadikaa *Great Basin NA*
Kuungkari *Australia*
Kuvalan *SE Asia*
Kuvale *S Africa*
Kuy (Co Sung, Lahu) *SE Asia*
Kuyani *Australia*
Kvens *N Europe*
Kwa Wa Aineuk *Northwest Coast NA*
Kwahu *W Africa*
Kwaio *Melanesia*
Kwajalein *Micronesia*
Kwakiutl (Kwakwaka'wakw) *Northwest Coast NA*
Kwakwaka'wakw (Kwakiutl) *Northwest Coast NA*
Kwamatwi *S Africa*
Kwandu *S Africa*
Kwangali *S Africa*
Kwangare *S Africa*
Kwankhwala *C Africa*

Kwantari *Australia*
Kwanyama *S Africa*
Kwarandji *Australia*
Kware *Melanesia*
Kwatkwat *Australia*
Kwayhquitlum *Northwest Coast NA*
Kwena *S Africa*
Kwengo *S Africa*
Kwepe *S Africa*
Kwera *S Africa*
Kwere *E Africa*
Kwiakah *Northwest Coast NA*
Kwiambal *Australia*
Kwicksutaineuk Ah Kwaw Ah Mish *Northwest Coast NA*
Kwinti *Orinoco Basin*
Kwisi *S Africa*
Kwoma *Melanesia*
Kxoe (Makwengo) *S Africa*
Kyaka *Melanesia*
Kyerepong *W Africa*
Kyuquot *Northwest Coast NA*

L
La *W Africa*
La Ve *SE Asia*
La Ven *SE Asia*
La Vy *SE Asia*
Labbai *S Asia*
Labu *SE Asia*
Labwor *E Africa*
Lacandon *Mesoamerica*
Ladakhi *S Asia*
Ladin *S Europe*
Laguna Pueblo *Southwest NA*
Lagunero *Mesoamerica*
Laheiwat (Safaiha) *Middle East*
Lahiwapa *Melanesia*
Lahu (Co Sung, Kuy) *SE Asia*
Laia *Australia*
Laiapo *Melanesia*
Lak *Melanesia*
Lak *Caucasus*
Laka *C Africa*
Laka *E Africa*
Lakahis *Melanesia*
Lakalai *Melanesia*
Lakalzap *Northwest Coast NA*
Lakandon *Mesoamerica*
Lake Northwest *Coast NA*
Lakher *SE Asia*
Laki *SE Asia*
Lakmiut *Northwest Coast NA*
Lakota Sioux (Teton Sioux) *Plains NA*
Lala *C Africa*
Lali *C Africa*
Lalundwe *C Africa*
Lalung *S Asia*

Lama *E Asia*
Lamaholot *SE Asia*
Lamba *E Asia*
Lambadi *S Asia*
Lambayeque *Andes*
Lambya *E Africa*
Lamet *SE Asia*
Lamisto *Andes*
Lamotrek *Micronesia*
Lamut (Even) *Arctic*
Landogo (Loko) *W Africa*
Landuma *W Africa*
Langamar *Melanesia*
Langi *E Africa*
Lango *E Africa*
Lanima *Australia*
Lano *E Asia*
Lanoh *SE Asia*
Lao Isan (Thai Lao) *SE Asia*
Lao Loum *SE Asia*
Lao Soung *SE Asia*
Lao Theung *SE Asia*
Lapps (Sami) *N Europe*
Laragia *Australia*
Larakia *Australia*
Larantuka *SE Asia*
Lardiil *Australia*
Larteh *W Africa*
Lashi *E Asia*
Lassik *Far West NA*
Lati *E Asia*
Latjilatji *Australia*
Latvians *E Europe*
Lavongai *Melanesia*
Lawa (Lua) *SE Asia*
Lax Kw'alaams *Northwest Coast NA*
Laz *Middle East*
Lebe *W Africa*
Lebou *W Africa*
Leco *Amazon Basin*
Lega *C Africa*
Lele (Bashilele) *C Africa*
Lembu *S Africa*
Lemkos (Carpatho Ukrainians) *C Europe*
Lemkos *E Europe*
Lenca *Mesoamerica*
Lendu *C Africa*
Lengola *C Africa*
Lengua *Central SA*
Lenje *S Africa*
Leonese *W Europe*
Lepanto (Sagada Igorot) *SE Asia*
Lepcha *S Asia*
Lese *C Africa*
Lesu *Melanesia*
Leti *SE Asia*
Leu (Lue) *SE Asia*
Leya *S Africa*
Leyte *SE Asia*
Lezgins *Caucasus*
Lheit Lit'en *NW Coast NA*
Lhoba *S Asia*
Lhomi *E Asia*
Lhuya (Bugusu, Luyia) *E Africa*

Li *E Asia*
Liard *Northwest Coast NA*
Libido *E Africa*
Likouala *C Africa*
Lillooet *Plateau NA*
Limba *W Africa*
Limbang *SE Asia*
Limbu *S Asia*
Lingayat *S Asia*
Lionese *SE Asia*
Lipan Apache *Southwest NA*
Lipe *Andes*
Listuguj *Northeast NA*
Lisu *E, SE Asia*
Lisum *SE Asia*
Lithuanians *E Europe*
Little Lake *Plateau NA*
Little Russians (Ukrainians) *E Europe*
Little Saskatchewan *Plains NA*
Little Shuswap *Northwest Coast NA*
Litvins *E Europe*
Lo Lo *SE Asia*
Lobedu *S Africa*
Lobi *W Africa*
Lod *C Asia*
Lodagaba *W Africa*
Logauleng *Melanesia*
Logo *C Africa*
Logoli *E Africa*
Lohara *S Asia*
Loinang *SE Asia*
Loko (Landogo) *W Africa*
Lokono *Orinoco Basin*
Loma *W Africa*
Lomami *C Africa*
Lomwe *E Africa*
Long Plain *Plains NA*
Loridja *Australia*
Loritcha *Australia*
Losso *W Africa*
Lotiga *Australia*
Lotuko *E Africa*
Loven *SE Asia*
Lower Brule Sioux *Plains NA*
Lower Chinook *Northwest Coast NA*
Lower Creek *Southeast NA*
Lower Elwha Klallam *Northwest Coast NA*
Lower Kootenay *Northwest Coast NA*
Lower Muskogee Creek *Southeast NA*
Lower Nicola *North-west Coast NA*
Lower Similkameen *Northwest Coast NA*

Lower Sioux *Plains NA*
Lower Umpqua *Northwest Coast NA*
Lowiili *W Africa*
Lowland Maya *Mesoamerica*
Lowland Scots *N Europe*
Lowwe *E Africa*
Loyality Islanders *Melanesia*
Lozi *S Africa*
Lu *SE Asia*
Lua (Lawa) *SE Asia*
Luano *S Africa*
Luapula *C Africa*
Luba *C Africa*
Lubale (Lwena) *S Africa*
Lue (Leu) *SE Asia*
Luena *C Africa*
Lufa *Melanesia*
Lugat *SE Asia*
Lugbara *E Africa*
Lugsiatsiak *Arctic*
Luhya *E Africa*
Luilang *SE Asia*
Luimbe *C Africa*
Luiseno *Far West NA*
Lukshuamiut *Northeast NA*
Lule *Central SA*
Lulua *C Africa*
Lumad *SE Asia*
Lumbee *Southeast NA*
Lummi *Northwest Coast NA*
Lunda *C Africa*
Lungga *Australia*
Lungu *C Africa*
Luntu *C Africa*
Luo *E Africa*
Lupaca *Andes*
Lur *Middle East*
Lur *C Asia*
Lurabunna *Australia*
Lushai (Mizo) *S Asia*
Lushange *S Africa*
Luyia (Bugusu, Lhuya) *E Africa*
Lwena (Lubale) *S Africa*
Lyangalile *E Africa*
Lytton Pomo *Far West NA*

M
Ma *SE Asia*
Ma'aza *N Africa*
Maanyan *SE Asia*
Mabinza *C Africa*
Macassarese *SE Asia*
Macedonian *S Europe*
Machia Lower Creek *Southeast NA*
Machiguenga (Matsigenka) *Amazon Basin*
Machis Creek *Southeast NA*
Mackinac *NENA*

Macorize *Caribbean*
Macuna *Amazon Basin*
Mada *W Africa*
Madang *SE Asia*
Madawaska Maliseet *Northeast NA*
Madeirans *W Europe*
Madhhij *Middle East*
Madi *E Africa*
Madiri *Melanesia*
Madjandji *Australia*
Madngela *Australia*
Madoitja *Australia*
Madurese *SE Asia*
Maduwongga *Australia*
Mae *Melanesia*
Mafulu *Melanesia*
Magar *S Asia*
Magatige *Australia*
Magh (Marmas) *S Asia*
Magnetawan *Northeast NA*
Magon *S Africa*
Maguana *Caribbean*
Maguindanao *SE Asia*
Maguzawa *W Africa*
Magyars (Hungarians) *C Europe*
Mahafaly *E Africa*
Mahar *S Asia*
Maharashta (Maratha) *S Asia*
Mahei *E Africa*
Mahi *W Africa*
Mahican (Mohican) *Northeast NA*
Mahmeri *SE Asia*
Mahra *Middle East*
Mahura *S Africa*
Maia *Australia*
Maiawali *Australia*
Maid *Middle East*
Maidu *Far West NA*
Maijabi *Australia*
Maikudunu *Australia*
Maikulan *Australia*
Mailu *Melanesia*
Maisin *Melanesia*
Maithakari *Australia*
Maiva *Melanesia*
Maji *E Africa*
Majuro *Micronesia*
Maka *Central SA*
Makaa *C Africa*
Makah *Northwest Coast NA*
Makassar *SE Asia*
Makhanya *S Africa*
Makianese *SE Asia*
Makiewahin *Melanesia*
Makin *Micronesia*
Makiritare (Yekuana) *Orinoco Basin*
Makka *C Africa*
Maklew *Melanesia*
Mako *C Africa*
Mako (Maku) *Amazon Basin*
Makoma (Bamakoma) *S Africa*
Makonde *E Africa*

Makong *SE Asia*
Makoua *C Africa*
Maku (Mako) *Amazon Basin*
Makua *E Africa*
Makuna *Amazon Basin*
Makushi *Orinoco Basin*
Makwa Sahgaiehcan *Plains NA*
Makwengo (Kxoe) *S Africa*
Malagasy *E Africa*
Malaita Islanders *Melanesia*
Malantji *Australia*
Malay (Bumiputra) *SE Asia*
Malayalam *S Asia*
Malayali *S Asia*
Malayo *Caribbean Coast SA*
Malecites *Northeast NA*
Maleku *Mesoamerica*
Malekula *Melanesia*
Malemiut *Arctic*
Malgana *Australia*
Malgaru *Australia*
Mali *Melanesia*
Malinke (Manding) *W Africa*
Maliseet *Northeast NA*
Maljangapa *Australia*
Malngin *Australia*
Malnkanidji *Australia*
Maloh *SE Asia*
Maltese *S Europe*
Mam *Mesoamerica*
Mamaleleqala Qwe Qwa Sot Enox *Northwest Coast NA*
Mamanua *SE Asia*
Mamassani *Middle East*
Mamboe (Mbowe) *S Africa*
Mambwe *E Africa*
Mamean *Mesoamerica*
Mamikons *Melanesia*
Mamprusi *W Africa*
Mamu *Australia*
Mamumba *W Africa*
Man (Mien, Yao) *SE Asia*
Manadra *W Africa*
Manala *S Africa*
Manam *Melanesia*
Manao *Amazon Basin*
Manar *C Asia*
Manasi *Amazon Basin*
Manawan *Northeast NA*
Manchu *E Africa*
Manda *E Africa*
Mandak *Melanesia*
Mandan *Plains NA*
Mandandanji *Australia*
Mandara *Australia*
Mandarese *SE Asia*
Mandari *C Africa*

Mandaya *SE Asia*
Mande (Mandinka) *W Africa*
Mandi *Australia*
Mandika *W Africa*
Manding (Malinke) *W Africa*
Mandinka (Mande) *W Africa*
Mandja *C Africa*
Mandjildjara *Australia*
Mandjindja *Australia*
Mandyak *W Africa*
Mang *E Asia*
Mangala *Australia*
Mangarai *Australia*
Mangareva *Polynesia*
Mangaridji *Australia*

Mangarrayi *Australia*
Mangbetu *C Africa*
Manggarai *SE Asia*
Mangyan *SE Asia*
Manhuy *Central SA*
Manie *Melanesia*
Maniema *C Africa*
Manihiki *Polynesia*
Manipos *Andes*
Manja *C Africa*
Mankanya *W Africa*
Manmit *E Asia*
Mano *W Africa*
Manobo *SE Asia*
Mansi *Subarctic*
Mansim *Melanesia*
Mansoanka *W Africa*
Manta *Andes*
Mantions *Melanesia*
Manus *Melanesia*
Manuvu *SE Asia*
Manx *N Europe*
Manyika *S Africa*
Manzanita *Far West NA*
Maonan *E Asia*
Maopityan *Orinoco Basin*
Maori *Polynesia*
Mapounou *C Africa*
Mappila *S Asia*
Mapuche *Andes*
Maputa *S Africa*
Maquindanao *SE Asia*
Mara *Australia*
Maragatos *W Europe*
Maranao *SE Asia*
Maranganji *Australia*
Maratha (Maharashtra) *S Asia*

Marathi *S Asia*
Marati *S Asia*
Maraura *Australia*
Marawa *Amazon Basin*
Marazig *N Africa*
Marditjali *Australia*
Mardudjara *Australia*
Mardudunera *Australia*
Mariamo *Australia*
Mariana Islanders *Micronesia*
Maricopa *SW NA*
Maridan *Australia*
Maridjabin *Australia*
Marien *Caribbean*
Marijedi *Australia*

Marimanindji *Australia*
Marinahua *Amazon Basin*
Marind Anim *Melanesia*
Maring *Melanesia*
Maringar *Australia*
Marinunggo *Australia*
Maris (Cheremis) *E Europe*
Marisi *Caribbean*
Marithiel *Australia*
Mariu *Australia*
Mariusa *Caribbean Coast SA*
Mariwunda *Australia*
Marka *W Africa*
Marlgu *Australia*
Marmas (Magh) *S Asia*
Maroni Carib *Orinoco Basin*
Maronites *Middle East*
Marquesas Islanders *Polynesia*
Marrago *Australia*
Marrakwet *E Africa*
Marshallese *Micronesia*
Maru *E Asia*
Marubo *Amazon Basin*
Marulta *Australia*
Marungu *C Africa*
Masa'id *Middle East*
Masai *E Africa*
Masbatemo *SE Asia*
Mascoy *Amazon Basin*

Mashantucket Pequot *Northeast NA*
Mashco *Amazon Basin*
Mashi *S Africa*
Mashpee Wampanoag *Northeast NA*
Masikoro *E Africa*
Masset Haida *Northwest Coast NA*
Matachewan *Northeast NA*
Mataco *Central SA*
Matagalpa *Mesoamerica*
Matakam *W Africa*
Matawai *Orinoco Basin*
Match c be nash she wish Pottawatomi *Northeast NA*
Matengo *E Africa*
Mathabathe *S Africa*
Mathias Colomb *Plains NA*
Matlazinca *Mesoamerica*
Matsigenka (Matsigenka) *Amazon Basin*
Mattagami *Northwest NA*
Mattaponi *SE NA*
Mattole *Far West NA*
Matuntara *Australia*
Mau *W Africa*
Maue (Mawe) *Amazon Basin*
Maundan *W Africa*
Maung *Australia*
Mawe (Maue) *Amazon Basin*
Maxakali *Central SA*
Maxinje *C Africa*
May *SE Asia*
Maya *Mesoamerica*
Mayaguez *Caribbean*
Maylayali *S Asia*
Mayo *Mesoamerica*
Mayop *Orinoco Basin*
Mayoruna *Amazon Basin*
Mazahua *Mesoamerica*
Mazandarani *C Asia*
Mazatec *Mesoamerica*
Mazhi *E Africa*
Mazidi *Middle East*

Mba *E Africa*
Mbaka *C Africa*
Mbala *C Africa*
Mbam *W Africa*
Mbanderu *S Africa*
Mbata *C Africa*
Mbay *C Africa*
Mbeere *E Africa*
Mbegua *Central SA*
Mberenzabi *C Africa*
Mbete *C Africa*
Mbewum *Australia*
Mbo *C Africa*
Mboko *W Africa*
Mbonggu *Melanesia*
Mboshi (Boubangi)
    C Africa
Mboum *W Africa*
Mbowe (Mamboe)
    S Africa
Mbudja *C Africa*
Mbui *C Africa*
Mbukushu *S Africa*
Mbum *C Africa*
Mbunda (Bamileke)
    S Africa
Mbundu *S Africa*
Mbunga *E Africa*
Mbuti (Bambuti)
    C Africa
Mbwei *Melanesia*
Mbwela *S Africa*
Mbwera *S Africa*
Mbya *Central SA*
Mdewakanton
    Dakota *Plains NA*
Me Wuk *Far West
    NA*
Meanambu
    Melanesia
Medzan *C Africa*
Meena *S Asia*
Meganin *N Africa*
Megarha *N Africa*
Megiar *Melanesia*
Meherrin *Southeast
    NA*
Mehinaku *Amazon
    Basin*
Mehni *Middle East*
Meintangk *Australia*
Mejbrat *Melanesia*
Mekeo *Melanesia*
Mekranoti *Amazon
    Basin*
Mekwa *S Africa*
Melabugan *SE Asia*
Melanau *SE Asia*
Melates *Caribbean*
Melochundum
    Tolowa *Far West
    NA*
Melpa *Melanesia*
Membertou
    Northeast NA
Mende *W Africa*
Mendi *Melanesia*
Mendrio *SE Asia*
Mendriq *SE Asia*
Menghua *E Asia*
Mennonites *Plains
    NA*
Menominee
    Northeast NA
Mentawai *SE Asia*

Mentaweian *SE Asia*
Menthajangal
    Australia
Menya *Melanesia*
Meo (Hmong, Miao,
    Mong, Tai) *S,
    SE Asia*
Meriam (Murray
    Islanders) *Australia*
Merina *E Africa*
Meru *E Africa*
Mesa Grande
    Far West NA
Mescalero Apache
    Southwest NA
Meshki/Osman Turks
    (Meskhetians) *C
    Asia*
Meskhetians (Os-
    man/Meshki Turks)
    C Asia
Methow *Northwest
    Coast NA*
Metis *Subarctic*
Metoac *Northeast
    NA*
Metoko *C Africa*
Mextitlaneca
    Mesoamerica
Meyach *Melanesia*
Mfengu *S Africa*
Miami *Plains NA*
Mian *Australia*
Miana *C Asia*
Miao (Hmong, Meo,
    Mong, Tai) *S, SE
    Asia*
Miawpukek
    Northeast NA
Miccosukee
    Southeast NA
Michigamea *Plains
    NA*
Michikamau
    Northeast NA
Michipicoten
    Northeast NA
Micmac (Mikmac)
    Northeast NA
Middle Sepik River
    Peoples *Melanesia*
Midob *N Africa*
Mien (Man, Yao)
    SE Asia
Miji *S Asia*
Mijikenda (Nyika)
    E Africa
Mikea *E Africa*
Mikir *S Asia*
Mikisew Cree *Plains
    NA*
Mikmac (Micmac)
    Northeast NA
Mikud *Melanesia*
Mikwok *Far West NA*
Millcayac *Andes*
Milpulko *Australia*
Milpulo *Australia*
Mimika *Melanesia*
Mimungkum
    Australia
Min (Hakka,
    Formosans) *E Asia*
Mina *S Asia*
Minahasa *SE Asia*

Minang *Australia*
Minangkabau
    SE Asia
Mingan *Northeast
    NA*
Mingendi *Melanesia*
Mingin *Australia*
Mingrelian *Caucasus*
Minjambuta *Australia*
Minjungbal *Australia*
Minnesota Chippewa
    Plains NA
Minuane *Central SA*
Minung *Australia*
Minyong *S Asia*
Miri (Mishming) *S
    Asia*
Miring *Australia*
Miriwung *Australia*
Mirning *Australia*
Mishars *E Europe*
Mishkeegogamang
    Northeast NA
Mishming (Miri) *S
    Asia*
Mishulundu *S Africa*
Miskito (Mosquitos)
    Mesoamerica
Missanabe Cree
    Northeast NA
Mississauga
    Northeast NA
Mississippi
    Anishinabe *Plains
    NA*
Mississippi Choctaw
    Southeast NA
Missouri *Plains NA*
Mistawasis *Plains NA*
Mistissini *Northeast
    NA*
Mitaka *Australia*
Mitjamba *Australia*
Mittu *C Africa*
Miwa *Australia*
Miwok *Far West NA*
Mixe *Mesoamerica*
Mixtec *Mesoamerica*
Miyanmin *Melanesia*
Mizo (Lushai) *S Asia*
Mlabri *SE Asia*
Mmalebogo
    (Gananwa) *S Africa*
Mmamabolo *S Africa*
Mnjikaning *Northeast
    NA*
Mnong *SE Asia*
Moando *Melanesia*
Moapa Paiute *Great
    Basin NA*
Moba *W Africa*
Mocha *E Africa*
Mocovi *Central SA*
Modang *SE Asia*
Modeki *Caucasus*
Modoc *Northwest
    Coast NA*
Morotai *SE Asia*
Morowari *Australia*
Mogoboya *S Africa*
Mohave (Mojave)
    Southwest NA
Mohawk *Northeast
    NA*
Mohegan *Northeast
    NA*

Mohican (Mahican)
    Northeast NA
Moinba *E Asia*
Moisie *Northeast NA*
Mojave (Mohave)
    Southwest NA
Mojo *Amazon Basin*
Moken *SE Asia*
Molalla *Northwest
    Coast NA*
Moldovans *E Europe*
Molet e *S Africa*
Moluccans *SE Asia*
Mompox *Caribbean
    Coast SA*
Mon *SE Asia*
Monacan *Southeast
    NA*
Monache *Far West
    NA*
Mondari *E Africa*
Moneton *Southeast
    NA*
Mong (Hmong, Meo,
    Miao, Tai) *SE Asia*
Mongo (Baloulou)
    C Africa
Mongols *E Asia*
Mongondow *SE Asia*
Monguor (Tu) *E Asia*
Moni *Melanesia*
Mono *Far West NA*
Monom *SE Asia*
Monpa *S Asia*
Montagnais
    Northeast NA
Montagnards
    SE Asia
Montana *Plains NA*
Montauk *Northeast
    NA*
Montenegrins
    C Europe
Moolukurumbas
    S Asia
Moorang (Mro,
    Tipura) *S Asia*
Moose Cree
    Northeast NA
Mopan *Mesoamerica*
Mopndomise *S Africa*
Moquegua *Andes*
Moraori *Melanesia*
Moratuc *Southeast
    NA*
Mordovians
    E Europe
Mordvins *C Asia*
More (Itene) *Amazon
    Basin*
Mori *SE Asia*
Moro (Ayoreo)
    Central SA
Morongo *Far West
    NA*
Morotai *SE Asia*
Morowari *Australia*
Moru *C Africa*
Mosakahiken Cree
    Plains NA
Moses *Northwest
    Coast NA*
Moseten *Amazon
    Basin*

Mosopelea
    Southeast NA
Mosquitos (Miskito)
    Mesoamerica
Mossi *W Africa*
Motilones (Yukpa)
    *Caribbean Coast
    SA*
Motu *Melanesia*
Mou Xoe (Museu)
    SE Asia
Moundan *C Africa*
Moundang *W Africa*
Mountain *Subarctic*
Mourdia *N Africa*
Movima *Amazon
    Basin*
Mowa Choctaw
    Southeast NA
Mowachaht
    *Northwest Coast
    NA*
Mphahlele *S Africa*
Mpondo *S Africa*
Mpondomise *S Africa*
Mpongwe *C Africa*
Mro (Moorang,
    Tipura) *S Asia*
Mru *S Asia*
Mtitamba *Australia*
Muchic *Andes*
Muckleshoot
    *Northwest Coast
    NA*
Mudbara *Australia*
Mugharbah *N Africa*
Muhajireen (New
    Sindhi) *C Asia*
Mukjarawaint
    Australia
Muklasa *Southeast
    NA*
Mulam *E Asia*
Mulluk Mulluk
    Australia
Multnomah
    *Northwest Coast
    NA*
Muluridji *Australia*
Mum *W Africa*
Muna *SE Asia*
Muncie *Plains NA*
Munda *S Asia*
Mundu *E Africa*
Mundugumor
    Melanesia
Mundurucu
    Amazon Basin
Mungo *W Africa*
Mungoobra *Australia*
Munkibura *Australia*
Munsee *Northeast
    NA*
Munyabora *Australia*
Muong *SE Asia*
Mur *Polynesia*
Mura *Amazon Basin*
Muragan *Australia*
Murias *S Asia*
Murik *Melanesia*
Murilo *Micronesia*
Murinbata *Australia*
Muringura *Australia*
Murmis *S Asia*

Murngin (Yolngu)
    Australia
Murray Islanders
    (Meriam) *Australia*
Murubura *Australia*
Murunitja *Australia*
Murut *SE Asia*
Muscogee Creek
    Plains NA
Muscowpetung
    Plains NA
Museu (Mou Xoe)
    SE Asia
Muskoday *Plains NA*
Muskogee Creek
    Southeast NA
Muskowekwan *Plains
    NA*
Musqueam
    *Northwest Coast
    NA*
Mutabura *Australia*
Mutair *Middle East*
Muthimuthi *Australia*
Mutjati *Australia*
Mutpura *Australia*
Mutsun (Costanoan)
    Far West NA
Mutumui *Australia*
Muyu *Melanesia*
Muyuw *Melanesia*
Muzeina *Middle East*
Mvura (Doma,
    VaDema) *S Africa*
Mwanga *S Africa*
Mwenyi *S Africa*
Mwera *E Africa*
Mwila *S Africa*
Myene *C Africa*
Mzab *N Africa*

N

Naath (Nuer) *E Africa*
Nabaloi *SE Asia*
Nabesna *Northwest
    Coast NA*
Nabesna *Arctic*
Nacho Nyak Dun
    Subarctic
Nadobo (Guariba)
    Amazon Basin
Nafar *Middle East*
Nagarwapuna
    Melanesia
Nagas (Konyak) *S
    Asia*
Nagot (Yoruba)
    W Africa
Nagyuktogmiut
    Arctic
Nahane *Arctic*
Nahd *Middle East*
Nahua *Mesoamerica*
Nahuatl
    Mesoamerica
Nahuatlato
    Mesoamerica
Naicatchewenin
    Northeast NA
Naichen (Naiken,
    Nayaka) *S Asia*
Naikda *S Asia*
Naiken (Naichen,
    Nayaka) *S Asia*
Nakako *Australia*

Nakanai *Melanesia*
Nakara *Australia*
Nakota Sioux *Plains NA*
Nalu *W Africa*
Nama *S Africa*
Namau *Melanesia*
Nambe Pueblo *Southwest NA*
Nambicuara *Amazon Basin*
Namoluk *Micronesia*
Namonuito *Micronesia*
Nana *Australia*
Nanai *Subarctic*
Nanaians *E Asia*
Nanaimo *Northwest Coast NA*
Nanaticoke *Northeast NA*
Nanaticoke Lenni Lennapes *Northeast NA*
Nanda *Australia*
Nande *C Africa*
Nandi *E Africa*
Nangatadjara *Australia*
Nangatara *Australia*
Nanggikorongo *Australia*
Nanggumiri *Australia*
Nango *Australia*
Nanoose *Northwest Coast NA*
Nanoptaim *Arctic*
Nansemond *Southeast NA*
Nanticoke *Southeast NA*
Nanumba *W Africa*
Napore *E Africa*
Nara *E Africa*
Narak *Melanesia*
Narangga *Australia*
Narene *S Africa*
Narinari *Australia*
Narinyeri *Australia*
Naron *S Africa*
Narragansett *Northeast NA*
Narrinyeri (Kukabrak, Ngarrindjeri, Yaraldi) *Australia*
Narunga *Australia*
Nasioi *Melanesia*
Naskapis *Northeast NA*
Nass Gitksan *Northwest Coast NA*
Natashquan *Northeast NA*
Natchez *Plains NA*
Naualko *Australia*
Nauo *Australia*
Nauruan *Micronesia*
Nauset *Northeast NA*
Nauthars *C Asia*
Nava *Melanesia*
Navajo (Dine) *Southwest NA*
Nawagi *Australia*
Nawash Chippewa *Northeast NA*
Naxi *E Asia*

Nayaka (Naichen, Naiken) *S Asia*
Nayaks *S Asia*
Nayar *S Asia*
Nbomve *C Africa*
Ndali *E Africa*
Ndaonese *SE Asia*
Ndau *S Africa*
Ndebele *S Africa*
Ndembu *C Africa*
Ndenges *C Africa*
Ndere *C Africa*
Ndereko *E Africa*
Ndibu *C Africa*
Ndjiband *Australia*
Ndogo *C Africa*
Ndombe *S Africa*
Ndongo *C Africa*
Ndop *W Africa*
Ndowe *C Africa*
Ndu *C Africa*
Nduga *Melanesia*
Ndundulu *S Africa*
Ndzundza *S Africa*
Nee Tahi Buhn *Northwest Coast NA*
Negidal *Subarctic*
Nekaneet *Plains NA*
Nemadi *N Africa*
Nemaska *Northeast NA*
Nenets (Samoyed) *Arctic*
Nentsy *Arctic*
Nentz *Arctic*
Nepali *S Asia*
Neskonlith *Northwest Coast NA*
Nespelem *Northwest Coast NA*
Nestorians *Middle East*
Netcetumiut *Northeast NA*
Netsilik Eskimos *Arctic*
Neua *SE Asia*
Neusiok *Southeast NA*
Neva *Amazon Basin*
New Caledonians *Melanesia*
New Georgia Islanders *Melanesia*
New Sindhi (Muhajireen) *C Asia*
Newar *S Asia*
Nez Perce *Plateau NA*
Ngada *SE Asia*
Ngadadjara *Australia*
Ngadi *Australia*
Ngadju *SE Asia*
Ngadjunmaia *Australia*
Ngadjuri *Australia*
Ngaiawang *Australia*
Ngaiawongga *Australia*
Ngaku *Australia*
Ngala *Australia*
Ngalakan *Australia*
Ngalea *Australia*
Ngalia *Australia*

Ngalik *Melanesia*
Ngaliwuru *Australia*
Ngalong *S Asia*
Ngalop (Bhota) *S Asia*
Ngaluma *Australia*
Ngamba *Australia*
Ngambwe *S Africa*
Ngameni *Australia*
Nganasan (Nia) *Arctic*
Nganda *Australia*
Ngandangara *Australia*
Ngandi *Australia*
Ngangela *C Africa*
Nganguruku *Australia*
Ngapou *C Africa*
Ngarabal *Australia*
Ngaralta *Australia*
Ngardi *Australia*
Ngardok *Australia*
Ngarigo *Australia*
Ngarinjin *Australia*
Ngarinman *Australia*
Ngarkat *Australia*
Ngarla *Australia*
Ngarlawongga *Australia*
Ngaro *Australia*
Ngarrindjeri (Kukabrak, Narrinyeri, Yaraldi) *Australia*
Ngatatjara *Australia*
Ngathokudi *Australia*
Ngatjara *Australia*
Ngaun *Australia*
Ngawait *Australia*
Ngawbe (Guaymi) *Mesoamerica*
Ngbaka *C Africa*
Ngbandi *C Africa*
Nge *SE Asia*
Ngeh *SE Asia*
Ngemba *Australia*
Ngere *W Africa*
Ngewin *Australia*
Nggamadi *Australia*
Ngindo *E Africa*
Ngintait *Australia*
Ngoborindi *Australia*
Ngoika *S Africa*
Ngolibardu *Australia*
Ngolokwangga *Australia*
Ngomane *S Africa*
Ngombal *Australia*
Ngonde *E Africa*
Ngoni *E Africa*
Ngormbur *Australia*
Ngouan *SE Asia*
Ngugan *Australia*
Ngugi *Australia*
Ngulu *E Africa*
Ngulungbara *Australia*
Ngumbo *E Africa*
Nguna *Melanesia*
Ngunawal *Australia*
Ngundjan *Australia*
Nguni (Xhosa) *S Africa*
Nguoi Kinh (Vietnamese) *SE Asia*
Ngurawola *Australia*
Ngurelban *Australia*

Nguri *Australia*
Ngurlu *Australia*
Ngurunta *Australia*
Ngwaketse *S Africa*
Ngwato *S Africa*
Nhang *E Asia*
Nharo *S Africa*
Nhlangwini *S Africa*
Nhuon (Nyouan) *SE Asia*
Ni Mi Win Ojibwas *Plains NA*
Ni Vanuatu *Melanesia*
Nia (Nganasan) *Arctic*
Niabali *Australia*
Niantic *Northeast NA*
Niasan *SE Asia*
Nibinamik *Northeast NA*
Nicickousemenecaning *Northeast NA*
Nicobarese *S Asia*
Nicomen *Northwest Coast NA*
Nilotes *C Africa*
Nimanburu *Australia*
Ninanu *Australia*
Ningebul *Australia*
Ningerum *Melanesia*
Ningo *W Africa*
Ninzam *W Africa*
Nipmuc *Northeast NA*
Nippising *Northeast NA*
Niquiran *Mesoamerica*
Nisenan *Far West NA*
Nishis *S Asia*
Niska *Northwest Coast NA*
Nisqually *Northwest Coast NA*
Nissan *Melanesia*
Nistrovyans *E Europe*
Niue Islanders *Polynesia*
Nivacle *Central SA*
Nivkh *Subarctic*
Njakinjaki *Australia*
Njamal *Australia*
Njangamarda *Australia*
Njikena *Australia*
Njinin *Australia*
Njulnjul *Australia*
Njunga *Australia*
Njuwathai *Australia*
Nkansi *E Africa*
Nkole (Ankole, Banykole) *E Africa*
Nkomi *C Africa*
Nkosi *S Africa*
Nkoya *S Africa*
Nkumbi *S Africa*
Nkutu *C Africa*
Nngalik *Melanesia*
Noahonirmiut *Arctic*
Noala *Australia*
Noanama *Andes*
Noarma *N Africa*
Nogay *Caucasus*
Nokon *Melanesia*
Nole *E Africa*
Nomlaki *Far West NA*

Nomoi *Micronesia*
Nongait *Australia*
Nongatl *Far West NA*
Nontagnais *Northeast NA*
Noo Wha Ha *Northwest Coast NA*
Nooaitch *Northwest Coast NA*
Nooksack *Northwest Coast NA*
Nootka (Nuu chah nulth aht) *Northwest Coast NA*
Noquet *Northeast NA*
Nor El Muk Wintu *Far West NA*
Norague *Orinoco Basin*
Northeast Alabama Cherokee *Southeast NA*
Northeastern Miami *Northeast NA*
Northeastern Paiute *Great Basin NA*
Northern Cherokee *Northeast NA*
Northern Cheyenne *Plains NA*
Northern Chicamunga Cherokee *Plains NA*
Northern Irish *N Europe*
Northern Islanders *N Europe*
Northern Maidu *Far West NA*
Northern Mono *Far West NA*
Northern Paiute *Plateau NA*
Northern Piegan *Plains NA*
Northern Tehuelche *Central SA*
Northern Tepehuan *Mesoamerica*
Northern Thai (Yuan) *SE Asia*
Northern Tungus (Evenki) *E Asia*
Northwestern Shoshone *Great Basin NA*
Norwegians *N Europe*
Nsenga *E Africa*
Nso *W Africa*
Nsula *N Africa*
Ntwane *S Africa*
Nu *E Asia*
Nuba *E Africa*
Nubians *N Africa*
Nuchatlaht *Northwest Coast NA*
Nuer (Naath) *E Africa*
Nugsuak *Arctic*
Nukak *Amazon Basin*
Nukubura *Australia*
Nukulo *C Africa*
Nukunu *Australia*

Numfor *Melanesia*
Numic *Great Basin NA*
Nunamiut *Arctic*
Nunatagmiut *Arctic*
Nunenumiut *Northeast NA*
Nung (Giai, Whang) *SE Asia*
Nunggubuju *Australia*
Nunukul *Australia*
Nupe *W Africa*
Nuristanis *C Asia*
Nusu *Melanesia*
Nuu chah nulth aht (Nootka) *Northwest Coast NA*
Nuvugmiut *Arctic*
Nuxalk *Northwest Coast NA*
Nya Heun *SE Asia*
Nyaanyadjarra *Australia*
Nyaginyagi *Australia*
Nyakyusa *E Africa*
Nyala *Australia*
Nyamal *Australia*
Nyamb *E Africa*
Nyamwezi *E Africa*
Nyaneka *C Africa*
Nyanga *C Africa*
Nyangamada *Australia*
Nyangbara *E Africa*
Nyanja (Chewa) *S Africa*
Nyaturu *E Africa*
Nyemba *S Africa*
Nyengo *S Africa*
Nyeri *E Africa*
Nygengo *S Africa*
Nyiabali *Australia*
Nyigena *Australia*
Nyiha *E Africa*
Nyika (Mijikenda) *E Africa*
Nyikina *Australia*
Nyinba *S Asia*
Nyining *Australia*
Nyoongah (Nyungah) *Australia*
Nyoro (Bunyoro, Kitara) *E Africa*
Nyouan (Nhuon) *SE Asia*
Nyungah (Nyoongah) *Australia*
Nzakara *C Africa*
Nzima *W Africa*

O

O'Chiese *Plains NA*
O Chi Chak Ko Sipi *Plains NA*
Oatchi *W Africa*
Oaycas *Caribbean Coast SA*
Obedjiwan *Northeast NA*
Obi *SE Asia*
Ocaina *Amazon Basin*
Ocale *Southeast NA*
Occitans *W Europe*
Ochapowace *Plains NA*

Ochiichagwe'babigo'ining (Dalles) *Northeast NA*
Odanak *Northeast NA*
Odawa *Northeast NA*
Odul (Yukaghir) *Arctic*
Ogadein *E Africa*
Ogan Besemah *SE Asia*
Oglala Sioux *Plains NA*
Ogoni *W Africa*
Ohekwe *S Africa*
Ohindo *C Africa*
Ohio Alleghenny *Northeast NA*
Ohlone Muwekma *Far West NA*
Oitbi *Australia*
Ojibwa (Chippewa) *Northeast NA*
Ojman *Middle East*
Ok *Melanesia*
Okanagan *Northwest Coast NA*
Okanese *Plains NA*
Okebo *E Africa*
Okiek (Dorobo) *E Africa*
Okinawans (Ryukyu Islanders) *E Asia*
Okkaliga *S Asia*
Oklewaha Seminole *Southeast NA*
Ola *Australia*
Old Believers *C Asia, E Europe, Northwest NA*
Olkolo *Australia*
Olongbura *Australia*
Omagua *Amazon Basin*
Omaguaca *Central SA*
Omaha *Plains NA*
Ombila *Australia*
Ometo *E Africa*
Omotik *E Africa*
Ona (Selknam) *Patagonia*
Onabasulu *Melanesia*
Ondo *W Africa*
Onegaming Ojibway (Sabaskong) *Northeast NA*
Oneida (Onyota'a:ka) *Northeast NA*
Ongbe *E Africa*
Onge *SE Asia*
Ongkarango *Australia*
Ongkomi *Australia*
Ongona *S Africa*
Onondaga *NE NA*
Ontonagon Chippewa *Northeast NA*
Ontong Java Islanders *Melanesia*
Onyota'a:ka (Oneida) *Northeast NA*

Opaskwayak Cree *Plains NA*
Opata *Mesoamerica*
Opau *Melanesia*
Opaye Shavante *Central SA*
Opetchesaht *Northwest Coast NA*
Opolyans *E Europe*
Ora *W Africa*
Orambul *Australia*
Orang Ambon *SE Asia*
Orang Asli *SE Asia*
Orang Babian *SE Asia*
Orang Darat *SE Asia*
Orang Glai *SE Asia*
Orang Kepor *SE Asia*
Orang Laut *SE Asia*
Orang Lom *SE Asia*
Orang Maluka Selatan *SE Asia*
Orang Mapor *SE Asia*
Orang Melayu *SE Asia*
Orang Rawas *SE Asia*
Orang Timor Asli *SE Asia*
Orang Utan *SE Asia*
Orangkanaq *SE Asia*
Oraon *S Asia*
Orcadians *N Europe*
Orejon (Coto) *Amazon Basin*
Oremano *Orinoco Basin*
Oriots *E Asia*
Oriwa *Melanesia*
Oriya *S Asia*
Ormut *Melanesia*
Ornoray *Caribbean*
Oroche *E Asia*
Orochi *Subarctic*
Orochons *E Asia*
Oroimo *Melanesia*
Orok *Subarctic*
Orokaiva *Melanesia*
Orokolo *Melanesia*
Oromo (Galla) *E Africa*
Oromocto *NE NA*
Oroqen *E Asia*
Orotina *Mesoamerica*
Oru *W Africa*
Osage *Plains NA*
Oser *Melanesia*
Osman/Meshki Turks (Meskhetians) *C Asia*
Osochi *Southeast NA*
Osoyoos *Northwest Coast NA*
Osprey Cherokee *Northeast NA*
Ossetes *Caucasus*
Ostyk (Ket) *Subarctic*
Ot Danom *SE Asia*
Otati *Australia*
Otavalenos *Andes*
Otavalo *W Europe*
Oto *Plains NA*

Otoe Missouria *Plains NA*
Otomac *Orinoco Basin*
Otomi *Mesoamerica*
Ottawa *Northeast NA*
Otuke *Central SA*
Ouachita *Southeast NA*
Ouarsenis *N Africa*
Ouchestigouek *Northeast NA*
Ouiba *Orinoco Basin*
Ouje Bougoumou *Northeast NA*
Oulad Djerir *N Africa*
Oumamiouek *Northeast NA*
Ounie *N Africa*
Ouria *N Africa*
Ovambo (Ambo) *S Africa*
Ovatijimba *S Africa*
Ovimbundu *C Africa*
Owland *C Asia*
Oy *SE Asia*
Oyampi (Wayapi) *Orinoco Basin*
Oyana *Orinoco Basin*
Oybea *Melanesia*
Ozette *Northwest Coast NA*

P

P'u Noi *SE Asia*
Pa Ko *SE Asia*
Pa O *SE Asia*
Pabineau *Northeast NA*
Pacaas Novas *Amazon Basin*
Pacaguara *Amazon Basin*
Pacaja *Amazon Basin*
Pacaje *Andes*
Pacheenaht *NW Coast NA*
Pacific Eskimos (Alutiiq) *Arctic*
Padam *S Asia*
Padaung *SE Asia*
Padebu *W Africa*
Padhola *E Africa*
Padlimiut *Arctic*
Padouca *Plains NA*
Paez *Andes*
Pahari *S Asia*
Pahouin *C Africa*
Pahrump Paiute *Great Basin NA*
Pai *S Africa*
Pai Tavytera *Central SA*
Paikoneka *Amazon Basin*
Paipai (Akwa'ala) *Mesoamerica*
Paiute (Piute) *Great Basin NA*
Paiute Shoshone *Great Basin NA*
Paiwan *E Asia*
Pak Thai (Southern Thai) *SE Asia*

Pakadji *Australia*
Pakaguara *Amazon Basin*
Pakhtun (Pashai, Pashtun, Pathan) *C Asia*
Pakoh Hoe *SE Asia*
Pakua Shipi *Northeast NA*
Pala *Far West NA*
Palauans *Micronesia*
Palaung *SE Asia*
Palawa *Australia*
Palawan *SE Asia*
Palenque (Guarine) *Orinoco Basin*
Palestinians *Middle East*
Palikur *Orinoco Basin*
Paliyan *S Asia*
Pallirmiut *Arctic*
Pallisa *E Africa*
Palouse *Plateau NA*
Palta *Andes*
Palu'e *SE Asia*
Pambia *C Africa*
Pame *Mesoamerica*
Pamiagikuk *Arctic*
Pamirian Tajiks (Pamirians) *C Asia*
Pamirians (Pamirian Tajiks) *C Asia*
Pampangan *SE Asia*
Pamunkey *Southeast NA*
Panag *E Asia*
Panare (E'napa) *Orinoco Basin*

Pancenu *Caribbean Coast SA*
Panche *Andes*
Pandaram *S Asia*
Pande *C Africa*
Pandit *S Asia*
Pandjima *Australia*
Pangan *SE Asia*
Pangasinan *SE Asia*
Pangerang *Australia*
Pangkala *Australia*
Pangwa *E Africa*
Paniyan *S Asia*
Pantagoro *Caribbean Coast SA*
Panzaleo *Andes*
Paoan *E Asia*
Papago (Tohono O'odham) *Southwest NA*
Papel *W Africa*
Papinachos *Northeast NA*

Papua New Guineans (Papuan) *Melanesia*
Papuan (Papua New Guineans) *Melanesia*
Paraitiry *Amazon Basin*
Parakana *Orinoco Basin*
Paramaka *Orinoco Basin*
Paraujano *Caribbean Coast SA*
Pare *E Africa*
Paressi *Amazon Basin*
Paringnoga *Australia*
Pariri *Orinoco Basin*
Parnkalla *Australia*
Paroja *S Asia*
Parsi *S Asia*
Parundji *Australia*
Pascua Yaqui *Southwest NA*
Pase *Amazon Basin*
Pashai (Pakhtun, Pashtun, Pathan) *C Asia*
Pashtun (Pakhtun, Pashai, Pathan) *C Asia*
Pasiegos *W Europe*
Paskenta Nomlaki *Far West NA*
Pasqua *Plains NA*
Passamaquoddy *Northeast NA*
Pasto *Andes*

Patamona *Orinoco Basin*
Patasho *Central SA*
Patelia *S Asia*
Pathan (Pakhtun, Pashai, Pashtun) *C Asia*
Patwin *Far West NA*
Paucatuck Eastern Pequot *Northeast NA*
Paugussett *Northeast NA*
Pauingassi *Plains NA*
Pauishana *Amazon Basin*
Pauma *Far West NA*
Paumari *Amazon Basin*
Pauquachin *NW Coast NA*
Pauserna *Amazon Basin*

Paushiana *Amazon Basin*
Pavagua *Central SA*
Pavivan *S Asia*
Pawaia *Melanesia*
Pawnaka *Amazon Basin*
Pawnee *Plains NA*
Pawumwa *Amazon Basin*
Paya (Pech) *Mesoamerica*
Payanso *Andes*
Pays Plat *Northeast NA*
Pear *SE Asia*
Pech (Paya) *Mesoamerica*
Pechanga *Far West NA*
Peda *W Africa*
Pedi (Sotho) *S Africa*
Pee Dee *Southeast NA*
Peepeekisis *Plains NA*
Peguis *Plains NA*
Pehuenche (Aravcanian) *Andes*
Peigan *Plains NA*
Peki *W Africa*
Peloponnesians *S Europe*
Pembina Chippewa *Plains NA*
Pemon (Taulipang) *Orinoco Basin*
Penan *SE Asia*

Pend d'Oreilles *Northwest NA*
Pende *C Africa*
Penelakut *Northwest Coast NA*
Penobscot *NE NA*
Pensacola *Southeast NA*
Pentecost Islanders *Melanesia*
Peoria *Plains NA*
Pepeha *Melanesia*
Pequot *NE NA*
Perak Jahai *SE Asia*
Peramangk *Australia*
Peranakan *SE Asia*
Pericu *Mesoamerica*
Persians *Middle East*
Petamini *Melanesia*
Petitsikapau *Northeast NA*
Peul (Fulani, Fulbe) *W Africa*

Dance wins a wife but does not keep the house.

DOGON PROVERB, WEST AFRICA

Pewenche *Andes*
Phalaborwa *S Africa*
Phoenix Islanders
  Polynesia
Phoka *E Africa*
Phong *SE Asia*
Phou Noy *SE Asia*
Phou Thay *SE Asia*
Phuan *SE Asia*
Pianokoto *Orinoco*
  Basin
Piapoco *Amazon*
  Basin
Piapot *Plains NA*
Piaroa *Orinoco Basin*
Pibelmen *Australia*
Pic Mobert *Northeast*
  NA
Picayune Chukchansi
  Far West NA
Picunche *Andes*
Picuris Pueblo
  Southwest NA
Piegan *Plains NA*
Piemontese *S Europe*
Pijao *Andes*
Pikangikum *NE NA*
Pikelot *Micronesia*
Pilaga *Central SA*
Pilatapa *Australia*
Pima *Southwest NA*
Pima Bajo
  Mesoamerica
Pinde *C Africa*
Pindiini *Australia*
Pindjarup *Australia*
Pine Creek *Plains NA*
Pingangnaktogmiut
  Arctic
Pini *Australia*
Pinoleville Pomo *Far*
  West NA
Pintubi *Australia*
Pipil *Mesoamerica*
Piqual Sept Shawnee
  Northeast NA
Piraha *Amazon Basin*
Piriou *Orinoco Basin*
Piro *Southwest NA*
Piro *Amazon Basin*
Pisa *Melanesia*
Piscataway *NE NA*
Piscataway Conoy
  Northeast NA
Pisigsarifik *Arctic*
Pit River Tribe *Far*
  West NA
Pitapita *Australia*
Pitcairn *Polynesia*
Pitjantatjara
  Australia
Pitjara *Australia*
Piute (Paiute) *Great*
  Basin NA
Plains Apache (Kiowa
  Apache) *Plains NA*
Plains Cree *Plains NA*
Plawi *W Africa*
Poarch Creek
  Southeast NA
Pocoman
  Mesoamerica
Poconchi
  Mesoamerica
Podzo *E Africa*
Pogoro *E Africa*

Pohey *Caribbean*
Pohlik *Far West NA*
Pohnpei Islanders
  Micronesia
Pohoy *Southeast NA*
Pojoaque Pueblo
  Southwest
Pojulu *E Africa*
Pokagon Potawatomi
  Northeast NA
Pokomam
  Mesoamerica
Pokomo *E Africa*
Pokot (Suk) *E Africa*
Polar Eskimos
  Arctic
Poles *C Europe*
Polishchuk *E Europe*
Pomaks *Middle East*
Pomo *Far West NA*
Pomouik *SE NA*
Ponape *Micronesia*
Ponca *Plains NA*
Pongaponga
  Australia
Pongo *W Africa*
Pontic *S Europe*
Pontunj *Australia*
Poospatuck
  Northeast NA
Popayanense *Andes*
Popoloca
  Mesoamerica
Popoluca
  Mesoamerica
Poqomam
  Mesoamerica
Poqomchi'
  Mesoamerica
Portaruwutj
  Australia
Portaulun *Australia*
Portuguese
  W Europe
Potano *Southeast NA*
Potawatomi *Plains*
  NA
Potidjara *Australia*
Potiguara *Amazon*
  Basin
Potter Pomo
  Far West NA
Poven *Arctic*
Powhatan *Southeast*
  NA
Powhatan Renape
  Northeast NA
Poya *Andes*
Poyndu *Australia*
Pozo *Andes*
Prairie Potawatomi
  Plains NA
Pranje *Melanesia*
Premingana *Australia*
Provencal *W Europe*
Pshav *Caucasus*
Pueblo *Southwest NA*
Puelche (Guennakin)
  Central SA
Puinave *Amazon*
  Basin
Puiplirmiut *Arctic*
Puisortok *Arctic*
Pukapuka *Polynesia*
Pulana *S Africa*
Pulap *Micronesia*

Pulayan *S Asia*
Pulusuk *Micronesia*
Puman *E Asia*
Pume (Yaruro)
  Orinoco Basin
Pumi *E Asia*
Pun *S Asia*
Punaba *Australia*
Punan *SE Asia*
Puneitja *Australia*
Punjabi *S Asia*
Punthamara
  Australia
Punu *C Africa*
Punu *E Asia*
Puraneters *Australia*
Purepecha (Tarascans)
  Mesoamerica
Puri *Central SA*
Purigoto *Orinoco*
  Basin
Purik *E Asia*
Puruha *Andes*
Purum *S Asia*
Pusht I Kuh *Middle*
  East
Puthai *SE Asia*
Puthlavamiut
  Northeast NA
Puyallup *Northwest*
  Coast NA
Puyuma *E Asia*
Pwo *SE Asia*

Q

Q'anjob'al (Kanjobal)
  Mesoamerica
Q'eqchi (Kekchi)
  Mesoamerica
Q'eros *Andes*
Qaernermiut *Arctic*
Qahatika *Southwest*
  NA
Qahtan *Middle East*
Qalandar *S Asia*
Qararsha *Middle East*
Qashqai *Middle East*
Qaumauangmiut
  Arctic
Qazaq (Kazakhs)
  C, E Asia
Qiang *E Asia*
Qimant *E Africa*
Qinguamiut *Arctic*
Qizilbash *C Asia*
Quakers *Northeast*
  NA
Qualicum *Northwest*
  Coast NA
Quamauangmiut
  Northeast NA
Quapaw (Akansa)
  Plains NA
Quda'a *Middle East*
Quechan *SW NA*
Quechua (Runa)
  Andes
Queets *Northwest*
  Coast NA
Querandi *Central SA*
Quero *Mesoamerica*
Qui (Dulong, Qui) *E*
  Asia
Quiang *E Asia*
Quiche (K'iche')
  Mesoamerica

Quichua *Andes*
Quienjiang *E Asia*
Quileute *Northwest*
  Coast NA
Quiligua (Kiliwi)
  Mesoamerica
Quillaca *Andes*
Quillacinga *Andes*
Quimbaya *Andes*
Quinault *Northwest*
  Coast NA
Quindio *Andes*
Qyrghyz (Kirgiz)
  E Asia

R

Rabai *E Africa*
Rabha *S Asia*
Racha *Caucasus*
Raglai *SE Asia*
Rahanwayn *E Africa*
Rai *S Asia*
Raiapu *Melanesia*
Rainbarngo *Australia*
Raintana *Melanesia*
Rais *Middle East*
Rajput *S Asia*
Rakhines *SE Asia*
Rakkaia *Australia*
Rama *Mesoamerica*
Ramindjeri *Australia*
Ramkokamekra
  (Canela) *Amazon*
  Basin
Ramona *Far West NA*
Rana *S Asia*
Rapa *W Europe*
Rapa Nui (Easter
  Islanders)
  Polynesia
Rappahannock
  Southeast NA
Raroia *Polynesia*
Rashid *Middle East*
Rastafarians
  Caribbean
Ratagnon *SE Asia*
Rathawa *S Asia*
Red Karen (Kayah)
  SE Asia
Red Thai (Tai Deng)
  SE Asia
Reddi *S Asia*
Redjang *SE Asia*
Regeibat *N Africa*
Rela *N Africa*
Rembarunga
  Australia
Remo *Andes*
Rendille *E Africa*
Rengao *SE Asia*
Rennell Islanders
  Melanesia
Resighini Yurok
  Far West NA
Reyesano *Amazon*
  Basin
Rhade *SE Asia*
Riang *S Asia*
Ribe *E Africa*
Rif *N Africa*
Rijal Al Ma *Middle*
  East
Rincon *Far West NA*
Ringaringa *Australia*
Ristebura *Australia*

Ritarngo *Australia*
Riyam *Middle East*
Rizegat *C Africa*
Roanoke *Southeast*
  NA
Roboda *Melanesia*
Rocky Cree *Northeast*
  NA
Roglai *SE Asia*
Rohingya (Arakanese)
  SE Asia
Roka *S Africa*
Rolong *S Africa*
Rom *Mesoamerica*
Roma (Gypsies)
  Europe
Romanians *E Europe*
Roro *Melanesia*
Rosebud Sioux *Plains*
  NA
Roshanis *C Asia*
Rossel Islanders
  Melanesia
Rotinese *SE Asia*
Rotumans *Polynesia*
Roucouyenne
  (Wayana) *Orinoco*
  Basin
Rozvi *S Africa*
Rucana *Andes*
Rucuyen *Amazon*
  Basin
Rufiji *E Africa*
Rukai *E Asia*
Rukuba *W Africa*
Rumai *E Asia*
Rumelian Turks
  Middle East
Rumsey Wintun *Far*
  West NA
Runa (Quechua)
  Andes
Runbubura *Australia*
Rungarungawa
  Australia
Rungus *SE Asia*
Rushan *C Asia*
Russians *C, E Asia,*
  E Europe
Rutuls *Caucasus*
Ryukyu Islanders
  (Okinawins) *E Asia*

S

Sa Dang *SE Asia*
Saar *Middle East*
Sabaneque
  Caribbean
Sabaskong
  (Onegaming
  Ojibway) *NE NA*
Saberi *Melanesia*
Sabras *Middle East*
Sac (Sauk) *Plains NA*
Sadhu *S Asia*
Saek (Xek) *SE Asia*
Safaiha (Laheiwat)
  Middle East
Safwa *E Africa*
Sagada Igorot
  (Lepanto) *SE Asia*
Sagamok
  Anishnawbek
  Northeast NA
Sagara *E Africa*
Sagdlirmiut *Subarctic*

Saginaw Chippewa
  Northeast NA
Saharwais *N Africa*
Sahi *W Africa*
Saho *E Africa*
Sahtu Dene *Arctic*
Said Atba *N Africa*
Saisiat *E Asia*
Sakalava *E Africa*
Sakha (Yakut) *Arctic*
Sakimay *Plains NA*
Sakuye *E Africa*
Sala *E Africa*
Salajar *SE Asia*
Salakahadi *Melanesia*
Salar *E Asia*
Salasaka *Andes*
Salawati *Melanesia*
Salinan *Far West NA*
Salish *NW Coast NA*
Salishan Bella Coola
  NW Coast NA
Saliva *Orinoco Basin*
Salor *C Asia*
Saluan *SE Asia*
Sam Tao *SE Asia*
Samaal *E Africa*
Samahquam *NW*
  Coast NA
Samal *SE Asia*
Samalek *Melanesia*
Samaritans *Middle*
  East
Samarzakan
  Caucasus
Sambaa *E Africa*
Sambal *SE Asia*
Sambas *SE Asia*
Sambia *Melanesia*
Sambioa *Amazon*
  Basin
Samburu *E Africa*
Sami (Lapps) *N*
  Europe
Samia *E Africa*
Samish *Northwest*
  Coast NA
Samo *W Africa*
Samoans *Polynesia*
Samoyed (Nenets)
  Arctic
Sampits *Plains NA*
Samre *SE Asia*
Samtal *S Asia*
San (Basarwa,
  Bushmen) *S Africa*
San Cristobal
  Islanders
  Melanesia
San'ha *Caribbean*
  Coast NA
Sanapana *Central SA*
Sandawe *E Africa*
Sandia Pueblo
  Southwest NA
Sanei *E Africa*
Sanema *Caribbean*
  Coast SA
Sangha *C Africa*
Sangil *SE Asia*
Sangir *SE Asia*
Sango *C Africa*
Sangu *E Africa*
Sanhaja *N Africa*
Sanpoil *Northwest*
  Coast NA

Sansu *E Asia*
Santa Cruz Islanders *Melanesia*
Santal *S Asia*
Santandar *W Europe*
Santee Sioux *Plains NA*
Santiam *Northwest Coast NA*
Sanye *E Africa*
Saoch *SE Asia*
Sapara *Melanesia*
Sapo *W Africa*
Saponi *Southeast NA*
Sapotaweyak Cree *Plains NA*
Sar *C Africa*
Sara *C Africa*
Saraguro *Andes*
Sarakatsani *S Europe*
Saramaka *Amazon Basin*
Sarcee *Plains NA*
Sardinians *S Europe*
Sarikoli *C Asia*
Sariq *C Asia*
Sarnia Chippewas *Northeast NA*
Sarsi *NW Coast NA*
Sart (Tajiks) *C Asia*
Sasak *SE Asia*
Satar *S Asia*
Satsup *Northwest Coast NA*
Saturiwa *SE NA*
Saugeen *NE NA*
Saui *Melanesia*
Sauiana *Amazon Basin*
Sauk (Sac) *Plains NA*
Sauk Suiattle *Northwest Coast NA*
Saulteaux *Plains NA*
Saumingmiut *Arctic*
Savara *S Asia*
Savunese *SE Asia*
Sawai *SE Asia*
Sawos *Melanesia*
Sayisi Dene *Plains NA*
Sayyid *Middle East*
Scandinavians *N Europe*
Scaticook *Northeast NA*
Schaghticoke *Northeast NA*
Schamatairi *Orinoco Basin*
Schiriana *Orinoco Basin*
Scots *N Europe*
Scugog Mississaugas *Northeast NA*
Sebei *E Africa*
Sebuano *SE Asia*
Sechelt *Northwest Coast NA*
Secotan *Southeast NA*
Secoya *Amazon Basin*
Sedang (Xo dang) *SE Asia*
Segeju *E Africa*

Seharia *S Asia*
Sek *SE Asia*
Sekani *Northwest Coast NA*
Sekele *S Africa*
Selepet *Melanesia*
Seletz *Northwest Coast NA*
Selknam (Ona) *Patagonia*
Selkup *Subarctic*
Selung *SE Asia*
Semai *SE Asia*
Semalai *SE Asia*
Semang *SE Asia*
Semariji *Melanesia*
Semelai *SE Asia*
Semiahmoo *NW Coast NA*
Seminole *Plains, Southeast NA*
Semoq Beri *SE Asia*
Sena *E Africa*
Seneca *NE NA*
Seneca Cayuga *Plains NA*
Senga *E Africa*
Sengseng *Melanesia*
Senoi *SE Asia*
Sentinelese *S Asia*
Senufo *W Africa*
Sephardic Jews *Middle East*
Serahuli *W Africa*
Seramina *Melanesia*
Serbs *C Europe*
Sere *E Africa*
Serer *W Africa*
Seri *Mesoamerica*
Serrano *Far West NA*
Sese *E Africa*
Sewa *C Africa*
Sgaw *SE Asia*
Shabar *S Asia*
Shackan *Northwest Coast NA*
Shacriaba *Central SA*
Shaderli *Caucasus*
Shahsevan (Ilsaven) *Caucasus*
Shake *C Africa*
Shakopee Sioux *Plains NA*
Shamatari *Amazon Basin*
Shamattawa *Plains NA*
Shambaa *E Africa*
Shamran *Middle East*
Shanafir *Middle East*
Shangana *S Africa*
Shanjo *S Africa*
Shans *E, SE Asia*
Sharanahua *Amazon Basin*
Shararat *Middle East*
Sharchop *S Asia*
Shashi *E Africa*
Shasta *Far West NA*
Shawanaga *Northeast NA*
Shawiya *N Africa*
Shawnee *Plains NA*
She *E Asia*
Sheguiandah *NE NA*
Sheikh *C Asia*

Shenabla *C Africa*
Sherbro *W Africa*
Sherente *Amazon Basin*
Sherpa *S Asia*
Sheshegwaning *Northeast NA*
Shetebo *Andes*
Shetlanders *N Europe*
Shewa *E Africa*
Shi *C Africa*
Shila *C Africa*
Shilluk (Collo) *C Africa*
Shinans *C Asia*
Shinnecock *Northeast NA*
Shipaya *Amazon Basin*
Shipibo *Amazon Basin*
Shiriana *Amazon Basin*
Shleuh *N Africa*
Shluh *N Africa*
Shokleng *Central SA*
Shona *S Africa*
Shors *C Asia*
Shoshone (Shoshoni) *Great Basin NA*
Shoshone Bannock *Great Basin NA*
Shoshone Paiute *Great Basin NA*
Shoshoni (Shoshone) *Great Basin NA*
Shua (Tshwa, Tyua) *S Africa*
Shuar (Jivaro) *Amazon Basin*
Shubenacadie *Northeast NA*
Shucuru (Shukuru) *Amazon Basin*
Shugnan *C Asia*
Shui *E Asia*
Shukuru (Shucuru) *Amazon Basin*
Shuma *Plains NA*
Shuswap *Northwest Coast NA*
Shuwa *W Africa*
Siamese (Thai) *SE Asia*
Sian *SE Asia*
Siane *Melanesia*
Sibea *Middle East*
Sicilians *S Europe*
Sidama *E Africa*
Sidamo *E Africa*
Sidi *S Asia*
Sierra Miwok *Far West NA*
Sihanaka *E Africa*
Sikaianan Islanders *Melanesia*
Sikanese *SE Asia*
Sikon *W Africa*
Siksika *Plains NA*
Sikuani *Orinoco Basin*
Sila (Sy La) *SE Asia*
Silesians *C Europe*
Siletz *Northwest Coast NA*

Simaa *S Africa*
Simba *Central SA*
Simong *S Asia*
Simore *Melanesia*
Sinabo *Amazon Basin*
Sindagua *Andes*
Sindhi *S Asia*
Singmun (Xing Moun) *SE Asia*
Sinhalese *S Asia*
Sio *Melanesia*
Siona *Amazon Basin*
Sioux *Plains NA*
Sipacapa *Mesoamerica*
Sipakapense *Mesoamerica*
Siraya *SE Asia*
Siriono *Central SA*
Sise *C Africa*
Siska *Northwest Coast NA*
Sisseton Wahpeton Sioux *Plains NA*
Sitka *Northwest Coast NA*
Siuai (Siwai) *Melanesia*
Siuslaw *Northwest Coast NA*
Siwai (Siuai) *Melanesia*
Siwang *SE Asia*
Skagit *Northwest Coast NA*
Skawahlook *Northwest Coast NA*
Skeetchestn *Northwest Coast NA*
Skilloot *Northwest Coast NA*
Skokomish *Northwest Coast NA*
Skolt Lapps *N Europe*
Skookumchuk *North-west Coast NA*
Skowkale *Northwest Coast NA*
Skuppah *Northwest Coast NA*
Slavey *Subarctic*
Slavs *C Europe*
Sleb *Middle East*
Sliammon *Northwest Coast NA*
Slovaks *C Europe*
Slovenes *C Europe*
Snake *Great Basin NA*
Snausi *N Africa*
Snohomish *Northwest Coast NA*
Snoqualmie *Northwest Coast NA*
So *SE Asia*
Sobo *W Africa*
Soboba *Far West NA*
Society Islanders *Polynesia*
Soda Creek *NW Coast NA*

Soga *E Africa*
Sokaogon Chippewa *Northeast NA*
Soli *S Africa*
Soligaru *S Asia*
Soliman *Amazon Basin*
Solomon Islanders *Melanesia*
Solorese *SE Asia*
Somali Boni (Aweer, Kilii) *E Africa*
Somalis *E Africa*
Sombra *W Africa*
Songhai *W Africa*
Songhees *Northwest Coast NA*
Songish *Northwest Coast NA*
Songo *C Africa*
Songu *Melanesia*
Songye *C Africa*
Soninke *W Africa*
Sooke *Northwest Coast NA*
Sop *SE Asia*
Sora *S Asia*
Sorbs (Wends) *W Europe*
Sork *SE Asia*
Sorol *Micronesia*
Sorongo *C Africa*
Sotaks *E Europe*
Sotatipo *E Asia*
Sotho (Pedi) *S Africa*
Sou *SE Asia*
Souei (Xouay) *SE Asia*
Soungor *N Africa*
Souninke *W Africa*
Southeast Alabama Cherokee *Southeast NA*
Southern Cherokee *Southeast NA*
Southern Cheyenne *Plains NA*
Southern Paiute *Great Basin NA*
Southern Piegan *Plains NA*
Southern Sierra Miwuk *Far West NA*
Southern Tehuelche *Patagonia*
Southern Tepehuan *Mesoamerica*
Southern Thai (Pak Thai) *SE Asia*
Southern Ute *Great Basin NA*
Spallumcheen *Northwest Coast NA*
Spanish *W Europe*
Spokane *Northwest Coast NA*
Spuzzum *Northwest Coast NA*
Squamish *Northwest Coast NA*
Squaxin *Northwest Coast NA*
Sraghna *N Africa*
Ssingo *E Africa*

Stalo *Northwest Coast NA*
Stanjikoming *Northeast NA*
Star Creek *SE NA*
Steilacoom *NW Coast NA*
Stieng (X. Tieng) *SE Asia*
Stikine *Northwest Coast NA*
Stillaguamish *NW Coast NA*
Sto:lo *Northwest Coast NA*
Stockbridge *NE NA*
Sua *C Africa*
Suau *Melanesia*
Subanun *SE Asia*
Subi *E Africa*
Subiya *S Africa*
Sufrai *Melanesia*
Suhul *Middle East*
Suk (Pokot) *E Africa*
Suka *Melanesia*
Suki *Melanesia*
Sukkertoppen *Arctic*
Suku *C Africa*
Sukuma *E Africa*
Sula *SE Asia*
Sulod *SE Asia*
Sumba *SE Asia*
Sumbanese *SE Asia*
Sumbawans *SE Asia*
Sumbwa *E Africa*
Sumu *Mesoamerica*
Sundanese *SE Asia*
Sundi *C Africa*
Sunwar *S Asia*
Suquamish *NW Coast NA*
Suri *E Africa*
Surui *Amazon Basin*
Susquehana *Northeast NA*
Susu *W Africa*
Sutenai *Plains NA*
Sutrai *Melanesia*
Suwarka *Middle East*
Suya *Amazon Basin*
Svans *Caucasus*
Swahili *E Africa*
Swaka *C Africa*
Swampy Cree *Northeast NA*
Swangla *S Asia*
Swazi *S Africa*
Swedes *N Europe*
Swinomish *Northwest Coast NA*
Swiss *W Europe*
Sy La (Sila) *SE Asia*
Sycuan *Far West NA*
Szeklers *E Europe*

T

T'en *E Asia*
T'in (Htin, Thin) *SE Asia*
Ta Liang *SE Asia*
Ta Oy *SE Asia*
Tabasarans *Caucasus*
Tabtulabal *Far West NA*

Tabun *SE Asia*
Tabwa *C Africa*
Tacana *Amazon Basin*
Tacarigua *Caribbean Coast SA*
Tacatacura *Southeast NA*
Tado *Andes*
Tadoussac *NE NA*
Tadvi *S Asia*
Tadyawan *SE Asia*
Tagabili *SE Asia*
Tagakaolo *SE Asia*
Tagal *SE Asia*
Tagalag *Australia*
Tagalog *SE Asia*
Tagbanoua *SE Asia*
Tagin *S Asia*
Tagish *Subarctic*
Tagoman *Australia*
Tahitians *Polynesia*
Tahltan *Northwest Coast NA*
Tai (Hmong, Meo, Miao, Mong) *S, SE Asia*
Tai Dam (Black Thai) *SE Asia*
Tai Deng (Red Thai) *SE Asia*
Tai Khao (White Thai) *SE Asia*
Taimanis (Taimuri) *C Asia*
Taimoro *E Africa*
Taimuri (Taimanis) *C Asia*
Taino *Caribbean*
Taior *Australia*
Taira *Orinoco Basin*
Tairora *Melanesia*
Taisaka *E Africa*
ITaise *S Africa*
Tajiks (Sart) *C Asia*
Taku *Northwest Coast NA*
Talamanca *Mesoamerica*
Talandji *Australia*
Tali *Southeast NA*
Tallanes *Andes*
Tallcree *Plains NA*
Tallensi *W Africa*
Talysh *Caucasus*
Tama *N Africa*
Tamacheq (Tuareg) *N Africa*
Tamanaco *Orinoco Basin*
Tamang *S Asia*
Tamathli *Southeast NA*
Tamaulipeco *Mesoamerica*
Tamaya *Melanesia*
Tamazight *N Africa*
Tambahoaka *E Africa*
Tambaro *E Africa*
Tambo *E Africa*
Tamils *S Asia*
Tamong *S Asia*
Tamoyo *Central SA*
Tanacross *Subarctic*
Tanaina *Subarctic*
Tanala *E Africa*

Tandroy *E Africa*
Tang *W Africa*
Tanga *C Africa*
Tanga Islanders *Melanesia*
Tanganekald *Australia*
Tangara *Australia*
Tanggum *Melanesia*
Tangu *Melanesia*
Tanikutti *Australia*
Tanimbar *Melanesia*
Tankarana *E Africa*
Tankas *E Asia*
/Tannekwe *S Africa*
Tannese *Melanesia*
Tanosy *E Africa*
Tanumuku *Amazon Basin*
Taonkawa *Plains NA*
Taos Pueblo *Southwest NA*
Tapajo *Amazon Basin*
Taparito *Orinoco Basin*
Tape *Central SA*
Tapiete *Central SA*
Tapirape *Amazon Basin*
Tapko *C Asia*
Tapoaja *Amazon Basin*
Tarahumara *Southwest NA*
Tarahumara *Mesoamerica*
Tarariu *Central SA*
Tarascans (Purepecha) *Mesoamerica*
Tareumiut *Arctic*
Targari *Australia*
Tariana *Amazon Basin*
Taribelang *Australia*
Tarma *Andes*
Taro *Melanesia*
Tarubura *Australia*
Taruma *Amazon Basin*
Tarumbul *Australia*
Tasaday *SE Asia*
Tasetsaut *Northwest Coast NA*
Tashilhit *N Africa*
Tasiusak *Arctic*
Tatars *E Asia*
Tatitati *Australia*
Tats *Caucasus*
Tatsanuttine *Arctic*
Tatungalung *Australia*
Tatuyo *Amazon Basin*
Tau *S Asia*
Tauade *Melanesia*
Taulipang (Pemon) *Orinoco Basin*
Taungthu *SE Asia*
Taungurong *Australia*
Tausug *SE Asia*
Taveta *E Africa*
Tavgi Yakut *Arctic*
Tawahka *Mesoamerica*
Tawakonie *Plains NA*
Tawana *S Africa*
Tawara *E Africa*
Tay *SE Asia*

Tayy *Middle East*
Tchambuli *Melanesia*
Tchinouk *Northwest Coast NA*
Te Moak *Great Basin NA*
Tebranuykuna *Australia*
Tebu *N Africa*
Teco (Cuitlatec) *Mesoamerica*
Teda *N Africa*
Tedei *Australia*
Tedong *SE Asia*
Teglin *Northwest Coast NA*
Tehatchapi *Far West NA*
Teheulche (Tsoneca) *Patagonia*
Teita *E Africa*
Tekasta *Southeast NA*
Teke *C Africa*
Tekesta *Caribbean*
Tekke *C Asia*
Tekna *N Africa*
Telefolmin *Melanesia*
Telugu *S Asia*
Temagami *Northeast NA*
Temba *W Africa*
Tembe *Amazon Basin*
Temiar *SE Asia*
Temne (Timmannee) *W Africa*
Temoq *SE Asia*
Temuan *SE Asia*
Tenana *Subarctic*
Tene *W Africa*
Tenetehara *Amazon Basin*
Tenggarese *SE Asia*
Tenino *Northwest Coast NA*
Tenma *Australia*
Teochiu *E Asia*
Tepecano *Mesoamerica*
Tepehuan *Mesoamerica*
Tepeth *E Africa*
Tepiti *Australia*
Teppathiggi *Australia*
Teque *Caribbean Coast SA*
Tequistlatec *Mesoamerica*
Terabin *Middle East*
Teralinak *Australia*
Terecuma *Amazon Basin*
Teremembe *Amazon Basin*
Terena *Central SA*
Teribe *Mesoamerica*
Terik *E Africa*
Ternatan *SE Asia*
Terraba *Mesoamerica*
Terrabura *Australia*
Teslin Tlingit *Arctic*
Teso *E Africa*
Tesuque Pueblo *Southwest NA*
Teton Sioux (Lakota Sioux) *Plains NA*
Tetum *SE Asia*

Teuesh *Patagonia*
Teve *S Africa*
Tewa *Plains NA*
Tewa Pueblo *Southwest NA*
Tewelche *Patagonia*
Tewi *W Africa*
Th wene *S Africa*
Thadou *S Asia*
Thagicu *E Africa*
Thai (Siamese) *SE Asia*
Thai Lao (Lao Isan) *SE Asia*
Thakali *S Asia*
Thakur *S Asia*
Thapa *S Asia*
Thaqif *Middle East*
Tharaka *E Africa*
Tharawal *Australia*
Tharu *S Asia*
Thaua *Australia*
Theddora *Australia*
Thembu *S Africa*
Thereila *Australia*
Thessalon *Northeast NA*
Thin (Htin, T'in) *SE Asia*
Thlalerwa *S Africa*
Thlopthlocco Creek *Plains NA*
Tho *SE Asia*
Thug *S Asia*
Thuri *C Africa*
Thuribura *Australia*
Tiak *Melanesia*
Tiatinagua *Amazon Basin*
Tibetans *E Asia*
Tidog *SE Asia*
Tidong *SE Asia*
Tidorese *SE Asia*
Tigray *E Africa*
Tigre *E Africa*
Tigua *Plains NA*
Tikar *W Africa*
Tikeramiut *Arctic*
Tikopia Islanders *Melanesia*
Tikuna *Amazon Basin*
Tilbabura *Australia*
Tillamook *Northwest Coast NA*
Timanambondro *E Africa*
Timba Sha Shoshone *Great Basin NA*
Timbaro *E Africa*
Timbira *Amazon Basin*
Timbu *Central SA*
Timiskaming *Northeast NA*
Timmannee (Temne) *W Africa*
Timorini *Melanesia*
Timote *Caribbean Coast SA*
Timucua *Southeast NA*
Tingaian *SE Asia*
Tingamitmiut *Arctic*
Tio *C Africa*
Tiononati *NENA*

Tipai (Campo) *Far West NA*
Tipura (Moorang, Mro) *S Asia*
Tirari *Australia*
Tiriki *E Africa*
Tirio (Trio) *Amazon Basin*
Tiris *N Africa*
Tiruray *SE Asia*
Tiv *W Africa*
Tiwa *Southwest NA*
Tiwi *Australia*
Tiyaha *Middle East*
Tjalkadjara *Australia*
Tjapukai *Australia*
Tjapwurong *Australia*
Tjeraridjal *Australia*
Tjial *Australia*
Tjingili *Australia*
Tjongkandji *Australia*
Tjuroro *Australia*
Tjuundji *Australia*
Tl'etinqox t'in *Northwest Coast NA*
Tla o qui aht *Northwest Coast NA*
Tlapanec *Mesoamerica*
Tlhaping *S Africa*
Tlhara *S Africa*
Tlingit *Northwest Coast NA*
Tlowitsis Mumtagila *Northwest Coast NA*
Toakas *SE Asia*
Toala *SE Asia*
Toaripi *Melanesia*
Toba *Central SA*
Tobajara *Amazon Basin*
Tobelorese (Tobolese) *SE Asia*
Tobique *Northeast NA*
Tobolese (Tobelorese) *SE Asia*
Tobosos *Plains NA*
Tocobaga *Southeast NA*
Toda *S Asia*
Tofalar *C Asia*
Togeman *Australia*
Tohono O'odham (Papago) *Southwest NA*
Tojolab'al *Mesoamerica*
Toka *S Asia*
Tokelauns *Polynesia*
Tolai *Melanesia*
Tolowa *Far West NA*
Tolupan (Jicaque, Torrupanes) *Mesoamerica*
Toma *W Africa*
Tomagra *N Africa*
Tombema *Melanesia*
Tomini *SE Asia*
Tonawanda Seneca *Northeast NA*
Tonga *S Africa*

Tongans *Polynesia*
Tongareva *Polynesia*
Tongass *Northwest Coast NA*
Tongwe *E Africa*
Tonkawa *Plains NA*
Tonkawa *Mesoamerica*
Tonocote *Central SA*
Tonto Apache *Southwest NA*
Toosey *Northwest Coast NA*
Tootinaowaziibeeng *Plains NA*
Topachula *Southeast NA*
Toposa *E Africa*
Toquaht *Northwest Coast NA*
Tor *Melanesia*
Toradja *E Africa*
Toraja *SE Asia*
Tori *W Africa*
Toro *E Africa*
Toromona *Amazon Basin*
Torres Strait Islanders *Australia*
Torres Martinez *Far West NA*
Torrupanes (Jicaque, Tolupan) *Mesoamerica*
Tory Islanders *N Europe*
Tosks *S Europe*
Tosto *Caribbean Coast SA*
Totbosos *Mesoamerica*
Totela *S Africa*
Totj *Australia*
Totok *SE Asia*
Totonac *Mesoamerica*
Toubouri *W Africa*
Toubous *N Africa*
Toucouleur (Tukulor) *W Africa*
Toum (Tum) *SE Asia*
Towa Pueblo *Southwest NA*
Tralakumbina *Australia*
Trinitario *Amazon Basin*
Trio (Tirio) *Amazon Basin*
Trique *Mesoamerica*
Trobrianders *Melanesia*
Trukese (Chuuk Islanders) *Micronesia*
Trumai *Amazon Basin*
Try (Chli) *SE Asia*
Ts'kw'aylaxw *Northwest Coast NA*
Tsakhurs *Caucasus*
Tsartlip *Northwest Coast NA*
Tsatchela (Colorado) *Andes*
Tsattine *Northwest Coast NA*

Tsaukwe *S Africa*
Tsawataineuk
 Northwest Coast NA
Tsawout *Northwest Coast NA*
Tsay Keh Dene *NW Coast NA*
Tsega *S Africa*
Tseku *E Asia*
Tserekwe *S Africa*
Tseshaht *Northwest Coast NA*
Tseycum *Northwest Coast NA*
Tshasi *S Africa*
Tshwa (Shua, Tyua)
 S Africa
Tsimihety *E Africa*
Tsimshian *Northwest Coast NA*
Tsnungwe *Far West NA*
Tsogo *C Africa*
Tsoneca (Teheulche)
 Patagonia
Tsongaa *S Africa*
Tsou *E Asia*
Tsuu T'ina *Plains NA*
Tswa *C Africa*
Tswana *S Africa*
Tu (Monguor) *E Asia*
Tualatin *Northwest Coast NA*
Tuamotu *Polynesia*
Tuareg (Tamacheq)
 N Africa
Tuareg Kel Ahaggar
 N Africa
Tuareg Kel Ajjer
 N Africa
Tuareg Kel Ferouan
 N Africa
Tuareg Kel Iforas
 N Africa
Tuareg Uraren
 N Africa
Tubar *Mesoamerica*
Tubatulabal
 Far West NA
Tubuai *Polynesia*
Tucano *Amazon Basin*
Tugen *E Africa*
Tuirimnainai *Orinoco Basin*
Tujen *E Asia*
Tujia *E Asia*
Tukkongo *C Africa*
Tukulor (Toucouleur)
 W Africa
Tukylor *W Africa*
Tulu *S Asia*
Tulua *Australia*
Tum (Toum) *SE Asia*
Tumbez *Andes*
Tumbuka *E Africa*
Tumbwe *C Africa*
Tumereha *Central SA*
Tunebo *Andes*
Tung *SE Asia*
Tungus (Evenk) *Arctic*
Tunica *Southeast NA*
Tununimiut *Arctic*
Tununirusirmiut
 Arctic

Tunuvivi *Australia*
Tuolumne Me Wuk
 Far West NA
Tupari *Amazon Basin*
Tupi *Central SA*
Tupinamba *Central SA*
Tupinambarana
 Amazon Basin
Tura *W Africa*
Turkana *E Africa*
Turkish Cypriots
 S Europe
Turkmen (Yomut)
 C Asia
Turks *Middle East*
Turrbal *Australia*
Tuscans *S Europe*
Tuscarora *NE NA*
Tuscola Cherokee
 Southeast NA
Tushetian *Caucasus*
Tuskegee *SE NA*
Tutchone *Subarctic*
Tutsi (Watutsi)
 C, E Africa
Tuvaluans *Polynesia*
Tuvans *C Asia*
Tuyuneri *Amazon Basin*
Twa *W Africa*
Twana *Northwest Coast NA*
Txikao *Amazon Basin*
Txukahamai *Amazon Basin*
Tyavikwa *S Africa*
Tyokwe *S Africa*
Tyrolians *C Europe*
Tyua (Shua, Tshwa)
 S Africa
Tzeltal *Mesoamerica*
Tzotzil *Mesoamerica*
Tzutuhil *Mesoamerica*

U
Uaka *Orinoco Basin*
Uakhanis *C Asia*
Ualarai *Australia*
Uanan *Amazon Basin*
Uashat Mak Mani
 Utenam *NE NA*
Ubina *Andes*
Uchecklesaht *NW Coast NA*
Ucluelet *Northwest Coast NA*
Udam *W Africa*
Udege *E Asia*
Udegei *Subarctic*
Udis *Caucasus*
Udmurts (Votyak)
 E Europe
Ugarung *Australia*
Uhunduni *Melanesia*
Ukit *SE Asia*
Ukonongo *E Africa*
Ukrainians (Little
 Russians) *E Europe*
Ul'che *E Asia*
Ulad Yihya *N Africa*
Ulchi *Subarctic*
Ulithi *Micronesia*
Ulkatcho *Northwest Coast NA*
Umanak *Arctic*

Umatilla *Northwest Coast NA*
Umbandu *C Africa*
Umede *Australia*
Umotina *Amazon Basin*
Umpqua *Northwest Coast NA*
Unaligmut *Arctic*
Unangan *Arctic*
Uncompahgre *Plains NA*
Undanbi *Australia*
Unga *C Africa*
Ungarinyin *Australia*
Unghi *Australia*
Ungorri *Australia*
Unjadi *Australia*
Unkechaug
 Poospatuck
 Northeast NA
Untsuri Shuar
 Amazon Basin
Upernavik *Arctic*
Upila *W Africa*
Upper Kiskopo
 Shawnee
 Northeast NA
Upper Kuskokwim
 Subarctic
Upper Mataponi
 Southeast NA
Upper Nicola *NW Coast NA*
Upper Similkmeen
 NW Coast NA
Upper Sioux *Plains NA*
Upper Skagit *NW Coast NA*
Upper Umpqua *NW Coast NA*
Urali *S Asia*
Urama *Melanesia*
Urapmin *Melanesia*
Urarina *Amazon Basin*
Urhobo *W Africa*
Uru (Chipaya) *Andes*
Urubu (Kaapor)
 Amazon Basin
Urupa *Amazon Basin*
Ushi *E Africa*
Usino *Melanesia*
Uspantec
 Mesoamerica
Usukuma *E Africa*
Utaibah *Middle East*
Ute *Great Basin NA*
Utina *Southeast NA*
Utu Utu Gwaitu
 Paiute *Great Basin NA*
Utuado *Caribbean*
Uveans *Polynesia*
Uygurs *C, E Asia*
Uzbeks *C Asia*

V
Vacaros de el Zada
 W Europe
VaDema (Doma,
 Mvura) *S Africa*
Vadeyeu Nganasans
 Arctic
Vai *W Africa*

Vaisi *Middle East*
Vale *S Africa*
Valunka *W Africa*
Vanatinai *Melanesia*
Varli *S Asia*
Vasava *S Asia*
Vatwa *S Africa*
Vedda (Wanniyala)
 S Asia
Vellala *S Asia*
Venda *S Africa*
Vezo *E Africa*
Vidunda *E Africa*
Viejas *Far West NA*
Vietnamese (Nguoi
 Kinh) *SE Asia*
Vilela *Central SA*
Vili *C Africa*
Vinza *E Africa*
Visayan *SE Asia*
Vlachs *E Europe*
Volga Tatars *C Asia*
Volokhs *E Europe*
Voltaic *W Africa*
Vonoma *E Africa*
Voto *Mesoamerica*
Votyak (Udmurts)
 E Europe
Vugusu *E Africa*

W
Wa *SE Asia*
Waagai *Australia*
Waata *E Africa*
Wabaga *Melanesia*
Wabasseemoong
 (Islington)
 Northeast NA
Wabauskang
 Northeast NA
Wabigoon *NE NA*
Wabo *Melanesia*
Waccamaw Sioux
 Southeast NA
Waco *Plains NA*
Wadai *N Africa*
Wadaman *Australia*
Wadandi *Australia*
Wadere *Australia*
Wadija *Australia*
Wadikali *Australia*
Wadjabangai
 Australia
Wadjalang *Australia*
Wadjari *Australia*
Wagera *C Africa*
Waggumbura
 Australia
Wagmatcook
 Northeast NA
Wagoman *Australia*
Wahgoshig
 Northeast NA
Wahnapitae
 Northeast NA
Wahpeton Dakota
 Plains NA
Wahta Mohawk
 Northeast NA
Waica (Yanomami)
 Amazon Basin
Waicuri *Mesoamerica*
Waigeo *Melanesia*
Waiiemi *Melanesia*
Wailaki *Far West NA*
Wailbri *Australia*

Wailpi *Australia*
Waimiri *Amazon Basin*
Wairacu *Amazon Basin*
Waiwai *Amazon Basin*
Waiyana *Amazon Basin*
Waiyarikule *Amazon Basin*
Waka *Melanesia*
Wakabunga *Australia*
Wakaja *Australia*
Wakaman *Australia*
Wakara *Australia*
Wakawaka *Australia*
Wakelbura *Australia*
Wakhan *C Asia*
Wakhi *C Asia*
Wakuenai *Amazon Basin*
Wala *W Africa*
Walamo *E Africa*
Walangama *Australia*
Walapai *SW NA*
Walbanga *Australia*
Walbiri (Walpiri,
 Warlpiri) *Australia*
Walgalu *Australia*
Waljen *Australia*
Walla Walla *NW Coast NA*
Wallirmiut *Arctic*
Walloons *W Europe*
Walmadjari *Australia*
Walmadje *Australia*
Walmbaria *Australia*
Walpiri (Walbiri,
 Warlpiri) *Australia*
Walu *Australia*
Waluwar *Australia*
Wama *Amazon Basin*
Wambaia *Australia*
Wamira *Melanesia*
Wampanoag
 Aquinnah
 Northeast NA
Wanamara *Australia*
Wanano *Amazon Basin*
Wanapam *Northwest Coast NA*
Wanda *E Africa*
Wandandian
 Australia
Wandarang *Australia*
Wandjira *Australia*
Waneiga *Australia*
Wangan *Australia*
Wangara *W Africa*
Wangkajunga
 Australia
Wanji *Australia*
Wanjiwalku *Australia*
Wanjuru *Australia*
Wanki *Mesoamerica*
Wanman *Australia*
Wanniyala (Vedda)
 S Asia
Wantoat *Melanesia*
Wao (Auca,
 Huaorani, Waorani)
 Amazon Basin
Waorani (Auca,
 Huaorani, Wao)

Amazon Basin*
Wape *Melanesia*
Wapekeka *NE NA*
Wapisiana *Orinoco Basin*
Wappo *Far West NA*
War *W Africa*
Warabul *Australia*
Warakamai *Australia*
Waramanga *Australia*
Waranbura *Australia*
Warao *Orinoco Basin*
Waray Waray *SE Asia*
Warbaa *Australia*
Wardal *Australia*
Wardaman *Australia*
Wardandi *Australia*
Ware *Melanesia*
Warei *Australia*
Wariangga *Australia*
Wariperidakena
 Orinoco Basin
Warjawa *W Africa*
Warkawarka
 Australia
Warki *Australia*
Warlpiri (Walbiri,
 Walpiri) *Australia*
Warndarrang
 Australia
Waropen *Melanesia*
Warroad Chippewa
 (Kah Bay Kah
 Nong) *Plains NA*
Warrumungu
 Australia
WARURA *Amazon Basin*
Warungu *Australia*
Warwa *Australia*
Wasagamack *Plains NA*
Wasauksing
 Northeast NA
Wasco *Northwest Coast NA*
Washoe *Great Basin NA*
Waskaganish
 Northeast NA
Wasongola *C Africa*
Wasteko (Huastec)
 Mesoamerica
Waswanipi *NE NA*
Waterhen *Plains NA*
Wathaurung
 Australia
Watiwati *Australia*
Watta *Australia*
Watutsi (Tutsi)
 C, E Africa
Watyi *W Africa*
Waura *Amazon Basin*
Wauzhushk Onigum
 Northeast NA
Wawakapewin
 Northeast NA
Wayana
 (Roucouyenne)
 Orinoco Basin
Wayapi (Oyampi)
 Orinoco Basin
Wayoro *Amazon Basin*
Wayumara *Amazon Basin*

Wayuu (Guajiro) *Caribbean Coast SA*
Waywayseecappo *Plains NA*
Wazimba *C Africa*
We Wai Kai *North-west Coast NA*
We Wai Kum *North-west Coast NA*
Weapemeoc *SE NA*
Webequie *Northeast NA*
Weber Ute *Great Basin NA*
Weenusk *NE NA*
Weilwan *Australia*
Welamo *E Africa*
Welega *E Africa*
Weli *Melanesia*
Welsh (Cymry) *N Europe*
Wembawemba *Australia*

White Thai (Tai Khao) *SE Asia*
Whitecap Dakota *Plains NA*
Whycocomagh *Northeast NA*
Wichita *Plains NA*
Widekum *W Africa*
Widi *Australia*
Widjabal *Australia*
Wiilman *Australia*
Wiimbaio *Australia*
Wik *Australia*
Wik kalkan *Australia*
Wikampama *Australia*
Wikanji *Australia*
Wikapatja *Australia*
Wikatinda *Australia*
Wikepa *Australia*
Wikmean *Australia*
Wikmunkan *Australia*
Wiknantjara *Australia*
Wiknatanja *Australia*
Wikwemikon

Wogeo Islanders *Melanesia*
Wola *Melanesia*
Wolamo *E Africa*
Woleai *Micronesia*
Wolf Cherokee *NW Coast NA*
Wolgal *Australia*
Wolinak *NE NA*
Wollaroi *Australia*
Wolof *W Africa*
Wom *Melanesia*
Wongaibon *Australia*
Wongkadjera *Australia*
Wongkamala *Australia*
Wongkanguru *Australia*
Wongkumara *Australia*
Wongo *C Africa*
Wonnarua *Australia*
Wontoat *Melanesia*
Woodland Cree

Xavante *Amazon Basin*
Xek (Saek) *SE Asia*
Xeni Gwet'in *North-west Coast NA*
Xerente *Amazon Basin*
Xesibe *S Africa*
Xeta (Heta) *Central SA*
Xhosa (Nguni) *S Africa*
Xibe *E Asia*
Xikrin (Kayapo) *Amazon Basin*
Xinca *Mesoamerica*
Xing Moun (Singmun) *SE Asia*
Xixime *Mesoamerica*
Xo dang (Sedang) *SE Asia*
Xokleng *Central SA*
!Xoo (!Ko) *S Africa*
Xouay (Souei) *SE Asia*
Xu *S Africa*

Y
Yab Anim *Melanesia*
Yadsi *W Africa*
Yae (Ye) *SE Asia*
Yafi *Middle East*
Yagnob *C Asia*
Yagua *Amazon Basin*
Yaguabo *Caribbean*
Yahgan (Yamana) *Patagonia*
Yaiwai *Australia*
Yaka *C Africa*
Yakan *SE Asia*
Yakima *Northwest Coast NA*
Yako (Ekoi) *W Africa*
Yakoma *C Africa*
Yakut *E Asia*
Yakut (Sakha) *Arctic*
Yamadi *Amazon Basin*
Yamamadi *Amazon Basin*
Yamana (Yahgan) *Patagonia*
Yameo *Amazon Basin*
Yamhill *NW Coast NA*
Yami *E Asia*
Yamiaca *Amazon Basin*
Yaminahua *Amazon Basin*
Yana *Far West NA*
Yanadi *S Asia*
Yandjinung *Australia*
Yang *SE Asia*
Yanghere *C Africa*
Yangman *Australia*
Yangoru Boiken *Melanesia*
Yanguro *Melanesia*
Yankibura *Australia*
Yankton Sioux *Plains NA*
Yanomami (Waica) *Amazon Basin*
Yans Mbun *C Africa*
Yantruwunta *Australia*
Yanzi *C Africa*
Yao *E Africa*

Yao (Man, Mien) *SE Asia*
Yaoro *Australia*
Yap Islanders *Micronesia*
Yaqui *Southwest NA*
Yaqui *Mesoamerica*
Yaraldi (Kukabrak, Narrinyeri, Ngarrindjeri) *Australia*
Yargo *Australia*
Yarmbura *Australia*
Yaro *Central SA*
Yaruro (Pume) *Orinoco Basin*
Yasa *C Africa*
Yate *Melanesia*
Yaulapiti *Amazon Basin*
Yaurorka *Australia*
Yauyo *Andes*
Yavapai *SW NA*
Yavapai Apache *Southwest NA*
Yawani *Orinoco Basin*
Yazgulem *C Asia*
Yazidi (Yezidi) *Middle East*
Ye (Yae) *SE Asia*
Yei *S Africa*
Yeke *C Africa*
Yekooche *Northwest Coast NA*
Yekuana (Makiritare) *Orinoco Basin*
Yela *Melanesia*
Yelmek *Melanesia*
Yelyuyendi *Australia*
Yemai *Melanesia*
Yemici *Caribbean Coast SA*
Yemreli *C Asia*
Yenadi *S Asia*
Yeraki *Melanesia*
Yerava *S Asia*
Yesey *Subarctic*
Yesibe *S Africa*
Yeskwa *W Africa*
Yeti *Melanesia*
Yezidi (Yazidi) *Middle East*
Yhamad *Middle East*
Yi *E Asia*
Yimas *Melanesia*
Yir Yoront *Australia*
Yokaghir *Subarctic*
Yokayo *Far West NA*
Yokuts *Far West NA*
Yolngu (Murngin) *Australia*
Yomba Shoshone *Great Basin NA*
Yombe *C Africa*
Yomud *C Asia*
Yomut (Turkmen) *C Asia*
Yoncalla *Northwest Coast NA*
Yonggom *Melanesia*
Yoruba (Nagot) *W Africa*
Yoruk *Middle East*
Yosko *Mesoamerica*
Youghiogheny Shawnee *NE NA*

Ysabel *Melanesia*
Ysleta del Sur Pueblo *Southwest NA*
Yuan (Northern Thai) *SE Asia*
Yuanzhumin (Gaosazhu) *E Asia*
Yucatan Maya *Mesoamerica*
Yuchi *Plains NA*
Yued *Australia*
Yugul *Australia*
Yugur *E Asia*
Yuin *Australia*
Yuit *Arctic*
Yukaghir (Odul) *Arctic*
Yukateko *Mesoamerica*
Yuki *Far West NA*
Yuko *Caribbean Coast SA*
Yukpa (Motilones) *Caribbean Coast SA*
Yukuna *Amazon Basin*
Yulbaridja *Australia*
Yuma *Amazon Basin*
Yumbo *Amazon Basin*
Yumbri *SE Asia*
Yungar *Australia*
Yunnan *SE Asia*
Yupiat (Yupik) *Arctic*
Yupik (Yupiat) *Arctic*
Yuqui *Andes*
Yuracare *Amazon Basin*
Yuraks *Arctic*
Yuri *Amazon Basin*
Yurok *NW Coast NA*
Yuruna *Amazon Basin*
Yustaga *SE NA*
Yusufzai *C Asia*

Z
Zacatec *Mesoamerica*
Zafisoro *E Africa*
Zaghawa *N Africa*
Zambales *SE Asia*
Zamindar *S Asia*
Zamuco *Central SA*
Zande (Azande) *C Africa*
Zapotec *Mesoamerica*
Zaramo *E Africa*
Zaraniq *Middle East*
Zarma *W Africa*
Zayr *N Africa*
Zemmur *N Africa*
Zentan *N Africa*
Zezhru *S Africa*
Zhongjia *E Asia*
Zhuang *E Asia*
Zia Pueblo *Southwest NA*
Zigula *E Africa*
Zimakani *Melanesia*
Zimba *S Africa*
Zinza *E Africa*
Zombo *C Africa*
Zoque *Mesoamerica*
Zoroastrians *Middle East*
Zulu *S Africa*
Zuni *Southwest NA*
Zuwayah *N*

He who plays the role of redeemer ends up getting crucified.

MEXICAN PROVERB

Wemindji *NE NA*
Wenamba *Australia*
Wenambal *Australia*
Wenatchee *Northwest Coast NA*
Wends (Sorbs) *W Europe*
Weraerai *Australia*
Werigha *N Africa*
West Greenlanders *Arctic*
Western Apache *Southwest NA*
Western Lamoot *Subarctic*
Western Mongols (Kalmyks) *C Asia*
Western Penan *SE Asia*
Western Shoshoni *Great Basin NA*
Wetar *SE Asia*
Weymontachie *Northeast NA*
Whadjuk *Australia*
Whang (Giai, Nung) *SE Asia*
Whapmagoostui *Northeast NA*
Whilkut *Far West NA*
White Karen *SE Asia*
White Russians (Belarusians) *E Europe*
White Tai *E Asia*

Northeast NA
Wilawila *Australia*
Wilingura *Australia*
Wiljakali *Australia*
Willara *Australia*
Wilmen *Australia*
Wilya *Australia*
Wimmarao *Australia*
Winduwinda *Australia*
Winnebago *NE NA*
Wintu *Far West NA*
Wintun *Far West NA*
Wiradjuri *Australia*
Wiram *Melanesia*
Wirangu *Australia*
Wirdanja *Australia*
Wiri *Australia*
Wirngir *Australia*
Wiru *Melanesia*
Wisconsin Potawatomi *Northeast NA*
Wishram *Plateau NA*
Witboois *S Africa*
Witoto (Huitoto) *Amazon Basin*
Witsuwit'en *NW Coast NA*
Wiya *W Africa*
Wiyot *NW Coast NA*
Wobe *W Africa*
Woda *Melanesia*
Wodiwodi *Australia*
Wogaidj *Australia*
Wogait *Australia*
Wogeman *Australia*

Subarctic
Worimi *Australia*
Workia *Australia*
Woror *Australia*
Wotjobaluk *Australia*
Wounaan *Mesoamerica*
Wovan *Melanesia*
Wowoni *SE Asia*
Wudjari *Australia*
Wulgurukaba *Australia*
Wulili *Australia*
Wulpura *Australia*
Wulwulam *Australia*
Wunambal *Australia*
Wuningag *Australia*
Wuradjeri *Australia*
Wurango *Australia*
Wurugu *Australia*
Wurundjeri *Australia*
Wuskwi *Plains NA*
Wute *W Africa*
Wyana *Orinoco Basin*
Wyandotte *Plains NA*
Wynoochee *NW Coast NA*

X
Xam *S Africa*
Xanekwe *S Africa*
Xaray *Amazon Basin*
Xarirawi *Melanesia*
Xaruma *Orinoco Basin*

CONTRIBUTORS

WADE DAVIS, an explorer-in-residence at the National Geographic Society, is an anthropologist and ethnobotanist whose ten books include the international bestseller *The Serpent and the Rainbow* and, most recently, *The Lost Amazon.* When not in the field, he divides his time between Washington, D.C., Vancouver, and a remote fishing lodge in the Stikine Valley of northern British Columbia.

K. DAVID HARRISON is a linguist who specializes in endangered languages and is cofounder of the Living Tongues Institute for Endangered Languages. He has conducted field expeditions to remote locations in Siberia, Mongolia, India, Bolivia, and Australia. His book, *When Languages Die,* examines the causes and consequences of global language loss. He lives in Philadelphia and teaches at Swarthmore College.

CATHERINE HERBERT HOWELL is a freelance writer with an M.A. in anthropology. She has conducted field research among urban women in India and Indian immigrants in New York City. A former National Geographic staff member, she has contributed to dozens of Society publications, including the first edition of *Peoples of the World, Wonders of the Ancient World,* and the *Expeditions Atlas.* She was the editor of *Out of Ireland,* a companion volume to the PBS documentary. She lives in Arlington, Virginia.

JASON BLUE-SMITH, research fellow for National Geographic's Genographic Project, studied population genetics at Stanford and Oxford. He now resides in the South Pacific, where he is studying the genetic impact of the first Polynesian migrations. He has conducted bird research in the Peruvian rain forest and has undertaken field expeditions in the Sahara in Chad, the Pamir Mountains in Tajikistan, the Peruvian highlands, Brazil's Amazon Basin, and the Society Islands of French Polynesia.

ROBERT E. HART trained in linguistics at Swarthmore College. He spent two years helping to research, edit, and design K. David Harrison's book, *When Languages Die.* His fascination with indigenous information systems, fostered during fieldwork in the Himalaya, has led him to pursue graduate study in ethno-ecology.

ELIZABETH KAPU'UWAILANI LINDSEY is a filmmaker and anthropologist who was raised by native Hawaiian elders. Her documentary film, *Then There Were None,* chronicles Hawaiian history. Her mentors include Mau Piailug, the Satawalese master navigator; ethno-astronomer Von Del Chamberlain; and her father, Henry Lindsey, an inventor and genealogist. A former Miss Hawaii, she serves as an advisor to Kamehameha Schools, the University of Hawaii-Hilo, and the 'Imiloa Astronomy Center.

MIRANDA WEINBERG is a student at Swarthmore College, where she is majoring in linguistics and minoring in history and music. She played violin for seven years in the elite Boston Youth Symphony Orchestra. She is currently studying Nepali language and culture in Kalimpong, India.

ILLUSTRATIONS CREDITS

FRONT MATTER
pp. 2-3, Randy Olson; pp. 4-5, National Geographic Photographer Jodi Cobb; p. 7, Kenneth Garrett; p. 8, Maria Stenzel; p. 11, Medford Taylor/NGS Image Collection.

SUB-SAHARAN AFRICA
pp. 18-19, Bob Krist/CORBIS; p. 21, Frans Lanting; p. 22, Angela Fisher and Carol Beckwith/Robert Estall Agency; p. 23, Owen Franken/CORBIS; p. 25, Chris Johns, NGS; p. 26, David C. Turnley; p. 27, David Doubilet; p. 29 & pp. 30-31, Ed Kashi; p. 33, Jose Azel; p. 34, Finbarr O'Reilly/Reuters/CORBIS; p. 35, Angela Fisher and Carol Beckwith/Robert Estall Agency; p. 37, Gordon Gahan: p. 38, Robb Kendrick; p. 39, Sarah Leen; p. 40, Michael Kirtley and Aubine Kirtley; p. 41, Paul Almasy/ CORBIS; p. 43, National Geographic Photographer Michael Nichols; p. 45, Michael Nichols/NGS Image Collection; p. 47, Randy Olson; p. 48, Sarah Leen; p. 49, Randy Olson; p. 50, Michael S. Lewis/NGS Image Collection; p. 52, Lynn Johnson; p. 53, George F. Mobley; p. 54, Randy Olson; p. 56, Michael Yamashita; p. 57, Robert Caputo/Aurora/Getty Images; p. 59, Farah Nosh/Getty Images; p. 61, K. David Harrison.

NORTH AFRICA & THE MIDDLE EAST
pp. 62-63, Steve McCurry; p. 65, Peter Turnley/CORBIS; p. 66, REZA; p. 67, Randy Olson; p. 69, National Geographic Photographer Jodi Cobb; p. 70 & p. 73, Alexandra Boulat; p. 74, Kenneth Garrett; p. 75, Thomas J. Abercrombie; p. 77, Annie Griffiths Belt; p. 78, Lynsey Addario/CORBIS; p. 80, Stephanie

Sinclair/CORBIS; p. 81, Ed Kashi; p. 82, Khaled El-Fiqi/epa/ CORBIS; p. 83, Alexandra Avakian; p. 84, James L. Stanfield; p. 86, David Evans/NGS Image Collection; p. 87, Karen Kasmauski/NGS Image Collection; p. 88 (upper), Behrouz Mehri/AFP/Getty Images; p. 88 (lower), Kelly James Richardson; p. 89, Karen Kasmauski/NGS Image Collection.

ASIA

pp. 90-91, David Guttenfelder, AP/Wide World Photos; p. 93, Stephen Shaver/AFP/Getty Images; p. 94, Bobby Model/NGS Image Collection; p. 95, Radhika Chalasani; p. 97, REZA; p. 98, Alexandra Avakian; p. 99, George F. Mobley; p. 101, Jonathan Blair; p. 102, Newsha Tavakolian; p. 103, David Edwards/NGS Image Collection; p. 105, Alexandra Avakian; p. 106 & p. 107, REZA; p. 109, Palani Mohan/Getty Images; p. 110, National Geographic Photographer Jodi Cobb; p. 111, Pamela Chen; p. 113, David Guttenfelder, AP/Wide World Photos; pp. 114-115, David Edwards/NGS Image Collection; p. 116, Gordon Wiltsie; p. 117, David Keaton/CORBIS; p. 119, National Geographic Photographer William Albert Allard; p. 120, Lindsay Hebberd/ CORBIS; p. 121 & p. 123, Pamela Chen; p. 124 & p. 126, Radhika Chalasani; p. 127, Pamela Chen; p. 129, Peter Essick; p. 130, Saurabh Das, AP/Wide World Photos; p. 133, Janet Jarman/ CORBIS; p. 135, Steve Raymer; p. 137, Earl and Nazima Kowall/ CORBIS; p. 139 & p. 140, Maria Stenzel; p. 142, Nicholas DeVore III/NGS Image Collection; p. 143, David S. Boyer; p. 144, Anders Ryman/CORBIS; p. 145, Alvis Upitis/Getty Images.

OCEANIA

pp. 146-147, Randy Olson; pp. 149-151, National Geographic Photographer Jodi Cobb; p. 153, Randy Olson/NGS Image Collection; p. 154 & p. 157, Sam Abell; p. 158, Annie Griffiths Belt/NGS Image Collection; p. 159, Randy Olson; p. 161, John Van Hasselt/CORBIS; p. 162, Sam Abell; p. 165, Danny Lehman/CORBIS; p. 166, Paul Chesley/NGS Image Collection; p. 167, James L. Stanfield; pp. 168-169, Peter Essick; p. 170, Peter Essick/Aurora/Getty Images; p. 171, Carsten Peter/NGS Image Collection; p. 172, Peter Essick; p. 173, Peter Essick/Aurora/ Getty Images; p. 175, Steve Raymer; p. 177, Frans Lanting; p. 178, Randy Olson; p. 181, National Geographic Photographer Jodi Cobb; p. 183, David Doubilet; p. 184, James P. Blair; p. 187, Charles O'Rear; p. 189, Hamid Sardar/CORBIS; p. 190, Catherine Karnow/CORBIS; p. 191, Anders Ryman/CORBIS.

EUROPE

pp. 192-193 & p. 195, Tomasz Tomaszewski; p. 196, Sisse Brimberg; p. 197, James L. Stanfield; p. 199, Ed Kashi; p. 200, Gerd Ludwig; p. 201 & p. 202, Julie Denesha; p. 204, James P. Blair; p. 205, Carlos Cazalis/CORBIS; pp. 206-207, Sisse Brimberg; p. 209, Gerd Ludwig; p. 210, James L. Stanfield; p. 212, Catherine Karnow; p. 213, David Turnley/CORBIS; p. 214, Massimo Borchi/Atlantide Phototravel/CORBIS; p. 215, Ed Kashi; p. 216, Melissa Farlow; p. 219, Alexandra Boulat; pp. 220-221, Massimo Borchi; p. 223, National

Geographic Photographer Jodi Cobb; p. 225, Lynn Johnson; p. 226, Jim Richardon; p. 228, Barry Lewis; p. 229, Reuters/ CORBIS; p. 230, Owen Franken/CORBIS; p. 231, William Coupon/CORBIS; p. 232, Andrew Fox/CORBIS; pp. 234-235, Medford Taylor; p. 236, Marco di Lauro/Getty Images; p. 237, Tomasz Tomaszewski; p. 239, Dean Conger; p. 240, Annie Griffiths Belt; p. 241, Adam Woolfitt/Robert Harding World Imagery/CORBIS; p. 243, Guido Cozzi/Atlantide Phototravel/ CORBIS; p. 244, Bo Zaunders/CORBIS; p. 245, Sisse Brimberg; pp. 246-247, George F. Mobley; p. 249, Annie Griffiths Belt/ NGS Image Collection; p. 250, Jim Richardson; p. 253, Prakash Singh/AFP/ Getty Images; p. 254, Jeffrey L. Rotman/CORBIS; p. 255, Viviane Moos/CORBIS.

NORTH AMERICA

pp. 256-257, Catherine Karnow/CORBIS; p. 259, Louie Psihoyos/CORBIS; p. 260, Randy Olson; p. 261, Annie Griffiths Belt; p. 263, Karen Kasmauski; p. 264, Richard Olsenius/ NGS Image Collection; p. 265, Dave Bartruff/CORBIS; p. 266, Galen Rowell/CORBIS; p. 267, Natalie Fobes; p. 269, James L. Stanfield; p. 271, Catherine Karnow/CORBIS; p. 272, Susanne Anderson; p. 273, Michael Melford/NGS Image Collection; p. 274, Stephen Trimble; p. 277, Joel Sartore; pp. 278-279, David Alan Harvey; p. 281, Chris Johns, NGS; p. 283, Peter Turnley/ CORBIS; p. 284, Joel Sartore; p. 287, Joel Sartore/NGS Image Collection; p. 288, Christopher J. Morris/CORBIS; p. 289, Maria Stenzel; p. 290, Andy Clark/Reuters/CORBIS; p. 291, Nathan Benn/CORBIS; p. 293, Annie Griffiths Belt; p. 294, Kevin Fleming/CORBIS; p. 297, Raymond Gehman/CORBIS; p. 299, Annie Griffiths Belt/CORBIS; p. 301, Jason Gutierrez/AFP/ Getty Images; p. 302, Kazuyoshi Nomachi/CORBIS; p. 303, Dean Conger.

SOUTH & CENTRAL AMERICA

pp. 304-305, Pablo Corral Vega/NGS Image Collection; p. 307, David Evans/NGS Image Collection; p. 308, Michael Nichols/NGS Image Collection; p. 309, Steve Winter; p. 311, Steve Winter/NGS Image Collection; p. 312, David Alan Harvey; p. 313, Steve Raymer/CORBIS; p. 315, James P. Blair; p. 316, Bojan Brecelj/CORBIS; p. 317, Dave G. Houser/COR-BIS; p. 318 & p. 319, Stephen Ferry; p. 321, David Alan Harvey; p. 322, Susie Post Rust; p. 323, Nicolas Reynard/NGS Image Collection; pp. 324-325, Patricia Dominguez/epa/CORBIS; p. 327, Stephen L. Alvarez; p. 328, Klea McKenna; p. 329, David Alan Harvey; p. 331, Alex Webb; p. 333, Bruce Dale; p. 335, Otis Imboden; p. 336, Danny Lehman/CORBIS; p. 338, Robert Caputo/Aurora/Getty Images; p. 339, Rodrigo Buendia/AFP/ Getty Images; p. 341, Robert Caputo/Aurora/Getty Images; p. 342, Michael Nichols/NGS Image Collection; p. 343, Cristina Mittermeier/NGS Image Collection; p. 345, Pablo Corral Vega/NGS Image Collection; p. 346, David Alan Harvey; p. 347, Stuart Franklin; p. 348, Susie Post Rust; p. 351, Fernando Bizerra, Jr./EFE/CORBIS; p. 352 & p. 353, James P. Blair; p. 355, Stuart Franklin; p. 356, Galen Rowell/CORBIS; p. 357, Janet Jarman/CORBIS.

READINGS & RESOURCES

Bennett, Linda, ed. *Encyclopedia of World Cultures.* G.K. Hall & Co., 1992.

Blunden, Caroline, and Mark Elvin. *Cultural Atlas of China.* Checkmark Books, 1998.

The CIA World Factbook, www.cia.gov/cia/publications/factbook/

Coe, Michael, et al. *Atlas of Ancient North America.* Facts on File, 1986.

Countries and Their Cultures, www.everyculture.com/

Cultural Survival, www.cs.org/

Cultures on the Edge, www.culturesontheedge.com/

Davis, Wade. *Light at the Edge of the World: A Journey Through the Realm of Vanishing Cultures.* National Geographic Society, 2002.

The Ethnologue, www.ethnologue.org/

Fitzhugh, William W., and Aron Crowell. *Crossroads of Continents: Cultures of Siberia and Alaska.* Smithsonian Institution Press, 1988.

Fitzpatrick, Judith M., ed. *Endangered Peoples of Oceania: Struggles to Survive and Thrive.* Greenwood Press, 2000.

Freeman, Milton M. R., ed. *Endangered Peoples of the Arctic: Struggles to Survive and Thrive.* Greenwood Press, 2000.

Gall, Timothy L., ed. *Encyclopedia of Cultures and Daily Life.* Gale Group, 1998.

Gerner, Deborah J., ed. *Understanding the Contemporary Middle East.* Lynne Rienner Publisher, 2000.

Gonen, Amiram, ed., *The Encyclopedia of the Peoples of the World.* Henry Holt and Co., 1993.

Harrison, K. David. *When Languages Die: The Extinction of the World's Languages and the Erosion of Human Knowledge.* Oxford University Press, 2007.

Hirschfelder, Arlene, and Martha Kreipe de Montaño. *The Native American Almanac.* Prentice Hall General Reference, 1993.

Hopkirk, Kathleen. *Central Asia: A Traveller's Companion.* John Murray Publishers Ltd., 1994.

Human Relations Area Files (HRAF), www.yale.edu/hraf/

Johnson, Gordon. *Cultural Atlas of India: India, Pakistan, Nepal, Bhutan, Bangladesh, and Sri Lanka.* Facts on File, 1996.

Language Hotspots, www.languagehotspots.org/

Lee, Richard B., and Richard Daly, eds. *The Cambridge Encyclopedia of Hunters and Gatherers.* Cambridge University Press, 1999.

Levinson, David. Ethnic *Groups Worldwide: A Ready Reference Handbook.* NetLibrary, Inc., 1998.

———. *The Encyclopedia of World Cultures.* Macmillan Publishing Company, 1995.

Lewis, Bernard. *The Multiple Identities of the Middle East.* Schocken Books, 1999.

Malinowski, Sharon, and Anna Sheets, eds. *The Gale Encyclopedia of Native American Tribes.* Gale Group, 1998.

Maybury-Lewis, David. *Millennium: Tribal Wisdom and the Modern World.* Viking Press, 1992.

Olson, James S. *The Peoples of Africa: An Ethnohistorical Dictionary.* Greenwood Press, 1996.

Palin, Michael. *Sahara.* New York: St. Martin's Press, 2003.

———. *Himalaya.* New York: St. Martin's Press. 2004.

Paxman, Jeremy. *The English.* Woodstock, New York: The Overlook Press, 2000.

Pfannmuller, Gunter, and Wilhelm Klein. *In Search of Dignity.* Aperture, 2005.

Price, David H. *Atlas of World Cultures: A Geographical Guide to Ethnographic Literature.* Sage Publications, 1989.

Pritzker, Barry M. *Native American Encyclopedia: History, Cultures, and Peoples.* New York: Oxford University Press, 2000.

Reader, John. *Africa: A Biography of the Continent.* Knopf, 1998.

Rogozinski, Jan. *A Brief History of the Caribbean: From the Arawak and the Carib to the Present.* Facts on File, 1999.

Sponsel, Leslie E., ed. *Endangered Peoples of Southeast and East Asia: Struggles to Survive and Thrive.* Greenwood Press, 2000.

Sturtevant, William C., ed. *Handbook of North American Indians.* Smithsonian Institution Press, 1990.

Wilson, David J. *Indigenous South Americans of the Past and Present.* Westview Press, 1999.

INDEX

Boldface indicates illustrations.

Aborigines 148, 150, 152–153, **154,** 155–156, **158,** 158–161, **162,** 163; art 159–160, **161,** 163; storytelling 255
Acadians 292
Achuar people 339
Afghan people **90–91**
Afghanistan: peoples 82–83, 85, **90–91,** 100, 104, 106, 107, 117
Africa: emigrants 261; genetic diversity 12; human origins 158; languages 20, 234. see also Central; East; North; Southern; Sub-Saharan; West
African Americans 296
African Caribbean: peoples 310–311
Africans 306, 308
Afrikaners 24–25, **26,** 28
Afro-Asiatic languages 46, 70
Agaw (language) 49
Ainu people 108–109, 112
Aka people 42
Akan people 22, 37
Alaska: languages 267; peoples **59,** 258, 262–265, **265, 266, 267,** 269
Alaskan Eskimos 262–263, **265, 266**
Albania: peoples 218–219; religion 197
Albanian language family 196, 218–219, 222
Albanians 214, 218–219, **219**
Aleut language family 263–265
Aleut people **263,** 263–265
Algeria: peoples 70–71, 75, **75**
Algonquian language family 258, 276–277, 279, 288–290, 296, 298
Alyawarre people 152
Amahuaca people 330
Amazon Basin, South America: languages 58, 61; map 330; peoples 330–343
American Indians see Native Americans
American Samoa: peoples 178–179
Amerind languages 267
Amerindians 311–313
Amhara people 46–47; proverb 48
Amharic (language) 46, 47, 49
Amish 261, 286–288, **287**
Anabaptists see Mennonites
Anasazi people 297
Anatolian Turks 85
Andes, South America: map 344; peoples 88, **307,** 309, 344–349, **345**
Andorra: peoples 227
Angola: languages 20; peoples 25–26, 43
Animism: Africa 51; Asia 104, 122, 140; Europe 200; North America 266, 290; Oceania 187
Anmatyerre people 152
Apache Indians 258, 260, 270–271
Apalachee Indians 295
Arabian Peninsula: peoples 66, 69
Arabic (language) 57, 64, 66, 68–69, 71, 72, 77, 81, 154
Arabs 64, 66, 67, 68–71, 76, 79, 80, 81, 82
Aramaic (language) 64
Aranda people see Arrernte people
Arapesh people 170
Araucanian language family 346
Arawak Indians 312, 313, 317, 332, 333

Arawak (language) 321
Arawakan language family 320–321
Architecture 300–303
Arctic regions: houses 300; languages 267; map 262; peoples 262–266, 267
Argentina: peoples 349, 351–356, **352, 353, 355, 357**
Argentines 354–356
Arikara Indians 281
Armenia: peoples 77, 96, **98**
Armenian language family 96
Armenians 79, 96, **98**
Arrernte people **11,** 152–153
Aruak language family 318
Aruba: languages 308
Arunta people see Arrernte people
Aryans 133
Asante (language) 32–33
Asante people 20, 32–33, **35**
Ashanti people see Asante people
Ashkenazic Jews 76, 77
Asia: languages 234; migrations 148, 261; music 188–190. see also Central; East; North; South; Southeast
Athabaskan-Eyak-Tlingit language family 269
Athabaskan language family 270–271, 274
Athapaskan Indians 258, 290
Australia: colonization 127, 148, 152, 156, 163; genetics 158; map 152; peoples 148, 152–163, **154, 157, 158, 161;** petroglyphs **11;** proverb 155; stations **153;** storytelling 255
Australians **153,** 153–155, 166, 172
Austria: alliance with Hungary 212
Austronesian languages 181, 185, 186
Aymara Indians 88, 191, 344–345, **345**
Aymara (language) 347
Aymaran language family 344–345
Azerbaijan: peoples 85, **97,** 97–98, **99**
Azerbaijanis see Azeri people
Azeri people **88, 97,** 97–98, **99**
Aztec 306, 325, 326, 327
Baganda people 47–48, **48**
Baha'i faith 82
Bahamas 308, 312
Bahrain: peoples 82
Bai people 109–110
Bali (island), Indonesia: music **190;** peoples 118–119; religion **120**
Balinese 118–119
Balochi people see Baluchi people
Baltic language family 199–200
Baluchi (language) 100
Baluchi people 100, **105**
Bamana (language) 33
Bambara people 33–34
Bangladesh: peoples 128, **130**
Bantu language family 26–28, 31, 35, 43, 44, 52, 56–57, 321
Bantu people 25, 26, 28
Barama Caribs 333
Basque (language) 196, 224, 236
Basques 224–225, **225;** proverb 233
Baule society 23
Bedouin 64, 66, 68–70, **69,** 72, **254**
Belarusans 213
Belize: peoples 313, 320–321
Bengali (language) 128
Bengalis 128
Benin: peoples 41
Benue-Congo language family 37–38, 40, 41
Berber language family 70–71, 75
Berber people **70,** 70–71, **73,** 76

Beta Israel people 48–49, 51
Bhutan: peoples 116
Bislama pidgin (language) 172
Black Caribbeans see African Caribbeans
Black Caribs see Garifuna people
Blackfeet Indians 276
Blood Indians 276
Bodi people 87–88
Boers see Afrikaners
Bolivia: carnival **304;** music **191;** peoples **8,** 88, 344–346, **345,** 349, 351–353
Borneo (island), Indonesia: early agriculture 127; peoples 119–120
Bororo language family 330–331
Bororo people 330–331
Bosnia: peoples 208–209, 214, 218; religion 197
Bosniaks 208–209
Bosnian Muslims see Bosniaks
Botswana: peoples **25,** 25–26, **27,** 28
Brazil: languages 332; music **191;** peoples 233–234, 236, 253, **308,** 330–332, **331,** 333, **334,** 335–336, 340, 341–343, **343,** 350–351, **351,** 353; storytelling 253
Brazilians 331–332
Breton (language) 227
Bretons 225, **226,** 227
British Isles: genetics 243
British people see English people
British West Indies 313
Buddhism: development 94; East Asia 109, 111, 112, 113, 115, 116; Europe 198, 199, **200,** 230; North Asia 140; South Asia 131, 134–135; Southeast Asia 122, 124, 125, 126
Budidjarra language group 155
Bulgaria: peoples 85; proverb 203
Burkina Faso: peoples 34, 75
Burundi: languages 57; peoples 44
Burushaski (language) 101
Burusho people 101, **101**
Bushmen see San people
Cajun French (language) 292
Cajun Indians **293**
Cajuns 292–293
Cakchiquel people 321
California Indians 260, 274–275
Cambodia: peoples 124–125
Cambodians 133
Cameroon: peoples 35
Canada: igloos 302; languages 229; peoples 58, 214, 229–230, 232, 240–241, 258, 260–261, 265–266, 268–269, **288,** 289–290, **290**
Cann, Rebecca 53
Cape York peoples **154,** 155, **157**
Carbon 14 297
Cargo cults 150, 172
Carib Indians 312–313, 320, 332–333, **333**
Cariban language family 332–333, 335
Caribbean region: map 310; peoples 310–319
Caribbean region: map 310; peoples 310–319
Caribou Eskimos 265
Caroline Islands: navigation 143
Caste system 129, 131–132, 133
Castilian (language) 237, 354
Catalan (language) 227, 236
Catalans 227–228
Catholicism see Roman Catholicism
Caucasus region, Asia-Europe: map 96; peoples 96–99
Cave art 6–7, **7**
Cayuga Indians 290–291

Celestial navigation **142,** 142–143, **144**
Celtic language family 225, 227, 238, 245, 249
Celtic peoples 225, 227, 244
Central Africa: map 42; peoples 42–44, **43**
Central and South New Guinea Kutuban language family 169–170
Central Asia: houses 300–301; map 100; migrations to Europe 198, 231; peoples 76, 100–107
Central Eskimos 265
Central Europe: map 208; peoples 208–217
Central South America: map 350; peoples 350–353
Central Sudanic language family 42, 44
Chad 158
Chadic language family 36–37
Chamorro language famly 182
Chamorro people 182–183
Chechens 98–99
Chehalis people 252–253
Cherewan Indians 296
Cherokee Indians **294,** 295, 296, **297**
Cherokee (language) 295
Cheyenne Indians 276–277, 279, 280
Chickasaw Indians 295
Chile: archaeology 297; peoples 346, **346,** 356
Chimbu people 164–165, **165**
China, People's Republic of: early agriculture 127; food 163; peoples 85, **86,** 102, 107, 109–111, **110, 111,** 115–117, **116,** 120–121, 125, 137–138
Chinese (language) 109, 110–111, 113, 126
Chinese people 112, 166, 177. see also Han people
Chipaya people **8**
Chippewa Indians 280, 288–289, **289,** 290
Chiricahua Apache 270–271
Choctaw Indians 295
Cholan-Tzeltalan language family 321–323
Chon language family 356
Christians: Australia 152, 162, 163; Caribbean region **311,** 316; Caucasus 93–94, 96; Central Africa 43; Central Europe 208, 211, 213, 214, 217; Central South America 350; East Africa 46, 48, 49; East Asia 112; Eastern Europe 198, 204, 206; Europe 196–197, 211, 213–214, 233; Fiji **166,** 167; Melanesia 151, **166,** 167, 170; Mesoamerica **323;** Micronesia 183, 184, 185; Middle East 64, 67, 79, 81, 82; North Africa 67, 71, 72; North America 298, 299; Northern Europe 245–246; Polynesia 179, 180; South Asia 131, 134; Southeast Asia 120, 126; Southern Africa 28, 31; Southern Europe 218; West Africa 38; Western Europe 233, 234, 236. see also Amish; Coptic Christians; Eastern Orthodoxy; Greek Orthodox Church; Lutherans; Mennonites; Protestants; Roman Catholicism; Russian Orthodox Church
Chukchi people 136–137
Chukotko-Kamchatkan language family 136–137

Chuuk Islanders 184–185
Ciboney people 311, 312
Clovis culture 297
Colombia: peoples 318–319, 333, 335, 336
Comanche Indians 270
Comoran people: proverb 51
Congo, Democratic Republic of the: languages 57; marriage 20, 22; peoples 42, 43, 44
Congo, Republic of: peoples 43
Copper Eskimos 265
Coptic Christians 46, **65**, 67, 71–72, **82**
Cora Indians 323
Cornish people 238
Cossacks **103**
Côte d'Ivoire: peoples 23, **40**
Cree Indians **288**, 289–290
Creek Indians 295–296
Creole languages 308; African-based 298–299; English-based 160–161, 317–318, 336, 338–339; French-based 314, 316–317
Creole people 292, 293
Crimeans **199**
Cro-Magnon people 194, 224, 231
Croatia: peoples 209–210, 214
Croatian (language) 210
Croatoan Indians 296
Croats 208, 209–210, 214, 217
Crow Indians 279–280, 302
Csángó people **195**
Cuba: peoples 311
Cuna people **337**
Curaçao: proverb 314
Cushitic language family 49, 55–56
Cypriots 222
Cyprus: peoples 85, 219, 221–222
Cyrillic alphabet 204, 205, 214
Czech (language) 211, 215
Czech Republic: Austrian domination 197; peoples **197, 210,** 210–211
Czechs **197, 210,** 210–211, 216, 217
Czigany see Roma
Dacians 203
Dakota Indians 260, **278–279,** 280–281, **281**
Danes 239–240
Danish (language) 239
Dayak people 119–120
Deitsch see Amish
Denmark: peoples 239–240, 241–242
Desana people 333, 335
Dine people see Navajo Indians
Dinka people **49,** 51
Djibouti: peoples 56
DNA: Africa 29, 53, 73, 158; Australia 158; Central Asia 12; Europe 231, 248; Genographic Project uses 12; markers 243; Middle East 73, 82; mitochondrial 29, 53; nonfunctional 337; South Asia 127
Dogon language family 34–35
Dogon people **33, 34,** 34–35, 303
Dolgan people 141
Dong people 110
Dravidian language family 135
Dravidians 133
Dreaming (belief system) 152, 155, 159, 160, 163
Drukpas 116
Druze people 79, 81
Dutch (language) 228
Dutch people **228,** 228–229, **231,** 336, 338
East Africa: map 46; peoples **22,** 46–52, 53, 54, 57, 130
East Asia: early agriculture 127, 181; map 108; peoples 108–117

East-Fijian Polynesian language family 174, 175, 178, 179, 180
East Indians 166, 313–314
East New Guinea Highlands language family 164–165
East Slavic languages 204, 205
Easter Island, South Pacific Ocean 181
Eastern Baltic languages 200
Eastern Band 295
Eastern Europe: map 198; migrations to North America 261; peoples 198–207
Eastern (Muskogean stock) language family 295–296
Eastern Orthodoxy: Europe 196, 203, 204–205, 206, 208, 210, 218, 242
Eastern Sudanic language family 72, 74
Ecuador: peoples **339,** 339–340, 346, 348, 349
Efe people 10, 20, 42
Egypt: peoples 66, 69, 71–72, 74, 76, 80; religions 67, **82**
Egyptians 71–72, **74**
Enga people 165–166
England: peoples 240
English (language) 20, 58, 81, 131, 134, 154, 171, 174, 186, 221, 228, 238, 239, 240, 245, 251, 272, 292, 296, 298–299, 306, 311–314, 317, 321; poetic devices 254; writings 255
English people 153, 177, **240,** 240–241
Equatorial Guinea: peoples 35
Eritrea: religions 64, **65**
Eskimo-Aleut languages 267
Eskimo language family 262–263, 265–266
Eskimos 262–263, **265,** 265–266, **266**
Estonian (language) 196
Ethiopia: peoples 46–47, 48–49, 51, 55–56, 56, 76; proverb 72
Ethiopian Orthodox Church 46
Euro-Caribbean people 314
Europe: genetics 231; languages 196; music 191; peoples 78, 117, 192–255. see also Central; Eastern; Northern; Southern; Western
European Union 197, 200, 242, 245, 251
Europeans 166, 192–255
Euskera (language) 224
Evangelical Christianity 134, 211, 218, 239, 242, 246
Evenk people 87, **137,** 137–138, 140, 302
Eyak people 258
Falasha people see Beta Israel people
Fang people 35
Fante people: proverb 36
Faroese people **241,** 241–242
Farsi (language) 100
Fiji, South Pacific Ocean: colonization 181; peoples 135, **166,** 166–167, **167,** 169; political system 151
Fijians 166–167, 169, 172, 178
Finland: peoples 242, 248
Finnish (language) 196, 242
Finno-Ugric languages 211, 242, 248
Finns 242, 250
First Nations 260–261, **288,** 290, **290.** see also specific peoples
Fortunato, Don **191**
France: cave paintings 231; emi-

grants to North America 261; peoples 200, 224–225, **225,** 227, 229–230, **230,** 232, 286
French Guiana: peoples 313, 338
French (language) 20, 54, 75, 79, 196, 222, 224, 229, 292, 314, 321
French people 229–230, **230,** 232, 292
French Polynesia: peoples 179–180, **181**
Frisian (language) 229
Frisians 228–229
Frum, John 172
Fuegian Indians 356
Fulani people 33, 36, 37
Gabon: peoples 35
Galician (language) 236
Gamelan music 188–189, **190**
Ganda (language) 47
Gandhi, Mohandas K. 129–130
Garifuna people 320–321
Gê-Kaingang language family 341–343
Geechee people see Gullah people
Ge'ez (language) 48
Genetic drift 337
Genetics see DNA
Genographic Project 12–13, 158, 231, 243
Genome 29, 337
Georgia (republic): music 191
German (language) 154, 171, 222, 232–233, 239, 286
Germanic language family 24–25, 153–155, 174–175, 176–177, 228–229, 232–233, 239–242, 244–246, 248–251, 286–288, 314
Germans 213, **232,** 232–233
Germany: emigrants to North America 261; peoples 85, 200, **232,** 232–233, 286
Gers see Yurts
Ghana: peoples 22, 32–33, **35,** 254
Ghers see Yurts
Gitanes see Roma
Giyadjarra language group 155
Global warming: impact **264**
Gould, Stephen Jay 82
Great Basin, U.S.: map 282; peoples 282–285
Greater Antilles: peoples 312
Greece: ancient history 196; peoples 218, 219, **220–221,** 221–222
Greek Cypriots 222
Greek language family 154, 219, 221–222
Greek Orthodox Church 221, 222
Greeks 219, **220–221,** 221–222
Greenland: igloos 302; peoples 265–266
Grenada, West Indies: peoples 313
Guadeloupe, West Indies: peoples 313
Guaicuruan language family 350–351
Guam (island), Mariana Islands, North Pacific Ocean: peoples 182–183
Guaraní people 350, **351**
Guaraúnos see Warao people
Guatemala: peoples **309,** 320–323
Guinea: peoples 36
Gujaratis 129–130; proverb 131
Gullah (language) 298–299
Gullah people **261,** 298–299, **299**
Gurkhas 132
Guyana: peoples 313, 333
Gwichin people see Kutchin people
Gypsies see Roma
Haida Indians **59,** 269
Haiʟʟom people 252
Haiti: languages 308, 311; peoples

311, 314, **315,** 316–317; proverb 319; religions **311,** 316
Haitians 314, **315,** 316–317
Halkomelem (language) 58, 60
Han people 110–111
Haudenosaunee see Iroquois people
Hausa (language) 37, 75
Hausa people 22, 32, 36–37, **37**
Havasupai Indians **271,** 271–272
Havel, Václav 211, 216
Hawaii: colonization 181; navigation 142, 143, 144, **145;** peoples **150, 175,** 179, 185
Hawaiian (language) 174
Hawaiians 174–175
Hebrew (language) 46, 64, 66, 76, 77, 81
Hidatsa Indians 281
Highland Maya **321,** 321–323, **323**
Hindi (language) 58, 131, 132, 135, 313–314
Hinduism: Caribbean region **312, 313;** sacred texts **253;** South Asia 94, 128, 129, 130, 131, 132, 133, 134, 135, **253;** Southeast Asia 95, 118, **120,** 122, 124
Hispaniola (island), West Indies 314; peoples 312
Hmong-Mien language family 120–121
Hmong people **110,** 120–121
Hokan language stock see Pomoan language family
Holocaust 200, 201, 203, 213, 216, 233
Honduras: peoples 320–321
Hopi Indians **272,** 272–273
Houses 300–303, **301**
Hualapi people see Walapai people
Huichol Indians 323, 325
Huli people **151,** 166
Human origins 12, 29, 53
Hungarian (language) 196
Hungarians see Magyars
Hungary: control of Transylvania 203; peoples 200, 211–212, **212, 213**
Hunzakuts see Burusho people
Hutterites 261
Hutu people 44
Iatmul people 170
Ibo people see Igbo people
Iceland: peoples 242, 244, **244**
Icelanders 242, 244, **244**
Icelandic (language) 244
Ifugao (language) 122
Ifugao people 121–122
Igbo people 37–38, 40
Igloos 302
Iglulik Eskimos 265
Imazighen people 70, 71
Inca 309, 346, 347, 349; festival reenactment **347**
Indentured servants 314
India: agriculture **129, 133;** caste system 129, 133; emigrations 200–201, 203, 261; geography 128; houses 300; influence on other cultures 313–314; languages 200–201, 229, 255; music 189–190, 191; peoples **95,** 96, 116, 128–131, 132–134, 135, **253;** storytelling 255
Indian Removal Act (1830) 295, 296
Indic languages 200–201
Indo-Aryan language family 129–130, 131–133, 134–135
Indo-Caribbean culture 313–314
Indo-European language family 96, 128, 196, 200–201, 203, 204, 218, 221, 228

Indo-Europeans: migrations 196
Indo-Fijians 166, **167**
Indo-Iranian languages 100
Indonesia: early agriculture 127; food 163; languages 54; music 188–189, **190**, 191; peoples 118–120, 122, 125, 169–170; religions 120
Ingush 98–99
Introgression 127
Inuit **264,** 265–266, **267,** 302
Inupiat 262, 263
Iran: peoples 64, 66, 76, 77–79, 82–83, **83,** 85, **88,** 97, 100, **102,** 106–107; religion 67
Iranian language family 77–79, 82–83, 100, 104, 106
Iraq: peoples 66, 69, 76, 77–79, **78,** 106
Ireland: peoples 245, **249**
Irish Gaelic (language) 245
Irish people 245, **249**
Iroquoian language family 290–291, 295
Iroquoian-speaking peoples 258, 296
Iroquois League 290–291
Iroquois people 290–291, **291**
Islam *see* Muslims
Israel: peoples 48–49, 51, 64, 66, 69, 76–77, 80–82, 203
Italian (language) 154, 196, 222, 223, 354
Italians 222–223, **223**; proverb 237
Italic language family 196, 203–204, 222–223, 227–228, 229–230, 233–234, 236–237, 292–293, 331–332, 354–356
Italy: peoples 222–223, **223**
Itzá (language) 323
Jamaica, West Indies: languages 311; peoples 313, **317,** 317–318; religions **316,** 317–318
Jamaicans 317–318
Japan: early agriculture 127; peoples 108–109, 111–112, **113**
Japanese (language) 112, 113, 186
Japanese language family 111–112
Japanese people 111–112, 186
Java (island), Indonesia: peoples 122
Javanese (language) 122
Javanese people 122
Jews: Africa 22, 48–49; Europe 197, 200, 203, 213, 216, 218, 223, 230, 233; Middle East 64, 66, 67, 76–77, **77,** 80; South America 354. *see also* Beta Israel people
Jicarilla Apache 270
Jívaro Indians *see* Shuar people
Jivaroan language family 339–340
Jordan: peoples 69, 80
Joseph, Chief (Nez Percé) 283, 285
Judaism *see* Jews
Kadiwéu people 350–351
Kalahari Desert, Botswana 73; peoples 20, **25,** 26
Kallawaya Indians 345–346
Kalmyk (language) 199
Kalmyks 198–199, **200**
Kam-Sui language family 110
Kanjobalan-Chujean language family 321–323
Kayapó Indians *see* Xikrín Indians
Kazakh (language) 103
Kazakhs 102–103, **103, 114–115;** proverb 104
Kazakhstan: peoples 85, 102–103, 107, 116
Kente cloth 32, **35**
Kenya: museums 53; peoples **50,** 52, **53,** 55, 56–57
Khalkhs *see* Mongols

Khmers 124–125, **127**
Khoi people 29
Khoisan language family 25–26
KiKongo (language) 311
Kikuyu people **50,** 52
Kimbangu, Simon 43
Kinh *see* Vietnamese people
Kiowa-Apache 260, 271
Kiowa Indians 271
Kiribati: navigation 142
Klamath Indians 282–283
Kogi people **318,** 318–319, **319**
Koita people 170
Kombai people 302
Kongo people 43; proverb 28
Koorie people *see* Wurundjeri people
Korea: emigrants to North America 261; peoples 112–113
Korean (language) 113
Koreans 112–113
Korowai people 302
Koryak people 136–137, **255**
Koyukon people 258
Kreyol (language) 308, 311, 314
Krio (language) 298
Kuikuru people 335
Kurdish (language) 77, 78
Kurds **66,** 77–79, **78**
Kutchin people 258
Kutenai Indians 276
Kwa language family 32–33
Kwakiutl Indians 268–269
Kwoma people 170
Kyrgyz (language) 103, 104
Kyrgyz people 103–104
Kyrgyzstan: houses 300–301; peoples 85, 103–104; storytelling 252
Lacandon Indians 323
Lacandon (language) 323
Ladakhis 116
Ladino culture 322
Ladino (language) 77
Lake Mungo 3 (human skeleton) 158
Lakota Sioux 260, 279, 280, 302
Language Hotspots 59; map 60
Language isolates 101, 108–109, 112–113, 224–225, 340, 356
Languages: loss of 9, 58–60
Laos: peoples **110,** 120–121, 125
Lapita people 181
Lapps *see* Sami people
Latin (language) 203, 236, 255
Latvian (language) 200
Lebanese people 79–80, 177
Lebanon: peoples 69, 79–80
Lese people 20, 22, 42
Lesser Antilles: peoples 312, 320–321, **333**
Lévi-Strauss, Claude 330–331
Libya: peoples 66, 69, 70–71, 75
Lipan Apache 270
Lithuania: peoples 199–200
Lithuanian (language) 200
Lithuanians 199–200, 213
Louisiana: peoples 292–293, **293**
Lowland Maya 323, **327**
Lowry, Henry Berry 296, 298
Luganda (language) 47, 48
Lumbee people 296, 298
Lutherans: Europe 211, 239, 241–242, 246, 250; Melanesia 164
Luzon (island), Philippines: peoples 121
Maasai people *see* Masai people
Macedonia: peoples 218, **219**
Madagascar: market **21**; peoples 52, 54–55
Madurese 119, 120
Magyar (language) 211

Magyars 203, 211–212, **213,** 216
Maize 327
Makah people 261
Maku language family 336
Maku people 334
Malagasy (language) 52, 54
Malagasy people 52, **52,** 54–55
Malayo-Polynesian language family 166–167, 169; Bali-Sasak 118–120; Chamorro 182–183; East Barito 52, 54–55; East-Fijian Polynesian 174–176, 178–180; Javanese 122; Malayic 125; Micronesian 184–185; New Ireland 173; Northern Philippine 121–122; Palauan 185–186; Papuan Tip 173; South Vanuatu 171–172; Yapese Oceanic 186–187
Malaysia: early settlements 127; genetics 127; peoples 119–120, 135
Mali: Dogon people **34**; houses 303; mosque **39**; peoples **18–19,** 33–35, 70, 71, 75
Manambu people 170
Mandan Indians 260, 281
Mandarin Chinese (language) 58, 110, 116
Mande language family 33–34
Mandjildjarra language group 155
Mangbetu people 44
Maori people 175–176, 177
Maoris 148, **177**
Maps: human migrations 13; language hotspots 60; world regions 16–17
Mapuche Indians 346, **346**
Mardu people 155–156
Mariana Islands, North Pacific Ocean: peoples 182–183
Marind-anim people 169–170
Maronites 79
Maroons 311, 314, 320; descendants **338**
Marquesas: colonization 181
Marshall Islands, North Pacific Ocean: colonization 181; peoples 185
Marshallese **184,** 185; proverb 160
Martinique, West Indies: peoples 313
Masai people **47, 53, 54,** 55
Masterpiece of Oral and Intangible Heritage of Humanity 122
Mataco Indians 351–353, **352, 353**
Mataco language family 351–353
Mauritius (island), Indian Ocean: festivals **135**; peoples 135, **135**
Maya **321,** 321–323, **323,** 327
Mayan language family 321–322
Maybury-Lewis, David 10
Mbayá people 350–351
Mbuti people 20, 42
McJunkin, George 297
Mead, Margaret 11
Melanesia: cargo cults 150; colonization 181; colony 164; migrations 148; peoples 164–173; political system 150–151
Melanesians 172
Mende (language) 298
Mende people: proverb 41
Mennonites **260,** 286
Meo people *see* Hmong people
Merina people 52, 54
Mescalero Apache 270
Mesoamerica: map 320; peoples 306, 308, 320–326, 327, 328–329
Métis people 289–290, **290**
Mevlevi Sufis **84,** 85
Mexica *see* Aztec
Mexicans 258, **259**

Mexico: music 191; peoples 270, 275, 321–323, **323, 324–325,** 325–326, 327, **328,** 328–329, **329**; proverbs 326, 353
Miao people *see* Hmong people
Miccosukee Indians 296
Micronesia: colonization 181; definition 148; map 182; navigation **144,** 145; nuclear testing 151; peoples 182–187, **183**
Micronesian language family 184, 185
Middle East: map 76; peoples 64, 68–70, 73, 76–85, 96; religions 66
Middle Sepik peoples 170
Migrations, human: Africa to Australia 158; Americas 337; Asia 127; Asia to Melanesia 148; Central Asia to Europe 231; Central Asia to North America 267; DNA tracking 12, 73, 82, 102, 158, 243; Europe 243; map 13; Middle East 82; Middle East to Central Asia 102; North Africa to Middle East 73; Polynesia 181; recent 243
Minangkabau people 125
Mississippian cultures 258, 295
Mixtec Indians 306, 325–326
Mixtecan language family 325–326
Modoc Indians 282–283
Mohawk Indians 290–291
Moldova: peoples 203–204
Moldovan (language) 204
Moldovans 203–204
Mon-Khmer language family 124–125, 126
Mon-Khmer peoples 133
Monchak (language) **61**
Monchak people **61**
Mongolia: houses 300–301, **303**; peoples **61,** 86, 88–89, **93,** 102, **114–115,** 115–116, 138, **189**; storytelling 252
Mongolian (language) 61, 199
Mongolian language family 198–199
Mongolic language family 115–116
Mongols 97, 102, 103, 107, 115–116, **189,** 198
Montenegro: peoples 214–215
Moravia 261
Morocco: peoples **70,** 70–71
Motu people 170–171
Motuan (language) 171
Mozambique: languages 20; peoples 26–28, 57
Munda language family 133–134
Mundurucú people 335–336
Munduruku language family 335–336
Music 188–191
Muskogee Indians 295
Muslims: Africa 22, 33, 36, 37, 40, 51, 56, 75; Asia 92; Caribbean region 312, 313; Caucasus 97, **97,** 98; Central Asia 100, 101, 103–104, 106, 107; Central Europe 208, 209, 211–212, 214, 215; East Africa 46, 51, 56, 57; East Asia 117; Eastern Europe 201; Europe 197; Middle East 64, 66, 67, **67,** 71, 72, 77, 78, 79, 80, 81, 82, 83, 85; North Africa 22, 64, 66, 68, 69, **70,** 71, 72, 75; South Asia 128, 132, 133; Southeast Asia 118, 120, 122, 125; Southern Europe 218, 219, 222, 223; West Africa 22, 33, 37, 40, 41; Western Europe 230
Musqueam people 60
Myanmar: peoples 125
Na-Dene languages 267

Naga people 130–131
Nahua people 326
Nahuatl (language) 325, 326
Nakh language family 98–99
Nakota Sioux 280
Namau people 171
Namibia: peoples 25–26, 28, 252
Nampeyo (Hopi-Tewa artist) 273
Natchez Indians 254–255
Native Americans 58, 260, 261, **277**, 292, 302. see also specific peoples
Navajo Indians **256–257**, 258, 260, 270, **273**, 274; proverb 275
Navigation **142**, 142–145, **144, 145**
Neandertals 6, 231
Nelson, Michael Jagamara **161**
Nenets people 138, **139, 140**
Nentsy people see Nenets
Nepal: peoples 116, 131–132
Nepali (language) 131
Nepalis 131–132
Netherlands: peoples **228**, 228–229
Netsilik Eskimos 265
New Caledonia, South Pacific Ocean 172
New Guinea (island), Indonesia-Papua New Guinea: genetics 127; languages **149, 151**, 164–166, **165, 168–169**, 169–171
New Ireland language family 173
New Zealand: colonialism 148; peoples 175–177, **177**, 179
New Zealanders 166, 176–177
Nez Percé Indians 283, **283, 284**, 285, 302
Ngarrindjeri people 156
Nicaragua: peoples 320
Niger: houses 301–302; peoples 36–37, **37**, 70, 75, **87, 89**
Nigeria: peoples 22, **23**, 36–38, **37**, 40, 41, **41**, 75
Niles, Eldridge 82
Nilo-Saharan language family 72
Nilotic language family 51, 55
Nobiin (language) 72
Nomads **83, 86**, 86–89, **87, 303**
Noongar people 156
North Africa: emigrants 229–230; map 68; peoples 64, 68–72, 73, 74–75, 76; religions 66
North America: languages 267; peoples 82, 96, 117, 130, 245, 256–299
North Asia: map 136; peoples 136–141
North Korea: peoples 112–113
Northeast (region), North America: map 286; peoples 286–291
Northern Athapaskan people 258
Northern Cheyenne Indians 277, 279
Northern Europe: genetics 243; map 238; peoples 238–251
Northern Ireland **243**, 245
Northern Mariana Islands: peoples 182–183
Northern Paiute Indians 285
Northern Piegan Indians 276
Northern Pomo Indians 275
Northwest Coast Indians 282
Northwest coast (region), North America: map 268; peoples 260, 268–269
Norway: houses 302; music 191; peoples 245–246, **246–247**, 248; sheep **245**
Norwegian (language) 246
Norwegians 245–246, 248
Nuba people: houses **302**
Nubians 72, 74

Nukak people 336
Nunamiut people 263
Nyoongah people see Noongar people
Nyungah people see Noongar people
Oceania: colonization 148, 150, 181; navigation 142–145; peoples 146–187
Odul people see Yukaghir people
Ogoni people 10
Ojibwa Indians see Chippewa Indians
Old Believers 261
Old Church Slavonic (language) 204
Olmec 327
Ona Indians see Selknam Indians
Ona language family see Chon language family
Oneida Indians 290–291
Onondaga Indians 290–291
O'odham (language) 275
Orinoco Basin, South America: map 330; peoples 330–336, 337, 338–343, **341**
Oriya (language) 134
Oromo people 47
Otavaleño Indians 346, 348
Otomí Indians 191, 326, 328
Otomian language family 326, 328
Ottoman Turks 85, 208. see also Turks
Pacific Islanders 175
Pakhtun people see Pashtun people
Pakistan: peoples 100, 101, **101**, 104, **105**, 106, **107**, 117, 132–133
Palau: peoples 185–186; political system 150
Palauan language family 185
Palauans 185–186
Palawa people 156, 159
Palestine 66, 80
Palestinian Territory: peoples 80–82
Palestinians 80–82, **81**
Pama-Nyungan language family 152–153, 155–156, 159–160, 161, 163
Pamiri people 102
Panama: peoples **337**
Panoan language family 330
Papago Indians see Tohono O'odham Indians
Papiamento (language) 308, 311
Papua New Guinea: genetics 127; houses 300, 302; languages 171; peoples **149, 151**, 164–166, **165, 168–169**, 169–171, 173
Papuan Tip language family 173
Papuans 160
Paraguay: peoples 350
Pashtu (language) 104
Pashtun people 104, 106, **107**
Patagonia (region), Argentina **356**; map 354; peoples 354–356
Pathan people see Pashtun people
Patois languages 311, 317
Pawnee Indians 260
Pennsylvania Dutch see Amish
Persian (language) 77, 78
Persians 64, 82–83, 97
Peru: archaeology 347; houses 300, 302–303; languages 61; music 191; peoples 330, 339, 344–346, **345**, 347, **347**, 348–349
Petroglyphs **11**
Philippines: emigrants 261; houses **301**; peoples 121–122
Piailug, Pius "Mau" **144**, 145, **145**
Pintubi people 159–160
Plains Apache see Kiowa-Apache

Plains Indians 260, 261, 270, 271, 282, 289–290
Plains (region), North America: map 276; peoples 276–281
Plateau Penutian language family 282–283, 285
Plateau (region), U.S.: map 282; peoples 282–285
Poland: peoples 96, 212–214
Polar Eskimos 265
Poles 177, 200, 212–214; proverb 211
Polish (language) 213
Polynesia: colonization 181; definition 148; map 174; peoples **150**, 174–180; political system 150
Polynesians: navigation **142**, 142–145
Pomo Indians 274–275
Pomoan language family 274–275
Portugal: colonies 331–332, 335, 353; peoples 233–234, **234–235**, 236
Portuguese (language) 20, 196, 234, 331–332
Portuguese people 233–234, 236
Powwows **277, 284**
Protestants: Caribbean region 316, 317; Central Europe 211, 216, 217; East Africa 48; Eastern Europe 203; Europe 211; Micronesia 184, 185; North America 296; Northern Europe 197, 240, 245, 251; Polynesia 174–175, 176, 177, 180; South America 341, 354; Western Europe 228, 229, 233
Provençal (language) 227
Pueblo Indians 260, 270
Puebloan peoples 260, 297
Puerto Rico: peoples **312**, 313
Punctuated equilibrium 82
Punjabi (language) 132
Punjabis 132–133
Purépecha Indians see Tarascan Indians
Pygmies 42, **43**, 44
Qashqai people 83, **83**, 85
Q'eros people 348–349
Quechua Indians 349
Quechua (language) 347
Quechua-Paquina language family 345–346
Quechuan language family 346, 348–349
Quiché Indians 321, 322
Quichean-Mamean language family 321–323
Radiocarbon dating 297
Rastafarianism **316**, 318
Roma 200–201, **201, 202**, 203, **237**
Roman Catholicism: Australia 160; Caribbean region 307, 308, 316; Caucasus 96; Central Europe 208, 210, 211, 213–214, 216, **216**, 217; East Africa 48; East Asia 113; Eastern Europe 200, 203; Melanesia 164; Mesoamerica 307, 325, 329; Micronesia 183, 184, 187; Middle East 79; North America 290, 292–293; Northern Europe 239, 240, 245; Polynesia 177, 179, 180; South America 309, 332, 333, 340, 341, 342, 346, 348, 349, 352, 353, 354; Southeast Asia 126; Southern Europe 196, 218, 223; West Africa 23; Western Europe 196, 201, 224, 227, 228, 229, 233, 234, 236, 237
Romance languages 222, 227, 234

Romani see Roma
Romania: peoples 96, **195**, 203–204
Romanian (language) 196, 203, 204
Romanians 203–204
Romany (language) 200–201
Russia: emigrants 261; peoples 98–99, 102, **103**, 108, 116, 136–138, 140–141, 198–199, **200, 204**, 204–205, 248, **255**, 263
Russian (language) 77, 98, 103, 104, 204, 205
Russian Orthodox Church 141, 199, 204–205, 242
Russians 97, 102, 104, 199, **199**, 200, 204–205, 265
Rwanda: languages 57; peoples 44, **45**
Saami people see Sami people
Sahara, Africa: climate 73, 158; houses 300, 301–302; peoples 75
Sahel, Africa: peoples 75
St. Croix (island), U.S. Virgin Islands: peoples 313
St. Kitts (island), West Indies: peoples 313
St. Vincent, West Indies: peoples 313, 320–321
Sakha people see Yakut people
Sami (language) 248
Sami language family 248
Sami people **239**, 242, **246–247**, 248, 250, 302
Samoa, South Pacific Ocean 180, 181; peoples 178–179
Samoans 172, **178**, 178–179
Samoyed people see Nenets
Samoyedic language family 138
San people 20, **25**, 25–26, **27**, 29
Sanskrit (language) 253
Santee Indians see Dakota Indians
Saramaka people 336, **338**, 338–339; proverb 340
Sarsi people 258
Satawalese people 143, 145
Saudi Arabia: peoples **69**, 117; religion 67
Savara people see Sora people
Scandinavia: languages 239, 246
Scandinavians 242, 243, 244
Scotland: government 238, 249; peoples 248–249, **250**
Scots English (language) 249
Scots Gaelic (language) 249
Scots people 177, 248–249, **250**; proverb 251
Sea Islanders see Gullah people
Sekani people 258
Selknam Indians 356
Seminole Indians **259**, 295–296
Semitic language family 37, 46–47, 48–49, 51, 64, 66, 68–70, 71–72, 76–77, 79–82
Seneca Indians 290–291
Senegal: languages 229; peoples **2–3**, 36, **38**, 40–41
Sephardic Jews 76, 77
Sequoyah (Cherokee) 295
Serbia: alliance with Bosnian Serbs 209; peoples 214–215, **215**, 219
Serbian (language) 214
Serbian Orthodox Church 214
Serbo-Croatian (language) 154, 208
Serbo-Croatian language family 103–104, 128
Serbs 208, 209–210, 214–215, **215**
Shaka (Zulu founder) 28
Shamanism: Amazon and Orinoco Basins 330, 335, 336, 340, 341, 342, 343; Asia **110**, 113;

Caribbean 312; Central South America 350, 352; East Asia 115; Europe 248; Mesoamerica **323**, 325; North America 266, 282, 290; North Asia 136–137, 138, 140, 141; Patagonia 356; South America 9, 309; Southeast Asia 121
Shan people 125
Shenouda III, Pope **82**
Sherpas **94**, 116, 132
Shiites 79, 82, 83
Shona (language) 27
Shona people 20, 26–28, 190
Shoshoni Indians 276
Shuar people **339**, 339–340
Siberia (region), Russia: houses 300, 302; languages 58, 60–61; peoples 60–61, 87, 88, 116, 136–138, 140–141, 198–199, **255**, 263
Siboney people *see* Ciboney people
Sicilian (language) 223
Sicilians **196**, 223; proverb 222
Sierra Leone: languages 298; peoples 298, 299
Sikkim: peoples 116
Simbu people *see* Chimbu people
Singapore: peoples 135
Sinhala (language) 134
Sinhalese people 134–135
Sinitic language family 110–111
Siouan Indians 296
Siouan language family 279–281
Sioux Indians *see* Dakota Indians
Six Nations Iroquois Confederacy 290–291
Slave trade: Americas 261, 308; Caribbean region 310, 311, 312, 313, 314; Central Africa 43; East Africa 54, 57; Mesoamerica 258, 306, 320; North Africa 75; North America 261, 269, 282, 295–296, 298; South America 332, 336, 338, 351, 354; West Africa 32, 35, 40
Slavic language family 204–206, 208–211, 212–217
Slavic peoples 217
Slovak (language) 211, 215, 216
Slovakia: peoples **201**, 203, 215–217
Slovaks 203, 210, 211, **214**, 215–217
Slovene (language) 217, 222
Slovenes **216**, 217
Slovenia: peoples 217
Somali people 55–56, **56**
Somalia: peoples 55–56, 57, 87–88
Somaliland 55–56
Sora (language) 134
Sora people 133–134
South Africa: peoples 24–26, 28, **29**, 31, 135
South America: languages 234, 337; music 191; peoples 308–309, 312, 337
South Asia: map 128; peoples 128–135; population genetics 127
South Korea: peoples 112–113
South Slavic languages 214, 217
Southeast Asia: genetics 127; map 118; peoples 118–126
Southeast (region), U.S.: map 292; peoples 292–296
Southern Africa: map 24; peoples 24–28, 31
Southern Cheyenne Indians 277
Southern Europe: map 218; peoples 218–223
Southern Piegan Indians 276
Southwest (region), U.S.: map 270;

peoples 261, 270–275
Spain: cave art 7; peoples 71, 77, 224–225, **225**, 227–228, **229**, **236**, 236–237, **237** Spanish (language) 58, 77, 196, 224, 236, 306, 321, 323, 354
Spanish people 236–237, 292, 293
Sri Lanka: peoples 134–135
Storytelling 252–255, **254**, **255**, **271**
Sua people 42
Sub-Saharan Africa: human origins 53; peoples **18–61**
Sudan: houses **302**; peoples 20, **49**, 51, 72, 74
Sufism 208
Sumatra (island), Indonesia: early agriculture 127; peoples 125
Sunnis 79, 81, 208
Suriname: peoples 313, 333, 336, **338**, 338–339; proverbs 332, 336
Suyá people 191
Swahili (language) 57, 321
Swahili people 56–57, **57**
Sweden: peoples **192–193**, 248, 249–251
Swedes **192–193**, 249–251
Swedish (language) 250
Switzerland: emigrants 261; peoples 286
Syncretic religions 317–318
Syria: peoples 69, 77, 78, 80, 106; proverbs 79, 80, 85
Tahitians 175, 179–180, **181**
Taic language family 125–126
Taino Indians 313
Taiwan: early agriculture 127; peoples 110, **121**, **123**, 181
Tajikistan: peoples 82
Tamasheq (language) 75
Tamil (language) 135
Tamils 134, 135, **135**
Tannese **171**, 171–172
Tanzania: peoples **47**, 52, 55, 56–57
Tapirapé people 340
Tarascan Indians 328–329
Tarascan language family 328–329
Telugu (language) 134
Tepehuans 323
Teton Indians *see* Lakota Sioux
Tewa people 273
Thai people 110, **119**, 125–126
Thailand: monks **4–5**; peoples **110**, **119**, 125–126
Thraco-Illyrian languages 196
Three Affiliated Tribes 281
Tibet **109**, 115, **117**
Tibetan Buddhism **109**, 116, 198
Tibetans 116, 131; proverb 121
Tibeto-Burman language family 109–110, 116, 130–131
Timucua Indians 295
Tito, Josip Broz 208, 209, 214
Tiwian language family 160
Tiwis **159**, 160
Tlinglit Indians 269, **269**
Tofa (language) 58, 60–61
Tofa people 60–61
Togo: peoples 41
Tohono O'odham Indians **274**, 275
Tok Pisin (language) 171
Tolai (language) 171
Tolai people 173
Tonga: colonization 181; peoples 180
Tongans 178, 180
Torres Strait Islanders 160–161
Totzil people 321
Touareg people *see* Tuareg people
Trail of Tears 295, 296
Trans-New Guinea language stock 165
Trinidad (island), Trinidad and

Tobago, West Indies: peoples 312, 313, **313**
Trobrianders 151, **168–169**, **172**, 173
Trukese *see* Chuuk Islanders
Tswana people 20, 26, 28
Tuareg people 70, 71, 75, **75**; houses 301–302
Tucanoan language family 333, 335
Tungus people *see* Evenk people
Tungusic language family 137–138
Tunisia: peoples 71
Tupí-Guaraní (language) 332
Tupí-Guaraní language family 340, 350, 353
Tupinambá people 353
Turkey: peoples 64, **66**, **67**, 76, 77–79, 85, 106, 117; religion 197
Turkic language family 83, 85, 97–98, 102–103, 106–107, 116–117, 138, 140–141
Turkic people 103; proverb 99
Turkish Cypriots 222
Turkish (language) 77, 85, 107, 221
Turkmen (language) 106
Turkmen people **106**, 106–107
Turkmenistan: peoples 85, 106–107
Turks 64, 85, 96, 97, 107, 211–212, 214. *see also* Ottoman Turks
Tuscarora Indians 290–291, 296
Tutsi people 20, 44, **45**
Tuvan (language) 88, 140, 254
Tuvan people 88, 138, 140, 252, 254, 255
Twa people 44
Twi languages 32
Tzotzil Maya 322
Uganda: peoples 47–48, **48**, 52
Ugric language family 211–212
Uighurs *see* Uygurs
Ukraine: peoples **199**, **205**, 205–206, **206–207**
Ukrainian (language) 204, 205
Ukrainians 199, **205**, 205–206, **206–207**, 213
United Arab Emirates: peoples 82
United Kingdom: peoples 130, 214, 238, **240**, 240–241, **243**, 248–249, 251
United States: music 191; peoples 58, 76, 78, 130, 174–175, 185, 199, 214, 240–241, 243, 245, 252–253, 260, 261, 262–265, 269–289, 290–296, 298–299, 320, 321; religious groups 261; storytelling 252–253. *see also* Great Basin; Northeast; Northwest coast; Plains; Southeast; Southwest; West
Untsuri Shuar people 339
Upland Yuman people 272
Ural-Altaic languages 85
Uralic languages 196
Urarina (language) 58, 61
Urdu (language) 100, 132
Uros people 302–303
Uto-Aztecan language family 275, 285, 323, 325, 326
Uto-Aztecan languages 272–273
Uygurs **116**, 116–117
Uzbek (language) 107
Uzbekistan: peoples 85, 102, 107
Uzbeks 107
Vai (language) 298
Vanuatu, South Pacific Ocean: languages 59; peoples **171**, 171–172
Venezuela: peoples **307**, 332–333, 340–341, **341**, 343
Vietnam: peoples **110**, 120–121, **124**, 125, 126, **126**
Vietnamese (language) 126, 154

Vietnamese people 126; proverb 132
Vikings 242, 243, 245, 249
Virgin Islands, West Indies: peoples 312
Wakashan language family 268–269
Walapai people 272
Wales: government 238, 251; peoples 251
Walpiri people **161**
Warao language family 340–341
Warao people 340–341, **341**
Warlpiri people 161, 163
Warrau people *see* Warao people
Watutsi people *see* Tutsi people
Wayampi people 253
Wayfinding 142–145
Wells, Spencer 12, 13
Welsh (language) 251
West Africa: map 32; peoples 32–41, 71, 75, 298
West Indies: peoples 308
West (region), U.S.: map 270; peoples 261, 270–275
West Slavic languages 215
Western Apache 260, 270
Western Arrernte people 152
Western Europe: genetics 231; map 224; peoples 82, 96, 224–237
Wichí Indians *see* Mataco Indians
Wik people 155
Wodaabe people 36, **87**
Wolof people 40–41
World War II 218; Holocaust 200, 201, 203, 213, 216, 233; refugees 250
Wurundjeri people 163
Xikrín Indians 341–343, **343**
Yahgan Indians *see* Yámana Indians
Yahooskin Indians 282–283
Yakut people 140–141
Yámana Indians 356
Yámana language family 356
Yankton Indians *see* Nakota Sioux
Yanomam language family 343
Yanomami Indians 10, **308**, **342**, 343
Yap Islands: peoples **183**
Yapese (language) 186
Yapese Oceanic language family 186
Yapese people **183**, 186–187, **187**
Yavapai people 272
Yazidi (religion) 78
Yemen: peoples 76
Yemeni people **62–63**
Yiddish (language) 77
Yolngu people 163
Yoruba (language) 311, 321
Yoruba people 20, 41, **41**
Yucatec (language) 323
Yucatec people 323
Yucatecan language family 323
Yugoslavia, Federal Republic of 214
Yugoslavia (former country) 208, 209–210, 214, 217
Yukaghir language family 141
Yukaghir people 141
Yuman lanugage family 271–272
Yupiat people 262
Yupik Eskimos *see* Yupiat people
Yupik-speaking Eskimos 263
Yurak people *see* Nenets
Yurts 300–301, **303**
Zapotec Indians 306, 325–326, 329, **329**
Zapotecan language family 329
Zigeuner *see* Roma
Zimbabwe: music 190–191; peoples 26–28, 28
Zoroastrianism 82–83, 97, 129
Zulus 20, 26, 28, **29**, **30–31**, 31, 43

BOOK OF PEOPLES OF THE WORLD
Edited by Wade Davis and K. David Harrison
with Catherine Herbert Howell

Published by the National Geographic Society
John M. Fahey, Jr., *President and Chief Executive Officer*
Gilbert M. Grosvenor, *Chairman of the Board*
Nina D. Hoffman, *Executive Vice President;*
 President, Book Publishing Group

Prepared by the Book Division
Kevin Mulroy, *Senior Vice President and Publisher*
Leah Bendavid-Val, *Director of Photography Publishing*
 and Illustrations
Marianne R. Koszorus, *Director of Design*
Barbara Brownell Grogan, *Executive Editor*
Elizabeth Newhouse, *Director of Travel Publishing*
Carl Mehler, *Director of Maps*

Staff for This Edition
Susan Tyler Hitchcock, *Project and Text Editor*
Garrett Brown, *Consulting Editor*
Kevin Eans, *Illustrations Editor*
Carol Farrar Norton, *Art Director*
Trudy Walker Pearson, *Researcher*
Hicks Wogan, *Editorial Assistant*
Matthew Chwastyk, Steven D. Gardner,
 Map Research, Edit, and Production
Susan Straight, *Contributing Writer*
Richard Wain, *Production Project Manager*
Meredith Wilcox, *Illustrations Specialist*
Connie D. Binder, *Indexer*
Jennifer A. Thornton, *Managing Editor*
Gary Colbert, *Production Director*

Staff for the First Edition
K. M. Kostyal, *Project Editor*

Beebe Bahrami, Patrick Booz, Brian Fagan,
Trudy Griffin-Pierce, Roy Richard Grinker, Catherine
Herbert Howell, Robert Lee Humphrey, Ian McIntosh,
Eugene Ogan, Philip Scher, George Stuart, Keith and
Elisabeth Ward, James F. Weiner, *Contributing Writers*

The staff wishes especially to thank Evan Howell for
his contributions to this edition.

Manufacturing and Quality Management
Christopher A. Liedel, *Chief Financial Officer*
Phillip L. Schlosser, *Vice President*
John T. Dunn, *Technical Director*
Chris Brown, *Director*
Maryclare Tracy, *Manager*
Nicole Elliott, *Manager*

Founded in 1888, the National Geographic Society is one
of the largest nonprofit scientific and educational organizations in the world. It reaches more than 285 million
people worldwide each month through its official journal,
NATIONAL GEOGRAPHIC, and its four other magazines; the
National Geographic Channel; television documentaries;
radio programs; films; books; videos and DVDs; maps;
and interactive media. National Geographic has funded
more than 8,000 scientific research projects and supports
an education program combating geographic illiteracy.

For more information, please call
1-800-NGS LINE (647-5463)
or write to the following address:

National Geographic Society
1145 17th Street N.W.
Washington, D.C. 20036-4688 U.S.A.

Visit us online at www.nationalgeographic.com/books

For information about special discounts
for bulk purchases, please contact
National Geographic Books Special Sales:
ngspecsales@ngs.org

For rights or permissions inquiries,
please contact National Geographic Books Subsidiary
Rights: ngbookrights@ngs.org

Library of Congress Cataloging-in-Publication Data

Book of peoples of the world: a guide to cultures /edited by Wade Davis and
K. David Harrison; with text by Catherine H. Howell.
 p. cm.
 Rev. ed. of: Peoples of the world. c2001.
 Includes index.
 ISBN 978-1-4262-0238-4 (regular ed.)--ISBN 978-1-4262-0239-1 (deluxe ed.)
1. Ethnology. 2. Ethnology--Pictorial works. I. Davis, Wade. II. Harrison, K.
David. III. Howell, Catherine Herbert. IV. National Geographic Society (U.S.)
V. Peoples of the world.
GN378.P4616 2007
305.8--dc22

 2007037598

ISBN 978-1-4262-0238-4 (regular ed.)
ISBN 978-1-4262-0239-1 (deluxe ed.)

Printed in Hong Kong.
10/THK/3